AF745344

Subscription Service Filing Record

RELEASE NUMBER 1
March 1991

has been filed in

HANDBOOK OF GATT DISPUTE SETTLEMENT

Filed ________________ Date ______________

NOTE: In order to assist subscribers in assuring themselves that their looseleaf sets are and continue to be complete and up to date, the Publisher has instituted a system of sequential numbering of all subscription service releases for each publication. The accompanying material is designated "Release Number 1" for Handbook of Gatt Dispute Settlement. Subsequent releases, in sequence, will each call for a check of the preceding Service Filing Record sheet to ensure the continuity of filing releases.

For information or assistance in connection with service for this volume please contact

Transnational Juris Publications, Inc.
P.O. Box 7282
Ardsley-on-Hudson, NY 10503 - USA
914/693-0089 - Fax 914/693-8776

or

Kluwer Law & Taxation Publishers
P.O.Box 23
7409 GA Deventer, The Netherlands
31 5700 47261 - Fax 315700 22244

FILE THIS SHEET IN THE VERY FRONT OF YOUR VOLUME, RETAIN THIS RECORD IN YOUR VOLUME FOR FUTURE REFERENCE UNTIL RELEASE NUMBER 2 IS ISSUED.

HANDBOOK OF GATT DISPUTE SETTLEMENT

Pierre Pescatore
William J. Davey
Andreas F. Lowenfeld

WITHDRAWN FROM STOCK + UNIV DUNELM +

Transnational Juris Publications, Inc.
Ardsley-on-Hudson, New York
Kluwer Law & Taxation Publishers
Deventer

UNIV DUNELM
24 NOV 1992

382.92
PES

For information or assistance in connection with service for this volume please contact

Transnational Juris Publications, Inc.
P.O. Box 7282
Ardsley-on-Hudson, NY 10503
(914) 693-0089 - Telephone
(914) 693-8776 - Telefax

Kluwer Law & Taxation Publishers
P.O. Box 23
7409 GA Deventer
The Netherlands
31 5700 47261 - Telephone
31 5700 22244 - Telefax

Copyright © 1991 by Transnational Juris Publications, Inc.

All rights reserved.
Printed in the United States of America
Library of Congress Catalog Number: 91-11795

ISBN 0-929179-48-X Transnational Juris Publications, Inc.
ISBN 90 6544 9531 Kluwer Law & Taxation Publishers

337.91
PES

ATO 809

CONTENTS

PART TWO—THE REPERTORY

PART THREE—TEXTS

EDITOR'S NOTE

This Handbook is based on the research of Professor Pierre Pescatore, who analyzed the complete set of the GATT decisions in the field of dispute settlement as they have been published in the official series of GATT *Basic Instruments and Selected Documents*. He established the secondary law on dispute settlement, the formal data on the panel reports, the summaries, the key-words and the excerpts, as well as the different indexes: chronological, alphabetical, by articles, by countries and by panel members' names. Professor Pescatore explained the purpose of his work and the method applied by him in his Introduction: "Drafting and Analyzing Decisions on Dispute Settlement".

Professor William J. Davey contributed an Introduction aimed at giving a general idea of GATT: Its aims, its structure and the place of dispute settlement in the whole of the system under the title: "An overview of the General Agreement on Tariffs and Trade". He took care moreover of the editorial presentation of the whole material composing this volume. He will also be responsible for the future updating of this Handbook, which is planned to take place on an annual basis.

Professor Andreas Lowenfeld consented to write a Preface to the whole from the perspective of his large experience in the field of international economic law and litigation.

Pierre Pescatore

PREFACE
SOME OBSERVATIONS ON DISPUTE SETTLEMENT IN GATT

Andreas F. Lowenfeld

As this volume goes to press (January 1991), the international trading community is uncertain whether the Uruguay Round of GATT negotiations is merely temporarily side-tracked or permanently derailed. If it turns out, however, that the agenda of the Uruguay Round was too ambitious, or the divisions too deep, for resolution in 1990–91, that does not mean, as some press reports have suggested, that the rules and achievements of nearly a half century of GATT have become irrelevant. On the contrary, the more difficult negotiations become, the more critical is the availability and smooth functioning of formal dispute settlement, as an alternative to "trade wars" that benefit no one. How such dispute settlement has worked up to now is the focus of the present book.

This handbook, so far as I am aware, is the first comprehensive collection of decided cases about and within the institutions of the General Agreement on Tariffs and Trade. Some of the General Agreement's early builders might be discontent that the lawyers have gotten hold of the GATT, which they preferred to view as a forum for economic diplomacy rather than as a set of obligations coupled with remedies for breach. I recall that in one of the early disputes between the United States and the European Economic Community, the so-called "Chicken War" of 1962-63, the United States team, representing the complaining party, arrived in Geneva armed with legal briefs, econometric studies, and, of course, counsel to present them. The Executive Secretary of the GATT[1], however, preferred to have the presentation made by the Permanent Representatives to the organization—diplomats by profession and one might say "members of the club." Regardless of the legal

[1] The title reflects the provisional character of the institution at the outset. In 1965, the title was changed to Director General. Three persons, an Englishman and two Swiss nationals have occupied the post at the head of the organization. See Overview, p. 15-16 infra.

arguments, or the intricate economic analyses, the best solution was one that could be acceptable to the disputing parties. And the less exploration of legal principles, the more likely it was that such a solution could be fashioned.[2]

Those days, I believe are gone. More and more, the GATT is perceived not only as a code of conduct, but as a system of rules, which can be interpreted in light of specific facts in a proceeding not very different from a law suit. The GATT has still not adopted the principle of separation of functions in that the conclusions of dispute panels—the "cases" collected and summarized are subject to unanimous approval by the GATT Council, i.e., the assembly of all the contracting states. Thus, in theory, a state that loses a case before a panel can block the adoption of the panel report; in practice dealy is more likely than outright veto, if only because the state (or group of states) that loses today may win in another dispute tomorrow, and will have an interest in the tradition that panel reports are adopted.

The arrangement for recommended decisions by panels subject to formal adoption by the Council has several effects. On the one hand, states seem more willing to submit their disputes to panels if they know they have another chance at the end of the process to ask the Council to disapprove all or part of a report. On the other hand, the knowledge that their report is subject to review in a political body, including not only the states were parties to the controversy but other states that may have adopted trade measures similar to the one condemned in the Report, tends to make reports narrow, more focused on particular facts of a case than might otherwise be true.

One of the interesting opportunities afforded by this book is that it allows the reader to compare the GATT rules, as set forth in clear and concise form in the Overview by Professor Davey, with the body of decisions, as collected and analyzed by Judge Pescatore. The fit is not perfect, of course: both the GATT itself—a kind of constitution for the regulation of international trade by states—and the dispute settlement process have evolved over the more than four decades plus of the institution's existence. But considering what has happened to the world at large in this period—the birth of a hundred new states, most of which

[2] It is fair to point out that despite its nickname in the popular press, the Chicken War was brought under Article XXVIII and not under the more adversarial Article XXIII, under which most of the cases collected here have been brought. The GATT Panel's disposition of the dispute from which almost nothing can be gleaned, is summarized as Case 21, p. CS21/1 infra; for a fuller account of the episode, see Chayes, Ehrlich and Lowenfeld, *International Legal Process,* ch. IV (1968-69).

became parties to GATT; the rise of Japan as an economic superpower; and the end of the system of fixed exchange rates based on a stable dollar/gold parity—the basic principles have remained reasonably constant.[3] While it is true that a significant amount of international trade has moved outside of GATT, and that other types of international exchange, notably in services and intellectual property, have not, at this writing, been brought under the General Agreement, the great bulk of world trade—oil, textiles, and agriculture apart—moves in accordance with the basic rules of GATT. GATT in other words, matters, and so I believe, do the cases collected here.

For the most part, the controversies under GATT that have gone as far as formal dispute settlement have been about interpretation, not about basic principle. The complainant state has asserted that a given practice adopted or continued by the respondent state violates a provision of the General Agreement or otherwise nullifies or impairs benefits to which the complaining state is entitled under the Agreement.[4] Typically, the respondent state has contended that its practice was misunderstood, or comes within an exception, or has not injured the complainant state. Generally, the complainant state has been successful before the Panel, but not always, and often not as completely or unambiguously as it hoped. Of the cases reported here, fewer than 10 have can be said to have been defeats for the complaining party.

These results, as well as the increasing amount of detail, analysis, and legal interpretation come out in the summaries that constitute the principal part of the volume. What does not, perhaps, come through, is how the process works. There is no single answer, and the process of dispute resolution has changed substantially over time. The early procedure, for instance, was that once a decision had been taken to convene a disputes panel, the members of the panel would be chosen by the Executive Secretary (Director General) from among permanent representatives to the GATT not involved in the dispute. Subsequently it was decided to enlarge the pool of panelists and to pick the states that would nominate

[3] In cataloguing the momentous developments of the post-war years I do not mean to fail to mention the rise and decline of the "cold war" between competing blocs. However, while some of the East European states joined (or remained in) GATT, East-West trade has been carried out largely outside of GATT, and only two of the cases here collected (Case 1, Czechoslovakia v. USA, and Case 55, Nicaragua v. USA) can be said to have their origin in the cold war. Neither case resulted in development of GATT law.

[4] For an explanation of the claim of nullification or impairment, sometimes referred to as the doctrine of reasonable expectations of contracting parties, see Overview, Section IV (A), also Cases 5 (Chile v. Australia) and 7 (Norway v. Germany).

members of the panel, generally from among their trade officials. More recently, the practice has been for the secretariat to choose panel members directly, and frequently go outside the ranks of government. Generally, panel members have been nationals of contracting states not involved in the dispute; in some instances, however, it has been felt that at least one member of a panel (but not a government official) should be familiar with the laws and procedures of the country whose measure is challenged, balanced by a national of the complainant state.

It has always been clear that panel members are supposed to act independently of the interests of their government; a party (i.e., a government) may object to the appointment of a member of the panel; once the person is chosen, however, no instructions to panel members may be given or taken. My impression is that this understanding has been upheld; there seems to be no counterpart in GATT to the suspicion often voiced about the International Court of Justice that the judges take instructions from or are influenced by the interests of their government.[5]

The analogy between a GATT panel and international arbitration is obvious.[6] Three is an agreed (sometimes negotiated) question or set of questions; each side makes written submissions accompanied by documentary annexes, and usually a reply submission as well; there are oral earings at which the parties respond to each other and to questions from the panel; and the whole proceeding is held behind closed doors.[7] But GATT panel procedure differs from international arbitration—both state-to-state and commercial—in several respects.

(1) Perhaps the most striking difference to one long familiar with international arbitration is the important role of the secretariat, i.e., members of the permanent professional staff of GATT, which in the past decade has included a legal section. The staff members assigned to a case not only assemble the facts and documents and prepare drafts of the report, but they adduce precedents, share their knowledge of present and past GATT practice, and teach panel members the "GATT language." One may argue about the roles of the secretariat and the

[5] I hasten to add that I think the suspicion about the World Court is exaggerated; nevertheless it is widely held, which has led to an increased use of the so-called "Chamber procedure" of the World Court, in which the parties select the members of the panel from among members of the Court.

[6] I note that Judge Pescatore, at pp. 89-90, emphasizes the differences between international arbitration and GATT dispute settlement more than I do.

[7] It is interesting to note that representatives of intervening states may be heard by the panel, but they are asked to leave after their own presentation and do not receive copies of the submissions of the parties.

panel; the architects of the Canada-United States Free Trade Agreement, which makes provision for similar dispute settlement (though primarily in the context of reviewing decisions of national administrative tribunals), opted for a secretariat with only a post office function. The GATT practice, I think, does introduce continuity in a procedure based on a series of ad hoc panels.

(2) After a draft of the report is completed, its factual or descriptive sections, including a summary of the contentions of the parties, is distributed to the parties with a view to submission by each party with proposed corrections. I have not seen this practice in other types of arbitration with which I am familiar, but it has obvious advantages. In the one GATT panel proceeding in which I participated, however, one side said an argument that it had made was not reflected in the draft report, the other side said the argument had never been made, and the panel had one more subsidiary question to decide.

(3) Following completion of the final draft of the Report, it is submitted to the two parties ten days prior to being circulated to all members of the GATT Council. The theory is that this affords the parties one more short period to settle "out of court." The problem with this practice is that the outcome of the case may leak to the press even before it has been submitted to the organ authorized to adopt the decision.

(4) Once the ten-day period expires, the chairman of the panel makes a brief oral summary of the Report to the Council, but does not participate in the debate on the Report. There is no guarantee that the Report will be adopted. Though only one panel report has been expressly rejected, adoption of others has been delayed, often at the insistence of the party whose measures have been found to be unjustified.

(5) Since the parties are governments, panels are not as tough as they would be with private litigants in their demand for documents, enforcement of deadlines, and conduct of proceedings generally. More important for the global trading system, panels do not usually go beyond stating that a given practice is unjustified and should be terminated. Panels rarely address the question of remedies. Though retaliation may be authorized by the contracting parties if a state fails to carry out an approved report, in only one case, so far as I am aware (case 11), was the question of retaliation discussed by a panel. The assumption, again in keeping with the quasi-diplomatic character of the procedure, is that member states will in due time comply with panel reports once they have been approved by the GATT Council.

No one, it is fair to say, regards the dispute settlement procedure as perfect. Although the increased resort to the procedure, after a lull of close to a decade, suggests that it is regarded as a useful way to resolve all but the most serious trade controversies, i.e., those that engage heads of state or government. A number of revisions of the procedure have been suggested, not only in law reviews and trade journals, but also in the Uruguay Round of Trade Negotiations. One proposal, favored for a time by the United States, would be to submit panel reports for approval by "GATT minus two," i.e., by all member states except those involved in the dispute. Another proposal would provide that panel reports go into effect automatically *x* months after their issuance, *unless* the GATT Council had in the meantime voted (by majority or some qualified majority) to disapprove the report or to postpone its implementation. Still another proposal would authorize panels to include in their reports an indication or recommendation of a remedy that the prevailing party could resort to if the respondent state did not discontinue the challenged measure or practice within a stated period. Proposals for private interested parties to make submissions and to attend hearings of panels have also been made from time to time. Such a procedure was adopted in the Canada-United States Free Trade Agreement, and thus far seems to have worked well.

It may well be that some of these proposals, or others that may be suggested will be accepted by the Contracting Parties. It seems clear, however, that the panel procedure for dispute settlement is here to stay, and that understanding of its work to date, as set out in this volume, is essential for all those who particpate in it or would look to improve it.

One final thought, by no means original but nevertheless worth repeating: The GATT dispute mechanism should not be judged only by the cases collected here. In almost every country, there is continuing pressure for protectionism of one kind or another. Trade officials seek to resist such pressures, often with the argument that a given proposal is "GATT-illegal." Not uncommonly, such an argument is met with. In addition to its role as an authoritative source of interpretation of the General Agreement, the GATT dispute settlement mechanism supplies an answer to that question: If we (country *X*) adopt a proposed measure, country *Y* may bring a complaint to GATT; if the measure is found inconsistent with the General Agreement or one of the GATT codes, we will be condemned, and if we do not promptly repeal the measure, country *Y* will be authorized to take a retaliatory measure against us. Moreover, if we want to complain against a measure of country *Z* that is hurting our industries, the fact that we have just adopted the measure you propose will be used against us.

There are no statistics about how often this argument has prevailed. There is little doubt, however, that a system of remedies, including some kind of adjudication, serves to sustain the rules and institutions of international trade. Without such a system, the General Agreement on Tariffs and Trade would be in continuing jeopardy.

AN OVERVIEW OF THE GENERAL AGREEMENT ON TARIFFS AND TRADE

Outline of Contents

PART ONE - INTRODUCTION

PART ONE - INTRODUCTION

AN OVERVIEW OF THE GENERAL AGREEMENT ON TARIFFS AND TRADE

William J. Davey

INTRODUCTION

The General Agreement on Tariffs and Trade (GATT)[1] is the principal international agreement regulating trade between nations. Together with its several side agreements,[2] GATT covers almost all aspects of trade in goods. In addition, GATT serves as the principal international forum for the negotiation of trade issues and for the settlement of trade disputes. Current negotiations under GATT's auspices in the so-called

[1] The agreement as originally signed is found in 61 Stat. (pt. 5) A3, T.I.A.S. No. 1700, 55 U.N.T.S. 188. The text of the agreement as amended to date is reproduced infra at page GATT 1 and has been published by the Contracting Parties to the General Agreement on Tariffs and Trade as volume IV of its collection of Basic Instruments and Selected Documents (hereinafter BISD). Supplements to BISD are published annually. The most recent supplement is the 35th Supplement, which was published in June 1989 and which is typically cited as BISD 35S/xx. The basic analysis of the General Agreement is J. Jackson, World Trade and the Law of GATT (1969) (hereinafter "Law of GATT"). See also J. Jackson, The World Trading System (1989) (hereinafter "World Trading System"); J. Jackson & W. Davey, Legal Problems of International Economic Relations (2d ed. 1986); E. McGovern, International Trade Regulation (2d ed. 1986); K. Dam, The GATT: Law and International Economic Organization (1970); G. Curzon, Multilateral Commercial Diplomacy (1965). The term "GATT" is used herein to refer both to the General Agreement and the organization and trading system that has evolved under the General Agreement.

[2] In addition to the General Agreement, there are side agreements on, inter alia, government procurement, customs valuation, technical standards, import licensing, antidumping duties, subsides and countervailing duties, civil aircraft and textiles. The latest version of the textiles agreement, known as the Multi-Fibre Arrangement, is published in BISD 33S/7 (1987). The other agreements are published in BISD 26S/8 et seq (1980). The relationship between the General Agreement and the various other GATT agreements and decisions is discussed in the text accompanying notes 37–40 infra. The GATT members that adhere to each side agreement are indicated in the annual publication "GATT Activities 19XX".

Uruguay Round[3] are considering proposals to subject trade in services and certain trade related aspects of intellectual property rights and foreign direct investment to regulation in the GATT system. Virtually all of the major trading nations are GATT contracting parties or are seeking to join GATT.[4] As a consequence, GATT now plays an extremely important role in international economic relations, a role that may grow considerably in the future as the volume of world trade continues to grow faster than the output of national economies and as the GATT system expands to regulate more aspects of trade.[5]

The Origins of GATT[6]

The General Agreement on Tariffs and Trade was signed in 1947 during the course of broader negotiations aimed at the establishment of an entity to be called the International Trade Organization (ITO). The ITO was to be the third leg of an international economic triad consisting also of the International Bank for Reconstruction and Development (World Bank) and the International Monetary Fund (IMF). The aim of these organizations was to be the promotion of economic development, the reconstruction of Europe and the expansion of world trade. In particular, the existence of the IMF to provide liquidity to countries running trade deficits was intended to enable the ITO to work for the reduction of tariffs and other trade barriers.

The General Agreement itself was intended to implement and protect the results of certain tariff reductions that had been agreed upon during the ITO negotiations.[7] It was expected that the General Agreement would promptly be subsumed under the mantle of the ITO once the ITO

[3] GATT has sponsored eight rounds of trade negotiations: Geneva (1947), Annecy (1948), Torquay (1950), Geneva (1956), the Dillon Round (1960–61), the Kennedy Round (1964–67), the Tokyo Round (1973–79) and the Uruguay Round (ongoing). The rounds initially focused on tariff reduction, but more recently they have dealt with a very broad range of trade issues. The Uruguay Round, which is scheduled for completion at the end of 1990, was launched at Punta del Este in 1986. See Ministerial Declaration on the Uruguay Round, BISD 33S/7.

[4] See text accompanying notes 23–24 infra.

[5] From 1983 to 1988, world trade grew at a rate of 6% annually, while national outputs grew at a rate of 4%. GATT Doc. GATT/1477, at 6 (March 14, 1990).

[6] See generally W. Brown, The United States and the Restoration of World Trade (1950); J. Jackson, Law of GATT, note 1 supra, ch. 2.

[7] See W. Brown, note 6 supra, at 131–134.

came into existence.[8] Unfortunately, it never did. The ITO negotiators produced a draft charter, known as the Havana Charter,[9] but the U.S. Congress failed to implement it, even though the United States had been a prime mover in the negotiations. Consequently, GATT was orphaned at the very beginning. Fortunately, however, the General Agreement, because it was intended to protect the integrity of tariff reduction commitments, did include most of the trade related provisions of the Havana Charter, albeit in some cases not in their final form. The principal differences between the General Agreement and the Havana Charter were that only the Havana Charter contained provisions (i) regulating restrictive business practices, (ii) regulating the use of export subsidies, (iii) regulating inter-governmental commodity agreements, (iv) calling for the promotion of full employment and economic development and reconstruction and (v) establishing detailed governance provisions.[10] Nevertheless, although no organization or secretariat was established in the General Agreement, there were some general governance provisions that enabled the GATT contracting parties to cobble together a workable, even if shaky, governance structure.

The tentative nature of GATT is also evidenced by the fact that the General Agreement has never come into effect on a definitive basis. It came into effect on January 1, 1948, pursuant to the terms of the Protocol of Provisional Application.[11] This protocol provided that parts I (containing the most-favored-nation obligation and the tariff concessions) and III (containing the customs union exception and various organizational provisions) of the General Agreement would come into effect on a preliminary basis and that part II of the agreement, where most of the substantive obligations are found (such as the quota prohibition, the national treatment obligation, the various rules applicable to customs law and the general exceptions to GATT obligations), would also come into effect provisionally, but would be subject to a clause that allows the contracting parties to maintain in force indefinitely existing legislation inconsistent with their part II obligations. To qualify as

[8] See GATT Art. XXIX, which deals with the relationship between the General Agreement and the Havana Charter of the ITO.

[9] The Havana Charter of the International Trade Organization is formally known as the Final Act of the United Nations Conference on Trade and Employment, March 24, 1948, UN Doc. E/Conf.2/78. It was published by the U.S. Dept. of State as Havana Charter for an International Trade Organization, Commercial Policy Series 113 (Pub. No. 3117, 1948) and Commercial Policy Series 114 (Pub. No. 3206, 1948).

[10] Some of the Havana Charter's provisions on export subsidies were later added to GATT's Article XVI. See text accompanying notes 157 infra.

[11] Reproduced in IV GATT, BISD 76–77 (1969) and at p. GATT 87 infra.

"existing legislation," a measure must be legislation in the formal sense, predate the Protocol[12] and be mandatory in character.[13] The number of such GATT-inconsistent provisions is believed to have decreased significantly with the passage of time, but the exception is still available, although there have been proposals to abolish it in the Uruguay Round.

The Objectives of GATT

The General Agreement on Tariffs and Trade was negotiated against the background of the Great Depression and World War II. Many of those involved in the GATT negotiations believed that the trade wars of the 1930's, provoked in part by the adoption of the so-called Smoot-Hawley tariff in the United States, had prolonged the depression, thereby creating an atmosphere favorable to the outbreak of World War II. According to one U.S. official:

> Nations have more often than not undertaken economic discriminations and raised up trade barriers with complete disregard for the damaging effects on the trade and livelihoods of other peoples, and, ironically enough, with similar disregard for the harmful resultant effects upon their own export trade. . . . The resultant misery, bewilderment, and resentment, together with other equally pernicious causes, paved the way for the rise of those very dictatorships which have plunged almost the entire world into war.[14]

One hope of the negotiators was that an agreement promoting freer trade and restricting the use of trade restrictions would encourage better relations among nations, thereby promoting world peace. Of course, another hope was that freer international trade would promote economic well being. As economist Paul Samuelson once wrote: "[T]here is essentially only one argument for free trade or freer trade, but it is an

[12] In the case of countries that become contracting parties pursuant to an accession protocol other than the Protocol of Provisional Application, the relevant date is typically the date of their accession protocol.

[13] Among the more important recent cases to analyze the terms of the existing legislation clause in detail are Norway—Restrictions on Imports of Apples and Pears, BISD 36S/306 (Case 71); United States—Manufacturing Clause, BISD 31S/75 (Case 56). See generally J. Jackson, Law of GATT, note 1 supra, at 60-63 and J. Jackson & W. Davey, note 1 supra, at 298–306.

[14] Speech by Under Secretary of State Wells, U.S. Dept. of State, Commercial Policy Series No. 71 (Pub. No. 1660, 1941).

exceedingly powerful one, namely: Free trade promotes a mutually profitable division of labor, greatly enhances the potential real national product of all nations, and makes possible higher standards of living all over the globe."[15]

Both of these goals find expression in the objectives that are set out in the brief preamble to the General Agreement. According to the preamble, GATT seeks to increase economic well being throughout the world and increase international trade by (i) substantially reducing tariffs and other trade barriers and (ii) eliminating discriminatory treatment in international commerce. These two mechanisms for achieving increased economic well being encapsulate the basic provisions of the General Agreement.

The discussion of GATT in this overview will be organized as follows: The next section will describe the organizational structure of GATT. The succeeding sections will describe the basic provisions of the General Agreement and the GATT dispute settlement system.

I. THE ORGANIZATIONAL STRUCTURE OF GATT

GATT was intended to be subsumed under the International Trade Organization, and as a consequence, the General Agreement provides no real organizational structure for GATT. It does not provide for a central secretariat or any specific governing bodies, except for the possibility of having all of the contracting parties meet and take decisions. Over time, however, GATT has evolved pragmatically so that some organizational structure exists in fact.

Four aspects of this structure merit attention: First, the development of the GATT secretariat and its role in GATT affairs; second, the powers and activities of the contracting parties; third, the creation of the GATT Council; and finally, the process by which countries become members of GATT.

The GATT Secretariat

GATT is now headquartered in Geneva in Centre William Rappard, the former International Labor Organization building overlooking Lake Geneva. The GATT Secretariat is headed by a Director General, who is

[15] P. Samuelson, Economics 692 (9th ed. 1973).

Arthur Dunkel of Switzerland at the present time. His predecessors were Eric Wyndham-White (1947–1968) and Oliver Long (1968–1980). The staff of the secretariat numbers some 400.[16] It produces studies of international trade and provides support services for the various GATT activities: negotiations on trade issues, oversight committees, dispute settlement proceedings and trade policy courses for officials from developing countries.

The role of the secretariat has tended to be a relatively passive one, rather than one that leads the world community on international trade issues. Perhaps because of its uncertain treaty status, it seems to act as a facilitator for negotiations between the contracting parties and as a service organization, rather than an active proponent of reforms in international and national trade policies. In this, it stands in contrast to the International Monetary Fund, which exerts considerable pressure on countries to put their financial affairs in order. In the future, however, the GATT secretariat may play an increasing role in promoting international trade. One preliminary outcome of the Uruguay Round is an agreement that the GATT secretariat will periodically review the trade policies of the various contracting parties, with the more significant countries being reviewed every two years.[17] Over time, this may give the secretariat more of an opportunity to highlight objectionable trade practices that should be changed and to take a more active role in pressing for reforms.

The Powers and Activities of the Contracting Parties[18]

As has already been noted, the General Agreement does not create any organizational structure within which GATT activities are to be undertaken. Nonetheless, several GATT provisions envision action by the contracting parties. In particular, Article XXV:1 provides that "the Contracting Parties shall meet from time to time for the purpose of giving effect to those provisions of this Agreement which involve joint action and, generally, with a view to facilitating the operation and

[16] Because GATT does not exist as an organization, the staff is technically employed by the Interim Commission of the International Trade Organization (ICITO). ICITO was intended to pave the way for the establishment of the ITO. It exists today only to appoint the Director-General and to serve as the legal entity through which GATT hires employees and enters into certain contracts.

[17] See GATT Doc. MTN.TNC/7(MIN) at 34–39 (1989), reproduced in GATT, GATT Activities 1988, at 160–162 (1989).

[18] See generally J. Jackson, Law of GATT, note 1 supra, at 119–144.

furthering the objectives of this Agreement." Article XXV provides further that each Contracting Party shall have one vote and that decisions shall be taken by majority vote. In fact, as discussed below in respect of dispute settlement, the practice in GATT is to take action almost exclusively by consensus.[19]

The exact parameters of the powers of the contracting parties under Article XXV:1 are not clear, but many GATT activities are undertaken pursuant to the authority of this provision. In some cases, other provisions lay out what the contracting parties may do. For example, Article XXV:5 provides that the contracting parties may waive an obligation imposed by the General Agreement by a two-thirds vote, provided that more than one-half of the contracting parties have voted to do so. Over the years, a number of waivers have been granted.[20]

Under Article XXX, the contracting parties may also vote to amend the General Agreement, again by a two-thirds vote, except in the case of Part I (the most-favored-nation clause and the tariff concessions) where unanimity is required. This power was exercised several times early in GATT's history, but for many years it was considered impractical to amend the General Agreement. This is in part because Article XXX provides that an amendment applies only to a country that accepts it. This makes unanimity necessary as a practical matter for any effective amendment, something that is difficult to attain in an international organization with 100 members. As a consequence, in recent years there has been a proliferation of side agreements, applicable only to those contracting parties that adhere to them.There were a dozen or so such agreements negotiated in the Tokyo Round and others will probably be added in the Uruguay Round.[21]

The contracting parties traditionally meet once a year. An annual meeting is, however, clearly inadequate to deal with the large volume of regular business that comes before GATT each year. Consequently, the contracting parties have delegated or assigned much work to the GATT Council and various committees.

[19] See text accompanying notes 206–207 infra.

[20] One which is particularly controversial was granted to the United States in 1955 and permitted the United States to impose quotas on many agricultural products. Waiver Granted to the United States in Connection with Import Restrictions Imposed Under Section 22 of the United States Agricultural Adjustment Act (of 1933), as amended, BISD 3S/32.

[21] Despite the difficulty of amending the General Agreement, a number of proposed amendments are under consideration in the Uruguay Round, where one negotiating group has the specific charge of considering changes in the General Agreement. See Ministerial Declaration, note 3 supra, at 24.

The GATT Council and the Committees

The GATT Council was established in 1960 and is open to any contracting party that is willing to serve on it. The contracting parties delegated all of their powers to the Council, except for the power to grant waivers under Article XXV:5. Typically the Council meets monthly and considers any matter that needs action by the contracting parties. Decisions of the Council may be appealed to the contracting parties.[22]

In addition to the Council, there are many GATT committees and working parties that oversee operation of various aspects of the GATT system. In particular, there is a committee of signatories for each of the various side agreements, which acts as the governing body of the side agreement. In addition, there are a number of GATT committees and working parties dealing with such topics as textiles, trade and development, balance of payments restrictions, review of free trade areas, review of waivers and accessions of new members. In the course of trade negotiating rounds, there are various negotiating groups.

GATT Membership

As of October 1990, there were 100 contracting parties to General Agreement. The three principal nonmembers, in terms of international trade volume, are the Soviet Union, China and Taiwan. China and Taiwan have applied for membership (or in the case of China, to renew its former membership status) and the Soviet Union has recently been granted observer status and reportedly hopes to accede to GATT in due course.

Article XXXIII allows for the accession of new members, provided that two-thirds of GATT's membership approves.[23] As a practical matter, it is necessary for the prospective member to negotiate the terms of its accession protocol with existing GATT members. Normally, in order to gain the benefits that 40 years of trade negotiations have produced for GATT members, a prospective member may have to make significant changes in the way it treats imports from GATT members. Under

[22] BISD 9S/8–9. There is also a smaller group, the so-called Consultative Group of 18, which now has 22 members, that is supposed to function as a steering committee for GATT. Although established in 1975 it has yet to play an important role in GATT. J. Jackson & W. Davey, note 1 supra, at 320.

[23] Separate customs territories of a country may become GATT members, even though they are not independent national states. Hong Kong, for example, is a GATT member.

Article XXXV, an existing member may opt out of a GATT relationship with a new member, something that the United States has done in connection with a number of Communist countries.[24]

There is an easier path to GATT membership applicable to some countries. Under Article XXVI:5(c), a country that gains its independence from a GATT member may become a GATT member automatically if its parent country applied GATT to the territory in question and sponsors the admission. This method is easier because no terms of accession have to be negotiated and it is usually the case that few of the sponsored territory's tariffs will be subject to GATT bindings. Consequently, former colonies may gain the benefits of GATT membership without undertaking significant obligations under the General Agreement, and many have done so. Under current GATT practice, GATT members apply the General Agreement on a de facto basis to 28 former colonies that have not yet decided whether to join GATT.

GATT's Structural Problems

As discussed in this section, GATT was given only a very rudimentary organizational structure when it was negotiated because it was expected to be subsumed under the aegis of the International Trade Organization (ITO). Consequently, the structure that has been cobbled together is not altogether satisfactory and has hindered GATT in playing a role comparable to such organizations as the International Monetary Fund and the World Bank, organizations that were intended to be sister organizations of the ITO. Moreover, the General Agreement is still applied only on a provisional basis and some GATT-inconsistent national legislation still benefits from the "existing legislation" provision of the Protocol of Provisional Application after over 40 years. While GATT manages to function, it would potentially be more effective if these temporary or ad hoc arrangements were regularized. In addition, the interrelationship between the General Agreement and the various side agreements is complex and confusing, and problems have arisen, inter alia, in respect of (i) claims that a side agreement has modified the General Agreement and (ii) whether certain disputes should be processed in light of the provisions of and under the procedures of the General Agreement or one of the side agreements.[25] All of these issues

[24] See GATT Doc. L/3619 (Romania); GATT Doc. L/3911 (Hungary). In 1985, the GATT secretariat reported 17 operative invocations of Article XXXV, most of which were quite old.

[25] See, e.g., EEC—Payments and Subsidies Paid to Processors and Procedures of Oilseeds and Related Animal-Feed Proteins, GATT Doc. L/6627, adopted 25 January 1990 (Case 77).

are potentially ripe for consideration in the Uruguay Round, particularly as part of the package by which the new subjects such as services are brought under GATT regulation, and there have been some specific suggestions on how GATT's structure could be improved in this context.[26]

II. THE BASIC PROVISIONS OF THE GENERAL AGREEMENT

The preamble to the General Agreement states that the objectives of GATT are to increase economic well being worldwide and to increase international trade. GATT aims to achieve these objectives by reducing barriers to world trade and eliminating discrimination in world trade. The basic substantive provisions of the General Agreement can accordingly be grouped into two categories: one containing those designed to reduce discrimination in international trade and the other containing those aimed at reducing trade barriers. Each category will be examined in turn. Subsequently, GATT's rules on unfair trade practices will be considered, followed by a brief description of potential new areas of applicability for GATT that are the subject of negotiations in the Uruguay Round. At the very outset, however, it is necessary to consider the sources and scope of GATT law.

The Sources of GATT Law

The basic source of GATT rules is, of course, the General Agreement on Tariffs and Trade, as amended, including the interpretative notes that are attached to it[27] and the Protocol of Provisional Application.[28] In interpreting the General Agreement, the contracting parties and the GATT dispute settlement panels have often relied on the drafting history of the General Agreement and the Havana Charter. That drafting history is found in the records of the meetings of the Preparatory Committee of the United Nations Conference on Trade and Employment, which were held in London in 1946, in New York in 1947 and in Geneva in 1947 (where the General Agreement was finalized),[29] and of the United Nations Conference on Trade and Employment, which was

[26] See J. Jackson, Restructuring the GATT System (Royal Institute of International Affairs 1990).

[27] GATT Art, XXXIV.

[28] See text accompanying notes 11–13 supra.

[29] The records of these meetings can be found in collections of United Nations documents under the general heading of "EPCT" or "E/PC/T". They are

held in Havana in 1947 and 1948 and which resulted in the Havana Charter.[30]

Each GATT contracting party is subject to some rules that are applicable only to it. The principal examples are the tariff schedules pursuant to which a country agrees to maximum tariff levels. These levels vary from country to country, but are binding on the country to which they apply by virtue of Article II. These tariff schedules change over time, as a result of formal negotiating rounds and ad hoc renegotiations. The main modifications to the tariff schedules have occurred as a result of tariff negotiating rounds, of which there have been eight: Geneva (1947), Annecy (1948), Torquay (1950), Geneva (1956), the Dillon Round (1960–61), the Kennedy Round (1964–47), the Tokyo Round (1973–79) and the Uruguay Round (ongoing).

In addition, for those countries that joined GATT pursuant to individual accession protocols, there may be special rules or exemptions applicable to those countries as a consequence of specific provisions in the accession protocols.[31] For example, Switzerland was exempted in part from the operation of Article XI on its accession to allow it to operate certain agricultural support programs;[32] and the accession protocols of several East European state trading countries imposed special

included in the set of microfiche GATT documents available from the GATT secretariat. Many relevant passages from these documents are quoted or cited in the Analytical Index, a GATT publication that analyzes each article of the General Agreement on a provision-by-provision and phrase-by-phrase basis through quoting GATT material (i.e. drafting history, dispute settlement reports and other reports) relevant to the interpretation of the particular provision or phrase.

[30] The records of the Havana Conference are also found in United Nations documents collections, under the heading "E/Conf.2" and in the GATT Secretariat's microfiche collection of GATT documents. They are also quoted extensively in the Analytical Index. See note 29 supra. It is generally agreed in GATT that work done at the Havana Conference is relevant to interpret those GATT provisions that are substantially the same as those that appear in the Havana Charter. The Havana Charter cannot be used, however, to reduce or limit the scope of obligations found in the General Agreement. See Canada—Administration of the Foreign Investment Review Act (FIRA), BISD 30S/140 (Case 54).

[31] For a recent example of a protocol of accession, see BISD 33S/3 (Mexico). Individual accession protocols typically have an "existing legislation" clause (see text accompanying notes 11–13 supra) tied to the date of the accession protocol.

[32] BISD 14S/6 (para. 4). This special Swiss accession protocol provision is subject to periodic review by the contracting parties. The most recent review is described in Working Party on Paragraph 4 of the Protocol for the Accession of Switzerland, BISD 33S/151.

provisions concerning their obligations to increase imports from other GATT members and authorized existing GATT members to maintain restrictions on their trade during a transitional period.[33] Some developing countries have been given grace periods in which they are allowed to maintain non GATT-conforming measures.[34] In addition, many GATT members benefit from individual waivers, which exempt them from complying with specific GATT provisions in certain circumstances.[35]

Finally, there are the decisions of the contracting parties. These include the dispute settlement panel reports that have been adopted by the contracting parties, as well as many working party and committee reports on various subjects that have been so adopted.[36] While most of these latter reports do not discuss the interpretation of the General Agreement, some do, while virtually all of the dispute settlement reports do so. These reports are traditionally adopted by consensus of the contracting parties, and as such, they represent the views of the contracting parties on a particular issue at a given point of time. Because dispute settlement panels and other GATT groups frequently refer to past reports to justify a particular interpretation of the General Agreement, they have an important persuasive impact and significantly influence future interpretations of GATT rules. Although the contracting parties could agree to adopt a report that was inconsistent with past reports, that could happen only if there is a consensus that the new report is the better interpretation of the General Agreement. Given the difficulty of developing a new consensus, the corpus of GATT dispute settlement reports represents a fairly stable body of precedent.

In addition to the foregoing sources of GATT law, there are also the various side agreements, particularly those of the Tokyo Round, many

[33] BISD 20S/3 (Hungary); BISD 15S/46 (Poland); BISD 18S/5 (Romania). See generally M. Kostecki, East-West Trade and the GATT System (1978). For a recent review of the Hungarian accession protocol, see BISD 33S/136; for a recent review of the Romanian protocol, see BISD 35S/337. The Polish accession protocol has not been reviewed recently. See BISD 24S/139.

[34] See, e.g., BISD 29S/3 (Thailand); BISD 17S/2 (Egypt).

[35] See text accompanying note 20 supra.

[36] All of the adopted reports of dispute settlement panels are published in the supplements to the BISD series. The supplements also contain many other important working party and committee reports. Additional material concerning the activities of the contracting parties, including minutes and reports of meetings, can be found in GATT documents. These are generally declassified after two years, but they are not easily accessible, except through the GATT secretariat's microfiche series, which has only recently become available to libraries and which is found in only a relatively few.

of which interpret or build on provisions of the General Agreement.[37] The side agreements have their own governing bodies—typically a committee of all signatories—and dispute settlement systems. The side agreements are binding on those countries that have joined them, but many GATT members have not. Consequently, the exact relationship between the side agreements and the General Agreement and the extent to which non-members have rights under the side agreements is somewhat unclear.[38] The contracting parties did state at the conclusion of the Tokyo Round:

> The Contracting Parties also note that existing rights and benefits under the GATT of contracting parties not being parties to these [Tokyo Round] Agreements, including those derived from Article I [the most-favored-nation clause], are not affected by these Agreements.[39]

Thus, to the extent that the side agreements deal with GATT provisions, non-members may benefit indirectly from the provisions of those agreements since treatment accorded to countries under the side agreement may have to be given to all GATT members pursuant to Article I. Of course, to the extent that the side agreements deal with matters not subject to Article I, non-members do not benefit.[40]

As the foregoing makes clear, the determination of applicable GATT rules can be a complex task for dispute settlement panels.

[37] See note 2 supra.

[38] For example, in one case involving subsidies, the panel established under Article XXIII of the General Agreement noted that it was appointed to consider the matter in light of relevant GATT provisions and it declined to propose interpretations of the Subsidies Code. It did note, however, that it felt that the Subsidies Code should be interpreted consistently with decisions interpreting the General Agreement. See EEC—Payments and Subsidies Paid to Processors and Producers of Oilseeds, GATT Doc. L/6627, adopted 25 January 1990 (Case 77).

[39] Action by the Contracting Parties on the Multilateral Trade Negotiations, BISD 26S/203.

[40] An example of an agreement where non-members do not benefit is the Government Procurement Code, since government procurement is not subject to Article I because of the government procurement exemption of Article III:8(a). See text accompanying notes 84–87 infra. On the other hand, the side agreements dealing with duties, such as the Subsidies Code and the Antidumping Code, may provide benefits to non-members since Article I does apply to the levying of all duties. Cf. United States—Countervailing Duties, BISD 28S/113 (Case 49).

The Territorial Scope of GATT Law

The General Agreement applies to "the metropolitan customs territories" of the contracting parties and to any other customs territories in respect of which the Agreement has been accepted.[41] There has been some controversy as to the application of the General Agreement to regional and local governments. Article XXIV:12 provides:

> Each contracting party shall take such reasonable measures as may be available to it to ensure observance of the provisions of this Agreement by the regional and local governments and authorities within its territory.

The issues are how much must a contracting party do and who is to judge the reasonableness of its measures.[42] One panel suggested in 1985, in a report that was *not* adopted by the GATT Council, that in the case of a provincial rule that violated the General Agreement, Canada had an obligation to provide compensation to the injured party and to continue to seek withdrawal of the offending rule by the province.[43] Canada blocked the adoption of the report. In a 1988 case, also involving Canada, the panel simply found that Canada had an obligation to use reasonable measures in light of the panel's findings that the challenged provincial actions violated the General Agreement. The panel seemed to feel that evaluation by anyone of the reasonableness of Canada's measures to ensure compliance could not be undertaken until the provincial actions were found to violate the General Agreement and Canada had time to take measures in light of that finding.[44] Thus, the exact scope of Article XXIV:12 remains uncertain. It would seem, however, that a contracting party, at a minimum, has a bona fide obligation to do its best to have the General Agreement observed and its objectives not undercut by regional and local authorities.

An Overview of the General Agreement

As a brief overview, it is useful to consider the basic structure of the General Agreement. The most important provisions are Articles I (the most-favored-nation clause), II (the tariff binding provision), III (the

[41] GATT Art. XXIV:1. Cf. United States Tax Legislation (DISC), BISD 23S/98 (Case 31).

[42] See generally J. Jackson, Law of GATT, note 1 supra, at 302–304.

[43] Canada—Measures Affecting the Sale of Gold Coins, GATT Doc. L/5863 (1985) (not adopted by the GATT Council).

[44] Canada—Distribution and Sale of Alcoholic Drinks, BISD 35S/37 (Case 65).

national treatment clause) and XI (the ban on non-tariff restrictions). In these four provisions, the General Agreement closely regulates the kind of restrictions that may be imposed on foreign products. It allows the imposition of tariff and other charges at the border (so long as they do not exceed limits agreed upon pursuant to Article II), but it prohibits any other restrictions on imports in Article XI. Article I is designed to prevent a country from discriminating among foreign producers at the border and in its internal tax and sales regulations. Article III is designed to prevent discrimination against foreign products once they have entered the country, through discriminatory taxes or sales regulations. These provisions effectively implement the basic philosophy of the General Agreement, which is that, subject to a few exceptions, restrictions on international trade should be in the form of tariffs only and that those tariffs should be nondiscriminatory.

* * *

With these preliminary issues disposed of, it is now appropriate to turn to a detailed examination of the basic provisions of GATT law, looking first at GATT's rules against discrimination in international trade and then its provisions on the reduction of trade barriers and unfair trade practices.

A. ELIMINATION OF DISCRIMINATION IN INTERNATIONAL TRADE

The first method by which GATT attempts to achieve its objective of increasing international trade and economic well being is to eliminate discrimination in world trade. It does this through two provisions: Article I—the most-favored-nation clause—which prohibits discrimination among foreign countries in certain trade matters, and Article III—the national treatment clause—which prohibits discrimination between national and foreign products in certain trade matters.

1. The Most-Favored-Nation Clause[45]—Article I

a. The Basic Provision

Article I:1 provides:

> With respect to customs duties and charges of any kind imposed on or in connection with importation or exportation or

[45] See generally Pescatore, La clause de la nation la plus favorisée dans les conventions multilaterales, 53–I Institut de Droit International—Annuaire (1969); J. Jackson, World Trading System, note 1 supra, ch. 6; E. McGovern, note 1 supra, at 254–268.

> imposed on the international transfer of payments for imports or exports, and with respect to the method of levying such duties and charges, and with respect to all rules and formalities in connection with importation and exportation, and with respect to all matters referred to in paragraphs 2 and 4 of Article III, any advantage, favor, privilege or immunity granted by any contracting party to any product originating in or destined for any other country shall be accorded immediately and unconditionally to the like product originating in or destined for the territories of all other contracting parties.[46]

Essentially Article I bans discrimination based on the source of the goods with respect to customs matters, internal taxes and internal sales regulations. The most-favored-nation concept is very basic to the General Agreement and numerous other GATT provisions contain most-favored-nation or similar non-discrimination rules.[47] The principal purpose of the MFN clause is to ensure equality of opportunity for exporters in all countries at the highest level of trade liberalization.

There are a number of rationales for this rule, two of which are of particular importance. First, if imports from all countries are treated the same with respect to duties, taxes and so on, then it is to be expected that the most efficient producing country will be the most successful in gaining access to the domestic market. If there is discrimination between imports on the basis of their source, it could happen that the most efficient producer would be frozen out of the market if higher duties or taxes were applied to its products. Thus, the basic GATT objective of increasing economic well being is best achieved if there is a ban on discrimination based on the origin of goods.

Second, the MFN rule is supported by political considerations. Countries resent being discriminated against. As noted in the introduction, one of the concerns of those who were instrumental in shaping the General Agreement was that trade tensions can lead to political conflicts

[46] Paragraphs 2–4 of Article I allowed the continuation of so-called colonial preferences. These preferences were quite controversial at the time the General Agreement was negotiated, and a major goal of the United States in the initial GATT negotiations was to end the British preferences. The United States succeeded only in limiting the preferences, not eliminating them. Overtime, these preferences have been replaced by free trade areas and customs unions and the generalized scheme of preferences for developing countries (see text accompanying notes 57–66 infra).

[47] See J. Jackson, Law of GATT, note 1 supra, at 255.

and destabilize international relations.[48] Prohibiting such discrimination is therefore a desirable political goal.

b. Interpretative Problems

The MFN clause is fairly straightforward but it does present some interpretative problems. If the measure in question is covered by the clause, then discrimination between like products is prohibited. The two obvious issues are: What measures are covered by the clause; and what are like products?

Covered Measures. Article I prohibits discrimination in tariffs, internal taxes and internal sales regulations based on the origin of foreign products. If certain favorable treatment is given to the products of one country with respect to those matters, it must be given to the products of all GATT members. Generally, there has not been much controversy as to the type of measure covered by Article I. The question of what measures are covered by the MFN clause is usually not difficult; they are specified in the text of the clause. The coverage issue may arise, however, when countries are invoking a GATT exception. For example, can Article XIX escape clause measures discriminate between products coming from different countries? Suppose the United States felt that imports of Japanese, but not European, cars were seriously injuring the U.S. domestic automobile industry. Could the U.S. impose duties or quotas only on Japanese cars and exempt identical European cars? While the answer is somewhat debatable, the better view would seem to be that it cannot.[49] Some countries have argued that such selective measures ought to be permitted and the dispute is one major reason why no code on safeguard measures was agreed upon in the Tokyo Round or in the following years.[50] A similar issue arises in the application of antidumping and countervailing duties. While the facts concerning dumped or subsidized exports usually differ on a country-by-country basis, where all relevant facts are the same, a GATT committee concluded that there should be no discrimination.[51]

Like Products. The most difficult interpretative problem with respect to Article I concerns the concept of like products. If the two foreign products at issue are only similar or competing, but not technically like products, then there may be no bar to discriminatory treatment. Thus,

[48] See text accompanying note 14 supra.

[49] See Norway—Restrictions on Imports of Textiles, BISD 27S/119 (Case 41). See also materials collected in J. Jackson & W. Davey, note 1 supra, at 595–606.

[50] See text following note 139 infra.

[51] BISD 9S/196.

the effectiveness of Article I as a broad-based ban on discrimination is linked to the definition of like product.[52] In the context of Article I, the like product issue has arisen in two situations. First, there has been one case where a contracting party changed its system of tariff classification so that products formerly treated the same were distinguished. In that case, a panel was faced with a Spanish decision to reclassify coffee from one into five separate tariff classifications, with differing duties. Brazil, whose coffees largely fell into the higher tariff categories, claimed that it was being denied MFN treatment—the lower duties charged on other kinds of coffee. The panel decided that coffee was coffee and found that Spain had violated Article I, even though there were flavor and other distinctions between the five different categories. The panel seemed to have been influenced by the fact that other countries did not differentiate coffee in the Spanish manner and that the Spanish classification was a new one.[53]

A different situation is presented when a contracting party challenges the general classification structure of another contracting party's tariff. In such cases, panels have rejected the argument that admittedly distinct products should nonetheless be treated as like products.[54] Panels have seemed to support the view that as long as there are real differences between the products, it is legitimate for a country to distinguish them if it chooses to do so for trade policy purposes. There are limits, however, to a country's freedom of action. The products distinguished must really be different; it would not be permissible to distinguish between like products on the basis that they came from countries having differing

[52] The term "like product" is used in several provisions of the General Agreement, and it is generally agreed that it must be interpreted in the context in which it appears in each of those provisions. For example, some panels found products not to be "like" when they were classified differently in a country's longstanding tariff classification system (see generally cases cited in note 54 infra). One other panel, however, in a detailed consideration of the like product issue in an Article III case, concluded that it would be appropriate to take into consideration "not only objective criteria (such as composition and manufacturing processes of products) but also the more subjective consumers' viewpoint (such as consumption and use by consumers)." Japan—Customs Duties, Taxes and Labelling Practices on Imported Wines and Alcoholic Beverages, BISD 34S/83, 116 para. 5.7 (Case 63). The panel cited a GATT working party report on border taxes to support its position. Id. at 115, citing BISD 18S/102, para. 18.

[53] Spain—Tariff Treatment of Unroasted Coffee, BISD 28S/102 (Case 48).

[54] See, e.g, Japan—Imports of SFP Dimension Lumber, BISD 36S/167 (Case 73); EEC—Measures on Animal Feed Proteins, BISD 25S/49 (Case 35); Germany—Imports of Sardines, BISD 1S/53 (Case 7); Brazilian Internal Taxes (II), II BISD 186 (Case 6); Australian Subsidy on Ammonium Sulphate, II BISD 188 (Case 5).

characteristics.[55] Moreover, such distinctions cannot be unilaterally introduced without running the risk that a panel will find that although no GATT provision was violated, the complainant is entitled to relief because its reasonable expectations of benefits under the General Agreement have been nullified or impaired. For example, in one early case involving a German decision to apply different tariff rates to closely related species of fish, a GATT panel concluded that, even though there was no violation of Article I because the different species were not like products, the injured party's benefits under the General Agreement had been nullified or impaired under Article XXIII because it had been led to expect that the products that were treated differently—three varieties of related fish—would be treated the same.[56]

c. *Exceptions to the MFN Clause*

There are two major exceptions to the MFN obligation.[57] First, it does not apply in the case of free trade areas and customs unions qualifying under Article XXIV of the General Agreement. Second, it does not preclude granting differential and more favorable treatment to developing countries.

Free trade areas and customs unions. Article XXIV establishes a general exception to the MFN clause of the General Agreement for free trade areas and customs unions.[58] For the exception to apply, (i) substantially all the trade between the constituent members must not be subject to duties or other restrictions, (ii) the requirement in phrase (i) must be met within a reasonable length of time in the case where the agreement is phased in, which is the usual case, and (iii) the duties and

[55] Cf. Belgian Family Allowances, BISD 1S/59 (Case 10). J. Jackson, Law of GATT, note 1 supra, at 259.

[56] Germany—Imports of Sardines, BISD 1S/53 (Case 7). See Australian Subsidy on Ammonium Sulphate, II BISD 188 (Case 5); text accompanying notes 185–192 infra.

[57] Most exceptions to the General Agreement impose some form of MFN requirement. See text accompanying notes 111–112 infra (Article XVII—state trading), 134–135 infra (Article XIX—escape clause) and 165 infra (Article XX—general exceptions).

[58] A free trade area is a group of two or more customs territories in which duties and other restrictive regulations of commerce are eliminated on substantially all the trade between the constituent members as to goods originating therein. A customs union is a free trade area that applies substantially the same duties and other regulations of commerce to the trade of nonconstituents. GATT, Art. XXIV:8. See generally H. Steinberger, GATT und regionale Wirschaftzusammenschlusse (1963).

commercial regulations applied by the constituents to third parties must not be higher or more restrictive than those before formation of the area or union.

Article XXIV has long been controversial. When it was drafted in the 1940's it was apparently not anticipated that free trade areas and customs unions would become as common as they have. In addition, at the time the General Agreement was negotiated prevailing tariff rates in the industrialized countries were around 40%. Thus, any device to cut tariffs to zero was viewed as obviously beneficial. As tariff levels have fallen, the benefits from such areas and unions have seemed less impressive. Moreover, closer economic analyses of free trade areas and customs unions, largely done after 1947, have raised general questions about whether their trade creation effects (benefitting the constituents) offset the trade diversion effects (suffered by the rest of the world as internal trade replaces external trade).[59]

The unanticipated extensive use of Article XXIV and these theoretical questions about the desirability of free trade areas and customs union have affected their reception in GATT. When free trade area and customs union agreements have been submitted to GATT for analysis to see if they comport with the terms of Article XXIV, the typical result has been an inconclusive working party report. In particular, the European Community was never given a clean bill of health. Thus, there are no precise answers to the questions of how much trade is "substantially all" or what interim period is a "reasonable length?"

Differential and More Favorable Treatment for Developing Countries.[60] In a number of ways, GATT allows derogations from the MFN provision that favor developing countries. Probably the best known derogation permits developed countries to adopt generalized preference systems that impose lower tariffs on products from developing countries than on those from other countries. These systems were initially permitted under a general ten-year waiver granted to such schemes that was adopted in 1970.[61] Since the conclusion of the Tokyo Round, GSP arrangements have been legitimized by an open-ended action adopted by the contracting parties, often referred to as the Enabling Clause.[62]

[59] See K. Dam, note 1 supra, ch. 16.

[60] See generally R. Hudec, Developing Countries in the GATT Legal System (1987).

[61] Generalized System of Preferences, BISD 18S/24.

[62] Differential and More Favorable Treatment, Reciprocity and Fuller Participation of Developing Countries, BISD 26S/203.

In addition to the Enabling Clause, there are a number of other provisions of the General Agreement that give special treatment to developing countries. In particular, Article XVIII provides developing countries, inter alia, the right to protect infant industries, and Part IV of the General Agreement, which was added in 1966, calls for special consideration to be given to developing countries on a variety of matters of interest to them, although its provisions are basically hortatory. There are also particular GATT provisions that in practice are of particular use to developing countries: The balance of payments exceptions of Articles XII and XVIII are ones that many developing countries can invoke.[63] Moreover, since many developing countries became members through "sponsorship" of their former colonial power, and consequently did not negotiate any particular terms of membership, they frequently have made very few tariff bindings.[64]

Beyond these provisions of the General Agreement, there are a number of provisions in Tokyo Round agreements that establish less rigorous obligations for developing countries. For example, the ban on export subsidies on nonprimary products does not apply to developing countries, although they are not to use such subsidies in a way that causes serious prejudice.[65] Similarly, there are relaxed obligations placed upon developing countries in the Customs Valuation Code.[66]

These special provisions are controversial. Even for those that agree that some developing countries may need this sort of assistance, there is the question of "graduation." At what point does a developing country that has been relatively successful, such as one of the East Asian countries, no longer merit special treatment. Moreover, there are many that argue that special treatment generally is undesirable for developing countries and works to undermine their development by encouraging inefficient and inappropriate industries. Others argue that even more special provisions are needed to enable developing countries to progress toward economic parity with the developed world. This is not the place to rehearse and debate these arguments, but it is important to note that there are deep divisions with the GATT membership on some of these issues.

[63] See text accompanying notes 121–125 infra.
[64] See text following note 24 supra.
[65] Subsidies Code, BISD 26S/56, art. 14.
[66] Customs Valuation Code, BISD 26S/116, art. 21, protocol.

2. The National Treatment Clause[67]—Article III

a. An Overview

The national treatment clause of Article III establishes the general principle that contracting parties should not distinguish between products of domestic origin and those of foreign origin with respect to (i) internal taxes and charges, (ii) laws, regulations and requirements affecting the internal sale, offering for sale, purchase, transportation, distribution or use of products or (iii) internal quantitative regulations requiring the mixture, processing or use of products in specific amounts or proportions. The basic idea underlying Article III and the national treatment clause is that once goods have cleared border controls (tariffs paid, other entry conditions satisfied), they should be treated no differently than domestically produced goods.

In Article III, paragraph I, there is a general statement that the contracting parties recognize that the above measures "should not be applied to imported or domestic products so as to afford protection to domestic production." This is a broad, sweeping statement, that expresses the underlying rationale of Article III as a whole. Although, it phrased in terms of what countries should do, not in terms of what they are obligated to do, it is specifically incorporated into two of the mandatory provisions of Article III—those dealing with taxes and mixing requirements.

b. Internal Taxes

Article III, paragraph 2 provides that imported products "shall not be subject, directly or indirectly, to internal taxes or other internal charges of any kind in excess of those applied, directly or indirectly, to like domestic products." Paragraph 2 goes on to provide that internal taxes shall not be applied contrary to the principles of paragraph 1, thus incorporating that paragraph's sweeping language into paragraph 2.

There have not been many recent GATT cases involving Article III:2, probably because the basic obligation is fairly straightforward. A number of observations can be made, however. First, Article III:2 has the object and purpose of promoting non-discriminatory competition

[67] See generally J. Jackson, Law of GATT, note 1 supra, ch. 12; J. Jackson, World Trading System, note 1 supra, ch. 8; E. McGovern, note 1 supra, at 245–254.

among imported and like domestic products. It was designed with the intention that internal taxes on goods should not be used as a means of protection.[68] As such, Article III:2 has been given a very broad interpretation.[69] This can be seen most clearly in the following example from the drafting history in respect of the interaction of paragraphs 1 and 2. If a country produces apples and places a large excise tax on oranges, one could argue that it is trying to protect its domestic apple industry through the use of internal taxes in violation of the principles of paragraph 1.[70] This example highlights that, while the basic obligation of paragraph 2 is expressed in terms of giving national treatment to like products, Article III's provisions on taxation go further and prohibit the use of indirect taxation to protect a domestic industry, whether or not it is a producer of like products.

Second, Article III is concerned with taxes on products. Thus, it would not seem to apply to income or other direct taxes, even if they are applied in a discriminatory manner.[71] It would be possible to argue that the "directly or indirectly" language is so broad as to cover the effects of discriminatory direct taxes, but such an interpretation is one that the framers of GATT probably did not have in mind, as they generally drew a clear distinction between indirect, product-related taxes and other, direct taxes, such as income taxes.[72]

Finally, it should be noted that it is permissible to apply taxes on importation that are equivalent to domestic taxes that a particular domestic product bears.[73] For example, the United States was permitted to collect a tax on certain imported chemical products that were derived from chemicals subject to an internal U.S. excise tax. The aim of the tax was to ensure that the imported products bore the same amount of U.S. excise tax as would the like U.S. products.[74]

[68] Japan—Imported Wines and Alcoholic Beverages, BISD 34S/83, 114 para. 5.5 (Case 67).

[69] See id.

[70] Cited in J. Jackson, Law of GATT, note 1 supra, at 282.

[71] Rules relating to direct taxes (e.g., tax credits, deductions, exemptions) may constitute subsidies, however, and violate GATT rules on subsidies (see, e.g., United States Tax Legislation (DISC), 23S/98 (Case 31)) or attract offsetting countervailing duties imposed under Article VI.

[72] See J. Jackson, Law of GATT, note 1 supra, at 284–285.

[73] GATT Art. II:2(a).

[74] United States—Taxes on Petroleum and Certain Chemical Products, BISD 34S/136 (Case 62).

c. *Internal Sales Regulations*

Paragraph 4 of Article III requires that imported products "be accorded treatment no less favorable than that accorded to like products of national origin in respect of all laws, regulations and requirements affecting their internal sale, offering for sale, purchase, transportation, distribution or use." Paragraph 4 does *not* specifically incorporate the principles of paragraph 1, as do paragraphs 2 and 5.

Article III, paragraph 4 has been the subject of a number of important GATT panel decisions. Generally, it has been given a broad reading by the panels. For example, in a relatively early GATT decision, the panel found that an Italian law providing government-subsidized, below-market interest rates on loans to Italian farmers to buy domestically produced agricultural machinery violated Article III:4.[75] In doing so, it rejected arguments by the Italian government that Article III:4 should be read narrowly, essentially as a ban on quantitative restrictions, and that such subsidies were permitted by the General Agreement.[76] Instead, the panel gave a expansive reading to paragraph 4, focusing in particular on the word "affecting". According to the panel the law, regulation or requirement at issue did not have to govern directly the sale, etc. of agricultural machinery, it was sufficient for it to affect the sale of such machinery by adversely modifying the conditions of competition between domestic and imported products, which the Italian law clearly did by providing cut-rate financing to purchasers of domestic products.

More recently, another GATT panel interpreted Article III:4 broadly in a case where the European Community challenged a U.S. law that established a procedure pursuant to which a U.S. firm could bring a patent infringement action in respect of an imported product, but not a domestically produced product, before the United States International Trade Commission.[77] Generally speaking there were certain advantages that a U.S. firm would gain in doing this compared to bringing such an action in federal district court, where actions against domestic infringers

[75] Italian Discrimination Against Imported Agricultural Machinery, BISD 7S/60 (Case 16).

[76] As noted below, Article III, paragraph 8(b) permits the payment of subsidies to domestic *producers*, but in this case the subsidies went to the buyers. The panel rejected the argument that since Italy could have achieved the same result by subsidizing producers as by subsidizing buyers, it should be allowed to do either.

[77] United States—Section 337 of the Tariff Act of 1930, BISD 36S/345 (Case 74).

have to be brought. For example, (i) an ITC proceeding would in general be faster than a district court proceeding, (ii) respondents in an ITC proceeding could not bring counterclaims in an ITC proceeding as they could in a district court proceeding and (iii) the result of a successful claim in an ITC proceeding is usually an order excluding the infringing goods from the United States that is enforced by the Customs Service, whereas a successful suit in district court must be enforced by the plaintiff in individual injunctive actions. While the panel suggested that Article III:4 did not require that imported and domestic products be treated identically, the panel felt that it was incumbent on party applying differential measures to demonstrate that those measures did not result in less favorable treatment of imported products, which it felt the United States had not done. The panel also rejected the U.S. claim that the measures were saved by the Article XX(d) exception for measures securing patent rights.[78]

GATT panels have also given a very broad reading to the word "requirements" as it is used in Article III:4. In one case, which involved Canadian investment regulations, the panel found that contractual commitments entered into by foreign investors in Canada to favor use of Canadian origin goods in the operation of their investments constituted "requirements" in the sense of Article III:4 and discriminated against imported products. The commitments were made in order to obtain the necessary Canadian government approvals for investments in Canada.[79] In another case, the panel found that certain undertakings to limit use of Japanese-origin parts in EC assembly plants, which were made by Japanese companies to avoid application of anti-circumvention duties under the EC's antidumping regulation, were "requirements" subject to Article III:4 and that they discriminated against imported products.[80]

All of these decisions together give Article III:4 a very wide field of application.

d. Mixing Requirements

Paragraph 5 of Article III bans any "internal quantitative regulation relating to the mixture, processing or use of products in specified amounts or proportions which requires, directly or indirectly, that any

[78] See text accompanying notes 165–166 infra.

[79] Canada—Administration of the Foreign Investment Review Act (FIRA), BISD 30S/140 (Case 54).

[80] EEC—Regulation of Imports of Parts and Components, GATT Doc. L/6657, adopted 16 May 1990 (Case 79). See note 152 infra and accompanying text.

specified amount or proportion of any product which is the subject of the regulation must be supplied from domestic sources." Like paragraph 2, paragraph 5 incorporates paragraph 1 by providing that internal quantitative regulations shall not be applied contrary to paragraph 1's principles.

A GATT panel in 1978 considered an EC regulation that required farmers who bought certain imported animal feed to also buy specified amounts of EC produced dried milk, which could also be used as animal feed.[81] The panel viewed this as using an internal quantitative regulation so as to afford protection to a domestic industry and therefore violative of Article III:5. It is likely that domestic content requirements, such as that 80% of the value of a car's components must be of domestic origin, would violate Article III:5.[82]

e. Exceptions to the National Treatment Clause

There are two important exceptions to the national treatment clause that are contained in Article III.[83] These exceptions permit discrimination against imported goods in the case of government procurement policies and permit the payment of subsidies exclusively to domestic producers.

Government Procurement. Article III, paragraph 8(a) provides an exception to Article III for government regulations governing the procurement by government agencies of products purchased for governmental purposes and not with a view to commercial resale or with a view to use in the production of goods for commercial resale. This exception may be somewhat limited by the provisions of Article XVII on state trading companies.[84]

[81] EEC—Measures on Animal Feed Proteins, BISD 25S/49 (Case 35).

[82] See Canada—Administration of the Foreign Investment Review Act, BISD 30S/140 (Case 54) (requiring domestic producers to buy domestic inputs violates Article III:4).

[83] Article III also exempts from its coverage internal quantitative regulations relating to exposed cinematograph film that meet the requirements of Article IV, which permits the use of screen quotas subject to certain conditions.

[84] It is disputed, however, whether the principles of nondiscrimination referred to in paragraph 1 of Article XVII include the national treatment clause, although that clause certainly establishes one of the two main nondiscrimination principles in the General Agreement. See Canada—Distribution and Sale of Alcoholic Drinks, BISD 35S/37, 63–64 paras. 3.47–3.48 (Case 65); Canada—Administration of the Foreign Investment Review Act, BISD 30S/140, 163 para. 5.16 (Case 54); J. Jackson, Law of GATT, note 1 supra, at 346–347.

In the Tokyo Round there was agreement reached on a Government Procurement Code, pursuant to which the signatories agreed to apply the national treatment principle to certain government procurement.[85] The coverage of the Code is fairly limited. It applies only to contracts worth an amount in excess of 130,000 SDRs ($176,000);[86] it does not cover local governments at all and it covers only those national government entities that are specified by the signatory in question. Consequently, the Code has not opened a great deal of government procurement to international trade. Nonetheless, it is expected that over time the coverage of the Code will be expanded and that it will have a significant effect on trading opportunities. Indeed, between the Tokyo Round and the start of the Uruguay Round, the Code was amended to broaden its coverage.[87]

Domestic Subsidies. Article III, paragraph 8(b) allows subsidies paid exclusively to domestic producers.[88] Other GATT rules may, however, limit the freedom of a country to grant domestic subsidies.[89]

f. The Problem of Disguised Discrimination

One of the more difficult areas of international trade law involves the problem of national rules and regulations that are facially neutral, but that in fact have a trade distorting effect in favor of national producers. Regulations imposing technical standards are probably the most common type of such rules. The General Agreement does not explicitly deal

[85] Agreement on Government Procurement, BISD 26S/33; amended by Protocol Amending the Agreement on Government Procurement, BISD 34S/12.

[86] The original limit was 150,000 special drawing rights. It was reduced to 130,000 SDRs in 1987. In the only dispute settlement case to date under the Code, it was decided that the applicable value-added tax should be included in determining whether a contract exceeds the Code's threshold. Panel on Value-Added Tax and Threshold, BISD 31S/247 (Case 58).

[87] See note 85 supra.

[88] This provision has been interpreted narrowly by GATT panels. For example, the fact that the effects of subsidizing purchasers might be the same as subsidizing producers does not mean that Article III:8(b) can be relied upon to justify subsidies to purchasers. See Italian Discrimination Against Imported Agricultural Machinery, BISD 7S/60 (Case 16). Similarly, the requirement that the subsidies be paid exclusively to producers means that the exception cannot be relied upon if the subsidies are paid to processors, particularly where the processors retain part of the economic benefits generated by the subsidies. See EEC—Payments and Subsidies Paid to Producers and Processors of Oilseeds, GATT Doc. L/6627, adopted 25 January 1990 (Case 77).

[89] See text accompanying note 110 supra.

with this problem,[90] although there was agreement reached on a Standards Code in the Tokyo Round.[91] The Code does not impose many concrete obligations, but it lays out a framework in which future negotiations can more effectively reduce the use of supposedly neutral standards to impede trade flows. The Code already indicates the direction in which progress may be made by its promotion of the establishment of international instead of national standards, the use of performance rather than design criteria and the recognition of testing in foreign laboratories. Eventually, the GATT rules may follow those that have evolved to deal with this problem within the EC.[92]

B. REDUCTION OF TRADE BARRIERS

The General Agreement attempts to realize its second goal—the reduction of barriers to international trade—by limiting the use of tariffs and quotas, which are the two principal instruments used by nations to keep out imports. It implements these limitations by creating a procedure for establishing maximum tariff rates and by prohibiting quotas and other nontariff barriers generally.

The preference for tariffs over quotas, which is seen in the fact that quotas are banned and tariffs only limited, is based on economic considerations.[93] Tariffs are thought to be a more transparent trade barrier and one that is not insurmountable so long as the tariffs are not at excessive levels. If a foreign supplier is sufficiently more efficient that a domestic producer, it may still sell in domestic market. Thus, access to the domestic market is, in principle, not eliminated. That is not the case with quotas. Once the quota limit is reached, there is no possibility for

[90] In one case, however, the panel recognized that "there may be cases where application of formally identical legal provisions would in practice accord less favorable treatment to imported products and a contracting party might thus have to apply different legal provisions to imported products to ensure that the treatment accorded them is in fact no less favorable." The panel noted that the "underlying objective is to guarantee equality of treatment." See U.S.—Section 337 of the Tariff Act of 1930, BISD 36S/345, 386, para. 5.11 (Case 74).

[91] Agreement on Technical Barriers to Trade, BISD 26S/8.

[92] See, e.g., Rewe-Zentral AG v. Bundesmonopololverwaltung fur Branntwein, Case No. 120/78, 1979 ECR 649 (the "Cassis de Dijon" decision) (goods lawfully produced and marketed in one member state may be sold in other member states, even if they do not meet standards applicable therein).

[93] J. Jackson & W. Davey, note 1 supra, at 366.

the foreign supplier to expand its sales in the domestic market. Moreover, the administration of quotas often raises problems for economists. The distribution of import permits, which are typical in a quota system, may lead to relatively inefficient foreign producers obtaining access rights to the domestic market since the permits are unlikely to be distributed to the most efficient producers, but rather on a first come, first served basis or on the basis of past trading patterns or even as a result of bribery. With a tariff that is applied generally to all imports at the same rate (as is required by Article I of the General Agreement), the most efficient foreign producer is the one that gains access to the domestic market. Consequently, GATT generally favors the use of tariffs over quotas, although it works to limit tariffs.

1. Limiting Tariffs

a. Binding Tariffs—Article II

The Basic Provision. In many ways the heart of the General Agreement is Article II, which obligates GATT members not to charge tariffs in excess of maximum levels that they have negotiated for specific products.[94] In GATT jargon, countries "bind" their tariffs on specific products. As was mentioned above, the General Agreement came into existence initially to embody the results of tariff-cutting negotiations held in 1947. To further its tariff-cutting goal, GATT has sponsored seven "rounds" of tariff negotiations and an eighth round—the so-called Uruguay Round—is now in progress. The results of these rounds of tariff negotiations have been spectacular. Average tariff rates in industrial countries have fallen from the 30–40% range to the 5–10% range, with a further significant cut expected in the Uruguay Round.[95]

The GATT tariff negotiations are based upon the idea of reciprocity, i.e. that each contracting party will offer tariff reductions so that a mutually acceptable balance is achieved. The General Agreement does not guarantee, however, the achievement of any particular balance.[96] It

[94] See Panel on Newsprint, BISD 31S/114, 132 para. 52 (Case 59) ("The panel shared the view expressed before it relating to the fundamental importance of the security and predictability of GATT tariff bindings, a principle which constitutes a central obligation in the system of the General Agreement.")

[95] J. Jackson & W. Davey, note 1 supra, at 9.

[96] EEC—Imports of Beef from Canada, 28S/92 (Case 45).

only protects the negotiated results (and parties' reasonable expectations in respect thereof).[97]

The success that GATT has had in cutting tariffs is impressive, but it is not unqualified. First, many developing countries have agreed to bind relatively few of their tariff classifications and the bindings are at relatively high levels. Indeed, even some industrialized countries have not bound significant parts of their tariff schedules and most continue to charge much-higher-than-average tariffs on some products. For example, the EC has only a few bound tariffs on agricultural products; U.S. tariffs on textile and apparel products are typically high compared to average U.S. tariff levels.

Second, because the MFN clause guarantees that everyone benefits when a country reduces its tariffs, there is a free-rider problem, especially with respect to smaller industrialized countries. Since they are on the margin of the tariff negotiations between the major economic powers, i.e. the United States, the European Community and Japan, they have traditionally lowered their tariffs less than the major powers. This situation has not greatly improved in recent rounds because of the use of tariff cutting formulae that cut all tariffs by about the same percentage amount.[98] It is important not to overemphasize the free-rider problem, however. The normal consequence of the MFN principle is to generalize benefits. It would surely not be worth sacrificing that general principle and returning to the days of conditional MFN in order to correct this relatively minor problem.[99]

Renegotiation of Tariff Bindings. The tariff bindings contained in a country's schedule of concessions are not fixed in stone. The General Agreement provides for the renegotiation of bindings in Article XXVIII. A detailed examination of the procedure is not necessary for our purposes. Suffice it to note that such renegotiations can and do occur from time to time, that Article XXVIII establishes procedures with respect to which countries must be involved in the renegotiation (those who negotiated the concession originally, those with a principal supplying interest and those with a substantial interest all have rights) and that Article XXVIII:2 provides that the parties concerned shall endeavor to maintain a general level of concessions not less favorable to trade than that previously in effect. It should also be mentioned that renegotiations of tariff bindings are sometimes necessitated by the creation of customs unions and the modification of tariff classification rules.

[97] See note 56 supra and accompanying text.

[98] The formulae have provided for deeper cuts in higher tariffs, but the depth of the greater cuts has not eliminated the problem.

[99] See Pescatore, note 45 supra, at 28–32.

b. Protecting the Integrity of Tariff Bindings

When a country agrees to lower tariffs, it does not necessarily mean that imports will flow easily into that country. There are a number of indirect ways that the effect of a tariff reduction can be offset. The General Agreement contains a number of provisions designed to prevent the use of these indirect methods.

Customs Rules: Classification, Valuation, Origin, Fees and Formalities. In the customs laws of most countries, the customs authorities possess considerable administrative discretion, which can be used arbitrarily to prevent imports from entering the country. For example, almost every entry of goods through customs requires the completion of certain formalities, such as the filing of certain documents with the authorities, and the determination of several basic facts concerning the good, i.e. its classification (what is it?), its value (how much is it worth?) and its origin (where did it come from?). Proper classification is necessary to know what part of the tariff schedule is applicable. An origin determination is essential so that it can be determined whether the good is subject to the normal tariff rate or a preferential tariff rate or a discriminatory rate applicable to non-GATT states. Valuation is required because most tariffs are ad valorem. That is to say that the imported goods are valued and an import duty equal to a certain percentage of the value is assessed as a tariff or duty.

Arbitrary action in respect of these determinations could thwart the expected effects of a tariff binding. For example, the good could be classified into a tariff heading to which a higher duty rate is applicable or it could be assigned non-GATT origin. An agreement to cut tariffs from 20% to 10% could be frustrated if the rules on valuation allowed a country to offset the decline in duties by arbitrarily doubling the value of all imports.

The General Agreement does not deal directly with issues of classification.[100] In fact, most major GATT contracting parties have joined the Harmonized Commodity Description and Coding System,[101] which provides a mechanism for resolving disputes over classification, with an aim toward standardizing international practice. In addition, GATT dispute settlement panels have dealt with this problem indirectly by holding in one case that a parties' reclassification nullified and impaired the bene-

[100] See, however, GATT Art. II:5.

[101] International Convention on the Harmonized Commodity Description and Coding System, done at Brussels on June 14, 1983, and the Protocol thereto, done at Brussels on June 24, 1986.

fits of another by defeating the reasonable expectations of that party[102] and in another case that reclassification violated Article I's most-favored-nation provision.[103]

With respect to determination of origin, the General Agreement contains no specific rules.[104] Some GATT members are parties to the Kyoto Convention, an international agreement that deals with origin determination, but which does not lay down detailed mandatory rules on the subject.[105] Most countries in fact have several rules for origin determinations. For normal customs purposes, origin is in the last country where a substantial transformation of the goods took place (or a similar rule). Because that rule is relatively easy to meet (most assembly operations would arguably meet it), countries may apply stricter origin rules to determine if imports are entitled to preferential treatment, such as would be provided to developing countries or to members of a free trade area, or in some cases because they want to prevent a simple assembly operation from conferring origin. Because these strict origin requirements are being used more and more frequently, origin rules have become a subject of negotiation in the Uruguay Round.

The General Agreement does deal more concretely with the problem of valuation. First, Article II:3 prohibits changes to valuation rules that impair tariff concessions. Second, Article VII prohibits the use of arbitrary or fictitious values. Moreover, the signatories of the Tokyo Round Valuation Code agreed to use, if possible, the "transaction value" as the basis for customs valuation.[106] The transaction value is essentially the invoice value—the price actually paid by the buyer for the imported goods—with certain adjustments.[107]

[102] Germany—Imports of Sardines, BISD 1S/53 (Case 7).

[103] Spain—Tariff Treatment of Unroasted Coffee, BISD 28S/102, (Case 48), *but see* Japan—Imports of SPF Dimension Lumber, BISD 36S/167 (Case 73).

[104] Article IX requires nondiscriminatory treatment in respect of origin marketing requirements and limits the extent to which such requirements can be applied arbitrarily.

[105] International Convention on the Simplification and Harmonization of Customs Procedures, done at Kyoto, March 13, 1973 (The origin rules are in the subsequently agreed upon Annex D.1.).

[106] Agreement on the Implementation of Article VII and Protocol, BISD 26S/116.

[107] The Code established alternative methods of valuation that may be used if the transaction value is inappropriate. Such a situation could arise if the buyer and seller are related parties. But the Code then requires the use of the transaction value in identical or similar transactions, or, if that cannot be done, the use of constructed or deductive cost.

There are many formalities to be accomplished and documents to be filed to enter goods through customs. One obvious way to offset negotiated tariff reductions would be to impose fees for customs inspections or other services. GATT Article VIII permits this, but limits the amount of such charges to the cost of the services. A recent attempt by the United States to recover the budget of the U.S. Customs Service through a "customs user fee" was found to violate Article VIII.[108]

The General Agreement also attempts to prevent arbitrary enforcement of customs rules. Article X requires their publication and the possibility of appealing lower-level administrative decisions.

Domestic Subsidies. Another indirect method to offset the effect of lowering tariffs is to subsidize the domestic producer so as to neutralize the impact of the lower tariffs. The General Agreement has always required the reporting of domestic subsidies, but it has never restricted their use per se.[109] However, early in GATT's history, it became accepted that the use of domestic subsidies in respect of goods subject to bound tariffs could amount to the nullification and impairment of benefits that the exporter reasonably expected under the General Agreement because the subsidies would alter the competitive relationship between the domestic and imported products, and thereby entitle the exporter to compensation in order to right the balance of concessions.[110]

State Trading Operations. In the case of import monopolies (whether for specific products or global in extent), the level of tariffs may not be the most important factor determining import levels. Because of the monopoly position of the importer, it is possible that a tariff reduction would have no effect because the reduction might not be passed along in the form of lower prices to buyers by the monopoly. Moreover, since the monopoly makes all relevant purchasing decisions, it may decide not to increase imports above prior levels regardless of their prices or the existence of demand. Indeed, the government that negotiated a tariff concession could effectively offset it through its control of the import monopoly. The General Agreement attempts to regulate this problem

[108] See United States—Customs User Fee, BISD 35S/245 (Case 64). The fee was assessed on the basis of the value of imports rather than the cost of processing import transactions. Thus, a high-value import was charged a higher fee than a low-value import, even if the same processing time and cost were involved.

[109] See GATT Art. XVI.

[110] The Australian Subsidy on Ammonium Sulphate, II GATT, BISD 188 (Case 5). This position was recently reiterated in EEC—Payments and Subsidies Paid to Processors and Producers of Oilseeds and Related Animal-Feed Proteins, GATT Doc. L/6627, adopted 25 January 1990 (Case 77).

in two ways. First, it provides in Article II:4 that an import monopoly shall not operate so as to provide greater protection to a product subject to a tariff binding than is provided for in that binding.[111] Second, and more generally, it provides that a state monopoly must act "in a manner consistent with the general principles of non-discriminatory treatment prescribed in this Agreement," and that "such enterprises shall . . . make any such purchases or sales solely in accordance with commercial considerations."[112] These latter provisions, which are found in Article XVII, are generally not thought to be particularly effective and have been the subject of proposed amendments in the Uruguay Round.

Exchange Rates. Article XV:4 provides that GATT parties shall not use exchange rates to frustrate the intent of the provisions of the General Agreement.

2. Prohibiting Quotas and Other Non-Tariff Barriers—Article XI[113]

a. The Basic Provision

The second method by which the General Agreement seeks to reduce trade barriers is through its prohibition on the use of quotas and other nontariff barriers. Article XI:1 of the General Agreement provides:

> No prohibitions or restrictions other than duties, taxes or other charges, whether made effective through quotas, import or export licenses or other charges, shall be instituted or maintained by any contracting party on the importation of any product of the territory of any other contracting party or on the exportation or sale for export of any product destined for the territory of any other contracting party.

[111] See generally Canada—Distribution and Sale of Alcoholic Drinks, BISD 35S/37 (Case 65).

[112] The principal discussion of Article XVII by a GATT panel is found in Canada—Distribution and Sale of Alcoholic Drinks, BISD 35S/37 (Case 65). See also Japan—Restrictions on Imports of Certain Agricultural Products, BISD 35S/163 (Case 67); Republic of Korea—Restriction on Imports of Beef, BISD 36S/268 (Case 75).

[113] See generally J. Jackson, Law of GATT, note 1 supra, ch. 13.

This provision has been the subject of more GATT dispute settlement panel reports than any other. Generally, it has been interpreted strictly by the panels.[114]

The language of the Article XI goes beyond prohibiting quotas and applies by its terms to any "restriction" "on importation" "other than duties, taxes or other charges." It applies by its terms to export controls as well as import restrictions.[115] The word "restrictions" has been interpreted broadly. For example, a GATT panel has held that Article XI's prohibition of quotas and other non-tariff restrictions applies to a system of minimum import prices.[116] The same panel concluded that a system of automatic import licensing did not violate Article XI, but non-automatic licensing systems have been found to violate Article XI.[117] In another case, a panel found that a series of Japanese measures restricting the export of certain semiconductors at below-cost prices violated Article XI, even though those measures did not formally prohibit exports.[118] Because of the nature of the Japanese controls, the panel's reasoning suggests that Article XI:1 bans voluntary export restraints and export price controls if the government is somehow involved.[119] The ban on non-tariff restrictions is one that may in the future be subject to even broader interpretations, as parties become more aware of such restrictions as tariffs fall. It should be noted, however, that the aim of

[114] See e.g., EEC—Quantitative Restrictions Against Imports from Hong Kong, BISD 30S/129 (Case 53) (panel emphatically rejected arguments that quotas violating Article XI could be justified by their longstanding existence or the special circumstances of the industry protected).

[115] Canada—Export of Unprocessed Herring and Salmon, BISD 35S/98 (Case 66).

[116] EEC—Imports of Processed Fruits and Vegetables, BISD 25S/68 (Case 38).

[117] Japan—Trade in Semi-Conductors, BISD 35S/116 (Case 68) (three months' delay in issuing export licenses).

[118] Japan—Trade in Semi-Conductors, BISD 35S/116 (Case 68). The panel rejected a claim by Japan that its measure merely prohibited dumping and thus was permissible under Article VI. In the view of the panel, Article VI authorized actions only in respect of injurious dumping and only by the importing country.

[119] See note 139 infra and accompanying text. In considering whether a challenged quota was administered in accordance with Article XIII's rules on the non-discriminatory administration of quotas, VRAs (voluntary restraint agreements) applicable to the product in question have been treated as quantitative restrictions. See Norway—Restrictions on Imports of Certain Textile Products, BISD 27S/119 (Case 41); EEC Restrictions on Imports of Apples from Chile, BISD 27S/98 (Case 43).

Article XI is to regulate measures applicable to imports at the border; measures affecting imports after they have passed the border, such as a requirement that a company give preference to the purchase of domestic products over imported products, have been held to be regulated by Article III:4.[120]

Despite these broad interpretations, historically, Article XI has not been as effective in controlling trade barriers as one might suspect. This is because there are a number of exceptions to Article XI's ban.

b. The Formal Exceptions

The Balance of Payments Exception. First, there is the Article XII exception for measures taken for balance of payments reasons. For the first decade or so of GATT's existence, most GATT members qualified for this exception, and even as they corrected their balance of payments problems in the 1950's and 1960's, many contracting parties did not move rapidly to remove all of the quantitative restrictions they had in effect. Although it was eventually found that these so-called "residual restrictions" violated Article XI and should be removed forthwith without delay or compensation, they disappeared slowly because cases were not often brought to challenge them.[121]

Today, the Article XII exception (and the similar provisions of Article XVIII applicable to developing countries) is still of critical importance because most developing countries have balance of payments problems and use quotas to help combat them. Even a country such as South Korea, which moved into a significant balance of payments surplus situation several years ago, has only recently conceded that the exception no longer applies to it and started to remove its quotas

[120] See Canada—Adminstration of Foreign Investment Review Act (FIRA), BISD 30S/140 (Case 54) and text accompanying notes 75–80 supra. It should be noted, however, that an interpretative note to Article XI–XIV and XVIII provides that the terms "import restrictions" or "export restrictions" include restrictions made effective through state-trading companies. Relying on this note, one panel found that restrictions on the number of sales outlets for imported alcoholic beverages violated Article XI:1. Canada—Distribution and Sale of Alcoholic Drinks, BISD 35S/37 (Case 65).

[121] See J. Jackson, Law of GATT, note 1 supra, at 707–710; EEC—Quantitative Restrictions against Imports of Certain Products from Hong Kong, BISD 30S/129 (Case 53).

generally.[122] But for most developing countries the balance of payments exceptions continue to exempt them from the most significant GATT obligations. A GATT committee reviews the operation of Articles XII and XVIII, but has not exercised particularly effective control over their use.

Two further comments on the balance-of-payments exception are appropriate. First, Article XII only allows quotas, not tariffs, to be used to correct balance of payments problems. This rule is inconsistent with the general GATT preference for using tariffs instead of quotas,[123] and has been criticized and ignored from time by countries, such as the United Kingdom and the United States, who have imposed tariff surcharges to correct balance of payments problems.[124] Second, Article XV provides for coordination between GATT and the IMF in respect of balance of payment measures.[125]

The Agricultural Quotas Exception.[126] The second exception to GATT's quota prohibition is found in paragraph 2 of Article XI and is largely concerned with agricultural products. Although the exception is narrowly drawn—it applies principally to quotas used to help enforce government programs that operate to restrict domestic production or marketing of agricultural products, and despite the fact that it has usually been applied restrictively by GATT panels to strike down trade barriers,[127] for many years agricultural restrictions were simply not attacked in GATT. This is probably due to the fact that the United States

[122] The Korean balance of payments controls were the subject of a GATT dispute settlement proceeding in which the panel found that the improvement in the Korean balance of payments was such that they should be phased out. Korea—Restrictions on Imports of Beef, BISD 36S/268 (Case 75).

[123] See text accompanying notes 93 infra.

[124] See J. Jackson and W. Davey, note 1 supra, at 874–879. The action of the United Kingdom was examined in United Kingdom—Temporary Import Charges, BISD 15S/113 (Case 25) in which the working party seemed tacitly to approve of the use of import charges in lieu of quotas.

[125] See Republic of Korea—Restrictions on Imports of Beef, BISD 36S/268 (Case 75).

[126] See generally Davey, Article XI of the General Agreement on Tariffs and Trade: A Legal Analysis of the Agricultural Exceptions, published by Sistema Económico Latinoamericano as Technical Paper on the Uruguay Round, No. 19 (1989).

[127] The principal case on the exception is Japan—Restrictions on Imports of Agricultural Products, BISD 35S/163 (Case 67). See also EEC—Restrictions on Imports of Dessert Apples, BISD 36S/93 (Case 69) (Noting that the exception has never been successfully invoked).

obtained a waiver of Article XI in 1955 in respect of a number of agricultural commodities in respect of which the U.S. applied quotas not in accordance with Article XI's terms. Thus, although the argument was never accepted by a GATT panel, it has been suggested by many, in dispute settlement proceedings and elsewhere, that it was inappropriate to apply Article XI strictly (or at all) to other countries' agricultural product quotas. In recent years, however, the United States and others have started to invoke Article XI, particularly where the offender has a large trade surplus, such as is the case with Japan and South Korea. The quota prohibition has been applied in other situations as well, for example, against Canada, Norway and the European Community, such that there have been proposals in the Uruguay Round to rewrite it so as to expand the scope of the Article XI:2 exceptions.

Administration of Quotas. In cases where the General Agreement permits the use of quotas, Article XIII requires that the quotas be administered on a non-discriminatory basis.[128] The basic aim of Article XIII is to create a trade pattern under a quota regime that reflects the relative market shares that countries would have held in the absence of quotas. Quotas are usually administered pursuant to a licensing system and in the Tokyo Round a side agreement on the use of import licensing was reached.[129]

c. The Informal Exemptions—Agriculture and Textiles

The General Agreement does not formally exempt any sectors from the quota rules, except as outlined above. Nonetheless, over time trade in agriculture and textiles seems to have become largely conducted outside of GATT rules.

Article XI in fact has certain special provisions applicable only to *agriculture.*[130] Over the years, however, GATT rules have not been rigorously applied to agricultural trade, on either the import or export side. In the case of agricultural imports, the United States obtained a waiver from the Article XI quota ban for certain of its agricultural programs in 1955.[131] Although few other formal waivers have been granted in respect of agricultural products, other countries have some-

[128] Article XIV contains several exceptions to Article XIII's nondiscrimination requirements.

[129] Agreement on Import Licensing Procedures, BISD 26S/154.

[130] See text accompanying notes 126–127 supra.

[131] Decision of March 5, 1955, BISD 3S/32.

times acted as if they view the U.S. waiver as generally applicable. This lack of discipline is also exemplified by the agricultural trade policies of the European Community. In constructing its Common Agricultural Policy (CAP), the EC unbound most of its agricultural tariffs, which means that it is free to charge any import duty it wishes. In fact, the EC has often implemented the CAP by using variable levies, which are flexible import charges set (and adjusted regularly) so as to make imported agricultural products more expensive than the comparable EC product. They effectively keep imports out of the European market. Developing countries, of course, can usually impose quotas on agricultural products pursuant to the balance of payments exceptions of Articles XII and XVIII. As noted above, GATT panel decisions in recent years have strictly enforced Article XI and found many agricultural quotas GATT illegal,[132] but the fact that there is little discipline exercised over U.S., EC and developing countries quota policies has meant that a very significant proportion of agricultural trade is not subject to the rules intended to be applied to it under the General Agreement.

International trade between the developed and developing countries in *textiles and apparel products* is mainly conducted under the Multi-Fibre Arrangement (MFA), which is administered by the GATT Textiles Committee.[133] Under the MFA, developed countries are permitted to negotiate specific quotas for the myriad textile and apparel products subject to the MFA. In theory, the MFA provides that these quotas will grow steadily over time and that the developed countries will assist their textiles industries to adjust structurally to import competition, i.e. to become competitive or to turn to other pursuits. The MFA also permits special trade restrictive measures to be taken by developed countries to deal with market disruption, such as a sudden surge in developing country imports. By and large, the developing countries are very dissatisfied with the MFA. They feel that little structural adjustment has taken place in the developed world and that the quotas for developing countries are not large enough. One goal of the Uruguay Round is to reach agreement on how and when this sector could be brought back under regular GATT rules. It has been suggested that if progress satisfactory to the developing countries is not made on this topic, they will not participate in the finalization of the Uruguay Round results.

[132] See note 127 supra and accompanying text.

[133] Arrangement Regarding International Trade in Textiles, BISD 21S/3; extended by Protocols appearing in id. at 24S/5; id. at 28S/3; id. at 33S/7.

3. The Escape Clause: An Exception to the Tariff Bindings and Quota Ban[134] for Seriously Injured Industries

There is essentially one general exception to the bound tariff levels and the ban on quotas and other restrictions and that is the so-called Escape Clause of Article XIX. It is a basic tenet of GATT that expanded international trade is desirable. It has long been recognized, however, that international trade, even if beneficial overall, produces winners and losers within a national economy. As lower-priced or higher-quality imports gain market share, consumers obviously benefit, but the domestic producer of competing products loses market share and may have to lay off workers or even close down. Recognizing this reality, the General Agreement in Article XIX provides that

> [i]f, as a result of unforeseen developments and of the effect of the obligations incurred by a contracting party under this Agreement, including tariff concessions, any product is being imported in the territory of that contracting party in such increased quantities and under such conditions as to cause or threaten serious injury to domestic producers of like or directly competing products, the contracting party shall be free . . . to suspend the obligation in whole or in part or to withdraw or modify the concession.

Article XIX provides that in the normal case the party wishing to avail itself of Article XIX should notify GATT and allow interested parties to consult with it in respect of its proposed action. If action is taken without consultation, consultations should occur thereafter promptly. Affected parties have the right, subject to disapproval by the Contracting Parties, to suspend substantially equivalent concessions to compensate themselves for their losses. Since Article XIX is a general exception to GATT obligations, the importing country may raise its tariffs in excess of the Article II bound levels or impose import quotas that would otherwise be banned by Article XI or take other trade restrictive action. Although the language of Article XIX is not explicit, it is generally accepted that Article XIX measures would have to be imposed without discrimination as to the origin of the injurious products.[135] Furthermore,

[134] See generally J. Jackson, Law of GATT, note 1 supra, ch. 23; J. Jackson, World Trading System, note 1 supra, ch. 7; J. Jackson & W. Davey, note 1 supra, ch. 9.

[135] Norway—Restrictions on Imports of Textiles, BISD 27S/119 (Case 41). See materials collected in J. Jackson & W. Davey, note 1 supra, at 595–606.

Article XIX provides that restrictions should be maintained only to the extent and for such time as may be necessary to prevent or remedy injury.

The standards applied to invocations of Article XIX are not particularly rigorous.[136] Nonetheless, it is often ignored by GATT members seeking to protect their domestic industries. Particularly in recent years, parties seeking to restrict imports have often informally contacted the relevant exporting country and prevailed upon that country to curtail its exports "voluntarily," so as to avoid formal action by the importing country.[137] These voluntary restraint agreements (VRAs) or safeguards, as they are often called, have become particularly common in the automobile, steel and electronics industries.[138] Although such export restraints have not been authorized by GATT waivers and probably violate the ban on export quotas contained in GATT Article XI (if the exporter's government is involved), neither of the directly affected countries is likely to complain and no such cases have been brought in GATT to date by third parties.[139]

[136] In an early case, the contracting parties seemed to say that if a country acted in good faith, they would not second guess that country on the applicability of Article XIX. See "Hatters Fur Case" in J. Jackson & W. Davey, note 1 supra, at 556.

[137] See generally J. Jackson, World Trading System, note 1 supra, ch. 7.

[138] Japan has restrained exports of automobiles, steel and electronic products to the United States and most European countries. Exports of steel to the United States and the EC are generally restrained by a whole network of restraint agreements.

[139] One very important panel decision dealt with these issues in a somewhat indirect manner in a case involving the alleged dumping by Japanese companies of semiconductors. (The problem of dumping and GATT's provisions with respect thereto are discussed in the text accompanying notes 140–152 infra.) In 1985, the United States prevailed upon Japan to agree (i) to stop dumping semiconductors in the U.S. market, (ii) to grant foreign companies more effective access to the Japanese market for semiconductors and (iii) to stop dumping semiconductors in other markets. The European Community challenged items (ii) and (iii) of this arrangement in GATT. The panel found that item (ii) was permissible because the undertaking by the Japanese government to promote imports was nondiscriminatory (i.e. it benefitted all exporters, not just U.S. exporters) and that item (iii) violated Article XI's ban on export restrictions and quotas because the Japanese government had effectively regulated the price of semiconductor exports. Although the case involved dumping, item (iii) of the agreement was similar to a voluntary restraint agreement (VRA) and the panel's reasoning could be extended to hold that VRAs distort trade in a manner that infringes the GATT rights of third countries. Japan—Trade in Semi-Conductors, BISD 35S/116 (Case 66).

VRAs are favored by governments of the importing countries because, inter alia, (i) they are informal and easily adaptable (no GATT review is had and they can be changed quickly), (ii) no compensation needs to be provided directly to the exporting country, as is provided for under Article XIX, and (iii) they can be selective, i.e. aimed at only one country, whereas Article XIX seems to require MFN treatment, which would require controlling imports from all producing countries. Exporting countries accept VRAs in lieu of action under Article XIX because if the importing country implements formal trade restrictions, it may be difficult to get rid of them later, whereas VRAs can be terminated by the exporting country. Furthermore, because an export restraint limits supply, it typically raises prices of imports, which redounds to the benefit of the exporters (in contrast to a tariff, which would also cut imports by raising their price, but which benefits the importing country's government by increasing tax revenue). Thus compensation is provided indirectly—by raising prices to consumers instead of affording the exporting country broader access to other domestic markets.

One of the major issues in the Tokyo Round and one that continues to be controversial in the Uruguay Round, is the extent to which new rules on safeguards are necessary. The developing countries in particular have been pressing for the negotiation of a safeguards code. Among the issues under consideration in the Uruguay Round are the question of whether safeguards should be permitted to be selective, whether their use should require compensation to be given to affected parties, the extent to which GATT should supervise or review the application of safeguards measures and whether use of safeguards should be tied to structural adjustment efforts.

C. REGULATION OF UNFAIR TRADE PRACTICES

The General Agreement does not have general provisions regulating the use of unfair trade practices. This is in contrast to the Havana Charter of the ITO, which had a separate section dealing with restrictive

There have also been two cases where a country that declined to agree to a VRA has contested quotas applied to its products. In considering whether the challenged quota was administered in accordance with Article III's rules on the nondiscriminatory administration of quotas, the other VRAs applicable to the product in question have been treated as quantitative restrictions. See Norway—Restrictions on Imports of Certain Textile Products, BISD 27S/119 (Case 41); EEC Restrictions on Imports of Apples from Chile, BISD 27S/98 (Case 43).

business practices. Under Chapter V of the Havana Charter, ITO member states would have been under an obligation to take appropriate measures to prevent private business practices affecting international trade that restrained competition, limited access to markets or fostered monopolistic control *if* such practices had harmful effects on the expansion of production and trade and interfered with the achievement of the objectives of the Charter. In particular, the following business practices were mentioned as possible subjects of regulation: price fixing, territorial or customer allocation agreements, discrimination against particular enterprises, production limits or quotas, agreements restricting development or use of technology, and the extension of rights under intellectual property laws to matters not within the scope of such laws. The Charter had procedures for handling claims by one member that the foregoing business practices were having the proscribed harmful effects.

None of these provisions on restrictive business practices appears in the General Agreement. It does have some provisions, however, dealing with business practices, and, in particular, the practice of dumping and the export of subsidized products. First, GATT condemns, but does not prohibit, dumping and authorizes antidumping duties to be imposed to offset dumping if a country's domestic industry is materially injured. Second, it regulates the use of subsidies and authorizes the imposition of countervailing duties to offset them if a country's domestic industry is materially injured by subsidization.

1. Dumping and Antidumping Duties[140]

Article VI authorizes a GATT contracting party to apply duties in excess of the Article II bound rates to offset the effects of dumping. Such an action can be taken unilaterally, but is permitted only if the domestic industry producing like products in the importing country has been materially injured.[141] Although the General Agreement does not define material injury or compare it to Article XIX's serious injury standard, it is commonly accepted that the material injury standard should be easier to meet because the imports at issue are unfairly

[140] For a recent review of the procedures and substance of antidumping law in the four countries that most frequently apply antidumping duties, see J. Jackson & E. Vermulst (eds.), Antidumping Law and Practice: A Comparative Study (1989).

[141] The determination of dumping and material injury can be reviewed in GATT. See, e.g., New Zealand—Imports of Electric Transformers, BISD 32S/54 (Case 59) (insufficient evidence of injury found).

traded. During the Tokyo Round, a side agreement was negotiated with respect to antidumping actions.[142]

Dumping is the sale of a product for export at a price below that charged in the home market or below that necessary to recover the cost of producing the product.[143] Antidumping actions are common in the United States, the European Community, Canada and Australia, and, recently, a number of other countries have adopted antidumping laws or have started to use pre-existing laws. By and large, in the past few years the principal targets of antidumping actions have been the exporting countries of the Pacific Rim and the nonmarket economies of Eastern Europe.

In considering antidumping issues, three topics merit discussion: The validity of the rationale for antidumping laws; the procedures used to conduct antidumping investigations and the substantive rules applied to determine whether or not dumping has occurred.

The rational of antidumping laws.[144] Antidumping laws were adopted at a time when price discrimination was thought to be undesirable. More recent economic theory suggests that in the absence of predatory behavior, which is probably quite rare, dumped imports should be treated like any other imports in analyzing their effect on a national economy.[145] This is also true of imports priced below cost, as normal antitrust principles would not penalize such practices absent predatory intent. Since imports are generally beneficial, serious questions are raised as to whether antidumping laws are justified. This is particularly true to the extent that national laws do not penalize price discrimination or below-cost sales in

[142] Agreement on the Implementation of Article VI, BISD 26S/171. The agreement is often referred to as the GATT Antidumping Code.

[143] Prior to 1974, dumping was generally thought to be limited to exporting below home market prices. However, since a 1974 change in the U.S. antidumping law and the adoption of the Tokyo Round Antidumping Code, most countries have accepted that below-cost export prices also constitute dumping.

[144] See generally Davey, Antidumping Laws: A Time for Restriction, in 1988 Fordham Corp. L. Inst., at page 8–1 (B. Hawk ed.).

[145] Sporadic dumping, that is dumping that occurs for a while and then ceases but resumes thereafter, might cause adjustment costs in the importing country as its industry had to expand and contract its output in response to the ebb and flow of dumped imports. Arguably, these adjustments costs might outweigh the benefits of low prices received by the importing country's consumers, but it is unclear (i) that that would in fact be the case typically and (ii) that the exporting dumper would easily abandon newly won markets. See id. at page 8–13.

domestic transactions, which is generally the case.[146] To penalize imports in such a case would be discriminatory. Nonetheless, even without a persuasive economic rationale, antidumping laws may serve a legitimate function. In times of economic stress, they provide a means by which domestic firms can seek some respite from import competition. This function may be a useful one for easing world progress toward freer international trade.[147]

Investigation procedures. The GATT Antidumping Code outlines minimum procedural requirements for antidumping investigations. Generally speaking, once an antidumping action is initiated, the administrative authority undertakes two investigations: one to determine if dumping has occurred; one to determine if material injury has been suffered. In the dumping investigation, the exporters are requested to supply information about their domestic and export prices (and their costs if below-cost sales are alleged). The administrative authority reviews the responses to its questionnaires and verifies them, usually by on-site visits to the companies involved. If an exporter does not cooperate, the "best information available" may be used, which is often the allegations of the domestic industry.

Based on the price data, adjusted to make the sales comparable, a dumping margin is calculated and translated into a duty rate that offsets the dumping margin.[148] This duty will be collected on a prospective basis because the GATT Antidumping Code prohibits use of retroactive duties except in rare cases. In the United States, this duty rate is collected at the time of importation as an estimate of the antidumping duties owed. Later, in annual reviews, the actual dumping margin and duty owed are calculated and a refund is given or additional duties collected, as appropriate. In the EC, the rate serves as the definitive

[146] There are some national laws that prohibit price discrimination, such as the Robinson-Patman Act in the United States. However, it appears that such laws are (i) often not enforced with much rigor and (ii) much more narrowly drawn than antidumping statutes in respect of conduct covered and defenses permitted. See id. at pages 8–16 to 8–21.

[147] J. Jackson, World Trading System, note 1 supra, at 244.

[148] Typically, the price of each export transaction is compared to the average domestic price, calculated over the investigative period (e.g. six months in the United States). So-called "negative margins," i.e. export sales prices above the domestic average price, are treated as if the export price and the domestic average price were equivalent. This means that if prices have changed in the six month period, some dumping will likely be found, even if, on a day-to-day basis, identical prices are charged in the domestic and export markets, a result that some find objectionable and unfair. See Davey, note 144 supra, at 8–25 to 8–29.

duty for imports, subject to a refund procedure that is seldom successfully invoked. Exporters may be permitted to settle dumping cases by undertaking to stop their dumping.[149]

While the dumping investigation is proceeding, the question of material injury is also considered. Duties are imposed only if both dumping and injury are found. In the EC, to the extent that the injury found can be redressed with a duty rate below the dumping margin, such a lesser duty is imposed. Although the GATT Code encourages such provisions, it does not require them and the U.S. law affords the administering authority *no* discretion in this regard at all, largely because Congress felt that prior to the 1979 changes in the law, such discretion had been too freely exercised to the detriment of U.S. industry.

Substantive issues. There are many substantive issues that arise in the administration of antidumping laws. They cannot be discussed in any detail here, but several of the more important issues will be highlighted. First, what adjustments are necessary to make the home market and export prices comparable? The terms of sales (e.g. FOB or CIF, warranties), the level of sale (wholesale or retail) and even the products themselves may differ between the home and export markets. It is therefore necessary to make adjustments to the prices actually charged in order to eliminate legitimate factors that explain differences in home market and export prices. The adjustment process is one of the most controversial aspects of antidumping law since there will always be adjustments that arguably should be made and often the extent of the adjustments allowed will have a significant effect on the outcome of the investigation.[150]

Second, in cases alleging below-cost sales, there is considerable controversy over how the cost of a product should be calculated. In the case of products that require extensive research and development or plant investment, whether they will be deemed to have been sold below cost is largely determined by how those R & D and investment costs are allocated over time.

A third difficult set of issues revolves around the problem of causation. The 1967 GATT Antidumping Code (now superceded by the Tokyo Round Antidumping Code) required that before antidumping

[149] Undertakings are common in the EC, but seldom occur in the United States because Congress has so tightly conditioned their use as to make them an unattractive option.

[150] For a discussion of the types of adjustments made and how adjustment practices may tilt in favor of finding dumping, see J. Jackson & E. Vermulst, note 140 supra, at 451–452.

duties could be imposed, it had to be established that the dumped imports were the principal cause of the injury suffered by the domestic industry.[151] The Tokyo Round Code only requires that the dumped imports be a cause of the injury and that other causes of injury not be attributed to dumping. It is left unclear what connection must be shown between dumping and injury. For example, if the dumping margin is 5%, but it is clear that the imports would still be able to underprice the domestic producers even if there were no dumping, has dumping caused the injury suffered by domestic industry? In other words should one consider the dumping margin in the injury analysis? If the investigation covers allegedly dumped imports form several countries, should the effects of the dumped imports from each country be cumulated to assess whether material injury has been suffered?

A fourth issue concerns the problem of circumvention. The General Agreement authorizes antidumping duties to be imposed if the domestic makers of like products are suffering injury. Generally, product definitions in an antidumping order are fairly narrow. What rules should apply if a company changes the features of its product so that it is no longer described by the terms of the antidumping order? What if the company decides to shift part of its assembly or manufacturing operations so that the product arguably no longer originates in the country whose products are subject to the antidumping order? To what extent can these "new" products be subject to the preexisting antidumping findings without the need to go through a new investigation. The United States and the EC have taken different approaches to this issue, and it is currently unclear whether the approaches will be found compatible with GATT rules or if the Uruguay Round negotiations will legitimize such measures.[152]

[151] Agreement on Interpretation of Article VI, BISD 15S/74, art. 3.

[152] The EC anticircumvention rule applied a charge on a product assembled in the EC if (i) the product was subject to an antidumping duty, (ii) the assembly operation was operated by a party related to the dumper and had been commenced after the dumping investigation began and (iii) less than 40% of the value of the materials used in the product was from sources other than the dumping country. On a Japanese complaint, a panel concluded that the EC provision violated Article III:2 because it was an internal tax not applied to EC origin like products. ECC—Regulation of Imports of Parts and Components, GATT Doc. L/6657, adopted 16 May 1990) (Case 79). The U.S. law would apply the antidumping duty applicable to the product in question to the imported components of the product in certain circumstances. Since the U.S. measure is applied at the border as an antidumping duty, it would not be subject to the panel's reasoning, but it might be attacked on other grounds, such as the fact that no separate dumping and injury investigation of the components is undertaken.

In those countries in which antidumping proceedings are common they have become viewed as inherent rights of domestic industry, at least in the eyes of some. Whether that view will remain is uncertain. As other countries make more frequent use of such measures, exporters may start pressing for international restrictions on their use, as has already occurred in the Uruguay Round where Pacific Rim exporters are pressing for such limits. Moreover, as trade barriers fall, particularly in free trade areas and customs unions, antidumping actions are often abolished since it is assumed that low priced exports will flow back to compete on the higher priced domestic market, thus effectively eliminating the possibility of dumping. Thus, in the future it is possible that antidumping actions may become less of a factor in international trade, particularly as tariffs and other barriers to trade fall.

2. Regulation of Subsidies

Although the General Agreement did not initially restrict the use of subsidies by explicit language, later practice and amendments have resulted in GATT provisions and practices that do so. Regulation of subsidies is a controversial topic.[153] One of the principal reasons for the controversy is that many countries feel that it is entirely appropriate for governments to provide certain kinds of subsidies to industry. These subsidies are typically motivated by domestic political and economic considerations, not by desires to increase exports. Consequently, they are not thought to be unfair. Moreover, for economists, the importing country would seem to be the beneficiary of subsidies granted by other countries. Thus, the application of increased duties would seem to be unwise as any harm is to the subsidizing country.

It may be necessary, however, to have some limits on the use of subsidies. For example, export subsidies, i.e. subsidies conditioned on the export of products, may be viewed as unfair since the domestic industry has to compete with the treasury of the exporter's country. Recognizing this problem, GATT has generally restricted export subsidies.[154] Moreover, even domestic subsidies can be used in a way that may increase trade tensions if the subsidies effectively lead to increased exports through, for example, support of companies in recessions or targeting, by which some industries are selected by the government for special treatment, incentives and assistance. Even if motivated by

[153] See G. Hufbauer & J. Erb, Subsidies in International Trade 5–6 (1984). See generally J. Jackson, World Trading System, note 1 supra, at 249–273.

[154] See text accompanying notes 157–160 infra.

domestic considerations, these sorts of subsidies may well promote countersubsidization and bad feelings since they will likely lead to the displacement of workers in the importing country. Such countersubsidization would in the end make everyone worse off. Consequently, unlike antidumping laws, rules limiting the use of subsidies are likely to be a permanent feature of international trade law. Indeed, customs unions and free trade areas typically try to control the use of subsidies by the constituent elements for the reasons mentioned above.

Subsidies are subject to regulation under GATT rules in three ways. First, use of domestic subsidies may constitute nullification or impairment under Article XXIII. Second, export subsidies are strictly controlled. Third, certain subsidies may be offset by countervailing duties.

a. Domestic Subsidies as Nullification or Impairment

GATT rules restrict the use of domestic subsidies insofar as they negate the value of negotiated bindings.[155] The Subsidies Code negotiated in the Tokyo Round also provides that its signatories shall seek to avoid using domestic subsidies so as to cause serious prejudice to the interests of another signatory.[156]

b. Export Subsidies

Under Article XVI, paragraphs 3 and 4 and the Subsidies Code, articles 9 and 10, the use of export subsidies on non-primary products is prohibited and the use of such subsidies on primary products is limited in that their use is not to result in the subsidizing country obtaining "a more than equitable share of world export trade" in that product.[157] The Subsidies Code does not explicitly define what is an export subsidy, but it does contain an illustrative list of export subsidies.[158] The use of export

[155] See text accompanying note 110 supra.

[156] Agreement on Interpretation and Application of Articles VI, XVI and XXIII (the "Subsidies Code"), BISD 26S/56, art. II(2).

[157] The ban on export subsidies on nonprimary products is applicable only to those GATT members that accepted a cut-off date when Article XVI was added to the General Agreement, generally the OECD countries (see BISD, 9S/32), or to those developed country GATT members that acceded to the Subsidies Code. The Subsidies Code allows developing countries to use export subsidies so long as their use does not result in serious prejudice to the interests of others. Subsidies Code, art. 14.

[158] Article XVI:4 suggests that an export subsidy is one that results in a product being sold for export at a price below that at which it is sold domestically.

subsidies on primary products has not been effectively controlled by the "equitable share" language. While one early, pre-Subsidies Code GATT decision suggested that this standard could be used to control effectively the use of export subsidies,[159] a more recent decision by a panel appointed under the Subsidies Code essentially concluded that the language was too imprecise to be applied to world wheat trade.[160] Consequently, there has been an increase in the use of export subsidies on certain products, particularly wheat, by the EC and the United States, much to the displeasure of other exporters such as Argentina, Australia and Canada which do not engage and cannot afford to participate in subsidy wars. Improving GATT control of export subsidies is one of the more controversial topics for negotiation in the Uruguay Round.

c. Subsidies and Countervailing Duties

Article VI of the General Agreement allows countervailing duties to be imposed in excess of Article II bound rates to the extent necessary to offset the injurious effects of subsidized imports. Like antidumping procedures, countervailing duty actions are subject to a Tokyo Round code.[161] Although a number of countries have countervailing duty statutes, only the United States frequently applies such duties.[162]

Countervail procedures. The procedures followed in a countervail case are essentially the same as those followed in an antidumping case. The basic difference is that the non-injury part of the investigation is focussed on the existence and amount of a countervailable subsidy, not the measurement of a dumping margin.

[159] French Assistance to Exports of Wheat and Wheat Flour, BISD 7S/46 (Case 17). See also EEC—Refunds on Exports of Sugar, BISD 26S/290 (Case 39).

[160] European Economic Community—Subsidies on Exports of Wheat Flour, GATT Doc. SCM/42. See GATT, BISD 31S/259. The text of the report can be found in 18 BNA U.S. Export Weekly 899–916 (1983). The panel was criticized by some for having abdicated its responsibility, and its report has not been adopted by the Subsidies and Countervailing Measures Committee, which is the body responsible for dispute settlement under the Subsidies Code. Indeed, one result of the decision was that dispute settlement under the Subsidies Code broke down completely as one or more signatories have blocked the adoption of all subsequent panel reports issued under the Code's dispute settlement provisions.

[161] Agreement on Interpretation and Application of Articles VI, XVI and XXIII (the "Subsidies Code"), BISD 26S/56.

[162] J. Jackson & W. Davey, note 1 supra, at 727.

Substantive issues in countervail cases. The principal substantive issue in a countervail case is whether the challenged subsidies are countervailable. At the moment there is a not an international agreement on what kinds of subsidies are countervailable. This is, of course, disturbing since one can imagine very broad definitions of subsidies, including one that would require the calculation of all benefits of government received by an exporter, from police and fire protection to national defense, from the education of its workers to infrastructure benefits such as roads and sewers. If such a definition were adopted, international trade could be completely choked off, as there is at present no requirement that countervailing duties be reduced by an amount equal to similar subsidies received by the domestic competitors of a subsidized exporter. Negotiations in the Tokyo Round and in the Uruguay Round have attempted to establish a list of prohibited subsidies, the use of which would violate GATT rules; permitted subsidies, the use of which would not be subject to trade remedies; and other subsidies, the use of which would not violate those rules, but would be subject to countervailing duties. So far, no such agreement has been reached.

In the Untied States, which is the principal user of countervailing duties, there is an administrative practice, which is supported by some statutory language, that provides that only "specific," as opposed to "generally available," subsidies are countervailable.[163] While there is some uncertainty where the line is to be drawn, subsidies that are in fact generally used by several industries are not countervailed, while those that are in theory available generally, but in fact only used by one industry, are countervailable.[164]

There are also difficult measurement issues in calculating countervailing duties. First, it is necessary to decide what the amount of a subsidy is. For example, should the focus be on the cost to the government of the subsidy or the amount of benefit received by the subsidized company? Second, it is necessary to allocate the subsidy over time and units produced so that the amount of the offsetting duty can be calculated.

D. THE GENERAL EXCEPTIONS TO GATT OBLIGATIONS—ARTICLES XX AND XXI

Article XX provides a general exception to the provisions of the General Agreement for measures that are (i) not applied in an arbitrary or unjustifiably discriminatory manner between countries, (ii) not a

[163] See 19 U.S.C. sec. 1677(5).
[164] See Cabot Corp. v. United States, 620 F. Supp. 722 (CIT 1985).

disguised restriction on international trade and (iii), inter alia, necessary to protect public morals or health or to secure compliance with GATT consistent regulations, such as those relating to customs enforcement, enforcement of government authorized import monopolies, protection of patents, trademarks and copyrights and the prevention of deceptive practices.[165] Generally speaking, GATT panels have strictly enforced the conditions imposed in Article XX. In particular, they have narrowly construed the requirement that measures be "necessary."[166] For example, in a case involving EC anticircumvention duties, which were designed to prevent technically legal "evasion" of antidumping duties,[167] the panel concluded that GATT-inconsistent measures designed to enforce the *objectives* of GATT-consistent rules were not permitted, and that such measures would be permitted only if necessary for the actual enforcement of the rules.[168]

Article XXI—the so-called national security exception—provides that the General Agreement does not prevent any contracting party from taking any action which it considers necessary for the protection of its essential security interests (i) relating to fissionable materials, (ii) relating to arms traffic and traffic in goods carried on for the purpose of military supply and (iii) taken in time of war or other emergency in international relations.[169] A Nicaraguan challenge to a U.S. trade embargo against it in the mid-1980s left unclear what the proper interpretation of Article XXI is and the question of whether a panel can review its invocation by a contracting party.[170]

[165] The exception also allows for measures relating to gold and silver imports and exports, products of prison labor, national treasures, export or distribution of products in short supply, and conservation of exhaustible natural resources, as well as measures relating to intergovernmental commodities agreements.

[166] See, e.g., United States—Section 337 of the Tariff Act of 1930, BISD 36S/345 (Case 74); Japan—Restrictions on Imports of Certain Agricultural Products, BISD 35S/163 (Case 67); Canada—Administration of the Foreign Investment Review Act (FIRA), BISD 30S/140 (Case 54). Panels have also narrowly construed the exception for conservation of exhaustible resources. See Canada—Export of Unprocessed Herring and Salmon, BISD 35S/98 (Case 66); United States—Prohibition of Imports of Tuna, BISD 29S/91 (Case 50).

[167] The case is described in note 152 supra.

[168] EEC—Restriction of Imports of Parts and Components, GATT Doc. L/6657, adopted 16 May 1990 (Case 79).

[169] Article XXI also allows a country to refuse to disclose information based on security grounds and to take action required by the United Nations charter, such as imposing economic sanctions at the direction of the Security Council.

[170] See GATT, GATT Activities 1986, at pages 58–59; GATT, GATT Activities 1987, at pages 69–70.

E. THE URUGUAY ROUND NEGOTIATIONS: OLD AND NEW ISSUES

One of the principal functions of GATT is to sponsor periodic rounds of trade negotiations in which trade problems can be discussed by its members and hopefully resolved. As noted in the foregoing sections, there are a number of areas in which the General Agreement or its side agreements need improvement. For example, there is a need (i) for improvement of the GATT institutional structure, (ii) to bring greater discipline to such sectors as agriculture and textiles, (iii) to regulate safeguards that are now being implemented outside of the GATT framework, (iv) to reach agreement on appropriate rules for the use of subsidies and countervailing duties, (v) to consider reforms to the anti-dumping rules and (vi) to otherwise improve the functioning of GATT. In addition, as will be discussed in the next section, there is room for improvement in the GATT dispute settlement system. For these and other reasons, the GATT membership launched the Uruguay Round.[171] As the negotiations will not be completed until December 1990 (if the current schedule is met), no attempt will be made here to predict the outcome of the negotiations. This section will instead highlight some of the problems facing GATT and new issues under discussion in the negotiations that have not been treated elsewhere.

The Problem of Economic Diversity.[172] One problem that faces GATT is how to handle the fact that the various contracting parties have different ideas of how a national economy should operate and, in particular, how much government intervention in an economy is appropriate. This problem will not be treated by a separate negotiating group in the Uruguay Round, but some of the more difficult issues under negotiation there and elsewhere in GATT stem from this problem. For example, negotiations under the Subsidies Code are difficult because different countries have different perceptions of what is an appropriate economic role for government. The United States tends not to subsidize industry as much as some other countries and therefore tends to take a

[171] The Uruguay Round is the eighth round of trade negotiations sponsored by GATT. It was launched in September 1986 at Punta del Este, Uruguay, whence its name. The organization of the negotiations and the subjects to be discussed are outlined in Ministerial Declaration and related documents, BISD 33S/19–52. The progress of the negotiations was reviewed in Montreal in December 1988 and in Geneva in April 1989. See GATT, GATT Activities 1988, at 138–167 (1989).

[172] See J. Jackson & W. Davey, note 1 supra, chs. 21, 22 & 23.

broader view of what sorts of subsidies ought to be controlled internationally or subject to national countervailing duties. For European countries and Japan a more expansive government role in the economy is seen as appropriate and beneficial.

More difficult problems of diversity arise in considering how GATT should deal with nonmarket economies that wish to join. In the past, a number of East European countries joined GATT pursuant to special accession protocols that took account of their nonmarket economy status.[173] By and large, these protocols have not been viewed as successful. As these countries become more market oriented in the 1990's, the problems may disappear, but the issue remains as both China and the Soviet Union have expressed interest in becoming GATT members.[174] These countries have large, state-controlled economic sectors and China is a rather poor developing country as well. Article XVII of the General Agreement is designed to deal with state trading monopolies and would seem to apply to nonmarket economies, but it is was not designed to do so in a comprehensive fashion and is generally viewed as inadequate to the tasks faced by GATT today in this regard.[175]

An additional related problem, which has been discussed in other contexts,[176] is how to bring the developing world into GATT on a more meaningful basis. At the moment, developing countries often view GATT as a club for rich countries in which they have little influence and receive little benefit.[177]

Bilateralism and Trading Blocs. In recent years, there has been a growth in the use of free trade areas and customs unions and in bilateral negotiations on trade issues. This has meant that GATT's basic principle—the most-favored-nation clause—is in fact applicable less and less often. This problem is not a specific subject of negotiations in the Uruguay Round, but it is one that worries GATT experts. Its practical

[173] See generally M. Kostecki, East-West Trade and the GATT System (1978).

[174] China has applied to renew its membership. See text accompanying note 23 supra. The Soviet Union has recently been granted observer status.

[175] See generally J. Jackson, World Trading System, note 1 supra, ch. 13. The Uruguay Round group negotiating changes in GATT articles is considering proposals to revise Article XVII.

[176] See text accompanying notes 60–66 supra. J. Jackson, World Trading System, note 1 supra, ch. 12.

[177] See generally J. Jackson, World Trading System, note 1 supra, ch. 12.

effect is to put considerable pressure on GATT to conclude the Uruguay Round successfully and to implement GATT rules on a more widespread basis or face the possibility that its multilateral approach will be abandoned as major trading blocs form and negotiate special relationships with each other. This general concern has been heightened by the tendency of the United States in recent years to try and solve trade disputes, especially with Japan, on a bilateral basis outside of the GATT system.

The New Issues: Services, Investment and Intellectual Property. Finally, it should be mentioned that the Uruguay Round encompasses negotiations on a number of issues that GATT has traditionally not dealt with: services and trade related aspects of investment measures and intellectual property. These new issues were included on the agenda at the insistence of the developed countries, particularly the United States. While there is not space to discuss these issues in any depth, a few comments are in order. In the case of *services,* the aim is to agree on an umbrella agreement for trade in services that will resemble the General Agreement in that it will establish general principles such as requiring most-favored-nation and national treatment in international services trade. Side agreements will then be negotiated with special provisions for various specific service industries. The aim of the talks on *trade related investment measures* (TRIMs) is to restrict the use of national investment rules that distort trade patterns through the use of local content or export performance requirements. The negotiations on *trade related aspects of intellectual property* (TRIPs) involve attempts to agree on provisions that effectively ban counterfeit goods in international trade and that provide for recognition and enforcement by GATT members of certain basic intellectual property rights. The developing world has not joined these talks with enthusiasm and it is unclear how much of it will participate in the agreements produced by the talks, particularly if progress is not made in other areas of particular interest to it, such as the negotiations on textiles and apparel, safeguards and certain product groups, such as tropical products and natural-resource based products.

Summary. The Uruguay Round is an extremely broad undertaking. The range of subjects under negotiation is immense. In addition to those mentioned above, there are negotiations on tariffs, on the various Tokyo Round codes and on other issues. Although much remains to be done, the Round is scheduled to conclude in Brussels in December 1990.

III. DISPUTE SETTLEMENT IN GATT[178]

The GATT system provides extensive rights and duties with respect to the international trade of its contracting parties. A key question to consider is how GATT goes about enforcing those rights and duties. Without an effective system to consider disputes over compliance with the rules of the GATT system, the elaborate structure of rights in GATT would mean little. This section reviews briefly the history and operation of the GATT dispute settlement system and examines a number of problems in that system and possible solutions to them.

A. ARTICLE XXIII: THE BASIC DISPUTE SETTLEMENT PROVISION

The General Agreement contains many provisions designed to resolve trade disputes between its contracting parties.[179] Most of them provide initially, and sometimes exclusively, for consultations between the contending parties.[180] If the parties are unable to settle their differences through negotiations, however, they may resort to Article XXIII, which is GATT's basic dispute settlement mechanism.

Article XXIII may be invoked when one GATT member claims that a benefit accruing to it under the General Agreement has been nullified or impaired by another member or that the attainment of any objective of the Agreement is being impeded.[181] In such a case, the contracting parties, acting jointly, are required to investigate the matter and make appropriate recommendations or rulings.[182] If the contracting parties

[178] This section is derived in part from Davey, Dispute Settlement in GATT, 11 Fordham Intl. L. J. 55 (1987), and is reproduced with the permission of the Fordham International Law Journal. The leading authority on GATT dispute settlement is Professor Hudec. See R. Hudec, The GATT Legal System and World Trade Diplomacy (1975) (hereinafter "The GATT Legal System"); R. Hudec, Adjudication of International Trade Disputes (1978) (hereinafter "Adjudication").

[179] J. Jackson, Law of GATT, note 1 supra, at 164–66.

[180] See, e.g, GATT, Art. VII:1, Art. VIII:2, Art. XIX:2, Art. XXII. Other provisions of the General Agreement that may play a role in dispute settlement include those allowing for waiver of obligations, Art. XXV:5, and periodic renegotiation of concessions, Art. XXVIII:1.

[181] Art. XXIII:1. No GATT panels have yet decided a case on the grounds that an objective of the Agreement is being impeded.

[182] Art. XXIII:2.

find that the circumstances are serious enough, they may authorize the complainant to take compensatory action against the respondent to reestablish the balance of concessions between the two parties.

Unlike the organic documents of some other international organizations, such as the United Nations or the EC, the General Agreement does not establish a specialized organ to rule on disputes. Instead, the task is entrusted to the contracting parties (now acting through the Council), which is a political body that makes policy decisions, conducts negotiations and so forth. Under the Havana Charter, there were provisions for disputes not satisfactorily resolved within the ITO to be referred to the International Court of Justice.[183] One consequence of this situation is that it is sometimes difficult to distinguish the Council's role as adjudicator and its role as mediator/negotiator.[184]

The scope of Article XXIII is extremely broad and panels have generally interpreted it accordingly. Under Article XXIII, one party's benefits under the General Agreement may be nullified or impaired not only by another party's violation of the General Agreement but also by "any measure" taken by another party, even if not in violation of the General Agreement.[185]

GATT dispute settlement practice distinguishes between cases alleging violations of the General Agreement and those alleging what is referred to as nonviolation nullification or impairment. In the case of a GATT violation, it is accepted that the violation constitutes prima facie evidence of nullification or impairment.[186] The assumption is that a violation of the agreement has an adverse impact and it is incumbent on the respondent party in such a case to rebut that assumption.[187] In practice, GATT panels have been unwilling to rule that violators have demonstrated a lack of nullification or impairment. For example, in a case involving Article III, the panel held:

[183] Havana Charter, note 9 supra, art. 96.

[184] See text accompanying notes 211–221 infra.

[185] Art. XXIII:1(b). It may also be caused by the "existence of any other situation." Art. XXIII:1(c).

[186] Understanding Regarding Notification, Consultation, Dispute Settlement and Surveillance, Annex, para. 5, BISD 26S/210, 216 (hereinafter "1979 Understanding"). This concept of prima facie nullification or impairment was introduced in Uruguayan Recourse to Article XXIII, BISD 11S/95 (Case 20).

[187] It has been suggested by one panel that the issue of rebuttal may be relevant only to whether countermeasures should be authorized, and is not relevant to the issue of whether the Contracting Parties (or the Council) should rule that a violation exists or recommended its termination. United States—Taxes on Petroleum and Certain Imported Products, BISD 34S/136 (Case 62).

> An acceptance of the argument that measures which have only an insignificant effect on the volume of exports do not nullify or impair benefits under Article III:2, first sentence, implies that the basic rationale of this provision—the benefit it generates for the contracting parties—is to protect expectations of export volumes. That is not the case. . . . [I]t protects expectations on the competitive relationship between imported and domestic products. A change in the competitive relationship contrary to that provision must consequently be regarded *ipso facto* as a nullification or impairment of benefits accruing under the General Agreement.[188]

This conclusion makes sense. As the panel quoted above noted, it is important that competitive relationships be maintained so that the predictability to plan for future trade flows exists. Thus, in the case of a GATT violation, it is virtually a foregone conclusion that nullification or impairment will be found.

In the case of an alleged nullification or impairment where the measures complained of are not claimed to violate the General Agreement, the complainant has the burden of providing a "detailed justification" of the allegations.[189] A greater burden is placed on the complainant in a nonviolation case because (i) there is no violation and (ii) because some GATT parties have at times been uncomfortable with the idea that a GATT-legal act could lead to finding of nullification or impairment, thereby entitling the injured party to compensation.[190] This burden has

[188] Id at 158 Para. 5.1.9.

[189] 1979 Understanding, para. 5. In fact, two types of cases involving nonviolation nullification or impairment claims have been viewed by some as cases where there is prima facie nullification or impairment. The two cases are (i) the granting of subsidies on products subject to a tariff binding and (ii) the use of otherwise GATT permissible quotas on such products. See J. Jackson, Law of GATT, note 1 supra, at 182–183. In a case not yet adopted by the GATT Council, a GATT panel held that a detailed justification was required if the quotas were imposed pursuant to a waiver under Article XXV. United States—Restrictions on the Importation of Sugar and Sugar-Containing Products, GATT Doc. L/6631 (not yet adopted).

[190] This concern is seen in the 1982 Declaration on Dispute Settlement, where it is stated "It is understood that decisions in [the dispute settlement] process cannot add to or diminish rights and obligations provided in the General Agreement." BISD, 29S/13, 16 (hereinafter "1982 Declaration"). One panel faced with this concern noted that allowing non-violation cases did not result in GATT-legal actions being somehow deemed illegal. Indeed, the panel noted that the GATT practice was not to ask that such a measure be modified. Instead,

been in practice eased for parties contesting actions that impair the value of Article II tariff concessions. For example, in a 1989 decision in a case challenging the use of domestic subsidies to favor domestic production of products subject to a tariff binding, the panel found that a showing that the competitive relationship between the domestic and imported products had been altered was sufficient to establish nullification or impairment.[191] In doing so, the panel followed longstanding GATT precedents that the reasonable expections of the parties should be honored.[192]

Consequently, because of these expansive decisions by dispute settlement panels, the GATT dispute settlement system affords considerable protection to GATT parties from the effects of GATT violations and any unexpected, GATT-legal actions that adversely affect the competitive balance between their exports and the products of other countries.

B. THE OPERATION OF GATT DISPUTE SETTLEMENT PANELS

Article XXIII only outlines how disputes are to be processed in the GATT system; it does not establish any formal procedures for handling them. From the outset it was evident that a general meeting of all contracting parties would be ill-suited to consider disputes. Although the procedures actually used have varied somewhat over the years, it has become the standard practice for the contracting parties to appoint a panel of individuals to consider a dispute and prepare a report so that the contracting parties can take appropriate action.[193]

if the measure unbalances competitive relationships, the injury party may be authorized to take offsetting, compensatory action to right the balance. EEC—Payments and Subsidies Paid to Processors and Producers of Oilseeds and Related Animal-Feed Proteins, GATT Doc. L/6627, adopted 25 January 1990 (Case 77).

[191] EEC—Payments and Subsidies Paid to Processors and Producers of Oilseeds and Related Animal-Feed Proteins, GATT Doc. L/6627, adopted 25 January 1990 (Case 77).

[192] See, e.g., GATT Report, Other Barriers to Trade, BISD 3S/222, 224 (1955); Germany—Imports of Sardines, BISD 1S/53 (Abstract 7); The Australian Subsidy on Ammonium Sulphate, II BISD 188 (Abstract 5).

[193] See generally R. Hudec, The GATT Legal System, note 178 supra, at 66–83. Initially, some disputes were resolved by a ruling of the chairman of the contracting parties. Most, however, were considered by working parties, consisting of the contending nations and several other GATT members. Working

By the early 1970s, there were increased complaints about many aspects of the panel process and a general disagreement among GATT members over whether the principal role of GATT dispute settlement panels should be to render judicial-like decisions or to promote negotiated settlements through conciliation.[194] As a result of these concerns, the dispute settlement system was the subject of extensive discussion in the Tokyo Round, which led to the adoption of an Understanding on Dispute Settlement at the conclusion of that Round.[195] The Understanding mainly summarized the dispute settlement procedures that had traditionally been used in GATT and indicated that they would continue to be used.[196] Despite continued dissatisfaction with the operation of the panel process, a 1982 GATT Ministerial Declaration on Dispute Settlement largely reiterated the 1979 decision.[197] The system appeared on the agenda of the Uruguay Round and several reforms were instituted (on a temporary basis for the duration of the Round) in 1989 as a result of an agreement reached at the Montreal midterm review session.[198]

As a result of these actions, the dispute settlement system as it currently operates can be summarized as follows:[199] Following the inability of two contracting parties to resolve a dispute through consultations

party reports typically stated the views of each member of the working party and did not reach decisions on the merits of the dispute, although the views of the majority were often evident and over time the reports were often treated as having reached definitive decisions. Id. In the early 1950s, use of panels became the standard practice in Article XXIII cases.

[194] For a description of the problems of the panel system as of the mid-1970s, see R. Hudec, Adjudication, note 178 supra, at 11–23.

[195] Understanding Regarding Notification, Consultation, Dispute Settlement and Surveillance, BISD 26S/210.

[196] Although the 1979 Understanding made no significant changes in GATT dispute settlement procedures (except for specifying certain time limits in which various actions ought to be taken), it was viewed as noteworthy because it indicated that the contracting parties were willing to continue the system as it had developed. Given the system's problems, the negotiations might well have left it in a more weakened state. See Hudec, GATT Dispute Settlement After the Tokyo Round: An Unfinished Business, 13 Cornell Intl. L.J. 145, 158–159 (1980).

[197] Ministerial Declaration, Dispute Settlement Procedures, BISD 29S/13, 16. The 1982 Declaration was followed by the 1984 Action by Contracting Parties on Dispute Settlement Procedures, BISD 31S/9–10.

[198] Dispute Settlement, GATT, GATT Activities 1988, at 152–158 (1989) (hereinafter "1989 Improvements"). See Davey, GATT Dispute Settlement: The 1988 Montreal Reforms, in R. Dearden, M. Hart & D. Steger, Living With Free Trade (1990).

[199] See also Judge Pescatore's introduction infra.

and negotiations, the aggrieved party may request the establishment of a panel to adjudicate the dispute. The request is made to the GATT Council. There is no absolute right to have a panel established, but the 1989 Improvements provide that if a contracting party so requests, a panel will be established at the second meeting of the Council at which the request appears on the Council's agenda, unless the Council decides otherwise. Since the Council's decisions are traditionally by consensus, it is arguable that a panel must be established at that meeting unless the petitioner agrees to the delay. The respondent is given the right to respond to the complaint made and may argue that the appointment of a panel would be premature or otherwise inappropriate. By doing so it may persuade the petitioner not to insist on the immediate establishment of a panel. In fact, however, panels have virtually always been established if requested, assuming the request is pursued.[200]

The decision to establish a panel means that a panel must be appointed. This may occasion some delay because the contending parties are consulted on the composition of the panel. The 1989 Improvements explicitly provide that the Director-General may appoint a panel if there is no agreement by the parties on panel membership within 20 days. It appears, however, that the Director-General has usually sought to obtain consent of the parties, even if that requires more time than provided for in the procedures. In the past, most panel members have been national officials responsible for GATT and international trade matters, particularly those based in Geneva who represent their countries at GATT. Prior to 1989, there was a stated preference for use of governmental experts over private individuals. No such preference is provided for in the 1989 Improvements, and in recent years, there has been a substantial increase in the use of private individuals on panels. Moreover, a roster of qualified panelists is now maintained by the GATT secretariat which aids in the process of panel formation.

Once the panel has been appointed, its task is typically to examine the dispute and make such findings as will assist the contracting parties in making recommendations or rulings as provided for in Article XXIII.[201] The panel receives written and oral submissions from the contending parties and may receive submissions from other interested parties. It

[200] See U.S. Intl. Trade Comm. Pub. No. 1793, Review of the Effectiveness of Trade Dispute Settlement under the GATT and the Tokyo Round Agreements 57 (1985) [hereinafter ITC Dispute Settlement Study] (Report to the Committee on Finance, U.S. Senate, on Investigation No. 332–212 under Section 332(g) of the Tariff Act of 1930).

[201] Panel procedures are summarized in the 1979 Understanding.

then issues a proposed report on which the contending parties comment. Following its consideration of the comments, the panel submits its report to the GATT Council. The report normally resolves the major disputed issues raised by the contending parties (or at least those necessary to reach a decision) and, if nullification or impairment is found, recommends, in order of preference: that the offending measure be removed; or, if that is not possible, that the injured party be compensated; or, as a last resort, that the injured party be authorized to retaliate against the offending party.[202] In fact, panels typically recommend only that the offending measure be removed and the losing party is traditionally afforded a reasonable (but undefined) period to bring the offending measure into compliance with GATT rules.[203] As a consequence, retaliation, which can be authorized under the terms of Article XXIII only if the circumstances are "serious enough," has been authorized only once, 35 years ago.[204] Throughout the panel procedure, the disputants are urged to resolve the matter amicably.[205]

A panel report in and of itself has no force. It is only the opinion of the panel members. It must be adopted by the Council on behalf of the contracting parties. Although the issues discussed in the report are not relitigated in the Council, in recent years it has not been unusual for individual contracting parties to express disagreement with specific aspects of a panel report. The meaning of these reservations is unclear, assuming that the Council in fact adopts the report because the Council traditionally does not act absent consensus.[206] Thus, the reserving party in a sense accepts the report despite the reservations expressed. In any event, the practice of requiring consensus means that the "losing" party (at least an important losing party) may hold up adoption of a panel report interminably while it purports to analyze it and to explore possible negotiated solutions with the prevailing party.[207]

[202] 1979 Understanding, Annex, para. 4.

[203] 1979 Understanding, para. 23.

[204] Netherlands Measures of Suspension of Obligations to the United States, BISD 1S/32, 62 (Case 11).

[205] See, e.g., 1979 Understanding, paras. 16, 18.

[206] Although the General Agreement establishes a one-nation/one-vote system, GATT, Art. XXV:3, it has traditionally operated on the basis of consensus. Thus, if any contracting party is strongly opposed to a proposed GATT action, that action will not be taken. See E. McGovern, supra note 1, at 24.

[207] ITC Dispute Settlement Study, note 200 supra, at 58–61. The 1982 Ministerial Declaration stated, "The Contracting Parties reaffirmed that consensus will continue to be the traditional method of resolving disputes; however, they agreed that obstruction in the process of dispute settlement shall be avoided."

Each of the Tokyo Round agreements has a provision on dispute settlement. Generally, these provisions either incorporate or closely follow the procedures described above. The main differences are that there is usually an unqualified right to have a panel appointed under the agreements, time limits for completion of certain stages are sometimes stricter and more precisely defined, and the panel report is adopted (or not) by the appropriate agreement's committee of signatories.[208]

C. PROBLEMS IN THE OPERATION OF THE GATT DISPUTE SETTLEMENT SYSTEM

The basic structure and operating procedures of the GATT dispute settlement system have not changed greatly since the early 1950s. Nonetheless, perceptions of the system's effectiveness and usefulness have varied widely over the years. It was generally viewed as effective during the first decade or so of GATT's existence, but prior to and during the Tokyo Round negotiations, there was much dissatisfaction with it.[209] This sentiment was particularly evident in the United States, where Congressional committees complained that the system's ineffectiveness prevented the United States from enforcing its rights under GATT, thereby indirectly suggesting that perhaps the United States should not participate in GATT.[210] Among the many criticisms leveled at the system, the principal charges were that the system:

a) was inappropriate and ill-conceived because it stressed judicial solutions to problems that were really resolvable only through negotiations.

b) was defective because of weaknesses in the panel process;

1982 Declaration, para. 10. The 1989 Improvements provide: "[T]he delaying of the process of dispute settlement shall be avoided." 1989 Improvements, para. G.3.

[208] This overview will not separately consider the dispute settlement procedures under the Tokyo Round codes except where they are particularly relevant to the matter under discussion. For analyses of the differences in the procedures adopted in those codes, see Hudec, note 196 supra, at 174–77; see also Jackson, The Birth of the GATT-MTN System: A Constitutional Appraisal, 12 L. & Poly. Intl. Bus. 21, 44–47 (1980).

[209] The first two phases are comprehensively analyzed in R. Hudec, The GATT Legal System, note 178 supra.

[210] See H.R. Rep. No. 571, 93d Cong., 1st Sess. 66–67 (1973).

c) was inefficient because of long delays; and

d) was ineffective because of its inability to ensure implementation of its decisions.

The first of these criticisms is philosophical in nature: How should GATT approach dispute settlement? Should third parties issue decisions on whether countries have violated the General Agreement or should they limit their role to conciliation? The other criticisms focus on operational aspects of the system: Who uses it? How long does it take? What results are produced? These criticisms will be analyzed in light of post-Tokyo Round experiences with the system. It appears that at least some of the criticisms of the past are no longer valid and that the current—third—phase of the dispute settlement system's history has been relatively successful.

1. The Philosophical Debate: Adjudication or Negotiation?[211]

As it has operated over the years, the GATT dispute settlement system has resembled a judicial system in important aspects: neutral decision-makers have determined whether a contracting party has violated the General Agreement and have usually recommended that the violation, if one is found, be terminated. Some critics of the system have argued that it should be made more judicial so as to promote more precise decisions on the merits of disputes and more effective implementation of decisions.[212] At the same time, other critics have argued that the nature and basic philosophy of GATT dictate that the system should be used only to the extent it facilitates negotiated settlements of trade disputes. The decline in the use of the system in the 1960's and 1970's probably reflected the influence of these latter critics since their position has been subscribed to by some leading GATT officials and parties.[213]

These two conflicting viewpoints are often referred to as the "legalistic" model, which stresses adjudication, and the "antilegalistic" model, which emphasizes negotiation and consensus.[214] Put simply, the legalistic

[211] For fuller development of this issue, see Davey, note 178 supra, at 65–81.

[212] See especially Davey, note 178 supra.

[213] A classic example is given by Professor Lowenfeld in his Preface supra. See, e.g., O. Long, Law and Its Limitations in the GATT Multilateral Trade System (1985) (Mr. Long was Director-General of GATT from 1968 to 1980); Phan van Phi, A European View of the GATT, 14 Intl. Bus. Law. 150 (1986) (Mr. Phan van Phi was in charge of GATT relations for the EC).

[214] ITC Dispute Settlement Study, note 200 supra, at 68.

view is that the General Agreement is a code of conduct and embodies a balance of concessions. If a contracting party violates the code or tips the balance, it is appropriate to penalize such behavior and put pressure on that party to conform to the code or right the balance, if necessary by allowing the petitioning party to take offsetting countermeasures. On the other hand, the antilegalistic position is that the General Agreement is not a code of conduct *per se,* but more of a commitment by the contracting parties to deal with each other in trade matters so as to work out a mutually acceptable solution to any disagreement. The United States is generally perceived to have supported the legalistic position, while Japan and the EC have been considered supporters of the opposing position. Most developing countries and non-European developed countries have tended to support the legalistic position because they see it as a more effective protector of small-country rights.[215]

The text of Article XXIII does not mandate adoption of either approach, although the grant of the power to determine the existence of nullification and impairment and to authorize retaliatory measures certainly suggests a judicial model was intended. In any event, the basic questions would seem to be: What are the goals of the GATT dispute settlement system, and would they be better achieved by emphasizing adjudication or negotiation?

The first question seems easy to answer. Clearly the goal of the dispute settlement system should be to promote compliance with GATT rules. Any lesser goal would have the effect of undermining the GATT system in the long run.[216] Thus, the question is whether a more adjudicative system would promote greater compliance with GATT rules.

Critics of the adjudicative approach suggest that it will not result in better compliance in the long run for essentially two reasons. First, they argue that disputes in the end must be resolved by negotiated settlement. Even in cases where a panel makes a recommendation, the implementation of that recommendation will be the subject of negotiations as to form and timing. A more contentious, adjudicative approach, they argue, will poison the atmosphere for these negotiations and ultimately undermine the system. As this author has argued elsewhere, the arguments in support of this position are not compelling.[217] Indeed, emphasis on a negotiation approach is likely to result in more powerful countries dominating the process to the detriment of weaker countries

[215] Id.
[216] See Davey, note 178 supra, at 67–69.
[217] Id. at 70–73.

and the integrity of GATT rules. This result is more likely to poison the GATT atmosphere in the long run than a system that only asks countries to comply with the obligations they freely undertook in the past.

Second, it is argued that a more legalistic system will encourage the filing of complaints and that some of these actions will be what could be called "wrong" cases.[218] A wrong case is one that may overwhelm the system because of political considerations. For example, the complaining party may be correct in alleging a violation, but because of domestic political considerations the violator may not be in a position to comply with GATT rules. In this author's view, such cases are likely to be rare and GATT has the strength to deal with them. Even if compliance cannot be assured, the violator still may be in a position to right the balance of concessions by taking other action.[219]

Thus, the criticisms of the adjudicative approach do not seem to be valid. The basic question remains, however. Will the adjudicative approach lead to better compliance with GATT rules? In this author's view, it is likely that it will for two reasons.[220] First, an adjudicative system discourage rule violations because a potential violator knows it is likely that it will be called to account if it ignores GATT rules. This is particularly true if counterbalancing action is authorized. In such a case, the violator suffers from the violation. In the negotiation model, the only detriment to the violator would be unpleasant diplomatic encounters. Second, because panel reports are usually implemented in the long run, more panel decisions—which is a likely result of an adjudicative system—will result in closer compliance with GATT rules. As the GATT system has grown stronger over time,[221] it has become better able to operate a more adjudicative dispute settlement system. In fact, it would seem that the trend in GATT today is clearly in the direction of making the dispute settlement system stronger and more adjudicative in nature.

2. Operational Criticisms

Critics of the GATT dispute settlement system have also raised a number of operational issues. Among the major problems cited have been (i) various defects in the panel process, (ii) delays in processing cases and (iii) failure to ensure implementation of panel decisions.

[218] See Hudec, note 192 supra, at 159–166.
[219] See Davey, note 178 supra, at 73–76.
[220] Id. at 76–81.
[221] See id. at 79–81.

Among the defects in the panel process, critics point to the use of inexperienced panelists, the potential bias inherent in using government officials as panelists and the poor quality of panel decisions. In the view of this author, these criticisms relate more to the past than the present. Recent years have seen a substantial increase in the use of independent, non-governmental experts on panels, as well as a tendency to reappoint such individuals to future panels. In addition, the establishment in the 1980's of a legal staff in the secretariat, which advises panels, has improved the quality and consistency of panel decisions. While some further improvements could be made, by and large the panel process seems to be now working relatively well.[222]

As to delays, the various reforms in the last decade and the establishment of time limits for panel action have meant that delays are usually not a problem today. The GATT secretariat reported in 1988 that most panel decisions are rendered within a year or so of the decision to establish a panel.[223]

The final criticism is more serious. It is often the case that several years elapse before a panel decision is implemented. There are a number of reasons for this. First, there may be considerable delay while the losing party studies the panel decision. Under the tradition of requiring consensus to adopt the panel decision, until the losing party consents to lose, no action will be taken. Even after adoption of the decision, negotiations between the parties over how compliance will be implemented may drag on for months or years. While the decisions usually are implemented to the satisfaction of the petitioner, there is considerable room for improving the timeliness of compliance.

All in all, it seems that the dispute settlement system works rather well, except at the very end of the process when panel report adoption and implementation often take too long. The following section suggests some useful improvements that could be made.

D. REFORM OF THE GATT DISPUTE SETTLEMENT SYSTEM[224]

The problems of the GATT dispute settlement system seem to revolve around delays in implementation and a nagging fear of difficult cases being mishandled by an individual panel.

[222] See id. at 88–89.

[223] Petersmann, Strengthening the GATT Dispute Settlement System, in E.-U. Petersmann & M. Hilf (eds.), The New GATT Round of Multilateral Trade Negotiations: Legal and Economic Problems 323, 334–335 (1988).

[224] See Davey, note 178 supra, at 90–109.

Delays in implementation could be significantly reduced by two reforms. First, a rule should be adopted that the panel report will be adopted at the second meeting at which it appears on the Council's agenda, absent an affirmative decision by the Council not to adopt it or to postpone consideration of it. The presumption should be that the panel, to which the decision of the dispute was delegated by the Council, is correct, not that the loser has some inherent right to consent to its loss. Proposals that would change the consensus rule to a "consensus minus the two parties" rule are inadequate because several contracting parties not formally involved in the dispute may have the same interests at stake as the loser. They should not be able to block adoption of the report either. Automatic adoption of panel reports would eliminate the delay associated with the loser dragging its feet before consenting to adoption of the report, delay which sometimes amounts to a year or so.

Second, there should be a greater willingness on the part of GATT to authorize countermeasures by the prevailing party in the event that the loser does not promptly implement the recommendations of the panel report. At present, there is no cost incurred for delay. If the violator has to incur costs if it fails to implement the recommendation promptly, implementation will be more likely. While such a change in practice will annoy parties when they lose, such a rule is appropriate because it is fairer than the present system, where the cost of non-compliance is borne by the prevailing party. Surely that party deserves to have the balance of concessions righted promptly, either through the losing party's compliance with the decision or by its own countermeasures.

The fear that a panel might mishandle a difficult case could be allayed, perhaps, by creating a system of appellate review in GATT. One way to do this would be to create a relatively short roster of panelists to decide cases. Appeals from a panel could then be made to the entire roster or the senior members of the roster in terms of experience. In addition to solving fears of a bad decision, the use of a shorter roster of panelists would increase the experience and expertise of the panelists and would probably lead to a more coherent body of GATT decisions.[225] While GATT panels tend to consider the decisions of prior panels in their decisions, they do not always do so and it is not completely clear under GATT practice the extent to which prior panel decisions have precedential value.[226] A smaller group of panelists and an

[225] It is, of course, possible for a new panel to reconsider an issue previously decided. See, e.g., United States—Section 337 of the Tariff Act of 1990, BISD 36S/345 (Case 74).

[226] See EEC—Restrictions on Imports of Chilean Apples (II), BISD 36S/93 (Case 69). See also text following note 36 supra.

appellate process would probably tend to create a body of precedent. This would be very desirable from the standpoint of the contracting parties as they would then be more certain whether their actions could be successfully challenged in GATT and could thereby avoid GATT-illegal actions. Care would have to be taken, however, to ensure that an appeals process did not subvert the GATT dispute settlement process by injecting into it unnecessary delays or inappropriate political considerations.

It is unclear whether additional reforms will be agreed upon in the Uruguay Round but reforms such as those discussed above have been put forward on a tentative basis to the negotiating group on dispute settlement.

PART TWO - THE REPERTORY

PART TWO - THE REPERTORY

PART TWO
THE REPERTORY

DRAFTING AND ANALYZING DECISIONS ON DISPUTE SETTLEMENT

Pierre Pescatore

OUTLINE OF CONTENTS

This handbook has a dual purpose. First it is intended to give practical assistance to all those involved in GATT dispute settlement: public servants, government representatives, Secretariat officials, legal practitioners, and, of course, panel members. The tables, key-words, and summaries provide a "short-hand" access to material that previously involved lengthy research. In addition, the book allows the reader to check that nothing essential has escaped his/her attention as well as giving a guide to the most important precedents. The second purpose of the handbook is to show all students of GATT law how to analyze and best understand GATT decisions in the critical field of dispute settlement.

GATT RULES ON DISPUTE SETTLEMENT (ARTICLE XXIII)

As the Overview by William Davey points out, all aspects of dispute settlement are concentrated in a single article of the General Agreement, Article XXIII. This article contains the essential components of the system: the causes for action, and the authority to resolve disputes—including indications on the legal implications of decisions.

Causes for Action

Paragraph 1 of Article XXIII defines the scope of complaints in broad and flexible terms by making reference to "nullification and impairment of benefits" under the Agreement, and to actions impeding "the attainment of any objective." Injury to the benefits thus defined, or impediment to the Agreement's objectives may flow from an action of any one of the contracting parties, be it through

(a) the failure to carry out any obligation assumed under the Agreement, or

(b) the application of any national measure, whether or not it conflicts with the Agreement or

(c) the existence of "any other situation."

It appears, therefore, that the central concept of the GATT dispute settlement mechanism is not primarily violation of the General Agreement, or of obligations assumed thereunder. It is curtailment, in the broadest sense of the word, of the benefits flowing from the Agreement, or of the objectives pursued by the entire Agreement or by individual provisions of it.

With regard to this central concept of the GATT dispute settlement mechanism, much attention has been devoted to a particular category derived from Article XXIII:1(b), conveniently called "non-violation impairment", since this provision appears to imply that a claim may be raised even in cases of impairment caused by a measure which does *not* conflict with any GATT obligation. This seems to be a legal paradox. Subsidies are a good example of how such a case may arise, because the granting of subsidies is not prohibited in principle by GATT. But the payment of subsidies distorts competition and may devalue or even offset tariff concessions. Thus, there may well be a case for impairment without there being a clear violation of any GATT rule.[1]

The emphasis placed on this legal category and the conclusions sometimes drawn from it (in the sense of less consideration being given to non-violation claims) are due to a misunderstanding of the GATT system of litigation, a system in which protection of trade benefits and the integrity of the General Agreement's objectives are the central values to be protected.[2] From this perspective it does not matter whether a measure causing impairment is consistent or inconsistent with the General Agreement, or whether it falls into some "gray area," legally speaking. The consequences, as they are set out by Article XXIII:2, are identical in all cases. The sole tangible difference in practice is that in the case of infringement of GATT rules (paragraph 1(a)) impairment of benefits is presumed, whereas it has to be established if it derives from measures not conflicting with GATT obligations (paragraph 1(b)).[3]

Strangely enough, the various possibilities for action under Article XXIII:1 are far from exhausted. All decided cases have concerned impairment of benefits in the strict sense of the word. A complaint for impediment of the General Agreement's objectives has never been brought—much to the detriment, it must be said, of a more systematic development of GATT law. Similarly, states have not had resort to the rather nebulous concept of "any other situation" under Article XXIII:1(c).

Authority for Dispute Settlement

When a dispute arises, Article XXIII requires the parties to first seek a solution on a voluntary basis. If no satisfactory compromise is reached, the matter may be referred to the Contracting Parties under

[1] The report on the "Soya Panel" (Case 77) is an example of the correct handling of this kind of issue.

[2] The report on the Uruguayan Recourse (Case 20) led to a false perception of so-called "non-violation impairments" when it recommended that in such cases there should be only "sympathetic consideration" of the complainant's representations, which was a ludicrous proposition. Under Article XXIII an impairing measure, if established, calls for compensation "whether or not" it conflicts with the General Agreement.

[3] 1979 Understanding, Annex, point 5.

paragraph 2. If this provision is resorted to, the Contracting Parties must promptly "investigate" the matter and issue appropriate "recommendations", or "give a ruling" on the matter. It is recognized by customary practice that the benefit of these provisions cannot be denied to a party seeking the settlement of an unresolved dispute.[4]

Again, practice demonstrates a striking feature with regard to the consequences of actions envisaged by Article XXIII. Numerous recommendations have been issued under Article XXIII:2, but until now there has never been a "ruling."[5] However, as we shall see, recommendations issued under the provisions on dispute settlement mean much more than the word "recommendation" might seem to imply. In fact, recommendations may come close to what a ruling could be, as they might result in retaliatory measures if they are disregarded by those concerned.

If an impairment of a party's benefits, or an infringement of any of the GATT rules or obligations, or an impediment to any of the General Agreement's objectives has been established, the complainant party maybe authorized to suspend "such concessions or other obligations" to a defendant as the Contracting Parties determine to be appropriate, if they consider that the circumstances are "serious enough to justify such action". These clauses of Article XXIII:2 call for two comments.

First, they imply that in the GATT system there is no room for self-help.[6] As a multilateral system, GATT makes no allowance for unilateral threats or countermeasures: resort to retaliatory action is reserved for the Contracting Parties. The real problem, as yet unresolved, is whether a contracting party may resort to unilateral retaliatory action

[4] This is one of the crucial points of the whole system. It is to be noted that after having stated that the matter "may" be referred to the Contracting Parties, Article XXIII:2 continues by saying that the Contracting Parties "shall" promptly investigate the matter and "shall" make appropriate recommendations, or give a ruling on the matter. This is strong legal language. Accordingly, the 1979 Understanding states the following: "It is agreed that if a contracting party invoking Article XXIII:2 requests the establishment of a panel to assist the Contracting Parties to deal with the matter, the Contracting Parties should decide on its establishment in accordance with standing practice" (point 10).

[5] This matter was touched on briefly in the report on the Uruguayan Recourse (Case 20).

[6] This again is a fundamental matter. Unilateral action has been declared incompatible with GATT in several panel reports. The question first came up in relation to the splitting of a tariff item in the German tariff: Treatment by Germany of Imports of Sardines (Case 7). An energetic condemnation of unilateral measures resulted from the reports on the French Special Temporary Compensation Tax on Imports (Case 13), on US-Imports of Sugar from Nicaragua (Case 55), and on EEC Restrictions on Import of Newsprint (Case 59).

if the Contracting Parties fail to take collective action, according to Article XXIII, by refusing to open a procedure under Article XXIII:2, second phrase, by unduly blocking the progress or outcome of a regular procedure, or by not allowing retaliatory action under Article XXIII:2, fourth phrase, after a contracting party's liability has been duly established. If the multilateral system fails to play its role, it cannot be said that unilateral action is illegitimate under general international law.

Second, it must be noted that, although there are only one or two examples of retaliatory measures authorized by the Contracting Parties,[7] the mere threat of such action has a highly persuasive effect. This makes the GATT dispute settlement system one of the most efficient means of conflict resolution in international life.

II. ESSENTIALS OF DISPUTE SETTLEMENT PROCEDURE

Historically, the conflict-resolving function was at first exercised directly by the Contracting Parties. But within a short period of time the preparation of the Contracting Parties' decisions in this field was entrusted to "working parties" which appear to have been open-ended bodies in which the parties to the dispute also had a seat and a voice. The record shows that the working parties were not entirely satisfactory. As the parties to a dispute took a direct role in the working party's proceedings, a unanimous settlement of the dispute was, by definition, out of reach. Conflict resolution by working parties was therefore in the nature of conciliation rather than dispute settlement.

Institution of Panels

From the mid-fifties onwards, practice switched from working-parties to independent "panels." Initially, these panels were mostly five-member groups. Later, three-member panels prevailed. This preference has been clearly expressed in the 1989 Improvements.[8] Indeed, three-

[7] In fact, there is only one clear case on record: the Netherlands Action under Article XXIII:2, initiated in response to US restrictions imposed on import of dairy products (see Case 11). But the so-called "Chicken War," about which GATT sources contain little information (see Case 21), is also relevant.

[8] See point F, letter (c)4, which states that "Panels shall be composed of three members unless the parties to the dispute agree . . . to a panel composed of five members".

member panels proved to be a much better device because, apart from speed, their very nature promotes mutual understanding and consensus. It must also be noted that from 1960 on, the Contracting Parties acting as a permanent body have assumed the title of "Council."[9] Since then, the Council and the various panels, together with the Director General and the Secretariat, are the main protagonists of the GATT dispute settlement system.

A rather elaborate customary practice evolved, which was codified by the 1979 Understanding on Dispute Settlement. This Understanding was supplemented by several ministerial decisions: the 1982 Declaration (rather unfavorable to the process), the 1984 Action (which is of little moment), and the well-named 1989 Improvements. This collection of secondary GATT law is the equivalent of the rules of procedure of other international judicial bodies. It must be added that, together with the 1979 Understanding, the Contracting Parties established a whole set of particular systems of dispute settlement in the framework of the so-called "Codes" adopted as an outcome of the Tokyo-Round of negotiations. Up to now, these rules have not yielded any noteworthy results. Only two reports have been adopted on the basis of these Codes.[10] Recent panel reports have emphasized the "all-embracing" scope of the Article XXIII procedure which seems to be preferred by the Contracting Parties, even in cases where the Codes are involved.[11] It must not be overlooked, in this respect, that the Article XXIII procedure is conducive to precedents which become automatically relevant to all contracting parties, whereas decisions reached on the basis of one of the codes are of concern only to the states that have adhered to that particular code.[12]

[9] The relevant decision has been published in BISD, 9S/7.

[10] The text of these rules is to be found in the respective Codes, all of which have been published in the 26th Supplement of BISD. The reduced practical value of these provisions did not warrant their inclusion in this Handbook: since the establishment of the Codes only two reports have been adopted (see Cases 58 and 61). The first report contains some interesting ideas on interpretation of secondary GATT law. The second is a purely formal document.

[11] See the report on Korea, Restriction on Imports of Beef (Case 75), where the panel had to determine its jurisdiction in relation to the specific provisions on balance of payments difficulties of developing countries (part B of Article XVIII). The "Soya Panel" had to cope with a similar problem in relation to the Subsidies Code (Case 77).

[12] Again, the "Soya Panel" report (Case 77) is a good example. The parties insisted on resolving their dispute in the framework of the General Agreement rather than in the narrow bounds of the Subsidies Code. This report is even more pertinent since the matter was inextricably linked to the question of the effect of tariff concessions.

Adoption of Panel Reports by the GATT Council

According to standing practice, approval of panel reports is by consensus.[13] Approval is normally unqualified, but under the consensus procedure there is ample room for the expression of particular opinions by single contracting parties. According to the nature of consensus, such opinions are, however, blurred by the final consent. Reservations or restrictions to a given report can have legal value only if they are also approved by consensus. In some rare cases, there have been agreed understandings qualifying the Council's approval.[14]

The general idea that inspires the system of dispute settlement in GATT was expressed in the following way in the opening provision of the mid-term Uruguay-Round resolution on Dispute Settlement Procedures Improvement adopted in 1989:

> "Contracting parties recognize that the dispute settlement system of GATT serves to preserve the rights and obligations of the contracting parties under the General Agreement and to clarify the existing provisions of the General Agreement. It is a central element in providing security and predictability to the multilateral trading system."[15]

As we shall see, all these features of the GATT dispute settlement system strongly influence the content and style of panel reports.

It appears from the text of Article XXIII that disputes can only be settled by decisions of the Contracting Parties. Panels are not mentioned in the provision since they are a product of the Contracting Parties practice whose importance was established through the Council's approach to dispute settlement long after the article was written.

[13] This was echoed in point X of the 1982 Ministerial Declaration. Until now, nobody seems to have thought of applying Article XXV:4 which provides as follows: "Except as otherwise provided for *in this Agreement*, decisions of the Contracting Parties shall be taken by a majority of the votes cast" (emphasis added).

[14] See the "DISC-Panel" report (Case 31) and the understanding thereto, which was established five years after the report had been presented to the Council. The report on the Automotive Spring Assemblies issue (Case 52) was approved on condition that the decision would not constitute a precedent, and that the matter of principle would be reexamined by another panel at a suitable later date. This reexamination came up in Section 337 of the US Tariff Act issue (Case 74), where as results of point 5.6, the panel overruled the former decision.

[15] 1989 Improvements, point A(1). This is the most remarkable description of the GATT dispute settlement system ever made.

Once they were instituted, however, panels became central to the dispute settlement process because the arguments supporting the Council's decisions could be inferred only from the respective panel's reports. The reader should keep in mind, however, that the panel reports have no authority of their own. They acquire legal authority only if they are adopted by the Council.

III. PANEL WORK IN PRACTICE

As appears from the foregoing, even though panels do not have the authority to resolve conflicts, they are nonetheless central to the dispute settlement procedure. The Council has authority to open and to conclude the proceedings, but it is the panels' role and responsibility to determine the substance of solutions to a given conflict. Therefore, no matter how panels are appointed, their terms of reference and internal procedures are of paramount importance.

Appointment of Panels

Panels are appointed by the Council upon proposal of the Director General.[16] The Director General's proposal is carefully prepared in consultation with the parties to the dispute. This procedure is quite unlike setting up an arbitral body, because panel members are neither proposed nor chosen by the parties. There is, therefore, nothing resembling "party arbitrators" in the GATT panels. At the end of his consultation, the Director General submits the list of panel members to the Contracting Parties and a mandate is conferred by the Council on the panel as a whole. Thus, the process of selection and appointment ensures that the panel is vested with the undivided confidence, not only of the parties to the dispute, but also of the Contracting Parties assembled in the Council. This selection process gives the panels a strong sense of independence and also of responsibility towards GATT as a whole.

Formerly panel members were drawn from national delegations, including government services connected to GATT. Serving on panels

[16] This is clearly expressed in point 11 of the 1979 Understanding: "When a panel is set up, the Director General, after securing the agreement of the contracting parties concerned, should propose the composition of the panel . . ." This prerogative of the Director General is an essential for the system to function and it should be kept unimpaired at all costs.

was considered to be part of the representative functions of national delegations and services. As a welcome consequence, panels were not financed by the organization's budget. Panel members were selected from countries which could be considered to have a "neutral" position towards the parties to a given dispute. In practice, this resulted in a de-facto ostracism of nationals from the major trading nations, such as the US, the EEC, and Japan, since these parties had an interest in most of the disputes. It also meant excluding some of the most prominent GATT specialists from participation in dispute settlement.

The 1984 Action departed from this practice by providing for a permanent "roster" of qualified persons willing to serve on panels. Since then, the national identity of panel members has disappeared from reports.

The typical panel today consists of both members of national delegations and outside members. Care is also taken to call on qualified lawyers to work alongside experts on the trade problems to be resolved. Each panel is assisted by a member of the GATT Secretariat acting as panel secretary and by a representative of GATT's legal department. As this handbook demonstrates, this practice has resulted in a marked improvement in reports from the early 1980's on, when, at long last, a legal department was established in GATT.

Terms of Reference

Under the practice codified in the 1989 Dispute Settlement Procedures Improvement, the task of panels is normally described in accordance with the "standard terms of reference" which are worded as follows:

> "To examine, in the light of the relevant GATT provisions, the matter referred to the CONTRACTING PARTIES by (name of contracting party) in document L/ . . . and to make such findings that will assist the CONTRACTING PARTIES in making the recommendations or in giving the rulings provided for in Article XXIII:2".

This standard formula is remarkable in several respects.

First, it shows that cases are introduced in the terms defined by the complainant party. Combined with the customary right of contracting parties to have proceedings instituted on unilateral request, the standard terms of reference emphasize complaints brought under Article XXIII. Under these terms it is the complainant party which unilaterally defines the subject-matter of the dispute. This goes far beyond the *compromis* as it is used in international arbitration, where terms of reference assigned to the arbitrators are fixed basically by mutual agreement.[17] By virtue of its standard terms of reference, the GATT system, therefore, comes closer to international adjudication than to arbitration.

Second, the panel is empowered to examine the complaint in the light of "the relevant GATT provisions." This is a very broad mandate since each panel has to examine the dispute not only in the light of the provisions specifically referred to by the parties, but also in reference to all GATT provisions it may consider relevant to the issue.[18] Even though it is good practice to have the parties address all provisions the panel intends to consider in order to resolve the dispute, the reference to "the relevant GATT provisions" in the terms of reference forestalls objections of *ultra vires* in a case in which a panel chooses to base its findings on GATT provisions not specifically relied upon by the parties.

Third, the reference to "GATT provisions" has always been construed in a broad sense by the panels to mean not only the General Agreement but also the whole GATT legal system, including secondary and complementary GATT law as it appears in agreements arrived at within the framework of GATT, such as in tariff protocols, in decisions taken by the Contracting Parties and in customary practice. Though no general theory has been worked out in this respect, panel reports contain numerous examples of such references to legal elements which have grown out of GATT practice over the years.

Fourth, the standard terms of reference invite panels to propose to the Council "recommendations" or "rulings" that they think appropriate. The General Agreement does not suggest a sharp distinction between these two types of possible solutions. It may be said that, whereas recommendations allow for flexibility (a feature which in fact appears in many variations in the panel reports), rulings have to be conceived of as

[17] See Karin Oellers-Frahm, *Compromis* in Bernhardt (ed.), Encyclopedia of Public International Law, Instalment 1 (1981).

[18] The panel appointed to resolve the second dispute on EEC Restrictions on Imports of Chilean Apples (Case 69) construed its terms of reference to mean that it was auhorized to examine the matter referred to it in the light of *all* relevant provisions of GATT law, i.e. of the General Agreement itself, and of provisions related to its interpretation and implementation.

authoritative legal decisions. Though panels have so far never resorted to suggesting the latter type of solution, it must be remembered that under the standard terms of reference they are also invited to explore this avenue.

Finally a *caveat* should be expressed in relation to the standard terms of reference. The substantive part of these terms contains a reference to an internal GATT document which remains inaccessible to the ordinary reader, even after the panel report has been approved and published. As the terms of reference are the basic premise from which the arguments used in each case and the solution reached can be understood, panels should take care either to quote the full content of the document referred to in the terms of reference or to append it to their findings.

Panel Procedure

Once a panel has been set up and its terms of reference have been defined, the procedure evolves within the framework of a tightly determined schedule which provides for the speedy presentation of written submissions by the parties and an oral hearing by the panel. This is followed by a second set of submissions and a second hearing. Unlike most judicial and arbitral proceedings, the presentation of submissions to GATT panels by the parties is simultaneous. Each of the two procedural phases thus has a particular significance. During the first phase the parties take note of each other's arguments. This is also the ideal time for the panel and its members to ask questions and require submission of documents and expert opinions. The second phase allows for a more thorough adversarial discussion of the material produced during the first stage. There has been a tendency on the part of the Council to set deadlines for the completion of each panel's work. In fact, panel proceedings are generally wound up within a period of six to nine months, but much depends on the difficulties encountered in the process.

Panel proceedings are strictly confidential, but panels and the GATT Secretariat can do nothing about information being leaked by the parties themselves. The danger of these leaks increases as proceedings advance, and no defence against them can be upheld after a panel report has been circulated among the Council members. It would be more realistic to declassify documents at that moment.

Third party states are permitted to present written and oral arguments if they have indicated their interest to do so when the panel was constituted by the Council. They have no access to the file of the proceedings, unless the parties to the dispute allow it. The participation of third parties is vital, not only because they add to the information available to the panel, but also, and foremost, because they make the panel aware of the multilateral dimension of the conflicts inside GATT. The limited access of third parties to the documents submitted to the panel is a product of the rule of confidentiality, but runs contrary to the rules in judicial proceedings, and is a source of misgivings for third parties. In discussions concerning reform of panel procedure rules, the question of increasing third party rights is a perennial subject of debate.

The internal deliberations of the panel go on throughout the proceeding, informally and in strict secrecy. Drafting of the report is conducted on two parallel tracks simultaneously. On the one hand, the panel prepares the "descriptive part" of its report, which is submitted in advance to the parties. The parties may, and do, present their response to the proposed finding of facts and their reflections on the panel's summary of their arguments, but the panel makes its own "findings" and "conclusions." A panel is required by the 1979 Understanding to "set out the rationale behind any findings and recommendations it makes", i.e., to give a reasoned opinion as any court of law would do.[19]

Final Stages of Dispute Settlement Procedure

When the report has been finally approved by the panel, it is first presented to the parties by the chairman. Under standing practice, he may on this occasion add his personal comments in order for the parties to understand the position of the panel and to help them in presenting the report in their respective capitals. From the date of this presentation, the parties are given a "reasonable period of time" to find a voluntary settlement of their dispute.[20] To be frank, the secret hope of all panels is that this will not happen because a voluntary settlement would make the report superfluous: Nobody would know whether a voluntary settlement had been arrived at on the basis of the report or in order to avoid the report's approval by the Council. In fact, the cases of voluntary settlement at this advanced stage are extremely rare.

[19] This provision, which is particularly important from the legal point of view, is to be found in point 17 of the said Understanding.

[20] 1979 Understanding, point 18. The "reasonable period of time" is estimated to be two weeks in practice.

In the normal course of events, if the parties are unable to reach a settlement, the report is circulated to all Contracting Parties. It receives a serial number and a date in the official GATT documents at this time but, as we shall see, both this number and date are deceptive with regard to the solution of the conflict.

A period of thirty days is left to Council members before the report comes up for discussion, and parties having objections are required to explain their objections in writing at least ten days prior to the Council meeting.[21] The panel chairman is first invited to make a short presentation of the report. Following this, the parties to the dispute are called to speak; there is then a general discussion which may well extend over several sessions of the Council before a decision is reached. The report and its conclusions become legally effective when they are adopted by the Council. It should be remembered that the date of the report, which is of primary importance legally, is not the date of the panel report, but the date on which the report was adopted by the Council. It is important that this be a precise date and not merely a reference to a given session, which may last for several days.

The report becomes a public document once it has been adopted by the Council. It will eventually be published in BISD under the date of its adoption. There is thus a delay of one to two years between the adoption of reports by the Council and their general availability in printed form, a highly regrettable situation which could be improved only by the creation of a regular official GATT journal. Reports that have not been adopted by the Council have no legal authority whatsoever. It is therefore bad legal practice to create a semblance of authority by quoting such reports in later cases or for academic purposes.

It also follows from the foregoing that panel reports adopted by the Council should be quoted exclusively by the date of their approval and by reference to the supplements of BISD. All other forms of citation are confusing because they do not distinguish between adopted and non-adopted reports. Of course, as long as reports have not appeared in BISD there is no other solution than to quote them by their serial number, but in this case it is important to warn the reader that the report has not yet been published.

[21] This results from the 1989 Improvements, points G(1) and G(2).

IV. STYLE AND STRUCTURE OF PANEL REPORTS

The style and structure of panel reports are determined, to a large extent, by the distribution of powers in conflict resolution and by the procedural rules and their application as they have been explained above.

General Style of Reports

GATT panel reports are not literary pieces, far from it. But before speaking of style, a word must be said about the use of languages. The choice of languages in international life is not neutral, because each language contains a world of idiosyncrasies. This is also true of legal language: here the choice of language implies an inescapable preference for a given legal system and for its characteristic methods of thought.

GATT has three official languages, English, French and Spanish, which may of course be used freely in the proceedings. Moreover, simultaneous interpretation allows for the use of still other languages during the panels' hearings. Despite this linguistic flexibility, internal deliberations of the panels are conducted exclusively in English, which is the original language in which panel reports are drafted. From the point of view of academic research, the English version of panel reports is therefore the primary source and the basis for analysis. The other versions, in French and Spanish, are the work of translators, not of the panels themselves. They may serve for the purpose of information, but their value for scientific research is nil. This is a fair description of the real situation, not a judgment on what is desirable.

The primary objective of panel reports is not to resolve a dispute directly (though this ultimate aim is, of course, uppermost in the minds of panel members) but to gain approval of the GATT Council for the solution worked out by the panel. Panel reports are therefore basically persuasive, not prescriptive documents. This accounts for the strange narrative character of reports which distinguishes them from judgments and arbitral awards. Panels are given to "noting", "recalling" or "considering" whatever occurs in the course of a given dispute. They refrain from giving authoritative opinions and their conclusions read as "suggestions" for action by the Council. This use of language makes the task of extracting the legal rationale from panel reports difficult. The art of reporting on GATT panel findings is therefore a much more arduous task than traditional law reporting. Writing summaries of GATT panel reports sometimes requires guesswork rather than extraction of solid legal principles from genuine decisions.

Structure of Reports

Since the early 1980's, when more attention was paid to the legal structure of panel reports, a certain *ordo scribendi* has established itself. Whereas formerly the facts of the case, the arguments of the parties and the panels' own considerations appeared together, the more recent reports fall into two major parts: first, the "descriptive part," which is prepared with the knowledge that it will be exposed to the criticism of the parties, as was explained above, and, second, the panel's own reasoning, the so-called "findings," which arrive at a "conclusion," in the form of a proposal for action by the Council.

The descriptive section of the report is divided into three or four chapters, beginning with an introduction which sets out the origin of the dispute and the procedure followed. In this introduction one finds a record of the institution of the panel and of its terms of reference. In the second chapter the panels set out the objective facts of the case, as they are required to do by the 1979 Understanding.[22] This chapter also often includes a description of national legislative, administrative or judicial acts which are the origin of the dispute. Next comes a reasoned and systematic account of the arguments put forward by the parties to the dispute. Here the panel is at pains to give an accurate and fair account of each party's position, an effort which does not always earn praise from those concerned. If there has been participation of third parties, their positions are likewise recorded.

Thus, ideally a well drafted report will have the following structure:

1. Introduction (origin of the dispute and procedure followed).
2. Factual aspects of the dispute.
3. Arguments of the parties.

[22] It is said in point 16 of the Understanding that ". . . a panel should make an objective assessment of the matter before it, including an objective assessment of the facts of the case and the applicability of and the conformity with the General Agreement . . .".

4. Submissions of third parties (if any).
5. Panel's findings (legal reasoning).
6. Panel's conclusions (recommendations and rulings proposed to Council).

It should be noted that the summaries, constituting the basis of this handbook, are mainly drawn from the panels' findings and conclusions. The descriptive parts of reports have only been referred to when uncertainties in the findings had to be cleared up. The full presentation of the parties' arguments would have required much more extensive, but ultimately inconclusive research. In some cases the findings include lengthy technical analyses which could only be recorded in a cursory way.[23]

Examples of Good Report Writing

Drafters of panel reports seeking inspiration might turn most profitably to the more recent cases, all of which are drafted in the "new style." Amongst these, the report on Trade in Semi-Conductors constitutes an outstanding example of analytical report-writing, whereas the report on Norwegian Restrictions on Imports of Apples and Pears—which concerned the "existing legislation clause" in the Protocol of Provisional Application of GATT—shows that concise report-writing also has a place in the best GATT tradition.[24]

Beyond the questions of style, certain reports have to be commended for their content and legal value. The 1958 report on the Italian Discrimination against Imported Agricultural Machinery, for instance, explained in simple and convincing arguments one of the fundamental principles of GATT: national treatment on internal legislation.[25] In 1984, a panel produced the Nicaragua Sugar Quota report which demonstrated strong resolve in a critical situation, but the United States refused to implement its findings as long as the political regime remained unchanged in Nicaragua.[26] The report of the Panel on Newsprint

[23] This relates to three reports: on the Uruguayan Recourse (Case 20), on the Taxation of Alcoholic Beverages in Japan (Case 63) and on Japanese Restrictions on Import of Agricultural Products (Case 67). Each of these reports contains extensive analysis of a great number of national measures in the fields of taxation and trade law.

[24] Japan, Trade in Semi-Conductors (Case 68) and Norway, Restrictions on Imports of Apples and Pears (Case 71).

[25] Case 16.

[26] Case 55.

is also a good example of a short and pertinent analysis leading to a strong conclusion, in this instance as a reaction against unilateral action of the EEC.[27]

The report on the Uruguayan Recourse to Article XXIII was an early landmark in the history of dispute settlement for two reasons. First, its general section contains some useful clarifications of the system for dispute settlement despite its inaccuracies regarding the so-called "non-violation impairments." Second, this report displays the effort made by a panel which, on the basis of a rather vaguely formulated complaint by a developing country, was at pains to examine in minute detail some 350 individual trade measures in 15 countries. It should be noted that this recourse was submitted to a Panel prior to the negotiation of Part IV of the General Agreement. This report, often cited, inspired a number of later determinations, especially with regard to agricultural markets.[28]

Several reports may be singled out for their attempts at defining some *principles of GATT law* beyond the letter of the General Agreement: that the GATT-system does not allow for self-redress;[29] that long-term tolerance of illegal practices does not eliminate the rights and duties of the contracting parties;[30] that the heritage of the Havana Charter is to help GATT, not to detract from its obligations;[31] that the "force of circumstances" may not allow a party to take liberties with its commitments;[32] that there must be transparency, security, and predictability in

[27] Case 59.

[28] Case 20. The importance of this report should not be underestimated because it was a turning point in the history of dispute settlement. But it must also be said that it has been counterproductive in several respects. Thus the lengthy considerations of procedure contained in the general part of the report turned out to be mostly theoretical and premature. It has already been noted that this report also gave credit to an entirely wrong idea of the so-called "non-violation impairments." As for its considerations of *onus probandi*, the panel diverted itself and many future panels from their primary task, which is to ascertain the facts, by dwelling on preconcieved ideas of the burden of proof (the latter is a typical device of judges who try to eschew the substance of the problems to be resolved). Time has come to get rid of this cumbersome precedent.

[29] See the cases quoted in note 6 above.

[30] This has been brought out quite forcefully in the report on EEC Quantitative Restrictions Against Imports from Hong Kong (Case 53), in fact French so-called "historic" or "residual" restrictions sustained by the EEC.

[31] This remark is to be found in the report on the Canadian FIRA Legislation (Case 54).

[32] This distasteful reasoning had been used by the EEC in the Hong Kong dispute (Case 53). It was rejected by the panel, with excessive courtesy in this author's opinion, as this argument smells of the "Normative Kraft des Faktischen" ideology which has played a most sinister role in European history.

international trade relations, even "law and order;"[33] that reasonable expectations must be honored beyond the letter of the law;[34] that GATT is based on certain fundamental principles including multilateralism,[35] non-discrimination,[36] and national treatment[37] and that we are travelling, with a view to these ends, on a "one-way street" from which there is no return.[38]

[33] As indicated above, "security and predictability" has been recognized as one of the main objectives of conflict resolution in the 1989 Improvements. These concepts are closely connected to the numerous provisions of the General Agreement on notification and publication of trade measures, which can be grouped together under the title of "transparency." This complex of rules has been prominent in quite a number of panel reports, including: The first Chile Apple dispute (Case 43); the report on the Distribution of Alcoholic Drinks in Canada (Case 65); the report on Japanese Restrictions on Import of Agricultural Products (Case 67); and, most importantly, in the report on the second Chile Apple dispute (Case 69). The "law and order" argument appears, quite unnecessarily, in the report on New Zealand, Import of Electrical Tranformers (Case 60).

[34] Protection of "reasonable expectations" is an old theme in GATT panel reports. See: Australian Subsidy on Ammonium Sulphate (Case 5); Germany, Imports of Sardines (Case 7); German Import Duties on Starch (Case 15); Norway, Import of Textiles (Case 41); EEC Panel on Vitamins (Case 51).

[35] Surprisingly, this principle, which is one of GATT's foundations, has hardly found expression in the practice of GATT panels. This is probably due to the fact that dispute settlement has so far been contained in a basically bilateral scheme. Consciouness of this multilateral context has been expressed only incidentally in some reports. See in this respect: the third report on the Uruguayan Recourse, where the panel recommends multilateral consultations on health regulations (Case 22); the report on the EEC, Import of Beef, where the panel draws attention to the fact that concessions granted in tariff negotiations must be extended to all contracting parties (Case 45); and the report on US Restrictions on Import of Sugar, where the panel explains that third party interests are safeguarded by the general bearing of the panel's findings (Case 72). The report on Japan, Trade in Semi-Conductors (Case 68) can be considered as a reaction against the reintroduction of bilateralism in a multilateral trade system.

[36] This principle has been strongly expressed in several panel reports. See: EEC, Import of Beef (Case 45); EEC Quantitative Restrictions against Imports from Hong Kong (Case 53); Canada, FIRA Legislation (Case 54); and Japan, Restrictions on Import of Agricultural Products (Case 67).

[37] The systematic study of panel reports shows, rather surprisingly, that the cases resolved on the basis of the principle of national treatment in Article III are much more numerous than those concerning the application of the MFN principle of Article I. Several important cases have been settled on the basis of the national treatment principle. The pattern has been set by the report on Italian Discrimination against Imported Agricultural Machinery (Case 16), which in retrospect appears to have been one of the most constructive early decisions. In recent practice, the principle has been central in the reports on the Canadian FIRA Legislation (Case 54), on Section 337 of the US Tariff Act

V. SHORTCOMINGS OF REPORT WRITING

The legal shortcomings of reports on dispute-settlement are unfortunately numerous and conspicuous. No one is to be blamed for this because these deficiencies are essentially due to the weakness of the basis upon which the process of dispute settlement rests in GATT. The General Agreement does not even mention "dispute settlement," which explains why for a long time GATT practice did not distinguish between conciliation and genuine dispute settlement.[39] Panels are created ad-hoc by the Contracting Parties and their reports acquire legal authority only if they are approved by the Council. They do not enjoy the standing of international judicial bodies, even though they do a job which is equal to formal dispute settlement at the international level.

Legal Shortcomings

This is the basic cause of the hesitancy in older reports which aimed at a mutual adjustment of divergent interests rather than at a principled solution of conflicts. Conclusions of *non liquet* (ie, not proven) were frequent during this period. Its positive features aside, the Uruguayan Recourse offers a striking example of this attitude.[40] The adoption of the 1979 Understanding on dispute settlement has done much to strengthen the system of conflict resolution, especially by requiring the panels to express the rationale underlying their findings. The panels' understanding of their role has changed since this adoption from conciliation to genuine dispute-settlement.

(Case 74), on EEC Subsidies to Processors and Producers of Oilseeds ("Soya Panel", Case 77) and on EEC, Regulation on Imports of Parts and Components ("Screwdriver-Factories Panel", Case 79).

[38] This telling expression was coined in the report on the US Manufacturing Clause (Case 56), in reference to the "existing legislation clause"—often called also the "grandfather clause"—in the Protocol of Provisional Application of the General Agreement. It was also used in the report on Norway, Restrictions on Imports of Apples and Pears (Case 71).

[39] Decisions on dispute settlement invariably appear in the tables of BISD under the word "Conciliation." Only the 31st Supplement uses the words "Dispute settlement" but in the following volumes "Conciliation" is used once again. The editor of BISD does not seem to be aware of the real character of decisions taken on the basis of Article XXIII.

[40] In that case the panel refrained from examining the compatibility of the variable levies imposed by the EEC on the import of cereals with GATT law, because this question was the subject of negotiations in another body of GATT (see Case 20). The matter remained there for the next thirty years.

From the lawyer's point of view, the major limitation in the older reports is the lack of any recognizable legal structure. Most of these reports are quite obviously the work of non-lawyers—which is not meant to be a reflection on the soundness of their conclusions. But the legal value of these reports is low because they do not contain the essential ingredients for the advancement of the law: the structured expression of legal principles. The first thing to be done with a document containing the solution of a dispute is to identify the legal problems raised by each case. The problems must then be addressed and solved in a logical order, which means putting preliminaries before merits, separating procedural from substantive issues and, as far as the substance is concerned, putting the expression of legal principles before particulars such as deductions, applications and exceptions.[41]

As the primary concern of panels is to obtain the Council's approval, their tendency is to avoid any arguments which might arouse objections by delegations. Panels must be mindful of the warning expressed in the 1982 Ministerial Declaration which states that the Contracting Parties are not prepared to accept new obligations by dispute settlement.[42] Contentious problems are therefore often played down and reports thus become exercises in understatement. They are a legal slalom in which panels do their best to get around the obstacles which stand in the way of reaching the finish line, which is to obtain the much desired consensus.

Technical Defects

On a more technical level it must be said that many reports are crowded with statistical data, tables and graphics which break the continuity of the legal argument and which generally do little to advance the report's conclusions.[43] Sometimes reports have been adorned with footnotes. It must be said in this respect that footnotes are a scientific, not a

[41] An example of a total lack of legal structure is to be found in the report on Automotive Spring Assemblies (Case 52). In this report the panel considered the question of legal protection of patents under the Article XX exceptions without first examining the principles which underlie these exceptions. This is primarily a matter of logic and not of law. As a result, the issues which that panel could have addressed came back a few years later in the Section 337 Case – Case 74.

[42] It was said in this Declaration that decisions taken in the process of dispute settlement "cannot add to or diminish the rights and obligations provided in the General Agreement" (point X).

[43] For an example of a report crowded with tables and statistics, see EEC Refunds on Exports of Sugar (Case 39).

legal device, since the legal status of a footnote is unclear: is it meant to be explanatory, extensive, or restrictive?[44] In a legal document footnotes, whatever their content or purpose, should be part of the main body of the text.

Another confusing feature is reference to unpublished documents. Such documents may be part of the file and thus accessible to the parties at the time of the proceedings. But once the dispute has been settled reports become public documents. Therefore reference should only be made to documents which are accessible to all, that is, published in the BISD series, or published together with the report through either being quoted in full or added as an appendix.

References to precedents, which may be an important part of a panel's reasoning, tend to be extremely short and cryptic, the sole reference often being the page number where the quoted phrases or words are to be found. It must be said in this respect, that precedents are not legislative texts and that they cannot be treated as such. Precedents have a significance only by reference to their factual context, which must be somehow represented whenever a precedent is relied upon.

A special mention must be made of panel's frequent recourse to the drafting history of the General Agreement, which means, in fact, the drafting history of the Havana Charter. At first sight, this method might seem to provide convincing arguments by referring governments to their own intentions. In fact, however, the excessive use of these materials is out of place and even counterproductive for several reasons. *First*, it prompts the panels to shift their attention from the analysis of substantive problems and from the consideration of GATT's objectives to textual research of a purely semantic character. *Second*, arguments based on textual history tend to foster a retrospective interpretation of an Agreement which, in the wake of the Havana Charter, was meant to be a forward-looking instrument aimed at creating a basis for the solution of the trade problems of the future, not at perpetuating past ideas about international trade. *Third*, attention must be drawn to the fact that only a small number of GATT's membership were involved in drafting the Havana Charter. The newer members of GATT have accepted the General Agreement at face-value but they cannot be engaged *a posteriori* in the meanderings of preparatory work in which they had no part. Thus, panels would be well advised to turn away from

[44] The worst example of this kind of report is the one on the US Customs User Fee (Case 64). This report, which was adopted on 2 February 1988, is hopefully the last remnant of antiquated report writing.

the drafting history of the General Agreement, to look ahead to the "objectives" of GATT as mentioned in Article XXIII:1, which is only another way of saying the "object and purpose" of the General Agreement according to the language of the Vienna Convention on the Law of Treaties.

VI. ANALYSIS OF PANEL REPORTS

The purpose of this Handbook is to provide easy access to GATT dispute settlement since its inception in 1947. The work began from scratch as practically nothing had been done on this during GATT's forty year history. There was no reliable record of existing decisions, no systematic analysis, nor an index.

Record of Cases, Summaries, Key-words

Even though the decisions on dispute settlement are not very numerous, it appeared rather difficult initially to establish a reliable record, a fact made even more complicated because dispute settlement decisions can sometimes hardly be distinguished from decisions, such as emergency actions and security exceptions, made under other provisions of the General Agreement. Fortunately, all decisions affected by Article XXIII seem to have been published in BISD. Unpublished material and, more particularly, panel reports which did not meet with the Contracting Parties' approval, have been left out since they have no legal authority. Authors who rely on such material are misleading their readers.

The next step, in fact the essential one, was to make summaries of all the reports. This proved to be a delicate task because of the descriptive style of the reports and the reluctance of so many panels to express clearly the legal principles upon which they relied. In other words, summing up required interpreting the intentions of several panels to some extent. The summaries, which are the central part of this volume, try to give an easily understandable synopsis of the various reports. But these summaries should be checked against the full text (the most important parts of which have been reprinted in this volume) if there are any doubts.

At a later stage, key-words are selected from the summaries and an alphabetical index compiled from them. This again was a troublesome task, as it appeared that GATT has never attempted to analyze and classify its own legal production. There is no index or data-bank so there is no standard legal vocabulary in GATT. An elementary conceptual framework had to be created which allowed for both the specific concepts found in the various decisions and the broader categories they fell into. The latter proved to be of particular importance because they provided a way of grouping specific aspects under some general ideas. It is hoped that this will be the Handbook's main contribution toward constructing a more coherent system of GATT law.

The primary references retained for the key-words and for the construction of the alphabetical index had to be, of course, the words of the General Agreement, including the titles of the various Articles. Through these words, the reasonings of the panels can, in most cases, be easily cross referenced with the pertinent Articles and clauses of the General Agreement. There are even "magic" numbers in GATT, such as Articles I:1, III:2 and 4, XI:1, XXIII:1 and 2, each of which designates a legal galaxy of its own. A lawyer can approach these matters only with a sense of sacred awe. There are also legal *infernos*, such as Article XI:2(c)(i) dealing with import restrictions on agricultural products which, as a panel noted recently, nobody has managed to pass unscathed so far.[45]

GATT System and General Concepts of Law

Apart from specific rules and words derived from the text of the General Agreement, panel reports also refer, sometimes explicitly but more often in a veiled form, to general principles of law or to standards of legal thinking and legal method.

Thus many questions are touched upon in relation to the *sources of GATT law*, such as secondary GATT law, GATT custom or practice, and the system of the General Agreement. No reference has been made so far to the rules of general international law, which is a pity. Possibly recent international events will make GATT more conscious of its role in retaining universal order in the economic field. In contrast, there is constant recourse, though mostly implicit, to the rules and methods of *interpretation*. Obviously Article 31 of the Vienna Convention on the

[45] EEC Restrictions on Imports of Chilean Apples (Case 69). The report on Japan, Restrictions on Imports of Agricultural Products (Case 67), is the origin of the "seven conditions doctrine" which, contrary to the intentions of those who framed GATT, has rendered Article XI:2(c) virtually inapplicable. The consideration of the principle of *effet utile* might have inspired a more convincing approach from the authors of this report.

Law of Treaties inspired some report drafters, but this provision has never been explicitly quoted. In some cases panels had recourse to what maybe called the *comparative law method*, though this promising vein has not been explored in depth.[46] At times, questions had to be resolved in relation to *GATT jurisdiction*, whenever disputes appeared to be part of a broader issue, political or other.[47] Similar problems arose, at a lower level, in relation to some panels' competence. They appear under the key-word *terms of reference*. Finally, it appeared that the panels have to cope quite frequently with all kinds of questions on *procedure*, including presumptions and rules of evidence, well beyond the directions found in the Council's understandings on dispute settlement. The corresponding key-word gives an interesting insight into the internal working of the panels.

Appropriate words had to be chosen to describe the general elements of law found in many panel reports that go beyond those expressed in the language of the General Agreement. Each one of the key-words in this area constitutes a convenient focus for reflection on the fundamentals of GATT. These theoretical indicators may be helpful not only to students of GATT law who are in search of the principles governing the action of this great world-trade organization; they might also provide some inspiration to future panels that desire to arrive at solutions based on principles rather than pragmatic on considerations.

The otherwise unlimited facility of the English language offered no ready solution, however, for one fundamental problem which is currently expressed in French as the "*qualification juridique*" of facts or rules.[48] Panels are faced with this quandary whenever they have to determine the rules applicable to given facts or in given circumstances.

[46] An interesting example of the comparative method is to be found in the report on the Tariff Treatment of Coffee by Spain (Case 48). In this report the panel established that the Spanish method of classifying coffee for tariff purposes had no equivalent in other countries' tariff schedules by comparing the Spanish approach with those of other countries.

[47] Questions of jurisdiction were treated in the reports on US Import of Sugar from Nicaragua (Case 55) and on Canada, Export of Unprocessed Herring and Salmon (Case 66). In the first case, the backdrop was a political conflict, in the second, a conflict on fisheries. The panels consistently restricted their examination to the trade issues involved, which they resolved in light of ordinary GATT rules.

[48] "Qualification" in the English language refers to the qualities fitting a person for an office or employment. "Classification" or "Characterization" is a better translation for the French word, which in the sense here used is a false cognate.

Thus in more than one instance the question arose whether a particular trade restriction was subject to Article I:1 (MFN treatment), to Article II (tariff concessions and bindings), to Article III (national treatment), to Article XI:1 (non-tariff barriers) or whether it was more correct to turn to the exceptions of Article XX. The problem arises from the fact that the choice of the legal base from which to start is not neutral since some types of trade restrictions are definitely prohibited, others are permitted (such as customs duties), and still others are tolerated only if they are applied on a MFN or non-discriminatory basis. The choice of the connecting factor may thus implicitly decide the issue.

Solutions to that intra-GATT *choice-of-law problem* have been recorded in the index under two complementary sets of words: "Classification of national measures" and "Scope of GATT provisions." The examples given under these headings show that there has been much empiricism and even arbitrariness in this respect on the part of some panels.[49]

Once the pertinent words had been chosen to identify legal concepts inherent in GATT which are not in the General Agreement, some foundation had still to be found for each of them within the system of the GATT Articles. Since all the problems referred to have emerged in the course of contentious proceedings, Article XXIII:2 appeared to be the most appropriate connection. Possibly this Article has been overburdened because of this, but there was no other provision which could serve the purpose.

[49] Again, the Automotive Spring Assemblies report (Case 52) is an example of arbitrariness in choice involving Articles II, III, XI and XX of GATT.

LEGAL AND PROCEDURAL ANALYSIS

CONTENTS

ABBREVIATIONS

GA	General Agreement
PPA	Protocol of Provisional Application of the GA
CP	CONTRACTING PARTIES, acting as a body (GA, art. XXV)
cp, cps	contracting party, contracting parties
BISD	GATT, Basic Instruments and Selected Documents (quoted by volume – only Volume II being relevant – and supplements (1S/etc.))
IMF	International Monetary Fund
MFN	Most-Favored-Nation (clause, principle, treatment)
VAT	Value Added Tax
WP	Working Party

US Export Restrictions

DECISION BY CP

adopted on June 8, 1949

Parties Czechoslovakia / US

Published in BISD II/28

Key Words

MFN treatment. Rules and formalities relating to exportation (Article I:1). Security exceptions (Article XXI).

Summary

Contention of Czechoslovakia that the US had failed to carry out its obligations under the GA through its practice in relation to the issuance of export licenses rejected.

Conclusion

Complaint rejected.

Remarks

No reasons indicated.

Brazilian Internal Taxes (first report)

WP REPORT

adopted on June 30, 1949

Parties	France / Brazil
WP Membership	not indicated
Published in BISD	II/181
Related documents	See also 2nd report of December 13, 1950 (Case 6), final report of October 24, 1953 (Case 12), and note on outcome (BISD 75/68).

Key Words

(1) "Existing Legislation" clause in paragraph 1(b) of PPA. Applicable only to mandatory legislation preceding date of PPA. No extension of existing discrimination allowed by subsequent legislation.

(2) National treatment on internal taxation. Like products. Products not produced domestically. Trade effects. Damage, prevention of, redress of. Differential taxes on imported products inherently protective, irrespective of damage caused or of volume of trade affected. (Article III:2 and interpretative note).

Summary

(1) "Existing Legislation" clause of PPA. Mandatory character of Brazilian tax law 7404 of 1945. Application of the Law was permitted, although it was discriminatory and hence contrary to Article III. Tax Law 494 of 1948 was not covered by PPA since it contained an expansion of the existing margin of discrimination.

(2) National treatment on internal taxation (Article III). Examination of particular products. Brazilian "conhaque" different from French cognac. Clocks and watches. Discrimination to be eliminated, including on watches, for which there was no domestic production. Taxes on imported products in excess of those levied

on like domestic products inherently protective, whether or not damage shown. Article III intended to prevent damage and not merely to provide means of redress. Article III equally applicable whether imports from other cps were substantial, small or non-existent.

Conclusion

Brazilian Government willing to seek amendment of tax legislation.

Remarks

Some divergencies of views in WP were recorded, rendering conclusions on various points uncertain. Status of France as claimant party can be established indirectly through the resolution of October 24, 1953.

Notification of Existing Measures and Procedural Questions (paragraphs 97-103 on measures permitted by the PPA and the Annecy Protocol)

WP REPORT

adopted on August 10, 1949

Published in BISD II/49

Key Words

(1) Notification of "existing legislation" covered by PPA or Annecy Protocol. Notification not compulsory.

(2) "Existing legislation" eligible under subparagraph 1(b) of the PPA or subparagraph 1(a)(ii) of the Annecy Protocol only if mandatory by its terms or expressed intent.

Summary

(1) No obligation for cp to notify "existing legislation" covered by paragraph 1(b) of the PPA or paragraph 1(a)(ii) of the Annecy Protocol.

(2) A national measure is covered by paragraph 1(b) of the PPA or paragraph 1(a)(ii) of the Annecy Protocol "provided that the legislation on which it is based is by its terms or its expressed intent of a mandatory character—that is, it imposes on the executive authority requirements which cannot be modified by executive action".

Date of Reference for the phrase "Existing legislation" in paragraph 1(b) of PPA

CHAIRMAN OF THE CP

Ruling of August 11, 1949

Published in BISD II/35

Key Words

"Existing legislation" clause in paragraph 1(b) of PPA referrs to legislation predating the signature of the Protocol on October 30, 1947.

Summary

The phrase "existing legislation" in paragraph 1(b) of the PPA "refers to legislation existing on October 30, 1947, the date of the Protocol as written at the end of its last paragraph".

The Australian Subsidy on Ammonium Sulphate

WP REPORT

adopted on April 3, 1950

Parties	Chile / Australia
WP Membership	not indicated
Published in BISD	II/188
Related documents	Note on outcome (BISD 7S/68)

Key Words

(1) "Like products" (Article I:1). Comparative tariff classification used as a criterion. Tariff treatment of competing products.

(2) Classification of a national measure. Removal of subsidy. Articles XI:1 and III:2 not relevant in case of a measure not involving any prohibition or restriction of imports and not instituting any tax or internal charge.

(3) "Non-violation" complaint. Impairment of benefits. (Article XXIII:1).

(4) Subsidies. Notification obligation. (Article XVI:1)

Summary

(1) Removal by Australia of sodium nitrate from the pool of nitrogenous fertilizers subsidized by the Australian Government. Differential customs treatment of both ranges of fertililzers. Sodium nitrate and ammonium sulphate, whether or not "directly competitive", are not to be considered "like products" within the terms of Article I:1, taking account of the fact that both products are listed separately in the tariff of Australia and in the tariff of "other countries", such as the UK.

(2) Articles XI:1 and III:2 not relevant in the case of a measure (removal of a subsidy) not involving any prohibition or restriction of imports of sodium nitrate and not instituting any tax or internal charge.

(3) Though no infringement by Australia of any obligation under the GA could be established, it appeared from the circumstances that impairment of concessions granted to Chile had taken place, within the meaning of Article XXIII:2, as a result of a measure which did not conflict with the GA, but which had created "reasonable expectations" for Chile in view of previous arrangements.

(4) Article XVI:1 covers financial aid given by a government to support domestic production or improve its competitive position on domestic or foreign markets. Notification of subsidies required only after imposition of measure. No injury from failure to notify, given other opportunities for consultation.

Conclusion

Recommendations were addressed to Australia with a view to obtaining removal of any "competitive inequality" between nitrate of soda and sulphate of ammonia. Reservations of Australia were expressed in a Statement annexed to the Report (BISD II/195).

Remarks

Agreement was reached between the governments of Australia and Chile. See note published in BISD 7S/68.

Brazilian Internal Taxes (2nd report)

WP REPORT

adopted on December 13, 1950

Parties France / Brazil

WP Membership not indicated

Published in BISD II/186

Related documents See first report of June 30, 1949 (Case 2), final report of October 24, 1953 (Case 12) and note on outcome (BISD 7S/98).

Key Words

(1) Complaint. Forfeiture of right of complaint. Review of draft legislation of a cp does not prejudice right of any other cp to raise subsequently a question as to the consistency of such legislation with the provisions of the GA. (Article XXIII).

(2) Origin. Goods originating from a cp imported after transit through a third country do not lose their GATT origin. (Article I:1. Article III).

(3) Customs duties. Incorporation of internal taxes (Article III, issue not resolved).

Summary

(1) Review by WP of draft law modifying legislation on consumption taxes with a view to eliminating margins of discrimination exceeding those existing on October 30, 1947. WP satisfied with Brazilian draft apart from specific exceptions. Brazil willing to propose amendments necessary with a view to obtaining elimination of increased margins of discrimination. Review of draft legislation does not prejudice right of any cp to raise subsequently any question as to the consistency of such legislation with the provisions of the GA.

(2) Elimination of discrimination only with respect to products imported from cp. The same treatment would have to be accorded to products entering Brazil after coming in transit through a third country.

(3) Incorporation of margins of discrimination into customs duties is permissible only by using the procedures of the GA for modification of tariff concessions (opinion expressed by France, Greece, the UK and the US). Question considered to be not within the Panel's terms of reference.

Conclusion

No formal conclusion was reached.

Treatment by Germany of Imports of Sardines

PANEL REPORT

adopted on October 31, 1952

Parties Norway / Germany

Panel Membership "Panel on complaints", membership not specified

Published in BISD 1S/53

Related document CP Recommendation of October 31, 1952 (BISD 1S/30). Note on outcome (BISD 7S/69).

Key Words

(1) Tariff classification. Differentiation of tariff positions in tariff negotiations not amounting to "unilateral splitting-up". "Like products" (Articles I:1 and XIII:1). Products closely related treated as if they were "like products".

(2) Non-violation complaint. Injury resulting from measures not inconsistent with the GA. Frustration of "reasonable anticipations derived from former tariff relationship. Impairment of benefits accruing to a cp under the GA. Alteration of competitive relationship. (Article XXIII:1).

Summary

(1) Competitive inequality between preparations of clupea pilchardus and other varieties of clupea as a consequence of classification change in the German tariff. Definition of "like products" within the meaning of Articles I:1 and XIII:1 of the GA (not conclusive). Consistent treatment of various types of clupea as separate products in tariff negotiations. No "unilateral splitting-up" of a tariff item by Germany. No failure by Germany to carry out its obligations under the GA.

(2) Reasonable expectations of Norway deriving from tariff negotiations conducted with Germany on the basis of equal tariff treatment of two items closely related. Impairment of benefits deriving

from the GA within the meaning of Article XXIII:1 by alteration of pre-existing competitive relationship. Statistical evidence of damage not required.

Conclusion

Germany was invited by CP Resolution "to remove the competitive inequality" between the preparations of clupea pilchardus and other varieties of the clupeoid family, in consultation with Norway.

Remarks

The dispute was settled by mutual agreement. See note on outcome published in BISD 7S/69.

Special Import Taxes Instituted by Greece

PANEL REPORT

adopted on November 3, 1952

Parties	France / Greece
Intervening	UK. Participation of IMF representatives
Panel Membership	"Panel on complaints", membership not specified
Published in BISD	1S/48
Related documents	Note on outcome (BISD 7S/69)

Key Words

(1) Jurisdiction. Legal classification of contribution levied on allocation of foreign exchange. Tax system possibly constituting charge within the meaning of Article II, or an internal tax subject to Article III or a multiple currency practice liable to determination by the IMF and subject to Article XV:4. Exchange actions frustrating the intent of the GA provisions.

(2) Procedure. Request for additional information from the defendant and from the IMF (Article XXIII). Final conclusion deferred.

(3) Interpretation of the GA. Preparatory work of the Havana Charter relevant to the interpretation of GATT provisions. (Article XXIII).

Summary

(1) Greek "contribution" levied on foreign exchange allocated for the importation of goods. Greek tax system examined with a view to determining whether it must be considered an "internal tax or charge" within the meaning of Article III or a "multiple currency practice". In the former case the Greek tax would be subject to the provisions of Article III, whatever might have been the underlying intent of the Greek authorities. In the latter case, the matter

would be for determination by the IMF. In that event, Article XV:4 would be relevant insofar as this provision debars cp from frustrating the intent of the GA provisions by exchange action.

(2) The Panel found itself insufficiently informed on the nature of the tax system and its method of application and unable to determine whether the Greek tax fell within the terms of Article III or whether it constituted an additional import charge under Article II.

(3) Interpretation of Article III. Reference was made to the preparatory work of the Havana Charter (Article 31).

Conclusion

Additional information was requested from Greece on the nature of the contested tax system.

An inquiry was addressed to the IMF with a view to establishing whether the Greek "contribution" (a) was a multiple currency practice and, if so, (b) whether it was in conformity with the Articles of Agreement of the IMF.

Remarks

It appears from the note on the outcome that following the Greek devaluation of the drachma in 1953 the special import taxes were abolished (BISD 7S/69).

Increase of Import Duties on Products Included in Schedule XXV (Greece)

PANEL REPORT

adopted on November 3, 1952

Parties UK / Greece

Panel Membership "Panel on complaints", membership not specified

Published in BISD 1S/51

Related documents CP Recommendation of November 3, 1952 (BISD 1S/23). Note on outcome (BISD 7S/69).

Key Words

Increase of coefficients for currency conversion bound in tariff negotiations. Infringement of Article II:1.

Summary

Increase of coefficients for currency conversion of pre-war metallic drachmae notes of customs duties into paper drachmae notes bound in tariff negotiations. The measure was taken as an emergency measure to meet acute financial difficulties. The inconsistency of the measure with Article II:1 recognized by Greece. A time-limit was suggested for removal of the measure.

Conclusion

The inconsistency of the measure was established and a time-limit for elimination was fixed.

Remarks

Measure in question was rescinded by Greece shortly after time-limit set by CP (BISD 7S/69).

Belgian Family Allowances

PANEL REPORT

adopted on November 7, 1952

Parties	Norway and Denmark / Belgium
Panel Membership	"Panel on Complaints", membership not specified
Published in BISD	1S/59
Related documents	CP Recommendation of November 7, 1952 (BISD 2S/18). Note on outcome (BISD 7S/68)

Key Words

(1) Import charge tied to legislation on family allowances. Classification of levy doubtful. Levy incompatible either with Article I:1 or Article III:2 and in any case inconsistent with the "spirit of the GA".

(2) Exemption from levy granted to certain cp to be unconditionally extended to all cp. (Article I:1).

(3) "Existing legislation" clause of paragraph 1(b) of PPA. Legislation applicable only to legislation having mandatory character. Legislation not of mandatory character if practice shows a case of exemption granted by the executive.

(4) Government procurement. Exception in Article III:8(a) for government procurement not applicable to internal taxes and charges subject to the National Treatment clause. Article III:2.

(5) State trading. Exception to rules applicable to state trading enterprises in Article XVII:2 for governmental use appears to refer only to Article XVII:1 and not to extend to matters dealt with in the National Treatment clause.

Summary

(1) Belgian levy of a charge on foreign goods purchased by public bodies when these goods originate in a country whose system of

family allowances does not meet specific requirements. Classification of Belgian levy appeared doubtful. Inconsistency with Article I and "possibly" with Article III:2 established. Levy "based on a concept which was difficult to reconcile with the spirit of the GA".

(2) Exemption from levy granted to certain countries (Luxembourg, Netherlands, France, Italy, Sweden and UK) must be extended unconditionally to other cp.

(3) "Existing legislation" clause of paragraph 1(b) of PPA applicable only to legislation having mandatory character. The mandatory character of the Belgian legislation could not be recognised in view of the fact that an exemption had been granted by the Belgian executive to a country whose system of family allowances did not fully meet the requirements of the law.

(4) The panel felt that the exception in Article III:8(a) for government procurement was not applicable to internal taxes and charges subject to the National Treatment clause of Article III:2.

(5) It appeared to the panel that the exception to rules applicable to state trading enterprises in Article XVII:2 for governmental use referred only to Article XVII:1 and did not extend to matters dealt with in the National Treatment clause.

Conclusion

Belgium was invited to take the necessary measures, including a possible amendment of the Belgian legislation, with a view to removing the discrimination complained of (see CP recommendation).

Remarks

Discriminatory application of the tax was terminated by a new law which entered into force on March 6, 1954 (see note on outcome).

Netherlands Action under Article XXIII:2 to Suspend Obligations to the US

WP REPORT

adopted on November 8, 1952

Parties Netherlands / US

WP Membership not indicated

Published in BISD 1S/62

Related documents CP Determination of November 8, 1952 (BISD 1S/31). See also Resolution of November 8, 1952 on US import restrictions on Dairy Products (BISD 1S/31). Suspension of obligations extended by virtue of WP Report of December 1, 1955, paragraph 11 (BISD 4S/96); WP Report of November 16, 1956, paragraph 13 (BISD 5S/136) and CP Determination of November 28, 1957 (BISD 6S/14); WP Report of November 20, 1958, paragraph 14 (BISD 7S/124) and CP Determination of November 20, 1958 (BISD 7S/23).

Key Words

(1) Damage suffered by a cp due to import restrictions on dairy products. (Article XI:1). Authorization granted by CP to suspend certain obligations according to Article XXIII:2.

(2) Impairment of benefits (Article XXIII:1). Assessment of damage having regard to the value of trade involved and to the broader elements of impairment. Equivalence between the impairment suffered and the countermeasures authorized by the CP. (Article XXIII:2).

Summary

(1) Damage suffered by the Netherlands through limitations on its ability to sell its dairy products in the US market owing to the restrictions imposed by the US under Section 104 of the Defense

Production Act. Request by the Netherlands to be authorized to suspend the application to the US of obligations equivalent to the impairment suffered as a result of the US restrictions, according to Article XXIII:2.

(2) Criteria to be used in assessing volume of trade affected by measures and countermeasures. A purely statistical test not sufficient. Consideration of broader economic elements appropriate, such as claim that US restrictions had adverse effects beyond the products directly concerned on the solution of Dutch balance-of-payments difficulties. "Reasonable" character of proposed measures recognized in principle, but magnitude somewhat reduced. Willingness of the Netherlands to resolve the matter in accordance with the objectives and the spirit of the GA.

Conclusion

The Netherlands was authorized to impose an upper limit of 60,000 tons on import of wheat flour from the US.

Brazilian Internal Taxes (3rd report)

CP RESOLUTION

adopted on October 24, 1953

Parties France / Brazil

Published in BISD 2S/25

Related documents See reports of June 30, 1949 (Case 2) and December 13, 1950 (Case 6). Note on outcome (BISD 7S/68).

Key Words

Tax legislation discriminating between imported and domestic products (Article III:2).

Summary

The Resolution urged Brazil to bring existing tax laws into conformity with the GA as early as possible.

Remarks

Note on outcome published in BISD 7S/68 recorded that tax discrimination had been abolished in August 1958 and that the CP had accordingly noted the settlement of the complaint.

French Special Temporary Compensation Tax on Imports

CP DECISION

adopted on January 17, 1955

Parties Italy / France

Published in BISD 3S/26

Related documents Note on outcome (BISD 7S/68)

Key Words

(1) Tax increased the incidence of bound customs rates (Article II) and of permissible preference margins (Article I:4). Motives for action irrelevant. Unilateral action without prior consultation of CP regrettable.

(2) Infringement of Articles I and II allows cp whose trade is adversely affected to propose compensatory action under Article XXIII:2.

Summary

(1) "Compensation tax" increased the incidence of customs charges in excess of the maximum rates bound under Article II and increased the preference margins permissible under Article I. Tax said by France to facilitate removal of quantitative restrictions. The incidence of the tax was to be considered in itself and not the reasons which may have motivated its introduction. Regret expressed at unilateral action by France without prior presentation to the CP.

(2) Action of France justified recourse to the provisions of Article XXIII and allowed any cp whose trade is adversely affected to propose compensatory action as appropriate under Article XXIII:2.

Conclusion

Note was taken of France's undertaking to remove the tax as soon as possible. Intersessional Committee was to follow the matter closely.

Remarks

The tax was abolished on August 10, 1957 and replaced by other measures. CP considered matter as having been settled. (BISD 7S/68)

Swedish Anti-Dumping Duties

PANEL REPORT

adopted on February 26, 1955

Parties	Italy / Sweden
Panel Membership	"Panel on complaints", membership not specified
Published in BISD	3S/81
Related documents	Note on outcome (BISD 7S/69)

Key Words

(1) Dumping. Levy of anti-dumping duties based on "normal value". "Basic price system" by Sweden, though not inconsistent with Article VI, liable to lead to inconsistencies by creating general protection against low-cost producers. Burden of proving existence of dumping lies with the importing country. Excessive delays and administrative difficulties create uncertainties for trade. Exemption and refund of internal taxes on export.

(2) Impairment of benefits under Article XXIII:1. Obligation for a cp having recourse to anti-dumping measures to show to the CP the legitimacy of the use made of that right. Cooperation of parties in establishing "normal value" of goods.

(3) Article VI does not impose an obligation to act in case of dumping. Material injury to domestic industry is a condition for application of anti-dumping duties.

Summary

(1) Anti-dumping duties on importation of nylon stockings. "Normal value" criterion to be applied to calculation of anti-dumping duties according to Article VI. Anti-dumping duties levied in Sweden according to a "basic price", determined by the Swedish authorities. "Basic price system" in itself not inconsistent with Article VI, so long as the basic price is equal to or lower than the actual price

on the market of the lowest-cost producer. If that condition is not fulfilled, the "basic price system" might easily run into conflict with the obligation flowing from Article VI, since it serves to reverse the burden of proving dumping against the importer and may thus be turned into a general protection against low-cost producers, even in the absence of dumping practices. Swedish "basic price" system associated moreover with undue delay and administrative difficulties creating uncertainties for trade. Parties agreed on the obligation to take account of legitimate refund of duties and taxes on export, according to Article VI:4.

(2) Assessment of impairment of benefits under Article XXIII:2. Rights of national authorities in establishing the existence of dumping practices were not restricted by GA, but any cp making use of that liberty was obliged to show to the CP that it exercised its rights consistently with the GA. In case of divergencies on the establishment of correct "normal value", facts on which determination of dumping were based must be ascertained in cooperation with the cp concerned.

(3) General indications given on the interpretation of Article VI. Article VI does not oblige a cp to levy anti-dumping duties in case of dumping. Anti-dumping duties may be levied only in case of material injury caused to domestic industry.

Conclusion

The Panel's recommendation required: (a) Sweden to improve the administration of dumping control so as to minimize delays and other impediments; (b) both parties to facilitate an enquiry by Swedish authorities with a view to establishing whether nylon stockings are being exported from Italy at a price less than their normal value.

Remarks

The findings of the Panel were generally not conclusive. Swedish regulations abrogated on July 10, 1955 and the complaint was considered settled. (BISD 7S/69)

German Import Duties on Starch and Potato Flour

PANEL REPORT

adopted on February 16, 1955

Parties Benelux / Germany

Panel Membership "Panel on complaints", membership not specified

Published in BISD 3S/77

Summary

Promises given by Germany at the Torquay negotiation, as a part of the balance of concessions granted. Offer made by Germany considered by the Benelux countries to provide a satisfactory adjustment for the time being. (Article II).

Conclusion

The matter was considered disposed of.

Italian Discrimination Against Imported Agricultural Machinery

PANEL REPORT

adopted on October 23, 1958

Parties	UK / Italy
Intervening	Denmark
Panel Membership	"Panel for Conciliation", membership not specified
Published in BISD	7S/60
Related documents	CP Recommendation of October 23, 1958 (BISD 7S/22)

Key Words

(1) National treatment on internal regulation. Laws and regulations "affecting" internal sale. Article III:4 refers not only to laws and regulations governing directly conditions of sale or purchase, but also laws and regulations modifying adversely conditions of competition between imported and domestic products.

(2) Interpretation (Article XXIII:2). Divergencies between authentic versions of Article III:4 to be resolved by reference to "intention of the drafters". Equal treatment.

(3) Article III:8 applicable to production subsidies, not to credit facilities granted to purchasers.

(4) Measures fostering economic development or protecting domestic industry permitted if in accordance with the GA. Extension of credit exclusively for purchasers of domestic goods not permitted. (Article III:4).

(5) "Non-violation" complaint. Impairment of benefits. Not dependent on whether measures complained of are inconsistent with the GA. (Article XXIII:1).

Summary

(1) Special credit facilities granted by the provisions of Law No. 949 for purchase of agricultural machinery produced in Italy. Laws and regulations "affecting" internal sale, offering for sale, etc. in Article III:4 refer not only to laws and regulations governing directly the conditions of sale or purchase, but also to laws and regulations which might adversely modify the conditions of competition between domestic and imported products on the internal market.

(2) Difference between French and English versions of Article III:4 elucidated by reference to "intention of the drafters", which was to treat imported products in the same way as like domestic products once they had been cleared through customs.

(3) Article III:8 applyies only to production subsidies, not to credit facilities granted to the purchasers of agricultural machinery.

(4) It is not the intention of the GA to limit the right of a cp to adopt measures designed to foster economic development or protect a domestic industry, provided such measures are permitted by the terms of the GA. The GATT offers a number of possibilities to achieve such purposes through tariff measures or otherwise. Extension of credit exclusively for purchasers of domestically produced agricultural machinery is not permissible under the GA.

(5) Under Article XXIII:1 a case for impairment of benefits may be brought before the CP whether the impairment was a result of a measure conflicting with the provisions of the GA or of a measure which was not inconsistent with its provisions. Evaluation of prejudice not conclusive, but special credit facilities "had probably influenced a number of purchasers."

Conclusion

Italy was required to eliminate adverse effects of the provisions of Law No. 949 on imports of agricultural machinery, by making available to farmers the same credit facilities for imported as for domestically produced machinery, or by other appropriate means.

French Assistance to Exports of Wheat and Wheat Flour

PANEL REPORT

adopted on November 21, 1958

Parties	Australia / France
Intervening	Japan
Panel Membership	"Panel for conciliation", membership not specified
Published in BISD	7S/46
Related documents	CP Recommendation of November 21, 1958 (BISD 7S/22)

Key Words

(1) Subsidies on export of wheat and wheat flour. Definition of export subsidy. Partial financing of domestic price stabilization.

(2) Subsidies having the result of assuring a cp of a more than "equitable share" in world export trade (Article XVI:3).

(3) Impairment of benefits by displacement of Australia's normal share of wheat and wheat flour trade in Southeast Asia. (Article XXIII:1).

Summary

(1) French market organization for cereals managed by ONIC resulted in the grant of subsidies on the export of wheat and wheat flour within the terms of Article XVI:3. Exemption for domestic price stabilization system inapplicable because of partial government funding of system.

(2) Subsidies may not be applied in a manner which has the effect that the cp granting such subsidies obtains more than an "equitable share" of world export trade. "Equitable" share meant to refer to

"world" export trade of a particular product and not trade in individual markets. Desirability of satisfying world requirements in the most effective and economic manner with particular regard to the exporting country's share of world trade in a given product during a previous representative period. Subsidy arrangements found to have contributed to a large extent to the increase in France's exports of wheat and of wheat flour.

(3) Impairment of benefits. Displacement by French exports of normal Australian exports in Southeast Asia. Losses by Australia included not only direct damage to flour milling industry, but also reduction in domestic supply of by-products. (Article XXIII:2).

Conclusion

France was invited to revise the system of payments by ONIC to exporters of wheat and wheat flour so as to avoid adverse effects on normal Australian exports to Southeast Asian markets.

Exports of Potatoes to Canada

PANEL REPORT

adopted on November 16, 1962

Parties	US / Canada
Panel Membership	not indicated
Published in BISD	11S/88
Related documents	CP Recommendation of November 16, 1962 (BISD 11S/55)

Key Words

Canadian system of "value for duty" of imported potatoes. System resulted in additional import charge, incompatible with obligations deriving from Article II:1(a). Impairment of benefits. (Article XXIII:1).

Summary

Classification of Canadian system of "value for duty" applied to import of fresh potatoes. Article VII on customs value not relevant to issue. Conditions of Article VI:1(a) on anti-dumping and countervailing duties not fulfilled. System of "value for duty" resulted in imposition of an additional charge on imported potatoes inconsistent with Canada's obligations under Article II:1(a).

Conclusion

Canada was required to withdraw additional charge or effect any other satisfactory adjustment of the impaired benefit accruing to the US.

French Import Restrictions

PANEL REPORT

adopted on November 14, 1962

Parties	US / France
Interested	EEC
Panel Membership	not indicated
Published in BISD	11S/94
Related documents	CP Recommendation of November 14, 1962 (BISD 11S/55)

Key Words

(1) Tariff concessions granted by the EEC (Article II). French import restrictions inconsistent with Article XI:1.

(2) Impairment of benefits (Article XXIII:1). First objective of dispute settlement procedure is to secure withdrawal of measures inconsistent with the GA. Withdrawal to be sought prior to recourse to measures of retaliation allowed for by Article XXIII:2. (1955 Report on Organizational and Functional Questions).

Summary

(1) Import restrictions applied by France to products on which the EEC had given tariff concessions to the US. Inconsistency with Article XI not contested by France.

(2) Impairment of benefits accruing from tariff concessions received by the EEC. The first object in cases of this sort should be to secure the withdrawal of the measures inconsistent with the GA, prior to resorting to measures allowed for by Article XXIII:2, according to the view expressed in the 1955 Report on Organizational and Functional Questions.

Conclusion

France was required to withdraw measures inconsistent with Article XI. US was requested to refrain, for a reasonable period, from exercising its right, under the procedures of Article XXIII:2, to propose suspension of the application of equivalent obligations and concessions.

Uruguayan Recourse to Article XXIII

PANEL REPORT

adopted on November 16, 1962

Parties	Uruguay / Fifteen Countries [Austria, Belgium, Canada, Czechoslovakia, Denmark, Finland, France, FR of Germany, Italy, Japan, Netherlands, Norway, Sweden, Switzerland, US (see BISD 11S/97, note 1)]
Panel Membership	Campbell Smith (Canada), Biermann (Netherlands), Itan (Israel), Portello di Aguiar (Brazil), Schnebli (Switzerland)
Published in BISD	11S/95
Related documents	CP Recommendation of November 16, 1962 (BISD 11S/56). Report of March 3, 1965 (BISD 13S/35) (Case 22), Report of March 3, 1965 (BISD 13S/45) (Case 23)

Key Words

(1) Primary products. Import restrictions, types distinguished (see Remarks).

(2) Dispute settlement under Article XXIII. Panel's terms of reference. "Matter" to be dealt with. Matter to be defined by complainant party according to Article XXIII:1. Types of actions open to CP. "Rulings". "Recommendations". Suspension of concessions or obligations called for only if circumstances are "serious enough".

(3) Infringement of provisions of GA presumed to cause impairment of benefits. In case of "non-violation" complaint, burden of establishing impairment incumbent on claimant. (Article XXIII:1).

(4) "Existing legislation" clause of PPA, Annecy Protocol and Torquay Protocol to be taken account of.

(5) Variable import levies. EEC market organization for cereals. (Question reserved).

(6) Panel procedure. Two-stage procedure applied, leaving question of suspension of concessions or obligations to a later stage. Examination of complaints country by country. (Article XXIII:2).

Summary

(1) Complaint of Uruguay related to trade restrictions on temperate primary products that limited marketing opportunities in fifteen countries. Scope of Panel's work under Article XXIII:2. Twelve different types of restrictive measures applied to over thirty different products or groups of products reviewed by Panel with a view to establishing consistency or otherwise of the measures in question and impairment of benefits under the GA.

(2) The Panel declared itself competent to deal with any "matter" referred to it under Article XXIII, i.e. any measure considered by a cp to have either impaired a benefit accruing under the GA or impeded the attainment of an objective of the GA. Before being referred to the CP under Article XXIII:2, such matter must have been the subject of representations or proposals made pursuant to Article XXIII:1. Under Article XXIII:2 different kinds of actions are open to the CP, namely to make recommendations or give a ruling on the matter and to authorize the suspension of concessions or obligations. A "ruling" is called for only if there is a dispute on a point of fact or law. "Recommendations" should always be appropriate whenever they would lead to a satisfactory adjustment of the matter. Suspension of concessions or obligations is to be considered only if the circumstances are "serious enough", i.e. in cases where there is impairment of benefits.

(3) Nullification or impairment must relate to benefits accruing to a cp under the GA. In cases where there is a clear infringement of the provisions of the GA, the action would, *prima facie*, constitute a case of nullification or impairment and *ipso facto* require consideration of whether the circumstances are serious enough to justify the authorization of suspension of concessions or obligations. While it is not precluded that a case of impairment could arise even if there is no infringement of GATT provisions, it would be incumbent on the country invoking Article XXIII to demonstrate the grounds and reasons for its claim.

(4) A measure not consistent with the GA may be permitted under the terms of the PPA, the Annecy Protocol or the Torquay Protocol on account of its being applied pursuant to "existing legislation".

(5) Status of variable import levies or charges and, in particular, levies introduced by the EEC in its regulation on cereals under the common agricultural policy. These measures, though they raised serious questions, were not examined by the Panel, the matter being under consideration of the CP.

(6) Two-stage panel procedure applied, which left question of whether to recommend authorization of suspension of concessions or obligations to a later stage.

Remarks

The Panel did not indicate precisely the Articles of the GA under which the measures complained of by Uruguay were examined. It can be inferred from the content of the Report that the following provisions were relied upon : Article I (tariff preferences); Article II (tariff bindings); Article III (internal taxation, pricing, mixing regulations); Articles XI, XII and XIII; Article XVII (State trading); Article XX (health controls).

Negotiation on Poultry

DECISION ON ESTABLISHMENT OF PANEL

adopted on November 21, 1963

Parties US / EEC

Panel Membership not indicated

Published in BISD 12S/65

Key Words

Advisory opinion by Panel on value of US exports of poultry affected by customs unbindings. (Article II. Article XXIII:2).

Summary

Advisory opinion rendered on the basis of the rules and practices of the GATT on the value to be ascribed to US exports of poultry to the Federal Republic of Germany in the context of the unbinding concerning this product.

Conclusion

The parties concerned have complied with the Panel's conclusions.

Remarks

Date not indicated in BISD. Date drawn from Analytical Index, Article XXIII - 97. Opinion not published.

Uruguayan Recourse to Article XXIII (1963 Report)

PANEL REPORT

adopted on March 3, 1965

Parties	Uruguay / Seven countries (Austria, Belgium, France, FR of Germany, Italy, Norway, Sweden)
Panel Membership	see Report of November 16, 1962 (Case 20)
Published in BISD	13S/35
Related documents	Report of November 16, 1962 (Case 20); Report of March 3, 1965 (Case 23)

Key Words

(1) Compliance with CP recommendations. Action in case of non-compliance. (Article XXIII:2)

(2) Health regulations. Multilateral consultations recommended taking account of similarity of national provisions. (Article XXIII:2).

Summary

(1) Discussion by Panel of measures for which removal had been required by the Report of November 16, 1962. Compliance with former recommendations recorded in one case (Sweden). For all other defendant countries, the Panel recorded non-compliance or only partial compliance.

(2) Health regulations. Comparative appreciation. Multilateral consultations recommended in view of the similarity of the provisions complained of by Uruguay.

Conclusion

The matter was referred back to Uruguay for further consideration.

Uruguayan Recourse to Article XXIII (1964 Report)

PANEL REPORT

adopted on March 3, 1965

Parties	Uruguay / Six countries (Austria, Belgium, France, FR of Germany, Italy, Norway)
Intervening	Observer from Australia attending
Panel Membership	see Report of November 16, 1962 (Case 20)
Published in BISD	13S/45
Related documents	Report of November 16, 1962 (Case 20); Report of March 3, 1965 (Case 22)

Key Words

(1) Dispute settlement. Panel procedure. Follow-up of former reports (Article XXIII:2). Not conclusive.

(2) Terms of reference. New measures complained of in current Panel proceedings. Panel not competent to deal with matters which have not been dealt with under Article XXIII:1 and referred to it by the CP.

Summary

(1) Progress report on elimination of measures formerly found inconsistent with the provisions of the GA. Complete clearance recorded for one country (Italy). Outstanding measures noted for five other countries (Austria, Belgium, France, Germany, Norway). Matters to be held under revision according to the "two-stage procedure".

(2) New measures complained of by Uruguay. Panel not competent to deal with measures which have not been dealt with according to Article XXIII:1 and referred to it by the CP according to Article XXIII:2.

Conclusion

No conclusion was drawn.

Turkey—Consultation under Article XXII:2

WP REPORT

adopted on March 28, 1966

Parties	UK / Turkey
Intervening	EEC participating in WP
WP Membership	Donovan (Australia), Chairman
Published in BISD	14S/59

Key Words

Tariff increases due to be renegotiated under Article XXVIII. Coincidence with agreement preparatory to creation of a customs union under Article XXIV. Ankara Agreement Turkey/EEC.

Summary

Increases in Turkish tariff rates due to be renegotiated under Article XXVIII, coinciding in time with conclusion of Ankara Agreement preparatory to the formation of a customs union with the EEC on the basis of Article XXIV. Suggestion by the UK that no preference should be granted by Turkey to the EEC under the Ankara Agreement until tariff rates to be raised following Article XXVIII renogotiations had been reduced to their prior levels.

Conclusion

The dispute was settled by expression of goodwill by Turkey to the effect that a declaration would be included in the Article XXVIII renegotiations, saying that Turkey would give due consideration to the equitable rights of cp who are not parties to the Ankara Agreement when it comes to implementing differential tariff treatment in favor of the EEC.

UK Temporary Import Charges

WP REPORT

adopted on November 17, 1966

Parties	- / UK (no indication of claimant parties)
Intervening	IMF consulted on UK monetary situation
WP Membership	not indicated
Published in BISD	15S/113

Key Words

(1) Import charges. Balance-of-payments safeguard. Difficulties to be solved by recourse to quantitative restrictions, not by institution of a levy (Article XII, not conclusive). Application of levy to current contracts questioned.

(2) WP procedure. Consultation of IMF in WP procedure relating to balance of payments problems (Article XXIII:2).

Summary

(1) *Ad valorem* surcharge applied on all imports from all sources except certain foods and raw materials in view of correcting the UK balance-of-payments as a part of wider problems inherent in the underlying economic situation. Measure based on Article XII but not in the form of a quantitative restriction as permitted by Article XII. Temporary character of the measure. Criticisms addressed to the measure itself, its appropriateness and its application to goods imported under contracts concluded prior to the imposition of the levy.

Conclusion

The matter was abandoned in view of the discontinuation of the charge by UK.

US Subsidy on Unmanufactured Tobacco

WP REPORT

adopted on November 22, 1967

Parties	Malawi / US
Intervening	Canada, India, Jamaica; Turkey "associated"
WP Membership	Mahmood (Pakistan), Chairman
Published in BISD	15S/116

Key Words

Export subsidies on leaf tobacco. Subsidies alleged to assure the US of a more than equitable share of world trade (Article XVI:3) and to deprive less-developed countries of their chance to secure a share in the growth in international trade (Article XXXVI:3).

Summary

Article XXII:2 consultation on introduction by the US of a 5 cents per lb export subsidy on leaf tobacco. Malawi and other participating countries complained that the effect of the export subsidy was to assure the US of a more than equitable share in the world tobacco market in violation of Article XVI:3 and was at variance with the objective of Article XXXVI:3.

Conclusion

WP considered that the available evidence, having regard to the many factors which affect levels of exports and prices, did not demonstrate conclusively that the trade interests of Malawi and the other countries which had joined in the proceedings had been adversely affected. The US representative gave assurance of "sympathetic attention" to the Malawian complaint.

Jamaica—Margins of Preference/Base Date under Article I:4

PANEL REPORT

adopted on February 2, 1971

Parties	US / Jamaica
Panel Membership	Pasin (Turkey), Moerel (Netherlands), Samaranayake (Ceylon), Schnebli (Switzerland)
Published in BISD	18S/183
Related documents	CP Decision of March 2, 1971 (BISD 18S/33)

Key Words

(1) Accession to GATT of a formerly dependent territory under Article XXVI:5(c). Rights and obligations of acceding country maintained as established formerly by administering power. Base date for permitted preferences April 1, 1947 according to Article I:4. Base date legally applicable to preferences granted during the period preceding independence of Jamaica attained in 1962.

(2) Interpretation of the GA. Recognition of "uniqueness" of a particular situation. Waiver under Article XXV:5 making it possible to avoid "strained interpretation" liable to endanger integrity of GA.

Summary

(1) Accession of Jamaica to GATT and determination of base date to be taken into consideration for tariff preferences under Article I:4. Rights and obligations assumed by Jamaica upon accession were the rights and obligations resulting from the application of the GA to Jamaica by the UK as from August 1, 1962, including the provision of Article I:4 establishing the date of April 10, 1947 as the base date for permissible margins of preference. Independence of Jamaica was achieved on August 6, 1962. Accession under Article XXVI:5(c) was effective on December 31, 1963.

Changes in existing preferences made before August 1, 1962 therefore fell legally under the time-limit established by Article I:4.

(2) The Panel wishing to avoid a "strained interpretation" endangering the integrity of the GA, while taking account of the "uniqueness" of the Jamaican case, recommended a waiver on the basis of Article XXV:5, changing with respect to Jamaica the base date referred to by Article I:4 from April 10, 1947 to August 1, 1962.

Conclusion

A waiver was granted by CP on March 2, 1971

UK Import Restrictions on Cotton Textiles

PANEL REPORT

adopted on February 5, 1973

Parties Israel / UK

Panel Membership Eastham (Canada), Affolter (Switzerland), Colliander (Sweden), Eun Tak Lee (Korea)

Published in BISD 20S/237

Key Words

Emergency action. Market disruption by low-cost suppliers. Structural changes in Israel's cotton industry recognised (Article XIX). Voluntary settlement reached by parties (Article XXIII:2).

Summary

Market disruption by imports from low-cost suppliers. Israel considered by UK to be a low-cost, disruptive supplier of textiles. Structural changes in Israel's cotton textile industry. Unanimous view of the Executive Committee of the British Textile Confederation considered. Mutually acceptable settlement reached between the parties on treatment of Israel as an "unrestricted supplier" as of January 1, 1973.

Conclusion

The settlement was recorded by Panel.

Remarks

Reference to Article XIX inferred from context, not contained in report.

UK—Dollar Area Quotas

PANEL REPORT

adopted on July 30, 1973

Parties	US / UK
Intervening	Commonwealth Caribbean Countries, Cuba
Panel Membership	Sahlgren (Finland), Dunkel (Switzerland), Niyi (Nigeria), Tomic (Yugoslavia)
Published in BISD	20S/230 (Interim Report), 236 (Report)

Key Words

(1) Quantitative restrictions established for balance-of-payments reasons (Article XII). Restrictions maintained in favor of certain Commonwealth Caribbean countries. Restrictions inconsistent with Articles XI and XIII. Suspension of concessions or obligations under Article XXIII:2. Assessment of damage.

(2) Panel procedure. Voluntary settlement. Procedure suspended after finding of inconsistency. Invitation to parties to seek agreed settlement under Article XXIII:2. Reservations by third parties directly concerned by settlement reached. Matter dismissed by Panel following a declaration of goodwill by main parties in the spirit of Part IV of the GA.

Summary

(1) Maintenance by the UK of quantitative restrictions on certain products imported from the US and certain other "dollar area" countries. Restrictions had their origin in the exchange control and currency conservation measures adopted by the UK, maintained since as constituting a protection for the economic interests of the developing Commonwealth Caribbean countries. Examination by Panel of items of critical export interest to the US. Inconsistency of restrictions with GATT obligations (Articles XI and XIII) not contested. Possibility of assessment of damage to US

envisaged with the consequence of resulting suspension of concessions or obligations under Article XXIII:2 by the US. No direct interest of the UK involved.

(2) Procedure suspended with a view to giving parties an opportunity to seek satisfactory solution, having due regard for the interests of the Caribbean countries and territories (Interim Report). Agreement reached between UK and US, meeting with reservations on the part of Caribbean countries and territories. Declaration of goodwill by main parties in the spirit of Part IV of the GA allowed the Panel to dismiss the matter. (Final Report).

Conclusion

Agreement reached by parties recorded in final report. Agreement did not give the Caribbean countries full satisfaction. Assurances given by parties with a view to avoiding harm to export interests of the Caribbean countries "welcomed" by Panel.

Remarks

Interim and final reports were adopted under the same date.

Canadian Import Quotas on Eggs ("advisory ruling")

WP REPORT

adopted on February 17, 1976

Parties US / Canada

WP Membership Eggert (Finland), Chairman

Published in BISD 23S/91

Key Words

Import restrictions on an agricultural product necessary to the enforcement of governmental measures restricting domestic production (Article XI:2(c)(i). Previous representative period (Article XI:2, second part, final phrase).

Summary

The WP agreed that the Canadian supply management program for eggs met the requirements of Article XI:2(c)(i). The US did not accept that the present system was able to effectively control domestic production and considered therefore that it would not be in conformity with Article XI:2(c)(i). The Panel was unable to decide which "representative period" would meet the requirements of Article XI.

Conclusion

The parties were invited to come to a "pragmatic solution" in bilateral discussions. No conclusion was drawn on impairment of benefits.

US Tax Legislation (DISC)

PANEL REPORT

presented on November 12, 1976

Parties	EEC / US
Intervening	Canada
Panel Membership	Mariadason (Sri Lanka), Falconer (New Zealand), Forte (Italy), Gabrielsson (Sweden), Prest (UK)
Published in BISD	23S/98
Related documents	Reports presented on November 12, 1976 in the cases US/France (Case 32), US/Belgium (Case 33) and US/Netherlands (Case 34) and the Understanding of the Council of December 7/8, 1981, on adoption of the four Reports (BISD 28S/114)

Key Words

(1) Export subsidies. US "DISC legislation" had effects constituting export subsidies, not in accordance with Article XVI:4.

(2) Export subsidies. Remission of direct taxes and exemption of sales taxes constituted export subsidies (Report on Subsidies, Provisions of Article XVI:4, of November 19, 1960, BISD 9S/185, paragraph 5(c) and (d)).

(3) Notification of subsidization under Article XVI:1. Provision applicable to US DISC legislation.

(4) Principles of GATT law. Tax distortion not justified by the aim of correcting tax distortions created by other cp. Redress of violation of the GA may be sought only by recourse to the remedies offered by the GA. (Article XXIII:2).

(5) Principles of GATT law. Practices of cp in force for some time without being subject of complaints. No evidence of consensus on compatibility of such practices with the GA. (Article XXIII:2).

(6) Subsidies inconsistent with Article XVI:4 constituted *prima facie* case of impairment of benefits under Article XXIII:1.

(7) (a) Territorial scope of Article XVI:4. Economic processes located outside the territorial limits of exporting country not to be regarded as export activities. (Article XXIII:2).

(b) Prices considered for the purposes of Article XVI:4 to be prices charged between independent enterprises acting at arm's length.

(c) Article XVI:4 does not prohibit the adoption of measures to avoid double taxation.

Summary

(1) US tax legislation on Domestic International Sales Corporations (DISC) conferred a tax benefit essentially related to exports and intended to increase US exports. As such, the DISC legislation should be regarded as an export subsidy, having in some cases effects which were not in accordance with the US obligations under Article XVI:4.

(2) Deferral of tax for an indeterminate period under the DISC legislation constituted to some extent a partial exemption covered by paragraphs (c) and (d) of the illustrative list given in paragraph 5 of the 1960 report on Subsidies on remission, calculated in relation to exports, of direct taxes, or exemption of charges or taxes in relation to exported goods.

(3) The DISC legislation, by the fact that it constituted an export subsidy, was covered by the notification obligation contained in Article XVI:1.

(4) The DISC legislation was said to have been introduced with a view to correcting an existing distortion created by tax practices of other cp. Panel concluded that one distortion would not be justified by another one. If the US had considered that other cp were violating the GA it could have had recourse to the remedies offered by the GA.

(5) The fact that tax practices of certain other countries had been in force for some time without being the subject of complaints was not, in itself, conclusive evidence that there was a consensus that they were compatible with the GA.

(6) *Prima facie* case of nullification or impairment of benefits considered established.

(7) The Panel report was adopted on the following understandings and declarations:

(a) Economic processes located outside the territorial limits of the exporting country need not be subject to taxation by the exporting country and should not be regarded as export activities in terms of Article XVI:4.

(b) Article XVI:4 requires that prices for goods in transactions between exporting enterprises and foreign buyers under their control or the same control should for tax purposes be the prices which would be charged between independent enterprises at arm's length.

(c) Article XVI:4 does not prohibit the adoption of measures to avoid double taxation.

Conclusion

Impairment of benefits was presumed.

Income Tax Practices Maintained by France

PANEL REPORT

presented on November 12, 1976

Parties	US / France
Panel Membership	same as DISC Panel (Case 31)
Published in BISD	23S/114
Related documents	see Report of DISC Panel (Case 31)

Key Words

Export subsidies. French income tax practices based on territoriality principle constituted a subsidy to exports inconsistent with Article XVI:4.

Summary

French income tax practices based on the territoriality principle (including treatment of foreign dividends and use of principles other than arm's length pricing to allocate income between related entities) allowed some part of export activities, belonging to an economic process originating in the country, to be outside the scope of French taxes. However much such practices may have been an incidental consequence of French taxation principles rather than a specific policy intention, they constituted a subsidy on exports because the benefits to exports did not apply to domestic activities for the internal market.

Conclusion

Impairment of benefits was presumed.

Income Tax Practices Maintained by Belgium

PANEL REPORT

presented on November 12, 1976

Parties US / Belgium

Panel Membership same as DISC Panel (Case 31)

Published in BISD 23S/127

Related documents see Report of DISC Panel (Case 31)

Key Words

Export subsidies. Belgian income tax practices based on territoriality principle constituted a subsidy to exports, inconsistent with Article XVI:4.

Summary

Findings substantially identical to findings in French case (Case 32).

Conclusion

Impairment of benefits was presumed.

Income Tax Practices Maintained by The Netherlands

PANEL REPORT

presented on November 12, 1976

Parties	US / Netherlands
Panel Membership	same as DISC Panel (Case 31)
Published in BISD	23S/137
Related documents	see Report of DISC Panel (Case 31)

Key Words

Export subsidies. Netherlands income tax practices, based on world-wide principle in conjunction with exemption of foreign income of foreign dividends and use of principles other than arms' length pricing, constituted a subsidy to exports, inconsistent with Article XVI:4

Summary

Dutch income tax practices based on particular application of the world-wide principle (including treatment of foreign dividends and use of principles other than arm's length pricing to allocate income between related entities), in conjunction with the qualified exemption in respect of foreign income, allowed some part of export activities, belonging to an economic process originating in the country, to be outside the scope of the Netherlands taxes, constituting a subsidy on exports.

Conclusion

Impairment of benefits was presumed.

EEC Measures on Animal Feed Proteins

PANEL REPORT

adopted on March 14, 1978

Parties US / EEC

Panel Membership Kaarlehto (Finland), Barnett (Jamaica), Denis (Canada), Eberhard (Switzerland), Parman (Turkey)

Published in BISD 25S/49

Key Words

(1) "Like products" and products "directly competitive and substitutable" (Articles I:1 and III).

(2) Security deposits provided by EEC Regulations to be considered as an "enforcement mechanism", not as a financial burden (Articles I:1 and III).

(3) Internal regulations relating to the "mixture, processing or use of the products" (Article III:5, first sentence) and "internal quantitative regulations" applied in a manner contrary to the principles of Articles III:1 and III:5, second sentence.

(4) Exemption of domestic corn gluten from measures applicable to imported corn gluten inconsistent with Article III:4.

(5) Administrative requirements established by EEC Regulation not considered inconsistent with Article III:4.

(6) "Internal measures" (Article III) and "border measures" under Article II distinguished.

(7) Most-favored-nation treatment required for like products, but not directly competitive or substitutable products (Article I).

Summary

(1) EEC Council Regulation 563/76 of March 15, 1976 provided for grant of aid to domestic producers of oil seeds and dehydrated fodder and made free circulation in the EEC of imported oil seeds,

cakes and meals, dehydrated fodder, corn gluten and compound feeds subject to the presentation of a "protein certificate" issued upon production of a document of proof of the purchase and the denaturing of skimmed milk powder, allowance being made for the replacement of the latter document by the deposit of a security or a bank guarantee. Products that add proteins to animal feeds, taking account of the great variety of their tariff classifications, protein contents and origin, could not be considered "like products" within the meaning of Articles I and III. The Panel recognised however that vegetable proteins and skimmed milk powder could be considered to be directly competitive and substitutable products within the meaning of Article III.

(2) Provision of security deposits, including any associated costs, are to be regarded as an enforcement mechanism relating to the enforcement of the purchase obligation, not as a financial burden.

(3) The EEC Regulation was not to be regarded as an internal quantitative regulation "relating to the mixture, processing or use of products" in the sense of Article III:5, first sentence, but the Panel found that the obligation to buy skimmed milk powder was an internal quantitative regulation measure protecting this product in a manner contrary to the principles of Article III:1 and to the provision of Article III:5, second sentence.

(4) Exemption of domestic corn gluten from measures applicable to imported corn gluten was inconsistent with Article III:4.

(5) The various administrative requirements, including the "protein certificate", were found to be not inconsistent with the rule of Article III:4 relating to treatment not less favorable than the treatment accorded to "like products" of domestic origin.

(6) EEC measures to be regarded as "internal measures" under Article III, not as "border measures" under Article II.

(7) EEC measures treating directly competitive or substitutable products differently not found to be inconsistent with Article I:1. Article I obligations apply only to like products.

Conclusion

No formal conclusion was drawn by Panel, apart from the finding that the EEC Regulation was inconsistent with the principles of Article III:1 and the provisions of Article III:5, second sentence. The EEC Regulation had been withdrawn prior to the issuance of the panel report.

Canada—Withdrawal of Tariff Concessions (Lead and Zinc)

PANEL REPORT

adopted on May 17, 1978

Parties	EEC / Canada
Panel Membership	Ukawa (Japan), Greig (New Zealand), Hagfors (Finland)
Published in BISD	25S/42

Key Words

(1) Conversion of specific tariff rates into *ad valorem* rates. Maintenance of general level of concessions (Article XXVIII).

(2) Base period to be considered for conversion. Three-year period to be considered according to the general principle observed in Article XXVIII negotiations.

(3) Withdrawal of concessions. Value of total imports to be taken into account for purpose of determining *ad valorem* equivalents (Article XXVIII).

(4) Retaliation to be related to actual damage, with a view to maintaining the highest possible general level of concession (Article XXIII:2).

Summary

(1) In negotiations undertaken with the aim of converting specific rates of duty into *ad valorem* rates under Article XXVIII, the intention is to maintain a general level of concessions not less favorable to trade than that provided prior to negotiations.

(2) Base period for the purpose of converting specific into *ad valorem* rates of duty to be determined by reference to the most recent three-year period for which trade statistics were available, according to the general principle observed in Article XXVIII negotiations.

(3) Article XXVIII:2 required that account be taken of the value of total imports of lead and zinc for the purpose of determining the *ad valorem* equivalents. Since the Community offer of *ad valorem* equivalent exceeded this limit for zinc, Canada was entitled to withdraw concessions in order to restore balance of interests.

(4) Right of retaliation to be related to the actual damage suffered by Canada. In the interest of maintaining the highest possible general level of concessions Canada required to withhold retaliatory action pending reduction by the Community of its tariff on zinc or grant of concessions on other products of export interest to Canada of an equivalent value.

Conclusion

Action by Canada was justified in principle but excessive in volume. Canada was required to withhold retaliatory action pending grant of adequate concession or compensation by the EEC.

Japan Measures on Imports of Thrown Silk Yarn

PANEL REPORT

adopted on May 17, 1978

Parties US / Japan

Intervening EEC

Panel Membership Ekblom (Finland), Breckenridge (Sri Lanka), Hall (Australia)

Published in BISD 25S/107

Key Words

Voluntary settlement. Compromise proposed by Panel. Bilateral solution reached by parties. (Article XXIII:2).

Summary

Prior-permission system applied to the importation of thrown silk yarn with a view to ensuring the functioning of the State trading system for raw silk established by Japan. Oral presentation of the Panel's findings to the parties. Attempt by Panel to bring about a compromise. Bilateral solution reached by parties.

Conclusion

Panel procedure terminated.

EEC—Program of Minimum Import Prices, Licences and Surety Deposits for Certain Processed Fruits and Vegetables

PANEL REPORT

adopted on October 18, 1978

Parties US / EEC

Intervening Australia

Panel Membership Jagmetti (Switzerland), Breckenridge (Sri Lanka), Hagfors (Finland), Segalla (Austria), Sigmundsson (Iceland)

Published in BISD 25S/68

Key Words

(1) Procedure. Change of Panel members. Dissenting opinions. (Article XXIII:2).

(2) Agricultural products. EEC import regime for fruit and vegetables. Import certificates. Automatic licensing. Consistency with Article XI:1.

(3) Fees connected with importation. Import certificates. Lodging of security. Interest charges and costs. Consistency with Article VIII:1(a).

(4) Forfeiture of security. Enforcement mechanism, not a charge on import. (Article VIII:1(a)).

(5) Importation within period of validity of import certificate. Obligations assumed by importer did not exceed limit fixed by Article VIII:1(a).

(6) Suspension of issuing of import certificates pending decision on safeguard action not inconsistent with Article VIII:1.

(7) Costs of administration of import controls [Article II:2(c) and Article VIII:1(a)].

(8) Forfeiture of security to be considered as an enforcement mechanism, not a charge in the purview of Article II:1(b).

(9) Quantitative restrictions. Minimum price for imported tomato concentrates constituted an import restriction under Article XI:1.

(10) "Agricultural products" covers fresh products and products in an early stage of processing (Article XI:2(c)(i) and (ii)).

(11) Import restrictions "necessary to the enforcement" of restrictions on production (Article XI:2(c)).

(12) "Like domestic product" (Article XI:2(c)).

(13) Governmental measure restricting production. Community market organization for fresh tomatoes lacking effective enforcement, did not qualify under Article XI:2(c).

(14) Charges imposed in excess of the bound rate (Article II:1(b)). Interest charges and costs of security.

(15) Charges imposed in excess of the bound rate (Article II:1(b)). Forfeiture of security.

(16) Fees and formalities connected with importation. (Article VIII:1).

(17) MFN treatment under Article I:1. Dispensation of security in case of undertaking taken by country of origin on minimum price of tomato concentrate not discriminatory.

(18) Measures inconsistent with GATT obligations constituted *prima facie* impairment of benefits (Article XXIII:1).

Summary

(1) Procedure. Two Panel members changed during proceedings. Dissenting opinions on particular points.

(a) *Import certificate and associated security system*

(2) Minimum price system for tomato concentrates and import certificates issued for certain fruits and vegetables established under EEC Regulation 1927/75. Automatic licensing and associated security system operated by the Community were not inconsistent with Article XI:1.

(3) Interest charges and costs in connection with the lodging of the security were recognised to be limited in amount to the approximate costs of administration and, as such, not inconsistent with Article VIII:1(a).

(4) Forfeiture of security was not considered as a charge in connection with importation in the purview of Article VIII:1(a), but as part of an enforcement mechanism to which Article VIII had no relevance.

(5) Obligations to be assumed by importer with a view to completing the importation within the period of validity of the certificate not onerous enough to violate Article VIII.

(6) Authority of Member States to suspend issuance of import certificates pending Community action in response to a request for safeguard action not inconsistent with the Community's obligations under Article VIII.

(7) Interest charges and costs in connection with lodging the security associated with the import certificate, though in excess of the bound rate under Article II, found to be limited in amount to the approximate costs of administration in accordance with the provisions of Article VIII:1(a) and Article II:2(c) and therefore not considered to be inconsistent with Article II.

(8) Forfeiture of security considered as a part of the enforcement mechanism and not as a charge in the purview of Article II:1(b) and therefore not inconsistent with this provision.

(b) *Minimum import price and associated security system*

(9) Minimum price for tomato concentrates and associated additional security system was considered as constituting a restriction within the meaning of Article XI:1. Dissenting opinion.

(10) Meaning of "agricultural product imported in any form" in the sense of Article XI:2(c)(i) and (ii). Covers fresh products and products when in an early stage of processing and still perishable so as to compete directly with the fresh product. Tomato concentrate was recognised to compete directly with fresh tomatoes and to qualify as "agricultural product".

(11) Import restrictions "necessary to the enforcement" of measures restricting production or marketing of agricultural products. Necessity recognised for import restrictions on tomato concentrate

only in concert with corresponding restrictions on the production and marketing of fresh tomatoes. (Article XI:2(c)(i) and (ii)).

(12) Concept of "the like domestic product" within the meaning of Article XI:2(c)(i) and (ii). Imported tomato concentrate and domestic tomato concentrate found to be like products, but Panel unable to decide whether imported tomato concentrate and fresh tomatoes would be like products.

(13) Community market organization for fresh tomatoes lacking effective enforcement did not qualify as a "governmental measure" which operated "to restrict the quantities of the like domestic product permitted to be marketed or produced" in the sense of Article XI:2(c)(i) and (ii). Minimum import price and additional security system for tomato concentrates did not qualify for the exemptions provided by Article XI:2(c)(i) and (ii) and were considered inconsistent with Article XI.

(14) Interest charges and costs in connection with the lodging of the additional security associated with the minimum import price for tomato concentrates were considered to be charges imposed on or in connection with importation in excess of the bound rate within the meaning of Article II:1(b) and therefore inconsistent with this provision.

(15) Forfeiture of additional security associated with the minimum import price for tomato concentrates was considered to be part of an enforcement mechanism and not a charge imposed on and in connection with importation within the purview of Article II:1(b). Dissenting opinion.

(16) Article VIII on fees and formalities connected with importation was considered not relevant to interest charges and costs associated with lodging the additional security and not relevant to the forfeiture of the additional security.

(17) Dispensation of additional security for products originating in countries undertaking to guarantee observance of minimum price for tomato concentrate was not considered as constituting a discrimination within the meaning of Article I:1, so long as a guarantee was necessary for all imports from all potential third country suppliers not giving the same undertaking.

(18) In accordance with established GATT practice measures judged to be inconsistent with GATT obligations are considered *prima facie* to constitute a case of nullification or impairment of benefits (Article XXIII:1).

Conclusion

System of import certificates and associated security were not inconsistent with GATT obligations.

Minimum import price and associated security were inconsistent with GATT obligations.

European Communities—Refunds on Exports of Sugar

PANEL REPORT

adopted on November 6, 1979

Parties	Australia / EEC
Intervening	Brazil (see, however, report of November 10, 1980) (Case 44)
Panel Membership	Kaarlehto (Finland), Eberhard (Switzerland), Parman (Turkey)
Published in BISD	26S/290
Related documents	WP Report of March 10, 1981, Article XVI:1. Discussions on European Communities Refunds on Export of Sugar, BISD 28S/80. WP Report of March 31, 1982 on Sugar, BISD 29S/82. Panel Report of November 10, 1980 (Case 44).

Key Words

(1) Basic obligations under Article XVI on subsidies. EEC refunds on export of sugar considered to be a form of subsidy.

(2) Article XVI based on concept of "total world export trade".

(3) Representative period to be considered under Article XVI. Three most recent years for which market conditions could be considered "normal".

(4) Exports of primary products. Equitable market share determined on the basis of development of individual market shares and prices [Article XVI:3. International Sugar Agreement (1977)].

(5) Displacement of market shares (Article XVI:3). No effective limitation of exportable sugar surpluses under EEC market organization. Establishment of clear causal relationship required.

(6) Depressing effect of EEC system on world market price. Threat of prejudice according to Article XVI:1.

(7) Impairment of benefits. Impediment to GA objectives. (Article XXIII:1; no conclusion).

Summary

(1) Refunds on exports of sugar financed by the European Agriculture Guidance and Guarantee Fund under EEC Regulation 3330/74 of December 19, 1974, as amended, considered to be a form of subsidy subject to the provisions of Article XVI. Basic obligations of cp under Article XVI are (a) to notify the application of any subsidy (Article XVI:1), (b) to consult with any cp concerned in cases of serious prejudice caused or threatened (Article XVI:1), (c) to avoid the use of subsidies on the export of primary products and in any case not to apply such subsidies in a manner which results in a cp having more than an equitable share of world export trade (Article XVI:3).

(2) Question of consistency of EEC sugar refunds with Article XVI:3. Examination to be based not on the concept of "free market" (i.e. market not subject to bilateral agreements) but on the concept of "total world export trade".

(3) Determination of representative time period to be considered. Choice of period of the three most recent calendar years for which market conditions could be considered normal.

(4) Exports of primary products. Determination of equitable market share. No definition of "equitable share" provided by GA. Analysis of main reasons for development in individual market share and of market and price developments. Evolution of EEC share in world sugar market analysed. Incidence of coming into operation of the International Sugar Agreement (1977). Increase of Community sugar exports in 1978.

(5) Displacement of market shares. "More than equitable share of world export trade" means displacement of the exports of another signatory, bearing in mind the developments in world markets. In case of new markets, traditional pattern of supply to be considered. Comparative analysis of Australian and EEC sugar exports. Assessment of the effects of the operation of EEC sugar market organization. No effective limitation of exportable sugar surpluses nor of the amount of refund granted as a result of the Community system. No element in the system and its application prevented the Community from having more than an equitable share of world export trade in sugar.

(6) Depressing effect on world market prices for white and raw sugar of Community management of sugar market.

(7) Lack of detailed submissions as to what benefits accruing to Australia had been impaired or as to which objective of the GA had been impeded.

Conclusion

Community system for granting refunds on export of sugar was considered a form of subsidy subject to the provisions of Article XVI. In spite of various measures taken to limit Community sugar production, the Community regulations and their operation had not prevented a continuing increase of sugar production, but no clear causal relationship between this increase and development of Australian exports could be established. The Community system of granting refunds on sugar imports had contributed to depress world sugar prices and the lack of effective limitation in respect of production constituted a permanent source of uncertainty in world sugar markets, constituting a "threat of prejudice" in terms of Article XVI:1.

Japanese Measures on Imports of Leather

PANEL REPORT

adopted on November 6, 1979

Parties	US / Japan
Intervening	Australia, Canada, India, New Zealand
Panel Membership	Nettel (Austria), Furulyas (Hungary), Ostenfeld (Denmark)
Published in BISD	26S/320
Related documents	Panel Reports of November 10, 1980 (Case 42) and May 15/16, 1984 (Case 57)

Key Words

Dispute settlement. Consultation leading to withdrawal of complaint, all rights being reserved under GATT. (Article XXIII:2).

Summary

Quantitative restrictions on the importation of certain leather items in Japan. Measure established under Article XII, maintained in view of the backward character of Japanese enterprises due to the "Dowa problem". Clarification on certain points obtained by Panel. Bilateral consultations leading to withdrawal of complaint, rights under the GA reserved.

Conclusion

Agreement between the parties constituted a solution to the matter.

Norway—Restrictions on Imports of Certain Textile Products

PANEL REPORT

adopted on June 18, 1980

Parties UK on behalf of Hong Kong / Norway

Panel Membership Martin (Canada), Dass (Trinidad and Tobago), Gerber (Switzerland)

Published in BISD 27S/119

Key Words

(1) Long-term agreements on supply of textile constituted a partial allocation of quotas. Expectation of third cp of obtaining a share on a non-discriminatory basis. (Article XIII:2(d)).

(2) Emergency action under Article XIX subject to the provisions of Article XIII.

(3) Relationship of Part IV and Part II.

(4) Measures inconsistent with the GA considered *prima facie* to cause impairment of benefits. (Article XXIII:1).

Summary

(1) Long-term bilateral agreements concluded by Norway with six textile-supplying countries constituted—failing the accession of Norway to the Multi-Fibre Agreement—a partial allocation of quotas. This action conferred on Hong Kong the expectation of obtaining a share of the quotas according to Article XIII:2(d). Hong Kong having a substantial interest in supplying the Norwegian market, the action of Norway was inconsistent with Article XIII.

(2) Emergency action under Article XIX is subject to the provisions of Article XIII, which provides for non-discriminatory administration of quantitative restrictions.

(3) Part IV cannot be cited as justification for actions inconsistent with cp's Part II obligations.

(4) A measure inconsistent with the provisions of the GA in acccordance with established practice constitutes *prima facie* a case of nullification or impairment of benefits under Article XXIII.

Conclusion

Norway was required either to terminate its action taken under Article XIX or make it consistent with Article XIII.

Japan's Measures on Imports of Leather

PANEL REPORT

adopted on November 10, 1980

Parties	Canada / Japan
Panel Membership	Ewerlöf (Sweden), Furulyas (Hungary), Ostenfeld (Denmark)
Published in BISD	27S/118

Key Words

See Report of November 6, 1979, US/Japan (Case 40).

Summary

Idem.

Conclusion

Idem.

EEC Restrictions on Imports of Apples from Chile

PANEL REPORT

adopted on November 10, 1980

Parties	Chile / EEC
Panel Membership	El Gowhari (Egypt), Lemmel (Sweden), Wright (Canada)
Published in BISD	27S/98
Related documents	See Report of June 23, 1989 (Case 69)

Key Words

(1) Scope of GATT provisions. Import restrictions do not constitute a duty or charge. To be examined in the light of Articles XI and XIII, not Articles I and II.

(2) Import restrictions on apples. EEC market organization recognized to restrict quantities of apples permitted to be marketed. "Like products" under Article XI:2(c)(i) and (ii)). Apples of different varieties recognized to be "like products".

(3) Public notice of restrictive measures required by Article XI:2, last paragraph. Obligation applicable to voluntary restraint agreements.

(4) "Previous representative period" (Article XI:2, last paragraph, 3rd sentence). According to "normal GATT practice", refers to a three-year period preceding contested measure.

(5) Measure meets some but not all the criteria contained in Article XI:2(c)(i) and (ii), inconsistent with GA. "Temporary surplus" according to Article XI:2(c)(ii).

(6) Non-discriminatory distribution of trade shares according to Article XIII. Voluntary restraint agreements to be considered as quotas for the purposes of Article XIII:2.

(7) Distribution of trade according to Article XIII:2, first sentence. Establishment of global quota (Article XIII:2(a)). Requirement of public notice of restrictions (Article XIII:2(a) and 3(b)).

(8) "Special factors" under Article XIII:2(d). Expansion of exports to be considered as a special factor.

(9) "Retroactive measures" prevented by Article XIII:3(b), phrase 2. Exemption of products *en route* at the time of publication of restrictive measure.

(10) Objectives and commitments of Articles XXXVI and XXXVII. Avoidance of barriers to exports of less developed cp.

(11) Impairment of benefits presumed in case of infringement of GATT rules (Article XXIII:1). Established GATT practice.

Summary

(1) Restriction of importation of apples from Chile by EEC Regulation 687/79 of April 5, 1979, instituted in the framework of the common organization for the marketing of apples. Restrictive measures not being a duty or charge, the Panel considered it more appropriate to examine the matter in the context of Articles XI and XIII rather than in the context of Articles I and II.

(2) Restrictive measure considered to be a prohibition or restriction in terms of Article XI:1. Chilean apples, though of different varieties, qualified as "like products" for the purposes of Article XI:2(c)(i) and (ii). EEC market organization recognised to restrict quantities of apples permitted to be marketed.

(3) Measures taken under Article XI:2(c)(i) must also meet the criteria expressed in the last paragraph of Article XI:2 requiring public notice to be given of restrictions affecting importation of any product pursuant to subparagraph (c). No public notice was given by EEC of the quantities to be imported under the voluntary restraint agreements negotiated with other countries of the southern hemisphere. EEC restrictions did not conform to the proportion required by the second sentence of the last paragraph of Article XI:2.

(4) The term "previous representative period" in the third sentence of the last paragraph of Article XI:2, according to normal GATT practice, referred to a three-year period preceding the contested measure.

(5) EEC measures met some but not all the criteria contained in Article XI:2(c)(i) and (ii) in order to qualify as an exception to Article XI:1. Measures did not qualify under Article XI:2(c)(i) in that they did not fulfill the requirements of the last paragraph of Article XI:2. As regards paragraph XI:2(c)(ii), the EEC surplus of apples could not be considered "temporary" as it appeared year after year, with the exception of the year 1979 when the surplus was significantly higher than normal.

(6) Non-discriminatory distribution of trade shares required by Article XIII in case of import restrictions. Voluntary restraint agreements, in spite of their differences with unilaterally imposed import restrictions, to be considered as "quotas" for the purposes of Article XIII:2.

(7) Distribution of trade among cp should approach as closely as possible the shares which the various cp might be expected to obtain in the absence of restrictions (Article XIII:2, first sentence). There should be established, whenever practicable, a quota representing the total amount of permitted imports [Article XIII:2(a)]. Requirement of public notice of restrictions [Article XIII:2(a) and 3(b), first sentence] met in the case of Chile by publication in the Community's Official Journal, but not met in respect of the voluntary restraint agreements.

(8) "Special factors" must be taken account of under Article XIII:2(d). Expansion of Chilean exports was a special factor to be taken account of. Quota allocated to Chile was insufficient, taking account of this factor.

(9) EEC measure not found to be retroactive in the context of Article XIII:3(b), since Chilean apples bound for the EEC at the moment when the restrictive measure was published had been excluded from the import restriction.

(10) EEC not found to have violated Articles XXXVI and XXXVII, and particularly XXXVII:1(b), which requires developed cp to the fullest extent possible to refrain from imposing barriers to exports of less developed cp, in light of EEC consultations with Chile.

(11) Impairment of benefits. In accordance with "established GATT practice" an action judged to be inconsistent with the GATT obligations *prima facie* constitutes a case of impairment. (Article XXIII:1).

Conclusion

EEC restriction on imports of apples from Chile found to be a prohibition or restriction of imports in terms of Article XI:1 and to be inconsistent with Article XIII:1, 2(a) and (d) and 3(b), first sentence.

EEC and Chile were invited to consult bilaterally with a view to arriving at a mutually satisfactory solution.

European Communities—Refunds on Exports of Sugar—Complaint by Brazil

PANEL REPORT

adopted on November 10, 1980

Parties	Brazil / EEC
Panel Membership	Kaarlehto (Finland), Eberhard (Switzerland), Ki-Choo Lee (Korea)
Published in BISD	27S/69
Related documents	Report of November 6, 1979 (Case 39), Australia/EEC and documents quoted in connection with that report.

Key Words

See report of November 6 1979 (Case 39).

Obligations flowing for cp from Articles XXXVI and XXXVIII. Efforts at improvement of market situation made by parties to the International Sugar Agreement (ISA) thwarted by cp not party to that Agreement.

Summary

The Panel's analysis and conclusions were substantially identical to the November 6, 1979 report, save that the Brazilian complaint had questioned also the consistency of the EEC export refunds with Articles XXXVI and XXXVIII. The Panel found that although the EEC had abstained from joining the International Sugar Agreement, whereas Brazil and other developing countries had taken action through the ISA to improve the market situation, the magnitude of subsidized Community sugar exports together with the use of maximum export refunds had accentuated the detrimental effect on export earnings of other sugar exporters who had taken steps within the framework of the ISA.

Conclusion

See report of November 6, 1979. Add the statement that the EEC had not collaborated jointly with other cp to further the principles and objectives of Articles XXXVI and XXXVIII.

EEC—Imports of Beef from Canada

PANEL REPORT

adopted on March 10, 1981

Parties Canada / EEC

Panel Membership Berger (Norway), Contestabile (Switzerland), Rego Santos-Neves (Brazil)

Published in BISD 28S/92

Key Words

(1) MFN treatment for products irrespective of origin. Internal rule limiting access of one single cp to tariff concession incompatible with Article I:1.

(2) Conditions attached to the grant of levy-free tariff quota. Article II:1 does not allow for conditions reserving access to quota to the products of a particular country.

(3) Multilateral trade negotiations. Concessions to be implemented on the basis of the relevant provisions of the GA. Balance of concessions irrelevant. (Articles I and II).

(4) Infringement of GATT provisions constituting *prima facie* impairment of benefits (Article XXIII:1).

Summary

(1) Article I:1 provides for MFN treatment of like products irrespective of origin. Tariff concession granted by EEC for high-quality beef. Internal rules of EEC (Regulation 2972/79) limited certification of beef quality to one single US agency. Advantage was thus reserved to products of US origin. EEC Regulation having the effect of preventing access of "like products" from origin other than US was inconsistent with MFN principle in Article I.

(2) Levy-free tariff quota for beef accorded by EEC "subject to conditions to be determined by competent authorities". Article II:1(b) does not allow for conditions limiting a given concession to

the products of a particular country. The manner in which the EEC concession was implemented accorded less favorable treatment to Canada and was inconsistent with Article II:1.

(3) The idea of "Balance of concessions" is no reason for reserving a concession to a given cp. When a multilateral negotiation under the auspices of GATT has been completed the concessions have to be implemented as laid down in the Schedules and on the basis of the relevant provisions of the GA.

(4) Infringement of Articles I and II constitutes *prima facie* impairment of benefits accruing under the GA (Article XXIII:1).

Conclusion

EEC was required to take the necessary steps to make the implementation of the concession consistent with the provisions of the GA.

EEC-UK Application of EEC Directives to Imports of Poultry from the US

PANEL REPORT

adopted on June 11, 1981

Parties US/UK and EEC

Panel Membership Trucco (Chile), Ki-Choo Lee (Korea), Pullinen (Finland)

Published in BISD 28S/90

Key Words

(1) Dispute settlement. Withdrawal of complaint. (Article XXIII. 1979 Understanding on Dispute Settlement, paragraph 17).

(2) National treatment under Article III. Derogation from Directive granted by the EEC to a particular Member State (issue not resolved).

Summary

Complaint of US based on Article III, relating to a derogation granted by the EEC to the UK from Directives on marketing of poultry. Complaint withdrawn by US without prejudice to US rights under the GA.

Conclusion

Work of Panel was declared terminated in accordance with paragraph 17 of the 1979 Understanding on Dispute Settlement.

Japanese Restraints on Imports of Manufactured Tobacco from the US

PANEL REPORT

adopted on June 11, 1981

Parties US / Japan

Intervening Sweden

Panel Membership Kröyer (Iceland), Jara (Chile), Lautenberg (Switzerland)

Published in BISD 28S/100

Key Words

(1) Dispute settlement. Withdrawal of complaint. Agreement reached between parties. (Article XXIII).

(2) National treatment (Article III) and State trading (Article XVII). Discrimination against imported manufactured tobacco (issue not resolved).

Summary

Discriminatory treatment against imports of manufactured tobacco alleged to be inconsistent with Articles III and XVII. Agreement was reached between the parties and complaint withdrawn.

Conclusion

Proceedings were declared terminated.

Spain—Tariff Treatment of Unroasted Coffee

PANEL REPORT

adopted on June 11, 1981

Parties	Brazil / Spain
Panel Membership	Ewerlöf (Sweden), Daniel (Poland), Herrmann (Switzerland)
Published in BISD	28S/102

Key Words

(1) MFN Principle—Article I:1 applies equally to bound and non-bound tariff items. Tariff classification of goods. No obligation under the GA to follow a particular system for classifying goods. Right of cp to introduce new tariff positions as appropriate, provided such action does not violate an existing tariff concession (Article II:5).

(2) Tariff classification. Equal tariff treatment to be applied to "like products". Criteria to be used in order to establish likeness. End use is relevant criterion in case of a product like coffee, universally regarded as a single product. Regard should be had to tariff classification by other cp. Differentiation of tariff treatment of "mild coffee" and other varieties of coffee considered discriminatory for a country producing mainly the latter varieties. (Article I:1).

(3) Tariff regime found inconsistent with the GA, thereby constituting a *prima facie* case of impairment of benefits (Article XXIII:1).

Summary

(1) Tariff treatment of unroasted coffee by Spain, introducing duty free treatment in favor of "Colombian mild" and "other mild" coffee. Article I:1 applies equally to bound and non-bound tariff items. No obligation was found to exist under GATT to follow any particular system for classifying goods. The right of a cp to introduce in its tariff new positions or subpositions as appropriate was

recognised, provided that the reclassification subsequent to the making of a concession would not be a violation of the basic commitment regarding that concession under Article II:5.

(2) Whatever the tariff classification adopted by a cp, Article I:1 requires that the same tariff treatment be applied to "like products". Organoleptic differences of coffee resulting from geographic factors, cultivation methods, processing and genetic factors were found not to be relevant for a product sold mainly in blends, coffee in its end-use being universally regarded as a well-defined and single product. No other cp was found to apply different tariff rates to different types of coffee. Spanish tariff regime considered to be discriminatory vis-à-vis Brazil, taking account of the fact that Brazil exported to Spain mainly Arabica and Robusta coffee not enjoying the tariff exemption granted to Colombian mild and other mild coffees.

(3) Spanish tariff regime for unroasted coffee was not in conformity with Article I:1, thereby constituting a *prima facie* case of impairment of benefits within the meaning of Article XXIII.

Conclusion

Spain was required to take the necessary measures in order to make its tariff regime for unroasted coffee conform to Article I:1.

Panel on US Countervailing Duties

PANEL REPORT

adopted on November 3, 1981

Parties India / US

Panel Membership Ewerlöf, Curzon, Flory, Jara, Maggio

Published in BISD 28S/113

Key Words

Countervailing Duties. Material injury criteria (Article VI:6). MFN principle. Injury criteria applied in a discriminating way (Article I:1). Agreement reached by parties (Article XXIII:2).

Summary

The complaint by India was that the levy of countervailing duties by the US on certain imports from India without applying the injury criteria referred to in Article VI:6, while extending the benefit of such criteria to the imports from other cp, was inconsistent with the GATT rules, in particular Article I:1.

Conclusion

Matter was satisfactorily resolved between the parties. Proceedings under Article XXIII:2 terminated.

US—Prohibition of Imports of Tuna and Tuna Products from Canada

PANEL REPORT

adopted on February 22, 1982

Parties	Canada / US
Panel Membership	Williams (UK), Chau (UK, Hong Kong), Gerber (Switzerland)
Published in BISD	29S/91

Key Words

(1) Procedure. Agreement reached during proceedings. Matter not exhausted by agreement. Claim for damage not settled. GATT proceedings reserved by parties. Request for substantial report on the case justified. (Article XXIII:2. 1979 Understanding on Dispute Settlement, paragraph 17).

(2) Import restrictions. General import prohibition of tuna and tuna products not justified under Article XI:2 if national restrictions on fishing limited to some species only. Interpretation. Divergency of language in subparagraphs (a), (b) and (c) of Article XI:2 noted and interpreted.

(3) Restrictive measures under Article XX(g) relating to the conservation of exhaustible natural resources. Measures permitted only if made effective in conjunction with restrictions on domestic production.

(4) Jurisdiction of GATT. Complex fisheries issue. Naval incidents. Panel findings relevant only to trade aspects of fisheries, not to questions of fisheries jurisdiction. (Article XXIII).

(5) Compensation of damage. No conclusion drawn. (Article XXIII:2).

Summary

(1) Prohibition of imports of Canadian tuna and tuna products imposed pursuant to Section 205 of the US Fishery Conservation and

Management Act of 1976. Agreement reached between the parties in the course of proceedings. Matter not exhausted considering that, according to Canada, the agreement reached was not considered to be a completely satisfactory settlement by Canada, that the damage caused by the action of the US had not been satisfactorily repaired and that the agreement reached had expressly reserved the possibility of action before GATT.

(2) US import restriction constituted a prohibition in terms of Article XI:1. Limitations on the catch of some species of tuna by the US legislation did not justify, under the exceptions provided by Article XI:2, a general prohibition on imports of tuna and tuna products from Canada. Divergency of language in subparagraphs (a), (b) and (c) of Article XI:2 noted; only "restrictions," not "prohibitions" permitted by Article XI:2(c) exception.

(3) Question of justification of US catch under Article XX(g). Action did not constitute unjustifiable discrimination as similar actions had been taken against a number of other States. Action did not constitute a disguised restriction on trade as measures had been taken publicly as trade measures. Action did not qualify under paragraph (g) on protection of exhaustible natural resources, as US found itself unable to establish that import restrictions had been made effective in conjunction with equivalent restrictions on domestic production or consumption.

(4) Complex issue on fisheries. Arrest by Canada of US vessels fishing for tuna. Panel findings and conclusions relevant only to trade aspects of the matter under dispute and not to questions of fisheries' jurisdiction.

(5) Compensation of damage not considered by the Panel due to the relatively small amount involved and the lack of detailed submissions from Canada.

Conclusion

US embargo on imports of tuna and tuna products from Canada was not consistent with Article XI and was not justified under Article XX(g).

Panel on Vitamins

PANEL REPORT

adopted on October 1, 1982

Parties EEC / US

Panel Membership Nettel (Austria), Pullinen (Finland), Yeabsley (New Zealand)

Published in BISD 29S/110

Key Words

(1) Valuation for tariff purposes (Article VII). Transition from US ASP System to GATT Valuation Code (BISD 26S/116 and 151). Conversion of tariff rates. Loss by EEC of vitamin market as a consequence of conversion. Conversion based on average of duties collected considered fair and equitable.

(2) "Non-violation" impairment of benefits (Article XXIII:1). Unfavorable consequences of tariff conversion to be reasonably foreseen. Bilateral understanding. US invited to make in the course of current tariff negotiations such concessions as would re-establish traditional competitive position of B12 feed grade vitamins.

Summary

(1) Adjustment of US tariff rates upon transition from the American Selling Price (ASP) System to the Agreement on the Implementation of Article VII of GATT (Valuation Code). Bilateral understanding EEC/US of March 2, 1979 provided that "adjustment must remain neutral and shall not involve an arbitrary increase in customs duties". US offer relating to chemical products, which was accepted in principle by the EEC, reserved the right to raise "specific cases" which the US will examine on a case-by-case basis "with a view to finding a mutually acceptable basis". Rates formerly differentiated for feed grade vitamins and pharmaceutical grade vitamins B12 were merged in same tariff line bearing a customs duty calculated on the basis of average duties collected in

the past. Conversion resulted in loss by the EEC of the market for feed grade vitamins. Panel considered that the bilateral understanding did not create an obligation for the US to meet the requests of the EEC and that the US had no obligation to maintain the existing *de facto* tariff differentiation, provided that the method used for the conversion of the previous common bound rate was neutral and in principle fair and equitable.

(2) Although the method used by the US for the calculation of the base rate for vitamin B12 was in principle fair and equitable, the Panel considered that the result in respect of feed grade quality vitamins had excessively negative effects for the suppliers of this product. Though the EEC could reasonably have foreseen that the abolition of the ASP valuation system would lead to a less favorable tariff treatment for certain products, it had no reason to assume that tariff treatment of feed grade quality vitamins would be adversely affected to the extent experienced. In the light of the particular circumstances the US was invited to grant in the framework of current tariff negotiations a concession on feed grade vitamin B12 to such an extent that imported vitamins could again attain their traditional competitive position in the US market.

Conclusion

US action was found to be not inconsistent with obligations flowing from the GA or from the bilateral EEC/US Understanding. US was invited to grant concession on B12 feed grade vitamins to such an extent that imported vitamins could again attain their traditional competitive position in the US market.

US Imports of Certain Automotive Spring Assemblies

PANEL REPORT

adopted on May 26, 1983

Parties Canada / US

Panel Membership Reed, Siraj, McPhail

Published in BISD 30S/107

Key Words

(1) Laws and regulations relating to the protection of intellectual property rights (Article XX(d)). Provision given precedence over other provisions of the GA, such as Articles II:1(b), III: 1, 2 and 4, and XI:1.

(2) National laws and regulations expressly recognized by Article XX(d) as such not inconsistent with the GA.

(3) "Measure" in the sense of the opening words of Article XX. General exclusion order issued by the US International Trade Commission (ITC) did not constitute "arbitrary discrimination".

(4) "Measure" in the sense of the opening words of Article XX. General exclusion order issued by the US ITC was not considered to be a case of "disguised restriction" on international trade.

(5) Measure "necessary" to secure compliance with laws and regulations relating to the protection of patents. Action before the ITC. Action in ordinary courts was not considered to be a satisfactory alternative. Section 337 of the US Tariff Act was considered to provide the means "necessary" to secure compliance with US patent law. [Article XX(d)].

(6) Measure "necessary" to secure compliance with laws and regulations relating to the protection of patents. Assessment of necessity depends on characteristics of products and legal and court systems in manufacturing country. [Article XX(d)].

(7) Measures "necessary" to secure compliance with laws and regulations relating to the protection of patents. Features of Section 337 of the US Tariff Code went beyond the requirement of necessity. [Article XX(d)].

Summary

(1) Action of the US International Trade Commission (ITC) under Section 337 of the US Tariff Code in case of US patent infringement by imported goods. General exclusion order issued by the ITC. Canada complained on the basis of the National Treatment provision of Article III:4, considering that Section 377 of the US Tariff Code was a highly protective provision and that procedures before the ITC, an agency instituted by the Tariff Code, suspended judicial action in ordinary courts applicable in case of infringement of patents by domestic goods. The Canadian claim was based on Article III:4; US defense on Article XX(d), relating to protection of intellectual property rights. The Panel gave precedence to Article XX(d), considering that if this provision applied, then examining the consistency of the exclusion order with other GATT provisions (i.e. Articles II:1(b), III:1, 2 and 4 and XI:1) would not be required.

(2) National laws and regulations are expressly recognised by Article XX(d) and as such are not inconsistent with the GA.

(3) General exclusion orders by the ITC were to be considered as a "measure" in the sense of the opening words of Article XX. But such exclusion orders were not applied in a manner which could constitute "arbitrary discrimination", as they were applicable to imports of all sources, not only to imports from one particular country.

(4) Exclusion order by the ITC was not to be considered as a "disguised restriction" on international trade within the meaning of the opening words of Article XX since the validity of the patent and the issue of infringement had to be examined by the ITC before an exclusion order could be issued and since notice of the exclusion order had been published in the Federal Register.

(5) Exclusion order by the ITC was considered to be a "necessary" means to secure compliance with the US patent law as action in civil courts would not have been a satisfactory alternative, taking

into account the fact that such action would be ineffective against foreign infringers and against imports from unknown sources. Accordingly, an exclusion order issued by the ITC under Section 337 of the US Tariff Act was to be considered "necessary" under Article XX(d) to secure compliance with US patent law.

(6) The result reached by the Panel would be appropriate in respect of many cases of patent infringement, but the Panel admitted that the result might differ depending on many factors such as the characteristics of the products involved and the legal and judicial court system in the country of the manufacturer infringing the patent. The Panel therefore did not exclude that there might be situations (for example involving high-cost products of an advanced technical nature) where a procedure before a judicial court might provide the patent holder with a satisfactory and effective remedy which might render recourse to Article XX(d) unnecessary.

(7) The Panel added that some elements contained in Section 337 of the US Tariff Code appeared to be out of place in legislation used for the protection of private patent rights, such as the words "unfair methods of competition and unfair acts", the requirement of "substantial injury to a US industry" and the system of "dual procedures" which gave the US patent holder a choice of taking action through the ITC, through the civil courts, or both.

Conclusion

The exclusion order issued in the specific case fell within the provisions of Article XX(d) and was therefore consistent with the GA. Examination under other GATT provisions was therefore not required. The Panel considered however that there might be merit in simplifying and improving the legal procedures in the US for patent infringement cases.

Remarks

This Report was overruled by the Report of November 7, 1989 (Case 74) on Section 337 of the US Tariff Act of 1930.

EEC-Quantitative Restrictions against Imports of Certain Products from Hong Kong

PANEL REPORT

adopted on July 12, 1983

Parties	UK on behalf of Hong Kong / EEC
Interested	France
Panel Membership	Hochörtler, Dumont, Greenfield
Published in BISD	30S/129

Key Words

(1) "Residual restrictions". Quantitative import restrictions were established in 1944 by France and maintained with the consent of the EEC. Restrictions had not been notified as being covered by the "existing legislation" clause of the PPA. Restrictions also took the form of an "SLQ regime" (licensing without quantitative limitation). Regime liable to Article XI:1.

(2) Sources of the law to be applied by Panel. All relevant GATT provisions and all other "discussions" which have taken place in GATT to be considered. No obligation for Panel to consider provisions not invoked by parties. (Article XXIII:2).

(3) Social and economic conditions prevailing in the different product categories irrelevant for the purposes of Articles XI:1 and XIII.

(4) Right of complaint. Forfeiture (no). The fact that "residual restrictions" have been maintained for a long time without having been contested is not an excuse under Articles XI:1 and XIII and is not a tacit acceptance debarring a cp from recourse to Article XXIII.

(5) Principles of law. "Law-creating force derived from circumstances" does not prevail against provisions of GA. (Article XXIII:2).

(6) Procedure. Terms of reference. Coverage of items by terms of reference. Unilateral extension of claim in course of proceedings incompatible with equity. (Article XXIII:2).

(7) Restrictions found incompatible with Article XI. Examination of possible discrimination under Article XIII superfluous.

(8) Infringement of Article XI considered to be *prima facie* case of impairment of benefits. (Article XXIII:1).

Summary

(1) Quantitive import restrictions were established by a French Decree of November 30, 1944 and maintained with the consent of the EEC. Decree not notified to GATT as being covered by the PPA.

(2) Panel capable of discharging its obligations by examining the issue in the light of all relevant GATT provisions and all other relevant "discussions" which have taken place in GATT. The Panel recognized that situations existed in which quantitative restrictions might be justified under the GA, but since no appropriate provisions had been invoked by the EEC, it was not for the Panel to establish whether the present measures would be justified under any GATT provision.

(3) To justify the restrictions, the EEC relied on the social and economic conditions which prevailed in the various product categories and did not claim any GATT provision justified them. Such matters however did not come within the purview of Articles XI and XIII.

(4) The fact that for historical reasons residual restrictions had been maintained for a long time without Articles XI:1 or XIII being invoked by Hong Kong did not alter the obligations which cp had accepted under GATT provisions. The fact that a measure had not been subject to the procedures of Article XXIII over a number of years was not tantamount to its tacit acceptance by cp. Discussions on quantitative restrictions which had taken place in GATT over the years were without prejudice to the legal status of the measures concerned.

(5) The argument drawn by the EEC from a principle referred to as "the law-creating force derived from circumstances" could be relevant in the absence of law, but here the matter had to be considered strictly in the light of the provisions of the GA.

(6) Coverage of items by the Panel's terms of reference. Subsequent acceptance of an item not included in the terms of reference would introduce an element of inequity into the proceedings. Omission of an item due to an error. The item being of peripheral interest, it could be disregarded in view of the Panel's conclusion.

(7) Quantitative restrictions maintained by France having been found to be inconsistent with Article XI, a complaint relating to discriminatory application of the same restrictions, inconsistent with Article XIII, was not examined in view of the finding of inconsistency with Article XI.

Conclusion

Infringement of obligations under Article XI established. Infringement considered *prima facie* to constitute a case of impairment of benefits accruing to Hong Kong under the GA. France required to terminate the quantitative restrictions complained of by Hong Kong.

Canada—Administration of the Foreign Investment Review Act (FIRA)

PANEL REPORT

adopted on February 7, 1984

Parties US / Canada

Intervening Argentina

Panel Membership O'Brien, Feij, Ikeda

Published in BISD 30S/140

(1) Jurisdiction of GATT. Regime of foreign investments. Sovereign right of cp to regulate foreign investments. Competence of GATT solely in the light of a cp's trade obligations. Scope of Article XXIII on dispute settlement.

(2) Procedure. Terms of reference of Panel. Panel not competent for matters outside its terms of reference. (Article XXIII). Dealing with a developed country, Panel not competent to examine questions of investment in developing countries. (Article XVIII:C).

(3) Article III:4 not limited to "laws and regulations", in the sense of mandatory rules of general scope and bearing. Article III:4 extends to any "requirements" established by a cp, comprises measures applied on a case-to-case basis, such as "undertakings" imposed on individual investors. Purpose of Article III. Interpretation of GATT provisions in the light of the Havana Charter (Article XXIX). "Principles" of the Charter applied to reinforce the GA, not detract from its obligations. (Article XXIII).

(4) Private contractual obligations assumed by particular foreign investors vis-à-vis the government of a cp may not adversely affect the rights which other cp exercise on behalf of their exporters under Article III:4. Particular importance of "national treatment principle" in Article III:4.

(5) Competitive advantage. Undertaking imposed on investors to purchase preferably goods of domestic origin, even under condi-

tion of "competitive availability", inconsistent with standard of "treatment no less favorable" of Article III:4.

(6) Scope of Article XI:1. Article applicable to "import" of goods, not to internal treatment of "imported goods" under Article III:4.

(7) Applicability of provisions of Article XVII on state trading not determined.

(8) Scope of the provisions of the GA. Export of goods. Undertaking imposed on foreign investors in relation to export of goods not inconsistent with any provision of the GA.

(9) Undertaking to purchase domestic products imposed on foreign investors not "necessary" to secure compliance with FIRA [Article XX(d)]. Provision constituting exception. Burden of proof.

(10) Trade effects. Evaluation of the negative trade effects of a national measures not necessary to findings on impairment of benefits under Article XXIII:1.

(11) Limitation of a finding on inconsistency of national measures with GATT obligations (Article XXIII:2).

Summary

(1) Undertakings of foreign investors pursuant to Canadian FIRA requiring them to give preference to purchase of Canadian goods over imported goods and to meet certain export performance requirements. GA does not prevent Canada from exercising its sovereign right to regulate foreign direct investments. Purchase and export undertakings of investors were to be examined solely in the light of Canada's trade obligations under the GA.

(2) Terms of reference of Panel. Dealing with a developed country, the Panel was not to examine special rules applying to investment in developing countries, such as Article XVIII:C. The Panel was also not to examine undertakings to manufacture goods which would otherwise be imported, as the terms of reference related only to purchase and export of goods. The Panel was not to examine various other undertakings relating to establishment, employment, research and development not covered by the terms of reference.

(3) Article III:4 is not limited to "laws" and "regulations", in the sense of mandatory rules having general application. The term "requirements" in Article III:4 must be understood as adding something different to the preceding words. For the application of Article III:4 it is not relevant whether a measure applies across-the-board or only in isolated cases. Any interpretation which would exclude case-by-case action would defeat the purposes of Article III:4. Accordingly, individual undertakings assumed by investors by virtue of the FIRA, by the fact that they establish legally enforceable obligations, are properly described as "requirements" in the sense of Article III:4. The scope of the word "requirements" may not be narrowed by reference to the Havana Charter. The mention of the "general principles" of the Charter in Article XXIX refers to the principles which were reinforced or added to the obligations of the GA. The charter may therefore not be used to detract from the cp's obligations under the GA.

(4) Private contractual obligations of particular foreign investors vis-à-vis the Canadian Government should not adversely affect the rights which cp, including cp not involved in the dispute, possess under Article III:4 of the GA and which they can exercise on behalf of their exporters. This applies in particular to the national treatment principle which is aimed at preventing the use of internal measures "so as to afford protection to domestic production".

(5) Undertakings to purchase goods of Canadian origin constitute clearly, as regards imported goods, "treatment less favorable" than that accorded to like products of national origin. Even conditional undertakings on goods being "competitively available" entail a preference for domestic products. Undertakings to buy from Canadian suppliers, by excluding direct purchases from the foreign producer create a competitive disadvantage and therefore are inconsistent with Article III:4.

(6) As the GA distinguishes measures affecting directly the "importation" of products, which are regulated by Article XI:1, and those which affect "imported products", which are dealt with in Article III:4, Article XI:1 is not applicable to purchase undertakings under the FIRA.

(7) A finding on question of principle relating to the scope of Article XVII:1 on state trading was not necessary, considering the incon-

sistency already established under Article III:4. However, Panel saw great force to argument that the phrase "general principles of non-discriminatory treatment prescribed in this agreement" in Article XVII:1 refers to MFN treatment and not national treatment.

(8) Undertakings under the FIRA to export specified quantities or proportions were not found inconsistent with the GA which contains no provision forbidding requirements to sell goods in foreign markets rather than on the domestic market.

(9) Purchase undertakings are not "necessary", in the sense of Article XX(d), in view of compliance with the FIRA, as the aims of this Act could be achieved without requiring investors to give a preference to domestic products. Article XX(d) being an exception to the system of the GA, the burden of establishing necessity rests on the party invoking the exception.

(10) Under standing GATT practice a breach of rule is presumed to have an adverse impact on other cp's interests and to impair benefits accruing under the GA. Evaluation of trade effects of Canadian measure therefore not relevant to findings.

(11) Panel suggests that in the future FIRA could be administered consistently with the GA. With respect to past actions, i.e. the existing purchase undertakings, Canada is requested to bring existing purchase undertakings into conformity with its obligations under the GA, as soon as possible.

Conclusion

Purchase undertakings imposed on foreign investors under the Canadian Foreign Investment Review Act were found to be inconsistent with Article III:4.

Remarks

The last sentence of paragraph 5.14 of the Report contains an obvious printing error (as compared to sentence 3 of paragraph 6.1), insofar as it should be read as saying: ". . . that they are *not* inconsistent with Article XI.1". A corrigendum has been issued to this effect.

US—Imports of Sugar from Nicaragua

PANEL REPORT

adopted on March 13, 1984

Parties Nicaragua / US

Panel Membership Peren, Villar Saraillet, Manhusen

Published in BISD 31S/67

Key Words

(1) Jurisdiction of GATT. Dispute tied to a complex political situation. Panel competent to deal with the contested measures in the light of relevant GATT provisions, concerning itself solely with trade issues. (Article XXIII).

(2) Terms of reference limited to specific issue, not extending to system of US sugar import regime. (Article XI:1, US Waiver of March 5, 1955).

(3) Unilateral reduction of import sugar quota inconsistent with Article XIII:2 on non-discriminatory administration of quota regimes.

Summary

(1) Reduction by the US of the sugar quota allocated to Nicaragua under its sugar quota system. Measures taken by the US were but one aspect of a more general problem. The Panel was competent to examine the contested measures solely in the light of the relevant GATT provisions, concerning itself only with the trade issue under dispute.

(2) The sugar quota system of the US was challenged as such by Nicaragua as being inconsistent with Article XI:1 and not covered by the Waiver granted to the US on March 5, 1955 (BISD 3S/32). The Panel held that consideration of the US quota system fell outside the terms of reference of the Panel, which was called only to consider the sugar import quota allocated to Nicaragua.

(3) The reduction of Nicaragua's sugar quota was found not to be motivated by any factor which might have affected or might be affecting trade in sugar. The US having not provided any justification of its action in the context of GATT, the reduction of the quota was inconsistent with the obligations of the United States under Article XIII:2. This being established the Panel did not examine the consistency of the US measures with Article II and Part IV of the GA.

Conclusion

US was required to "promptly allocate to Nicaragua a sugar import quota consistent with the criteria set out in Article XIII:2".

US Manufacturing Clause

PANEL REPORT

adopted on May 15/16, 1984

Parties EEC / US

Panel Membership Rantanen, Haron, Kemmochi

Published in BISD 31S/75

Key Words

(1) US "Manufacturing Clause" inconsistent with Article XI:1.

(2) "Existing legislation" clause of the PPA. Amendments of existing legislation. Legislation does not lose its status under the PPA if amendments increase consistency with Part II of GA.

(3) "Existing legislation" clause of PPA opens a "one-way street" permitting no return of legislation to greater inconsistency. PPA provides a temporary dispensation from obligations of Part II. One of the basic aims of the GA is security and predictability in the trade relations among cp.

(4) Infringement of Article XI:1. *Prima facie* nullification or impairment.

Summary

(1) The US manufacturing clause (Section 601 of Title 17 of the US Code, as extended by Public Law 97-215 of July 13, 1982) prohibits the importation into or the distribution in the US of a copyrighted work consisting preponderately of non-dramatic literary material in the English language, the author of which is a US domiciliary, unless the portions consisting of such material have been manufactured in the US or in Canada. The origin of the legislation goes back to 1892, but the scope of the clause has been successively reduced by later amendments. An expiry date for the Manufacturing Clause was set by an amendment introduced in

1976 for 1982. Later on, this date was deferred to 1986. The prohibition provided for by the "manufacturing clause" was recognized to be inconsistent with Article XI:1.

(2) Question of eligibility of US legislation as successively amended under the "existing legislation" clause of the PPA. It was recognized that legislation inconsistent with Part II of the GATT could be modified without losing its status of "existing legislation", provided the degree of inconsistency with the GA was not increased. The Panel noted in this respect that one of the basic purposes of the provisional application of Part II had been to ensure that the value of tariff concessions was not undermined by new protective legislation. To permit changes to "existing legislation" that did not increase the degree of inconsistency of such legislation with the GA would thus be in accordance with the purpose of the PPA.

(3) The expiry date inserted in 1976 was not to be considered as a mere announcement of the possibility of a future change in policy, but had to be considered as an actual policy change. Thus the insertion of the expiry date of July 1, 1982 for the Manufacturing Clause by Public Law 94-553 had meant a move towards greater GATT conformity. Therefore the legislation of July 13 1982 postponing the expiry date had constituted a reversal of this move. The PPA had been conceived as providing a temporary dispensation to enable contracting parties to apply Part II of the GA without changing existing legislation or acting inconsistently with it. Given this purpose of the Protocol, once a cp had reduced the degree of inconsistency of "existing legislation" with the GA, there could be no justification for a move to increase the degree of GATT inconsistency of such legislation, albeit to a level not exceeding that which had existed on October 30, 1947. One of the basic aims of the GA was security and predictability in the trade relations among cp. The "existing legislation" clause was therefore to be interpreted as opening a "one-way street", permitting only movements to the situation required by Part II of the GATT, not the reverse. The Panel therefore found that the US legislation of July 13, 1982 postponing the expiry date of the US Manufacturing Clause could not be justified under the PPA.

(4) The extension of the Manufacturing Clause beyond July 1, 1982 had to be considered *prima facie* to impair benefits accruing to the EEC under GATT.

UNIV DUNELM

Conclusion

US Manufacturing Clause was found inconsistent with Article XI:1. Extension of the Manufacturing Clause beyond July 1, 1982 was not justified under the PPA.

The extension of the Manufacturing Clause had to be considered *prima facie* to impair benefits accruing to the EEC under the GA.

Japanese Measures on Import of Leather

PANEL REPORT

adopted on May 15/16, 1984

Parties	US / Japan
Intervening	Australia, EEC, India, New Zealand, Pakistan
Panel Membership	Huslid, Jayasekera, Reed
Published in BISD	31S/94
Related documents	Panel Reports of November 6, 1979 (Case 40) and November 10, 1980 (Case 42)

Key Words

(1) Trade restrictions inconsistent with Article XI:1. Special historical, cultural and socio-economic circumstances are no justification in the GATT system for maintenance of trade restrictions.

(2) Inconsistency of national measures with GATT provisions is *prima facie* case of impairment of benefits. Rising tendency of imports and inability of claimant to fill allocated quota is no rebuttal of presumption. (Article XXIII:1. 1979 Understanding on dispute Settlement, paragraphs 4 and 5).

(3) Procedure. Arguments raised by third parties going beyond the Panel's terms of reference were not considered but brought to attention of the Council. (Article XXIII:2).

(4) Implementation of council decision on dispute settlement to be delayed due to internal difficulties encountered by defendant party. (Article XXIII:2).

Summary

(1) Restrictions were maintained by Japan on the import of certain semi-processed and finished leather. The restrictions were inspired by internal socio-economic problems and in particular by the

desire to safeguard the interests of the "Dowa Population" for whom leather industry and footwear manufacturing was one of the main occupations. Quantitative restrictions are prohibited by Article XI.1. Japan did not invoke any justification recognized by GATT for maintaining quantitative restrictions. Special historical, cultural and socio-economic circumstances referred to by Japan provided no justification for quantitative restrictions under GATT rules. Japanese restrictions were inconsistent with Article XI:1.

(2) In accordance with established GATT practice restrictions recognized to be inconsistent with the GA constitute a *prima facie* case of impairment of benefits. The fact that US imports had increased and that the US had been unable to fill the quota allocated by Japan was not sufficient to rebut this presumption. The existence of a trade restriction should be presumed to cause nullification or impairment not only because of any possible effect it had on the volume of trade but also for other reasons such as increased transaction costs and uncertainties affecting investment plans.

(3) Arguments were raised by third parties on the basis of Articles XIII:1 and 2, which went beyond the complaint of the US and the Panel's terms of reference. No findings were made by the Panel thereon but the arguments were brought to the attention of the Council.

Conclusion

Japan was required to eliminate its trade restrictions. Taking account of the difficulties faced by Japan, Panel recommended that Japan be given a certain amount of time progressively to eliminate the import restrictions in question.

Panel on Value Added Tax and Threshold

PANEL REPORT

adopted on May 16, 1984
by the Committee on Government Procurement

Parties US / EEC

Panel Membership Berger, Contestabile, Sivam

Published in BISD 31S/247

Key Words

(1) Government procurement. "Contract value". Threshold established by Article I:1(b) of the Agreement on Government Procurement (BISD 26S/49). Exclusion of VAT (no).

(2) Interpretation. Absence of negotiating history. Natural meaning of terms.

(3) Interpretation. General practice of Parties. Necessity of uniform interpretation for all Parties. Specific provisions of internal legislation of one Party no reason to introduce exclusion of VAT into the terms of the Agreement.

(4) Interpretation. Number of imprecise and erratic factors to be considered in establishing "contract value" no reason for creating further differences in evaluation.

(5) Purpose of the Agreement on Government Procurement different from the requirements of a common market regime based on harmonized conditions of competition.

(6) "Contract value" to be interpreted as being the full cost of the contract including VAT.

(7) Inconsistency with Agreement on Government Procurement of EEC practice excluding the VAT from the contract value.

Summary

(1) The matter submitted to the Panel was the EC's practice, established in Council Directive 77/62/EEC of December 21, 1976, of

excluding value added tax (VAT) from the contract price of EC Member State government purchases in relation to the determination of whether such purchases fall under the Agreement on Government Procurement. It was recalled that Article I:1(b) of the Agreement provided that the Agreement applied to "any procurement contract of a value of SDR 150 000 or more . . ." and Parties were obligated to ensure that all purchases of goods by the entities subject to the Agreement having a contract value of this amount or more were advertised and awarded in accordance with the Agreement's requirements. The conformity of this practice with Article I:1(b) of the Agreement was challenged by the US.

(2) The Panel found that the case before it depended on an interpretation of the term "contract value". In view of the silence of the Agreement and the absence of negotiating history concerning this term, the Panel considered that for the purchasing entity what counted was the total price which the entity would have to pay in order to obtain the product in question and that therefore the natural interpretation of the term contract value would be the full cost to the entity and would therefore include any VAT payable.

(3) The Panel noted in this respect that in fact most Parties to the Agreement had, from the outset, included indirect taxes such as VAT when making threshold determinations. It considered also that whether any VAT payable was included or excluded in the context of threshold determination would make a clear difference in the number of contracts to which the Agreement would be applied and that the obligations flowing from the Agreement should be interpreted in a uniform way by all Parties with respect to this question.

(4) The fact that the EEC legislation explicitly excluding VAT for threshold determinations had already existed at the time of the negotiations was an indication that the term contract value in Article I:1(b) of the Agreement lacking an explicit provision to this effect, did not exclude the VAT element. The circumstance that threshold determinations had to be based on estimates which by their nature were imprecise and included erratic factors, such as fluctuations of exchange rates, was no reason to create a further difference in evaluation by admitting the exclusion of VAT.

(5) As to the absence of uniform VAT rates in the Community, the Panel considered that although an argument could be made for a "net of VAT rule" in the context of a common market which

aimed at harmonizing conditions of competition, this was not of decisive relevance for the interpretation of the Agreement. VAT rates as well as other elements that went into the total contract prices differed between the Parties to the Agreement other than the EEC and there was therefore no justification for excluding particular cost elements in the absence of provisions specifically excluding them.

Conclusion

The Panel concluded that the term contract value in Article I:1(b) of the Agreement on Government Procurement should be interpreted to be the full cost to the entity, taking into account all the elements that would normally enter into the final price and would therefore include any VAT payable.

The EEC practice of excluding the VAT was found to be not in conformity with this interpretation.

Panel on Newsprint

PANEL REPORT

adopted on November 20, 1984

Parties	Canada / EEC
Intervening	Finland, Norway, Sweden, New Zealand
Panel Membership	Patterson, Dumont, Shaton
Published in BISD	31S/114

Key Words

(1) Tariff quota opened under Article II. Any changes in tariff quotas, even if they are purely formal and if they did not affect the GATT rights of other countries, exceed quota "administration" in the sense of Article XIII and require renegotiation according to Article XXVIII and to long-standing GATT practice.

(2) Free-trade agreement. Incidence on duty-free tariff quota of free access to EEC market granted by free-trade agreements. Qualification or reservation under Article II:1(b) forgone by EEC.

(3) Fundamental importance of security and predictability of GATT tariff bindings. Principle constituting a central obligation in the system of the GA, disregarded by the EEC. Unilateral action by EEC constituting *prima facie* impairment of benefits. (Article II. Article XXIII:1. 1979 Understanding on Dispute Settlement, paragraph 5).

(4) Increase of value of concession of a duty-free quota for MFN suppliers, due to free access to EEC market of EFTA suppliers. Increased value justifying renegotiation under Article XXVIII with the objective of achieving reduction of quota by MFN suppliers without payment of compensation. (Article XXVIII).

(5) Maintenance of existing quota. Recording of all imports including EFTA countries incompatible with the nature of a duty-free quota. (Article II. Article XXVIII).

(6) Retaliatory action delayed in view of renegotiations under Article XXVIII. (Article XXIII:2).

Summary

(1) EEC Regulation 3684/83 opened a duty-free tariff quota of 500,000 tons for newsprint for the year 1984, whereas the commitment of the EEC in its GATT schedule LXXII provided for an annual duty-free quota of 1.5 million tons. EEC alleged that the volume of 500,000 tons was fixed "at a provisional level" and that the action taken was merely a change in the administration or the management of the tariff quota permissible under Article XIII and that therefore renegotiations under Article XXVIII were not called for. The Panel noted in this respect that under a long-standing GATT practice even purely formal changes in the tariff schedule of a cp, which may not affect the GATT rights of other countries, such as the conversion of a specific duty to an *ad valorem* duty, have been considered to require renegotiations.

(2) Duty-free access to the Community market for newsprint was accorded to EFTA countries from January 1, 1984 onwards. The EEC had not made the concession granted in 1973 subject to any qualification or reservation in the sense of Article II:1(b) although it was known at that time that agreement had been reached on this point with the EFTA countries. EEC Regulation 3684/83 did not in fact constitute a change in administration or management of the tariff quota from a global quota system to a system of country shares, as alleged by the EEC but the opening of a reduced quota, it being understood that imports would not be charged against this quota if they were already free of customs duties under other preferential tariff agreements. The Regulation did not provide an allocation of country shares to individual MFN suppliers, nor had a global quota been established as Article XIII required.

(3) The EEC in unilaterally establishing a reduced duty-free quota had not acted in conformity with its obligation under Article II of the GATT and had thus disregarded the fundamental importance of the security and predictability of GATT tariff bindings, a principle which constitutes a central obligation in the system of the GA. In accordance with established GATT practice the EEC action constituted a *prima facie* case of impairment of benefits which Canada was entitled to expect under the GA (1979 Understanding on Dispute Settlement, paragraph 5).

(4) As a result of the duty-free access of newsprint imports from EFTA countries under the terms of free-trade agreements, the value of the EEC concession had greatly increased for non-EFTA suppliers and especially for Canada as the most important MFN supplier. This increased value of the concession justifies the EEC engaging in renegotiations under Article XXVIII, in accordance with the customary procedures and practices, with the objective of achieving some reduction in size of the tariff quota, without payment of compensation, considering that Canadian exports never exceeded half of the quota.

(5) The EEC envisaged as an alternative the maintenance of a 1.5 million tons quota against which imports from all sources would be recorded, including the EFTA countries. Such action, though not specifically forbidden by GATT, would not be an appropriate solution and would create an unfortunate precedent. It is the nature of a duty-free quota to allow specified quantities of imports duty-free which would otherwise be dutiable, which is not the case of EFTA imports by virtue of the free-trade agreements. Imports which are already duty free, due to a preferential agreement, cannot by their very nature participate in an MFN duty-free quota.

Conclusion

The EEC was required to engage promptly in renegotiations under the procedures of Article XXVIII.

Pending renegotiation, the EEC was required to maintain the duty-free tariff quota of 1.5 million tons for MFN suppliers.

There was no need to rule on the request of Canada that it be authorized to suspend the application of application of appropriate concessions or other obligations under the GA.

New Zealand—Imports of Electrical Transformers from Finland

PANEL REPORT

adopted on July 18, 1985

Parties Finland/New Zealand

Panel Membership van Tuinen, Kaczurba, Stoler

Published in BISD 32S/55

Key Words

(1) Dumping. Anti-dumping duties on custom-built transformers. Definition of dumping. Absence of domestic price. Price elements drawn from other sources. (Article VI:1).

(2) Material injury. Determination by importing cp. Determination challengeable by any cp having an interest. Review of determination by GATT. Law and order in international trade relations. [Article VI:6(a)].

(3) Material injury. Evaluation related to total national output of importing country. Company representing 92 per cent of output satisfying this criterion. [Article VI:6(a). Report of the Group of Experts on Anti-Dumping, adopted on May 13, 1959, BISD 8S/145].

(4) Material injury. Not equivalent to profit lost. Imports insignificant in relation to overall sales do not cause injury. Imposition of anti-dumping duties inconsistent with Article VI:6(a).

(5) Measure inconsistent with GA constitutes *prima facie* case of impairment of benefits. (Article XXIII:1).

Summary

(1) Imposition by New Zealand of anti-dumping duties on custom-built electrical transformers from Finland. Definition of dumping in Article VI:1. In the absence of a domestic price for custom-built

transformers and the Finnish exporter having been unable to provide all the cost elements allowing for a meaningful cost-of-production calculation, according to Article VI:1(b)(ii), the New Zealand authorities had rightly made a calculation on the basis of price elements obtained from other sources.

(2) Though the responsibility to make a determination of material injury caused by dumped imports rested in the first place with the authorities of the importing cp, according to Article VI:6(a), such determination could be challenged by a cp having an interest in the matter. To conclude otherwise would give governments complete freedom and unrestricted discretion in deciding anti-dumping cases without any possibility to review the action taken in GATT. This would lead to an unacceptable situation under the aspect of law and order in international trade relations.

(3) Evaluation of material injury is to be related to the total national output of the like commodity concerned or a significant part thereof (1959 Report of the Group of Experts on Anti-Dumping). Complaining New Zealand company satisfied this criterion as it represented 92 per cent of the national production.

(4) Material injury in the sense of Article VI:1 is not equivalent with any given amount of profit lost. Imports from Finland, being insignificant in relation to the overall sales of transformers, could not be the cause of the poor economic situation of the corresponding branch of the New Zealand industry. For the same reason no threat of injury could be seen, New Zealand having been unable to demonstrate that injury suffered by its transformer industry had been caused by imports from Finland. Imposition of anti-dumping duties was therefore not consistent with Article VI:6(a).

(5) In accordance with established GATT practice a measure judged to be inconsistent with the provisions of the GA constituted a *prima facie* case of impairment of benefits.

Conclusion

New Zealand was required to revoke the anti-dumping determination and to reimburse the anti-dumping duty paid.

Panel on US Initiation of a Countervailing Duty Investigation into Softword Lumber Products from Canada

PANEL REPORT

of June 3, 1987
by the Committee on Subsidies and Countervailing Measures

Parties Canada / US

Panel Membership Cartland, Mohrmann, Wasescha

Published in BISD 34S/194

Key Words

(1) Subsidies on export constituted by preferential conditions granted to nationals in relation to harvesting softwood ("stumpage"). [Agreement on Interpretation and application of Articles VI, XVI and XXIII of the GA ("Subsidies Code")].

(2) Understanding constituting voluntary settlement. (Subsidies Code, Article 18:7).

Summary

(1) Investigation of the US authorities into programs of the Canadian provincial and federal authorities relating to the right to harvest softwood timber ("stumpage") allegedly involving preferential advantages to manufacturers, producers or exporters in Canada considered to imply a net subsidy estimated at 15 per cent *ad valorem*.

(2) Memorandum of understanding entered into by the Parties providing for withdrawal of US measures and for collection by Canada of an export charge of 15 per cent *ad valorem* of certain softwood lumber products.

Conclusion

Panel's mandate regarded as being completed in view of the mutually satisfactory resolution of the dispute reached by the parties.

US—Taxes on Petroleum and Certain Imported Substances ("Superfund Act")

PANEL REPORT

adopted on June 17, 1987

Parties Canada, EEC, Mexico / US

Intervening Australia, Indonesia, Kuwait, Malaisia, Nigeria, Norway

Panel Membership Cartland, Manhusen, Akasaka

Published in BISD 34S/136

Key Words

(1) Internal taxation. Excise tax levied on imported petroleum and on certain imported chemicals for the benefit of environmental programs. (Article III:2).

(2) Excise duty on imported petroleum. "Like products" in the sense of Article III:2. Rate on imported products higher than rate on domestic products. Taxation inconsistent with Article III:2. (WP Report on Border Tax Adjustments, BISD 18S/97).

(3) Infringement constituting *prima facie* impairment of benefits according to Article XXIII:1. (1979 Understanding on Dispute Settlement, Annex, paragraph 5). Presumption in practice irrefutable. Minimal margin of discrimination. Trade effects of infringement irrelevant. Rationale of Article III:2 (as of Article XI:1) is to protect competitive relationship between imported and domestic products, not expectations of trade volumes.

(4) Internal taxes. Proceeds of tax dedicated to environmental improvements in the importing country. Purpose of taxes levied directly on products irrelevant under Article III:2. Tax eligible for border tax adjustment. No infringement established.

(5) Border tax adjustment [note to Article III.2. Article II:2(a)]. Tax eligible if equivalent of tax levied domestically on chemicals and materials used for production of imported taxable product.

(6) Penalty tax provided for by US legislation potentially discriminatory. Assurance given by US Government. (Article XXIII).

Summary

(1) US "Superfund Act" of 1986 authorized a program for cleaning up hazardous waste sites and dealing with public health problems caused by hazardous waste, and provided for excise and corporate income taxes and appropriations to pay for the costs. Excise tax levied on certain imported and domestic goods, viz. (a) petroleum and (b) certain chemical substances. (See Remarks).

(a) *Tax on petroleum*

(2) Excise duty levied on imported petroleum and liquid hydrocarbon products was justified insofar as these products are identical to the corresponding national products or serve substantially identical end-uses (Article III:2 and 1970 WP Report on Border Tax Adjustments). However the tax applied to imported products was found to be inconsistent with Article III:2 insofar as the rate applied to imported products was 3.5 cents per barrel higher than the rate applied to domestic products, whether or not the products concerned are subject to a tariff concession.

(3) Where there is an infringement of the obligations assumed under the GA, the action is considered *prima facie* to constitute a case of impairment. (1979 Understanding on Dispute Settlement). The circumstance that the tax differential was so small that its trade effects were minimal or nil, as was alleged by the US, was no rebuttal of this presumption, which came close in practice to an irrefutable presumption. In any case, the impact of a measure inconsistent with the GA is not relevant for a determination of impairment, the basic rationale of Article III:2 (like the rationale of Article XI) being to protect expectations not of export volumes, but of the competitive relationship between imported and domestic products. Unlike some other provisions in the GA, Article III:2 does not refer to trade effects. A change in the competitive relationship contrary to that provision must consequently be regarded in that respect as an impairment of benefits in the sense of Article XXIII.

(b) *Tax on certain imported chemical substances*

(4) Considering the objection drawn by the claimants from the circumstance that the tax was not eligible for border tax adjustment, as it was designed to tax polluting activities that occurred in the US

and to finance environmental programs benefiting only US producers, the Panel held that the tax adjustment rules of the GA distinguished between taxes on products and taxes not directly levied on products. Taxes on products were eligible for border tax adjustment independently of the purpose served by the tax legislation, whether the tax was levied for general revenue purposes or for other ends, such as encouraging rational use of environmental resources.

(5) In spite of the circumstance that the Superfund Act established an internal tax on certain imported substances without imposing an equivalent burden on like domestic products, the tax was considered to qualify as a "border tax adjustment", as the tax on imported substances was found to equal the amount of the tax which would have been imposed on the chemicals used as materials in the manufacture or production of the imported substances, had these been used in the US. To that extent the tax on certain imported substances was recognized to be equivalent to the tax borne by like domestic substances. (Note ad Article III, Article II:2(a)).

(6) The penalty tax of 5% provided for where an importer fails to give adequate information was considered to entail potential discrimination. Inconsistency disregarded by Panel in view of assurance given by US that penalty would "in all probability" never be applied.

Conclusion

The US was required to adjust the tax on petroleum in conformity with its obligations under the GA.

The tax on certain imported substances constituting a tax adjustment corresponding to the tax on certain chemicals was recognized to be in principle consistent with Article III:2. Note was taken of US statement relating to the penalty rate.

Remarks

Chemical substances listed in Annexes I and II to Report.

Japan—Customs Duties, Taxes and Labelling Practices on Imported Wines and Alcoholic Beverages

PANEL REPORT

adopted on November 10, 1987

Parties	EEC / Japan
Intervening	Argentina, Canada, Finland, US, Yugoslavia
Panel Membership	Tello, Bondad, Kauter
Published in BISD	34S/83

Key Words

(1) Internal taxation. Large degree of freedom granted by GA to cp in deciding autonomously on the objectives, level, principles and methods of their internal taxation systems. In making use of this freedom, the cp are however bound to conform to the provisions of Article III.

(2) Object and purpose of Article III:2 is to assure "trade neutrality" of internal taxation and promote non-discriminatory competition among imported and like domestic products. Tax specialization liable to be discriminatory against like products.

(3) "Like products". Concept has different meanings according to context which are to be determined on a case-to-case basis (Article I:1. Article III:2. Drafting history. WP on Border Tax Adjustments (1970), BISD 19S/95).

(4) "Like products". Alcoholic beverages. Likeness to be determined in the light of objective criteria rather than on the basis of consumer habits. Consumer preferences liable to be crystallized by taxation. Flexibility in the use of alcoholic beverages and common characteristics of the same leading to high degree of competitive relationship and substitutability inside some broad categories (distilled liquors, liqueurs, wines, sparkling wines). (Article III:2).

(5) Strict character of prohibition of tax discrimination by Article III:2. Account to be taken not only of the rate of taxation but also of taxation methods and rules for tax collection.

(6) Japanese "grading system" and "mixed" system of specific and *ad valorem* tax resulted in discrimination against imported products, hardening consumer preferences for traditional home products. (Article III:2).

(7) As to the tax base assessment, objective reasons may justify or necessitate differences in the system of taxation for imported and domestic products. Evidence insufficient to make a finding on Japanese "fixed subtraction system". (Article III:2).

(8) Taxation according to alcoholic strength and "extract" content leads to tax discrimination. (Article III:2).

(9) Tax system found to afford protection to domestic "sotchu". No sufficient evidence to establish discrimination between traditional Japanese "saké" and "minin", and imported wines and liquors. (Article III:2).

(10) Taxation according to "tax-bearing ability" does not provide an objective standard for taxation. National tax policy and national policy of promoting domestic production of certain goods to be pursued in conformity with the GA without resorting to discriminatory taxation. (Article III:2).

(11) Use of trade names and true origin of products. Japanese labelling legislation and practice not found to be inconsistent with obligations of Article IX:6.

(12) Impairment of benefits. Increase of imports in spite of discriminatory tax treatment no refutation of impairment presumption. (Article XXIII:1).

Summary

(1) Japanese tax system, based on "tax-bearing ability", was found to involve a complex arrangement of categories and quality grades and a combination of specific and *ad valorem* taxes. Though the GA granted each cp a large degree of freedom to decide autonomously on the objectives, level, principles and methods of its internal taxation of goods and though the GA did not impose an obligation on cp to adopt a specific tax system or

specific taxation methods, in making use of this freedom the cp had to conform to the provisions of Article III.

(a) *General considerations on the interpretation of Article III*

(2) A comparison has to be made under Article III:2 in respect of taxation between "like products", i.e. not only between "identical" or "equal" products, but also between products having "similar qualities". Article III:2 has to be construed, by analogy with Article I:1, so as to protect the competitive benefits accruing from reciprocal tariff bindings, prohibiting "tax specialization" discriminating against "like products". Only this interpretation could make sure that competitive benefits accruing under tariff concessions would not be nullified or impaired by internal tax discrimination against like products. The philosophy behind Article III:2, according to the preparatory work of the UN Conference on Trade and Employment and a WP Report on Border Tax Adjustments established in 1970, was to ensure a certain "trade neutrality" of internal taxation and to provide equal conditions of competition once the goods had been cleared through customs. The object and purpose of Article III:2, which was to promote non-discriminatory competition among imported and like domestic products, could not be achieved if Article III:2 were construed in a manner allowing discriminatory and protective internal taxation of imported goods.

(b) *"Like products" in the field of alcoholic beverages*

(3) The concept of "like products", which occurs some sixteen times throughout the GA, may have different meanings in different contexts, as results from the GA's drafting history. The meaning of this concept should therefore be determined on a case-to-case basis using, *inter alia,* criteria such as end-uses in a given market; consumers' tastes and habits which change from country to country; and the products' properties, nature and quality.

(4) The Panel recognized that certain categories of alcoholic beverages, such as gin, vodka, whisky, brandy, certain "classic" liquors, wine and sparkling wine were recognized in their end-use to constitute each a well-defined and single product, and that minor differences in taste, colour and other properties did not prevent products qualifying as "like products". But it did not exclude that other alcoholic beverages could also be considered "like products". The Panel agreed that the "liquors" must be

examined taking into account not only objective criteria but also the more subjective consumer's viewpoint. It considered however that consumer habits are variable in time and space and that the aim of Article III:2, which was to ensure neutrality of internal taxation, could not be achieved if differential taxes could be used to crystallize consumer preferences for domestic products. Thus national Japanese consumer habits with regard to "sotchu" provided no reason for not considering vodka to be a "like" product. The Panel considered also the flexibility in the use of alcoholic drinks and their common characteristics, which often offered an alternative choice to consumers, leading to a competitive relationship and substitutability inside some broad categories, which the Panel identified as being: distilled liquors, wines and sparkling wines.

(c) *Analysis of the fiscal burden*

(5) The Panel noted that the prohibition of tax discrimination by Article III:2 was strict, account having to be taken not only of the rate of the applicable internal tax, but also of the taxation methods and the rules for tax collection.

(6) The Japanese "grading system" for whisky was found to result in differential taxation by imposing higher rates on imported whiskies while according to more than half of the domestic whiskies and brandies considerably lower rates. The "mixed" system of specific tax and *ad valorem* tax applying to wines, whiskies, brandies, spirits and liquors was found to be not as such inconsistent with Article III.2, but the introduction by Japan of non-taxable thresholds resulted in a considerably higher taxation of imported products as compared to domestic ones, hardening consumer preferences for traditional home products.

(7) As to the method of calculating *ad valorem* taxes it was admitted that Article III:2 does not prescribe the use of any specific method or system of taxation. The Panel also admitted that objective reasons proper to the tax in question could justify or necessitate differences in the system of taxation for imported and domestic products. Under Article III:2 it had to be examined whether the application of different taxation methods had a discriminatory or protective effect against imported products. The Panel did not dispose of sufficient evidence for concluding that the simplified method of tax base assessment ("fixed subtraction system") applied to domestic products had actually resulted,

or was likely to result, in tax discrimination against imported products.

(8) Taxation according to alcoholic strength and "extract" content (the latter reflecting the raw material contents) was found to result in differential taxation of like products, incompatible with Article III:2.

(9) The Japanese tax system was found to afford in particular protection to domestic "sotchu" by applying to this product an extremely favorable taxation, as compared to competing imported products such as whiskies and brandies. To the contrary, there was not sufficient evidence to establish that traditional Japanese products like "saké" or "minin" had been subjected to lower tax burdens than imported wines and liquors.

(10) The Japanese tax policy objective of "taxation according to tax-bearing ability of prospective consumers" did not offer an objective criterion for taxation, insofar as it relied on necessarily subjective assumptions about future competition and uncertain consumer responses. The implementation of this policy did not necessitate discriminatory or protective taxation of imported products and could be pursued in many ways in compliance with Article XIII:2. Likewise, a national policy of promoting the domestic production of certain goods could be pursued in conformity with the GA without resorting to discriminatory or protective taxation.

(d) *Use of trade names; true origin of products*

(11) The Panel found that Japanese labelling practice under the relevant internal legislation was not inconsistent with the obligations flowing from Article IX:6 and that the Japanese authorities had not failed to meet their obligations to cooperate pursuant to the same provision.

(e) *Impairment of benefits*

(12) Since it had been recognized in GATT practice that Article III:2 protects expectations as to the competitive relationship between imported and domestic products rather than expectations as to trade volumes, the Panel did not consider it necessary to examine the quantitative trade effects of tax discrimination. Likewise, an increase of imports could not refute the presumption that discriminatory or protective taxes had impaired competitive benefits

protected under Article III:2 because, *inter alia,* an increase in imports said nothing about what the trade might have been in the absence of the inconsistent trade restrictions.

Conclusion

Japan was required to bring its taxes on whiskies, brandies, other distilled spirits (such as gin and vodka), liquors, still wines and sparkling wines into conformity with its obligations under the GA.

US Customs User Fee

PANEL REPORT

adopted on February 2, 1988

Parties	Canada, EEC / US
Intervening	Australia, Hong Kong, India, Japan, New Zealand
Panel Membership	Donovan, Hudec, Roselli
Published in BISD	35S/245

Key Words

(1) Procedure. Single Panel examining parallel complaints. Individual rights of parties. (Article XXIII:2).

(2) Procedure. Terms of reference. Findings restricted to issues raised by parties. (Article XXIII:2).

(3) Fees or other charges commensurate with the cost of services rendered [Article II:2(c)]. Fees and charges imposed by cp on importation limited in amount to the approximate cost of services rendered. [Article VIII:1(a)]. Both provisions having substantially the same meaning. "Services" means not services in the economic sense, but government activities closely enough connected to the process of customs entry.

(4) "Cost of services rendered" to be understood as reflecting the approximate cost of customs processing for the individual entry concerned. *Ad valorem* levy was inconsistent with obligations of Article II:2(c) and VIII:1(a).

(5) Compatibility of fees with Articles II:2(c) and VIII:1(a) to be tested by the criteria of "proximity to the normal process of customs clearance" and "general applicability". Types of fees consistent and fees not consistent with the GA.

(6) Interpretation. Exceptional character of Articles II:2(c) and VIII:1(a), requires particularly strict interpretation. Burden of proof. Burden of justifying any governmental activity charged for

incumbent on government imposing the fee. Indirect protection of domestic products contrary to Article VIII:1(a) not established.

Summary

(1) Panel procedure. Single Panel instituted in view of examining parallel claims of several cp. Procedural rights of complaining parties as if separate panels had examined their complaints. Taking regard of the frequently overlapping positions of the parties the Panel did not find it necessary to separate the arguments brought forward.

(2) Panel procedure. Separate issues raised by intervening parties. According to GATT practice the Panel made findings only on the issues raised by the main parties to the dispute.

(3) Question of consistency with Articles II:2(c) and VIII:1(a) of the US merchandise processing fee, part of the "customs user fees" imposed for the processing by the Customs Service of passenger conveyances and merchandise entering the US. General meaning and mutual relationship of Articles II:2(c) and VIII:1(a). Though Article II:2(c) is a provision of a somewhat narrower scope, both provisions, taking account of their origin and drafting history, have in substance the same meaning, insofar as the central concept of "services rendered" is concerned. The term "services" in this context means not services in the economic sense, but government activities closely enough connected to the process of customs entry.

(4) "Cost of services rendered" must be understood as a charge reflecting the approximate cost of customs processing for the individual entry in question. The *ad valorem* structure of the US merchandise processing fee, causing fees to be levied in excess of these approximate costs, is therefore inconsistent with the obligations of Articles II:2(c) and VIII:1(a).

(5) "Proximity to the normal process of customs clearance" and "general applicability" to be used as criteria for analysis of consistency of fees with the GA. The Panel considered *inter alia* the following operations to be part of "normal customs activities" of "sufficiently general character" qualifying as such for cost of services rendered: investigation of customs fraud and counterfeit goods; collection of anti-dumping and countervailing duties; technical laboratories and centralized investigations; legal rulings; "clear-

ance of carriers"; executive management activities (international affairs excluded). Costs exceeding the "cost of services rendered" were identified as being: airport passenger processing; handling of exports; the "international affairs" item in the commercial operations budget of the US Customs Service; customs processing of exempt imports.

(6) Exceptional character of Articles II:2(c) and VIII:1(a), requires "particularly strict interpretation". Burden of justifying any government activity charged for was found to be incumbent on the government imposing the fee. "Indirect protection to domestic products" was not considered to have been established by complaining parties.

Conclusion

US merchandise processing fee was considered to nullify or impair benefits accruing to Canada and EEC.

US was required to bring the merchandise processing fee into conformity with its obligations under the GA.

Panel on Import, Distribution and Sale of Alcoholic Drinks by Canadian Provincial Marketing Agencies

PANEL REPORT

adopted on March 22, 1988

Parties EEC / Canada

Intervening Australia, US

Panel Membership Haran, Contestabile, Viganó

Published in BISD 35S/37

Key Words

(1) Import and distribution monopoly of provincial liquor boards of Canada (Articles II:4; III:4; XI; XVII; XXIV:12; "Provincial Statement of Intentions").

(2) Import monopolies under Article II;4. Amount of protection allowed depends either on Article II:4 or on specific agreement by interested parties. "Provincial Statement of Intentions" does not derogate from Canada's obligations under Article II:4.

(3) Revenue maximization by import and distribution monopoly and discriminatory price mark-ups inconsistent with standard of "reasonable margin of profit". (Article II:4, interpretative note and Article 31 of the Havana Charter). Impairment of benefits. Non-decline of imports no argument in favor of monopoly practice. (Article XXIII:1).

(4) Revenue-raising function of monopoly permitted, but liable to the provisions of the GA, in particular Article III:1 and 2. Mark-ups affording protection to domestic production. Mark-ups do not conform to Article X on publication of trade regulations.

(5) Restrictions resulting from limitations of points of sale and from listing practices inconsistent with Article XI:1. Article III:4 also probably applicable. Application of Article XVII on State trading not examined.

(6) "Existing legislation" clause of PPA applicable only to mandatory legislation.

(7) Action of alcohol monopoly under Article XX(d) unobjectionable if conforming to requirements of GA.

(8) Notification of State trading operations under Article XVII:4(a) and CP decisions of 1960 and 1962 (BISD 9S/182 and 11S/58).

(9) Obligations of cp in relation to local authorities under Article XXIV:12. Obligation of cp concerned to demonstrate that all reasonable measures had been taken. Measures taken by Canada clearly not conforming to the standard of Article XXIV:12.

Summary

(1) The complaint of the EEC related to the practices of the Provincial Liquor Boards of Canada which under the 1928 Importation of Intoxicating Liquors Act enjoy an import and sales monopoly for alcoholic beverages. The complaint of the EEC concerned

(a) mark ups on liquor prices (Article II:4);

(b) restrictions on the points of sale and discriminatory practices in the listing of beverages offered for sale (Articles III:4, XI or XVII);

(c) disregard of notification obligations under Article XVII:4(a).

(d) apart from the provisions of the GA, the matter was governed by the Provincial Statement of Intentions with Respect to Sales of Alcoholic Beverages by Provincial Marketing Agencies in Canada, negotiated by Canada with the EEC in the context of the Tokyo Round which had led to a binding of the Canadian tariff rates on all alcoholic beverages under Article II.

(a) *Mark-Ups*

(2) The Canadian marketing system of alcoholic beverages was found to qualify as an import monopoly under Article II:4. The amount of protection allowed was thus either the amount provided for in the Canadian Schedule or as otherwise agreed between the parties. The Panel held that the Provincial Statement of Intentions, considering its "non-contractual" nature and its content, did not modify Canada's obligations arising from the inclusion of alcoholic beverages in its GATT Schedule.

(3) Article II:4, interpreted in the light of Article 31 of the Havana Charter according to the corresponding note, allowed for a "reasonable margin of profits", i.e. a margin of profit that would have been obtained under normal conditions of competition (in the absence of the monopoly). The margin of profit on the average would have to be the same on both domestic and the like imported products so as not to undermine the value of tariff concessions under Article II. A monopoly profit-margin on imports resulting from policies of revenue maximization by provincial liquor boards could therefore not normally be considered a "reasonable margin of profit", especially if it were higher on imported products than on domestic products. Mark-ups which were higher on imported than on like domestic alcoholic beverages ("differential mark-ups") could only be justified to the extent that they represented additional costs necessarily associated with marketing of the imported products and the burden of proof would in this case be on Canada. The fact that the volume of imports from the EEC of the products in question had not declined was no argument as it did not say anything about what the imports would have been in the absence of a policy of monopolistic profit maximization.

(4) The conclusions on Article II:4 did not affect the right of Canada to use import monopolies to raise revenue for the provinces, but such action remained liable to the relevant provisions of the GA. In particular, under Article III: 1 and 2, the fiscal element of mark-ups could not be applied to imported products so as to afford protection to domestic production. Moreover, mark-ups would have to be administered in conformity with Article X dealing with the publication and administration of trade regulations.

(b) *Restrictions on the points of sale and on listing*

(5) The Panel considered that under the common note to Articles XI, XII, XIII, XIV and XVIII on State-trading operations the distinction normally made in the GA between restrictions affecting the importation of products and restrictions affecting imported products lost much of its significance since both types of restrictions could be made effective through decisions by the monopoly. Article XI was therefore relevant. The Panel considered that systematic discriminatory practices were among the "other measures" contrary to the provisions of Article XI:1. The Panel saw great force in the argument that Article III:4 was also applicable to State-trading enterprises, at least when the importation and the distribution monopolies in the domestic markets were combined.

In these circumstances, the Panel did not find it necessary to rule on Article XVII, on State-trading.

(6) The Importation of Intoxicating Liquors Act of 1928 was not eligible as "existing legislation" under the PPA, since this Act did not have a mandatory character in relation to the establishment of points of sale and discriminatory listing requirements.

(7) Nothing in the Panel's conclusions on points of sale and listing requirements affected the right of Canada to use import monopolies for the purposes of the protection of health of its population [Article XX(b)], provided it was done consistently with the relevant provision of the GA.

(c) *Notification requirements*

(8) The Panel recognized that Canada had complied with its obligations under Article XVII:4(a) on notification of State trading operations, but called on Canada to conform fully to the CP decisions of 1960 and 1962 (BISD 9S/182 and 11S/58).

(d) *Canada's obligations under Article XXIV:12*

(9) The Panel rejected the position of Canada that the Canadian Government was the only authority that could judge whether all reasonable measures had been taken under Article XXIV:12. According to the Panel, Canada had to demonstrate to the CP that it had taken all reasonable measures available and that it would then be for the CP to decide whether Canada had met its obligations under Article XXIV:12. The Panel concluded on this point that the measures taken by Canada were clearly not all the reasonable measures as might be available to it to ensure observance of the provisions of the GA. However, it was the Panel's view that the Government of Canada should be given a reasonable period of time to take such measures to bring the practices of the provincial liquor boards into line with the relevant provisions of the GA.

Conclusion

Canada was required to take such reasonable measures as may be available to it to ensure observance of Article II and XI by the provincial liquor boards in Canada. Canada was required to report to the CP before the end of 1988 on the action taken.

Canada—Measures Affecting Exports of Unprocessed Herring and Salmon

PANEL REPORT

adopted on March 22, 1988

Parties US / Canada

Panel Membership Nyerges, Groser, Sivertsen

Published in BISD 35S/98

Key Words

(1) Export restrictions (Article XI:1). Measure prohibiting export of salmon in unprocessed form incompatible with Article XI:1.

(2) Terms of reference. Panel mandate limited to examination of actual measures. Panel not competent to impose future action on respondent. (Article XXIII:2).

(3) Jurisdiction. Panel competence restricted to examining fisheries matters in the light of relevant provision of the GA. Panel competence does not extend to matters of fisheries jurisdiction. (Article XXIII).

(4) Export prohibitions "necessary" to the application of regulations for the marketing of commodities in international trade [Article XI:2(b)]. Not applicable to export restrictions on one commodity with a view to promoting sales of another commodity.

(5) Conservation of natural resources. Measures eligible under Article XX(g) only if they are aimed primarily at the conservation of natural resources, not if they limit access of only foreign processors or consumers to unprocessed products.

Summary

(1) Canadian measures prohibiting export of salmon and herring in unprocessed form admitted to be inconsistent with Article XI.1, but considered by Canada to be covered by the provision of Article XI:2(b) on export restrictions necessary to the application

of standards or regulations for the classification, grading or marketing of commodities in international trade and of Article XX(g) on the conservation of natural resources.

(2) Panel mandate was limited to the examination of Canada's present measure. Panel was incompetent to examine US claim asking the Panel to request Canada to refrain from replacing existing export prohibitions by other equivalent measures.

(3) Panel mandate was limited to the examination of Canada's measures in the light of the relevant provisions of the GA, and did not extend to questions on fisheries jurisdiction under international agreements on fisheries and the Convention on the Law of the Sea.

(4) Canada's measures could not be considered "necessary" to the application of quality standards within the meaning of Article XI:2(b), as they were found to apply also to fish meeting these standards. Nor could Canada's measures be considered to be "regulations for the marketing of commodities in international trade", as Article XI:2(b) permitted only export restrictions designed to promote foreign sales of the restricted product but not export restrictions on one commodity designed to promote sales of another commodity.

(5) The Panel recognized that salmon and herring stocks are "exhaustible natural resources" and that Canada maintained a variety of measures for the conservation of these stocks. But the measures contested by the US were not covered by the exception of Article XX(g) insofar as they could not be considered to be primarily aimed at the conservation of an exhaustible natural resource. It appeared that the restrictions established by Canada did not limit access to the species concerned for domestic processors and consumers and that they limited access for foreign processors and consumers only to unprocessed fish.

Conclusion

Canada was required to bring its measures affecting export of certain unprocessed salmon and unprocessed herring into conformity with the GA.

Japan—Restrictions on Imports of Certain Agricultural Products

PANEL REPORT

adopted on March 22, 1988

Parties US / Japan

Intervening Australia, EEC, Uruguay

Panel Membership Pasin, Feij, Simon

Published in BISD 35S/163

Key Words

(1) Import restrictions on agricultural products permitted by Article XI:2(c)(i). Conditions (seven-condition doctrine).

(2) Interpretation of Article XI:2(c)(i) according to Note attached to the GA (Article XXXIV). Drafting history of the Havana Charter relevant.

(3) "Governmental measure" according to Article XI:2(c)(i). Import restrictions permitted only if domestic measures effectively limit agricultural output. "Administrative guidance," relying on consensus leading to effective measures, equivalent to governmental measures. "Special factors" in the sense of Article XI:2, second subparagraph, exclude changes artificially brought about by means not permitted under the GA, but do not exclude production subsidies.

(4) The term "like products" to be interpreted according to the context of Article XI:2(c)(i). Like products imported in "any form" comprise products processed from agricultural products in the early stage of processing and still perishable, that compete directly with the fresh product. Article XI:2(c)(i) not applicable to products capable of being stocked.

(5) Import restrictions under Article XI:2(c)(i) must be "necessary" to the enforcement of the domestic supply restriction. (WP Report on Quantitative Restrictions, BISD 3S/190).

(6) Public notice to be given of restrictions (inference from Article XI:2, second subparagraph).

(7) Proportion between restriction on domestic production and restriction on imports. Previous "representative period" and "special factors" according to Article XI:2, second subparagraph. Article XI:2(c)(i) being an exception to the general ban of import restrictions, the burden of proof of all requirements of this provision has to be borne by the party claiming application of the exception.

(8) Article XI:1 covers all types of restrictions, including state-trading and import monopolies. (Note on Articles XI, XII, XIII, XIV and XVIII. Article II:4 and corresponding Note. Article 31 of Havana Charter).

(9) Article XX(d) on enforcement of monopolies covers only measures otherwise consistent with the GA.

(10) Analysis of 12 product groups leads to conclusion that none of the Japanese measures was consistent with Article XI:2(c)(i).

(11) Practice of other countries, current negotiations and underlying social, political and economic background no justification of practice inconsistent with the GA (Article XXIII:2).

(12) Impairment of benefits to be presumed in case of measures inconsistent with the GA (1979 Understanding on Dispute Settlement). Article XI protects expectations as to competitive conditions, not trade volumes. Presumption of impairment not refuted by arguments drawn from evolution of trade volumes. (Article XXIII:1).

Summary

(1) Quantitative import restrictions maintained by Japan on twelve categories of agricultural products and products derived from agricultural products. Under Article XI:2(c)(i) import restrictions are compatible with the GA only if they meet each and every one of seven conditions:

(i) a measure must be an import restriction, not amounting to a complete import prohibition;

(ii) a measure must be a restriction applicable to an agricultural or fisheries product;

(iii) there must be a governmental measure operating to restrict the quantities of a product to be marketed or produced;

(iv) import restriction and domestic supply restriction must apply to "like" products;

(v) an import restriction must be "necessary" to the enforcement of the domestic supply restriction;

(vi) public notice must be given of the total quantity or value of the quota for each product;

(vii) a reasonable proportion must be observed between the internal restriction and the restriction on imports.

(2) Interpretation of Article XI:2(c)(i). Interpretative notes attached to the GA are an integral part of the GA according to Article XXXIV. Drafting history of the Havana Charter is relevant to the interpretation of GATT provisions.

(3) Apart from requiring a "governmental measure", Article XI:2(c)(i) does not specify how a restriction on production or marketing is to be imposed, the essential point being that the measures of domestic restriction must effectively keep output below the level it would have attained in the absence of restrictions (see also point 11 below). "Special factors" recognised by Article XI:2, second subparagraph, exclude changes artificially brought about by means not permitted under the GA, but do not exclude production subsidies. Restrictions on production may coexist with the grant of subsidies. (Article XVI). It is therefore not necessary that the level of production be restricted below the level that could exist in the absence of all government support.

(4) The term "like products" has different meanings in different contexts. The mere fact that products are in competition with one another does not in itself make them like products. In the context of Article XI and taking account of the note to Article XI:2(c), the terms "imported in any form" make it possible to consider products processed from agricultural products, but only if they are in an early stage of processing and still perishable, and the processed product competes directly with the fresh product, and imports would tend to make the restriction on the fresh product ineffective. Article XI:2(c)(i) must therefore be interpreted as envisaging the perishable kind of processed product, not the kind that is capable of being stocked.

(5) The import restrictions must be necessary to the enforcement of the domestic supply restriction. (WP Report on Quantitative Restrictions).

(6) Under the last subparagraph of Article XI:2 public notice must be given of restrictions. This provision implies that only those quotas can be applied which define the quantity or value for each product subject to quota.

(7) The quotas under Article XI:2(c)(i) must be such as not to reduce the total of imports relative to domestic production as compared with the proportion which might reasonably be expected to obtain between the two in the absence of restrictions, during a previous "representative period" and taking account of "special factors". Among these special factors regard may be had to changes in relative productive efficiency, but not to changes resulting from measures not permitted under the GA. Where a cp invoked an exception to the GA the burden of proof was on the cp invoking the exception. The consequence of this allocation of the burden of proof was that Article XI:2(c)(i) could in practice not be invoked when, as in the case of Japan, the import restrictions had been maintained for a long time, so that it was impossible to determine a "previous period" free of restrictions. The Panel considered that it had no authority to change the burden of proof in order to make Article XI:2(c)(i) operational in case of long-term import restrictions, as this would have consequences equivalent to those of an amendment of this provision and affect the balance of existing tariff concessions. The burden of evidence that all requirements of Article XI:2(c)(i) had been met must therefore remain fully with the cp invoking that provision.

(8) Article XI:1 covers restrictions on the importation of any product whether made effective through quotas, import licenses or other measures. The wording of this provision is comprehensive, and comprises also restrictions made effective through an import monopoly. (Note to Article XI, XII, XIII, XIV and XVIII). The basic purpose of the Note is to extend to State-trading the rules of the GA governing private trade and to ensure that cp cannot escape their obligations by establishing State-trading operations. This solution is consistent with the provision in Article II:4 on State monopolies and the reference of the corresponding note to Article 31 of the Havana Charter. The import restrictions applied by Japan fall under Article XI:1 independent of whether they

were made effective through quotas or through import monopoly operations.

(9) Article XX(d) permits measures necessary to the enforcement of monopolies, including measures necessary to enforce the exclusive trade rights of the monopoly, but only under the condition that such measures are not inconsistent with the GA. Article XX(d) therefore does not permit cp to operate monopolies inconsistently with the other provisions of the GA. Therefore the enforcement of laws or regulations providing for an import restriction made effective through an import monopoly inconsistently with Article XI:1 was not covered by Article XX(d).

(10) Upon analysis of the 12 product groups retained under its terms of reference the Panel found that none of the Japanese restrictive measures satisfied the conditions inherent in Article XI:2(c)(i). (See Section 5.3 of the Panel report).

(11) In relation to some general arguments drawn from the practice of other countries, the status of the multilateral negotiations under way with a view to revising Article XI:2(c)(i) and the special characteristics of Japanese agriculture, the Panel ruled that neither the practice of others nor current negotiations could justify a departure from the provisions of the GA and that, according to the 1982 Ministerial Declaration, decisions in the dispute settlement process cannot add to or diminish the rights and obligations provided for in the GA. The vital role of the twelve items under consideration and the underlying social, political and economic background could not provide a justification for import restrictions under the GA. As to the nature of the contested measures, the GA was primarily concerned with the effectiveness of the measures, which in fact were governmental measures. The practice of "administrative guidance" was a traditional tool of Japanese Government policy based on consensus and peer pressure. The judgment of the Panel, in spite of the initial lack of transparency, was based on the effectiveness of the measures taken, though this approach could not be considered a precedent in other contexts. Thus these arguments of Japan could not be taken into consideration as being "pertinent elements" under the terms of reference.

(12) Impairment of benefits is to be presumed in case of measures inconsistent with the GA (1979 Understanding on Dispute Settlement). Since Article XI:1 protects expectations as to competitive

conditions, not trade volumes, impairment could not be refuted by arguments relating to export volumes.

Conclusion

Japan was required to eliminate or otherwise to bring into conformity with the GA its quantitative restrictions subject to the US complaint.

Japan—Trade in Semi-Conductors

PANEL REPORT

adopted on May 4, 1988

Parties	EEC / Japan
Intervening	Australia, Brazil, Canada, Hong Kong, Singapore. US participated in proceedings
Panel Membership	Lacarte-Muró, Falconer, Greenwald
Published in BISD	35S/116

Key Words

(1) Procedure. Bilateral agreement. Procedural rights of a cp not party to Panel proceedings. (Article XXIII).

(2) Procedure. Terms of reference. Limits of Panel competence. Findings restricted to issues raised by parties. Not to be extended to issues raised by third parties (Article XXIII).

(3) Quantitative restrictions. Article XI:1 to be broadly construed. Article XI:1 applicable to all measures restrictive of trade other than measures taking the form of customs duties or charges. Bilateral agreement establishing monitoring, by exporting country, of exports under a given price level is a restriction inconsistent with Article XI:1.

(4) Quantitative restrictions. "Other measures" in the sense of Article XI:1. Non-mandatory measure of government, entailing sufficient incentives or disincentives for producers or exporters to conform, is "measure" in the sense of Article XI:1.

(5) Quantitative restrictions. Monitoring of exports, entailing excessive delays in the issuing of export licences is inconsistent with Article XI:1.

(6) Dumping (Article VI). Prevention of dumping by exporting country does not justify export restrictions inconsistent with Article XI:1.

(7) MFN treatment (Article I:1). Bilateral agreement favoring access to market not inconsistent with GATT obligations if it does not prevent extension to other cp according to MFN principle.

(8) Impairment of benefits (Article XXIII:1). (a) Export restrictions on semi-conductors established by US/Japan bilateral agreement were inconsistent with GA. Restrictions presumed to have created a competitive disadvantage for the traders of other cp. (b) "Non-violation" complaint in relation to free access to Japanese market. Detailed justification required from the complainant country. (1979 Understanding on dispute settlement).

Summary

(1) Panel procedure. Bilateral agreement Japan/US. US was not a party to Panel proceedings. Adequate opportunity was given to US to participate in the work of Panel.

(2) Panel procedure. Findings of Panel must remain restricted to the issues raised by the main parties to the dispute. They may not extend to issues raised solely by third parties.

(3) Bilateral arrangement between Japan and the US on trade in semi-conductors. Arrangement providing for increased market access and prevention of dumping, including corresponding export controls extending to third countries. Question of compatibility of third-country market monitoring with Article XI:1 on elimination of restrictions on exportation. Comprehensive wording of Article XI:1, applies to all measures instituted or maintained by a cp, which prohibit or restrict the importation, the exportation or the sale for export of products, other than measures that take the form of duties, taxes or other charges. Restrictions on export of goods below a given price level constituted a restriction within the meaning of Article XI:1.

(4) Article XI:1 refers broadly to any "measures" irrespective of the status of these. Article XI:1 is applicable also to non-mandatory measures of governments entailing sufficient incentives or disincentives for producers and exporters to conform. Administrative structure created by Japan, which operated to exert maximum possible pressure on the private sector to cause exporting at a given price level, constituted a coherent system restricting export of semi-conductors at prices below a given level to markets other than the US market and was inconsistent with Article XI:1.

(5) Excessive delays in the issuing of export licences resulting from the system of monitoring of costs and export prices of semi-conductors were inconsistent with Article XI:1.

(6) National measures designed to prevent dumping do not justify export restrictions inconsistent with Article XI:1. Purpose of Article VI is to allow cp to levy a duty on dumped products where dumping causes or threatens material injury to domestic industry. Article VI is silent on actions by exporting countries. Article VI does not provide a justification for measures restricting the exportation or sale for export of a product inconsistently with Article XI:1.

(7) Bilateral arrangement favoring access to market is not inconsistent with GATT obligations if such arrangement contains nothing that would prevent extension of market-opening provisions on an MFN basis. (Article I:1).

(8) (a) Japanese measures relating to restrictions of exports of semi-conductors to third country markets and found to be inconsistent with Article XI:1 are presumed to have nullified or impaired benefits accruing to the EEC under the GA.
(b) A cp claiming that benefits accruing to it under the GA had been nullified or impaired as a consequence of a measure consistent with the GA would be called upon to provide a detailed justification [Understanding on dispute settlement (1979)]. The evidence submitted by the EEC relating to access to the Japanese market did not establish the existence of any measure by the Japanese authorities that had put EEC exporters at a competitive disadvantage vis-à-vis those of the US.

Conclusion

Japan was required to bring its measures relating to the sale for export of semi-conductors to cp other than the US into conformity with the GA.

Note was taken of the change introduced meanwhile by Japan into its export procedures with a view to avoiding excessive delays.

Note was also taken of Japan's statement that its policy was to improve access to the Japanese market for semi-conductors in conformity with the MFN principle. EEC contention of discrimination in favor of US products by measures improving access to Japanese market was not established.

EEC—Restrictions on Imports of Dessert Apples—Complaint by Chile

PANEL REPORT

adopted on June 22, 1989

Parties	Chile / EEC
Intervening	Argentina, Canada, South Africa
Panel Membership	Maciel, Liang, Cottier
Published in BISD	36S/93
Related documents	See Report of November 10, 1980, Chile/EEC (Case 43)

Key Words

(1) Import restrictions. EEC import restrictions on Chilean apples inconsistent with Article XI:1 if not covered by exceptions provided for by Article XI:2.

(2) Terms of reference. Panel authorized to consider all relevant provisions of the GA and those related to its interpretation and implementation. Authority of precedent. Legitimate expectations created by adoption of former report on the same matter. Panel not legally bound by details and legal reasoning of former report. Preliminary decision of Panel. (Article XXIII:2).

(3) Interpretation of the GA. A cp invoking an exception to the GA bears the burden of proving that it has met all the conditions of the exception. (Article XXIII:2). Exceptions to Article XI:1. Strict character of exceptions. Conditions to be fulfilled under Article XI:2(c)(i). Reference to work undertaken with a view to the revision of this provision considered to be irrelevant. Function of the Panel to apply existing provisions, not to propose changes to be made.

(4) Import restrictions and import prohibitions. Article XI:2(c)(i) allows restrictions, not total prohibition of imports.

(5) "Like products" under Article XI:2(c)(i). Differences in price, variety and quality of apples irrelevant.

(6) Production and marketing of apples. Restrictions bearing only on marketing. (Article XI:2(c)(i)).

(7) "Governmental measures" under Article XI:2(c)(i). EEC system of buying-in and withdrawal considered to qualify as a "governmental measure" though it combined elements of public and private responsibility.

(8) Article XI:2(c)(i) requires effective limitation on the quantity domestic producers are allowed to sell.

(9) A price-related system with no quantitative target defined does not justify import restrictions under Article XI:2(c)(i).

(10) Action under Article XI:2(c)(ii) allowed only in case of temporary, not of structural surpluses.

(11) Non-discriminatory administration of quantitative restrictions (Article XIII). "Representative period". "Special factors" to be taken account of: increase in production efficiency and export capacity [Article XIII:2(d)].

(12) Notification and publicity of quantitative restrictions [Article XIII:3(c) and Article X:1]. Back-dated quotas inconsistent with notification and publicity requirements. All goods *en route* to be exempted from restrictions [Article XIII:3(b). 1950 Standard Practices for Import and Export Restrictions and Exchange Controls, GATT Doc. CP. 5/30/Rev. 1, not published in BISD]

(13) Developing countries. Duty of developed countries to avoid trade restrictions on products of interest to developing countries. (Articles XXXVI and XXXVII). Obligation to consult. Failure to satisfy obligations. Inconclusive panel decision.

(14) Terms of reference. Stand-Still Commitment of Punta del Este Declaration. Provision of special forum. Not to be considered an obligation under Article XXIII:1(a).

(15) Terms of reference. GATT "custom". Request for specific compensation not envisaged by Article XXIII:2. Sanction in case of impairment restricted to withdrawal of equivalent obligations. (1979 Understanding on Dispute Settlement and 1965 Secretariat Note).

Summary

(1) EEC Regulation 1035/72 as amended, established a common organization for fruit and vegetables (including apples) and Regulation 2701/72 on the external regime. The common organization of the market was based on an internal system of prices maintained by an intervention system comprising buying-in by public agencies and withdrawal by producer groups with the financial help of the Community. Towards the outside, the system provided for a customs duty (bound in GATT) and for import licensing, made dependent on a "reference price". By Regulation 962/88 the EEC suspended the import of apples originating in Chile for the period April 15 to 22, 1988, extended by Regulation 984/88 to April 29, 1988 and by Regulation 1040/88 to August 31, 1988. The latter Regulation fixed a "reference quantity" which was deemed to have been already exceeded when it was determined. It was not contested that the restrictive licensing system was inconsistent with Article XI:1 but the EEC contended that it was covered by Article XI:2(c).

(2) The Panel construed its terms of reference to mean that it was authorized to examine the matter referred to it in the light of *all* relevant provisions of the GA and those related to its interpretation and implementation. As the same matter had already been examined, for an earlier period, in a Panel Report adopted on November 10, 1980 (BISD 27S/98), the Panel considered that it had to take into account the "legitimate expectations" created by the adoption of that report, but that it was not legally bound by all the details and legal reasoning of the 1980 report. This decision was communicated early in the proceedings to the parties to assist them in the presentation of their arguments.

(3) As to Article XI:2(c)(i), relating to import restrictions considered necessary to the enforcement of governmental measures which operate to restrict the quantities of the like domestic product permitted to be marketed or produced, the Panel recalled that a cp invoking an exception to the GA bears the burden of proving that it has met all the conditions of the exception. Referring to previous reports, the Panel singled out seven conditions to be fulfilled (see Report of February 2, 1988 on Japanese Restrictions on Imports of Certain Agricultural Products) which made this provision extremely difficult to comply

with. Though there existed widespread dissatisfaction with this provision, leading to work on a revision of the same, it was not the function of the panel to propose changes to the provisions of the GA, but to make findings regarding their interpretation and application. (1982 Ministerial Declaration).

(4) Article XI:2(c)(i) allows import restrictions, but not import prohibitions. A minimum quantity of imports must always be permitted.

(5) The import restriction and the domestic supply restriction must apply to "like products," in any form, or directly substitutable products if there is no substantial production of the like product. Notwithstanding differences in price, variety and quality Chilean and EEC apples performed a similar function for the consumer and were both marketed as substantially similar products. They were therefore to be considered to be "like products" for the purposes of Article XI:2(c)(i).

(6) It was not claimed that production of apples was restricted in the EEC. The EEC claimed that it effectively restricted the marketing of apples through a system of market withdrawals.

(7) After having recalled precedents relating to the concept of "governmental measures", the Panel noted that the EEC system was a hybrid one, with combined elements of public and private responsibility. But as the regime had been established by Community regulations and its operation depended on decisions fixing prices and on public financing, the Panel found that both buying-in and withdrawal systems could be considered to be "governmental measures" for the purposes of Article XI:2(c)(i).

(8) The Panel, interpreting Article XI:2(c)(i) according to its wording, its context and its purpose held that governmental measures, to be eligible under this provision must include an effective limitation on the quantity that domestic producers are allowed to sell. Article XI:2(c)(i) being an exception, this requirement had to be interpreted narrowly. The final paragraph of Article XI:2 allowed restrictions only in proportion to "domestic production". Thus schemes which prevent or discourage producers from selling their products beyond fixed amounts can reasonably be expected to have an effect on production. By contrast, a scheme which imposes no limitations on what producers may sell cannot, by itself, bring about a restriction of production. If Article XI:2(c)(i) could be used to justify import restrictions which were

not the counterpart of any governmental measure capable of limiting production the value of the GA as a legal framework for the exchange of tariff concessions would be seriously impaired.

(9) Judged in the light of these standards, the EEC system's operation and targets appeared to be essentially price-related, providing a price-floor to EC producers. There was no quantitative target or limit defined by the EEC and no ceiling on the quantity eligible for this guarantee. Thus, the system could in fact operate as an incentive for producers. The Panel found therefore that the EEC measures taken under the intervention system for apples did not constitute marketing restrictions of a type which could justify import restrictions under Article XI:2(c)(i).

(10) The Panel found moreover that the exception of Article XI:2(c)(ii), on removal of temporary agricultural surpluses, could not apply, since statistical evidence showed that the EEC had substantial structural surpluses.

(11) As to the non-discriminatory administration of quantitative restrictions, the measure taken in relation to Chile was found to be in several regards inconsistent with the obligations of the GA. Regulation 984/88, suspending the issue of import licenses only in relation to Chile, eight days before the publication of import quotas, constituted a discriminatory prohibition against Chile. Though the "reference period" had been correctly fixed, the EEC had not duly taken account under Article XIII:2(d) of the special factors which had characterized the position of Chile, viz. an increase in Chile's relative productive efficiency and export capacity.

(12) Concerning the notification of quotas and quota shares under Article XIII:3(b) and the publicity requirements of Article XIII:3(c) and Article X:1, the Panel considered that both the total quota and the shares allocated in it had to be publicly notified for a specified future. The EEC measure against Chile, consisting in the allocation of back-dated quotas, that is, quotas declared to have already been filled at the time of their announcement, did not conform to the requirements of Article XIII:3(b) and (c) and it resulted moreover in a violation of the rule of XIII:1 on non-discriminatory administration of restrictions. Moreover the provisions of Regulation 962/88, exempting from the import ban only products for which an import licence had been issued before sailing, were found to be contrary to the

stipulation of Article XIII:3(b) on goods *en route,* account being taken also of the Standard Practices for the Administration of Import and Export Restrictions approved by the CP in 1950. The Panel was aware of the interim decision of the President of the European Court of Justice, dated June 10, 1988, which suspended the operation of the corresponding EEC regulation.

(13) Chile argued that the EEC had an obligation under Part IV of the GA (Articles XXXVI and XXXVII) to avoid imposing trade restrictions on products of interest to developing countries and that it had an obligation to consult with Chile before it did so. Although the panel concluded that the EEC did not fully meet its obligations under Article XXXVII in that it had not made appropriate efforts to avoid taking protective measures, it concluded that it was not necessary to pursue the matter under Article XXXVII in light of its other rulings in the case.

(14) The terms of reference of the Panel could not extend to the Standstill Commitment of the Punta del Este Declaration. These commitments had their own special forum—the Surveillance Body established by the "Committee on Trade Negotiations". They could therefore not be considered to be obligations within the meaning of Article XXIII:1(a).

(15) Chile's arguments for an allocation of compensation against the EEC were not accepted, as it was "customary" for a Panel examining complaints under Article XXIII:2 to make a finding regarding impairment of benefits, the final sanction of which was withdrawal of equivalent obligations as provided for by Article XXIII:2. Specific compensation therefore was a matter for negotiation between the parties, not for recommendation by the Panel. (1979 Understanding on Dispute Settlement and 1965 Secretariat Note).

Conclusion

The EEC restrictions on apples were found to be inconsistent with Article XI:1 and not justified by Article XI:2.

The administration of the quotas resulted in a discriminatory application of import restrictions contrary to Article XIII.

The operation of back-dated import restrictions in respect of Chile was found to be inconsistent with Articles X and XIII.

EEC—Restrictions on Import of Apples—Complaint by the US

PANEL REPORT

adopted on June 22, 1989

Parties	US / EEC
Intervening	Canada
Panel Membership	Maciel, Liang, Cottier
Published in BISD	36S/135
Related documents	This report is in substance identical to the Report of the same date in the case Chile/EEC (Case 69), except that the considerations relating specifically to Chile were left out, the US coming under the quota opened to "other countries" by EEC Regulation 1040/88.

Key Words

See Chile/EEC, (1)-(10) and (12).

Impairment of benefits presumed in case of infringement of obligations under the GA (Article XXIII:1. 1979 Understanding on Dispute Settlement). Article XI:1 protected expectations as to competitive conditions, not trade volumes. Impairment of benefits did not depend on evolution of trade volumes.

Summary

See Chile/EEC, (1)—(10) and (12).

Impairment of benefits is to be presumed in case of infringement of obligations under the GA (Article XXIII). Article XI protected expectations of the cp as to competitive conditions, not trade volumes. Hence the presumption that a measure inconsistent with Article XI:1 had nullified or impaired a benefit accruing under that provision would stand irrespective of arguments concerning trade volumes.

Conclusion

The EEC restrictions on imports of apples were found to be inconsistent with Article XI:1 and were not justified by Article XI:2.

The operation of a back-dated import restriction in respect of "other countries" including the U.S. was found to be inconsistent with Articles X and XIII.

Norway—Restrictions on Imports of Apples and Pears

PANEL REPORT

adopted on June 22, 1989

Parties US / Norway

Panel Membership Pescatore, Ahmed, de la Peña

Published in BISD 36S/306

Key Words

(1) Quantitative restrictions. Restrictions on import of apples and pears inconsistent with Article XI:1.

(2) "Existing legislation" clause [Paragraph 1(b) of PPA]. Historical origin and purpose of clause. Clause not to be extended beyond those functions it was originally designed to serve.

(3) "Existing legislation" clause consistently interpreted by CP to be limited to "mandatory" legislation and to open a "one-way street" towards full application of the GA, basic aim of the GA being security and predictability in international trade.

(4) "Existing legislation" clause. To be eligible under the clause legislation must (a) be legislation in a formal sense, (b) predate the Protocol and (c) be mandatory in character.

(5) "Existing legislation" clause. Notification of legislation eligible under the clause. No legal obligation to notify. Note taken of failure of Norway to notify legislation actually relied upon.

(6) "Existing legislation" clause. Enabling legislation not eligible. Political documents not qualifying as legislation. Documents not having a specific relationship with contested measures and documents established after 1947 not relevant.

Summary

(1) Norway maintained a system of restrictive licensing for apples and pears, the inconsistency of which with Article XI:1 was not con-

tested. Norway claimed that this system was covered by the "existing legislation" clause of paragraph 1(b) of the PPA, as it was based on legislation predating the PPA.

(2) Historical origin and purpose of the PPA was to enable governments to accept the obligations of Part II of the GA without having to adjust their domestic legislation and to keep the way open for the ITO Charter. In the light of this purpose, it would not be justified to give the "existing legislation" clause four decades after the entry into force of the Protocol an interpretation that would extend its functions beyond those it was originally designed to serve.

(3) Paragraph 1(b) of the PPA had been interpreted consistently by the CP so as to further the full application of the GA. In particular, the CP had restricted application of the existing legislation clause to mandatory legislation and they had considered that the PPA had opened a "one-way street" permitting movements only to fuller application of the GA. The Protocol was designed to provide only a temporary dispensation from Part II. The basic aim of the GA was security and predictability in trade relations and it would be inconsistent with that aim if cp were free to reverse, at any time and at their discretion, the steps they had taken to bring their legislation into conformity with the GA.

(4) To be eligible as "existing legislation" under the Protocol, such legislation must:

(a) be legislation in a formal sense,

(b) predate the Protocol and

(c) be mandatory in character by its terms or expressed intent

(5) Notification in 1955 and 1958 upon request of the CP of legislation eligible under Paragraph 1(b) of the PPA. Although there was no legal obligation to make such notification, the Panel noted that Norway did not avail itself of the opportunity to notify on that occasion the acts and declarations cited in the present dispute.

(6) Analysis by the Panel of the legislation relied upon by Norway. The 1934 Act was considered to be not eligible as it was enabling, not mandatory in character. Political documents predating the 1947 Protocol were found not eligible as they were not legislation in a formal sense and had no specific relation to the measures complained of by the US. White Papers presented after 1947 to

the Norwegian Storting Parliament by the Government and corresponding resolutions irrelevant.

Conclusion

Norway's restrictions on apples and pears were not covered by the "existing legislation" clause of the PPA.

Norway was required to bring its measures into conformity with the GA.

US—Restriction on Imports of Sugar

PANEL REPORT

adopted on June 22, 1989

Parties Australia / US

Intervening Argentina, Brazil, Canada, Colombia, EEC, Nicaragua, Thailand

Panel Membership Broadbridge, Rosselli, Jozwiak

Published in BISD 36S/331

Key Words

(1) Quantitative restrictions (Article XI:1). US sugar quotas maintained under the authority of a Headnote in the US Schedule established under Article II:1(b).

(2) Tariff schedules. Terms, conditions or qualifications set forth in schedules may be related only to customs duties. They may not qualify obligations under other Articles of the GA [Article II:1(b)]. Purpose of the GA. Reduction of tariffs and other barriers to trade. Interpretation of Article II in the light of the Preamble.

(3) Interpretation of Article II in the light of Article XVII:3 on State trading, of a note to the same provision, of the practice of the CP as expressed in the 1955 Report of the WP on Other Barriers to Trade and of the drafting history of the Havana Charter.

(4) System of the GA. Article II:1(b) does not permit cp to qualify their obligations under other provisions of the GA.

(5) Terms of reference to be interpreted not only in the light of the interests of the parties to the dispute, but also of third parties. Panel not competent to deal with issues raised after its establishment (Article XXIII:2). Third party interests safeguarded by general bearing of Panel's finding, in the sense that Article II:1(b) does not permit cp to qualify their obligations under any other provision of the GA, including Article XIII.

(6) Terms of reference. Panel competent to deal with issues raised by parties, not with those raised solely by a third party. (Article XXIII:2).

Summary

(1) Maintenance by the US of quantitative restrictions on sugar imports based on a Headnote in the US Schedule of Concessions (Schedule XX) established under Article II:1(b). The Panel found that the restrictions were inconsistent with Article XI:1 but the question was whether the declaration was justified by the words "subject to the terms, conditions or qualifications set forth in that Schedule" in Article II:1(b).

(2) The Panel held that the words "subject to the terms, conditions or qualifications set forth in that Schedule" in Article II:1(b), read in conjunction with the reference by the same provision to customs duties, must be interpreted as permitting cp to qualify the obligation to exempt products from customs duties in excess of the levels specified in the Schedule, not however to qualify their obligations under other Articles of the GA. This interpretation was consistent with the purpose of the GA which, according to its Preamble, provided a legal framework enabling cp to enter into reciprocal and mutually advantageous arrangements directed to the substantial reduction of tariffs and other barriers to trade. Article II gives cp the possibility of incorporating into the legal framework of the GA commitments additional to those already contained in the GA and to qualify such additional commitments, but not to reduce their commitments under other provisions of that Agreement.

(3) This interpretation was confirmed by the context of Article II, viz. Article XVII:3 on State-trading, a note to that provision, and the practice of the CP, expressed in the 1955 Report of the WP on Other Barriers to Trade, and the drafting history of the Havana Charter.

(4) For these reasons, the Panel found that Article II:1(b) does not permit cp to qualify their obligations under other provisions of the GA and that the provisions of the US GATT Schedule of Concessions can consequently not justify the maintenance of quantitative restrictions on the importation of sugar inconsistent with the application of Article XI:1.

(5) In relation to a claim of Australia relating to the reallocation of a portion of Guyana's sugar quota to Belize, Jamaica, Trinidad and Tobago in disregard of Article XIII.2, the Panel said that although it had to interpret its terms of reference not only in the light of the interests of the parties to the dispute, but also in the light of the rights of third cp, the issue raised by Australia was not part of its mandate as the matter had arisen only after the establishment of the Panel. The Panel recalled however that it had found all restrictions established by the US on the importation of sugar under the Headnote in the US Tariff Schedules to be inconsistent with the GA independent of the quota allocation to specific countries. It also recalled its finding that Article II:1(b) does not permit cp to qualify their obligations under other provisions of the GA, including Article XIII.

(6) The issue raised by the EEC in relation to the agricultural waiver granted to the US in 1955 could not be examined by the Panel, as the practice was for panels to make findings only on those issues raised by the parties to the dispute, not on those raised solely by third parties.

Conclusion

The restrictions on the importation of sugar maintained by the US under the authority of the Headnote in the Tariff Schedule of the US are inconsistent with Article XI:1 and cannot be justified under the provisions of Article II:1(b).

The US was required either to terminate these restrictions or to bring them into conformity with the GA.

Tariff on Import of Spruce Pine Fir (SPF) Dimension Lumber

PANEL REPORT

adopted on July 19, 1989

Parties	Canada / Japan
Intervening	EEC, New Zealand
Panel Membership	Pescatore, de la Peña, Senti
Published in BISD	36S/167

Key Words

(1) Tariff treatment by Japan of spruce-pine-fir (SPF) lumber. "Like products" under the MFN clause of Article I.1. Arrangement of Japanese tariff classification relating to planed lumber. Treatment of Canadian SPF "Dimension Lumber".

(2) Structure of national tariffs and tariff classification of goods. Discretion left to cp in relation to tariff classification. Harmonized System not entailing any obligation as to ultimate details of tariff classification. Tariff classification going beyond the HS structure a legitimate means of trade policy. Abuse of discretion in tariff classification. Claim of "likeness" of products as a defense against abuse. (Article I:1).

(3) Abuse of tariff classification. Burden of proof on party alleging abuse (Article XXIII:2). Complaints relating to abuse to be examined considering protection interest involved and influence of classification on the pattern of imports from different sources. (Article I:1).

(4) "Like products" under Article I:1 to be determined on import by reference to national tariff of importing country. "Dimension lumber" not an appropriate basis for establishing likeness of products in relation to the Japanese tariff.

Summary

(1) Application of a tariff duty of 8 per cent on imports of spruce-pine-fir (SPF) "dimension lumber" by Japan considered by Canada to be not in conformity with the provisions of Article I:1, SPF dimension lumber (a standard applied by the Canadian lumber industry as to measurement, quality-grading and finishing of lumber) being a "like product" as compared with other types of dimension lumber entering Japan with zero duty. In substance Canada complained of the fact that Japan had arranged its tariff classification in such a way that a considerable part of Canadian exports of SPF dimension lumber to Japan was submitted to a customs duty of eight per cent, whereas other comparable types of dimension lumber enjoyed the advantage of a zero-tariff duty.

(2) The GA left wide discretion to the cp in relation to the structure of national tariffs and the classification of goods in the framework of such structure. The adoption of the Harmonized System had brought a large measure of harmonization in the field of customs classification of goods, but this system did not entail any obligation as to the ultimate detail in the respective tariff classifications. The Panel considered that under these conditions a tariff classification going beyond the Harmonized System's structure is a legitimate means of adapting the tariff scheme to each cp's trade policy interests, comprising both its protection needs and its requirements for the purposes of tariff and trade negotiations. It must, however, be borne in mind that such differentiations may lend themselves to abuse, in so far as they may serve to circumscribe tariff advantages in such a way that they are inductive to discrimination among like products originating in different cp. A cp prejudiced by such action may therefore request that its own exports be treated as "like products".

(3) Tariff differentiation being basically a legitimate means of trade policy, a cp which claims to be prejudiced by such practices bears the burden of establishing that such tariff arrangement has been diverted from its natural purpose so as to become a means of discrimination in international trade. Such complaints have to be examined in considering simultaneously the internal protection interest involved in a given tariff specification, as well as its actual or potential influence on the pattern of imports from different extraneous sources.

(4) The tariffs referred to by the GA being those of the individual cp, a claim of likeness raised by a cp in relation to the tariff treatment of its goods on importation by some other cp should be based on the classification of the importing country's tariff. "Dimension lumber" as defined by Canada being a concept extraneous to the Japanese tariff and to any internationally accepted customs classification, it was not an appropriate basis for establishing "likeness" of products under Article I:1 of the GA.

Conclusion

Canadian case was not established.

US—Section 337 of the Tariff Act of 1930

PANEL REPORT

adopted on November 7, 1989

Parties	EEC / US
Intervening	Canada, Japan, Korea, Switzerland
Panel Membership	Fortune, Lowenfeld, Pescatore
Published in BISD	36S/345
Related Documents	See Panel report of May 26, 1983, Canada/US, on US Imports of certain Automotive Spring Assemblies (Case 52).

Key Words

(1) Unfair trade practices. Section 337 of the US Tariff Act. Action of US International Trade Commission (US ITC) under Section 337. Consistency with Article III:4 and Article XX (d).

(2) Terms of reference of Panel. Particular case and general problem raised by national legislation. Settlement attained in particular case leaving open general problem. Patent rights treated as part of intellectual property rights. Amendment of national legislation in course of Panel proceedings. "Procedures" applied to imported products to be construed broadly. (Article XXIII).

(3) Former Panel report. Limits imparted to authority of precedent. (Article XXIII).

(4) Scope of alternative GATT Articles. Relationship of Article III:4 and Article XX. Situation to be determined under Article III before considering exceptions of Article XX.

(5) "Laws" and "regulations" affecting the internal sale of imported products include substantive as well as procedural laws and regulations. Enforcement procedures not to be separated from substantive rules. Application at the border of laws and regulations affecting internal sale covered by Article III:4. Product-related

rules of GA apply in respect of enforcement procedures applied to persons.

(6) "No less favorable treatment". Unqualified requirement. Expression of a principle of equality underlying both MFN standard in Article I and national treatment standard in Article III. No less favorable treatment calling not only for application of formally identical provisions but for effective equality of opportunities. The mere fact that imported products are subject to distinct provisions in itself not conclusive in establishing infringement of the no less favorable treatment principle, but burden of proof incumbent in that case to party applying differential treatment.

(7) Purpose of Article III:4 as well as of Article III:2 is to protect expectations on competitive relationship. Measures to be appraised in themselves and on their potential impact. Incidental effect of measures more favorable to imports does not offset elements of less favorable treatment.

(8) Comparative assessment of US ITC proceedings and judicial proceedings. Discriminatory features of US ITC proceedings. Discovery of business secrets. Time-limits. Counterclaims. Exclusion orders. Enforcement by Customs Service. Choice of forum and dual proceedings. (Article III:4).

(9) Decision making by administrative and judicial authorities. Standard of decision making. Structural difference. (Article III:4).

(10) Laws and regulations relating to the protection of intellectual property rights [Article XX (d)]. General conditions attached to the use of the Article XX (d) exception. Cumulative character of conditions.

(11) Necessity requirement in case of Article XX (d). Not applicable if alternative measure consistent with the GA available. In case of non-availability, cp bound to use measure which entails least degree of incompatibility.

(12) Necessity requirement in case of Article XX (d). Burden of proof incumbent on party having recourse to restrictive measures. Measures inconsistent with the necessity requirement not justified by their inclusion in a scheme containing permissible measures.

(13) System of determining allegation of violation of patent rights under Section 337 of the US Tariff Act not justified as being

necessary according to Article XX (d). Justification of certain border-measures necessary to ensure protection against infringing products from extraneous sources. Specific protective measures relating to process-patents not justified. Comparative appreciation.

(14) Level of protection accorded to patents and effectiveness of procedure to enforce such protection not specified by Article III:4 and Article XX (d).

Summary

(1) Consistency with the principle of national treatment in Article III:4 and with Article XX(d) of procedures instituted before the United States International Trade Commission (US ITC) under the Unfair Trade Practices Clause of Section 337 of the US Tariff Act 1930 in case of infringement of a US patent, as compared to procedures instituted before regular courts of law.

(2) Panel's terms of reference extended to both the application of Section 337 in general and its application in a particular case (Certain Aramid Fibre, Dupont de Nemours v. AKZO). Settlement by the parties of the particular case pending the Panel's proceedings leaves the general issue to be decided. Section 337 being applied to infringement of any intellectual property rights, the Panel's finding may be relevant to all such rights, though the Panel concentrated on patent-based cases. Section 337 having been amended during the Panel's proceedings, the findings relate to the law as it was at the time when the Panel was established. The Panel's terms of reference relating to "procedures" applied to imported products must be construed broadly so as to extend beyond legal procedure in a strict sense.

(3) A former precedent was considered by the Panel in the light of an understanding which limited its authority as a precedent.

(4) The relationship of Article III to Article II(d) was defined in such a way that the problems raised by Section 337 had to be determined first in the light of Article III:4 before the situation could be examined under the exceptions provided for by Article XX.

Article III:4

(5) The words "laws, regulations and requirements affecting" the internal sale of imported products are to be understood as covering both substantive and procedural laws which might adversely

modify the conditions of competition on the internal markets. In this respect, enforcement procedures cannot be separated from substantive provisions they serve to enforce. According to the interpretative note attached to Article III the fact that Section 337 is used as a means for the enforcement of patent law at the border does not provide an escape from the applicability of Article III:4. Nor could the applicability of Article III:4 be denied on the ground that enforcement procedures are applied to persons rather than to products.

(6) The "no less favorable" treatment requirement set out in Article III:4 is unqualified. The "no less favorable" treatment is an expression of a principle of equality underlying both the MFN standard and the national treatment standard of Article III. These words call for equality of opportunities for imported products, setting a minimum permissible standard as a basis. Such standard allows for more favorable treatment of imported products. It has to be recognized also that there may be cases where application of formally identical legal provisions would in practice lead to less favorable treatment. For these reasons the mere fact that imported products are subject to legal provisions different from those applying to products of national origin is in itself not conclusive in establishing inconsistency with Article III:4. But in such case it is incumbent on the party applying differential treatment to establish that in spite of such differences the no less favorable treatment standard is met.

(7) The purpose of Article III:4, as well as the purpose of Article III:2 is to protect expectations on the competitive relationship between imported and domestic products and to forestall any less favorable treatment. Measures must be therefore appraised in themselves and on their potential impact. Incidental elements of less favorable treatment may not be offset by elements of more favorable treatment of imported goods in certain cases. Such balancing would only be appropriate if such elements appeared necessarily in all individual cases.

(8) Considering the specific differences between Section 337 proceedings and those in federal district courts, the Panel noted that in the following respects Section 337 proceedings imparted less favorable treatment to imported goods:

(a) the requirements set by Section 337 involved the respondent in litigation, defense and discovery of business secrets unrelated to the underlying patent issue,

(b) time-limits were found to put the respondent in such proceedings in a significantly less favorable position,

(c) inadmissibility of counterclaims deprived the respondent of an option that was available in the federal courts,

(d) *in rem* exclusions orders gave the successful plaintiffs advantages not available in federal district courts, insofar as all such orders were automatically enforced by the US Customs Service and as general exclusion orders accorded relief against persons others than the parties to a proceeding,

(e) federal district courts and the US ITC having concurrent jurisdiction over matters of patent infringement, this arrangement conferred a choice of forum to domestic plaintiffs and exposed importers to double proceedings. Except as noted under (a), the Panel found that the techniques applied under Section 337 to the treatment of confidential information were not effectively different from those used in federal district courts.

(9) Though the standard of decision making and of review under Section 337 was not considered to be significantly different from the standard of legal protection in federal courts, the Panel wondered whether all the differences of treatment established could not be traced back to one common cause, this being the structure of the US ITC which is fundamentally not a court of law but an administrative agency, and whether this structural difference could be said to entail in itself treatment incompatible with the requirements of Article III. This question had to be left open, as the Community had not raised it in such general terms.

Article XX(d)

(10) Measures necessary to secure compliance with laws relating to the protection of intellectual property rights. General conditions attached to the use of Article XX(d): laws and regulations with which compliance is to be secured must be "not inconsistent" with the GA; measures must be "necessary" to secure compliance; measures must not entail arbitrary discrimination or disguised restriction on trade. A measure cannot be justified under Article XX(d) if it does not meet any one of these conditions. The Panel noted that the conformity of the substantive US patent laws with the GA was not challenged.

(11) As to the "necessary to secure compliance" condition, the Panel noted that a cp cannot justify a measure inconsistent with another GATT provision if an alternative measure not inconsistent with GATT is available. If no such alternative existed, a cp is bound to use that which entails the least degree of inconsistency.

(12) It is up to the cp seeking to justify measures under Article XX(d) to demonstrate that those measures are "necessary" within the meaning of that provision. Under this condition, the system of Section 337 could not be considered as a whole, as such a contention could permit a cp to introduce GATT inconsistencies that are not necessary for the purposes of Article XX(d) simply by making them part of a scheme which contained elements that are necessary. The Panel had therefore to examine each of the specific inconsistencies found to exist in the light of the requirements inherent in Article III:4.

(13) In the light of these considerations, the Panel found that on the whole the system of determining allegations of violation of US patent rights under Section 337 of the US Tariff Act cannot be justified as necessary within the meaning of Article XX(d) so as to permit an exception to the basic obligation contained in Article III:4, but that some of the inconsistencies with Article III:4 of individual aspects of procedures under Section 337 could be justified in certain circumstances. In this respect, the Panel singled out the following aspects.

(a) A special scheme for imports alleged to infringe process patents was not considered to be necessary, as it appeared possible to give civil courts jurisdiction over this matter, as was shown by the legislation of many countries and a recent amendment introduced into the US legislation.

(b) Presidential review as provided for by Section 337 did not appear to be a measure necessary to secure compliance with the US patent legislation.

(c) The Panel saw a justification for *in rem* exclusion orders as a defense against imports from extraneous sources as it was difficult to identify these sources and to secure enforcement in their respect. The enforcement of such orders by the customs authorities could under these circumstances be considered as a legitimate border measure.

(d) Finally the Panel considered that although Section 337 provided legitimately for expeditious prospective relief against infringing imports these provisions could not be justified as "necessary" beyond the limits of preliminary conservatory action.

Conclusion

The Panel concluded that Section 337 of the US Tariff Act of 1930 is inconsistent with Article III:4 in that it accords to imported products challenged as infringing US patents treatment less favorable than the treatment accorded to products of US origin similarly challenged, and that these inconsistencies cannot be justified in all respects under Article XX(d) and that the CP request the US to bring its procedure into conformity with its obligations under the GA.

While drawing these conclusions, the Panel stressed that neither Article III:4 nor Article XX(d) puts obligations on cp specifying the level of protection that they should accord to patents or the effectiveness of procedures to enforce such protection.

Republic of Korea—Restrictions on Imports of Beef—Complaint by the US

PANEL REPORT

adopted on November 7, 1989

Parties	US / Korea
Intervening	Australia, Canada, New Zealand
Panel Membership	Chew Tai Soo, Choi, Freyberg
Published in BISD	36S/268
Related Documents	Two identical reports have been adopted on the same day upon complaints by Australia and New Zealand BISD 36S/202 & 234.

(1) Import restrictions on beef in connection with operation of a producer-controlled import monopoly. Import restrictions maintained for purposes of balance of payments (BOP) safeguards (Articles XI:1, XV, XVIII:B).

(2) Admissibility of complaint. Preliminary decision by Panel. [Articles XXIII:2, XVIII:12(d)].

(3) General ban on import restrictions and import prohibitions by Article XI:1. Exemptions to be specifically justified.

(4) Inconsistency with Article XI:1 of restrictions on import of beef established for the purpose of protecting domestic cattle industry. No case for exemption under Article XI:2.

(5) Producer-controlled import monopoly subject to Article XVII on state-trading activities. Enterprises enjoying exclusive or special privileges. Mere existence of import monopoly not in violation of the GA. Operation of import monopoly subject to provisions of the GA, including Articles XVII and XI:1.

(6) Dispute settlement. Relationship between the general provisions of Article XXIII:2 and the special review procedures in paragraphs 12(b) and 12(d) of Article XVIII:B administered by BOP

Committee. Article XXIII is all-embracing and provides for dispute-settlement procedures applicable to all relevant articles of the GA, including Article XVIII:B. Difference of scope of procedures provided by Articles XXIII and XVIII:B.

(7) Scope of restrictions for safeguard of BOP difficulties limited to serious decline in monetary reserves. Relaxation required as conditions improve. (Article XVIII:9 and 11).

(8) Jurisdiction International Monetary Fund consultation required on BOP difficulties (Article XV:2). Need for elimination of Korean BOP restrictions recognized by IMF and BOP Committee.

(9) Bound Tariff rate (Article II:A, Interpretative note and Article 31 of Havana Charter). Provisions not applicable in case of quantitative restrictions. Mark-ups imposed by monopoly directly afforded by scarcity due to quantitative restrictions. Monopoly bound to respect tariff concession upon removal of quantitative restrictions.

(10) Public notice requirements (Articles X:1 and XIII:3).

Summary

(1) Import restrictions on beef maintained by Korea in connection with the operation of a producer-controlled import monopoly, partly for the purpose of protecting Korea's domestic cattle industry and partly for the purpose of Koreas's Balance-of-Payments (BOP).

(2) The complaint having been referred to the Panel on the basis of Article XXIII, the admissibility of the complaint was contested in a preliminary objection by Korea with reference to the special procedure provided for in Article XVIII:12(d). Korea having requested an immediate ruling on this matter, the Panel decided that it clearly had the mandate to examine the merits in the framework of the procedure provided for by Article XXIII:2, in the light of the relevant GATT provisions, according to its terms of reference.

(3) The Panel held that on principle Article XI:1 did not permit the use of either import restrictions or import prohibitions. Exemptions from this general prescription had to be specifically justified under other provisions of the GA. The Panel distinguished in this respects two sorts of measures taken by Korea, viz. restrictive

measures notified to and reviewed by the BOP Committee and restrictive measures amounting to a virtual suspension of imports neither notified to nor reviewed by the said Committee.

Restrictive Measures Not Notified

(4) Korea admitted that the restrictive measures not notified had been established for the purpose of protecting Korea's domestic cattle industry and that these matters were inconsistent with Article XI:1. Korea was not in a position to claim exemption of these measures under Article XI:2.

(5) As to the operation of the producer-controlled import monopoly, the Panel considered that it came under Article XVII on State-trading activities which includes enterprises enjoying exclusive or special privileges. The existence of such monopoly could not in itself be in violation of the GA, but it had to conform to a number of rules contained in the GA, including those of Articles XVII and XI:1. As the import restrictions administered by the monopoly had already been found to violate Article XI:1, the mere existence of the monopoly could not be considered as a separate restriction on trade.

Restrictive Measures Notified to BOP Committee

(6) In this respect the Panel had first to determine the relationship between the provisions on dispute settlement of Article XXIII and the special review procedures in paragraphs 12(b) and 12(d) of Article XVIII:B administered by the BOP Committee. The Panel considered that Article XXIII was all-embracing and provided for dispute settlement procedures applicable to all relevant articles of the GA, including Article XVIII:B. The Panel noted moreover that Article XXIII, in the light of paragraph 10 of the 1979 Understanding on Dispute Settlement, provided for the detailed examination of individual measures by a panel of independent experts, whereas Article XVIII:B provided for a general review of a country's BOP situation by a committee of government representatives. Anyhow, it resulted from the terms of reference that the parties had clearly chosen to proceed under Article XXIII.

(7) As to the justification for restrictions, the Panel noted that paragraph 9 of Article XVIII limited permissible restrictions to those necessary to forestall the threat of, or to stop a serious decline in

monetary reserves and that paragraph 11 required the progressive relaxation of such restrictions as conditions improve and their elimination when conditions no longer justify such maintenance.

(8) Article XV:2 of the GA provided in such cases for full consultation with the International Monetary Fund. It resulted from the latest consultation concerning Korea's BOP situation that the current situation and outlook for Korea were such that import restrictions could no longer be justified. As a consequence, the BOP Committee had stressed the need to establish a clear time-table for the early, progressive removal of Korea's restrictive trade measures. The Panel concluded in this respect that there was a need for the prompt establishment of a time-table for the phasing-out of Korea's BOP restrictions on beef.

(9) The Panel considered that the mark-ups imposed on imported beef by the import monopoly in combination with the import duties collected at a bound rate were not contrary to Article II:4, which was not applicable in view of the existence of quantitative restrictions. This interpretation resulted from Article 31:4 and 31:5 of the Havana Charter, to which reference was made in the interpretative note to Article II:4. The price premium obtained by the monopoly could be considered to be directly afforded by the situation of market scarcity arising from the quantitative restrictions. The Panel stressed however that once Korea's quantitative restrictions had been removed, the monopoly was not to afford protection in excess of the amount of protection provided for in the relevant schedule, as set out in Article II:4.

(10) The Panel finally recalled the provisions of Articles X:1 and XIII:3(b) requiring public notice of import restrictions, but did not find it necessary to address more fully these subsidiary issues.

Conclusions

Korea was required to eliminate or otherwise bring into conformity with the provisions of the GA the import measures on beef not notified.

Korea was moreover invited to hold consultations with the US and other interested cps to work out a time-table for the removal of import restrictions on beef justified for BOP reasons and report on the result of such consultations within a period of three months.

Canada—Import Restrictions on Ice Cream and Yogurt

PANEL REPORT

adopted on December 4, 1989

Parties	US / Canada
Intervening	EEC, Japan
Panel Membership	Anell, Bartlett, Luz Guarda
Published in BISD	BISD 36S/68

Key words

(1) Agricultural markets. Import restrictions on ice cream and yogurt inconsistent with Article XI:1 if not justified by exception of Article XI:2(c)(i).

(2) Interpretation of the GA. Exceptions to the principles of the GA. Burden of proof on parties invoking exception. Exceptions to be interpreted narrowly. Strict interpretation of Article IX:2(c)(i). Dissatisfaction with existing provisions and existence of discussions on revision no reason for altering interpretation. Authority of existing precedents. (Article XXIII:2).

(3) Article XI:2(c)(i) allows restrictions, not prohibitions of trade.

(4) Ice cream and yogurt considered to be agricultural products within the meaning of Article XI(c)(i).

(5) "Like products" in the framework of Article XI:2(c)(i). Primary products and processed products.

(6) "Like products". Criteria of comparison. Early stage of processing. "Still perishable". Direct competition with primary product. Impairment of effectiveness of domestic restrictions. (Article XI:2(c)(i)).

(7) Regulation of agricultural production and price stabilization programs are not an effective restriction of production within the meaning of Article XI:2(c)(i).

(8) "Necessary to the enforcement" criterion in Article XI:2(c)(i). No necessity established in case of minimal import shares.

(9) Public notification of restrictive measures (Articles X, XI:2, 2nd subparagraph and XIII:2(a).

Summary

(1) The issue concerned import restrictions maintained by Canada on yogurt and various ice cream products. It was not contested that the quotas applied by Canada were prohibited by Article XI:1. At issue was whether these measures could be justified under Article XI:2(c)(i).

(2) The Panel recalled some principles already established by previous Panel reports, viz. that a party invoking an exception to the GA bore the burden of proving that it had met all of the conditions of that exception; that exceptions were to be interpreted narrowly and that this argued against flexible interpretation of Article XI:2(c)(i); that the requirements of that provision made compliance extremely difficult in practice. The Panel recalled also that the widespread dissatisfaction with Article XI:2(c)(i) and the fact that its revision was under discussion provided no reason to diverge from its task to make findings on the interpretation and application of the law as it stood. Considering the existing precedents, the Panel analyzed the issue on the basis of the seven conditions singled out in the Panel report adopted on March 22, 1988 on Japan's Restrictions on Imports of Certain Agricultural Products (BISD 35S/163).

(3) The Panel recognized that Canada's measures constituted only a restriction, as required by Article XI:2(c)(i), and not a prohibition of trade.

(4) Considering that ice cream and yogurt were food products generally regarded by consumers and the industry to be agricultural products, the Panel found that ice cream and yogurt were agricultural products within the meaning of Article XI:2(c).

(5) Examining the issue of "like products imported in any form", the Panel considered that the relevant Canadian product subject to restrictions was raw milk. It was recognized in Article XI: 2(c)(i) that it might be necessary to restrict import not only the fresh product, but also some of its processed forms to the extent that

free importation of processed products would render ineffective the restrictions on the fresh product (interpretative note to Article XI and note to Article 20 of the Havana Charter).

(6) Examining the different elements which had to be considered in this context, the Panel found it was not necessary to make findings on the question as to whether ice cream and yogurt were still in the "early stage of processing" of raw milk and whether they could be considered to be "still perishable". But the Panel considered that ice cream and yogurt did not compete directly with raw milk in terms of Article XI:2(c)(i) and that there was no reason to broaden the scope of this requirement to include the concept of displacement or indirect competition. Relying on the preparatory work of the Havana Charter, the Panel did not consider either that there was an immediate threat of imports at such significantly increased levels as could render ineffective the Canadian dairy supply program.

(7) The Panel felt it was not in a position to determine whether the Canadian dairy management scheme constituted a government measure which effectively restricted total raw milk production in Canada within the meaning of Article XI:2(c)(i), but it recalled in this context that during the preparatory work of the UN Conference on Trade and Employment proposals to make the regulation of production, through price stabilization programs, an accepted criterion, were rejected. The Panel stressed in this respect that the requirement was for the effective restriction of production, not merely its regulation.

(8) Finally the Panel concluded that the criterion "necessary to the enforcement" of governmental measures restricting production was not fulfilled as imports of ice cream and yogurt had gained only a half percent share of the Canadian market and accounted for less than ten one-thousands of one percent of total raw milk production.

(9) Considering these findings, the Panel found it unnecessary to go into the question as to whether the operation of the quotas was in conformity with the requirements concerning public notification of restrictive measures under Articles X and XIII:2(a). As to the Canadian import permit system, the Panel considered that to the extent that the permit system was a mechanism for the administration of the quota system it had no justifiable basis. The Panel noted that a discretionary import licensing system could not meet the public notice requirements.

Conclusion

Canada's restrictions on the importation of ice cream and yogurt were found to be inconsistent with Article XI:1 and could not be justified under the provisions of Article XI:2(c)(i). Accordingly, Canada was requested either to terminate these restrictions or to bring them into conformity with the GA.

EEC—Payments and Subsidies Paid to Processors and Producers of Oilseeds and Related Animal-Feed Proteins ("Soya-Panel")

PANEL REPORT

adopted on January 25, 1990

Parties	US / EEC
Intervening	Argentina, Australia, Brazil, Canada
Panel Membership	Cartland, Nyerges, Pescatore
Published in BISD	(Not yet published; see Doc. L/6627)

Key Words

(1) Agricultural markets. EEC market organization for oilseeds. Price-system for marketing of oilseeds. Subsidies offsetting benefit of zero tariff bound concession. Producer subsidy and processor benefit. (Articles II and III). Tariff negotiations, general and Article XXIV:6 negotiations.

(2) National Treatment under Article III:4. Producer subsidies allowed by Article III:8 (a). Payment made "exclusively" to producers. Indirect payment not eligible. EEC price-system providing incentive for processors to give preference to domestic production.

(3) "Treatment no less favorable" under Article III:4. System implying risk of discrimination equivalent to actual discrimination.

(4) Tariff binding entered into by the EEC in 1962. Continuity of identical tariff bindings in successive negotiations under Article XXIV:6, upon enlargement of the Community.

(5) Effect of tariff concessions. Improved market access by improved price competition. Legitimate expectations flowing from bound tariff concessions. Price-mechanism and product specific subsidies completely offsetting value of tariff concessions. (Article II; "Other Barriers to Trade", Report adopted by the CP on March 3, 1955, BISD 3S/222, 224).

(6) Impairment of benefits frustrating legitimate expectations opens way of redress under Article XIII:2 whenever a cp cannot claim removal of a measure not inconsistent with the GA (Article XXIII:1(b).

(7) Tariff concessions are commitments on conditions of competition for trade, not on volumes of trade. Common concept underlying Articles II, III:2 and XI:1. Article XXIII:1(b) not workable on basis of consideration of volumes of trade.

(8) US embargo on export of soya (1973). Security of supplies valid issue but extraneous to matter before panel (XXIII:2).

(9) Subsidies Code of 1979, Article 8:4 not covered by mandate of Panel. Subsidies Code to be interpreted in conformity with decisions of CP.

(10) Redress for impairment under Article XXIII:1(b): delayed pending revision of Community Regulations found inconsistent with GA.

Summary

(1) The dispute concerned certain aspects of the EEC market organization for oilseeds established by Council Regulation 136/66, as amended, for rapeseed and sunflowerseed and extended to soyabeans by Regulation 1900/74, the latter being replaced by Regulation 1491/85. The market organization provided for a price system combined with the payment of considerable subsidies. Under Regulation 1594/83 (this being the regulation applicable at the time when the dispute arose), these subsidies were paid to the oilseed processors, but had to be passed on, under the mechanism of the market organization, at least partially to the producers. The complaint of the US was that the price system was arranged in such a way that (a) it left a benefit in the hands of the processors, creating a preference with respect of EC produced oilseeds, contrary to Article III and (b) the subsidies flowing back to the producers entailed a nullification and impairment of tariff concessions at zero-tariff level granted and bound by the Community in 1962 pursuant to Article II of the GA. The Panel established in the first place that the bindings, entered into the 1962 at the end of the "Dillon Round", were originally the result of general negotiations on the reduction of tariffs and of negotiations under Article XXIV:6 as a result of the creation of a common external tariff by

the Community. The concession had been continued on the occasion of each of the successive enlargements of the Community as a result of negotiations based exclusively on Article XXIV:6.

National treatment: Article III

(2) The Panel first ruled out application of Article III:8(a), under which Article III "shall not prevent the payment of subsidies exclusively to domestic producers". The Panel considered in this respect that a payment not made directly to producers is not made "exclusively" to them. The Panel considered that under the price system as it functioned in the framework of the market organization, which distinguished between "guide price" and "minimum price" on the internal market and which left a margin of discretion to the EEC authorities in determining "reconstructed" world-market prices, subsidy payments made to processors could be greater than the difference between the price processors actually paid to producers and the price that processors would have to pay for imported oilseeds. If the economic benefits generated by the payments granted by the Community can be at least partly retained by the processors of Community oilseeds, the payments generate a benefit conditional upon the purchase of oilseeds of domestic origin inconsistent with Article III.

(3) Even if this effect could not be established in each case, it was sufficient to establish that the system was capable of producing such result, the risk of discrimination constituting by itself a treatment incompatible with the standard of "treatment no less favorable" within the meaning of Article III:4.

Nullification or Impairment of Tariff Concessions: Article II

(4) The tariff concession relied upon by the US having been made in 1962 the Panel first examined whether there was continuity between the 1962 tariff binding and the bindings which came out of the negotiations conducted on the occasion of the successive enlargements of the Community on the basis of Article XXIV:6. The Panel found in this respect that the intent of the Article XXIV:6 negotiations was not to attain a new balance of concessions, but to extend the existing tariff concessions to new member States. The Panel found therefore that the benefits accruing to the US from the latest negotiations under Article XXIV:6 in 1986/87 included

the protection of the reasonable expectation the US had when these concessions were initially negotiated in 1962.

(5) The main value of a tariff concession is to assure better market access through improved price competition. The Panel considered that this effect was jeopardized by the price mechanism established in the framework of the Community's market organization for oilseeds and the related product specific subsidies, worked to protect Community producers completely from the movement of prices for imports and hence to prevent the lowering of import duties from having any impact on the competitive relationship between domestic and imported oilseeds. Recalling a report adopted by the CP in 1955, the Panel said that the US had a legitimate expectation that the price effect of the tariff concessions granted by the Community would not be systematically offset by the price system inherent in the market organization.

(6) The Panel made clear in this respect that though the legitimacy of expectations flowing from tariff concessions in no way prevented a cp from using production subsidies consistently with the GA, this did not permit the creation by a cp of a price regime the effect of which was that all domestically-produced oilseeds are disposed of in the internal market notwithstanding the availability of imports. Though in such circumstances a finding of impairment does not authorize the CP to request the impairing cp to remove a measure not inconsistent with the GA (Article XXIII:1(b), the cp frustrated in its expectations may request, in accordance with Article XXIII:2, an authorization to suspend the application of concessions or other obligations under the GA.

(7) The EEC having drawn attention to the fact that in spite of measures contested by the US imports of oilseeds into the Community had significantly risen, the Panel said that tariff concessions are commitments on conditions of competition for trade, not on volumes of trade. This was a concept common to tariff matters, to matters of taxation governed by Article III and to non-tariff restrictions coming under Article XI:1. Article XXIII:1(b), which opened a way of redress against any measures "whether or not it conflicts with the provisions of this Agreement", would be hardly workable if its application were made dependent on the volume of trade flows, instead of expectations on conditions of competition.

(8) As to an embargo imposed in 1973 by the US on export of soybeans, to which the Community had referred for its defense, the Panel said that though it recognized the legitimacy of the

Community's concern for the security of its supplies, this was a separate issue which the Community had been free to bring before the CP at the appropriate time.

(9) The Community having relied also on Article 8:4 of the Subsidies Code of 1979, the Panel said that having been established in view of making its findings "in the light of the relevant GATT provisions", it had no mandate to propose interpretations of the provisions of the Subsidies Code. The Panel remarked in this respect that the purpose of the Subsidies Code is, according to its preamble, "to apply fully and interpret" the provisions of the GA, which speaks in favor of interpreting Article 8:4 in conformity with the decisions of the CP.

Conclusion

The Community Regulations providing for payments to seed processors conditional on the purchase of oilseeds originating in the community were found to be inconsistent with Article III of the GA and the Community was requested to bring these Regulations into conformity with the GA.

Benefits accruing to the US under Article II of the GA in respect of the zero tariff bindings for oilseeds were found to have been nullified or impaired as a result of the introduction of production subsidy schemes which operate to protect Community producers of oilseeds completely from the movement of prices of imports and thereby prevent the tariff concessions from having any impact on the competitive relationship between domestic and imported oilseeds. It was accordingly suggested that the community consider ways and means to eliminate the impairment of its tariff concessions on oilseeds.

The Panel considered that the modification of the community Regulations in the light of Article III: 4 could simultaneously serve to eliminate the impairment of the tariff concessions. The Panel therefore recommended that the CP take no further action under Article XXIII:2 in relation to the nullification or impairment of the tariff concessions until the Community has had a reasonable opportunity to adjust its Regulations to conform to Article III:4.

EEC—Restrictions on Exports of Copper Scrap

PANEL REPORT

adopted on February 1990

Parties US / EEC

Panel Membership Kartajomena, Falconer, Simon

Published in BISD Not yet published, see GATT Doc. DS5/R, February 5, 1990

Key Words

(1) Export Restrictions. Article XI:1

(2) Settlement. Panel was informed of settlement and request for termination of panel process.

Summary

(1) The US asked that the Panel examine certain quantitative restrictions imposed by the EEC on the export of copper scrap, presumably under Article XI:1.

(2) The Panel was informed that the matter had been resolved through bilateral consultation and that the United States had requested that the dispute settlement proceedings be terminated.

Conclusion

None. Matter settled.

EEC—Regulation of Imports of Parts and Components

PANEL REPORT

adopted on May 16, 1990

Parties	Japan / EEC
Intervening	Australia, Canada, Hong Kong, Korea, Singapore, US
Panel Membership	Greenwald, Groser, Thomas
Published in BISD	Not yet published, see GATT Doc. L/6657, March 22, 1990

Key Words

(1) Categorization of anti-circumvention duties as customs duties or internal taxes. [Article II:1(b); Article III:2] Customs duties allowed if not in excess of bound rate; all other duties or charges on bound products prohibited. Discriminatory internal taxes prohibited on all products, bound or unbound.

(2) Anti-circumvention duties levied on products sold in EEC after assembly or production in EEC. For purpose of categorizing charge as customs duty or internal tax, the relevant fact is whether the charge is due on importation or at time or point of importation or whether it is collected internally.

(3) Purpose of charge irrelevant in determining whether charge is customs duty or internal charge.

(4) Categorization of charge under domestic law as duty is not determinative. Categorization of product on which charge is applied as not being in free circulation (i.e. as not having cleared customs) not determinative as to whether charge is customs duty or internal charge.

(5) Anti-circumvention duties levied on products sold in EEC after assembly or production in EEC are not levied on or in connection with importation and do not constitute customs duties.

(6) Anti-circumvention duties result in an internal charge being applied to imported products that is not applied to like domestic products and therefore violate Article III:2, first sentence. Consistency of duties with Article III:2, second sentence and Article I not considered.

(7) Procedure. Arguments raised only by third parties not considered by panel. Argument that anti-circumvention duties may be justified by Article VI not made by EEC and therefore not considered by panel.

(8) Exceptions to the GA. [Article XX(d)] Exception applies to measures, such as anti-circumvention provisions, necessary to secure compliance with laws or regulations that are not inconsistent with the GA.

(9) Exception for measures necessary to secure compliance with laws and regulations applies only to measures that would be illegal under those laws or regulations.

(10) Interpretation of GA. Relevance of negotiating history of Havana Charter provisions. Analogous provision in 1946 Suggested Charter for ITO allowed measures necessary to "induce" compliance. Use of word to "secure" compliance in the GA suggests the GA uses stricter language.

(11) Purpose of Article XX(d) would be broadened if interpreted to allow measures aimed at achieving objectives of laws and regulations, as opposed to the enforcement thereof. Such a broad interpretation not justified because the conditions to the exception would be made ineffective.

(12) Article XX(d) covers only measures necessary to secure compliance with GATT-consistent laws or regulations. Anti-circumvention duties do not serve to enforce the payment of antidumping duties, which are the only obligation necessary to be enforced. Article XX(d) does not apply to anti-circumvention duties as imposed by the EEC.

(13) National Treatment. Definition of laws, regulations and requirements affecting internal sale. Undertakings relating to the use of imported parts and materials voluntarily offered by enterprises in

order to obtain a governmental advantage (such as the avoidance of anti-circumvention duties) constitute "requirements" within the meaning of Article III:4. Since like domestic and other foreign products are not subjected to such a requirement, such undertakings in respect of Japanese products violate Article III:4.

(14) Most-Favored-Nation Treatment. Consistency of price undertakings with MFN clause not considered. (Article I)

(15) Dumping. Justification of price undertakings under Article VI not considered because not raised by EEC. See note (7) above.

(16) Exception to GA. Article XX(d) does not serve as a justification for price undertakings as such undertakings function as a substitute for anti-circumvention duties. See notes (8)-(11) above.

(17) Existence of legislation authorizing violation of the GA. Mere existence of such legislation does not violate the GA. EEC could meet its obligations under the GA by not applying the legislation, although it would be desirable for EEC to withdraw such legislation.

(18) Procedure. Having decided that the EEC's anti-circumvention duties and acceptance of undertakings violated the GA and were not justifiable under Article XX, the panel did not consider whether the EEC, in its administration thereof, violated Article X:1 and X:3.

(19) Procedure. Panel considered matter referred to it in light of existing provisions of the GA. Panel took note of ongoing negotiations on subject matter of the dispute.

Summary

(1) The EEC antidumping regulation contains anti-circumvention provisions designed to prevent the circumvention of antidumping duties on finished products through the importation of parts or materials for use in the assembly or production of like finished products within the EEC. The EEC regulation authorizes the imposition of anti-circumvention duties in such circumstances, subject to certain conditions, when the goods are introduced into EEC commerce. The regulation also provides for acceptance of undertakings, in which a manufacturer agrees to use not more than a certain level of imported parts and in return is not subjected to the anti-circumvention duty.

(2) The duties imposed by the EEC could arguably be considered either customs duties or internal taxes. The distinction in the GA between import duties and internal charges is of fundamental importance because duties and internal charges are regulated differently. Duties are allowed unless they exceed an applicable tariff binding; all other charges on imported items are prohibited in respect of bound items. [Article II:1(b)] Internal taxes that discriminate against imported products are prohibited. (Article III:2) For purposes of deciding how to categorize anti-circumvention duties, the relevant fact is whether the charge is due on importation or at the time or point of importation or whether it is collected internally.

(3) In determining whether the anticircumvention duty is an internal charge or a charge imposed in connection with importation, the purpose of the duty is irrelevant. It is frequently difficult to ascertain the purpose of a measure and measures may serve more than one purpose. To consider the purpose of the charge would create substantial legal uncertainty.

(4) In determining whether the anticircumvention duty is an internal charge or a charge imposed in connection with importation, the categorization of the charge under domestic law is not relevant. Allowing the country imposing the duty to determine itself whether the duty is an internal charge or a charge in connection with importation would prevent the achievement of the objectives of Articles II and III of the GA. Similarly, the fact that the EEC considers the imported parts and materials not to have entered free circulation within the EEC does not mean that the anti-circumvention duty is collected in connection with importation.

(5) In light of the above, the Panel concluded that the anti-circumvention duties are not levied on or in connection with importation within the meaning of Article II:1(b) and consequently do not constitute customs duties within the meaning thereof.

(6) The anti-circumvention duties are imposed in an amount equal to the antidumping duty rate applicable to the finished products of the exporter-assembler times the CIF value of the imported parts. Since such duties subjected the imported products to an internal charge in excess of that applied to like domestic products, the Panel concluded that the duties were contrary to Article III:2, first sentence. In light of that finding, the Panel did not

consider whether the duties were inconsistent with Article III:2, second sentence or Article I.

(7) The EEC did not defend the anti-circumvention duties as anti-dumping duties within the meaning of Article VI, but rather as measures designed to prevent the circumvention of such duties. Although a third party had suggested that anti-circumvention duties could be justified to a certain extent by Article VI, the Panel did not examine this argument because the EEC presented no arguments in justification of its measures under Article VI. The Panel noted that it was the practice of panels not to examine exceptions not invoked by the cp complained against and not to examine issues raised by other cp.

(8) Article XX(d) allows the adoption by a cp of measures necessary to secure compliance with laws or regulations which are not inconsistent with the GA. The Panel considered that for the purposes of Article XX(d) the "measures" at issue were the anti-circumvention duties and the laws or regulations not inconsistent with the GA were the EEC's antidumping regulations. The Panel assumed, for purposes of this proceeding, that the EEC's anti-dumping regulations were not inconsistent with the GA.

(9) In deciding whether the Article XX(d) exception would apply to a measure designed to prevent actions that are consistent with the underlying laws and regulations but undermine their objectives or would apply only to actions that are inconsistent with those laws and regulations, the Panel noted that the language of Article XX(d) did not refer to the objectives of laws or regulations, but rather to measures necessary to secure compliance with the laws and regulations. The panel further noted that the language of Article XX(d) referred to customs enforcement, the enforcement of monopolies, the protection of patents and the prevention of deceptive practices, which also suggested to the Panel that the exception only covers measures designed to prevent action that would be illegal under the relevant laws or regulations.

(10) The Panel referred to the negotiating history of the Havana Charter to assist in the interpretation of Article XX(d) and noted that the corresponding provision of the 1946 Suggested Charter the words "to induce compliance" were used in place of "to secure compliance". The panel felt that the stricter language of the GA indicated that its above conclusion was correct [see note (9)].

(11) The Panel then considered the alternative interpretations [see note (9)] in light of the purpose of Article XX(d). It felt that interpreting Article XX(d) to encompass measures aimed at the attainment of the objectives of GATT-consistent laws and regulations would allow GATT-inconsistent measures to be justified under Article XX(d) in a manner that would undermine the conditions normally applicable for invoking such GATT exceptions as those contained in Articles VI, XII and XIX.

(12) Accordingly, the Panel found that Article XX(d) covers only measures related to the enforcement of obligations under GATT-consistent laws or regulations. It further noted that the only obligation necessary to enforce in connection with antidumping duties was the payment of those duties, and that the anti-circumvention duties did not serve to enforce the payment of those duties. The Panel concluded that those duties could not be justified under Article XX(d).

(13) Article III:4 refers to all laws, regulations or requirements affecting the internal sale, etc. of goods. The Panel considered that the word "requirements" encompassed requirements that an enterprise voluntarily accepts in order to obtain an advantage from a government, and therefore encompassed the undertakings obtained by the EEC from certain Japanese companies in which they agreed to restrict their use of Japanese parts and materials in return for exemption from the anti-circumvention duties. Since the use of like products of EEC and other origins was not restricted, the use of undertakings is inconsistent with Article III:4.

(14) In light of its finding under Article III:4, the Panel did not consider whether the undertakings were inconsistent with Article I.

(15) Since the EEC did not invoke Article VI as a justification for the use of undertakings, the Panel did not consider whether the use of undertakings inconsistent with Article III:4 could be justified by Article VI.

(16) In light of its findings in respect of Article XX(d) and anti-circumvention duties, the Panel found that Article XX(d) could not serve as a justification for undertakings since they functioned as a substitute for anti-circumvention duties and could not be considered to secure compliance with the EEC's antidumping regulation.

(17) In its examination of the consistency of the provisions of the EEC regulation that authorized imposition of anti-circumvention duties and the acceptance of parts undertakings with the GA, the Panel concluded that the mere existence of such provisions was not inconsistent with the GA. While it would be desirable for the EEC to withdraw those provisions, the EEC could meet its obligations under the GA by not applying the provisions to other cp.

(18) In light of its foregoing decisions that the EEC use of anti-circumvention duties and undertakings was inconsistent with the GA, the Panel did not consider whether the EEC regulation was consistent with Article X.

(19) The Panel concluded by noting that it was aware of ongoing negotiations in GATT on the subject of circumvention of anti-dumping duties, but that its task was limited to considering the case in light of the relevant provisions of the GA invoked by the parties.

Conclusions

The anti-circumvention duties imposed by the EEC on certain Japanese products subject to antidumping duties are inconsistent with Article III:2 and not justified by Article XX(d).

The undertakings to limit use of imported parts, obtained by the EEC from Japanese enterprises so as to avoid application of anti-circumvention duties, violate Article III:4 and are not justified by Article XX(d).

KEY WORD INDEX

KEY WORD INDEX

GATT ARTICLE INDEX

INDEX OF ARTICLES OF THE GENERAL AGREEMENT

INDEX OF COUNTRIES

INDEX OF COUNTRIES

C = claimant; R = respondent; I = intervening or otherwise interested

PANELISTS INDEX

PANEL MEMBERS

UNIV DUNELM

PART THREE - TEXTS

PART THREE - TEXTS

PART THREE
TEXTS

GENERAL AGREEMENT ON TARIFFS AND TRADE AND PROTOCOL OF PROVISIONAL APPLICATION

THE GENERAL AGREEMENT ON TARIFFS AND TRADE*

The Governments of the COMMONWEALTH OF AUSTRALIA, the KINGDOM OF BELGIUM, the UNITED STATES OF BRAZIL, BURMA, CANADA, CEYLON, the REPUBLIC OF CHILE, the REPUBLIC OF CHINA, the REPUBLIC OF CUBA, the CZECHOSLOVAK REPUBLIC, the FRENCH REPUBLIC, INDIA, LEBANON, THE GRAND-DUCHY OF LUXEMBURG, the KINGDOM OF THE NETHERLANDS, NEW ZEALAND, the KINGDOM OF NORWAY, PAKISTAN, SOUTHERN RHODESIA, SYRIA, the UNION OF SOUTH AFRICA, the UNITED KINGDOM OF GREAT BRITAIN AND NORTHERN IRELAND, and the UNITED STATES OF AMERICA:

Recognizing that their relations in the field of trade and economic endeavour should be conducted with a view to raising standards of living, ensuring full employment and a large and steadily growing volume of real income and effective demand, developing the full use of the resources of the world and expanding the production and exchange of goods,

Being desirous of contributing to these objectives by entering into reciprocal and mutually advantageous arrangements directed to the substantial reduction of tariffs and other barriers to trade and to the elimination of discriminatory treatment in international commerce,

Have through their Representatives agreed as follows:

* Asterisks mark the portions of the text that should be read in conjunction with the notes and supplementary provisions in Annex I to the Agreement.

PART I

Article I

General Most-Favored-Nation Treatment

1. With respect to customs duties and charges of any kind imposed on or in connection with importation or exportation or imposed on the international transfer of payments for imports or exports, and with respect to the method of levying such duties and charges, and with respect to all rules and formalities in connection with importation and exportation, and with respect to all matters referred in paragraphs 2 and 4 of Article III,* any advantage, favor, privilege or immunity granted by any contracting party to any product originating in or destined for any other country shall be accorded immediately and unconditionally to the like product originating in or destined for the territories of all other contracting parties.

2. The provisions of paragraph 1 of this Article shall not require the elimination of any preferences in respect of import duties or charges which do not exceed the levels provided for in paragraph 4 of this Article and which fall within the following descriptions:

(*a*) Preferences in force exclusively between two or more of the territories listed in Annex A, subject to the conditions set forth therein;

(*b*) Preferences in force exclusively between two or more territories which on July 1, 1939, were connected by common sovereignty or relations of protection or suzerainty and which are listed in Annexes B, C and D, subject to the conditions set forth therein;

(*c*) Preferences in force exclusively between the United States of America and the Republic of Cuba;

(*d*) Preferences in force exclusively between neighboring countries listed in Annexes E and F.

3. The provisions of paragraph 1 shall not apply to preferences between the countries formerly a part of the Ottoman Empire and detached from it on July 24, 1923, provided such preferences are approved

under paragraph 5† of Article XXV, which shall be applied in this respect in the light of paragraph 1 of Article XXIX.

4. The margin of preference* on any product in respect of which a preference is permitted under paragraph 2 of this Article but is not specifically set forth as a maximum margin of preference in the appropriate Schedule annexed to this Agreement shall not exceed:

(*a*) in respect of duties or charges on any product described in such Schedule, the difference between the most-favored-nation and preferential rates provided for therein; if no preferential rate is provided for, the preferential rate shall for the purposes of this paragraph be taken to be that in force on April 10, 1947, and, if no most-favored-nation rate is provided for, the margin shall not exceed the difference between the most-favored-nation and preferential rates existing on April 10, 1947;

(*b*) in respect of duties or charges on any product not described in the appropriate Schedule, the difference between the most-favored-nation and preferential rates existing on April 10, 1947.

In the case of the contracting parties named in Annex G, the date of April 10, 1947, referred to in sub-paragraphs (*a*) and (*b*) of this paragraph shall be replaced by the respective dates set forth in that Annex.

Article II

Schedules of Concessions

1. (*a*) Each contracting party shall accord to the commerce of the other contracting parties treatment no less favorable than that provided for in the appropriate Part of the appropriate Schedule annexed to this Agreement.

(*b*) The products described in Part I of the Schedule relating to any contracting party, which are the products of territories of other contracting parties, shall, on their importation into the territory to which the Schedule relates, and subject to the terms, conditions or qualifications set forth in that Schedule, be exempt from ordinary customs duties in excess of those set forth and provided for therein. Such products shall also be exempt from all other duties or charges of any kind imposed on

† The authentic text erroneously reads "sub-paragraph 5 (*a*)".

or in connection with importation in excess of those imposed on the date of this Agreement or those directly and mandatorily required to be imposed thereafter by legislation in force in the importing territory on that date.

(*c*) The products described in Part II of the Schedule relating to any contracting party which are the products of territories entitled under Article I to receive preferential treatment upon importation into the territory to which the Schedule relates shall, on their importation into such territory, and subject to the terms, conditions or qualifications set forth in that Schedule, be exempt from ordinary customs duties in excess of those set forth and provided for in Part II of that Schedule. Such products shall also be exempt from all other duties or charges of any kind imposed on or in connection with importation in excess of those imposed on the date of this Agreement or those directly and mandatorily required to be imposed thereafter by legislation in force in the importing territory on that date. Nothing in this Article shall prevent any contracting party from maintaining its requirements existing on the date of this Agreement as to the eligibility of goods for entry at preferential rates of duty.

2. Nothing in this Article shall prevent any contracting party from imposing at any time on the importation of any product:

(*a*) a charge equivalent to an internal tax imposed consistently with the provisions of paragraph 2 of Article III* in respect of the like domestic product or in respect of an article from which the imported product has been manufactured or produced in whole or in part;

(*b*) any anti-dumping or countervailing duty applied consistently with the provisions of Article VI;*

(*c*) fees or other charges commensurate with the cost of services rendered.

3. No contracting party shall alter its method of determining dutiable value or of converting currencies so as to impair the value of any of the concessions provided for in the appropriate Schedule annexed to this Agreement.

4. If any contracting party establishes, maintains or authorizes, formally or in effect, a monopoly of the importation of any product described in the appropriate Schedule annexed to this Agreement, such monopoly shall not, except as provided for in that Schedule or as otherwise agreed between the parties which initially negotiated the

concession, operate so as to afford protection on the average in excess of the amount of protection provided for in that Schedule. The provisions of this paragraph shall not limit the use by contracting parties of any form of assistance to domestic producers permitted by other provisions of this Agreement.*

5. If any contracting party considers that a product is not receiving from another contracting party the treatment which the first contracting party believes to have been contemplated by a concession provided for in the appropriate Schedule annexed to this Agreement, it shall bring the matter directly to the attention of the other contracting party. If the latter agrees that the treatment contemplated was that claimed by the first contracting party, but declares that such treatment cannot be accorded because a court or other proper authority has ruled to the effect that the product involved cannot be classified under the tariff laws of such contracting party so as to permit the treatment contemplated in this Agreement, the two contracting parties, together with any other contracting parties substantially interested, shall enter promptly into further negotiations with a view to a compensatory adjustment of the matter.

6. (*a*) The specific duties and charges included in the Schedules relating to contracting parties members of the International Monetary Fund, and margins of preference in specific duties and charges maintained by such contracting parties, are expressed in the appropriate currency at the par value accepted or provisionally recognized by the Fund at the date of this Agreement. Accordingly, in case this par value is reduced consistently with the Articles of Agreement of the International Monetary Fund by more than twenty per centum, such specific duties and charges and margins of preference may be adjusted to take account of such reduction; *Provided* that the CONTRACTING PARTIES (*i.e.*, the contracting parties acting jointly as provided for in Article XXV) concur that such adjustments will not impair the value of the concessions provided for in the appropriate Schedule or elsewhere in this Agreement, due account being taken of all factors which may influence the need for, or urgency of, such adjustments.

(*b*) Similar provisions shall apply to any contracting party not a member of the Fund, as from the date on which such contracting party becomes a member of the Fund or enters into a special exchange agreement in pursuance of Article XV.

7. The Schedules annexed to this Agreement are hereby made an integral part of Part I of this Agreement.

PART II

Article III

National Treatment on Internal Taxation and Regulations

1. The contracting parties recognize that internal taxes and other internal charges, and laws, regulations and requirements affecting the internal sale, offering for sale, purchase, transportation, distribution or use of products, and internal quantitative regulations requiring the mixture, processing or use of products in specified amounts or proportions, should not be applied to imported or domestic products so as to afford protection to domestic production.

2. The products of the territory of any contracting party imported into the territory of any other contracting party shall not be subject, directly or indirectly, to internal taxes or other internal charges of any kind in excess of those applied directly or indirectly, to like domestic products. Moreover, no contracting party shall otherwise apply internal taxes or other internal charges to imported or domestic products in a manner contrary to the principles set forth in paragraph 1.

3. With respect to any existing internal tax which is inconsistent with the provisions of paragraph 2, but which is specifically authorized under a trade agreement, in force on April 10, 1947, in which the import duty on taxed product is bound against increase, the contracting party imposing the tax shall be free to postpone the application of the provisions of paragraph 2 to such tax until such time as it can obtain release from the obligations of such trade agreement in order to permit the increase of such duty to the extent necessary to compensate for the elimination of the protective element of the tax.

4. The products of the territory of any contracting party imported into the territory of any other contracting party shall be accorded treatment no less favorable than that accorded to like products of national origin in respect of all laws, regulations and requirements affecting their internal sale, offering for sale, purchase, transportation, distribution or use. The provisions of this paragraph shall not prevent the application of differential internal transportation charges which are based exclusively on the economic operation of the means of transport and not on the nationality of the product.

5. No contracting party shall establish or maintain any internal quantitative regulation relating to the mixture, processing or use of products in specified amounts or proportions which requires, directly or indirectly, that any specified amount or proportion of any product which is the subject of the regulation must be supplied from domestic sources. Moreover, no contracting party shall otherwise apply internal quantitative regulations in a manner contrary to the principles set forth in paragraph 1.

6. The provisions of paragraph 5 shall not apply to any internal quantitative regulation in force in the territory of any contracting party on July 1, 1939, April 10, 1947, or March 24, 1948, at the option of that contracting party; *Provided* that any such regulation which is contrary to the provisions of paragraph 5 shall not be modified to the detriment of imports and shall be treated as a customs duty for the purpose of negotiation.

7. No internal quantitative regulation relating to the mixture, processing or use of products in specified amounts or proportions shall be applied in such a manner as to allocate any such amount or proportion among external sources of supply.

8. (*a*) The provisions of this Article shall not apply to laws, regulations or requirements governing the procurement by governmental agencies of products purchased for governmental purposes and not with a view to commercial resale or with a view to use in the production of goods for commercial sale.

(*b*) The provisions of this Article shall not prevent the payment of subsidies exclusively to domestic producers, including payments to domestic producers derived from the proceeds of internal taxes or charges applied consistently with the provisions of this Article and subsidies effected through governmental purchases of domestic products.

9. The contracting parties recognize that internal maximum price control measures, even though conforming to the other provisions of this Article, can have effects prejudicial to the interests of contracting parties supplying imported products. Accordingly, contracting parties applying such measures shall take account of the interests of exporting contracting parties with a view to avoiding to the fullest practicable extent such prejudicial effects.

10. The provisions of this Article shall not prevent any contracting party from establishing or maintaining internal quantitative regulations relating to exposed cinematograph films and meeting the requirements of Article IV.

Article IV

Special Provisions relating to Cinematograph Films

If any contracting party establishes or maintains internal quantitative regulations relating to exposed cinematograph films, such regulations shall take the form of screen quotas which shall conform to the following requirements:

(*a*) Screen quotas may require the exhibition of cinematographic films of national origin during a specified minimum proportion of the total screen time actually utilized, over a specified period of not less than one year, in the commercial exhibition of all films of whatever origin, and shall be computed on the basis of screen time per theatre per year or the equivalent thereof;

(*b*) With the exception of screen time reserved for films of national origin under a screen quota, screen time including that released by administrative action from screen time reserved for films of national origin, shall not be allocated formally or in effect among sources of supply;

(*c*) Notwithstanding the provisions of sub-paragraph (*b*) of this Article, any contracting party may maintain screen quotas conforming to the requirements of sub-paragraph (*a*) of this Article which reserve a minimum proportion of screen time for films of a specified origin other than that of the contracting party imposing such screen quotas; *Provided* that no such minimum proportion of screen time shall be increased above the level in effect on April 10, 1947;

(*d*) Screen quotas shall be subject to negotiation for their limitation, liberalization or elimination.

Article V

Freedom of Transit

1. Goods (including baggage), and also vessels and other means of transport, shall be deemed to be in transit across the territory of a contracting party when the passage across such territory, with or without trans-shipment, warehousing, breaking bulk, or change in the mode of transport, is only a portion of a complete journey beginning and

terminating beyond the frontier of the contracting party across whose territory the traffic passes. Traffic of this nature is termed in this Article "traffic in transit."

2. There shall be freedom of transit through the territory of each contracting party, via the routes most convenient for international transit, for traffic in transit to or from the territory of other contracting parties. No distinction shall be made which is based on the flag of vessels, the place of origin, departure, entry, exit or destination, or on any circumstances relating to the ownership of goods, of vessels or of other means of transport.

3. Any contracting party may require that traffic in transit through its territory be entered at the proper custom house, but, except in cases of failure to comply with applicable customs laws and regulations, such traffic coming from or going to the territory of other contracting parties shall not be subject to any unnecessary delays or restrictions and shall be exempt from customs duties and from all transit duties or other charges imposed in respect of transit, except charges for transportation or those commensurate with administrative expenses entailed by transit or with the cost of services rendered.

4. All charges and regulations imposed by contracting parties on traffic in transit to or from the territories of other contracting parties shall be reasonable, having regard to the conditions of the traffic.

5. With respect to all charges, regulations and formalities in connection with transit, each contracting party shall accord to traffic in transit to or from the territory of any other contracting party treatment no less favorable than the treatment accorded to traffic in transit to or from any third country.*

6. Each contracting party shall accord to products which have been in transit through the territory of any other contracting party treatment no less favorable than that which would have been accorded to such products had they been transported from their place of origin to their destination without going through the territory of such other contracting party. Any contracting party shall, however, be free to maintain its requirements of direct consignment existing on the date of this Agreement, in respect of any goods in regard to which such direct consignment is a requisite condition of eligibility for entry of the goods at preferential rates of duty or has relation to the contracting party's prescribed method of valuation for duty purposes.

7. The provisions of this Article shall not apply to the operation of aircraft in transit, but shall apply to air transit of goods (including baggage).

Article VI

Anti-dumping and Countervailing Duties

1. The contracting parties recognize that dumping, by which products of one country are introduced into the commerce of another country at less than the normal value of the products, is to be condemned if it causes or threatens material injury to an established industry in the territory of a contracting party or materially retards the establishment of a domestic industry. For the purposes of this Article, a product is to be considered as being introduced into the commerce of an importing country at less than its normal value, if the price of the product exported from one country to another

(*a*) is less than the comparable price, in the ordinary course of trade, for the like product when destined for consumption in the exporting country, or,

(*b*) in the absence of such domestic price, is less than either
- (i) the highest comparable price for the like product for export to any third country in the ordinary course of trade, or
- (ii) the cost of production of the product in the country of origin plus a reasonable addition for selling cost and profit.

Due allowance shall be made in each case for differences in conditions and terms of sale, for differences in taxation, and for other differences affecting price comparability.*

2. In order to offset or prevent dumping, a contracting party may levy on any dumped product an anti-dumping duty not greater in amount than the margin of dumping in respect of such product. For the purposes of this Article, the margin of dumping is the price difference determined in accordance with the provisions of paragraph 1.*

3. No countervailing duty shall be levied on any product of the territory of any contracting party imported into the territory of another contracting party in excess of an amount equal to the estimated bounty or subsidy determined to have been granted, directly or indirectly, on the manufacture, production or export of such product in the country of

origin or exportation, including any special subsidy to the transportation of a particular product. The term "countervailing duty" shall be understood to mean a special duty levied for the purpose of offsetting any bounty or subsidy bestowed, directly or indirectly, upon the manufacture, production or export of any merchandise.*

4. No product of the territory of any contracting party imported into the territory of any other contracting party shall be subject to anti-dumping or countervailing duty by reason of the exemption of such product from duties or taxes borne by the like product when destined for consumption in the country of origin or exportation, or by reason of the refund of such duties or taxes.

5. No product of the territory of any contracting party imported into the territory of any other contracting party shall be subject to both anti-dumping and countervailing duties to compensate for the same situation of dumping or export subsidization.

6. (*a*) No contracting party shall levy any anti-dumping or countervailing duty on the importation of any product of the territory of another contracting party unless it determines that the effect of the dumping or subsidization, as the case may be, is such as to cause or threaten material injury to an established domestic industry, or is such as to retard materially the establishment of a domestic industry.

(*b*) The CONTRACTING PARTIES may waive the requirement of sub-paragraph (*a*) of this paragraph so as to permit a contracting party to levy an anti-dumping or countervailing duty on the importation of any product for the purpose of offsetting dumping or subsidization which causes or threatens material injury to an industry in the territory of another contracting party exporting the product concerned to the territory of the importing contracting party. The CONTRACTING PARTIES shall waive the requirements of sub-paragraph (*a*) of this paragraph, so as to permit the levying of a countervailing duty, in cases in which they find that a subsidy is causing or threatening material injury to an industry in the territory of another contracting party exporting the product concerned to the territory of the importing contracting party.*

(*c*) In exceptional circumstances, however, where delay might cause damage which would be difficult to repair, a contracting party may levy a countervailing duty for the purpose referred to in sub-paragraph (*b*) of this paragraph without the prior approval of the CONTRACTING PARTIES; *Provided* that such action shall be reported immediately to the CONTRACTING PARTIES and that the countervailing duty shall be withdrawn promptly if the CONTRACTING PARTIES disapprove.

7. A system for the stabilization of the domestic price or of the return to domestic producers of a primary commodity, independently of the movements of export prices, which results at times in the sale of the commodity for export at a price lower than the comparable price charged for the like commodity to buyers in the domestic market, shall be presumed not to result in material injury within the meaning of paragraph 6 if it is determined by consultation among the contracting parties substantially interested in the commodity concerned that:

(*a*) the system has also resulted in the sale of the commodity for export at a price higher than the comparable price charged for the like commodity to buyers in the domestic market, and

(*b*) the system is so operated, either because of the effective regulation of production, or otherwise, as not to stimulate exports unduly or otherwise seriously prejudice the interests of other contracting parties.

Article VII

Valuation for Customs Purposes

1. The contracting parties recognize the validity of the general principles of valuation set forth in the following paragraphs of this Article, and they undertake to give effect to such principles, in respect of all products subject to duties or other charges* or restrictions on importation and exportation based upon or regulated in any manner by value. Moreover, they shall, upon a request by another contracting party review the operation of any of their laws or regulations relating to value for customs purposes in the light of these principles. The CONTRACTING PARTIES may request from contracting parties reports on steps taken by them in pursuance of the provisions of this Article.

2. (*a*) The value for customs purposes of imported merchandise should be based on the actual value of the imported merchandise on which duty is assessed, or of like merchandise, and should not be based on the value of merchandise of national origin or on arbitrary or fictitious values.

(*b*) "Actual value" should be the price at which, at a time and place determined by the legislation of the country of importation, such or like merchandise is sold or offered for sale in the ordinary course of trade under fully competitive conditions. To the extent to which the price of such or like merchandise is governed by the quantity in a particular transaction, the price to be considered should uniformly be related to either (i) comparable quantities, or (ii) quantities not less favorable to importers than those in which the greater volume of the merchandise is sold in the trade between the countries of exportation and importation.

(*c*) When the actual value is not ascertainable in accordance with sub-paragraph (*b*) of this paragraph, the value for customs purposes should be based on the nearest ascertainable equivalent of such value.

3. The value for customs purposes of any imported product should not include the amount of any internal tax, applicable within the country of origin or export, from which the imported product has been exempted or has been or will be relieved by means of refund.

4. (*a*) Except as otherwise provided for in this paragraph, where it is necessary for the purposes of paragraph 2 of this Article for a contracting party to convert into its own currency a price expressed in the currency of another country, the conversion rate of exchange to be used shall be based, for each currency involved, on the par value as established pursuant to the Articles of Agreement of the International Monetary Fund or on the rate of exchange recognized by the Fund, or on the par value established in accordance with a special exchange agreement entered into pursuant to Article XV of this Agreement.

(*b*) Where no such established par value and no such recognized rate of exchange exist, the conversion rate shall reflect effectively the current value of such currency in commercial transactions.

(*c*) The CONTRACTING PARTIES, in agreement with the International Monetary Fund, shall formulate rules governing the conversion by contracting parties of any foreign currency in respect of which multiple rates of exchange are maintained consistently with the Articles of Agreement of the International Monetary Fund. Any contracting party may apply such rules in respect of such foreign currencies for the purposes of paragraph 2 of this Article as an alternative to the use of par values. Until such rules are adopted by the CONTRACTING PARTIES, any contracting party may employ, in respect of any such foreign currency, rules of conversion for the purposes of paragraph 2 of this Article which are designed to reflect effectively the value of such foreign currency in commercial transactions.

(*d*) Nothing in this paragraph shall be construed to require any contracting party to alter the method of converting currencies for customs purposes which is applicable in its territory on the date of this Agreement, if such alteration would have the effect of increasing generally the amounts of duty payable.

5. The bases and methods for determining the value of products subject to duties or other charges or restrictions based upon or regulated in any manner by value should be stable and should be given sufficient publicity to enable traders to estimate, with a reasonable degree of certainty, the value for customs purposes.

Article VIII

*Fees and Formalities connected with Importation and Exportation**

1. (*a*) All fees and charges of whatever character (other than import and export duties and other than taxes within the purview of Article III) imposed by contracting parties on or in connexion with importation or exportation shall be limited in amount to the approximate cost of services rendered and shall not represent an indirect protection to domestic products or a taxation of imports or exports for fiscal purposes.

(*b*) The contracting parties recognize the need for reducing the number and diversity of fees and charges referred to in sub-paragraph (*a*).

(*c*) The contracting parties also recognize the need for minimizing the incidence and complexity of import and export formalities and for decreasing and simplifying import and export documentation requirements.*

2. A contracting party shall, upon request by another contracting party or by the CONTRACTING PARTIES, review the operation of its laws and regulations in the light of the provisions of this Article.

3. No contracting party shall impose substantial penalties for minor breaches of customs regulations or procedural requirements. In particular, no penalty in respect of any omission or mistake in customs documentation which is easily rectifiable and obviously made without fraudulent intent or gross negligence shall be greater than necessary to serve merely as a warning.

4. The provisions of this Article shall extend to fees, charges, formalities and requirements imposed by governmental authorities in connexion with importation and exportation, including those relating to:

(*a*) consular transactions, such as consular invoices and certificates;

(*b*) quantitative restrictions;

(*c*) licensing;

(*d*) exchange control;

(*e*) statistical services;

(*f*) documents, documentation and certification;

(*g*) analysis and inspection; and

(*h*) quarantine, sanitation and fumigation.

Article IX

Marks of Origin

1. Each contracting party shall accord to the products of the territories of other contracting parties treatment with regard to marking requirements no less favorable than the treatment accorded to like products of any third country.

2. The contracting parties recognize that, in adopting and enforcing laws and regulations relating to marks of origin, the difficulties and inconveniences which such measures may cause to the commerce and industry of exporting countries should be reduced to a minimum, due regard being had to the necessity of protecting consumers against fraudulent or misleading indications.

3. Whenever it is administratively practicable to do so, contracting parties should permit required marks of origin to be affixed at the time of importation.

4. The laws and regulations of contracting parties relating to the marking of imported products shall be such as to permit compliance without seriously damaging the products, or materially reducing their value, or unreasonably increasing their cost.

5. As a general rule, no special duty or penalty should be imposed by any contracting party for failure to comply with marking requirements prior to importation unless corrective marking is unreasonably delayed or deceptive marks have been affixed or the required marking has been intentionally omitted.

6. The contracting parties shall co-operate with each other with a view to preventing the use of trade names in such manner as to misrepresent the true origin of a product, to the detriment of such distinctive regional or geographical names of products of the territory of a contracting party as are protected by its legislation. Each contracting party shall accord full and sympathetic consideration to such requests or representations as may be made by any other contracting party regarding the application of the undertaking set forth in the preceding sentence to names of products which have been communicated to it by the other contracting party.

Article X

Publication and Administration of Trade Regulations

1. Laws, regulations, judicial decisions and administrative rulings of general application, made effective by any contracting party, pertaining to the classification or the valuation of products for customs purposes, or to rates of duty, taxes or other charges, or to requirements, restrictions or prohibitions on imports or exports or on the transfer of payments therefor, or affecting their sale, distribution, transportation, insurance, warehousing, inspection, exhibition, processing, mixing or other use, shall be published promptly in such a manner as to enable governments and traders to become acquainted with them. Agreements affecting international trade policy which are in force between the government or a governmental agency of any contracting party and the government or governmental agency of any other contracting party shall also be published. The provisions of this paragraph shall not require any contracting party to disclose confidential information which would impede law enforcement or otherwise be contrary to the public interest or would prejudice the legitimate commercial interests of particular enterprises, public or private.

2. No measure of general application taken by any contracting party effecting an advance in a rate of duty or other charge on imports under an established and uniform practice, or imposing a new or more burdensome requirement, restriction or prohibition on imports, or on the transfer of payments therefor, shall be enforced before such measures has been officially published.

3. (*a*) Each contracting party shall administer in a uniform, impartial and reasonable manner all its laws, regulations, decisions and rulings of the kind described in paragraph 1 of this Article.

(*b*) Each contracting party shall maintain, or institute as soon as practicable, judicial, arbitral or administrative tribunals or procedures for the purpose, *inter alia,* of the prompt review and correction of administrative action relating to customs matters. Such tribunals or procedures shall be independent of the agencies entrusted with administrative enforcement and their decisions shall be implemented by, and shall govern the practice of, such agencies unless an appeal is lodged with a court or tribunal of superior jurisdiction within the time prescribed for appeals to be lodged by importers; *Provided* that the central administration of such agency may take steps to obtain a review of the matter in another proceeding if there is good cause to believe that the decision is inconsistent with established principles of law or the actual facts.

(*c*) The provisions of sub-paragraph (*b*) of this paragraph shall not require the elimination or substitution of procedures in force in the territory of a contracting party on the date of this Agreement which in fact provide for an objective and impartial review of the administrative action even though such procedures are not fully or formally independent of the agencies entrusted with administrative enforcement. Any contracting party employing such procedures shall, upon request, furnish the CONTRACTING PARTIES with full information thereon in order that they may determine whether such procedures conform to the requirements of this sub-paragraph.

Article XI*

General Elimination of Quantitative Restrictions

1. No prohibitions or restrictions other than duties, taxes or other charges, whether made effective through quotas, import or export licences or other measures, shall be instituted or maintained by any contracting party on the importation of any product of the territory of any other contracting party or on the exportation or sale for export of any product destined for the territory of any other contracting party.

2. The provisions of paragraph 1 of this Article shall not extend to the following:

(*a*) Export prohibitions or restrictions temporarily applied to prevent or relieve critical shortages of foodstuffs or other products essential to the exporting contracting party;

(*b*) Import and export prohibitions or restrictions necessary to the application of standards or regulations for the classification, grading or marketing of commodities in international trade;

(*c*) Import restrictions on any agricultural or fisheries product, imported in any form,* necessary to the enforcement of governmental measures which operate:

(i) to restrict the quantities of the like domestic product permitted to be marketed or produced, or, if there is no substantial domestic production of the like product, of a domestic product for which the imported product can be directly substituted; or

(ii) to remove a temporary surplus of the like domestic product, or, if there is no substantial domestic production of the like product, of a domestic product for which the imported product can be directly substituted, by making the surplus available to certain groups of domestic consumers free of charge or at prices below the current market level; or

(iii) to restrict the quantities permitted to be produced of any animal product the production of which is directly dependent, wholly or mainly, on the imported commodity, if the domestic production of that commodity is relatively negligible.

Any contracting party applying restrictions on the importation of any product pursuant to sub-paragraph (*c*) of this paragraph shall give public notice of the total quantity or value of the product permitted to be imported during a specified future period and of any change in such quantity or value. Moreover, any restrictions applied under (i) above shall not be such as will reduce the total of imports relative to the total of domestic production, as compared with the proportion which might reasonably be expected to rule between the two in the absence of restrictions. In determining this proportion, the contracting party shall pay due regard to the proportion prevailing during a previous representative period and to any special factors* which may have affected or may be affecting the trade in the product concerned.

Article XII*

Restrictions to Safeguard the Balance of Payments

1. Notwithstanding the provisions of paragraph 1 of Article XI, any contracting party, in order to safeguard its external financial position

and its balance of payments, may restrict the quantity or value of merchandise permitted to be imported, subject to the provisions of the following paragraphs of this Article.

2. (*a*) Import restrictions instituted, maintained or intensified by a contracting party under this Article shall not exceed those necessary:

(i) to forestall the imminent threat of, or to stop, a serious decline in its monetary reserves, or

(ii) in the case of a contracting party with very low monetary reserves, to achieve a reasonable rate of increase in its reserves.

Due regard shall be paid in either case to any special factors which may be affecting the reserves of such contracting party or its need for reserves, including, where special external credits or other resources are available to it, the need to provide for the appropriate use of such credits or resources.

(*b*) Contracting parties applying restrictions under sub-paragraph (*a*) of this paragraph shall progressively relax them as such conditions improve, maintaining them only to the extent that the conditions specified in that sub-paragraph still justify their application. They shall eliminate the restrictions when conditions would no longer justify their institution or maintenance under that sub-paragraph.

3. (*a*) Contracting parties undertake, in carrying out their domestic policies, to pay due regard to the need for maintaining or restoring equilibrium in their balance of payments on a sound and lasting basis and to the desirability of avoiding an uneconomic employment of productive resources. They recognize that, in order to achieve these ends, it is desirable so far as possible to adopt measures which expand rather than contract international trade.

(*b*) Contracting parties applying restrictions under this Article may determine the incidence of the restrictions on imports of different products or classes of products in such a way as to give priority to the importation of those products which are more essential.

(*c*) Contracting parties applying restrictions under this Article undertake:

(i) to avoid unnecessary damage to the commercial or economic interests of any other contracting party;*

(ii) not to apply restrictions so as to prevent unreasonably the importation of any description of goods in minimum commercial quantities the exclusion of which would impair regular channels of trade; and

(iii) not to apply restrictions which would prevent the importation of commercial samples or prevent compliance with patent, trade mark, copyright, or similar procedures.

(*d*) The contracting parties recognize that, as a result of domestic policies directed towards the achievement and maintenance of full and productive employment or towards the development of economic resources, a contracting party may experience a high level of demand for imports involving a threat to its monetary reserves of the sort referred to in paragraph 2(*a*) of this Article. Accordingly, a contracting party otherwise complying with the provisions of this Article shall not be required to withdraw or modify restrictions on the ground that a change in those policies would render unnecessary restrictions which it is applying under this Article.

4. (*a*) Any contracting party applying new restrictions or raising the general level of its existing restrictions by a substantial intensification of the measures applied under this Article shall immediately after instituting or intensifying such restrictions (or, in circumstances in which prior consultation is practicable, before doing so) consult with the CONTRACTING PARTIES as to the nature of its balance of payments difficulties, alternative corrective measures which may be available, and the possible effect of the restrictions on the economies of other contracting parties.

(*b*) On a date to be determined by them,* the CONTRACTING PARTIES shall review all restrictions still applied under this Article on that date. Beginning one year after that date, contracting parties applying import restrictions under this Article shall enter into consultations of the type provided for in sub-paragraph (*a*) of this paragraph with the CONTRACTING PARTIES annually.

(*c*) (i) If, in the course of consultations with a contracting party under sub-paragraph (*a*) or (*b*) above, the CONTRACTING PARTIES find that the restrictions are not consistent with the provisions of this Article or with those of Article XIII (subject to the provisions of Article XIV), they shall indicate the nature of the inconsistency and may advise that the restrictions be suitably modified.

(ii) If, however, as a result of the consultations, the CONTRACTING PARTIES determine that the restrictions are being applied in a manner involving an inconsistency of a serious nature with the provisions of this

Article or with those of Article XIII (subject to the provisions of Article XIV) and that damage to the trade of any contracting party is caused or threatened thereby, they shall so inform the contracting party applying the restrictions and shall make appropriate recommendations for securing conformity with such provisions within a specified period of time. If such contracting party does not comply with these recommendations within the specified period, the CONTRACTING PARTIES may release any contracting party the trade of which is adversely affected by the restrictions from such obligations under this Agreement towards the contracting party applying the restrictions as they determine to be appropriate in the circumstances.

(*d*) The CONTRACTING PARTIES shall invite any contracting party which is applying restrictions under this Article to enter into consultations with them at the request of any contracting party which can establish a *prima facie* case that the restrictions are inconsistent with the provisions of this Article or with those of Article XIII (subject to the provisions of Article XIV) and that its trade is adversely affected thereby. However, no such invitation shall be issued unless the CONTRACTING PARTIES have ascertained that direct discussions between the contracting parties concerned have not been successful. If, as a result of the consultations with the CONTRACTING PARTIES, no agreement is reached and they determine that the restrictions are being applied inconsistently with such provisions, and that damage to the trade of the contracting party initiating the procedure is caused or threatened thereby, they shall recommend the withdrawal or modification of the restrictions. If the restrictions are not withdrawn or modified within such time as the CONTRACTING PARTIES may prescribe, they may release the contracting party initiating the procedure from such obligations under this Agreement towards the contracting party applying the restrictions as they determine to be appropriate in the circumstances.

(*e*) In proceeding under this paragraph, the CONTRACTING PARTIES shall have due regard to any special external factors adversely affecting the export trade of the contracting party applying restrictions.*

(*f*) Determinations under this paragraph shall be rendered expeditiously and, if possible, within sixty days of the initiation of the consultations.

5. If there is a persistent and widespread application of import restrictions under this Article, indicating the existence of a general disequilibrium which is restricting international trade, the CONTRACTING PARTIES shall initiate discussions to consider whether other measures

might be taken, either by those contracting parties the balance of payments of which are under pressure or by those the balances of payments of which are tending to be exceptionally favorable, or by any appropriate intergovernmental organization, to remove the underlying causes of the disequilibrium. On the invitation of the CONTRACTING PARTIES, contracting parties shall participate in such discussions.

Article XIII*

Non-discriminatory Administration of Quantitative Restrictions

1. No prohibition or restriction shall be applied by any contracting party on the importation of any product of the territory of any other contracting party or on the exportation of any product destined for the territory of any other contracting party, unless the importation of the like product of all third countries or the exportation of the like product to all third countries is similarly prohibited or restricted.

2. In applying import restrictions to any product, contracting parties shall aim at a distribution of trade in such product approaching as closely as possible the shares which the various contracting parties might be expected to obtain in the absence of such restrictions, and to this end shall observe the following provisions:

(*a*) Wherever practicable, quotas representing the total amount of permitted imports (whether allocated among supplying countries or not) shall be fixed, and notice given of their amount in accordance with paragraph 3 (*b*) of this Article;

(*b*) In cases in which quotas are not practicable, the restrictions may be applied by means of import licences or permits without a quota;

(*c*) Contracting parties shall not, except for purposes of operating quotas allocated in accordance with sub-paragraph (*d*) of this paragraph, require that import licences or permits be utilized for the importation of the product concerned from a particular country or source;

(*d*) In cases in which a quota is allocated among supplying countries, the contracting party applying the restrictions may seek agreement with respect to the allocation of shares in the quota with all other contracting parties having a substantial interest in supplying the product concerned. In cases in which this method is not reasonably practicable, the contracting party concerned shall allot to contracting parties having a substantial interest in supplying the product shares based upon the proportions, supplied by such contracting parties during a previous representative period, of the total quantity or value of imports of the product, due account being taken of any special factors which may have affected or may be affecting the trade in the product. No conditions or formalities shall be imposed which would prevent any contracting party from utilizing fully the share of any such total quantity or value which has been allotted to it, subject to importation being made within any prescribed period to which the quota may relate.*

3. (*a*) In cases in which import licences are issued in connection with import restrictions, the contracting party applying the restrictions shall provide, upon the request of any contracting party having an interest in the trade in the product concerned, all relevant information concerning the administration of the restrictions, the import licences granted over a recent period and the distribution of such licences among supplying countries; *Provided* that there shall be no obligation to supply information as to the names of importing or supplying enterprises.

(*b*) In the case of import restrictions involving the fixing of quotas, the contracting party applying the restrictions shall give public notice of the total quantity or value of the product or products which will be permitted to be imported during a specified future period and of any change in such quantity or value. Any supplies of the product in question which were *en route* at the time at which public notice was given shall not be excluded from entry; *Provided* that they may be counted so far as practicable, against the quantity permitted to be imported in the period in question, and also, where necessary, against the quantities permitted to be imported in the next following period or periods; and *Provided* further that if any contracting party customarily exempts from such restrictions products entered for consumption or withdrawn from warehouse for consumption during a period of thirty days after the day of such public notice, such practice shall be considered full compliance with this sub-paragraph.

(*c*) In the case of quotas allocated among supplying countries, the contracting party applying the restrictions shall promptly inform all other contracting parties having an interest in supplying the product concerned of the shares in the quota currently allocated, by quantity or value, to the various supplying countries and shall give public notice thereof.

4. With regard to restrictions applied in accordance with paragraph 2 (*d*) of this Article or under paragraph 2 (*c*) of Article XI, the selection of a representative period for any product and the appraisal of any special factors* affecting the trade in the product shall be made initially by the contracting party applying the restriction; *Provided* that such contracting party shall, upon the request of any other contracting party having a substantial interest in supplying that product or upon the request of the CONTRACTING PARTIES, consult promptly with the other contracting party or the CONTRACTING PARTIES regarding the need for an adjustment of the proportion determined or of the base period selected, or for the reappraisal of the special factors involved, or for the elimination of conditions, formalities or any other provisions established unilaterally relating to the allocation of an adequate quota or its unrestricted utilization.

5. The provisions of this Article shall apply to any tariff quota instituted or maintained by any contracting party, and, in so far as applicable, the principles of this Article shall also extend to export restrictions.

Article XIV*

Exceptions to the Rule of Non-discrimination

1. A contracting party which applies restrictions under Article XII or under Section B of Article XVIII may, in the application of such restrictions, deviate from the provisions of Article XIII in a manner having equivalent effect to restrictions on payments and transfers for current international transactions which that contracting party may at that time apply under Article VIII or XIV of the Articles of Agreement of the International Monetary Fund, or under analogous provisions of a special exchange agreement entered into pursuant to paragraph 6 of Article XV.*

2. A contracting party which is applying import restrictions under Article XII or under Section B of Article XVIII may, with the consent of the CONTRACTING PARTIES, temporarily deviate from the provisions of Article XIII in respect of a small part of its external trade where the benefits to the contracting party or contracting parties concerned substantially outweigh any injury which may result to the trade of other contracting parties.*

3. The provisions of Article XIII shall not preclude a group of territories having a common quota in the International Monetary Fund from applying against imports from other countries, but not among themselves, restrictions in accordance with the provisions of Article XII or of Section B of Article XVIII on condition that such restrictions are in all other respects consistent with the provisions of Article XIII.

4. A contracting party applying import restrictions under Article XII or under Section B of Article XVIII shall not be precluded by Articles XI to XV or Section B of Article XVIII of this Agreement from applying measures to direct its exports in such a manner as to increase its earnings of currencies which it can use without deviation from the provisions of Article XIII.

5. A contracting party shall not be precluded by Articles XI to XV, inclusive, or by Section B of Article XVIII, of this Agreement from applying quantitative restrictions:

(*a*) having equivalent effect to exchange restrictions authorized under Section 3 (*b*) of Article VII of the Articles of Agreement of the International Monetary Fund, or

(*b*) under the preferential arrangements provided for in Annex A of this Agreement, pending the outcome of the negotiations referred to therein.

Article XV

Exchange Arrangements

1. The CONTRACTING PARTIES shall seek co-operation with the International Monetary Fund to the end that the CONTRACTING PARTIES and the Fund may pursue a coordinated policy with regard to exchange questions within the jurisdiction of the Fund and questions of quantitative restrictions and other trade measures within the jurisdiction of the CONTRACTING PARTIES.

2. In all cases in which the CONTRACTING PARTIES are called upon to consider or deal with problems concerning monetary reserves, balances of payments or foreign exchange arrangements, they shall consult fully with the International Monetary Fund. In such consultations, the CONTRACTING PARTIES shall accept all findings of statistical and other facts

presented by the Fund relating to foreign exchange, monetary reserves and balances of payments, and shall accept the determination of the Fund as to whether action by a contracting party in exchange matters is in accordance with the Articles of Agreement of the International Monetary Fund, or with the terms of a special exchange agreement between that contracting party and the CONTRACTING PARTIES. The CONTRACTING PARTIES, in reaching their final decision in cases involving the criteria set forth in paragraph 2(*a*) of Article XII or in paragraph 9 of Article XVIII, shall accept the determination of the Fund as to what constitutes a serious decline in the contracting party's monetary reserves, a very low level of its monetary reserves or a reasonable rate of increase in its monetary reserves, and as to the financial aspects of other matters covered in consultation in such cases.

3. The CONTRACTING PARTIES shall seek agreement with the Fund regarding procedures for consultation under paragraph 2 of this Article.

4. Contracting parties shall not, by exchange action frustrate* the intent of the provisions of this Agreement, nor, by trade action, the intent of the provisions of the Articles of Agreement of the International Monetary Fund.

5. If the CONTRACTING PARTIES consider, at any time, that exchange restrictions on payments and transfers in connexion with imports are being applied by a contracting party in a manner inconsistent with the exceptions provided for in this Agreement for quantitative restrictions, they shall report thereon to the Fund.

6. Any contacting party which is not a member of the Fund shall, within a time to be determined by the CONTRACTING PARTIES after consultation with the Fund, become a member of the Fund, or, failing that, enter into a special exchange agreement with the CONTRACTING PARTIES. A contracting party which ceases to be a member of the Fund shall forthwith enter into a special exchange agreement with the CONTRACTING PARTIES. Any special exchange agreement entered into by a contracting party under this paragraph shall thereupon become part of its obligations under this Agreement.

7. (*a*) A special exchange agreement between a contracting party and the CONTRACTING PARTIES under paragraph 6 of this Article shall provide to the satisfaction of the CONTRACTING PARTIES that the objectives of this Agreement will not be frustrated as a result of action in exchange matters by the contracting party in question.

(*b*) The terms of any such agreement shall not impose obligations on the contracting party in exchange matters generally more restrictive than those imposed by the Articles of Agreement of the International Monetary Fund on members of the Fund.

8. A contracting party which is not a member of the Fund shall furnish such information within the general scope of section 5 of Article VIII of the Articles of Agreement of the International Monetary Fund as the CONTRACTING PARTIES may require in order to carry out their functions under this Agreement.

9. Nothing in this Agreement shall preclude:

(*a*) the use by a contracting party of exchange controls or exchange restrictions in accordance with the Articles of Agreement of the International Monetary Fund or with that contracting party's special exchange agreement with the CONTRACTING PARTIES, or

(*b*) the use by a contracting party of restrictions or controls on imports or exports, the sole effect of which, additional to the effects permitted under Articles XI, XII, XIII and XIV, is to make effective such exchange controls or exchange restrictions.

Article XVI*

Subsidies

Section A—Subsidies in General

1. If any contracting party grants or maintains any subsidy, including any form of income or price support, which operates directly or indirectly to increase exports of any product from, or to reduce imports of any product into, its territory, it shall notify the CONTRACTING PARTIES in writing of the extent and nature of the subsidization, of the estimated effect of the subsidization on the quantity of the affected product or products imported into or exported from its territory and of the circumstances making the subsidization necessary. In any case in which it is determined that serious prejudice to the interests of any other contracting party is caused or threatened by any such subsidization, the contracting party granting the subsidy shall, upon request, discuss with the other contracting party or parties concerned, or with the CONTRACTING PARTIES, the possibility of limiting the subsidization.

*Section B—Additional Provisions on Export Subsidies**

2. The contracting parties recognize that the granting by a contracting party of a subsidy on the export of any product may have harmful

effect for other contracting parties, both importing and exporting, may cause undue disturbance to their normal commercial interests, and may hinder the achievement of the objectives of this Agreement.

3. Accordingly, contracting parties should seek to avoid the use of subsidies on the export of primary products. If, however, a contracting party grants directly or indirectly any form of subsidy which operates to increase the export of any primary product from its territory, such subsidy shall not be applied in a manner which results in that contracting party having more than an equitable share of world export trade in that product, account being taken of the shares of the contracting parties in such trade in the product during a previous representative period, and any special factors which may have affected or may be affecting such trade in the product.*

4. Further, as from 1 January 1958 or the earliest practicable date thereafter, contracting parties shall cease to grant either directly or indirectly any form of subsidy on the export of any product other than a primary product which subsidy results in the sale of such product for export at a price lower than the comparable price charged for the like product to buyers in the domestic market. Until 31 December 1957 no contracting party shall extend the scope of any such subsidization beyond that existing on 1 January 1955 by the introduction of new, or the extension of existing, subsidies.

5. The CONTRACTING PARTIES shall review the operation of the provisions of this Article from time to time with a view to examining its effectiveness, in the light of actual experience, in promoting the objectives of this Agreement and avoiding subsidization seriously prejudicial to the trade or interests of contracting parties.

Article XVII

State Trading Enterprises

1.* (*a*) Each contacting party undertakes that if it establishes or maintains a State enterprise, wherever located, or grants to any enterprise, formally or in effect, exclusive or special privileges,* such enterprise shall, in its purchases or sales involving either imports or exports, act in a manner consistent with the general principles of non-discriminatory treatment prescribed in this Agreement for governmental measures affecting imports or exports by private traders.

(*b*) The provisions of sub-paragraph (*a*) of this paragraph shall be understood to require that such enterprises shall, having due regard to the other provisions of this Agreement, make any such purchases or sales solely in accordance with commercial considerations,* including price, quality, availability, marketability, transportation and other conditions of purchase or sale, and shall afford the enterprises of the other contracting parties adequate opportunity, in accordance with customary business practice, to compete for participation in such purchases or sales.

(*c*) No contracting party shall prevent any enterprise (whether or not an enterprise described in sub-paragraph (*a*) of this paragraph) under its jurisdiction from acting in accordance with the principles of sub-paragraphs (*a*) and (*b*) of this paragraph.

2. The provisions of paragraph 1 of this Article shall not apply to imports of products for immediate or ultimate consumption in governmental use and not otherwise for resale or use in the production of goods* for sale. With respect to such imports, each contracting party shall accord to the trade of the other contracting parties fair and equitable treatment.

3. The contracting parties recognize that enterprises of the kind described in paragraph 1 (*a*) of this Article might be operated so as to create serious obstacles to trade; thus negotiations on a reciprocal and mutually advantageous basis designed to limit or reduce such obstacles are of importance to the expansion of international trade.*

4. (*a*) Contracting parties shall notify the CONTRACTING PARTIES of the products which are imported into or exported from their territories by enterprises of the kind described in paragraph 1 (*a*) of this Article.

(*b*) A contracting party establishing, maintaining or authorizing an import monopoly of a product, which is not the subject of a concession under Article II, shall, on the request of another contracting party having a substantial trade in the product concerned, inform the CONTRACTING PARTIES of the import mark-up* on the product during a recent representative period, or, when it is not possible to do so, of the price charged on the resale of the product.

(*c*) The CONTRACTING PARTIES may, at the request of a contracting party which has reason to believe that its interests under this Agreement are being adversely affected by the operations of an enterprise of the kind described in paragraph 1 (*a*), request the contracting party establishing, maintaining or authorizing such enterprise to supply information about its operations related to the carrying out of the provisions of this Agreement.

(*d*) The provisions of this paragraph shall not require any contracting party to disclose confidential information which would impede law enforcement or otherwise be contrary to the public interest or would prejudice the legitimate commercial interests of particular enterprises.

Article XVIII*

Governmental Assistance to Economic Development

1. The contracting parties recognize that the attainment of the objectives of this Agreement will be facilitated by the progressive development of their economies, particularly of those contracting parties the economies of which can only support low standards of living* and are in the early stages of development.*

2. The contracting parties recognize further that it may be necessary for those contracting parties, in order to implement programs and policies of economic development designed to raise the general standard of living of their people, to take protective or other measures affecting imports, and that such measures are justified in so far as they facilitate the attainment of the objectives of this Agreement. They agree, therefore, that those contracting parties should enjoy additional facilities to enable them (*a*) to maintain sufficient flexibility in their tariff structure to be able to grant the tariff protection required for the establishment of a particular industry and (*b*) to apply quantitative restrictions for balance of payments purposes in a manner which takes full account of the continued high level of demand for imports likely to be generated by their programs of economic development.

3. The contracting parties recognize finally that, with those additional facilities which are provided for in Sections A and B of this Article, the provisions of this Agreement would normally be sufficient to enable contracting parties to meet the requirements of their economic development. They agree, however, that there may be circumstances where no measure consistent with those provisions is practicable to permit a contracting party in the process of economic development to grant the governmental assistance required to promote the establishment of particular industries* with a view to raising the general standard of living of its people. Special procedures are laid down in Sections C and D of this Article to deal with those cases.

4. (*a*) Consequently, a contracting party the economy of which can only support low standards of living* and is in the early stages of development* shall be free to deviate temporarily from the provisions of the other Articles of this Agreement, as provided in Sections A, B and C of this Article.

(*b*) A contracting party the economy of which is in the process of development, but which does not come within the scope of sub-paragraph (*a*) above, may submit applications to the CONTRACTING PARTIES under Section D of this Article.

5. The contracting parties recognize that the export earnings of contracting parties, the economies of which are of the type described in paragraph 4 (*a*) and (*b*) above and which depend on exports of a small number of primary commodities, may be seriously reduced by a decline in the sale of such commodities. Accordingly, when the exports of primary commodities by such a contracting party are seriously affected by measures taken by another contracting party, it may have resort to the consultation provisions of Article XXII of this Agreement.

6. The CONTRACTING PARTIES shall review annually all measures applied pursuant to the provisions of Sections C and D of this Article.

Section A

7. (*a*) If a contracting party coming within the scope of paragraph 4 (*a*) of this Article considers it desirable, in order to promote the establishment of a particular industry* with a view to raising the general standard of living of its people, to modify or withdraw a concession included in the appropriate Schedule annexed to this Agreement, it shall notify the CONTRACTING PARTIES to this effect and enter into negotiations with any contracting party with which such concession was initially negotiated, and with any other contracting party determined by the CONTRACTING PARTIES to have a substantial interest therein. If agreement is reached between such contracting parties concerned, they shall be free to modify or withdraw concessions under the appropriate Schedules to this Agreement in order to give effect to such agreement, including any compensatory adjustments involved.

(*b*) If agreement is not reached within sixty days after the notification provided for in sub-paragraph (*a*) above, the contracting party which proposes to modify or withdraw the concession may refer the matter to the CONTRACTING PARTIES, which shall promptly examine it. If they find that the contracting party which proposes to modify or withdraw the concession has made every effort to reach an agreement and that the compensatory adjustment offered by it is adequate, that contracting party shall be free to modify or withdraw the concession if, at the same time, it gives effect to the compensatory adjustment. If the CONTRACTING PARTIES do not find that the compensation offered by a contracting party proposing to modify or withdraw the concession is adequate, but find that it has made every reasonable effort to offer adequate compensation, that contracting party shall be free to proceed with such modification or withdrawal. If such action is taken, any other contracting party referred to in sub-paragraph (*a*) above shall be free to modify or withdraw substantially equivalent concessions initially negotiated with the contracting party which has taken the action.*

Section B

8. The contracting parties recognize that contracting parties coming within the scope of paragraph 4 (*a*) of this Article tend, when they are in rapid process of development, to experience balance of payments difficulties arising mainly from efforts to expand their internal markets as well as from the instability in their terms of trade.

9. In order to safeguard its external financial position and to ensure a level of reserves adequate for the implementation of its programme of economic development, a contracting party coming within the scope of paragraph 4 (*a*) of this Article may, subject to the provisions of paragraphs 10 to 12, control the general level of its imports by restricting the quantity or value of merchandise permitted to be imported; *Provided* that the import restrictions instituted, maintained or intensified shall not exceed those necessary:

(a) to forestall the threat of, or to stop, a serious decline in its monetary reserves, or

(b) in the case of a contracting party with inadequate monetary reserves, to achieve a reasonable rate of increase in its reserves.

Due regard shall be paid in either case to any special factors which may be affecting the reserves of the contracting party or its need for reserves, including, where special external credits or other resources are available to it, the need to provide for the appropriate use of such credits or resources.

10. In applying these restrictions, the contracting party may determine their incidence on imports of different products or classes of

products in such a way as to give priority to the importation of those products which are more essential in the light of its policy of economic development: *Provided* that the restrictions are so applied as to avoid unnecessary damage to the commercial or economic interests of any other contracting party and not to prevent unreasonably the importation of any description of goods in minimum commercial quantities the exclusion of which would impair regular channels of trade; and *Provided* further that the restrictions are not so applied as to prevent the importation of commercial samples or to prevent compliance with patent, trade mark, copyright or similar procedures.

11. In carrying out its domestic policies, the contracting party concerned shall pay due regard to the need for restoring equilibrium in its balance of payments on a sound and lasting basis and to the desirability of assuring an economic employment of productive resources. It shall progressively relax any restrictions applied under this section as conditions improve, maintaining them only to the extent necessary under the terms of paragraph 9 of this Article and shall eliminate them when conditions no longer justify such maintenance; *Provided* that no contracting party shall be required to withdraw or modify restrictions on the ground that a change in its development policy would render unnecessary the restrictions which it is applying under this Section.*

12. (*a*) Any contracting party applying new restrictions or raising the general level of its existing restrictions by a substantial intensification of the measures applied under this Section, shall immediately after instituting or intensifying such restrictions (or, in circumstances in which prior consultation is practicable, before doing so) consult with the CONTRACTING PARTIES as to the nature of its balance of payments difficulties, alternative corrective measures which may be available, and the possible effect of the restrictions on the economies of other contracting parties.

(*b*) On a date to be determined by them,* the CONTRACTING PARTIES shall review all restrictions still applied under this Section on that date. Beginning two years after that date, contracting parties applying restrictions under this Section shall enter into consultations of the type provided for in sub-paragraph (a) above with the CONTRACTING PARTIES at intervals of approximately, but not less than, two years according to a program to be drawn up each year by the CONTRACTING PARTIES; *Provided* that no consultation under this sub-paragraph shall take place within two years after the conclusion of a consultation of a general nature under any other provision of this paragraph.

(*c*) (i) If, in the course of consultations with a contracting party under sub-paragraph (*a*) or (*b*) of this paragraph, the CONTRACTING PARTIES find that the restrictions are not consistent with the provisions of this Section or with those of Article XIII (subject to the provisions of Article XIV), they shall indicate the nature of the inconsistency and may advise that the restrictions be suitably modified.

(ii) If, however, as a result of the consultations, the CONTRACTING PARTIES determine that the restrictions are being applied in a manner involving an inconsistency of a serious nature with the provisions of this Section or with those of Article XIII (subject to the provisions of Article XIV) and that damage to the trade of any contracting party is caused or threatened thereby, they shall so inform the contracting party applying the restrictions and shall make appropriate recommendations for securing conformity with such provisions within a specified period. If such contracting party does not comply with these recommendations within the specified period, the CONTRACTING PARTIES may release any contracting party the trade of which is adversely affected by the restrictions from such obligations under this Agreement towards the contracting party applying the restrictions as they determine to be appropriate in the circumstances.

(*d*) The CONTRACTING PARTIES shall invite any contracting party which is applying restrictions under this Section to enter into consultations with them at the request of any contracting party which can establish a *prima facie* case that the restrictions are inconsistent with the provisions of this Section or with those of Article XIII (subject to the provisions of Article XIV) and that its trade is adversely affected thereby. However, no such invitation shall be issued unless the CONTRACTING PARTIES have ascertained that direct discussions between the contracting parties concerned have not been successful. If, as a result of the consultations with the CONTRACTING PARTIES no agreement is reached and they determine that the restrictions are being applied inconsistently with such provisions, and that damage to the trade of the contracting party initiating the procedure is caused or threatened thereby, they shall recommend the withdrawal or modification of the restrictions. If the restrictions are not withdrawn or modified within such time as the CONTRACTING PARTIES may prescribe, they may release the contracting party initiating the procedure from such obligations under this Agreement towards the contracting party applying the restrictions as they determine to be appropriate in the circumstances.

(*e*) If a contracting party against which action has been taken in accordance with the last sentence of sub-paragraph (*c*)(ii) or (*d*) of this paragraph, finds that the release of obligations authorized by the CONTRACTING PARTIES adversely affects the operation of its program and policy of economic development, it shall be free, not later than sixty days after such action is taken, to give written notice to the Executive Secretary[1] to the CONTRACTING PARTIES of its intention to withdraw from this Agreement and such withdrawal shall take effect on the sixtieth day following the day on which the notice is received by him.

(f) In proceeding under this paragraph, the CONTRACTING PARTIES shall have due regard to the factors referred to in paragraph 2 of this Article. Determinations under this paragraph shall be rendered expeditiously and, if possible, within sixty days of the initiation of the consultations.

Section C

13. If a contracting party coming within the scope of paragraph 4 *(a)* of this Article finds that governmental assistance is required to promote the establishment of a particular industry* with a view to raising the general standard of living of its people, but that no measure consistent with the other provisions of this Agreement is practicable to achieve that objective, it may have recourse to the provisions and procedures set out in this Section.*

14. The contracting party concerned shall notify the CONTRACTING PARTIES of the special difficulties which it meets in the achievement of the objective outlined in paragraph 13 of this Article and shall indicate the specific measure affecting imports which it proposes to introduce in order to remedy these difficulties. It shall not introduce that measure before the expiration of the time-limit laid down in paragraph 15 or 17, as the case may be, or if the measure affects imports of a product which is the subject of a concession included in the appropriate Schedule annexed to this Agreement, unless it has secured the concurrence of the CONTRACTING PARTIES in accordance with the provisions of paragraph 18; *Provided* that, if the industry receiving assistance has already started production, the contracting party may, after informing the CONTRACTING PARTIES, take such measures as may be necessary to prevent, during that period, imports of the product or products concerned from increasing substantially above a normal level.*

15. If, within thirty days of the notification of the measure, the CONTRACTING PARTIES do not request the contracting party concerned to consult with them,* that contracting party shall be free to deviate

[1] See Preface.

from the relevant provisions of the other Articles of this Agreement to the extent necessary to apply the proposed measure.

16. If it is requested by the CONTRACTING PARTIES to do so,* the contracting party concerned shall consult with them as to the purpose of the proposed measure, as to alternative measures which may be available under this Agreement, and as to the possible effect of the measure proposed on the commercial and economic interests of other contracting parties. If, as a result of such consultation, the CONTRACTING PARTIES agree that there is no measure consistent with the other provisions of this Agreement which is practicable in order to achieve the objective outlined in paragraph 13 of this Article, and concur* in the proposed measure, the contracting party concerned shall be released from its obligations under the relevant provisions of the other Articles of this Agreement to the extent necessary to apply that measure.

17. If, within ninety days after the date of the notification of the proposed measure under paragraph 14 of this Article, the CONTRACTING PARTIES have not concurred in such measure, the contracting party concerned may introduce the measure proposed after informing the CONTRACTING PARTIES.

18. If the proposed measure affects a product which is the subject of a concession included in the appropriate Schedule annexed to this Agreement, the contracting party concerned shall enter into consultations with any other contracting party with which the concession was initially negotiated, and with any other contracting party determined by the CONTRACTING PARTIES to have a substantial interest therein. The CONTRACTING PARTIES shall concur* in the measure if they agree that there is no measure consistent with the other provisions of this Agreement which is practicable in order to achieve the objective set forth in paragraph 13 of this Article, and if they are satisfied:

(a) that agreement has been reached with such other contracting parties as a result of the consultations referred to above, or

(b) if no such agreement has been reached within sixty days after the notification provided for in paragraph 14 has been received by the CONTRACTING PARTIES, that the contracting party having recourse to this Section has made all reasonable efforts to reach an agreement and that the interests of other contracting parties are adequately safeguarded.*

The contracting party having recourse to this Section shall thereupon be released from its obligations under the relevant provisions of the other Articles of this Agreement to the extent necessary to permit it to apply the measure.

19. If a proposed measure of the type described in paragraph 13 of this Article concerns an industry the establishment of which has in the initial period been facilitated by incidental protection afforded by restrictions imposed by the contracting party concerned for balance of payments purposes under the relevant provisions of this Agreement, that contracting party may resort to the provisions and procedures of this Section; *Provided* that it shall not apply the proposed measure without the concurrence* of the CONTRACTING PARTIES.*

20. Nothing in the preceding paragraphs of this Section shall authorize any deviation from the provisions of Articles I, II and XIII of this Agreement. The provisos to paragraph 10 of this Article shall also be applicable to any restriction under this Section.

21. At any time while a measure is being applied under paragraph 17 of this Article any contracting party substantially affected by it may suspend the application to the trade of the contracting party having recourse to this Section of such substantially equivalent concessions or other obligations under this Agreement the suspension of which the CONTRACTING PARTIES do not disapprove;* *Provided* that sixty days' notice of such suspension is given to the CONTRACTING PARTIES not later than six months after the measure has been introduced or changed substantially to the detriment of the contracting party affected. Any such contracting party shall afford adequate opportunity for consultation in accordance with the provisions of Article XXII of this Agreement.

Section D

22. A contracting party coming within the scope of sub-paragraph 4 *(b)* of this Article desiring, in the interest of the development of its economy, to introduce a measure of the type described in paragraph 13 of this Article in respect of the establishment of a particular industry* may apply to the CONTRACTING PARTIES for approval of such measure. The CONTRACTING PARTIES shall promptly consult with such contracting party and shall, in making their decision, be guided by the considerations set out in paragraph 16. If the CONTRACTING PARTIES concur* in the proposed measure the contracting party concerned shall be released

from its obligations under the relevant provisions of the other Articles of this Agreement to the extent necessary to permit it to apply the measure. If the proposed measure affects a product which is the subject of a concession included in the appropriate Schedule annexed to this Agreement, the provisions of paragraph 18 shall apply.*

23. Any measure applied under this Section shall comply with the provisions of paragraph 20 of this Article.

Article XIX

Emergency Action on Imports of Particular Products

1. *(a)* If, as a result of unforeseen developments and of the effect of the obligations incurred by a contracting party under this Agreement, including tariff concessions, any product is being imported into the territory of that contracting party in such increased quantities and under such conditions as to cause or threaten serious injury to domestic producers in that territory of like or directly competitive products, the contracting party shall be free, in respect of such product, and to the extent and for such time as may be necessary to prevent or remedy such injury, to suspend the obligation in whole or in part or to withdraw or modify the concession.

(b) If any product, which is the subject of a concession with respect to a preference, is being imported into the territory of a contracting party in the circumstances set forth in sub-paragraph *(a)* of this paragraph, so as to cause or threaten serious injury to domestic producers of like or directly competitive products in the territory of a contracting party which receives or received such preference, the importing contracting party shall be free, if that other contracting party so requests, to suspend the relevant obligation in whole or in part or to withdraw or modify the concession in respect of the product, to the extent and for such time as may be necessary to prevent or remedy such injury.

2. Before any contracting party shall take action pursuant to the provisions of paragraph 1 of this Article, it shall give notice in writing to the CONTRACTING PARTIES as far in advance as may be practicable and shall afford the CONTRACTING PARTIES and those contracting parties having a substantial interest as exporters of the product concerned an opportunity to consult with it in respect of the proposed action. When such notice is given in relation to a concession with respect to a preference, the notice shall name the contracting party which has requested

the action. In critical circumstances, where delay would cause damage which it would be difficult to repair, action under paragraph 1 of this Article may be taken provisionally without prior consultation, on the condition that consultation shall be effected immediately after taking such action.

3. *(a)* If agreement among the interested contracting parties with respect to the action is not reached, the contracting party which proposes to take or continue the action shall, nevertheless, be free to do so, and if such action is taken or continued, the affected contracting parties shall then be free, not later than ninety days after such action is taken, to suspend, upon the expiration of thirty days from the day on which written notice of such suspension is received by the CONTRACTING PARTIES, the application to the trade of the contracting party taking such action, or, in the case envisaged in paragraph 1 *(b)* of this Article, to the trade of the contracting party requesting such action, of such substantially equivalent concessions or other obligations under this Agreement the suspension of which the CONTRACTING PARTIES do not disapprove.

(b) Notwithstanding the provisions of sub-paragraph *(a)* of this paragraph, where action is taken under paragraph 2 of this Article without prior consultation and causes or threatens serious injury in the territory of a contracting party to the domestic producers of products affected by the action, that contracting party shall, where delay would cause damage difficult to repair, be free to suspend, upon the taking of the action and throughout the period of consultation, such concessions or other obligations as may be necessary to prevent or remedy the injury.

Article XX

General Exceptions

Subject to the requirement that such measures are not applied in a manner which would constitute a means of arbitrary or unjustifiable discrimination between countries where the same conditions prevail, or a disguised restriction on international trade, nothing in this Agreement shall be construed to prevent the adoption or enforcement by any contracting party of measures:

(a) necessary to protect public morals;

(b) necessary to protect human, animal or plant life or health;

(c) relating to the importation or exportation of gold or silver;

(d) necessary to secure compliance with laws or regulations which are not inconsistent with the provisions of this Agreement, including those relating to customs enforcement, the enforcement of monopolies operated under paragraph 4 of Article II and Article XVII, the protection of patents, trade marks and copyrights, and the prevention of deceptive practices;

(e) relating to the products of prison labor;

(f) imposed for the protection of national treasures of artistic, historic or archaeological value;

(g) relating to the conservation of exhaustible natural resources if such measures are made effective in conjunction with restrictions on domestic production or consumption;

(h) undertaken in pursuance of obligations under any intergovernmental commodity agreement which conforms to criteria submitted to the CONTRACTING PARTIES and not disapproved by them or which is itself so submitted and not so disapproved;*

(i) involving restrictions on exports of domestic materials necessary to ensure essential quantities of such materials to a domestic processing industry during periods when the domestic price of such materials is held below the world price as part of a governmental stabilization plan; *Provided* that such restrictions shall not operate to increase the exports of or the protection afforded to such domestic industry, and shall not depart from the provisions of this Agreement relating to non-discrimination;

(j) essential to the acquisition or distribution of products in general or local short supply; *Provided* that any such measures shall be consistent with the principle that all contracting parties are entitled to an equitable share of the international supply of such products, and that any such measures, which are inconsistent with the other provisions of this Agreement shall be discontinued as soon as the conditions giving rise to them have ceased to exist. The CONTRACTING PARTIES shall review the need for this subparagraph not later than 30 June 1960.

Article XXI

Security Exceptions

Nothing in this Agreement shall be construed

(a) to require any contracting party to furnish any information the disclosure of which it considers contrary to its essential security interests; or

(b) to prevent any contracting party from taking any action which it considers necessary for the protection of its essential security interests

(i) relating to fissionable materials or the materials from which they are derived;

(ii) relating to the traffic in arms, ammunition and implements of war and to such traffic in other goods and materials as is carried on directly or indirectly for the purpose of supplying a military establishment;

(iii) taken in time of war or other emergency in international relations; or

(c) to prevent any contracting party from taking any action in pursuance of its obligations under the United Nations Charter for the maintenance of international peace and security.

Article XXII

Consultation

1. Each contracting party shall accord sympathetic consideration to, and shall afford adequate opportunity for consultation regarding, such representations as may be made by another contracting party with respect to any matter affecting the operation of this Agreement.

2. The CONTRACTING PARTIES may, at the request of a contracting party, consult with any contracting party or parties in respect of any matter for which it has not been possible to find a satisfactory solution through consultation under paragraph 1.

Article XXIII

Nullification or Impairment

1. If any contracting party should consider that any benefit accruing to it directly or indirectly under this Agreement is being nullified or impaired or that the attainment of any objective of the Agreement is being impeded as the result of

(a) the failure of another contracting party to carry out its obligations under this Agreement, or

(b) the application by another contracting party of any measure, whether or not it conflicts with the provisions of this Agreement, or

(c) the existence of any other situation,

the contracting party may, with a view to the satisfactory adjustment of the matter, make written representations or proposals to the other contracting party or parties which it considers to be concerned. Any contracting party thus approached shall give sympathetic consideration to the representations or proposals made to it.

2. If no satisfactory adjustment is effected between the contracting parties concerned within a reasonable time, or if the difficulty is of the type described in paragraph 1 *(c)* of this Article, the matter may be referred to the CONTRACTING PARTIES. The CONTRACTING PARTIES shall promptly investigate any matter so referred to them and shall make appropriate recommendations to the contracting parties which they consider to be concerned, or give a ruling on the matter, as appropriate. The CONTRACTING PARTIES may consult with contracting parties, with the Economic and Social Council of the United Nations and with any appropriate inter-governmental organization in cases where they consider such consultation necessary. If the CONTRACTING PARTIES consider that the circumstances are serious enough to justify such action, they may authorize a contracting party or parties to suspend the application to any other contracting party or parties of such concessions or other obligations under this Agreement as they determine to be appropriate in the circumstances. If the application to any contracting party of any concession or other obligation is in fact suspended, that contracting

party shall then be free, not later than sixty days after such action is taken, to give written notice to the Executive Secretary to the CONTRACTING PARTIES of its intention to withdraw from this Agreement and such withdrawal shall take effect upon the sixtieth day following the day on which such notice is received by him.

PART III

Article XXIV

Territorial Application—Frontier Traffic—Customs Unions and Free-trade Areas

1. The provisions of this Agreement shall apply to the metropolitan customs territories of the contracting parties and to any other customs territories in respect of which this Agreement has been accepted under Article XXVI or is being applied under Article XXXIII or pursuant to the Protocol of Provisional Application. Each such customs territory shall, exclusively for the purposes of the territorial application of this Agreement, be treated as though it were a contracting party; *Provided* that the provisions of this paragraph shall not be construed to create any rights or obligations as between two or more customs territories in respect of which this Agreement has been accepted under Article XXVI or is being applied under Article XXXIII or pursuant to the Protocol of Provisional Application by a single contracting party.

2. For the purposes of this Agreement a customs territory shall be understood to mean any territory with respect to which separate tariffs or other regulations of commerce are maintained for a substantial part of the trade of such territory with other territories.

3. The provisions of this Agreement shall not be construed to prevent:

(a) Advantages accorded by any contracting party to adjacent countries in order to facilitate frontier traffic;

(b) Advantages accorded to the trade with the Free Territory of Trieste by countries contiguous to that territory, provided that such advantages are not in conflict with the Treaties of Peace arising out of the Second World War.

4. The contracting parties recognize the desirability of increasing freedom of trade by the development, through voluntary agreements, of closer integration between the economies of the countries parties to such agreements. They also recognize that the purpose of a customs union or of a free-trade area should be to facilitate trade between the

constituent territories and not to raise barriers to the trade of other contracting parties with such territories.

5. Accordingly, the provisions of this Agreement shall not prevent, as between the territories of contracting parties, the formation of a customs union or of a free-trade area or the adoption of an interim agreement necessary for the formation of a customs union or of a free-trade area; *Provided* that:

(a) with respect to a customs union, or an interim agreement leading to the formation of a customs union, the duties and other regulations of commerce imposed at the institution of any such union or interim agreement in respect of trade with contracting parties not parties to such union or agreement shall not on the whole be higher or more restrictive than the general incidence of the duties and regulations of commerce applicable in the constituent territories prior to the formation of such union or the adoption of such interim agreement, as the case may be;

(b) with respect to a free-trade area, or an interim agreement leading to the formation of a free-trade area, the duties and other regulations of commerce maintained in each of the constituent territories and applicable at the formation of such free-trade area or the adoption of such interim agreement to the trade of contracting parties not included in such area or not parties to such agreement shall not be higher or more restrictive than the corresponding duties and other regulations of commerce existing in the same constituent territories prior to the formation of the free-trade area, or interim agreement, as the case may be; and

(c) any interim agreement referred to in sub-paragraphs *(a)* and *(b)* shall include a plan and schedule for the formation of such a customs union or of such a free-trade area within a reasonable length of time.

6. If, in fulfilling the requirements of sub-paragraphs 5 *(a)*, a contracting party proposes to increase any rate of duty inconsistently with the provisions of Article II, the procedure set forth in Article XXVIII shall apply. In providing for compensatory adjustment, due account shall be taken of the compensation already afforded by the reductions brought about in the corresponding duty of the other constituents of the union.

7. *(a)* Any contracting party deciding to enter into a customs union or free-trade area, or an interim agreement leading to the formation of such a union or area, shall promptly notify the CONTRACTING PARTIES and shall make available to them such information regarding the proposed union or area as will enable them to make such reports and recommendations to contracting parties as they may deem appropriate.

(b) If, after having studied the plan and schedule included in an interim agreement referred to in paragraph 5 in consultation with the parties to that agreement and taking due account of the information made available in accordance with the provisions of sub-paragraph *(a)*, the CONTRACTING PARTIES find that such agreement is not likely to result in the formation of a customs union or of a free-trade area within the period contemplated by the parties to the agreement or that such period is not a reasonable one, the CONTRACTING PARTIES shall make recommendations to the parties to the agreement. The parties shall not maintain or put into force, as the case may be, such agreement if they are not prepared to modify it in accordance with these recommendations.

(c) Any substantial change in the plan or schedule referred to in paragraph 5*(c)* shall be communicated to the CONTRACTING PARTIES, which may request the contracting parties concerned to consult with them if the change seems likely to jeopardize or delay unduly the formation of the customs union or of the free-trade area.

8. For the purposes of this Agreement:

(a) A customs union shall be understood to mean the substitution of a single customs territory for two or more customs territories, so that
   (i) duties and other restrictive regulations of commerce (except, where necessary, those permitted under Articles XI, XII, XIII, XIV, XV and XX) are eliminated with respect to substantially all the trade between the constituent territories of the union or at least with respect to substantially all the trade in products originating in such territories, and,
   (ii) subject to the provisions of paragraph 9, substantially the same duties and other regulations of commerce are applied by each of the members of the union to the trade of territories not included in the union;

(b) A free-trade area shall be understood to mean a group of two or more customs territories in which the duties and other restrictive regulations of commerce (except, where necessary, those permitted under Articles XI, XII, XIII, XIV, XV and XX) are eliminated on substantially all the trade between the constituent territories in products originating in such territories.

9. The preferences referred to in paragraph 2 of Article I shall not be affected by the formation of a customs union or of a free-trade area but may be eliminated or adjusted by means of negotiations with contracting parties affected.* This procedure of negotiations with affected contracting parties shall, in particular, apply to the elimination of preferences required to conform with the provisions of paragraph 8 *(a)*(i) and paragraph 8 *(b)*.

10. The CONTRACTING PARTIES may by a two-thirds majority approve proposals which do not fully comply with the requirements of paragraphs 5 to 9 inclusive, provided that such proposals lead to the formation of a customs union or a free-trade area in the sense of this Article.

11. Taking into account the exceptional circumstances arising out of the establishment of India and Pakistan as independent States and recognizing the fact that they have long constituted an economic unit, the contracting parties agree that the provisions of this Agreement shall not prevent the two countries from entering into special arrangements with respect to the trade between them, pending the establishment of their mutual trade relations on a definitive basis.*

12. Each contracting party shall take such reasonable measures as may be available to it to ensure observance of the provisions of this Agreement by the regional and local governments and authorities within its territory.

Article XXV

Joint Action by the Contracting Parties

1. Representatives of the contracting parties shall meet from time to time for the purpose of giving effect to those provisions of this Agreement which involve joint action and, generally, with a view to facilitating the operation and furthering the objectives of this Agreement. Wherever reference is made in this Agreement to the contracting parties acting jointly they are designated as the CONTRACTING PARTIES.

2. The Secretary-General of the United Nations is requested to convene the first meeting of the CONTRACTING PARTIES, which shall take place not later than March 1, 1948.

3. Each contracting party shall be entitled to have one vote at all meetings of the CONTRACTING PARTIES.

4. Except as otherwise provided for in this Agreement, decisions of the CONTRACTING PARTIES shall be taken by a majority of the votes cast.

5. In exceptional circumstances not elsewhere provided for in this Agreement, the CONTRACTING PARTIES may waive an obligation imposed upon a contracting party by this Agreement; *Provided* that any such decision shall be approved by a two-thirds majority of the votes cast and that such majority shall comprise more than half of the contracting parties. The CONTRACTING PARTIES may also by such a vote

(i) define certain categories of exceptional circumstances to which other voting requirements shall apply for the waiver of obligations, and

(ii) prescribe such criteria as may be necessary for the application of this paragraph.†

Article XXVI

Acceptance, Entry into Force and Registration

1. The date of this Agreement shall be October 30, 1947.

2. This Agreement shall be open for acceptance by any contracting party which, on March 1, 1955, was a contracting party or was negotiating with a view to accession to this Agreement.

3. This Agreement, done in a single English original and in a single French original, both texts authentic, shall be deposited with the Secretary-General of the United Nations, who shall furnish certified copies thereof to all interested governments.

4. Each government accepting this Agreement shall deposit an instrument of acceptance with the Executive Secretary[1] to the CONTRACTING PARTIES, who will inform all interested governments of the date of

† The authentic text erroneously reads "sub-paragraph".

deposit of each instrument of acceptance and of the day on which this Agreement enters into force under paragraph 6 of this Article.

5. *(a)* Each government accepting this Agreement does so in respect of its metropolitan territory and of the other territories for which it has international responsibility, except such separate customs territories as it shall notify to the Executive Secretary to the CONTRACTING PARTIES at the time of its own acceptance.

(b) Any government, which has so notified the Executive Secretary under the exceptions in sub-paragraph *(a)* of this paragraph, may at any time give notice to the Executive Secretary that its acceptance shall be effective in respect of any separate customs territory or territories so excepted and such notice shall take effect on the thirtieth day following the day on which it is received by the Executive Secretary.

(c) If any of the customs territories, in respect of which a contracting party has accepted this Agreement, possesses or acquires full autonomy in the conduct of its external commercial relations and of the other matters provided for in this Agreement, such territory shall, upon sponsorship through a declaration by the responsible contracting party establishing the above-mentioned fact, be deemed to be a contracting party.

6. This Agreement shall enter into force, as among the governments which have accepted it, on the thirtieth day following the day on which instruments of acceptance have been deposited with the Executive Secretary to the CONTRACTING PARTIES on behalf of governments named in Annex H, the territories of which account for 85 per centum of the total external trade of the territories of such governments, computed in accordance with the applicable column of percentages set forth therein. The instrument of acceptance of each other government shall take effect on the thirtieth day following the day on which such instrument has been deposited.

7. The United Nations is authorized to effect registration of this Agreement as soon as it enters into force.

Article XXVII

Withholding or Withdrawal of Concessions

Any contracting party shall at any time be free to withhold or to withdraw in whole or in part of any concession, provided for in the appropriate Schedule annexed to this Agreement, in respect of which such contracting party determines that it was initially negotiated with a government which has not become, or has ceased to be, a contracting party. A contracting party taking such action shall notify the CONTRACTING PARTIES and, upon request, consult with contracting parties which have a substantial interest in the product concerned.

Article XXVIII*

Modification of Schedules

1. On the first day of each three-year period, the first period beginning on January 1, 1958 (or on the first day of any other period* that may be specified by the CONTRACTING PARTIES by two-thirds of the votes cast) a contracting party (hereafter in this Article referred to as the "applicant contracting party") may, by negotiation and agreement with any contracting party with which such concession was initially negotiated and with any other contracting party determined by the CONTRACTING PARTIES to have a principal supplying interest* (which two preceding categories of contracting parties, together with the applicant contracting party, are in this Article hereinafter referred to as the "contracting parties primarily concerned"), and subject to consultation with any other contracting party determined by the CONTRACTING PARTIES to have a substantial interest* in such concession, modify or withdraw a concession* included in the appropriate Schedule annexed to this Agreement.

2. In such negotiations and agreement, which may include provision for compensatory adjustment with respect to other products, the contracting parties concerned shall endeavor to maintain a general level of reciprocal and mutually advantageous concessions not less favorable to trade than that provided for in this Agreement prior to such negotiations.

3. *(a)* If agreement between the contracting parties primarily concerned cannot be reached before January 1, 1958 or before the expiration of a period envisaged in paragraph 1 of this Article, the contracting party which proposes to modify or withdraw the concession shall, nevertheless, be free to do so and if such action is taken any contracting party with which such concession was initially negotiated, any contracting party determined under paragraph 1 to have a principal supplying interest and any contracting party determined under paragraph 1 to

have a substantial interest shall then be free not later than six months after such action is taken, to withdraw, upon the expiration of thirty days from the day on which written notice of such withdrawal is received by the CONTRACTING PARTIES, substantially equivalent concessions initially negotiated with the applicant contracting party.

(b) If agreement between the contracting parties primarily concerned is reached but any other contracting party determined under paragraph 1 of this Article to have a substantial interest is not satisfied, such other contracting party shall be free, not later than six months after action under such agreement is taken, to withdraw, upon the expiration of thirty days from the day on which written notice of such withdrawal is received by the CONTRACTING PARTIES, substantially equivalent concessions initially negotiated with the applicant contracting party.

4. The CONTRACTING PARTIES may, at any time, in special circumstances, authorize* a contracting party to enter into negotiations for modification or withdrawal of a concession included in the appropriate Schedule annexed to this Agreement subject to the following procedures and conditions:

(a) Such negotiations* and any related consultations shall be conducted in accordance with the provisions of paragraphs 1 and 2 of this Article.

(b) If agreement between the contracting parties primarily concerned is reached in the negotiations, the provisions of paragraph 3*(b)* of this Article shall apply.

(c) If agreement between the contracting parties primarily concerned is not reached within a period of sixty days* after negotiations have been authorized, or within such longer period as the CONTRACTING PARTIES may have prescribed, the applicant contracting party may refer the matter to the CONTRACTING PARTIES.

(d) Upon such reference, the CONTRACTING PARTIES shall promptly examine the matter and submit their views to the contracting parties primarily concerned with the aim of achieving a settlement. If a settlement is reached, the provisions of paragraph 3 *(b)* shall apply as if agreement between the contracting parties primarily concerned had been reached. If no settlement is reached between the contracting parties primarily concerned, the applicant contracting party shall be free to modify or withdraw the concession, unless the CONTRACTING PARTIES determine that the applicant contracting party has unreasonably failed to offer adequate compensation.* If such action is taken, any contracting party with which the concession was initially negotiated, any contracting party determined under paragraph 4 *(a)* to have a principal supplying interest and any contracting party determined under paragraph 4 *(a)* to have a substantial interest, shall be free, not later than six months after such action is taken, to modify or withdraw, upon the expiration of thirty days from the day on which written notice of such withdrawal is received by the CONTRACTING PARTIES, substantially equivalent concessions initially negotiated with the applicant contracting party.

5. Before January 1, 1958 and before the end of any period envisaged in paragraph 1 a contracting party may elect by notifying the CONTRACTING PARTIES to reserve the right, for the duration of the next period, to modify the appropriate Schedule in accordance with the procedures of paragraphs 1 to 3. If a contracting party so elects, other contracting parties shall have the right, during the same period, to modify or withdraw, in accordance with the same procedures, concessions initially negotiated with that contracting party.

Article XXVIII bis

Tariff Negotiations

1. The contracting parties recognize that customs duties often constitute serious obstacles to trade; thus negotiations on a reciprocal and mutually advantageous basis, directed to the substantial reduction of the general level of tariffs and other charges on imports and exports and in particular to the reduction of such high tariffs as discourage the importation even of minimum quantities, and conducted with due regard to the objectives of this Agreement and the varying needs of individual contracting parties, are of great importance to the expansion of international trade. The CONTRACTING PARTIES may therefore sponsor such negotiations from time to time.

2. *(a)* Negotiations under this Article may be carried out on a selective product-by-product basis or by the application of such multilateral procedures as may be accepted by the contracting parties concerned. Such negotiations may be directed towards the reduction of duties, the binding of duties at then existing levels or undertakings that individual duties or the average duties on specified categories of products shall not

exceed specified levels. The binding against increase of low duties or of duty-free treatment shall, in principle, be recognized as a concession equivalent in value to the reduction of high duties.

(b) The contracting parties recognize that in general the success of multilateral negotiations would depend on the participation of all contracting parties which conduct a substantial proportion of their external trade with one another.

3. Negotiations shall be conducted on a basis which affords adequate opportunity to take into account:

(a) the needs of individual contacting parties and individual industries;

(b) the needs of less-developed countries for a more flexible use of tariff protection to assist their economic development and the special needs of these countries to maintain tariffs for revenue purposes; and

(c) all other relevant circumstances, including the fiscal,* developmental, strategic and other needs of the contracting parties concerned.

Article XXIX

The Relation of this Agreement to the Havana Charter

1. The contracting parties undertake to observe to the fullest extent of their executive authority the general principles of Chapters I to VI inclusive and of Chapter IX of the Havana Charter pending their acceptance of it in accordance with their constitutional procedures.*

2. Part II of this Agreement shall be suspended on the day on which the Havana Charter enters into force.

3. If by September 30, 1949, the Havana Charter has not entered into force, the contracting parties shall meet before December 31, 1949, to agree whether this Agreement shall be amended, supplemented or maintained.

4. If at any time the Havana Charter should cease to be in force, the CONTRACTING PARTIES shall meet as soon as practicable thereafter to agree whether this Agreement shall be supplemented, amended or maintained. Pending such agreement, Part II of this Agreement shall

again enter into force; *Provided* that the provisions of Part II other than Article XXIII shall be replaced, *mutatis mutandis,* in the form in which they then appeared in the Havana Charter; and *Provided* further that no contracting party shall be bound by any provisions which did not bind it at the time when the Havana Charter ceased to be in force.

5. If any contracting party has not accepted the Havana Charter by the date upon which it enters into force, the CONTRACTING PARTIES shall confer to agree whether, and if so in what way, this Agreement in so far as it affects relations between such contracting party and other contracting parties, shall be supplemented or amended. Pending such agreement the provisions of Part II of this Agreement shall, notwithstanding the provisions of paragraph 2 of this Article, continue to apply as between such contracting party and other contracting parties.

6. Contracting parties which are Members of the International Trade Organization shall not invoke the provisions of this Agreement so as to prevent the operation of any provision of the Havana Charter. The application of the principle underlying this paragraph to any contracting party which is not a Member of the International Trade Organization shall be the subject of an agreement pursuant to paragraph 5 of this Article.

Article XXX

Amendments

1. Except where provision for modification is made elsewhere in this Agreement, amendments to the provisions of Part I of this Agreement or to the provisions of Article XXIX or of this Article shall become effective upon acceptance by all the contracting parties, and other amendments to this Agreement shall become effective, in respect of those contracting parties which accept them, upon acceptance by two-thirds of the contracting parties and thereafter for each other contracting party upon acceptance by it.

2. Any contracting party accepting an amendment to this Agreement shall deposit an instrument of acceptance with the Secretary-General of the United Nations within such period as the CONTRACTING PARTIES may specify. The CONTRACTING PARTIES may decide that any amendment made effective under this Article is of such a nature that any contracting party which has not accepted it within a period specified by

the CONTRACTING PARTIES shall be free to withdraw from this Agreement, or to remain a contracting party with the consent of the CONTRACTING PARTIES.

Article XXXI

Withdrawal

Without prejudice to the provisions of paragraph 12 of Article XVIII, of Article XXIII or of paragraph 2 of Article XXX, any contracting party may withdraw from this Agreement, or may separately withdraw on behalf of any of the separate customs territories for which it has international responsibility and which at the time possesses full autonomy in the conduct of its external commercial relations and of the other matters provided for in this Agreement. The withdrawal shall take effect upon the expiration of six months from the day on which written notice of withdrawal is received by the Secretary-General of the United Nations.

Article XXXII

Contracting Parties

1. The contracting parties to this Agreement shall be understood to mean those governments which are applying the provisions of this Agreement under Articles XXVI or XXXIII or pursuant to the Protocol of Provisional Application.

2. At any time after the entry into force of this Agreement pursuant to paragraph 6 of Article XXVI, those contracting parties which have accepted this Agreement pursuant to paragraph 4 of Article XXVI may decide that any contracting party which has not so accepted it shall cease to be a contracting party.

Article XXXIII

Accession

A government not party to this Agreement, or a government acting on behalf of a separate customs territory possessing full autonomy in the conduct of its external commercial relations and of the other matters provided for in this Agreement, may accede to this Agreement, on its own behalf or on behalf of that territory, on terms to be agreed between such government and the CONTRACTING PARTIES. Decisions of the CONTRACTING PARTIES under this paragraph shall be taken by a two-thirds majority.

Article XXXIV

Annexes

The annexes to this Agreement are hereby made an integral part of this Agreement.

Article XXXV

Non-application of the Agreement between particular Contracting Parties

1. This Agreement, or alternatively Article II of this Agreement, shall not apply as between any contracting party and any other contracting party if:

(a) the two contracting parties have not entered into tariff negotiations with each other, and

(b) either of the contracting parties, at the time either becomes a contracting party, does not consent to such application.

2. The CONTRACTING PARTIES may review the operation of this Article in particular cases at the request of any contracting party and make appropriate recommendations.

PART IV*
TRADE AND DEVELOPMENT

Article XXXVI

Principles and Objectives

1. *The contracting parties,

(a) recalling that the basic objectives of this Agreement include the raising of standards of living and the progressive development of the economies of all contracting parties, and considering that the attainment of these objectives is particularly urgent for less-developed contracting parties;

(b) considering that export earnings of the less-developed contracting parties can play a vital part in their economic development and that the extent of this contribution depends on the prices paid by the less-developed contracting parties for essential imports, the volume of their exports, and the prices received for these exports;

(c) noting, that there is a wide gap between standards of living in less-developed countries and in other countries;

(d) recognizing that individual and joint action is essential to further the development of the economies of less-developed contracting parties and to bring about a rapid advance in the standards of living in these countries;

(e) recognizing that international trade as a means of achieving economic and social advancement should be governed by such rules and procedures—and measures in conformity with such rules and procedures—as are consistent with the objectives set forth in this Article;

(f) noting that the CONTRACTING PARTIES may enable less-developed contracting parties to use special measures to promote their trade and development;

agree as follows.

3. There is need for a rapid and sustained expansion of the export earnings of the less-developed contracting parties.

3. There is need for positive efforts designed to ensure that less-developed contracting parties secure a share in the growth in international trade commensurate with the needs of their economic development.

4. Given the continued dependence of many less-developed contracting parties on the exportation of a limited range of primary products,* there is need to provide in the largest possible measure more favorable and acceptable conditions of access to world markets for these products, and wherever appropriate to devise measures designed to stabilize and improve conditions of world markets in these products, including in particular measures designed to attain stable, equitable and remunerative prices, thus permitting an expansion of world trade and demand and a dynamic and steady growth of the real export earnings of these countries so as to provide them with expanding resources for their economic development.

5. The rapid expansion of the economies of the less-developed contracting parties will be facilitated by a diversification* of the structure of their economies and the avoidance of an excessive dependence on the export of primary products. There is, therefore, need for increased access in the largest possible measure to markets under favorable conditions for processed and manufactured products currently or potentially of particular export interest to less-developed contracting parties.

6. Because of the chronic deficiency in the export proceeds and other foreign exchange earnings of less-developed contracting parties, there are important inter-relationships between trade and financial assistance to development. There is, therefore, need for close and continuing collaboration between the CONTRACTING PARTIES and the international lending agencies so that they can contribute most effectively to alleviating the burdens these less-developed contracting parties assume in the interest of their economic development.

7. There is need for appropriate collaboration between the CONTRACTING PARTIES, other intergovernmental bodies and the organs and agencies of the United Nations system, whose activities relate to the trade and economic development of less-developed countries.

8. The developed contracting parties do not expect reciprocity for commitments made by them in trade negotiations to reduce or remove tariffs and other barriers to the trade of less-developed contracting parties.*

9. The adoption of measures to give effect to these principles and objectives shall be a matter of conscious and purposeful effort on the part of the contracting parties both individually and jointly.

Article XXXVII

Commitments

1. The developed contracting parties shall to the fullest extent possible—that is, except when compelling reasons, which may include legal reasons, make it impossible—give effect to the following provisions:

(a) Accord high priority to the reduction and elimination of barriers to products currently or potentially of particular export interest to less-developed contracting parties, including customs duties and other restrictions which differentiate unreasonably between such products in their primary and in their processed forms;*

(b) refrain from introducing, or increasing the incidence of, customs duties or non-tariff import barriers on products currently or potentially of particular export interest to less-developed contracting parties; and

(c) (i) refrain from imposing new fiscal measures, and
(ii) in any adjustments of fiscal policy accord high priority to the reduction and elimination of fiscal measures,

which would hamper, or which hamper, significantly the growth of consumption of primary products, in raw or processed form, wholly or mainly produced in the territories of less-developed contracting parties, and which are applied specifically to those products.

2. (a) Whenever it is considered that effect is not being given to any of the provisions of sub-paragraph *(a), (b)* or *(c)* or paragraph 1, the matter shall be reported to the CONTRACTING PARTIES either by the contracting party not so giving effect to the relevant provisions or by any other interested contracting party.

(b) (i) THE CONTRACTING PARTIES shall, if requested so to do by any interested contracting party, and without prejudice to any bilateral consultations that may be undertaken, consult with the

contracting party concerned and all interested contracting parties with respect to the matter with a view to reaching solutions satisfactory to all contracting parties concerned in order to further the objectives set forth in Article XXXVI. In the course of these consultations, the reasons given in cases where effect was not being given to the provisions of sub-paragraph *(a)*, *(b)* or *(c)* of paragraph 1 shall be examined.
(ii) As the implementation of the provisions of sub-paragraph *(a)*, *(b)* or *(c)* of paragraph 1 by individual contracting parties may in some cases be more readily achieved where action is taken jointly with other developed contracting parties, such consultation might, where appropriate, be directed towards this end.
(iii) The consultations by the CONTRACTING PARTIES might also, in appropriate cases, be directed towards agreement on joint action designed to further the objectives of this Agreement as envisaged in paragraph 1 of Article XXV.

3. The developed contracting parties shall:

(a) make every effort, in cases where a government directly or indirectly determines the resale price of products wholly or mainly produced in the territories of less-developed contracting parties, to maintain trade margins at equitable levels;

(b) give active consideration to the adoption of other measures* designed to provide greater scope for the development of imports from less-developed contracting parties and collaborate in appropriate international action to this end;

(c) have special regard to the trade interests of less-developed contracting parties when considering the application of other measures permitted under this Agreement to meet particular problems and explore all possibilities of constructive remedies before applying such measures where they would affect essential interests of those contracting parties.

4. Less-developed contracting parties agree to take appropriate action in implementation of the provisions of Part IV for the benefit of the trade of other less-developed contracting parties, in so far as such action is consistent with their individual present and future development, financial and trade needs taking into account past trade developments as well as the trade interests of less-developed contracting parties as a whole.

5. In the implementation of the commitments set forth in paragraphs 1 to 4 each contracting party shall afford to any other interested contracting party or contracting parties full and prompt opportunity for consultations under the normal procedures of this Agreement with respect to any matter or difficulty which may arise.

Article XXXVIII

Joint Action

1. The contracting parties shall collaborate jointly, within the framework of this Agreement and elsewhere, as appropriate, to further the objectives set forth in Article XXXVI.

2. In particular, the CONTRACTING PARTIES shall:

(a) where appropriate, take action, including action through international arrangements, to provide improved and acceptable conditions of access to world markets for primary products of particular interest to less-developed contracting parties and to devise measures designed to stabilize and improve conditions of world markets in these products including measures designed to attain stable, equitable and remunerative prices for exports of such products;

(b) seek appropriate collaboration in matters of trade and development policy with the United Nations and its organs and agencies, including any institutions that may be created on the basis of recommendations by the United Nations Conference on Trade and Development;

(c) collaborate in analysing the development plans and policies of individual less-developed contracting parties and in examining trade and aid relationships with a view to devising concrete measures to promote the development of export potential and to facilitate access to export markets for the products of the industries thus developed and, in this connexion, seek appropriate collaboration with governments and international organizations, and in particular with organizations having competence in relation to financial assistance for economic development, in systematic studies of trade and aid relationships in individual less-developed contracting parties aimed at obtaining a clear analysis of export potential, market prospects and any further action that may be required;

(d) keep under continuous review the development of world trade with special reference to the rate of growth of the trade of less-developed contracting parties and make such recommendations to contracting parties as may, in the circumstances, be deemed appropriate;

(e) collaborate in seeking feasible methods to expand trade for the purpose of economic development, through international harmonization and adjustment of national policies and regulations, through technical and commercial standards affecting production, transportation and marketing, and through export promotion by the establishment of facilities for the increased flow of trade information and the development of market research; and

(f) establish such institutional arrangements as may be necessary to further the objectives set forth in Article XXXVI and to give effect to the provisions of this Part.

ANNEX A

LIST OF TERRITORIES REFERRED TO IN PARAGRAPH 2*(a)* OF ARTICLE I

United Kingdom of Great Britain and Northern Ireland
Dependent territories of the United Kingdom of Great Britain and Northern Ireland
Canada
Commonwealth of Australia
Dependent territories of the Commonwealth of Australia
New Zealand
Dependent territories of New Zealand
Union of South Africa including South West Africa
Ireland
India (as on April 10, 1947)
Newfoundland
Southern Rhodesia
Burma
Ceylon

Certain of the territories listed above have two or more preferential rates in force for certain products. Any such territory may, by agreement with the other contracting parties which are principal suppliers of such products at the most-favored-nation rate, substitute for such preferential rates a single preferential rate which shall not on the whole be less favorable to suppliers at the most-favored-nation rate than the preferences in force prior to such substitution.

The imposition of an equivalent margin of tariff preference to replace a margin of preference in an internal tax existing on April 10, 1947 exclusively between two or more of the territories listed in this Annex or to replace the preferential quantitative arrangements described in the following paragraph, shall not be deemed to constitute an increase in a margin of tariff preference.

The preferential arrangements referred to in paragraph 5*(b)* of Article XIV are those existing in the United Kingdom on April 10, 1947, under contractual agreements with the Governments of Canada, Australia and New Zealand, in respect of chilled and frozen beef and veal, frozen mutton and lamb, chilled and frozen pork, and bacon. It is the intention, without prejudice to any action taken under sub-paragraph *(h)* † of Article XX, that these arrangements shall be eliminated or replaced by tariff preferences, and that negotiations to this end shall take place as soon as practicable among the countries substantially concerned or involved.

The film hire tax in force in New Zealand on April 10, 1947, shall, for the purposes of this Agreement, be treated as a customs duty under Article I. The renters' film quota in force in New Zealand on April 10, 1947, shall, for the purposes of this Agreement, be treated as a screen quota under Article IV.

The Dominions of India and Pakistan have not been mentioned separately in the above list since they had not come into existence as such on the base date of April 10, 1947.

ANNEX B

List of Territories of the French Union referred to in Paragraph 2*(b)* of Article I

France
French Equatorial Africa (Treaty Basin of the Congo[1] and other territories)
French West Africa
Cameroons under French Trusteeship[1]
French Somali Coast and Dependencies
French Establishments in Oceania
French Establishments in the Condominium of the New Hebrides[1]
Indo-China
Madagascar and Dependencies
Morocco (French zone)[1]
New Caledonia and Dependencies
Saint-Pierre and Miquelon
Togo under French Trusteeship[1]
Tunisia

† The authentic text erroneously reads "part I *(h)*"

[1]For imports into Metropolitan France and Territories of the French Union.

ANNEX C

LIST OF TERRITORIES REFERRED TO IN PARAGRAPH 2(*b*) OF ARTICLE I AS RESPECTS THE CUSTOMS UNION OF BELGUIM, LUXEMBURG AND THE NETHERLANDS

The Economic Union of Belgium and Luxemburg
Belgian Congo
Ruanda Urundi
Netherlands
New Guinea
Surinam
Netherlands Antilles
Republic of Indonesia

For imports into the territories constituting the Customs Union only.

ANNEX D

LIST OF TERRITORIES REFERRED TO IN PARAGRAPH 2(*b*) OF ARTICLE I AS RESPECTS THE UNITED STATES OF AMERICA

United States of America (customs territory)
Dependent territories of the United States of America
Republic of the Philippines

The imposition of an equivalent margin of tariff preference to replace a margin of preference in an internal tax existing on April 10, 1947, exclusively between two or more of the territories listed in this Annex shall not be deemed to constitute an increase in a margin of tariff preference.

ANNEX E

LIST OF TERRITORIES COVERED BY PREFERENTIAL ARRANGEMENTS BETWEEN CHILE AND NEIGHBORING COUNTRIES REFERRED TO IN PARAGRAPH 2(*d*) OF Article I

Preferences in force exclusively between Chile on the one hand, and

1. Argentina

2. Bolivia

3. Peru

on the other hand.

ANNEX F

List of Territories covered by Preferential Arrangements between Lebanon and Syria and Neighboring Countries referred to in Paragraph 2*(d)* of Article I

Preferences in force exclusively between the Lebano-Syrian Customs Union, on the one hand, and

1. Palestine

2. Transjordan

on the other hand.

ANNEX G

Dates establishing Maximum Margins of Preference referred to in Paragraph 4 † of Article I

Australia	October 15, 1946
Canada	July 1, 1939
France	January 1, 1939
Lebano-Syrian Customs Union	November 30, 1938
Union of South Africa	July 1, 1938
Southern Rhodesia	May 1, 1941

ANNEX H

Percentage Shares of Total External Trade to be Used for the Purpose of Making the Determination referred to in Article XXVI

(based on the average of 1949–1953)

† The authentic text erroneously reads "Paragraph 3".

ANNEX H

If, prior to the accession of the Government of Japan to the General Agreement, the present Agreement has been accepted by contracting parties the external trade of which under column I accounts for the percentage of such trade specified in paragraph 6 of Article XXVI, column I shall be applicable for the purposes of that paragraph. If the present Agreement has not been so accepted prior to the accession of the Government of Japan, column II shall be applicable for the purposes of that paragraph.

	Column I (Contracting parties on 1 March 1955)	*Column II* (Contracting parties on 1 March 1955 and Japan)
Australia	3.1	3.0
Austria	0.9	0.8
Belgium-Luxemburg	4.3	4.2
Brazil	2.5	2.4
Burma	0.3	0.3
Canada	6.7	6.5
Ceylon	0.5	0.5
Chile	0.6	0.6
Cuba	1.1	1.1
Czechoslovakia	1.4	1.4
Denmark	1.4	1.4
Dominican Republic	0.1	0.1
Finland	1.0	1.0
France	8.7	8.5
Germany, Federal Republic of	5.3	5.2
Greece	0.4	0.4
Haiti	0.1	0.1
India	2.4	2.4
Indonesia	1.3	1.3
Italy	2.9	2.8
Netherlands, Kingdom of the	4.7	4.6
New Zealand	1.0	1.0
Nicaragua	0.1	0.1
Norway	1.1	1.1
Pakistan	0.9	0.8
Peru	0.4	0.4
Rhodesia and Nyasaland	0.6	0.6
Sweden	2.5	2.4
Turkey	0.6	0.6
Union of South Africa	1.8	1.8
United Kingdom	20.3	19.8
United States of America	20.6	20.1
Uruguay	0.4	0.4
Japan	—	2.3
	100.0	100.0

Note: These percentages have been computed taking into account the trade of all territories in respect of which the General Agreement on Tariffs and Trade is applied.

ANNEX I

Notes and Supplementary Provisions

Ad Article I

Paragraph 1

The obligations incorporated in paragraph 1 of Article I by reference to paragraphs 2 and 4 of Article III and those incorporated in paragraph 2 *(b)* of Article II by reference to Article VI shall be considered as falling within Part II for the purposes of the Protocol of Provisional Application.

The cross-references, in the paragraph immediately above and in paragraph 1 of Article I, to paragraphs 2 and 4 of Article III shall only apply after Article III has been modified by the entry into force of the amendment provided for in the Protocol Modifying Part II and Article XXVI of the General Agreement on Tariffs and Trade, dated September 14, 1948.[1]

Paragraph 4

The term "margin of preference" means the absolute difference between the most-favored-nation rate of duty and the preferential rate of duty for the like product, and not the proportionate relation between those rates. As examples:

(1) If the most-favored-nation rate were 36 per cent *ad valorem* and the preferential rate were 24 per cent *ad volorem,* the margin of preference would be 12 per cent *ad valorem,* and not one-third of the most-favored-nation rate;

(2) If the most-favored-nation rate were 36 per cent *ad valorem* and the preferential rate were expressed as two-thirds of the most-favored-nation rate, the margin of preference would be 12 per cent *ad valorem;*

(3) If the most-favored-nation rate were 2 francs per kilogram and the preferential rate were 1.50 francs per kilogram, the margin of preference would be 0.50 franc per kilogram.

[1] This Protocol entered into force December 14, 1948.

The following kinds of customs action, taken in accordance with established uniform procedures, would not be contrary to a general binding of margins of preference:

(i) The re-application to an imported product of a tariff classification or rate of duty, properly applicable to such product, in cases in which the application of such classification or rate to such product was temporarily suspended or inoperative on April 10, 1947; and

(ii) The classification of a particular product under a tariff item other than that under which importations of that product were classified on April 10, 1947, in cases in which the tariff law clearly contemplates that such product may be classified under more than one tariff item.

Ad Article II

Paragraph 2(a)

The cross-reference, in paragraph 2(a) of Article II, to paragraph 2 of Article III shall only apply after Article III has been modified by the entry into force of the amendment provided for in the Protocol Modifying Part II and Article XXVI of the General Agreement on Tariffs and Trade, dated September 14, 1948.[1]

Paragraph 2(b)

See the note relating to paragraph 1 of Article I.

Paragraph 4

Except where otherwise specifically agreed between the contracting parties which initially negotiated the concession, the provisions of this paragraph will be applied in the light of the provisions of Article 31 of the Havana Charter.

Ad Article III

Any internal tax or other internal charge, or any law, regulation or requirement of the kind referred to in paragraph 1 which applies to an imported product and to the like domestic product and is collected or

[1] This Protocol entered into force December 14, 1948.

enforced in the case of the imported product at the time or point of importation, is nevertheless to be regarded as an internal tax or other internal charge, or a law, regulation or requirement of the kind referred to in paragraph 1, and is accordingly subject to the provisions of Article III.

Paragraph 1

The application of paragraph 1 to internal taxes imposed by local governments and authorities within the territory of a contracting party is subject to the provisions of the final paragraph of Article XXIV. The term "reasonable measures" in the last-mentioned paragraph would not require, for example, the repeal of existing national legislation authorizing local governments to impose internal taxes which, although technically inconsistent with the letter of Article III, are not in fact inconsistent with its spirit, if such repeal would result in a serious financial hardship for the local governments or authorities concerned. With regard to taxation by local governments or authorities which is inconsistent with both the letter and spirit of Article III, the term "reasonable measures" would permit a contracting party to eliminate the inconsistent taxation gradually over a transition period, if abrupt action would create serious administrative and financial difficulties.

Paragraph 2

A tax conforming to the requirements of the first sentence of paragraph 2 would be considered to be inconsistent with the provisions of the second sentence only in cases where competition was involved between, on the one hand, the taxed product and, on the other hand, a directly competitive or substitutable product which was not similarly taxed.

Paragraph 5

Regulations consistent with the provisions of the first sentence of paragraph 5 shall not be considered to be contrary to the provisions of the second sentence in any case in which all of the products subject to the regulations are produced domestically in substantial quantities. A regulation cannot be justified as being consistent with the provisions of the second sentence on the ground that the proportion or amount allocated to each of the products which are the subject of the regulation constitutes an equitable relationship between imported and domestic products.

Ad Article V

Paragraph 5

With regard to transportation charges, the principle laid down in paragraph 5 refers to like products being transported on the same route under like conditions.

Ad Article VI

Paragraph 1

1. Hidden dumping by associated houses (that is, the sale by an importer at a price below that corresponding to the price invoiced by an exporter with whom the importer is associated, and also below the price in the exporting country) constitutes a form of price dumping with respect to which the margin of dumping may be calculated on the basis of the price at which the goods are resold by the importer.

2. It is recognized that, in the case of imports from a country which has a complete or substantially complete monopoly of its trade and where all domestic prices are fixed by the State, special difficulties may exist in determining price comparability for the purposes of paragraph 1, and in such cases importing contracting parties may find it necessary to take into account the possibility that a strict comparison with domestic prices in such a country may not always be appropriate.

Paragraphs 2 and 3

1. As in many other cases in customs administration, a contracting party may require reasonable security (bond or cash deposit) for the payment of anti-dumping or countervailing duty pending final determination of the facts in any case of suspected dumping or subsidization.

2. Multiple currency practices can in certain circumstances constitute a subsidy to exports which may be met by countervailing duties under paragraph 3 or can constitute a form of dumping by means of a partial depreciation of a country's currency which may be met by action under paragraph 2. By "multiple currency practices" is meant practices by governments or sanctioned by governments.

Paragraph 6(b)

Waivers under the provisions of this sub-paragraph shall be granted only on application by the contracting party proposing to levy an anti-dumping or countervailing duty, as the case may be.

Ad Article VII

Paragraph 1

The expression "or other charges" is not to be regarded as including internal taxes or equivalent charges imposed on or in connexion with imported products.

Paragraph 2

1. It would be in conformity with Article VII to presume that "actual value" may be represented by the invoice price, plus any non-included charges for legitimate costs which are proper elements of "actual value" and plus any abnormal discount or other reduction from the ordinary competitive price.

2. It would be in conformity with Article VII, paragraph 2*(b)*, for a contracting party to construe the phrase "in the ordinary course of trade . . . under fully competitive conditions", as excluding any transaction wherein the buyer and seller are not independent of each other and price is not the sole consideration.

3. The standard of "fully competitive conditions" permits a contracting party to exclude from consideration prices involving special discounts limited to exclusive agents.

4. The wording of sub-paragraphs *(a)* and *(b)* permits a contracting party to determine the value for customs purposes uniformly either (1) on the basis of a particular exporter's prices of the imported merchandise, or (2) on the basis of the general price level of like merchandise.

Ad Article VIII

1. While Article VIII does not cover the use of multiple rates of exchange as such, paragraphs 1 and 4 condemn the use of exchange taxes or fees as a device for implementing multiple currency practices; if, however, a contracting party is using multiple currency exchange fees for balance of payments reasons with the approval of the International Monetary Fund, the provisions of paragraph 9*(a)* of Article XV fully safeguard its position.

2. It would be consistent with paragraph 1 if, on the importation of products from the territory of a contracting party into the territory of

another contracting party, the production of certificates of origin should only be required to the extent that is strictly indispensable.

Ad Articles XI, XII, XIII, XIV and XVIII

Throughout Articles XI, XII, XIII, XIV and XVIII, the terms "import restrictions" or "export restrictions" include restrictions made effective through state-trading operations.

Ad Article XI

Paragraph 2(c)

The term "in any form" in this paragraph covers the same products when in an early stage of processing and still perishable, which compete directly with the fresh product and if freely imported would tend to make the restriction on the fresh product ineffective.

Paragraph 2, last-sub paragraph

The term "special factors" includes changes in relative productive efficiency as between domestic and foreign producers, or as between different foreign producers, but not changes artificially brought about by means not permitted under the Agreement.

Ad Article XII

The CONTRACTING PARTIES shall make provision for the utmost secrecy in the conduct of any consultation under the provisions of this Article.

Paragraph 3(c) (i)

Contracting parties applying restrictions shall endeavor to avoid causing serious prejudice to exports of a commodity on which the economy of a contracting party is largely dependent.

Paragraph 4(b)

It is agreed that the date shall be within ninety days after the entry into force of the amendments of this Article effected by the Protocol Amending the Preamble and Parts II and III of this Agreement. However, should the CONTRACTING PARTIES find that conditions were not suitable for the application of the provisions of this sub-paragraph at the time envisaged, they may determine a later date; *Provided* that such date is not more than thirty days after such time as the obligations of Article VIII, Sections 2, 3 and 4, of the Articles of Agreement of the International Monetary Fund become applicable to contracting parties, members of the Fund, the combined foreign trade of which constitutes at least fifty per centum of the aggregate foreign trade of all contracting parties.

Paragraph 4(e)

It is agreed that paragraph 4*(e)* does not add any new criteria for the imposition or maintenance of quantitative restrictions for balance of payments reasons. It is solely intended to ensure that all external factors such as changes in the terms of trade, quantitative restrictions, excessive tariffs and subsidies, which may be contributing to the balance of payments difficulties of the contracting party applying restrictions, will be fully taken into account.

Ad Article XIII

Paragraph 2(d)

No mention was made of "commercial considerations" as a rule for the allocation of quotas because it was considered that its application by governmental authorities might not always be practicable. Moreover, in cases where it is practicable, a contracting party could apply these considerations in the process of seeking agreement, consistently with the general rule laid down in the opening sentence of paragraph 2.

Paragraph 4

See note relating to "special factors" in connexion with the last sub-paragraph of paragraph 2 of Article XI.

Ad Article XIV

Paragraph 1

The provisions of this paragraph shall not be so construed as to preclude full consideration by the CONTRACTING PARTIES, in the consultations provided for in paragraph 4 of Article XII and in paragraph 12 of Article XVIII, of the nature, effects and reasons for discrimination in the field of import restrictions.

Paragraph 2

One of the situations contemplated in paragraph 2 is that of a contracting party holding balances acquired as a result of current transactions which it finds itself unable to use without a measure of discrimination.

Ad Article XV

Paragraph 4

The word "frustrate" is intended to indicate, for example, that infringements of the letter of any Article of this Agreement by exchange action shall not be regarded as a violation of that Article if, in practice, there is no appreciable departure from the intent of the Article. Thus, a contracting party which, as part of its exchange control operated in accordance with the Articles of Agreement of the International Monetary Fund, requires payment to be received for its exports in its own currency or in the currency of one or more members of the International Monetary Fund will not thereby be deemed to contravene Article XI or Article XIII. Another example would be that of a contracting party which specifies on an import license the country from which the goods may be imported, for the purpose not of introducing any additional element of discrimination in its import licensing system but of enforcing permissible exchange controls.

Ad Article XVI

The exemption of an exported product from duties or taxes borne by the like product when destined for domestic consumption, or the remission of such duties or taxes in amounts not in excess of those which have accrued, shall not be deemed to be a subsidy.

Section B

1. Nothing in Section B shall preclude the use by a contracting party of multiple rates of exchange in accordance with the Articles of Agreement of the International Monetary Fund.

2. For the purposes of Section B, a "primary product" is understood to be any product of farm, forest or fishery, or any mineral, in its natural form or which has undergone such processing as is customarily required to prepare it for marketing in substantial volume in international trade.

Paragraph 3

1. The fact that a contracting party has not exported the product in question during the previous representative period would not in itself preclude that contracting party from establishing its right to obtain a share of the trade in the product concerned.

2. A system for the stabilization of the domestic price or of the return to domestic producers of a primary product independently of the movements of export prices, which results at times in the sale of the product for export at a price lower than the comparable price charged for the like product to buyers in the domestic market, shall be considered not to involve a subsidy on exports within the meaning of paragraph 3 if the CONTRACTING PARTIES determine that:

(a) the system has also resulted, or is so designed as to result, in the sale of the product for export at a price higher than the comparable price charged for the like product to buyers in the domestic market; and

(b) the system is so operated, or is designed so to operate, either because of the effective regulation of production or otherwise, as not to stimulate exports unduly or otherwise seriously to prejudice the interests of other contracting parties.

Notwithstanding such determination by the CONTRACTING PARTIES, operations under such a system shall be subject to the provisions of paragraph 3 where they are wholly or partly financed out of government funds in addition to the funds collected from producers in respect of the product concerned.

Paragraph 4

The intention of paragraph 4 is that the contracting parties should seek before the end of 1957 to reach agreement to abolish all remaining subsidies as from January 1, 1958; or, failing this, to reach agreement to extend the application of the standstill until the earliest date thereafter by which they can expect to reach such agreement.

Ad Article XVII

Paragraph 1

The operations of Marketing Boards, which are established by contracting parties and are engaged in purchasing or selling, are subject to the provisions of sub-paragraphs *(a)* and *(b)*.

The activities of Marketing Boards which are established by contracting parties and which do not purchase or sell but lay down regulations covering private trade are governed by the relevant Articles of this Agreement.

The charging by a state enterprise of different prices for its sales of a product in different markets is not precluded by the provisions of this Article, provided that such different prices are charged for commercial reasons, to meet conditions of supply and demand in export markets.

Paragraph 1(a)

Governmental measures imposed to ensure standards of quality and efficiency in the operation of external trade, or privileges granted for the exploitation of national natural resources but which do not empower the government to exercise control over the trading activities of the enterprise in question, do not constitute "exclusive or special privileges".

Paragraph 1(b)

A country receiving a "tied loan" is free to take this loan into account as a "commercial consideration" when purchasing requirements abroad.

Paragraph 2

The term "goods" is limited to products as understood in commercial practice, and is not intended to include the purchase or sale of services.

Paragraph 3

Negotiations which contracting parties agree to conduct under this paragraph may be directed towards the reduction of duties and other charges on imports and exports or towards the conclusion of any other mutually satisfactory arrangement consistent with the provisions of this Agreement. (See paragraph 4 of Article II and the note to that paragraph.)

Paragraph 4(b)

The term "import mark-up" in this paragraph shall represent the margin by which the price charged by the import monopoly for the imported product (exclusive of internal taxes within the purview of Article III, transportation, distribution, and other expenses incident to the purchase, sale or further processing, and a reasonable margin of profit) exceeds the landed cost.

Ad Article XVIII

The CONTRACTING PARTIES and the contracting parties concerned shall preserve the utmost secrecy in respect of matters arising under this Article.

Paragraphs 1 and 4

1. When they consider whether the economy of a contracting party "can only support low standards of living", the CONTRACTING PARTIES shall take into consideration the normal position of that economy and shall not base their determination on exceptional circumstances such as those which may result from the temporary existence of exceptionally favorable conditions for the staple export product or products of such contracting party.

2. The phrase "in the early stages of development" is not meant to apply only to contracting parties which have just started their economic development, but also to contracting parties the economies of which are undergoing a process of industrialization to correct an excessive dependence on primary production.

Paragraphs 2, 3, 7, 13 and 22

The reference to the establishment of particular industries shall apply not only to the establishment of a new industry, but also to the establishment of a new branch of production in an existing industry and to the substantial transformation of an existing industry, and to the substantial expansion of an existing industry supplying a relatively small proportion of the domestic demand. It shall also cover the reconstruction of an industry destroyed or substantially damaged as a result of hostilities or natural disasters.

Paragraph 7(b)

A modification or withdrawal, pursuant to paragraph 7*(b)*, by a contracting party, other than the applicant contracting party, referred to in paragraph 7*(a)*, shall be made within six months of the day on which the action is taken by the applicant contracting party, and shall become effective on the thirtieth day following the day on which such modification or withdrawal has been notified to the CONTRACTING PARTIES.

Paragraph 11

The second sentence in paragraph 11 shall not be interpreted to mean that a contracting party is required to relax or remove restrictions if such relaxation or removal would thereupon produce conditions justifying the intensification or institution, respectively, or restrictions under paragraph 9 or Article XVIII.

Paragraph 12(b)

The date referred to in paragraph 12*(b)* shall be the date determined by the CONTRACTING PARTIES in accordance with paragraph 4*(b)* of Article XII of this Agreement.

Paragraphs 13 and 14

It is recognized that, before deciding on the introduction of a measure and notifying the CONTRACTING PARTIES in accordance with paragraph 14, a contracting party may need a reasonable period of time to assess the competitive position of the industry concerned.

Paragraphs 15 and 16

It is understood that the CONTRACTING PARTIES shall invite a contracting party proposing to apply a measure under Section C to consult with them pursuant to paragraph 16 if they are requested to do so by a contracting party the trade of which would be appreciably affected by the measure in question.

Paragraphs 16, 18, 19 and 22

1. It is understood that the CONTRACTING PARTIES may concur in a proposed measure subject to specific conditions or limitations. If the measure as applied does not conform to the terms of the concurrence it will to that extent be deemed a measure in which the CONTRACTING PARTIES have not concurred. In cases in which the CONTRACTING PARTIES have concurred in a measure for a specified period, the contracting party concerned, if it finds that the maintenance of the measure for a further period of time is required to achieve the objective for which

the measure was originally taken, may apply to the CONTRACTING PARTIES for an extension of that period in accordance with the provisions and procedures of Section C or D, as the case may be.

2. It is expected that the CONTRACTING PARTIES will, as a rule, refrain from concurring in a measure which is likely to cause serious prejudice to exports of a commodity on which the economy of a contracting party is largely dependent.

Paragraphs 18 and 22

The phrase "that the interests of other contracting parties are adequately safeguarded" is meant to provide latitude sufficient to permit consideration in each case of the most appropriate method of safeguarding those interests. The appropriate method may, for instance, take the form of an additional concession to be applied by the contracting party having recourse to Section C or D during such time as the deviation from the other Articles of the Agreement would remain in force or of the temporary suspension by any other contracting party referred to in paragraph 18 of a concession substantially equivalent to the impairment due to the introduction of the measure in question. Such contracting party would have the right to safeguard its interests through such a temporary suspension of a concession; *Provided* that this right will not be exercised when, in the case of a measure imposed by a contracting party coming within the scope of paragraph 4*(a)*, the CONTRACTING PARTIES have determined that the extent of the compensatory concession proposed was adequate.

Paragraph 19

The provisions of paragraph 19 are intended to cover the cases where an industry has been in existence beyond the "reasonable period of time" referred to in the note to paragraphs 13 and 14, and should not be so construed as to deprive a contracting party coming within the scope of paragraph 4*(a)* of Article XVIII, of its right to resort to the other provisions of Section C, including paragraph 17, with regard to a newly established industry even though it has benefited from incidental protection afforded by balance of payments import restrictions.

Paragraph 21

Any measure taken pursuant to the provisions of paragraph 21 shall be withdrawn forthwith if the action taken in accordance with paragraph

17 is withdrawn or if the CONTRACTING PARTIES concur in the measure proposed after the expiration of the ninety-day time limit specified in paragraph 17.

Ad Article XX

Sub-paragraph (h)

The exception provided for in this sub-paragraph extends to any commodity agreement which conforms to the principles approved by the Economic and Social Council in its resolution 30(IV) of 28 March 1947.

Ad Article XXIV

Paragraph 9

It is understood that the provisions of Article I would require that, when a product which has been imported into the territory of a member of a customs union or free-trade area at a preferential rate of duty is re-exported to the territory of another member of such union or area, the latter member should collect a duty equal to the difference between the duty already paid and any higher duty that would be payable if the product were being imported directly into its territory.

Paragraph 11

Measures adopted by India and Pakistan in order to carry out definitive trade arrangements between them, once they have been agreed upon, might depart from particular provisions of this Agreement, but these measures would in general be consistent with the objectives of the Agreement.

Ad Article XXVIII

The CONTRACTING PARTIES and each contracting party concerned should arrange to conduct the negotiations and consultations with the greatest possible secrecy in order to avoid premature disclosure of details of prospective tariff changes. The CONTRACTING PARTIES shall be informed immediately of all changes in national tariffs resulting from recourse to this Article.

Paragraph 1

1. If the CONTRACTING PARTIES specify a period other than a three-year period, a contracting party may act pursuant to paragraph 1 or paragraph 3 of Article XXVIII on the first day following the expiration of such other period and, unless the CONTRACTING PARTIES have again specified another period, subsequent periods will be three-year periods following the expiration of such specified period.

2. The provision that on January 1, 1958, and on other days determined pursuant to paragraph 1, a contracting party "may . . . modify or withdraw a concession" means that on such day, and on the first day after the end of each period, the legal obligation of such contracting party under Article II is altered; it does not mean that the changes in its customs tariff should necessarily be made effective on that day. If a tariff change resulting from negotiations undertaken pursuant to this Article is delayed, the entry into force of any compensatory concessions may be similarly delayed.

3. Not earlier than six months, nor later than three months, prior to January 1, 1958, or to the termination date of any subsequent period, a contracting party wishing to modify or withdraw any concession embodied in the appropriate Schedule, should notify the CONTRACTING PARTIES to this effect. The CONTRACTING PARTIES shall then determine the contracting party or contracting parties with which the negotiations or consultations referred to in paragraph 1 shall take place. Any contracting party so determined shall participate in such negotiations or consultations with the applicant contracting party with the aim of reaching agreement before the end of the period. Any extension of the assured life of the Schedules shall relate to the Schedules as modified after such negotiations, in accordance with paragraphs 1, 2 and 3 of Article XXVIII. If the CONTRACTING PARTIES are arranging for multilateral tariff negotiations to take place within the period of six months before January 1, 1958, or before any other day determined pursuant to paragraph 1, they shall include in the arrangements for such negotiations suitable procedures for carrying out the negotiations referred to in this paragraph.

4. The object of providing for the participation in the negotiations of any contracting party with a principal supplying interest, in addition to any contracting party with which the concession was initially negotiated, is to ensure that a contracting party with a larger share in the trade affected by the concession than a contracting party with which the

concession was initially negotiated shall have an effective opportunity to protect the contractual right which it enjoys under this Agreement. On the other hand, it is not intended that the scope of the negotiations should be such as to make negotiations and agreement under Article XXVIII unduly difficult nor to create complications in the application of this Article in the future to concessions which result from negotiations thereunder. Accordingly, the CONTRACTING PARTIES should only determine that a contracting party has a principal supplying interest if that contracting party has had, over a reasonable period of time prior to the negotiations, a larger share in the market of the applicant contracting party than a contracting party with which the concession was initially negotiated or would, in the judgment of the CONTRACTING PARTIES, have had such a share in the absence of discriminatory quantitative restrictions maintained by the applicant contracting party. It would therefore not be appropriate for the CONTRACTING PARTIES to determine that more than one contracting party, or in those exceptional cases where there is near equality more than two contracting parties, had a principal supplying interest.

5. Notwithstanding the definition of a principal supplying interest in note 4 to paragraph 1, the CONTRACTING PARTIES may exceptionally determine that a contracting party has a principal supplying interest if the concession in question affects trade which constitutes a major part of the total exports of such contracting party.

6. It is not intended that provision for participation in the negotiations of any contracting party with a principal supplying interest, and for consultation with any contracting party having a substantial interest in the concession which the applicant contracting party is seeking to modify or withdraw, should have the effect that it should have to pay compensation or suffer retaliation greater than the withdrawal or modification sought, judged in the light of the conditions of trade at the time of the proposed withdrawal or modification, making allowance for any discriminatory quantitative restrictions maintained by the applicant contracting party.

7. The expression "substantial interest" is not capable of a precise definition and accordingly may present difficulties for the CONTRACTING PARTIES. It is, however, intended to be construed to cover only those contracting parties which have, or in the absence of discriminatory quantitative restrictions affecting their exports could reasonably be expected to have, a significant share in the market of the contracting party seeking to modify or withdraw the concession.

Paragraph 4

1. Any request for authorization to enter into negotiations shall be accompanied by all relevant statistical and other data. A decision on such request shall be made within thirty days of its submission.

2. It is recognized that to permit certain contracting parties, depending in large measure on a relatively small number of primary commodities and relying on the tariff as an important aid for furthering diversification of their economics or as an important source of revenue, normally to negotiate for the modification or withdrawal of concessions only under paragraph 1 of Article XXVIII, might cause them at such a time to make modifications or withdrawals which in the long run would prove unnecessary. To avoid such a situation the CONTRACTING PARTIES shall authorize any such contracting party, under paragraph 4, to enter into negotiations unless they consider this would result in, or contribute substantially towards, such an increase in tariff levels as to threaten the stability of the Schedules to this Agreement or lead to undue disturbance of international trade.

3. It is expected that negotiations authorized under paragraph 4 for modification or withdrawal of a single item, or a very small group of items, could normally be brought to a conclusion in sixty days. It is recognized, however, that such a period will be inadequate for cases involving negotiations for the modification or withdrawal of a larger number of items and in such cases, therefore, it would be appropriate for the CONTRACTING PARTIES to prescribe a longer period.

4. The determination referred to in paragraph 4*(d)* shall be made by the CONTRACTING PARTIES within thirty days of the submission of the matter to them unless the applicant contracting party agrees to a longer period.

5. In determining under paragraph 4*(d)* whether an applicant contracting party has unreasonably failed to offer adequate compensation, it is understood that the CONTRACTING PARTIES will take due account of the special position of a contracting party which has bound a high proportion of its tariffs at very low rates of duty and to this extent has less scope than other contracting parties to make compensatory adjustment.

Ad Article XXVIII bis

Paragraph 3

It is understood that the reference to fiscal needs would include the revenues aspect of duties and particularly duties imposed primarily for revenue purpose, or duties imposed on products which can be substituted for products subject to revenue duties to prevent the avoidance of such duties.

Ad Article XXIX

Paragraph 1

Chapters VII and VIII of the Havana Charter has been excluded from paragraph 1 because they generally deal with the organization, functions and procedures of the International Trade Organization.

Ad Part IV

The words "developed contracting parties" and the words "less-developed contracting parties" as used in Part IV are to be understood to refer to developed and less-developed countries which are parties to the General Agreement on Tariffs and Trade.

Ad Article XXXVI

Paragraph 1

This Article is based upon the objectives set forth in Article I as it will be amended by Section A of paragraph 1 of the Protocol Amending Part I and Articles XXIX and XXX when that Protocol enters into force.[1]

Paragraph 4

The term "primary products" includes agricultural products, *vide* paragraph 2 of the note ad Article XVI, Section B.

[1] This Protocol was abandoned on January 1, 1968.

Paragraph 5

A diversification program would generally include the intensification of activities for the processing of primary products and the development of manufacturing industries, taking into account the situation of the particular contracting party and the world outlook for production and consumption of different commodities.

Paragraph 8

It is understood that the phrase "do not expect reciprocity" means, in accordance with the objectives set forth in this Article, that the less-developed contracting parties should not be expected, in the course of trade negotiations, to make contributions which are inconsistent with their individual development, financial and trade needs, taking into consideration past trade developments.

This paragraph would apply in the event of action under Section A of Article XVIII, Article XXVIII, Article XXVIII *bis* (Article XXIX after the amendment set forth in Section A of paragraph 1 of the Protocol Amending Part I and Articles XXIX and XXX shall have become effective[1]), Article XXXIII, or any other procedure under this Agreement.

_Ad_ Article XXXVII

Paragraph 1(a)

This paragraph would apply in the event of negotiations for reduction or elimination of tariffs or other restrictive regulations of commerce under Articles XXVIII, XXVIII *bis* (XXIX after the amendment set forth in Section A of paragraph 1 of the Protocol Amending Part I and Articles XXIX and XXX shall have become effective[1]), and Article XXXIII, as well as in connexion with other action to effect such reduction or elimination which contracting parties may be able to undertake.

Paragraph 3(b)

The other measures referred to in this paragraph might include steps to promote domestic structural changes, to encourage the consumption of particular products, or to introduce measures of trade promotion.

[1] This Protocol was abandoned on January 1, 1968.

PROTOCOL OF PROVISIONAL APPLICATION OF THE GENERAL AGREEMENT ON TARIFFS AND TRADE

1. The Governments of the COMMONWEALTH OF AUSTRALIA, the KINGDOM OF BELGIUM (in respect of its metropolitan territory), CANADA, the FRENCH REPUBLIC (in respect of its metropolitan territory), the GRAND-DUCHY OF LUXEMBURG, the KINGDOM OF THE NETHERLANDS (in respect of its metropolitan territory), the UNITED KINGDOM OF GREAT BRITAIN AND NORTHERN IRELAND (in respect of its metropolitan territory), and the UNITED STATES OF AMERICA, undertake, provided that this Protocol shall have been signed on behalf of all the foregoing Governments not later than November 15, 1947, to apply provisionally on and after January 1, 1948:

(a) Parts I and III of the General Agreement on Tariffs and Trade, and

(b) Part II of that Agreement to the fullest extent not inconsistent with existing legislation.

2. The foregoing Governments shall make effective such provisional application of the General Agreement, in respect of any of their territories other than their metropolitan territories, on or after January 1, 1948, upon the expiration of thirty days from the day on which notice of such application is received by the Secretary-General of the United Nations.

3. Any other government signatory to this Protocol shall make effective such provisional application of the General Agreement, on or after January 1, 1948, upon the expiration of thirty days from the day of signature of this Protocol on behalf of such Government.

4. This Protocol shall remain open for signature at the Headquarters of the United Nations *(a)* until November 15, 1947, on behalf of any government named in paragraph 1 of this Protocol which has not signed it on this day, and *(b)* until June 30, 1948, on behalf of any other Government signatory to the Final Act adopted at the conclusion of the Second Session of the Preparatory Committee of the United Nations Conference on Trade and Employment which has not signed it on this day.

5. Any government applying this Protocol shall be free to withdraw such application, and such withdrawal shall take effect upon the expira-

tion of sixty days from the day on which written notice of such withdrawal is received by the Secretary-General of the United Nations.

6. The original of this Protocol shall be deposited with the Secretary-General of the United Nations, who will furnish certified copies thereof to all interested Governments.

IN WITNESS WHEREOF the respective Representatives, after having communicated their full powers, found to be in good and due form, have signed the Protocol.

DONE at Geneva, in a single copy, in the English and French languages, both texts authentic, this thirtieth day of October one thousand nine hundred and forty-seven.

DOCUMENTS RELATING TO DISPUTE SETTLEMENT PROCEDURES

1955 REPORT ON ORGANIZATIONAL AND FUNCTIONAL QUESTIONS BISD 3S/250

PROPOSALS RELATING TO VARIOUS ARTICLES AND LEGAL QUESTIONS

* * *

Article XXIII

62. The Working Party discussed proposals by the Governments of Denmark, Norway and Sweden to add an interpretative note to paragraph 2 of Article XXIII. The representative of the Scandinavian countries, when introducing the proposal, stressed that action by the CONTRACTING PARTIES under Article XXIII should be directed towards the maintenance of a general level of reciprocal and mutually advantageous concessions not less favorable to trade than that provided for in the original situation; it was, therefore, desirable that resort should be had to retaliatory action only when all other possibilities had been explored.

63. The proposal was withdrawn in the light of the agreement by the Working Party that, subject to the qualifications explained in the following paragraph the principle set out in the proposed interpretative note conformed with both the intention of the Article and the practice the CONTRACTING PARTIES had hitherto followed in applying its provisions. The Working Party considered that the requirement in paragraph 2 of the Article that the circumstances must be "serious enough" limits the possibility of authorizing a contracting party or parties to take appropriate retaliatory action to cases where endeavours to solve the problem through the withdrawal of the measures causing the damage, the substitution of other concessions, or some other appropriate action have not proved to be possible, and where there is considered to be a substantial justification for retaliatory action, as in cases in which such authorization appears to be the only means either of preventing serious economic consequences to the country for which a benefit has been nullified or impaired, or the only means of restoring the original situation.

64. Furthermore, the Working Party felt that any implication (such as had existed in the Scandinavian proposal) that the provision of appro-

priate compensation, on the one hand, and the removal of a measure inconsistent with the Agreement, on the other hand, are fully equivalent and satisfactory alternatives would not accord with the intent and spirit of the Article. In their view, the first objective if the CONTRACTING PARTIES decided, in the event of a complaint under Article XXIII, that certain measures were inconsistent with provisions of the Agreement, should be to secure the withdrawal of the measures. In such a case, the alternative of providing compensation for damage suffered should be resorted to only if the immediate withdrawal of the measures was impracticable and only as a temporary measure pending the withdrawal of the measures which were inconsistent with the Agreement.

1966 REPORT ON TRADE AND DEVELOPMENT
BISD 14S/139

IX. Legal Amendments to the General Agreement

40. On the instructions of the CONTRACTING PARTIES, the Committee has dealt with outstanding issues relating to the amendment of the General Agreement to meet the special trade and development needs of less-developed countries which were not finished by the former Committee on Legal and Institutional Framework. The Ad Hoc Group on Legal Amendments, established by the Committee in 1965 to deal with these matters, has submitted an interim report (COM.TD/F/4). The Committee has further discussed the various proposals in the light of the findings of the Group and wishes to report on the two subjects of:

(a) amendment of Article XXIII to take account of difficulties experienced by less-developed countries in using that Article, and

(b) amendment of Article XVIII to authorize the use of surcharges by less-developed countries for balance-of-payment reasons.

(a) Article XXIII

41. The work on this subject has been based on a proposal introduced by the Brazilian and Uruguayan delegations for amending Article XXIII. Their proposal had four elements: (i) the present arrangement for action under paragraph 2 of Article XXIII should be elaborated in a way which would give less-developed countries invoking the Article the option of employing certain additional measures; (ii) where it has been established that measures complained of have adversely affected the trade and economic prospects of less-developed countries and it has not been possible to eliminate the measure or obtain adequate commercial remedy, compensation in the form of an indemnity of a financial character would be in order; (iii) in cases where the import capacity of a less-developed country has been impaired by the maintenance of measures by a developed country contrary to the provisions of the GATT, the less-developed country concerned shall be automatically released from its obligations under the General Agreement towards the developed country complained of, pending examination of the matter in GATT; and (iv) in the event that a recommendation by the CONTRACTING

PARTIES to a developed country is not carried out within a given time-limit, the CONTRACTING PARTIES shall consider what collective action they could take to obtain compliance with their recommendation.

42. At an early stage of discussion, the Brazilian and Uruguayan delegations reformulated their proposals in the form of a draft decision, with a view to expediting its adoption since an amendment would have to go through long constitutional procedures in national legislatures.

43. The sponsors of the proposal explained that the intention behind the proposal was to streamline and to set out clearly the procedures so as to speed up action under that Article XXIII and to go some way towards redressing the unequal bargaining position of less-developed countries vis-à-vis developed countries in proceedings under that Article.

44. On the basis of the discussions in the Ad Hoc Group, the Committee has drawn up a revised draft decision which embodied the agreement reached in the Committee on procedures for more speedy and efficient use of the provisions of Article XXIII by less-developed contracting parties. This revised text is contained in Annex I to the report.[1]

45. Less-developed countries, while agreeing that the procedures embodied in the draft decision represented a positive step forward, felt that their fundamental concerns had not really been met. The Brazilian and Uruguayan delegations, in particular, stated that, while they would accept the compromise reached on point (iv) and reflected in paragraph 10 of the draft decision, they could agree to the proposed draft decision only on the understanding that further work would be done with a view to resolving the two issues mentioned in (ii) and (iii) above. The developed contracting parties had no objection to these issues being given further consideration in the Ad Hoc Group, but were unable to accept the proposed texts in question for various reasons which have been stated in the report of the Ad Hoc Group.

46. In agreeing that the annexed draft decision should be presented to the CONTRACTING PARTIES for adoption, the Committee also agreed that further work with regard to the two outstanding issues dealt with in the text of the two paragraphs reproduced in Annex II of the present report should be continued in the Ad Hoc Group on Legal Amendments.

[1] The Decision was adopted by the CONTRACTING PARTIES on April 5, 1966, and appears on page [D3/1]; accordingly, Annex I of the report is not reproduced [here.]

47. The Committee agreed that the phrase "shall consider what measures" in paragraph 10 of the draft decision is intended to mean that the CONTRACTING PARTIES shall consider the matter with a view to finding appropriate solution.[2]

[2] The Chairman of the Committee on Trade and Development, in presenting the draft decision to the CONTRACTING PARTIES for adoption, asked to be placed on record the following understanding regarding its provisions:

(1) In consultations to be carried out by the Director-General under paragraph 3 of the draft decision, the Director-General would, in addition to the entities mentioned in that paragraph, be free to consult such experts as he considered would assist him in studying the facts and in finding solutions.

(2) With respect to paragraph 6 of the draft decision, the CONTRACTING PARTIES may provide more particular terms of reference for any such panel in order to assist them to assess the relative impact of the measures complained of on the economics of the contracting parties concerned and to consider the adequacy of any measure which those contracting parties would be prepared to take to remedy the situation. In establishing such particular terms of reference, the CONTRACTING PARTIES or the Council should bear in mind the desirability of having such panels appraise, in particular,the following elements:

(a) the damage incurred through the incidence of the measures complained of upon the export earnings and economic effort of the less-developed contracting party;

(b) the compensatory or remedial measures which the contracting party whose measures are complained of would be prepared to take to make good the damage inflicted by their application;

(c) the effects of such measures as the injured contracting party would be prepared to take in relation to the contracting party whose measures have nullified or impaired the benefits deriving from the General Agreement which the former contracting party is entitled to expect.

1966 DECISION ON PROCEDURES UNDER ARTICLE XXIII
BISD 14S/18

The CONTRACTING PARTIES,

Recognizing that the prompt settlement of situations in which a contracting party considers that any benefits accruing to it directly or indirectly from the General Agreement are being impaired by measures taken by another contracting party, is essential to the effective functioning of the General Agreement and the maintenance of a proper balance between the rights and obligations of all contracting parties;

Recognizing further that the existence of such a situation can cause severe damage to the trade and economic development of the less-developed contracting parties; and

Affirming their resolve to facilitate the solution of such situations while taking fully into account the need for safeguarding both the present and potential trade of less-developed contracting parties affected by such measures;

Decide that:

1. If consultations between a less-developed contracting party and a developed contracting party in regard to any matter falling under paragraph 1 of Article XXIII do not lead to a satisfactory settlement, the less-developed contracting party complaining of the measure may refer the matter which is the subject of consultations to the Director-General so that, acting in an *ex officio* capacity, he may use his good offices with a view to facilitating a solution.

2. To this effect the contracting parties concerned shall, at the request of the Director-General, promptly furnish all relevant information.

3. On receipt of this information, the Director-General shall consult with the contracting parties concerned and with such other contracting parties or inter-governmental organizations as he considers appropriate with a view to promoting a mutually acceptable solution.

4. After a period of two months from the commencement of the consultations referred to in paragraph 3 above, if no mutually satisfying solution has been reached, the Director-General shall, at the request of one of the contracting parties concerned, bring the matter to the attention of the CONTRACTING PARTIES or the Council, to whom he shall

submit a report on the action taken by him, together with all background information.

5. Upon receipt of the report, the CONTRACTING PARTIES or the Council shall forthwith appoint a panel of experts to examine the matter with a view to recommending appropriate solutions. The members of the panel shall act [sic] a personal capacity and shall be appointed in consultation with, and with the approval of, the contracting parties concerned.

6. In conducting its examination and having before it all the background information, the panel shall take due account of all the circumstances and considerations relating to the application of the measures complained of, and their impact on the trade and economic development of affected contracting parties.

7. The panel shall, within a period of sixty days from the date the matter was referred to it, submit its findings and recommendations to the CONTRACTING PARTIES or to the Council, for consideration and decision. Where the matter is referred to the Council, it may, in accordance with Rule 8 of the Intersessional Procedures adopted by the CONTRACTING PARTIES at their thirteenth session[1], address its recommendations directly to the interested contracting parties and concurrently report to the CONTRACTING PARTIES.

8. Within a period of ninety days from the date of the decision of the CONTRACTING PARTIES or the Council, the contracting party to which a recommendation is directed shall report to the CONTRACTING PARTIES or the Council on the action taken by it in pursuance of the decision.

9. If on examination of this report it is found that a contracting party to which a recommendation has been directed has not complied in full with the relevant recommendation of the CONTRACTING PARTIES or the Council, and that any benefit accruing directly or indirectly under the General Agreement continues in consequence to be nullified or impaired, and that the circumstances are serious enough to justify such action, the CONTRACTING PARTIES may authorize the affected contracting party or parties to suspend, in regard to the contracting party causing the damage, application of any concession or any other obligation under the General Agreement whose suspension is considered warranted, taking account of the circumstances.

10. In the event that a recommendation to a developed country by the CONTRACTING PARTIES is not applied within the time-limit pre-

[1] BISD, Seventh Supplement, page 7.

scribed in paragraph 8, the CONTRACTING PARTIES shall consider what measures, further to those undertaken under paragraph 9, should be taken to resolve the matter.

11. If consultations, held under paragraph 2, of Article XXXVII, relate to restrictions for which there is no authority under any provisions of the General Agreement, any of the parties to the consultations may, in the absence of a satisfactory solution, request that consultations be carried out by the CONTRACTING PARTIES pursuant to paragraph 2 of Article XXIII and in accordance with the procedures set out in the present decision, it being understood that a consultation held under paragraph 2 of Article XXXVII in respect of such restrictions will be considered by the CONTRACTING PARTIES as fulfilling the conditions of paragraph 1 of Article XXIII if the parties to the consultations so agree.

1979 UNDERSTANDING ON DISPUTE SETTLEMENT
BISD 26S/210

1. The CONTRACTING PARTIES reaffirm their adherence to the basic GATT mechanism for the management of disputes based on Articles XXII and XXIII.[1] With a view to improving and refining the GATT mechanism, the CONTRACTING PARTIES agree as follows:

Notification

2. Contracting parties reaffirm their commitment to existing obligations under the General Agreement regarding publication and notification.

3. Contracting parties moreover undertake, to the maximum extent possible, to notify the CONTRACTING PARTIES of their adoption of trade measures affecting the operation of the General Agreement, it being understood that such notification would of itself be without prejudice to views on the consistency of measures with or their relevance to rights and obligations under the General Agreement. Contracting parties should endeavor to notify such measures in advance of implementation. In other cases, where prior notification has not been possible, such measures should be notified promptly *ex post facto*. Contracting parties which have reason to believe that such trade measures have been adopted by another contracting party may seek information on such measures bilaterally, from the contracting party concerned.

Consultations

4. Contracting parties reaffirm their resolve to strengthen and improve the effectiveness of consultative procedures employed by contracting parties. In that connexion, they undertake to respond to requests for consultations promptly and to attempt to conclude

[1] It is noted that Article XXV may, as recognized by the CONTRACTING PARTIES, *inter alia*, when they adopted the report of the Working Party on particular difficulties connected with trade in primary products (L/930) also afford an appropriate avenue for consultation and dispute settlement in certain circumstances.

consultations expeditiously, with a view to reaching mutually satisfactory conclusions. Any request for consultations should include the reasons therefor.

5. During consultations, contracting parties should give special attention to the particular problems and interests of less-developed contracting parties.

6. Contracting parties should attempt to obtain satisfactory adjustment of the matter in accordance with the provisions of Article XXIII:1 before resorting to Article XXIII:2.

Dispute settlement

7. The CONTRACTING PARTIES agree that the customary practice of the GATT in the field of dispute settlement, described in the Annex, should be continued in the future, with the improvements set out below. They recognize that the efficient functioning of the system depends on their will to abide by the present understanding. The CONTRACTING PARTIES reaffirm that the customary practice includes the procedures for the settlement of disputes between developed and less-developed countries adopted by the CONTRACTING PARTIES in 1966[1] and that these remain available to less-developed contracting parties wishing to use them.

8. If a dispute is not resolved through consultations the contracting parties concerned may request an appropriate body or individual to use their good offices with a view to the conciliation of the outstanding differences between the parties. If the unresolved dispute is one in which a less-developed contracting party has brought a complaint against a developed contracting party, the less-developed contracting party may request the good offices of the Director-General who, in carrying out his tasks, may consult with the Chairman of the CONTRACTING PARTIES and the Chairman of the Council.

9. It is understood that requests for conciliation and the use of the dispute settlement procedures of Article XXIII:2 should not be intended or considered as contentious acts and that, if disputes arise, all contracting parties will engage in these procedures in good faith in an effort to resolve the disputes. It is also understood that complaints and counter-complaints in regard to distinct matters should not be linked.

[1] BISD 14S/18.

10. It is agreed that if a contracting party invoking Article XXIII:2 requests the establishment of a panel to assist the CONTRACTING PARTIES to deal with the matter, the CONTRACTING PARTIES would decide on its establishment in accordance with standing practice. It is also agreed that the CONTRACTING PARTIES would similarly decide to establish a working party if this were requested by a contracting party invoking the Article. It is further agreed that such requests would be granted only after the contracting party concerned had had an opportunity to study the complaint and respond to it before the CONTRACTING PARTIES.

11. When a panel is set up, the Director-General, after securing the agreement of the contracting parties concerned, should propose the composition of the panel, of three or five members depending on the case, to the CONTRACTING PARTIES for approval. The members of a panel would preferably be governmental. It is understood that citizens of countries whose governments[1] are parties to the dispute would not be members of the panel concerned with that dispute. The panel should be constituted as promptly as possible and normally not later than thirty days from the decision by the CONTRACTING PARTIES.

12. The parties to the dispute would respond within a short period of time, i.e., seven working days, to nominations of panel members by the Director-General and would not oppose nominations except for compelling reasons.

13. In order to facilitate the constitution of panels, the Director-General should maintain an informal indicative list of governmental and non-governmental persons qualified in the fields of trade relations, economic development, and other matters covered by the General Agreement, and who could be available for serving on panels. For this purpose, each contracting party would be invited to indicate at the beginning of every year to the Director-General the name of one or two persons who would be available for such work.[2]

14. Panel members would serve in their individual capacities and not as government representatives, nor as representatives of any organization. Governments would therefore not give them instructions nor seek to influence them as individuals with regard to matters before a panel.

[1] In the case customs unions or common markets are parties to a dispute, this provision applies to citizens of all member countries of the customs unions or common markets.

[2] The coverage of travel expenses should be considered within the limits of budgetary possibilities.

Panel members should be selected with a view to ensuring the independence of the members, a sufficiently diverse background and a wide spectrum of experience.[1]

15. Any contracting party having a substantial interest in the matter before a panel, and having notified this to the Council, should have an opportunity to be heard by the panel. Each panel should have the right to seek information and technical advice from any individual or body which it deems appropriate. However, before a panel seeks such information or advice from any individual or body within the jurisdiction of a State it shall inform the government of that State. Any contracting party should respond promptly and fully to any request by a panel for such information as the panel considers necessary and appropriate. Confidential information which is provided should not be revealed without formal authorization from the contracting party providing the information.

16. The function of panels is to assist the CONTRACTING PARTIES in discharging their responsibilities under Article XXIII:2. Accordingly, a panel should make an objective assessment of the matter before it, including an objective assessment of the facts of the case and the applicability of and conformity with the General Agreement and, if so requested by the CONTRACTING PARTIES, make such other findings as will assist the CONTRACTING PARTIES in making the recommendations or in giving the rulings provided for in Article XXIII:2. In this connexion, panels should consult regularly with the parties to the dispute and give them adequate opportunity to develop a mutually satisfactory solution.

17. Where the parties have failed to develop a mutually satisfactory solution, the panel should submit its findings in a written form. The report of a panel should normally set out the rationale behind any findings and recommendations that it makes. Where a bilateral settlement of the matter has been found, the report of the panel may be confined to a brief description of the case and to reporting that a solution has been reached.

18. To encourage development of mutually satisfactory solutions between the parties and with a view to obtaining their comments, each panel should first submit the descriptive part of its report to the parties concerned, and should subsequently submit to the parties to the dispute its conclusions, or an outline thereof, a reasonable period of time before they are circulated to the CONTRACTING PARTIES.

[1] A statement is included in the Annex describing the current practice with respect to inclusion on panels of persons from developing countries.

19. If a mutually satisfactory solution is developed by the parties to a dispute before a panel, any contracting party with an interest in the matter has a right to enquire about and be given appropriate information about that solution in so far as it relates to trade matters.

20. The time required by panels will vary with the particular case.[1] However, panels should aim to deliver their findings without undue delay, taking into account the obligation of the CONTRACTING PARTIES to ensure prompt settlement. In cases of urgency the panel would be called upon to deliver its findings within a period normally of three months from the time the panel was established.

21. Reports of panels and working parties should be given prompt consideration by the CONTRACTING PARTIES. The CONTRACTING PARTIES should take appropriate action on reports of panels and working parties within a reasonable period of time. If the case is one brought by a less-developed contracting party, such action should be taken in a specially convened meeting, if necessary. In such cases, in considering what appropriate action might be taken the CONTRACTING PARTIES shall take into account not only the trade coverage of measures complained of, but also their impact on the economy of less-developed contracting parties concerned.

22. The CONTRACTING PARTIES shall keep under surveillance any matter on which they have made recommendations or given rulings. If the CONTRACTING PARTIES' recommendations are not implemented within a reasonable period of time, the contracting party bringing the case may ask the CONTRACTING PARTIES to make suitable efforts with a view to finding an appropriate solution.

23. If the matter is one which has been raised by a less-developed contracting party, the CONTRACTING PARTIES shall consider what further action they might take which would be appropriate to the circumstances.

Surveillance

24. The CONTRACTING PARTIES agree to conduct a regular and systematic review of developments in the trading system. Particular attention would be paid to developments which affect rights and obligations under the GATT, to matters affecting the interests of less-

[1] An explanation is included in the Annex that "in most cases the proceedings of the panels have been completed within a reasonable period of time, extending from three to nine months".

developed contracting parties, to trade measures notified in accordance with this understanding and to measures which have been subject to consultation, conciliation or dispute settlement procedures laid down in this understanding.

25. The technical assistance services of the GATT secretariat shall, at the request of a less-developed contracting party, assist it in connexion with matters dealt with in this understanding.

ANNEX

Agreed Description of the Customary Practice of the GATT in the Field of Dispute Settlement (Article XXIII:2)

1. Any dispute which has not been settled bilaterally under the relevant provisions of the General Agreement may be referred to the CONTRACTING PARTIES[1] which are obliged, pursuant to Article XXIII:2, to investigate matters submitted to them and make appropriate recommendations or give a ruling on the matter as appropriate. Article XXIII:2 does not indicate whether disputes should be handled by a working party or by a panel.[2]

2. The CONTRACTING PARTIES adopted in 1966 a decision establishing the procedure to be followed for Article XXIII consultations between developed and less-developed contracting parties[3]. This procedure provides, *inter alia*, for the Director-General to employ his good offices with a view to facilitating a solution, for setting up a panel with the task of examining the problem in order to recommend appropriate solutions, and for time-limits for the execution of the different parts of this procedure.

3. The function of a panel has normally been to review the facts of a case and the applicability of GATT provisions and to arrive at an objective assessment of these matters. In this connexion, panels have consulted regularly with the parties to the dispute and have given them

[1] The Council is empowered to act for the CONTRACTING PARTIES, in accordance with normal GATT practice.

[2] At the Review Session (1955) the proposal to institutionalize the procedures of panels was not adopted by CONTRACTING PARTIES mainly because they preferred to preserve the existing situation and not to establish judicial procedures which might put excessive strain on the GATT.

[3] BISD 14S/18.

adequate opportunity to develop a mutually satisfactory solution. Panels have taken appropriate account of the particular interests of developing countries. In cases of failure of the parties to reach a mutually satisfactory settlement, panels have normally given assistance to the CONTRACTING PARTIES in making recommendations or in giving rulings as envisaged in Article XXIII:2.

4. Before bringing a case, contracting parties have exercised their judgment as to whether action under Article XXIII:2 would be fruitful. Those cases which have come before the CONTRACTING PARTIES under this provision have, with few exceptions, been brought to a satisfactory conclusion. The aim of the CONTRACTING PARTIES has always been to secure a positive solution to a dispute. A solution mutually acceptable to the parties to a dispute is clearly to be preferred. In the absence of a mutually agreed solution, the first objective of the CONTRACTING PARTIES is usually to secure the withdrawal of the measures concerned if these are found to be inconsistent with the General Agreement. The provision of compensation should be resorted to only if the immediate withdrawal of the measure is impracticable and as a temporary measure pending the withdrawal of the measures which are inconsistent with the General Agreement. The last resort which Article XXIII provides to the country invoking this procedure is the possibility of suspending the application of concessions or other obligations on a discriminatory basis vis-à-vis the other contracting party, subject to authorization by the CONTRACTING PARTIES of such measures. Such action has only rarely been contemplated and cases taken under Article XXIII:2 have led to such action in only one case.

5. In practice, contracting parties have had recourse to Article XXIII only when in their view a benefit accruing to them under the General Agreement was being nullified or impaired. In cases where there is an infringement of the obligations assumed under the General Agreement, the action is considered *prima facie* to constitute a case of nullification or impairment. A *prima facie* case of nullification of impairment would *ipso facto* require consideration of whether the circumstances are serious enough to justify the authorization of suspension of concessions or obligations, if the contracting party bringing the complaint so requests. This means that there is normally a presumption that a breach of the rules has an adverse impact on other contracting parties, and in such cases, it is up to the contracting parties against whom the complaint has been brought to rebut the charge. Paragraph 1*(b)* permits recourse to Article XXIII if nullification or impairment results from measures taken by other contracting parties whether or not these conflict with the provisions of the General Agreement, and paragraph 1*(c)* if any other

situation exists. If a contracting party bringing an Article XXIII case claims that measures which do not conflict with the provisions of the General Agreement have nullified or impaired benefits accruing to it under the General Agreement, it would be called upon to provide a detailed justification.

6. Concerning the customary elements of the procedures regarding working parties and panels, the following elements have to be noted:

(i) working parties are instituted by the Council upon the request of one or several contracting parties. The terms of reference of working parties are generally "to examine the matter in the light of the relevant provisions of the General Agreement and to report to the Council". Working parties set up their own working procedures. The practice for working parties has been to hold one or two meetings to examine the matter and a final meeting to discuss conclusions. Working parties are open to participation of any contracting party which has an interest in the matter. Generally working parties consist of a number of delegations varying from about five to twenty according to the importance of the question and the interests involved. The countries who are parties to the dispute are always members of the Working Party and have the same status as other delegations. The report of the Working Party represents the views of all its members and therefore records different views if necessary. Since the tendency is to strive for consensus, there is generally some measure of negotiation and compromise in the formulation of the Working Party's report. The Council adopts the report. The reports of working parties are advisory opinions on the basis of which the CONTRACTING PARTIES may take a final decision.

(ii) In the case of dispute, the CONTRACTING PARTIES have established panels (which have been called by different names) or working parties in order to assist them in examining questions raised under Article XXIII:2. Since 1952, panels have become the usual procedure. However, the Council has taken such decisions only after the party concerned has had an occasion to study the complaint and prepare its response before the Council. The terms of reference are discussed and approved by the Council. Normally, these terms of reference are "to examine the matter and to make such findings as will assist the CONTRACTING PARTIES in making the recommendations or rulings provided for in paragraph 2 of Article XXIII". When a contracting party having recourse to Article XXIII:2 raised questions relating to the suspension of concessions or other obligations, the terms of reference were to examine the matter in accordance with the provisions of Article XXIII:2. Members of the panels are usually selected from permanent delegations or, less frequently, from the national administrations in the capitals amongst delegates who participate in GATT activities on a regular basis. The practice has been to appoint a member or members from developing countries when a dispute is between a developing and a developed country.

(iii) Members of panels are expected to act impartially without instructions from their governments. In a few cases, in view of the nature and complexity of the matter, the parties concerned have agreed to designate non-government experts. Nominations are proposed to the parties concerned by the GATT secretariat. The composition of panels (three or five members depending on the case) has been agreed upon by the parties concerned and approved by the GATT Council. It is recognized that a broad spectrum of opinion has been beneficial in difficult cases, but that the number of panel members has sometimes delayed the composition of panels, and therefore the process of dispute settlement.

(iv) Panels set up their own working procedures. The practice for the panels has been to hold two or three formal meetings with the parties concerned.The panel invited the parties to present their views whether in writing and/or orally in the presence of each other. The panel can question both parties on any matter which it considers relevant to the dispute. Panels have also heard the views of any contracting party having a substantial interest in the matter, which is not directly party to the dispute, but which has expressed in the Council a desire to present its views. Written memoranda submitted to the panel have been considered confidential, but are made available to the parties to the dispute. Panels often consult with and seek information from any relevant source they deem appropriate and they sometimes consult experts to obtain their technical opinion on certain aspects of the matter. Panels may seek advice or assistance from the secretariat in its capacity as guardian of the General Agreement, especially on historical or procedural aspects. The secretariat provides the secretary and technical services for panels.

(v) Where the parties have failed to develop a mutually satisfactory solution, the panel has submitted its findings in a written form. Panel reports have normally set out findings of fact, the applicability of relevant provisions, and the basic rationale behind any findings and recommendations that it has made. Where a bilateral settlement of the matter has been found, the report of the panel has been confined to a brief description of the case and to reporting that a solution has been reached.

(vi) The reports of panels have been drafted in the absence of the parties in the light of the information and the statements made.

(vii) To encourage development of mutually satisfactory solutions between the parties and with a view to obtaining their comments, each panel has normally first submitted the descriptive part of its report to the parties concerned, and also their conclusions, or an outline thereof, a reasonable period of time before they have been circulated to the CONTRACTING PARTIES.

(viii) In accordance with their terms of reference established by the CONTRACTING PARTIES panels have expressed their views on whether an infringement of certain rules of the General Agreement arises out of the measure examined. Panels have also, if so requested by the CONTRACTING PARTIES, formulated draft recommendations addressed to the parties. In yet other cases panels were invited to give a technical opinion on some precise aspect of the matter (e.g. on the modalities of a withdrawal or suspension in regard to the volume of trade involved). The opinions expressed by the panel members on the matters are anonymous and the panel deliberations are secret.

(ix) Although the CONTRACTING PARTIES have never established precise deadlines for the different phases of the procedure, probably because the matters submitted to panels differ as to their complexity and their urgency, in most cases the proceedings of the panels have been completed within a reasonable period of time, extending from three to nine months.

The 1966 decision by the CONTRACTING PARTIES referred to in paragraph 2 above lays down in its paragraph 7 that the Panel shall report within a period of sixty days from the date the matter was referred to it.

1982 MINISTERIAL DECLARATION ON DISPUTE SETTLEMENT BISD 29S/13

The CONTRACTING PARTIES:

Agree that the Understanding on Notification, Consultation, Surveillance and Dispute Settlement negotiated during the Tokyo Round (hereinafter referred to as the "Understanding") provides the essential framework of procedures for the settlement of disputes among contracting parties and that no major change is required in this framework, but that there is scope for more effective use of the existing mechanism and for specific improvements in procedures to this end;

And agree further that:

(i) With reference to paragraph 8 of the Understanding, if a dispute is not resolved through consultations, any party to a dispute may, with the agreement of the other party, seek the good offices of the Director-General or of an individual or group of persons nominated by the Director-General. This conciliatory process would be carried out expeditiously, and the Director-General would inform the Council of the outcome of the conciliatory process. Conciliation proceedings, and in particular positions taken by the parties to the dispute during conciliation, shall be confidential, and without prejudice to the rights of either party in any further proceedings under Article XXIII:2. It would remain open at any time during any conciliatory process for either party to the dispute to refer the matter to the CONTRACTING PARTIES.

(ii) In order to ensure more effective compliance with the provisions of paragraphs 11 and 12 of the Understanding, the Director-General shall inform the Council of any case in which it has not been found possible to meet the time-limits for the establishment of a panel.

(iii) With reference to paragraph 13 of the Understanding, contracting parties will co-operate effectively with the Director-General in making suitably qualified experts available to serve on panels. Where experts are not drawn from Geneva, any expenses, including travel and subsistence allowance, shall be met from the GATT budget.

(iv) The secretariat of GATT has the responsibility of assisting the panel, especially on the legal, historical and procedural aspects of the matters dealt with.

(v) The terms of reference of a panel should be formulated so as to permit a clear finding with respect to any contravention of GATT provisions and/or on the question of nullification and impairment of benefits. In terms of paragraph 16 of the Understanding, and after reviewing the facts of the case, the applicability of GATT provisions and the arguments advanced, the panel should come to such a finding. Where a finding establishing a contravention of GATT provisions or nullification and impairment is made, the panel should make such suggestions as appropriate for dealing with the matter as would assist the CONTRACTING PARTIES in making recommendations to the contracting parties which they consider to be concerned, or give a ruling on the matter, as appropriate.

(vi) Panels would aim to deliver their findings without undue delay, as provided in paragraph 20 of the Understanding. If a complete report cannot be made within the period foreseen in that paragraph, panels would be expected to so advise the Council and the report should be submitted as soon as possible thereafter.

(vii) Reports of panels should be given prompt consideration by the CONTRACTING PARTIES. Where a decision on the findings contained in a report calls for a ruling or recommendation by the Council, the Council may allow the contracting party concerned a reasonable specified time to indicate what action it proposes to take with a view to a satisfactory settlement of the matter, before making any recommendation or ruling on the basis of the report.

(viii) The recommendation or ruling made by the CONTRACTING PARTIES shall be aimed at achieving a satisfactory settlement of the matter in accordance with GATT obligations. In furtherance of the provisions of paragraph 22 of the Understanding the Council shall periodically review the action taken pursuant to such recommendations. The contracting party to which such a recommendation has been addressed, shall report within a reasonable specified period on action taken or on its reasons for not implementing the recommendation or ruling by the CONTRACTING PARTIES. The contracting party bringing the case may also ask the CONTRACTING PARTIES to make suitable efforts with a view to finding an appropriate solution as provided in paragraph 22 of the Understanding.

(ix) The further action taken by the CONTRACTING PARTIES in the above circumstances might include a recommendation for compensatory adjustment with respect to other products or authorization for the suspension of such concessions or other obligations as foreseen in Article XXIII:2, as the CONTRACTING PARTIES may determine to be appropriate in the circumstances.

(x) The Parties to a dispute would fully participate in the consideration of the matter by the CONTRACTING PARTIES under paragraph (vii) above, including the consideration of any rulings or recommendations the CONTRACTING PARTIES might make pursuant to Article XXIII:2 of the General Agreement, and their views would be fully recorded. They would likewise participate and have their views recorded in the considerations of the further actions provided for under paragraphs (viii) and (ix) above. The CONTRACTING PARTIES reaffirmed that consensus will continue to be the traditional method of resolving disputes; however, they agreed that obstruction in the process of dispute settlement shall be avoided.[1] It is understood that decisions in this process cannot add to or diminish the rights and obligations provided in the General Agreement.

[1] This does not prejudice the provisions on decision making in the General Agreement.

1984 ACTION ON DISPUTE SETTLEMENT
BISD 31S/9

I. The CONTRACTING PARTIES adopted the following proposal in L/5718/Rev.1:

At the 1982 Ministerial it was agreed that the Dispute Settlement "Understanding" provides the essential framework of procedures for the settlement of disputes among contracting parties and that no major change is required in this framework, but that there is scope for more effective use of the existing mechanism and for specific improvements in procedures to this end.

However, if improvement in the whole system is to be achieved, it is necessary not only to make specific procedural improvements, but also to obtain a clear-cut understanding by and commitment from the CONTRACTING PARTIES (or Signatories to the Codes) with respect to the nature and time-frame of (a) the panel process; (b) the decision on the dispute matter to be taken by the CONTRACTING PARTIES (or the Code Committee) on the basis of the panel's report; and (c) the follow-up to be given to that decision by the parties to the dispute.

A number of procedural problems related to the panel process have been encountered which can be addressed within the existing framework. Such problems include the formation of panels in a timely manner, and the timely completion of panel work. Although the "Understanding" provides guidelines for these procedures (thirty days for the formation of a panel and three to nine months to complete the panel's work), experience has shown these time targets are seldom met. These are only a couple of difficulties related to the dispute settlement mechanism, so addressing them alone will not cure all its deficiencies. However, procedural improvements can lead to improvements in the quality of panel reports. Therefore, the CONTRACTING PARTIES agree that, as a first step, the following approach should be adopted, on a trial basis, for a period of one year in order to continue the process of improving operation of the system.

Formation of Panels

1. Contracting parties should indicate to the Director-General the names of persons they think qualified to serve as panelists, who are not presently affiliated with national administrations but who

have a high degree of knowledge of international trade and experience of the GATT. These names should be used to develop a short roster of non-governmental panelists to be agreed upon by the CONTRACTING PARTIES in consultation with the Director-General. The roster should be as representative as possible of contracting parties.

2. The Director-General should continue the practice of proposing panels composed preferably of governmental representatives but may also draw as necessary on persons on the approved roster. The parties should retain the ability to respond to the Director-General's proposal, but shall not oppose nominations except for compelling reasons.

3. In the event that panel composition cannot be agreed within thirty days after a matter is referred by the CONTRACTING PARTIES, the Director-General shall, at the request of either party and in consultation with the Chairman of the Council, complete the panel by appointing persons from the roster of non-governmental panelists to resolve the deadlock, after consulting both parties.

Completion of Panel Work

1. Panels should continue to set their own working procedures and, where possible, panels should provide the parties to the dispute at the outset with a proposed calendar for the panel's work.

2. Where written submissions are requested from the parties, panels should set precise deadlines, and the parties to a dispute should respect those deadlines.

1989 DISPUTE SETTLEMENT PROCEDURES IMPROVEMENTS BISD 36S/61

Following the meetings of the Trade Negotiations Committee at Ministerial level in December 1988 and at the level of high officials in April 1989, the CONTRACTING PARTIES to the General Agreement on Tariffs and Trade

Approve the improvements of the GATT dispute settlement rules and procedures set out below and their application on the basis set out in this Decision:

A. General Provisions

1. Contracting parties recognize that the dispute settlement system of GATT serves to preserve the rights and obligations of contracting parties under the General Agreement and to clarify the existing provisions of the General Agreement. It is a central element in providing security and predictability to the multilateral trading system.

2. Contracting parties agree that all solutions to matters formally raised under the GATT dispute settlement system under Articles XXII, XXIII and arbitration awards shall be consistent with the General Agreement and shall not nullify or impair benefits accruing to any contracting party under the General Agreement, nor impede the attainment of any objective of the General Agreement.

3. Contracting parties agree that the existing rules and procedures of the GATT in the field of dispute settlement shall continue. It is further agreed that the improvements set out below, which aim to ensure prompt and effective resolution of disputes to the benefit of all contracting parties, shall be applied on a trial basis from May 1, 1989 to the end of the Uruguay Round in respect of complaints brought during that period under Article XXII or XXIII; it is also agreed to keep the application of these improvements under review during the remainder of the Round and to decide on their adoption before the end of the Round; to continue negotiations with the aim of further improving and strengthening the GATT dispute settlement system taking into account the experience gained in the application of these improvements.

4. All the points set out in this Decision shall be applied without prejudice to any provision on special and differential treatment for

developing contracting parties in the existing instruments on dispute settlement including the CONTRACTING PARTIES' Decision of April 5, 1966 (BISD 14S/18).

B. Notification

Mutually agreed solutions to matters formally raised under GATT Articles XXII and XXIII, as well as arbitration awards within GATT, must be notified to the Council where any contracting party may raise any point relating thereto.

C. Consultations

1. If a request is made under Article XXII:1 or XXIII:1, the contracting party to which the request is made shall, unless otherwise mutually agreed, reply to the request within ten days after its receipt and shall enter into consultations in good faith within a period of no more than thirty days from the date of the request, with a view to reaching a mutually satisfactory solution. If the contracting party does not respond within ten days, or does not enter into consultations within a period of no more than thirty days, or a period otherwise mutually agreed, from the date of the request, then the contracting party that requested the holding of consultations may proceed directly to request the establishment of a panel or a working party.

2. If the consultations under Article XXII:1 or XXIII:1 fail to settle a dispute within sixty days after the request for consultations, the complaining party may request the establishment of a panel or a working party under Article XXIII:2. The complaining party may request a panel or a working party during the sixty-day period if the parties jointly consider that consultations have failed to settle the dispute.

3. Requests for consultations under Article XXII:1 or XXIII:1 shall be notified to the Council by the party which requests consultations. Any request for consultations shall be submitted in writing and shall give the reasons for the request.

4. In cases of urgency, including those which concern perishable goods en route, parties shall enter into consultations within a period of no more than ten days from the date of the request. If the consultations have failed to settle the dispute within a period of thirty days after the request, the complaining party may request the establishment of a panel or a working party.

D. Good Offices, Conciliation, Mediation

1. Good offices, conciliation and mediation are procedures that are undertaken voluntarily if the parties to the dispute so agree. They may be requested at any time by any party to a dispute. They may begin at any time and be terminated at any time. Once terminated, the complaining party can then proceed with a request for the establishment of a panel or a working party under Article XXIII:2. When good offices, conciliation or mediation are entered into within sixty days of a request for consultations, the complaining party must allow a period of sixty days from the date of the request for consultations before requesting the establishment of a panel or working party. The complaining party may request a panel or a working party during the sixty days if the parties to the dispute jointly consider that the good offices, conciliation or mediation process has failed to settle the dispute.

2. If the parties to a dispute agree, procedures for good offices, conciliation or mediation may continue while the panel or working party process proceeds.

3. The Director-General may, acting in an *ex officio* capacity, offer his good offices, conciliation or mediation with the view to assisting contracting parties to settle a dispute.

E. Arbitration

1. Expeditious arbitration within GATT as an alternative means of dispute settlement can facilitate the solution of certain disputes that concern issues that are clearly defined by both parties.

2. Resort to arbitration shall be subject to mutual agreement of the parties which shall agree on the procedures to be followed. Agreements to resort to arbitration shall be notified to all contracting parties sufficiently in advance of the actual commencement of the arbitration process.

3. Other contracting parties may become party to an arbitration proceeding upon the agreement of the parties which have agreed to have recourse to arbitration. The parties to the proceeding shall agree to abide by the arbitration award.

F. Panel and Working Party Procedures

(a) Establishment of a Panel or a Working Party

The request for a panel or a working party shall be made in writing. It shall indicate whether consultations were held, and provide a brief summary of the factual and legal basis of the complaint sufficient to present the problem clearly. In case the applicant requests the establishment of a panel or a working party with other than standard terms of reference, the written request shall include the proposed text of special terms of reference. If the complaining party so requests, a decision to establish a panel or working party shall be taken at the latest at the Council meeting following that at which the request first appeared as an item on the Council's regular agenda, unless at that meeting the Council decides otherwise.*

(b) Standard Terms of Reference

1. Panels shall have the following terms of reference unless the parties to the dispute agree otherwise within twenty days from the establishment of the panel:

> "To examine, in the light of the relevant GATT provisions, the matter referred to the CONTRACTING PARTIES by (name of contracting party) in document L/ . . . and to make such findings as will assist the CONTRACTING PARTIES in making the recommendations or in giving the rulings provided for in Article XXIII:2".

2. In establishing a panel, the Council may authorize its Chairman to draw up the terms of reference of the panel in consultation with the parties subject to the provisions of the preceding paragraph. The terms of reference thus drawn up shall be circulated to all contracting parties. If other than standard terms of reference are agreed upon, any contracting party may raise any point relating thereto in the Council.

* References to the Council, made in this paragraph as well as in the following paragraphs, are without prejudice to the competence of the CONTRACTING PARTIES, for which the Council is empowered to act in accordance with normal GATT practice (BISD 26S/215).

(c) Composition of Panels

1. Contracting parties shall undertake, as a general rule, to permit their representatives to serve as panel members.

2. Panels shall be composed of well-qualified governmental and/or non-governmental individuals.

3. The roster of non-governmental panelists shall be expanded and improved. To this end, contracting parties may nominate individuals to serve on panels and shall provide relevant information on their nominee's knowledge of international trade and of the GATT.

4. Panels shall be composed of three members unless the parties to the dispute agree, within ten days from the establishment of the panel, to a panel composed of five members.

5. If there is no agreement on the members within twenty days from the establishment of a panel, at the request of either party, the Director-General, in consultation with the Chairman of the Council, shall form the panel by appointing the panelists whom he considers most appropriate, after consulting both parties. The Director-General shall inform the contracting parties of the composition of the panel thus formed no later than ten days from the date he receives such a request.

(d) Procedures for Multiple Complainants

1. Where more than one contracting party requests the establishment of a panel related to the same matter, a single panel may be established to examine these complaints taking into account the rights of all parties concerned. A single panel should be established to examine such complaints whenever feasible.

2. The single panel will organize its examination and present its findings to the Council so that the rights which the parties to the dispute would have enjoyed had separate panels examined the complaints are in no way impaired. If one of the parties to the dispute so requests, the panel will submit separate reports on the dispute concerned. The written submissions by each of the complainants will be made available to the other complainants, and each complainant will have the right to be present when one of the other complainants presents its view to the panel.

3. If more than one panel is established to examine the complaints related to the same matter, to the greatest extent possible the same persons shall serve as panelists on each of the separate panels and the timetable for the panel process in such disputes shall be harmonized.

(e) Third Contracting Parties

1. The interests of the parties to a dispute and those of other contracting parties shall be fully taken into account during the panel process.

2. Any third contracting party having a substantial interest in a matter before a panel, and having notified this to the Council, shall have an opportunity to be heard by the panel and to make written submissions to the panel. These submissions shall also be given to the parties to the dispute and shall be reflected in the panel report.

3. At the request of the third contracting party, the panel may grant the third contracting party access to the written submissions to the panel by those parties to the dispute which have agreed to the disclosure of their respective submission to the third contracting party.

(f) Time Devoted to Various Phases of a Panel

1. Panel procedures should provide sufficient flexibility so as to ensure high-quality panel reports, while not unduly delaying the panel process.

2. Panels shall follow the Suggested Working Procedures found in the July 1985 note of the Office of Legal Affairs unless the members of the panel agree otherwise after consulting the parties to the dispute. After consulting the parties, the panel members shall, as soon as practicable and whenever possible within one week after the composition and terms of reference of the panel have been agreed upon, fix the timetable for the panel process at least until its first substantive meeting.

3. In determining the timetable for the panel process, the panel shall provide sufficient time for the parties to the dispute to prepare their submissions.

4. Each party to the dispute shall deposit its written submissions with the Secretariat for immediate transmission to the panel and to the other party or parties to the dispute. The complaining party shall submit its first submission in advance of the responding party's first submission

unless the panel decides, in fixing the timetable referred to in the second paragraph of this section and after consultations with the parties to the dispute, that the parties should submit their first submissions simultaneously. When there are sequential arrangements for the deposit of first submissions, the panel shall establish a firm time period for receipt of the responding party's submission. Any subsequent written submissions shall be submitted simultaneously.

5. In order to make the procedures more efficient, the period in which the panel shall conduct its examination, from the time the composition and terms of reference of the panel have been agreed upon to the time when the final report is provided to the parties to the dispute, shall, as a general rule, not exceed six months. In cases of urgency, including those relating to perishable goods, the panel shall aim to provide its report to the parties within three months.

6. When the panel considers that it cannot provide its report within six months, or within three months in cases of urgency, it shall inform the Council in writing of the reasons for the delay together with an estimate of the period within which it will submit its report. In no case should the period from the establishment of the panel to the submission of the report to the contracting parties exceed nine months.

7. In the context of consultations involving a measure taken by a developing contracting party, the parties may agree to extend the periods established in paragraphs 2 and 4 of Section C. If, after the relevant period has elapsed, the parties cannot agree that the consultations have concluded, the Chairman of the Council shall decide, after consultation with the parties, whether to extend the relevant period and, if so, for how long. In addition, in examining a complaint against a developing contracting party, the panel shall accord sufficient time for the developing contracting party to prepare and present its argumentation. The provisions of paragraph 4 of Section G are not affected by any action pursuant to this paragraph.

G. Adoption of Panel Reports

1. In order to provide sufficient time for the members of the Council to consider panel reports, the reports shall not be considered for adoption by the Council until thirty days after they have been issued to the contracting parties.

2. Contracting parties having objections to panel reports shall give written reasons to explain their objections for circulation at least ten

days prior to the Council meeting at which the panel report will be considered.

3. The parties to a dispute shall have the right to participate fully in the consideration of the panel report by the Council, and their views shall be fully recorded. The practice of adopting panel reports by consensus shall be continued, without prejudice to the GATT provisions on decision-making which remain applicable. However, the delaying of the process of dispute settlement shall be avoided.

4. The period from the request under Article XXII:1 or Article XXIII:1 until the Council takes a decision on the panel report shall not, unless agreed to by the parties, exceed fifteen months. The provisions of this paragraph shall not affect the provisions of paragraph 6 of Section F(f).

H. Technical Assistance

1. While the Secretariat assists contracting parties in respect of dispute settlement at their request, there may also be a need to provide additional legal advice and assistance in respect of dispute settlement to developing contracting parties. To this end, the Secretariat shall make available a qualified legal expert within the Technical Co-operation Division to any developing contracting party which so requests. This expert shall assist the developing contracting party in a manner ensuring the continued impartiality of the Secretariat.

2. The Secretariat shall conduct special training courses for interested contracting parties concerning GATT dispute settlement procedures and practices so as to enable contracting parties' experts to be better informed in this regard.

I. Surveillance of Implementation of Recommendations and Rulings

1. Prompt compliance with recommendations or rulings of the CONTRACTING PARTIES under Article XXIII is essential in order to ensure effective resolution of disputes to the benefit of all contracting parties.

2. The contracting party concerned shall inform the Council of its intentions in respect of implementation of the recommendations or rulings. If it is impractable to comply immediately with the recommendations or rulings, the contracting party concerned shall have a reasonable period of time in which to do so.

3. The Council shall monitor the implementation of recommendations or rulings adopted under Article XXIII:2. The issue of implementation of the recommendations or rulings may be raised at the Council by any contracting party at any time following their adoption. Unless the Council decides otherwise, the issue of implementation of the recommendations or rulings shall be on the agenda of the Council meeting after six months following their adoption and shall remain on the Council's agenda until the issue is resolved. At least ten days prior to each such Council meeting, the contracting party concerned shall provide the Council with a status report in writing of its progress in the implementation of the panel recommendations or rulings.

4. In cases brought by developing contracting parties, the Council shall consider what further action it might take which would be appropriate to the circumstances, in conformity with paragraphs 21 and 23 of the 1979 Understanding regarding Notification, Consultation, Dispute Settlement and Surveillance (BISD 26S/214).

TEXTS OF DISPUTE SETTLEMENT DECISIONS

EDITOR'S NOTE

In this documents section, we have omitted those reports containing no substantive discussion of the General Agreement. The text of the reports has been taken from the Basic Instruments and Selected Documents series, except where the reports have not yet appeared in that series. We have attempted to reproduce the reports faithfully and have not corrected errors or stylistic inconsistencies, although we have marked gross errors with "[sic]". In particularly lengthy reports (including most recent reports), we have included a basic factual description of the dispute and the section of the report containing the reasoning of the panel. This means that we have eliminated extraneous background material and the separate sections describing the arguments of the parties and intervenors. (In most cases, the main arguments of the parties are restated by the panel.) We have omitted annexes to the reports, as well as most tables contained in the reports. We have eliminated some footnotes, but have kept most. Although we have not indicated the pagination of the reports in BISD, we believe that it would be adequate and proper to cite a report in this material with the initial page of the report in the BISD, followed by the relevant paragraph number. Thus, a cite to BISD XXS/yy, ¶zz will enable any reader to locate your reference precisely and quickly. (Where we have referred to two page numbers in our references to BISD, the first page number is always the initial page of the report.)

CONTENTS

Case No.

Case 1

OMITTED

BRAZILIAN INTERNAL TAXES

First Report adopted by the Contracting Parties on June 30, 1949
II BISD 181

1. The working party examined the question of internal taxes imposed by the Government of Brazil, in order to determine whether these were consistent with Brazil's obligations under the General Agreement.

2. Details of the taxes in question were furnished by the Brazilian delegation.

3. With the agreement of the Brazilian representative, the working party decided to adopt, as the basis for its examination, the text of Article III of the General Agreement as modified by the protocol amending Part II and Article XXVI. At the time of examination, Brazil was bound by the provisions of the original and not of the amended text, but it was understood that the Government of Brazil intended to accept the protocol in the near future.

4. The working party agreed that a contracting party was bound by the provisions of Article III whether or not the contracting party in question had undertaken tariff commitments in respect of the goods concerned. The delegates of Brazil and India qualified their agreement by the statement that the obligations of Article III applied only in respect of goods exported by other contracting parties.

5. The working party then considered the Brazilian law 7404 of 1945. The Brazilian delegate agreed that the law imposed taxes which discriminated between products of national origin and like products supplied by other contracting parties, but pointed out that, during the period of provisional application, the application of the provisions of Article III of the Agreement was limited by the Protocol of Provisional Application in the sense that contracting parties were obliged to apply the provisions of Part II of the Agreement only "to the fullest extent not inconsistent with existing legislation". The Brazilian delegate informed the working party that any change in the rates of tax established by this law could not have been effected by administrative action, but would have required amending legislation to be enacted by the Brazilian Congress. The working party therefore concluded that in view of the mandatory nature of law 7404 the taxes imposed by it, although discriminatory and hence contrary to the provision of Article III, were permitted by the terms of the

Protocol of Provisional Application and need not be altered so long as the General Agreement was being applied only provisionally by the Government of Brazil.

6. The working party then examined law No. 494 of 1948, and first considered two particular taxes established by it, relating to *conhaque* and clocks and watches respectively.

7. With reference to amendment No. 7 made to Brazilian internal taxes by article I of law No. 494 of 1948, the Brazilian delegate explained that this amendment concerned beverages containing aromatic or medicinal substances and known as tar, honey or ginger *conhaque,* which were quite different from French cognac. He gave an assurance that the authorities responsible for administering the taxes were able to distinguish between those products (which were of strictly local origin and subject to a tax of 3.60 cruzeiros per litre) and cognac imported from abroad. He made it clear that home-produced beverages similar to the cognac produced abroad were subject to the tax of 18 cruzeiros per litre. The members of the working party accepted this explanation, since the Brazilian delegate gave an assurance that careful instructions would be sent to the authorities administering the taxes, concerning the distinction to be drawn between these various products.

8. As regards alarm, table and wall or hanging clocks, the Brazilian delegate agreed that the law of 1948 had imposed a new discrimination which was not permitted by the terms of the Agreement even during the period of provisional application and agreed to recommend that the law should be modified in this respect. The delegate of Brazil pointed out that there was no domestic production of watches and that those imported into Brazil were supplied mostly by countries which were not contracting parties. He agreed, however, that watches would in future have a separate classification in the law and that the same rate of tax would be applied to the imported and to the (theoretical) domestic product.

9. The working party then considered as a whole the other taxes imposed by law No. 494 of 1948.

10. As regards cigarettes, the working party found that under the law No. 8538 of 1946 (which modified law 7404 of 1945 in respect of cigarettes) the difference between the highest tax charged on cigarettes of national origin and the tax charged on imported cigarettes was 2.70 cruzeiros per 20, whereas under the law of 1948 the tax on imported cigarettes was at the same level as the highest tax on cigarettes of national origin, and in both cases the tax had been raised to 8 cruzeiros per 20. The delegate of Brazil explained that the retail price on which the tax was based included the rate of tax itself.

11. In all the remaining cases the rates of tax on the domestic product had been increased, and the differential of 100 per cent on the rate imposed on imported products had been retained, with the result that the absolute difference between the two rates had been increased although the proportionate relationship had been retained. The Brazilian delegate, supported by one other member of the working party, took the view that, since this proportionate relationship had already been established by the law of 1945, any increase in the absolute difference in the rates was permitted during the period of provisional application, so long as this proportion was retained.

12. The other members of the working party, however, took the view that the Protocol of Provisional Application limited the operation of Article III only in the sense that it permitted the retention of an absolute difference in the level of taxes applied to domestic and imported products, required by existing legislation, and that no subsequent change in legislation should have the effect of increasing the absolute margin of difference. To take a case in point, the Brazilian law of 1945 required the tax on domestic liqueurs to be 3 cruzeiros and the tax on imported liqueurs 6 cruzeiros. The law of 1948 had raised the tax on domestic liqueurs to 18 cruzeiros and the tax on imported liqueurs to 36 cruzeiros. These members of the working party felt that while the Brazilian Government was entitled to raise the tax on the domestic product to 18 cruzeiros, the new tax on imported liqueurs could not in these circumstances exceed 21 cruzeiros if the increase were to be compatible with the requirements of Article III and the Protocol; it was evident to them that the structure of the law of 1945 (which imposed a margin of 100 per cent on imported products) could have been modified when the rates had been altered.

13. The Brazilian delegate adduced the further argument that the object of Article III was to prevent the protection of domestic products by the use of discriminatory taxes, and that therefore unless it could be shown that the effect of the law of 1948 had been to increase the protection of the national product, the law could not be held to be incompatible with the provisions of Article III. In support of this argument the Brazilian delegate said that Article III, paragraph 2, should be read in the light of paragraph 1 and of the interpretative note to paragraph 2.

14. Several members of the working party, on the other hand, took the view that the interpretative note to Article III, paragraph 2, modified the second sentence only of that paragraph, that taxes on imported products in excess of those on like domestic products were inherently protective and therefore in all cases contrary to Article III,

and that the second sentence, as explained by the interpretative note, merely referred to certain other types of taxes which were proscribed by Article III because of the protective results which might occur.

15. The Brazilian delegate supported by two other delegates, advanced the view that unless damage to other contracting parties could be demonstrated, a breach of Article III could not be alleged. Three other members of the working party took the view that, whether or not damage was shown, taxes on imported products in excess of those on like domestic products were prohibited by Article III, and that the provisions of Article III were intended to prevent damage and not merely to provide a means of rectifying such damage. The Cuban delegate supported the interpretation of the Brazilian delegate in cases where there was no domestic production of the like imported product.

16. The delegate for Brazil had stated at the meeting of the CONTRACTING PARTIES that in respect of some of the products on which internal taxes were imposed there were hardly any imports from other contracting parties. He laid particular emphasis on the interpretative note to Article III, paragraph 2, and stated that none of the contracting parties was either greatly interested or affected by the levy of these internal taxes. He did not feel that in such a situation contracting parties were materially affected and could lodge a complaint. In this connexion, the delegate of Brazil submitted the argument that if an internal tax, even though discriminatory, does not operate in a protective manner the provisions of Article III would not be applicable. He drew attention to the first paragraph of Article III, which prescribes that such taxes should not be applied "so as to afford protection to domestic production". His view of the obligations under Article III was, he said, borne out by the interpretative note to paragraph 2. The delegate for Brazil, supported by one delegate, suggested that where there were no imports of a given commodity or where imports were small in volume, the provisions of Article III did not apply. Another delegate took the view that the provisions of Article III applied in cases where there were small imports, but not in cases where there were no imports. The other members of the working party argued that the absence of imports from contracting parties during any period of time that might be selected for examination would not necessarily be an indication that they had no interest in exports of the product affected by the tax, since their potentialities as exporters, given national treatment, should be taken into account. These members of the working party therefore took the view that the provisions of the first sentence of Article III, paragraph 2, were equally

applicable whether imports from other contracting parties were substantial, small or non-existent.

17. In conclusion the working party noted that the Brazilian Government had already called the attention of the Brazilian Congress to all existing laws providing for different levels of taxation with respect to domestic and imported products, in order to bring those laws into conformity with Article III of the General Agreement. The working party also accepted the statement by the Brazilian delegation that the Government was willing to send a further message to the congress asking it to proceed as soon as possible with the amendment of all such laws and in particular the law of 1948.

18. It was understood that in view of the constitutional procedure of Brazil such action by the Brazilian Congress, even in respect of the law of 1948, could not have an effective result before 1 January 1950.

19. In view of these statements the working party recommends to the CONTRACTING PARTIES that no further action in this matter be undertaken at the present session, but that at the next session the question should be reviewed in the light of action taken by the Brazilian Government by that date.

NOTIFICATION OF EXISTING MEASURES AND PROCEDURAL QUESTIONS

Report Approved by the Contracting Parties on August 10, 1949
II BISD 49, 61

I. PROCEDURES UNDER ARTICLE XVII WITH RESPECT TO MEASURES PERMITTED BY THE PROTOCOL OF PROVISIONAL APPLICATION AND THE ANNECY PROTOCOL OF ACCESSION

97. At the fourth meeting of the CONTRACTING PARTIES the representative of Pakistan raised the question whether a contracting party need notify under Article XVIII any measure which, though contrary to the provisions of Part II of the Agreement, is permitted by the provisions of the Protocol of Provisional Application. At the fourteenth meeting of the CONTRACTING PARTIES, the representative of Pakistan, in connexion with the statement submitted by the Government of Ceylon, again raised the question of procedure under Article XVIII, both with respect to notification and to action by the CONTRACTING PARTIES in these circumstances. The working party was required by its terms of reference to take account of the points raised in the discussion at those meetings and to report thereon to the CONTRACTING PARTIES.

98. In considering this subject, the working party had the advantage of the participation of the representative of Pakistan, who also submitted a written statement setting forth the views of his delegation.

99. The Working Party directed its attention to the question of whether a government is obliged to notify the CONTRACTING PARTIES in accordance with the provisions of paragraph 6 or 11 of Article XVIII, if the measure in question is permitted during the period of provisional application by virtue of sub-paragraph 1(*b*) of the Protocol of Provisional Application or sub-paragraph 1(*a*)(ii) of the Annecy Protocol of Terms of Accession. The working party agreed that a measure is so permitted, provided that the legislation on which it is based is by its terms or expressed intent of a mandatory character—that is, it imposes on the executive authority requirements which cannot be modified by executive action. There was disagreement on the question of whether the date on which legislation was "existing" in terms of the Protocol of

Provisional Application was the date of the Protocol or the date of signature of the Protocol by individual governments.

100. The working party believed that there is no obligation on the part of a contracting party to notify a measure permitted by sub-paragraph 1 (*b*) of the Protocol of Provisional Application or sub-paragraph 1 (*a*) (ii) of the Annecy Protocol. On the other hand, the working party recognized that the provisions of Article XVIII should not be denied to a contracting party simply because the measure in question is permitted under either protocol, as such a contracting party should be allowed to ascertain whether it will be permitted to maintain a measure for economic development during a specified period even if that period extends beyond the time when the Agreement enters definitively into force pursuant to Article XXVI. Further, if a measure existing on the date prescribed in paragraph 11 were not notified under the provisions of that paragraph, it could be continued in force after the Agreement entered definitively into force only if it had been approved by the CONTRACTING PARTIES as a new measure under paragraph 7 or 8.

101. In addition, even where a release is not requested, there would be advantages if the contracting party concerned were to inform the CONTRACTING PARTIES of any existing or new measure.

102. The working party therefore concluded that during the period of provisional application:

(1) a contracting party need not notify a measure which is already exempted by virtue of sub-paragraph 1 (*b*) of the Protocol of Provisional Application or sub-paragraph 1 (*a*) (ii) of the Annecy Protocol;

(2) in case it chooses to notify the measure for the purpose of obtaining a release under paragraph 7, 8 or 12, as the case may be, the full procedures and the criteria of the relevant parts of Article XVIII would apply as if the Agreement were definitively in force. However, if as a result of examination the CONTRACTING PARTIES decide that the measure should be withdrawn or modified, the contracting party concerned would nevertheless be free to maintain the measure during the period of provisional application only; and

(3) it would be open to the contracting party to inform the CONTRACTING PARTIES of any measure for which it was not seeking a release under paragraph 7, 8 or 12, but which it was imposing or

retaining in accordance with sub-paragraph 1 (*b*) of the Protocol of Provisional Application or sub-paragraph 1 (*a*) (ii) of the Annecy Protocol.

103. The conclusions above relate both to existing measures under paragraphs 11 and 12 and to new measures under paragraphs 6, 7 and 8. However, the working party considered that in practice these conclusions were unlikely to affect new measures, because it is improbable that a future measure would have been required by "existing" legislation.

PROTOCOL OF PROVISIONAL APPLICATION

DATE OF REFERENCE FOR THE PHRASE "EXISTING LEGISLATION" IN PARAGRAPH I(b) OF THE PROTOCOL

Ruling by the Chairman on August 11, 1949
II BISD 35

On the question whether the phrase "existing legislation" in paragraph 1 (*b*) of the Protocol of Provisional Application refers to legislation existing on the date of the Protocol or on that of signature of the Protocol by the government concerned, the Chairman ruled that it refers to legislation existing on October 30, 1947, the date of the Protocol as written at the end of its last paragraph.

THE AUSTRALIAN SUBSIDY ON AMMONIUM SULPHATE

Report adopted by the Contracting Parties on April 3, 1950
II BISD 188

I. INTRODUCTION

1. The working party examined with the delegations of Australia and Chile the factual situation resulting from the removal, on July 1, 1949, of nitrate of soda from the pool of nitrogenous fertilizers which is subsidized by the Australian Government. It then considered whether the measure taken by the Australian Government constituted a failure by the Australian Government to carry out its obligations under the Agreement, within the terms of Article XXIII.

Having come to the conclusion that the measure taken by the Australian Government did not conflict with the provisions of the Agreement, the working party then examined whether the Australian measure had nullified or impaired the tariff concession granted by Australia to Chile on nitrate of soda in 1947, and agreed on the text of a recommendation which, in its opinion, would best assist the Australian and Chilean Governments to arrive at a satisfactory adjustment.

The Australian representative stated that his Government was unable to associate itself with the conclusions reached by the working party in paragraph 12 of this report; their views are reproduced in the annex to this report.

II. THE FACTS OF THE CASE

2. Prior to the outbreak of war in 1939, ammonium sulphate was distributed in Australia by a commercial pooling arrangement operated by Nitrogenous Fertilizers Proprietary, Ltd., a private enterprise; that corporation bought ammonium sulphate from the local producers (both by-product and synthetic sulphate) and from foreign sources of supply. The ammonium sulphate from all sources was sold to consumers at a uniform price. The distribution of imported sodium nitrate was effected by independent agencies.

3. In view of the scarcity of ammonium sulphate during the war, the

Australian Government purchased sodium nitrate from abroad and appointed Nitrogenous Fertilizers Proprietary, Ltd., to act as distributing agent for the Commonwealth for both such fertilizers, which were sold to consumers at a uniform price of £A16 10*s*. per ton. During the first year of the operation of the pooling arrangement, the company could supply the market without any loss; during the later years, the Australian Government undertook to meet the deficit of the company on the sales of both ammonium sulphate and sodium nitrate. This financial support by the Commonwealth Government had the effect of a subsidy on imported fertilizers.

4. As from July 1, 1949, Nitrogenous Fertilizers Proprietary, Ltd. ceased to distribute sodium nitrate, the trade of which reverted to the pre-war commercial channels. The Australian Government continued, however, to purchase abroad ammonium sulphate, which it sold to Nitrogenous Fertilizers Proprietary, Ltd., at landed cost. The retail price of ammonium sulphate, both domestic and imported, was no longer fixed by government control; the price therefore rose by stages to £A22 10*s*. per ton, but the Australian government agreed to meet any loss on procurement or distribution of sulphate which might be incurred by Nitrogenous Fertilizers Proprietary, Ltd., up to an amount of approximately £A500,000.

5. On the basis of information supplied by the Australian representative, the financial implications of that arrangement for 1949/50 may be summarized as follows:

	Tons	*(1) Estimated retail price on a commercial basis (£A)*	*(2) Retail price under subsidized pooling arrangement (£A)*	*(3) Gross difference between columns (1) and (2) (£A)*
(a) Domestic supply of sulphate				
By-products.......	15,000	15 10*s*.	22 10*s*.	+ 30,000
Synthetic products.	30,000	25		
(b) Foreign supply of sulphate				
Various sources ...	26,700	31 33	22 10*s*.	(approx.) −275,000

NOTE.—The weighted average of the quantities of ammonium sulphate listed under (*a*) and (*b*) above at the prices indicated in column (1) would give a selling price of £A25 12*s*. in the absence of a subsidy. However, as some elements of cost cannot be estimated with perfect accuracy, the figure of £A28 per ton was indicated by the Australian representative as a fair estimate of the maximum selling price of ammonium sulphate through the Nitrogenous Fertilizers Proprietary, Ltd., pooling arrangement if no subsidy were maintained.

6. The subsidy on sulphate of ammonia was maintained because, *inter alia,* users of that fertilizer would have been prevented, by domestic price control and long-term contracts, from increasing their selling price in order to take account of the increased cost of ammonium sulphate which would have resulted from the discontinuance of the subsidy. The same conditions did not exist in the case of sodium nitrate, as the agricultural producers who used most of that fertilizer were no longer subject to price control arrangements and adequate supplies to meet all demands were available. The unsubsidized retail price of nitrate of soda is estimated at £A33 10*s*. by the representative of Australia and at £A31 10*s*. by the representative of Chile. These prices may be compared with the price of £A28 per ton for ammonium sulphate referred to in the note above.

The Australian imports of sodium nitrate during the post-war period were limited to the amounts allocated by the International Emergency Food Council until June 1949. The total imports, mainly for industrial purposes, are estimated at about 14,000 tons for 1949/50, as compared with about 7,000 tons for 1948/49. However, the working party took note of the information supplied by the Australian representative that the agricultural demand for nitrate of soda had dropped from 6,300 tons in 1947/48 to 450 tons in 1948/49 (when nitrate of soda was sold under the pooling arrangement at the same price and under the same conditions as sulphate of ammonia), and the same amount will probably be used in agriculture in 1949/50 under the new arrangements. The Chilean representative stated that during 1948/49 nitrate of soda was not sold under the same conditions as sulphate of ammonia, as the whole allocation made that year by the IEFC to Australia was assigned by the Australian Government for industrial purposes, and it was due only to Chile's reiterated petitions that 450 tons were withdrawn from industrial stocks and given to agricultural uses, therefore leaving a demand of more than 3,000 tons without fulfillment.

III. CONSISTENCY OF THE AUSTRALIAN MEASURES WITH THE PROVISIONS OF THE GENERAL AGREEMENT

7. The removal of nitrate of soda from the pooling arrangements did not involve any prohibition or restriction on the import of sodium nitrate and did not institute any tax or internal charge on that product. The working party concluded, therefore, that the provisions of Article XI, paragraph 1, and of Article III, paragraph 2, were not relevant.

8. As regards the applicability of Article I to the Australian measure,

the working party noted that the General Agreement made a distinction between "like products" and "directly competitive or substitutable products". This distinction is clearly brought out in Article III, paragraph 2, read in conjunction with the interpretative note to that paragraph. The most-favored-nation treatment clause in the General Agreement is limited to "like products". Without trying to give a definition of "like products", and leaving aside the question of whether the two fertilizers are directly competitive, the working party reached the conclusion that they were not to be considered as "like products" within the terms of Article I. In the Australian tariff the two products are listed as separate items and enjoy different treatment. Nitrate of soda is classified as item 403 (C) and sulphate of ammonia as item 271 (B). Whereas nitrate of soda is admitted free both in the preferential and most-favored-nation tariff, sulphate of ammonia is admitted free only for the preferential area and is subject to a duty of 12½ per cent for the m.f.n. countries; moreover, in the case of nitrate of soda the rate is bound whereas no binding has been agreed upon for sulphate of ammonia. In the tariffs of other countries the two products are listed separately. In certain cases the rate is the same, but in others the treatment is different: for instance, in the case of the United Kingdom, nitrate of soda is admitted free, whereas a duty of £4 per ton is levied on ammonium sulphate.

9. In view of the fact that Article III, paragraph 4, applies to "like products", the provisions of that paragraph are not applicable to the present case, for the reasons set out in paragraph 8 above. As regards the provisions of paragraph 9 of the same article, the working party was informed that a maximum selling price for ammonium sulphate was no longer fixed by governmental action and, in any event, noted that Australia had considered the Chilean complaint and had made an offer within the terms of that paragraph. Since it was not found that any of the substantive provisions of Article III were applicable, the exception contained in paragraph 8 (*b*) is not relevant.

10. The working party then examined the question of whether the Australian Government had complied with the terms of Article XVI on subsidies. It noted that, although this Article is drafted in very general terms, the type of subsidy which it was intended to cover was the financial aid given by a government to support its domestic production and to improve its competitive position either on the domestic market or on foreign markets.

Even if it is assumed that the maintenance of the Australian subsidy on ammonium sulphate is covered by the terms of Article XVI, it does not seem that the Australian Government's action can be considered as justifying any claim of injury under this article. It is recognized that the CONTRACTING PARTIES have not been notified by the Australian Government of the maintenance of that subsidy, but the working party noted that the procedural arrangements for such notifications under Article XVI have been approved by the CONTRACTING PARTIES only at their present session, and that they require notification only after imposition of the measure. Moreover, the Chilean Government has not suffered any injury from this failure to notify the CONTRACTING PARTIES, as it is established that the Chilean Consul-General had an opportunity to discuss this matter with the Australian authorities before the decision to discontinue the subsidy on sodium nitrate had been enforced. The Australian Government has discussed with the Chilean Government the possibility of limiting the effects of the subsidization, and has also discussed the matter with the CONTRACTING PARTIES, in accordance with the provisions of Article XVI.

11. Within the terms of reference of the working party, the examination of the relevant provisions of the General Agreement thus led it to the conclusion that no evidence had been presented to show that the Australian Government had failed to carry out its obligations under the Agreement.

IV. NULLIFICATION OR IMPAIRMENT OF THE CONCESSION GRANTED TO CHILE ON SODIUM NITRATE

12. The working party next considered whether the injury which the Government of Chile said it had suffered represented a nullification or impairment of a benefit accruing to Chile directly or indirectly under the General Agreement and was therefore subject to the provisions of Article XXIII. It was agreed that such impairment would exist if the action of the Australian Government which resulted in upsetting the competitive relationship between sodium nitrate and ammonium sulphate could not reasonably have been anticipated by the Chilean Government, taking into consideration all pertinent circumstances and the provisions of the General Agreement, at the time it negotiated for the duty-free binding on sodium nitrate. The working party concluded that the Government of Chile had reason to assume, during these negotiations, that the war-time fertilizer subsidy would not be removed from sodium nitrate before it was removed from ammonium sulphate. In

reaching this conclusion, the working party was influenced in particular by the combination of the circumstances that:

(a) The two types of fertilizer were closely related;

(b) Both had been subsidized and distributed through the same agency and sold at the same price;

(c) Neither had been subsidized before the war, and the war-time system of subsidization and distribution had been introduced in respect of both at the same time and under the same war powers of the Australian Government;

(d) This system was still maintained in respect of both fertilizers at the time of the 1947 tariff negotiations.

For these reasons, the working party also concluded that the Australian action should be considered as relating to a benefit accruing to Chile under the Agreement, and that it was therefore subject to the provisions of Article XXIII. In reaching this conclusion, however, the Working Party considered that the removal of a subsidy, in itself, would not normally result in nullification or impairment. In the case under consideration, the inequality created and the treatment that Chile could reasonably have expected at the time of the negotiation, after taking into consideration all pertinent circumstances, including the circumstances mentioned above, and the provisions of the General Agreement, were important elements in the working party's conclusion.

The situation in this case is different from that which would have arisen from the granting of a new subsidy on one of the two competing products. In such a case, given the freedom under the General Agreement of the Australian Government to impose subsidies and to select the products on which a subsidy would be granted, it would be more difficult to say that the Chilean Government had reasonably relied on the continuation of the same treatment for the two products. In the present case, however, the Australian Government, in granting a subsidy on account of the war-time fertilizer shortage and continuing it in the post-war period, had grouped the two fertilizers together and treated them uniformly. In such circumstances it would seem that the Chilean Government could reasonably assume that the subsidy would remain applicable to both fertilizers so long as there remained a local nitrogenous fertilizer shortage. The working party has no intention of implying that the action taken by the Australian Government was unreasonable, but simply that the Chilean Government could not have been expected during the negotiations in 1947 to have foreseen such action or the reasons which led to it.

13. Having thus concluded that there was a *prima facie* case that the value of a concession granted to Chile had been impaired as a result of a measure which did not conflict with the provisions of the General Agreement, the working party came to the conclusion that there was no infringement of the Agreement by Australia. Since Chile had not applied for a release from any of its obligations, under the provisions of the last two sentences of Article XXIII, paragraph 2, and it was moreover hoped that an adjustment of the matter satisfactory to both parties could be reached (without prejudice to the views of either on the merits of the case), it was not necessary for the working party to consider whether the above-mentioned provisions were applicable to the case.

14. The Chilean representative stated that his Government did not press for a discussion of the question of the degree of damage sustained and would be satisfied if an arrangement could be made to remove the cause of the present competitive inequality between the two fertilizers. Such an arrangement would not necessarily involve the restoration of the previous method of subsidization. The Chilean representative suggested that no subsidy be granted for either fertilizer, or that, if the Australian Government wished to subsidize certain agricultural products, the subsidy might be paid on fertilizer used by the producers of those crops which it desires to subsidize, without distinction between types of fertilizer. Thus, wherever one nitrogenous fertilizer is subsidized for a particular crop, the other would receive equal subsidization.

15. As the declared intention of the Australian Government in maintaining the subsidy on ammonium sulphate was to give financial aid, not to the producers of a certain type of fertilizer, but to the producers of certain crops, whose selling price was limited by price control and who preferred to use ammonium sulphate for technical reasons, irrespective of price considerations, the working party came to the conclusion that a satisfactory adjustment would be achieved if the Australian Government could consider the possibility of modifying the present arrangements in such a way as to achieve that object while giving to the two types of fertilizers equal opportunity to compete on its market.

16. In the light of the considerations set out above, the working party wishes to submit to the CONTRACTING PARTIES the following draft recommendation, which, in its opinion, would best assist the Australian and Chilean Governments to arrive at a satisfactory adjustment. In making this recommendation the working party wishes to draw

attention to one point of particular importance. There is in their view nothing in Article XXIII which would empower the CONTRACTING PARTIES to require a contracting party to withdraw or reduce a consumption subsidy such as that applied by the Government of Australia to ammonium sulphate, and the recommendation made by the working party should not be taken to imply the contrary. The ultimate power of the CONTRACTING PARTIES under Article XXIII is that of authorizing an affected contracting party to suspend the application of appropriate obligations or concessions under the General Agreement. The sole reason why the adjustment of subsidies to remove any competitive inequality between the two products arising from subsidization is recommended is that, in this particular case, it happens that such action appears to afford the best prospect of an adjustment of the matter satisfactory to both parties.

17. The following is the text of the draft recommendation submitted by the working party to the CONTRACTING PARTIES:

RECOMMENDATION REGARDING THE COMPLAINT OF CHILE CONCERNING THE AUSTRALIAN SUBSIDY ON SULPHATE OF AMMONIA

The CONTRACTING PARTIES recommend that the Australian Government consider, with due regard to its policy of stabilizing the cost of production of certain crops, means to remove any competitive inequality between nitrate of soda and sulphate of ammonia for use as fertilizers which may in practice exist as a result of the removal of nitrate of soda from the operations of the subsidized pool of nitrogenous fertilizers and communicate the results of their consideration to the Chilean Government, and that the two parties report to the CONTRACTING PARTIES at the next session.

BRAZILIAN INTERNAL TAXES

Second Report adopted by the Contracting Parties on December 13, 1950 II BISD 186

1. The working party was asked to examine a draft law (No. 483-50) modifying the present legislation on consumption taxes which has been prepared by the Government of Brazil and submitted to its legislature, and to advise on the conformity of the draft with relevant provisions of the General Agreement and the Protocol of Provisional Application.

2. In commencing its deliberations, the working party noted that during discussions of this question by the CONTRACTING PARTIES the Brazilian government had indicated that it was prepared to ask Congress to proceed as soon as possible with the amendment of all existing laws providing for different levels of taxation with respect to domestic and imported products, and in particular law No. 494 of 1948, in order to bring them into conformity with Article III of the General Agreement. In a communication to the Executive Secretary following a further examination of the question at the fourth session, the Government of Brazil advised that a message had been sent to the Congress requesting action towards amending all existing laws which provide for different levels of taxation for domestic and imported products in order to bring them into conformity with Article III. The working party proceeded to examine the draft law, No. 483-50, in the light of the conclusions reached in previous discussions by the CONTRACTING PARTIES.

3. The Brazilian delegation informed the working party that the draft law was a first step in what would be a gradual process of removing all the discriminatory taxes. The draft law was intended to remove the new or increased discrimination between domestic and foreign products which had been introduced since October 30, 1947, and, in addition—although this was not required so long as the Agreement was being applied only on a provisional basis—it provided, on some commodities, for the removal of some of the discrimination which had existed prior to that date.

4. With reference to the removal of the margins of discrimination which existed prior to October 30, 1947, the Brazilian delegation stated that its Government reserved the right to incorporate such margins of discrimination into the customs duties. The delegation of Brazil ad-

vanced economic and legal arguments to support this view. The representative of Chile suggested that there might be justification in this case on various, and particularly economic, grounds for the conversion of the internal tax discrimination into customs duties. The representatives of France, Greece, the United Kingdom and the United States, on the other hand, pointed out that while a government would have the legal right to convert internal tax margins into customs duties in respect of tariff items not included in its schedule to the General Agreement, it would not have that right in respect of scheduled items except through the procedures of the Agreement for the modification of concessions. The Chairman expressed the view that the working party's terms of reference did not permit it to reach a conclusion on this matter. The majority of the working party agreed with his view, and felt that it would not be necessary to decide this issue in present circumstances. The representative of Brazil stated that in that event his Government would reserve the right to modify the draft law to retain only those provisions which are strictly necessary to eliminate the new or increased discrimination introduced since October 30, 1947.

5. The Brazilian delegation made available to the working party two documents containing, respectively, a translation of the draft law, and translations of extracts from laws and decrees at present in force in order that the amendments being introduced by the draft law might be more readily understood. Nevertheless, members of the working party found some difficulty in understanding the full significance of many provisions of the draft law and sought additional information and explanations from the representatives of Brazil.

6. On the basis of the information available to the working party in the form of written and oral statements, it appeared to the working party that, except in the respects noted below, the draft law would remove the new and increased internal tax discrimination introduced since October 30, 1947, and bring Brazil's consumption tax legislation into conformity with the General Agreement as applied under the Protocol of Provisional Application. The exceptions are as follows:

(a) The increase in the internal tax discrimination on playing cards resulting from legislation subsequent to October 30, 1947 (*i.e.*, decrees pursuant to law No. 494 of 1948) would not be removed by the draft law. The Brazilian representative stated that his delegation would recommend an appropriate amendment to take care of this.

(b) Most members of the working party were of the opinion that on cigars, cheroots, snuff, shredded and cut tobacco and tobacco in powder (sections 1, 3 and 4 of paragraph XXIV in schedule D of the consolidation of consumption taxes) the margins of discrimination had been increased since October 30, 1947. The representative of Brazil did not agree, but nevertheless stated that he was willing to propose the modifications necessary to eliminate the margins of discrimination which most members of the working party concluded had been introduced since October 30, 1947.

7. The working party noted that various provisions (paragraphs 8, 11, and 12 of article I of the draft law) would eliminate the discrimination in question only with respect to products imported from the contracting parties. The question was raised in the working party as to the treatment which would be accorded to products of the contracting parties which were not imported directly, but came to Brazil in transit through a third country. The representative of Brazil assured the working party that products of any contracting party which entered Brazil after coming in transit through a third country would receive the same treatment as if the goods in question had been imported directly from a contracting party.

8. Finally, the working party considers that the review of draft legislation by the CONTRACTING PARTIES with a view to determining whether such legislation is in conformity with the General Agreement in no way prejudices the right of any contracting party, subsequent to such review, to raise any question as to the consistency of such legislation with the provisions of the Agreement.

TREATMENT BY GERMANY OF IMPORTS OF SARDINES

Report adopted by the Contracting Parties on October 31, 1952
BISD 1S/53

I. INTRODUCTION

1. The Panel on Complaints examined with the delegations of the Federal Republic of Germany and Norway the factual situation resulting from (*a*) the imposition, as from October 1, 1951, of an import duty of 14 per cent on preparations of clupea pilchardus as compared with a duty of 20 per cent for clupea harengus and 25 per cent for clupea sprattus, (*b*) the application as from November 16, 1951 of a charge equivalent to the German turnover tax at a rate of 4 per cent on preparations of clupea pilchardus and of 6 per cent on preparations of clupea sprattus and clupea harengus, and (*c*) the removal of quantitative restrictions on preparations of clupea pilchardus while these restrictions were maintained on the preparations of the other varieties. It then considered whether the aforementioned measures taken by the Government of the Federal Republic of Germany constituted, within the terms of Article XXIII: 1 (*a*), a failure by that Government to carry out its obligations under the Agreement. Having come to the conclusion that the evidence produced by the parties was not such as to warrant a finding that the measures taken by the Government of the Federal Republic of Germany were in conflict with the provisions of Article I: 1 or of Article XIII: 1 of the General Agreement, the Panel then examined whether those measures had nullified or impaired the tariff concessions granted by Germany to Norway on sub-items 1604 C 1 (d)—sprats (clupea sprattus) and 1604 C 1 (*e*) herring, and agreed on the text of a recommendation which, in its opinion, would best assist the German and Norwegian Governments to arrive at a satisfactory adjustment of the question submitted by Norway to the CONTRACTING PARTIES.

II. FACTS OF THE CASE

2. Prior to the tariff negotiations conducted at Torquay between Germany and Norway within the framework of the General Agreement, canned products of clupea sprattus and clupea harengus enjoyed the

same customs treatment in Germany as the canned products of clupea pilchardus. This equality of treatment had been guaranteed by notes exchanged between the two Governments in 1925 and 1927.

3. The Torquay negotiations were conducted on the basis of the draft of a new German Customs Tariff, following the nomenclature elaborated in 1949 by the European Customs Union Study Group. The canned products of clupea pilchardus, clupea sprattus and clupea harengus were classified under separate sub-items of item 1604 C 1, but the duties proposed were uniformly at 30 per cent *ad valorem*. Requests for tariff reductions were submitted by two delegations regarding sub-item (*b*)—sardines (clupea pilchardus) and by Norway regarding sub-item (*d*) sprats and (*e*) herrings. The German delegation was not prepared to negotiate on sub-item (*b*), as the main supplier was not a contracting party, but agreed to enter into negotiations with Norway as regards the duties on "sprats" and "herrings". As a result of the Torquay negotiations, the duty on sardines remained unbound at 30 per cent and was not included in the German Schedule, whereas the duties on "sprats" were bound at 25 per cent and those on "herrings" at 25 per cent and 20 per cent.

4. The German Schedule and the Notes annexed to it do not contain any written commitment on the part of the German Government regarding the granting or continuance of equality of treatment as between the preparations of the various clupeae. Although no agreed minutes were kept in the course of the bilateral negotiations, the Panel was satisfied, on the basis of the evidence submitted, that the question of equality of treatment had been discussed between the two delegations at Torquay and that these conversations resulted in the basic assumption upon which the Norwegian delegation conducted its negotiations, i.e., that the Norwegian "Brisling" and "Silde" sardines would continue to be granted full customs equality with preparations of clupea pilchardus.

5. At the time when the Torquay concessions entered into force the import duty applicable to sardines (clupea pilchardus) had been reduced. The German Government considered that it was bound by the tariff concession granted to Portugal before the war for that product and applied a specific duty of RM. 30 per 100 kgs. as before the war; this duty was replaced soon after by an *ad valorem* duty of 14 per cent. As the duties on preparations of clupea sprattus and harengus remained at the level bound at Torquay, this change introduced a differential of 6 per cent in certain cases and of 11 per cent in other cases between the duties applicable to the preparations of various types of clupeae.

6. The German Government levies on imports a charge equivalent to the German turnover tax; the rates of this countervailing tax have been fixed in a law which entered into force after the conclusion of the Torquay negotiations. In the course of these negotiations, several delegations, including the Norwegian delegation, discussed this problem with the German delegation, but did not obtain definite information on the way in which this countervailing tax would operate. According to evidence submitted to the Panel, the rate of the countervailing tax is normally 4 per cent but this rate may be increased to 6 per cent if it is ascertained that the incidence of internal taxes on the like domestic products equals or exceeds that figure. In the computation of such incidence, the German authorities include not only the 4 per cent turnover tax on the finished product but also the so-called *Vorbelastung*, i.e. the incidence of the taxes which have been paid on the raw materials and semi-finished products at various stages of processing. As the German authorities estimated that the domestic preparations of clupea sprattus and clupea harengus were subject to a tax incidence of more than 6 per cent, the rate for the imported like products has been fixed at 6 per cent. As there is no domestic production of preparations of clupea pilchardus, the imports of such products are subject to the standard rate of 4 per cent. The tax differential of 2 per cent, as between the various types of imports, represents an additional adverse factor in the relative competitive position of the Norwegian product.

7. The Panel noted that the operation of the German countervailing tax in the circumstances described in paragraph 6 above, had the effect of subjecting the German preparations of clupea sprattus and clupea harengus to a turnover tax of 4 per cent (*if the Vorbelastung is not taken into account*), whereas the like imported products are subject to a 6 per cent countervailing charge and that an additional 1 per cent tax may be levied on them when they are sold by the importer to the wholesaler.

8. As a result of measures taken within the framework of the OEEC program of liberalisation, the German Government decided to place the preparations of clupea pilchardus on a free list as from April 1, 1952, whereas the products of clupea sprattus and clupea harengus remained subject to quantitative restrictions. Consequently, the preparations of clupea pilchardus, originating in the territories of the OEEC countries, are imported without limitation in Germany, whereas the imports of the preparations of other varieties cannot exceed the quotas that may be granted unilaterally by Germany or agreed in the course of bilateral trade agreements. This difference of treatment constitutes an additional

adverse factor in the relative competitive position of the Norwegian products.

9. According to the figures submitted by the parties, the exports of Norwegian preparations of clupea sprattus and clupea harengus to Germany have undergone a substantial decrease in the first seven months of 1952, as compared with the exports in the corresponding period of 1951. As, however, those export figures include the exports to United States military units in Western Germany, which are not subject to import duty and as the fluctuations in the volume of German imports of canned fish products from all sources in recent years have been particularly erratic, the Panel did not feel that an analysis of the recent trade statistics would lead to definite conclusions as regards the existence of any causal relationship between the measures taken by the German Government and the reduction in the volume of Norwegian exports of fish products to Germany. Nor did the Panel feel that it was necessary for a finding of nullification or impairment under Article XXIII first to establish statistical evidence of damage.

III. CONSISTENCY OF THE GERMAN MEASURES WITH THE PROVISIONS OF ARTICLE I: 1 AND ARTICLE XIII: 1.

10. The Panel considered whether, by failing to extend to particular preparations of the clupeoid family, of interest to Norway, the advantages, favors and privileges granted by Germany to other preparations of the same family, which are of interest to Portugal, Germany had acted inconsistently with the provisions of paragraph 1 of Article I and of paragraph 1 of Article XIII of the General Agreement.

11. The Panel noted that the difference of treatment was not based on the origin of the goods but on the assumption that preparations of clupea pilchardus, clupea sprattus and clupea harengus are not "like products" within the terms of Article I and Article XIII.

12. The Panel noted also that the General Agreement made a distinction between "like products" and "directly competitive or substitutable products" and that the most-favored-nation treatment clause in the General Agreement was limited to "like products". The Panel did not feel that it was called upon to give a definition of "like products" or that it was necessary for the consideration of the Norwegian complaint to

decide whether the preparations of clupea pilchardus, clupea sprattus and clupea harengus had to be generally treated as "like products". Although the Norwegian complaint rested to a large extent on the concept of "like products" as set out in the Agreement and the German reply addressed itself also to that concept, the Panel was satisfied that it would be sufficient to consider whether in the conduct of the negotiations at Torquay the two parties agreed expressly or tacitly to treat these preparations as if they were "like products" for the purposes of the General Agreement.

13. The evidence produced before the Panel shows that in the course of the Torquay negotiations the German delegation has consistently treated the preparation of the various types of clupeae as if they were separate products; the wording of item 1604 and its sub-items was not objected to by other delegations and separate negotiations were in effect conducted on the various sub-items. The Norwegian delegation tried without success to obtain that preparations of sprats and herrings should be treated as sardines for marketing purposes and, failing that, was content with assurances that equality of treatment in customs matters would be continued. It would seem, therefore, that the Norwegian Government, in order to secure the extension of advantages or privileges granted to preparations of clupea pilchardus to preparations of clupea sprattus and clupea herengus, relied on assurances which it considered it has obtained in the course of the negotiation rather than on the automatic operation of the most-favored-nation clause.

14. Since the draft German customs tariff was first submitted at Torquay, there has been no unilateral splitting-up of item 1604; one change has been introduced with the concurrence of the Norwegian delegation at Torquay in order to provide for a privileged treatment for certain preparations of herring.

15. The examination of the evidence submitted led the Panel to the conclusion that no sufficient evidence had been presented to show that the German Government had failed to carry out its obligations under Article I: 1 and Article XIII: 1. The Panel did not consider that it was necessary to consider whether the practical application of the German countervailing tax was inconsistent with the provisions of Article III: 2, or whether the failure to liberalise imports of preparations of clupea sprattus and clupea harengus, even though consistent with the provisions of Article XIII: 1 of the General Agreement, was inconsistent with other provisions of Articles XII to XIV.

IV. NULLIFICATION OR IMPAIRMENT OF THE CONCESSIONS GRANTED TO NORWAY ON PREPARATIONS OF CLUPEA SPRATTUS AND CLUPEA HARENGUS

16. The Panel next considered whether the injury which the Government of Norway claimed it had suffered represented a nullification or an impairment of a benefit accruing to Norway directly or indirectly under the General Agreement and was therefore subject to the provisions of Article XXIII. It agreed that such impairment would exist if the action of the German Government, which resulted in upsetting the competitive relationship between preparations of clupea pilchardus and preparations of the other varieties of the clupeoid family could not reasonably have been anticipated by the Norwegian Government at the time it negotiated for tariff reductions on preparations of clupea sprattus and clupea harengus. The Panel concluded that the Government of Norway had reason to assume, during these negotiations that preparations of the type of clupeae in which they were interested would not be less favorably treated than other preparations of the same family and that this situation would not be modified by unilateral action of the German Government. In reaching this conclusion, the Panel was influenced in particular by the following circumstances:

(a) the products of the various varieties of clupeae are closely related and are considered by many interested parties as directly competitive;

(b) that both parties agreed that the question of the equality of treatment was discussed in the course of the Torquay negotiations; and

(c) although no conclusive evidence was produced as to the scope and tenor of the assurances or statements which may have been given or made in the course of these discussions, it is reasonable to assume that the Norwegian delegation in assessing the value of the concessions offered by Germany regarding preparations of clupeae and in offering counter concessions, had taken into account the advantages resulting from the continuation of the system of equality which had prevailed ever since 1925.

17. As the measures taken by the German Government have nullified the validity of the assumptions which governed the attitude of the Norwegian delegation and substantially reduced the value of the

concessions obtained by Norway, the Panel found that the Norwegian Government is justified in claiming that it had suffered an impairment of a benefit accruing to it under the General Agreement.

18. In the light of the considerations set out above, the Panel suggests to the CONTRACTING PARTIES that it would be appropriate for the CONTRACTING PARTIES to make a recommendation to Germany and Norway in accordance with the first sentence of paragraph 2 of Article XXIII. This recommendation should aim at restoring, as far as practicable, the competitive relationship which existed at the time when the Norwegian Government negotiated at Torquay and which that Government could reasonably expect to be continued.

SPECIAL IMPORT TAXES INSTITUTED BY GREECE

Report adopted by the Contracting Parties on November 3, 1952
BISD 1S/48

1. The Panel on Complaints examined with the representatives of Greece and France the complaint of the French Government regarding the alleged inconsistency of a special "contribution" levied by the Greek Government on certain imported goods. Representatives of the International Monetary Fund participated in the discussions on this matter. The French delegation, supported by the United Kingdom delegation, contended that the tax was applied only on imported products and was contrary to the provisions of paragraph 2 of Article III of the General Agreement as no corresponding charge was levied on like domestic products. The United Kingdom delegation maintained also that, if it were found that the Greek "contribution" was not to be considered as an internal tax or charge within the meaning of Article III, it would nevertheless have to be treated as an import charge within the meaning of Article II, and, as that charge was in excess of those authorized by the provisions of that Article, it was contrary to those provisions insofar as it applied to products in Schedule XXV.

2. On the other hand, the Greek delegation stated that the contribution levied by its Government was, to all intents and purposes, a charge imposed on foreign exchange allocated for the importation of goods from abroad equivalent to a multiple currency practice, which measure was considered by the Greek Government as indispensable to cover the constantly widening gap between the official exchange rates of the drachma in relation to foreign currency and the effective purchasing power of the drachma. Accordingly, this contribution did not fall under Article III, the application of which was limited to internal taxes applied on imported products.

3. The Panel attempted to elucidate the factual situation and to analyse the complicated issues involved.

4. One of the main difficulties in this connection was the fact that the "contribution" against which the French Government complaint was directed has undergone substantial changes since it was introduced in

November 1951. It might be useful to record that the original measure was repealed on December 31, 1951 and replaced by new regulations which in turn were modified by a new order dated October 8, 1952. As the text of the new Decree has been available in Geneva only a few days, the delegations concerned were not in a position to examine the changes recently introduced.

5. It appeared to the Panel that the principal question arising for determination was whether or not the Greek tax was an internal tax or charge on imported products within the meaning of paragraph 2 of Article III. If the finding on this point were affirmative, the Panel considered that it would be subject to the provisions of Article III whatever might have been the underlying intent of the Greek Government in imposing the tax.

6. In this connection, the Panel took into account the comments of the Committee of the Havana Conference which drafted the text of Article 18 of the Havana Charter which, with a few verbal changes, replaced the original text of Article III of the General Agreement. These comments are as follows:

> "The Sub-Committee considered that charges imposed in connection with the international transfer of payments for imports or exports, particularly the charges imposed by countries employing multiple currency practices, where such charges are imposed not inconsistently with the Articles of Agreement of the International Monetary Fund, would not be covered by Article 18. On the other hand, in the unlikely case of a multiple currency practice which takes the form of an internal tax or charge, such as an excise tax on an imported product not applied on the like domestic product, that practice would be precluded by Article 18. It may be pointed out that the possible existence of charges on the transfer of payments insofar as these are permitted by the International Monetary Fund is clearly recognized by Article 16."

7. On the other hand, if the contention of the Greek Government were accepted that the tax was not in nature of a tax or charge on imported goods but was a tax on foreign exchange allocated for the payment of imports, the question would arise whether this was a multiple currency practice, and, if so, whether it was in conformity with the Articles of Agreement of the International Monetary Fund. These matters would be for the determination of the International Monetary

Fund. If the Fund should find that the tax system was a multiple currency practice and in conformity with the Articles of Agreement of the International Monetary Fund, it would fall outside the scope of Article III.

8. Even if it were found that the tax did not fall within the ambit of Article III the further question might arise under Article XV: 4 whether the action of the Greek Government constituted frustration by exchange action of the intent of the provisions of Article III of the General Agreement.

9. The Panel does not feel that sufficient information is available at the present time as to the nature of the tax system or method of its application to enable a determination to be made as to whether it falls within the terms of Article III, or constitutes additional import charges under Article II. It therefore recommends that the CONTRACTING PARTIES invite the interested contracting parties to submit additional information on these points. In particular, the Panel suggests that the CONTRACTING PARTIES should request additional information regarding the operation of the tax system introduced by the Greek Government on October 8, 1952, its form and its method of application.

10. The Panel suggest moreover that the CONTRACTING PARTIES should address an enquiry to the International Monetary Fund as to whether the Greek "contribution" in force since October 8, 1952 (*a*) is a multiple currency practice, and (*b*) whether or not it is in conformity with the Articles of Agreement of the International Monetary Fund.

11. If these steps are taken, the Panel considers that the CONTRACTING PARTIES, when they come to deal with the matter again, will have before them the necessary information to determine whether the Greek "contribution" is an internal tax or charge on imported goods within the meaning of Article III or an additional import charge under Article II, and at the same time the findings of the Fund.

12. At that time, the CONTRACTING PARTIES could also consider whether any question arose under Article XV: 4.

13. In suggesting that the CONTRACTING PARTIES defer a decision on this point pending the receipt of further information the Panel have taken into account that, although both the French and United Kingdom delegations have stated that they are suffering commercial damage as a result of the "contribution" imposed by Greece, this is not their major concern in having the matter brought before the CONTRACTING PARTIES. The desire of these two contracting parties is to obtain a decision

on principle from the CONTRACTING PARTIES and, in the event that the measures were judged inconsistent with the General Agreement, the withdrawal or modification of these measures by the Greek Government.

INCREASE IN IMPORT DUTIES ON PRODUCTS INCLUDED IN SCHEDULE XXV (GREECE)

Report adopted by the Contracting Parties on November 3, 1952
BISD 1S/51

1. The Panel on Complaints investigated, with the assistance of the delegations of the United Kingdom and Greece, the consistency of Decision No. 766 taken by the Greek Cabinet on July 10, 1952 with the obligations of the Greek Government under the General Agreement.

2. When the Greek Government conducted tariff negotiations at Annecy and Torquay within the framework of the General Agreement, it agreed to bind the coefficients applied before 1939 for the conversion of metallic drachmae rates of customs duty into paper drachmae notes on items included in Schedule XXV and those coefficients were specified in a note to that Schedule. The Decision of July 10 increased those coefficients on a number of products to levels in excess of those specified in the Greek Schedule. The new levels of these coefficients, as well as the levels at which they were bound in Schedule XXV, are listed in the Annex to this Report.

3. The United Kingdom Government, as well as other contracting parties interested, maintained that this Decision constituted an infringement of the provisions of paragraph 1 of Article II of the General Agreement. The Greek Government agreed that this emergency measure taken in last July was not consistent with its obligations under the General Agreement.

4. The Greek Government indicated that the measure had been taken as an emergency measure to meet acute financial difficulties and undertook to withdraw the Decision and to revert before July 1, 1953 to the levels bound under the General Agreement. The United Kingdom delegation, as well as the delegations of other contracting parties affected, stated that they recognized that the Greek Government had to encounter serious difficulties and that their Governments would be prepared to consider that the case would be settled to their satisfaction if the coefficients applied to the products described in Schedule XXV were brought down to the agreed levels specified in the Schedule before the date suggested by the Greek delegation.

5. In this connection, the Panel recommends that the CONTRACTING PARTIES take note of the undertaking given on behalf of the Greek Government to remove the measure within the time-limit suggested and to ask that Government to report on the measures taken to implement this undertaking.

6. Accordingly, the Panel submits a draft resolution to the CONTRACTING PARTIES for consideration and approval.

BELGIAN FAMILY ALLOWANCES (ALLOCATIONS FAMILIALES)

Report adopted by the Contracting Parties on November 7, 1952
BISD 1S/59

I. EXAMINATION OF THE LEGAL ISSUES INVOLVED

1. The Panel on Complaints examined the legal issues involved in the complaint submitted by the Norwegian and Danish delegations regarding the application of the Belgian law on the levy of a charge on foreign goods purchased by public bodies when these goods originated in a country whose system of family allowances did not meet specific requirements.

2. After examining the legal provisions regarding the methods of collection of that charge, the Panel came to the conclusion that the 7.5 per cent levy was collected only on products purchased by public bodies for their own use and not on imports as such, and that the levy was charged, not at the time of importation, but when the purchase price was paid by the public body. In those circumstances, it would appear that the levy was to be treated as an "internal charge" within the meaning of paragraph 2 of Article III of the General Agreement, and not as an import charge within the meaning of paragraph 2 of Article II.

3. According to the provisions of paragraph 1 of Article I of the General Agreement, any advantage, favor, privilege or immunity granted by Belgium to any product originating in the territory of any country with respect to all matters referred to in paragraph 2 of Article III shall be granted immediately and unconditionally to the like product originating in the territories of all contracting parties. Belgium has granted exemption from the levy under consideration to products purchased by public bodies when they originate in Luxemburg and the Netherlands, as well as in France, Italy, Sweden and the United Kingdom. If the General Agreement were definitively in force in accordance with Article XXVI, it is clear that that exemption would have to be granted unconditionally to all other contracting parties (including Denmark and Norway). The consistency or otherwise of the system of family allowances in force in the territory of a given contracting party with the requirements of the Belgian law would be irrelevant in this respect, and

the Belgian legislation would have to be amended insofar as it introduced a discrimination between countries having a given system of family allowances and those which had a different system or no system at all, and made the granting of the exemption dependent on certain conditions.

4. The Panel wishes to stress that this undertaking to extend an exemption of an internal charge unconditionally is not qualified by any other provision of the Agreement. The Panel did not feel that the provisions of paragraph 8 (*a*) of Article III were applicable in this case as the text of the paragraph referred only to laws, regulations and requirements and not to internal taxes or charges. As regards the exception contained in paragraph 2 of Article XVII, it would appear that it referred only to the principle set forth in paragraph 1 of that Article, *i.e.* the obligation to make purchases in accordance with commercial considerations and did not extend to matters dealt with in Article III.

5. The Panel then considered whether the fact that the General Agreement was applied only provisionally had a bearing on the Belgian obligations under Article I with regard to internal taxes. It recognised that the Interpretative Note to Article I allowed Belgium to observe those obligations "to the fullest extent not inconsistent with existing legislation", so long as Belgium was applying the Agreement pursuant to the Protocol of Provisional Application. The Belgian law on family allowances dated back to 1930, and the provisions now applicable were enacted in a Royal Decree of December 19, 1939, with the exception of the provision fixing the rate of the levy, which was amended on March 27, 1951.

6. The Panel noted, however, that, in another case, the CONTRACTING PARTIES agreed that the Protocol of Provisional Application had to be construed so as to limit the operation of the provisions of paragraph 1 (*b*) of the Protocol to those cases where "the legislation on which [the measure] is based is, by its tenor or expressed intent, of a mandatory character—that is, it imposes on the executive authorities requirements which cannot be modified by executive action".[1]

7. The Panel, although recognizing that the relevant provisions of the Belgian royal decree appeared to be of a mandatory character, noted that, as pointed out by the Danish and the Norwegian representatives and admitted by the Belgian representative, it had been possible for the Belgian executive authorities to grant an exemption to a country whose system of family allowances did not meet fully the requirements of the

[1]See Case 3.

law. Even if it might be difficult for the Belgian authorities to take similar action in similar cases, the Panel did not feel that it had been proved to its satisfaction that the Belgian legislation fulfilled all the conditions laid down by the CONTRACTING PARTIES to justify an exception under the Protocol of Provisional Application.

II. RECOMMENDATION

8. The Panel felt that the legal issues involved in the complaint under consideration are such that it would be difficult for the CONTRACTING PARTIES to arrive at a very definite ruling. On the other hand, it was of the opinion that the Belgian legislation on family allowances was not only inconsistent with the provisions of Article I (and possibly with those of Article III, paragraph 2), but was based on a concept which was difficult to reconcile with the spirit of the General Agreement and that the CONTRACTING PARTIES should note with satisfaction the statements made at the Sixth and Seventh Sessions by the Belgian representatives and should recommend to the Belgian Government to expedite the consideration and the adoption of the necessary measures, consistent with the General Agreement, including a possible amendment of the Belgian legislation, to remove the discrimination complained of, and to refer to the CONTRACTING PARTIES not later than the first day of the Eighth Session.

NETHERLANDS ACTION UNDER ARTICLE XXIII:2 TO SUSPEND OBLIGATIONS TO THE UNITED STATES

Report adopted by the Contracting Parties on November 8, 1952
BISD 1S/62

1. At the Sixth Session the CONTRACTING PARTIES decided that the import restrictions on dairy products maintained by the United States under Section 104 of the Defense Production Act were contrary to the provisions of the General Agreement and, under the circumstances, were sufficiently serious to justify recourse to paragraph 2 of Article XXIII, by the contracting parties affected. That paragraph provides in part that, if the CONTRACTING PARTIES consider that the circumstances are serious enough to justify such action, they may authorise a contracting party or parties to suspend the application to any other contracting party or parties of such obligations or concessions under the Agreement as the CONTRACTING PARTIES determine to be appropriate in the circumstances. Therefore, the Netherlands delegation requested the CONTRACTING PARTIES, in accordance with Article XXIII: 2, to authorise the Netherlands to suspend the application to the United States of its obligations under the Agreement to the extent necessary to allow the Netherlands to impose an upper limit of 57,000 metric tons on imports of wheat flour from the United States during the calendar year 1953. This would constitute an annual reduction of approximately 15,000 metric tons from the rate of current imports from the United States.

2. The Working Party was instructed by the CONTRACTING PARTIES to investigate the appropriateness of the measure which the Netherlands Government proposed to take, having regard to its equivalence to the impairment suffered by the Netherlands as a result of the United States restrictions.

3. The Working Party felt that the appropriateness of the measure envisaged by the Netherlands Government should be considered from two points of view: in the first place whether, in the circumstances, the measure proposed was appropriate in character, and secondly, whether the extent of the quantitative restriction proposed by the Netherlands government was reasonable, having regard to the impairment suffered.

4. Although the Working Party recognised that it was appropriate to consider calculations of the trade affected by the measures and counter-measures in question, it was aware that a purely statistical test would not, by itself, be sufficient and that it would also be necessary to consider the broader economic elements entering into the assessment of the impairment suffered. It was agreed therefore that it would be proper to take into account the contention of the Netherlands Government that the restrictions imposed by the United States had had serious effects on the efforts which were being made by the Netherlands to stimulate its exports to the United States not only of the products subject to the restrictions but of other products as well, and the further contention of the Netherlands government that the restrictions had affected its efforts to overcome balance-of-payments difficulties with which the country was confronted.

5. The meetings of the Working Party were conducted in a spirit of co-operation. The representatives of the Netherlands and the United States presented statements, including statistical information, for the guidance of the Working Party.

6. The Working Party recognised the difficulties inherent in fixing, with any real precision, the point at which any proposed measure could no longer be considered reasonable. The Working Party was of the view that the size of the measure proposed could not be regarded as unreasonable. However, on the basis of its independent review of the circumstances and of the considerations adduced at this Session, the Working Party decided to recommend a measure somewhat different in magnitude from that proposed by the Netherlands.

7. The Working Party submits to the CONTRACTING PARTIES a draft decision for their consideration and approval.

BRAZILIAN INTERNAL TAXES

Resolution of October 24, 1953
BISD 2S/25

Considering that the CONTRACTING PARTIES have had on their Agenda for six successive sessions the issue raised by the Government of France concerning the increased discrimination against imported products in the application of certain internal taxes maintained by the Government of Brazil,

Considering that on June 2, 1950 the Government of Brazil sent a message to the Brazilian Congress requesting action towards amending all existing laws which provide for different levels of taxation with respect to domestic and imported products in order to bring these laws into conformity with Article III of the General Agreement,

Considering that at their Fifth Session the CONTRACTING PARTIES examined a draft law prepared by the Brazilian Government for adoption by their Congress and found that it appeared to eliminate for the most part the discrimination in favor of domestic products which had been adopted or increased since October 30, 1947, and

Considering that the Brazilian Congress has not yet passed legislation to bring these laws into conformity with Article III of the General Agreement,

The CONTRACTING PARTIES

Urge the Government of Brazil to take all steps necessary to amend the existing laws so as to bring them into conformity with the General Agreement and to report, as early as possible and in any case not later than the Ninth Session, to the CONTRACTING PARTIES on action taken in this matter.

FRENCH SPECIAL TEMPORARY COMPENSATION TAX ON IMPORTS

Decision of January 17, 1955
BISD 3S/26

Having considered the complaint submitted by the Italian Government regarding a special temporary compensation tax imposed by the French Government on certain goods imported into its customs territory,

Having examined carefully, in the light of the provisions of Articles I and II of the General Agreement, the circumstances in which the French Government introduced the tax,

Having heard the explanation given by the French Government that its purpose has not been to replace the incidental protection afforded by the maintenance of quantitative restrictions under Article XII of the General Agreement by additional tariff protection, but solely to resort to a temporary and transitional device designed to facilitate the removal of quantitative restrictions on imports into France of the goods affected from the other countries members of the Organization for European Economic Co-operation, that the French Government would otherwise have felt entitled, under the provisions of the said Article XII, to maintain these restrictions, and that there was no question of charging the tax on any imports for which these restrictions were maintained,

The CONTRACTING PARTIES have reached the following conclusions:

1. whatever may have been the reasons which motivated the French Government's decision, and whatever may have been the French Government's interpretation of the relevant provisions of the General Agreement in respect of many of the goods affected, the tax has increased the incidence of customs charges in excess of maximum rates bound under Article II, and the application of the tax introduces, in respect of the products affected, an increase in the incidence of preferences in excess of the maximum margins permissible under Article I; and

2. it follows that the action of the French Government justifies the invocation of the provisions of Article XXIII and that any contracting party whose trade is adversely affected has grounds to

propose under paragraph 2 of that Article such compensatory action as it may think appropriate for authorization by the CONTRACTING PARTIES.

The CONTRACTING PARTIES regret, in view of the foregoing, that the French Government should have decided to impose the tax without first presenting its case to them for their consideration.

The CONTRACTING PARTIES

Take note of the action taken on November 16, 1954 by the French Government to reduce the incidence of the tax for a number of goods,

Take note further of the declaration in which the French Government

(a) has undertaken to remove the tax as soon as it is possible to do so, and

(b) has expressed its firm intention of adopting definite measures to assure effective progress towards a more liberal system of trade,

Instruct the Intersessional Committee to follow closely the measures taken by the French Government to implement the undertaking referred to in paragraph (*a*) of the above-mentioned declaration,

Recommend that the French Government take steps to reduce the present degree of discrimination against the trade of contracting parties whose exports are subject to the tax but to which the liberalization measures taken by the French Government do not apply,

Call upon the French Government to report to the Intersessional Committee on the measures taken by it to implement the undertaking and recommendation referred to above, the first report to be communicated to the Executive Secretary before April 1, 1955 and circulated forthwith to all contracting parties; and to participate in any consultations which the Ad Hoc Committee may initiate at the request of any contracting party or parties,

Decide to review this matter at the Tenth Session in the light of progress achieved in carrying out the aforesaid undertakings of the French Government and recommendation of the CONTRACTING PARTIES.

SWEDISH ANTIDUMPING DUTIES

Report adopted on February 26, 1955
BISD 3S/81

INTRODUCTION

1. The Panel on Complaints examined with the representatives of Italy and Sweden the complaint of the Italian Government that the Swedish anti-dumping regulations were not consistent with the obligations of Sweden under the General Agreement and that the administration of these regulations impaired the benefits which should accrue to Italy under that Agreement. The Panel heard statements from the two parties and obtained from them additional information to clarify a number of points. On the basis of that documentation, the Panel considered if and to what extent the Swedish Royal Decree of October 15, 1954 regarding the levying of anti-dumping duties with respect to the importation of ladies stockings of nylon or similar synthetic fibers was consistent with the provisions of the General Agreement. It considered further whether and to what extent the administration of that decree had actually impaired the benefits accruing directly or indirectly to the Government of Italy under the General Agreement. Finally, the Panel agreed on the text of a recommendation which, in its opinion, would best assist the Italian and Swedish Governments in arriving at a satisfactory adjustment of the question submitted by Italy to the CONTRACTING PARTIES.

FACTS OF THE CASE

2. On May 29, 1954, the Swedish Government introduced anti-dumping duties on the importation of nylon stockings. In accordance with this Decree, an anti-dumping duty was levied whenever the invoice price was lower than the relevant minimum price fixed by the Swedish Government, the importer being entitled to obtain a refund of that duty if the case of dumping was not established. The Italian complaint was

related to that Decree. However, a new decree was issued on October 15, 1954, i.e. before the Italian complaint was considered by the CONTRACTING PARTIES. The main difference between the new decree and the preceding one was that the basic prices were no longer a determining factor for the assessment of the anti-dumping duty but were retained as an administrative device enabling the Swedish Customs Authorities to exempt from anti-dumping enquiries any consignment the price of which was higher than the basic price; the actual determination of dumping policies and the levying of the anti-dumping duty were related to the concept of normal value which was defined in terms similar to those of Article VI of the General Agreement. The anti-dumping duty is assessed in relation to the basic price only when that price is lower than the normal value of the imported product.

3. In spite of the changes introduced in the Swedish regulations, the Italian Government maintained its complaint on the ground that, even though the basic prices had become an administrative device, the maintenance of that system was inconsistent with Article VI and other provisions of the Agreement and the administration of that system had in effect impaired benefits which should accrue to Italy under the General Agreement.

ALLEGED INCONSISTENCY OF THE SWEDISH DECREE WITH THE PROVISIONS OF PARAGRAPH 1 OF ARTICLE I AND OF ARTICLE VI

4. The Italian delegation contended that the system of basic prices, as an anti-dumping procedure, represented by itself an infringement of the provisions of the General Agreement for the following reasons:

(a) it discriminated against low-cost producers and deprived them of the competitive advantages to which they were entitled under the general most-favored-nation clause;

(b) that system did not take into account the differences existing in the various exporting countries or the actual price differences between the various qualities of goods on the exporting market; the fixing of uniform prices irrespective of the country of supply and the averaging of different prices of products could not be reconciled with the provisions of Article VI of the General Agreement;

(c) the official character of these basic prices would tend to influence unduly the decisions by the Customs Authorities and render ineffective the formal protection which the decree appeared to afford to exporters by providing that the levying and assessment of anti-dumping duties would be related to normal prices as defined in Article VI of the General Agreement;

(d) In those circumstances, the basic price system would tend to become a system by which minimum prices are imposed for the admission of imported goods whether there is dumping or not; this type of protection against efficient producers would deprive low-cost exporters of the price advantage which they enjoy when the protection is administered through a most-favoured-nation tariff, and change fundamentally the conditions of competition which Italy could reasonably have expected to be protected by the General Agreement.

5. In this connection, two further arguments were advanced by the Italian representative, namely that the Decree reverses the onus of the proof since the customs authorities are authorized to prevent the import of goods without establishing even a *prima facie* case of dumping. The importer is in effect prevented from clearing the goods without delay or added costs and is placed at a legal disadvantage by that administrative technique. Finally, the Swedish Decree does not provide for the exemption or refund of duties or taxes in the importing country as is required in paragraph 4 of Article VI of the General Agreement.

6. The Panel considered these various contentions in detail and came to the conclusions which are summarized in the following paragraphs.

7. Regarding the alleged discrimination against low-cost producers, the Italian argument was as follows: it is agreed that the cost of production of nylon stockings is different in the various supplying countries. In the absence of anti-dumping duties, the low-cost producer has a substantial price advantage as compared with the high-cost producer. If the high-cost producer subsidizes its exports to the extent necessary to bring down its export price to the level of the Swedish price, he would not be affected by the Swedish anti-dumping regulations. On the other hand, the low-cost producer, if his normal price was equal to or lower than the Swedish basic price, would have lost his price advantage if he were to sell without dumping. If, in order to meet the changed conditions of the competition, he were to resort to dumping practices, he would have to pay in full the anti-dumping duty, even if the amount of dumping in his case were much lower than in the case of the high-cost producer. The

Italian Government considered that this would amount to a discrimination against the low-cost producer.

8. The Panel considered that this argument was not entirely convincing. If the low-cost producer is actually resorting to dumping practices, he forgoes the protection embodied in the most-favored-nation clause. On the other hand, Article VI does not oblige an importing country to levy an anti-dumping duty whenever there is a case of dumping, or to treat in the same manner all suppliers who resort to such practices. The wording of paragraph 6 supports that view. The importing country is only entitled to levy an anti-dumping duty when there is material injury to a domestic industry or at least a threat of such an injury. If, therefore, the importing country considers that the imports above a certain price are not prejudicial to its domestic industry, the text of paragraph 6 does not oblige it to levy an anti-dumping duty on imports coming from high-cost suppliers, but, on the contrary, prevents it from doing so. On the other hand, if the price at which the imports of the low-cost producers are sold is prejudicial to the domestic industry, the levying of an anti-dumping duty is perfectly permissible, provided, of course, that the case of dumping is clearly established.

9. The Panel recognized however that the basic price system would have a serious discriminatory effect if consignments of the goods exported by the low-cost producers had been delayed and subjected to uncertainties by the application of that system and the case for dumping were not established in the course of the enquiry. The fact that the low-cost producer would thus have been at a disadvantage whereas the high-cost producer would have been able to enter his goods freely even at dumping prices would clearly discriminate against the low-cost producer.

10. As regards the second argument relating to the fact that the basic price system is unrelated to the actual prices on the domestic markets of the various exporting countries, the Panel was of the opinion that this feature of the scheme would not necessarily be inconsistent with the provisions of Article VI so long as the basic price is equal to or lower than the actual price on the market of the lowest cost producer. If that condition is fulfilled, no anti-dumping duty will be levied contrary to the provision of Article VI. The Swedish representative stressed that the basic prices were fixed in accordance with that principle. (See also paragraph 22 below.)

11. The second part of the Italian argument is to the effect that the basic price system groups the various types of stockings into categories and that the average price for each category differs from the actual price

for the various products included in the same category. As an example, the Italian representative indicated that the Swedish Decree provides for the price of 46 Sw. crowns for the 60 gauge stockings and for 40 crowns for the 51-54 gauges, a differential of 6 crowns which is substantially different from the actual price differential on the Italian market which does not exceed 2 Sw. crowns. In those circumstances, the administration of the system cannot guarantee that only consignments of dumped goods would be subjected to an enquiry. If the price of 40 crowns is correct for the 51-54 gauges, the price of 46 crowns for the 60 gauge would be too high, and the consignments of 60 gauge stockings would be delayed or subject to uncertainties for an indefinite period although the goods would have been exported at a normal price.

12. As regards the contention that the official character of the basic prices would unduly influence the actual decisions on alleged anti-dumping practices, the Panel was not in a position to come to any definite conclusion since no evidence was submitted by either party regarding the way in which individual cases have been settled. In view of the fact, however, that, before October, the basic price was actually used as a determining factor and of the statement by the Swedish representative that the basic prices have been fixed by the Swedish authorities as a result of an official enquiry, it would be reasonable to suppose that the customs authorities would be guided to a large extent by those basic prices. Since, however, the determining factor would be in any case the domestic price in the exporting country, if it is lower than the basic price, the Decree would not be inconsistent with the General Agreement if it were applied correctly.

13. The further contention that the basic prices would in effect prevent any import of the product except at a price which would be fixed arbitrarily by the Swedish authorities and might, therefore, nullify any price advantage which low-cost exporters should enjoy did not appear to the Panel to be conclusive if it is assumed that the system would apply to cases of dumping. Of course, if the system were to be applied when the case of dumping is not established, that particular technique might be more prejudicial to the interests of low-cost producers than other anti-dumping techniques.

14. In this connection, the Swedish representative pointed out that the ordinary customs duties for nylon stockings were comparatively low, and that the Swedish Government did not make use of its right to raise the rate to the level of 25 per cent at which it had been bound. The Italian representative pointed out that, if the Swedish industry were suffering from competition from low-cost producers, such as Italian

producers, the Swedish Government would be entitled, under the General Agreement, to raise its customs duties. The Italian Government would raise no objection to such a measure, as it would not deprive Italy of its competitive advantage over other suppliers.

15. The Panel then considered the argument developed by the Italian representative to the effect that the Swedish Decree reversed the onus of the proof since the customs authorities can act without being required to prove the existence of dumping practices or even to establish a *prima facie* case of dumping. The Panel considered that it was not competent to deal with the legal rules which may exist in Sweden regarding procedures before customs authorities or the courts. On the other hand, it was clear from the wording of Article VI that no anti-dumping duties should be levied unless certain facts had been established. As this represented an obligation on the part of the contracting party imposing such duties, it would be reasonable to expect that that contracting party should establish the existence of these facts when its action is challenged.

16. Finally, the Panel noted that there was no disagreement between the parties concerned regarding the obligation to take account of legitimate refund of duties or taxes. The Swedish representative indicated, on behalf of his Government, that the Decree would be applied in a manner fully consistent with the provisions of paragraph 4 of Article VI of the General Agreement. As soon as the Swedish Authorities come to a final conclusion regarding the applicability of paragraph 4 to the Italian refund of taxes and duties—and it is expected that this examination will be completed by the middle of March—the Swedish Government would be prepared to adjust its procedures to take into account such exemptions or refunds which were consistent with Article VI, for such case as may be outstanding and for any future case, provided that the Italian exporters indicate clearly the amount of these refunds on their involves.

17. The general conclusion of the Panel regarding the consistency of the Swedish Decree with the obligations of the Swedish Government under the General Agreement was:

(a) that the basic price system was not inconsistent with the most-favored-nation clause or with the provisions of Article VI,

(b) but that, in practice, the administration of that system might easily run into conflict with those obligations.

Unless the customs authorities were prepared to decide on the alleged cases of dumping in a matter of days after arrival of the consignment, and unless the basic prices were constantly kept under review to make sure that they did not exceed the actual prices prevailing for all the varieties of stockings on the domestic markets of the most efficient producer, there was a certain danger of discrimination against low-cost producers in individual cases. Constant supervision of the operation of the scheme would also be necessary in order to avoid that it might be turned into a general protection against low-cost producers, even in the absence of dumping practices.

ALLEGED NULLIFICATION OR IMPAIRMENT OF BENEFITS ACCRUING TO ITALY UNDER THE GENERAL AGREEMENT

18. The Panel next considered whether the administration of the Decree had actually caused a serious injury to Italian commercial interests, and whether such an injury represented an impairment of the benefits accruing to Italy under the General Agreement.

19. On the basis of the data submitted by the Italian representative, exports of Italian nylon stockings to Sweden decreased to an appreciable extent after the introduction of anti-dumping duties; the reduction affected more particularly the types of stockings which had been submitted to anti-dumping enquiries. Moreover, the amounts of stockings submitted to those enquiries represented about one half of the total export of Italian stockings to Sweden. The Italian representative indicated that the existence of the basic price system has had the effect, not only of causing delays in the clearing of consignments, but also of making Swedish importers reluctant to pass any orders in view of the delays and the uncertainties involved in the procedure.

20. The Italian representative stressed that it took a long time (up to 6 to 7 months) for the Swedish authorities to take a decision and assess the anti-dumping duty. Such delays of course made the operation of the system particularly damaging for exporting countries. The Swedish representative stated that those delays were due to the fact that the customs procedure was quite new and that the customs authorities as well as the importers had no previous experience in dealing with such cases, that some delay had also been occasioned by the changes made in the earlier Decree and the entry into force of a new Decree on October 15, 1954, but that most of the cases outstanding had now been settled.

21. The Panel recommended that the Swedish customs authorities

should endeavour to settle these cases within 20 days, on the understanding that such time limit would not cover the appeal proceedings before an ordinary court. The Swedish representative was prepared on behalf of his Government, to accept that recommendation.

22. Apart from the damage caused by those delays, the Italian delegation contended that the main injury suffered by exporters was due to the fact that the Swedish Government was levying an anti-dumping duty on Italian stockings although it had not established that the export prices of the Italian exporters were less than the normal value of those products as required in Article VI of the GATT. The Panel agreed that if the Swedish Decree was being applied in such a manner as to impose an anti-dumping levy in the absence of dumping practices, the Italian Government would be deprived of the protection it would reasonably expect from the terms of Article VI of the Agreement and that it could claim an impairment of benefits.

23. The Swedish representative stated that it appeared doubtful to his delegation that the CONTRACTING PARTIES could consider that question and that it was the right of the national authorities to decide whether dumping had really taken place. The Panel agreed that no provision of the General Agreement could limit in any way the rights of national authorities in that respect. But, for the reasons set forth in paragraph 15 above, it would be reasonable to expect from the contracting party which resorts to the provisions of Article VI, if such action is challenged, to show to the satisfaction of the CONTRACTING PARTIES that it had exercised its rights consistently with those provisions. The Panel felt therefore that, in order to decide whether Italy had suffered an impairment of benefits, it would be appropriate and necessary to examine whether a case had been made out that Italian stocking exporters had resorted to dumping practices.

24. The Swedish representative indicated that, on the basis of extensive investigations, "the Swedish authorities had established that the normal value of the stockings in question considerably exceeded the invoice prices charged for stockings exported to Sweden". As, however, no definite evidence had been brought forward to support that conclusion, the Panel tried to consider this question in detail on the basis of the factual data obtained from both parties.

25. The Italian representative submitted to the Panel the export prices charged for the "types" of stockings exported to Sweden as well as the official price lists for the sale of those types on the Italian market. These data showed that, if the comparison were limited to the same

types, the export prices to Sweden, even without allowing for any refund of duties or taxes, were not lower than the prices charged on the Italian market, but that both sets of prices were substantially lower than the Swedish basic prices.

26. The Swedish representative considered, however, that such a comparison was not justified for the following reasons: although the stockings exported to Sweden were of the so-called "unmarked" variety and stockings of the same variety were sold on the Italian market, the structure of the Italian market was such that those stockings, when they were sold with a trade-mark, fetched prices substantially higher than if they were "unmarked". Under those circumstances, the Swedish authorities felt that the Italian producers could afford to sell unmarked stockings on the domestic market at less than the normal price and recoup themselves with the additional profits which they could make on the sale of stockings with a trade mark, as the difference in prices was greater than would be justified by cost differences. Accordingly, they decided to calculate the normal price on the basis of a weighted average between the prices of the "unmarked" and "marked" stockings of the same variety.

27. The Italian delegation contended that it would not be consistent with Article VI to compare one product with another type of product, or with a group of like and unlike products. In any case, the Swedish argument would not apply to those producers who do not sell stockings with a trade mark in Italy. Since 9 out of the 15 producers who export to Sweden do not sell stockings with trade marks in Italy, those producers would not even have the means of indulging in the financial operation suggested by the Swedish authorities.

28. The Panel was of the opinion that if the Swedish authorities considered that it was not possible to find "a comparable price in the ordinary course of trade for the like product when destined for consumption in the exporting country", no provision in the General Agreement would prevent them from using one of the other two criteria laid down in Article VI.

29. The Swedish representative indicated that his Government could not rely on the second criterion which involved a comparison with the export prices to third countries as the Swedish delegation sent to Milan to enquire into this matter had not been in a position to obtain relevant data from the Italian manufacturers. The Italian representative explained that this lack of success was not surprising, since the Swedish delegation included two Swedish manufacturers and the Italian manu-

facturers were naturally reluctant to disclose confidential information to competitors.

30. The Panel concluded that, in effect, the Swedish authorities were relying on the third criterion which related to the cost of production. The Panel felt that the use by the Swedish authorities of a weighted average as between the Italian prices could only give a rough estimate of the normal price and that if this approach were retained, it would be reasonable to expect that, if the average included not only the "unmarked" and "marked" first choice stockings of a given type, but also the second and third choices of the same type, the results would be more accurate.

31. In order, however, to see what results the method of calculation adopted by the Swedish authorities would give in a specific instance, the Panel asked the Swedish representative if he could give the actual details of the calculation for one type of stockings. The Panel then compared the data used by the Swedish representative with the official price lists which were used for that calculation and came to the conclusion that, probably through some misunderstandings on a few points, the two sets of figures were difficult to reconcile and that these misunderstandings might explain to a certain extent the divergence of views between the two governments regarding the alleged existence of dumping practices.

32. The Panel felt, therefore, that before it could come to any definite conclusion regarding the difference, if any, between the Italian export prices and the comparable prices on the Italian market, it would be appropriate for the two delegations to try and clarify the facts on which the determination of dumping was based. In its opinion, the best way to arrive at some understanding on this point would be for the Swedish Government to send to Italy a responsible official who, by his functions, would be under an oath of secrecy, and to whom the Italian Government could guarantee free access to the books of the exporters. If such a procedure were acceptable to both parties, and if the Swedish authorities had arrived at definite conclusions regarding the extent to which allowance should be made for the refund of taxes or duties, when the enquiry suggested would be completed, the Panel believes that it would be comparatively easy for the two parties to agree on what is the correct normal price for stockings in Italy, and to determine whether there are any dumping practices as defined in Article VI of the General Agreement. If, however, disagreement should subsist, the Italian Government would be free to refer the matter again to the CONTRACTING PARTIES.

33. In the light of the considerations set out above, the Panel suggests to the CONTRACTING PARTIES that it would be appropriate for them to make a recommendation to Italy and Sweden in accordance with the second sentence of paragraph 2 of Article XXIII. That recommendation should aim at expediting the anti-dumping procedure in Sweden in order to minimize the adverse effects on Italian export trade and at improving the administration of the basic price system, in order to eliminate some of the objections raised by the Italian Government. Accordingly, the Panel submits the following recommendation to the CONTRACTING PARTIES for consideration and approval:

RECOMMENDATION[1]

Having investigated, in accordance with Article XXIII, the complaint of the Italian Government concerning the Swedish Decree regarding the levying of anti-dumping duties on nylon stockings and the manner in which this Decree has been applied with respect to Italian exports,

The CONTRACTING PARTIES

Approve the Report of the Panel and the suggestions contained therein, and

Recommend:

(*a*) that the Swedish Government consider ways and means of improving the administration of the Decree of October 15, 1954 so as to minimize the delays and other impediments to the exports of Italian nylon stockings to Sweden;

(*b*) that the Governments of Italy and Sweden make the necessary arrangements to facilitate an enquiry by the Swedish authorities to clarify the various points of fact on which the two governments hold different views, with a view to determining whether Italian nylon stockings are being exported to Sweden at a price less than their normal value and that they take such action as may be necessary in the light of those conclusions, and

(*c*) that the two parties report to the CONTRACTING PARTIES at the Tenth Session or, should it be necessary, to the Intersessional Committee which is hereby authorized to take such action as may be appropriate in the circumstances.

[1] Adopted together with the Report.

GERMAN IMPORT DUTIES ON STARCH AND POTATO FLOUR

Report noted by the Contracting Parties on February 16, 1955
BISD 3S/77

INTRODUCTION

1. The Panel on Complaints examined with the delegations of the Federal Republic of Germany and of the Benelux countries the complaint of the Benelux countries regarding the failure by Germany to bring down to the level of the Benelux rates the German duties on cereal starch and potato flour as well as on some derivatives. It examined the conditions under which the negotiations on these items were conducted at Torquay between the delegations concerned. It considered further to what extent the promises made by the German delegate at Torquay had been fulfilled so far and the prospects of a full implementation of these promises in a very near future. It was not necessary for the Panel to submit definite recommendations to the CONTRACTING PARTIES since the German delegation was in a position to make an offer which was considered by the Benelux delegations as providing a satisfactory adjustment of the matter for the time being.

FACTS OF THE CASE

2. In the course of the Torquay negotiations, the Benelux delegations requested the German delegation to agree on a reduction of the German import duties on the products specified in paragraph 1 above to the level of the Benelux tariff. The German delegation was only prepared to reduce the rates on cereal starch and potato flour to 25 per cent as compared with 15 per cent in the Benelux tariff, but agreed to give the assurance that further reductions would be contemplated in the near future, and the Chairman of the German delegation addressed a letter to that effect to the Benelux delegations on March 31, 1951. This letter, which is reproduced as an annex to this report, contained two promises which committed the German delegation acting on behalf of its government. The first promise was of a general character; it contained an

agreement by the German Government that the duties would be reduced "as soon as possible". The second was more specific, since the German Government accepted to enter into negotiations after the autumn of 1952 with the Benelux government to solve this problem.

3. The two parties agree that these promises formed part of the balance of concessions granted at Torquay and that the contemplated reduction of the German duties would be made without any further concession from the Benelux Governments. In accordance with the terms of the letter of March 31, 1951, negotiations took place in March 1953; no agreement was reached between the delegations concerned and discussions which took place between the industries concerned regarding potato flour were also inconclusive. Further negotiations took place in February 1954, but difficulties resulting from the direct and indirect effects of the price-support scheme applied in Germany for cereals prevented any progress from being made. Alternative suggestions put forward by the German delegation were not considered as satisfactory by the Benelux governments.

4. After hearing the additional statements and clarifications which the two parties were able to give to it on a number of facts, the Panel felt that there was little prospect of the German Government being able, in the immediate future, to bring down all the duties on the products in question to the level of the Benelux duties. The Chairman of the Panel, therefore, invited the two parties to resume bilateral contacts in order to see whether some alternative but constructive offer could be made by the German delegation and accepted by the Benelux Governments. If no such solution could be found, the Panel would have to adjudicate the matter.

5. At the second meeting of the Panel, the representative of the Federal Republic of Germany made the following offer: the German delegation, while pointing out that the German government was not in a position to modify the customs tariff without approval by Parliament and that the delegation was not therefore prepared to indicate a date for the reduction of the tariff rates, agree to "request the Federal Government to propose to Parliament, within three months after the end of the Ninth Session of the GATT, to grant the following tariff concessions:

1) For *potato starch* a general annual customs quota amounting to 20,000 tons at a tariff rate of 15 per cent;

2) For *maize* and *wheat starch* a reduction of the existing tariff rate from 25 per cent to 15 per cent;

3) The concessions for potato starch as well as for maize and wheat starch will be limited to a period of three years.

4) The German delegation will request the Federal Government to negotiate with the Benelux countries, within one year after the entry into force of these concessions, on the possibility of reducing the tariff rates for rice starch and starch derivatives (e.g. glucose under Item 1702; dextrines under item No. 3507 as well as glues on the basis of starch under item No. 3509 B)."

6. This offer was considered as acceptable by the Benelux representative, on the understanding that their governments reserved their right to bring the matter again before the CONTRACTING PARTIES if the proposals of reduction were not approved by the Parliament of the Federal Republic of Germany or if the concessions were withdrawn after the period of three years contemplated in the German offer.

7. The Panel took note of the agreement reached between the delegations concerned on the basis of the offer which, in the opinion of both parties, represents a first step toward the fulfillment of the promise contained in the letter of March 31, 1951, and noted also the assurance given by the German delegation that the global custom quotas envisaged for potato starch would be administered in accordance with the provisions of Article XIII of the General Agreement.

8. In those circumstances, the Panel recommends to the CONTRACTING PARTIES to take note of this report and to consider Item 12 (*r*) of the Agenda as being disposed of.

ITALIAN DISCRIMINATION AGAINST IMPORTED AGRICULTURAL MACHINERY

Report adopted on October 23, 1958
BISD 7S/60

I. INTRODUCTION

1. The Panel for Conciliation examined with the representatives of the United Kingdom and Italy the complaint of the United Kingdom Government that certain provisions of chapter III of Italian Law No. 949 of July 25, 1952, which provides special credit facilities to some categories of farmers or farmers' co-operatives for the purchase of agricultural machinery produced in Italy, were inconsistent with the obligations of Italy under Article III of the General Agreement and that the operation of this Law impaired the benefits which should accrue to the United Kingdom under the Agreement. The Panel heard statements from both parties and obtained additional information from them to clarify certain points. It also heard a statement by the observer of Denmark recording his Government's interest, as an exporter of agricultural machinery, especially of reaper binders, in the United Kingdom complaint. On the basis of these statements the Panel considered whether the provisions of the Italian Law of July 25, 1952 concerning the granting of special facilities for the purchase of domestic agricultural machinery had effects which were inconsistent with the provisions of the General Agreement. It considered further whether and to what extent the operation of these provisions impaired the benefits accruing directly or indirectly to the Government of the United Kingdom under the General Agreement. Finally, the Panel agreed on a recommendation which, in its opinion, would assist the Italian and United Kingdom Governments in arriving at a satisfactory adjustment of the case submitted by the United Kingdom to the CONTRACTING PARTIES.

II. FACTS OF THE CASE

2. In accordance with the Law of July 25, 1952, the Italian Government established a revolving fund which enabled the Ministry of Agriculture and Forestry to grant special credit terms *inter alia* for the purchase of Italian agricultural machinery. To this fund are allocated by

budgetary appropriations 25 thousand million lire a year for five fiscal years starting with the year 1952-53; out of these 25 thousand million lire, the Law provides that 7.5 thousand million would be assigned for the purchase of agricultural machinery, an amount which may be modified by the Italian authorities. The loans are granted at 3 per cent, including fees to the Credit Institute, for a period of five years to finance up to 75 percent of the cost of the machinery. The interest and repayments of the loans are paid into the revolving fund and may be used for further loans. The revolving fund will remain in existence until 1964. Eligible purchasers may benefit from these favorable terms when they buy Italian agricultural machinery; if, on the other hand, they wish to buy foreign machinery on credit the terms would be less favorable. The United Kingdom delegation indicated that loans on commercial terms were presently available at the rate of about 10 per cent while the Italian delegation stated that farmers could obtain from agricultural credit institutions five-year loans on terms substantially more favorable than 10 per cent.

3. The Italian delegation estimated that during the period 1952-1957 the purchasers of about half of the Italian tractors sold in Italy (i.e. about one-third of all tractors sold in the country) benefitted from the credit facilities provided under Law No. 949.

4. In 1949, i.e. before the entry into force of Law No. 949, the import duties on various types of tractors and other agricultural machinery, were bound under the GATT and, in particular, the duties on wheeled tractors with internal combustion engines of cylinder capacity up to 7,000 c.c. (Italian tariff item ex 1218-a-1), which are of particular interest to the United Kingdom, were bound at a rate of 40 per cent ad valorem; in the course of the 1956 tariff negotiations, further concessions were granted by Italy, including a reduction of the rate on these tractors to 32 per cent ad valorem.

III. ALLEGED INCONSISTENCY OF THE EFFECTS OF THE PROVISIONS OF THE ITALIAN LAW WITH THE PROVISIONS OF PARAGRAPH 4 OF ARTICLE III

5. The United Kingdom delegation noted that Article III:4 of the General Agreement provided that products imported into the territory of any contracting party "shall be accorded treatment no less favorable than that accorded to like products of national origin in respect of all laws, regulations and requirements affecting their internal sale, offering

for sale, purchase, transportation. . ." etc. As the credit facilities provided under the Italian Law were not available to the purchasers of imported tractors and other agricultural machinery these products did not enjoy the equality of treatment which should be accorded to them. The fact that these credit facilities were reserved exclusively to the purchasers of Italian tractors and other agricultural machinery represented a discrimination and the operation of the Law involved an inconsistency with the provisions of Article III of the General Agreement which provides that laws, regulations and requirements affecting internal sale should not be applied to imported products so as to afford protection to domestic producers. The United Kingdom would not challenge the consistency with the General Agreement of subsidies which the Italian Government might wish to grant to domestic producers of tractors and other agricultural machinery in accordance with the terms of paragraph 8 (b) of Article III. However, in the case of the Italian Law the assistance by the State was not given to producers but to the purchasers of agricultural machinery, a case which is not covered by the provisions of paragraph 8 (b). Even in the case of subsidies granted to producers the rights of the United Kingdom under Article XXIII of the General Agreement would be safeguarded as was recognized by the CONTRACTING PARTIES in paragraph 13 of the report on other barriers to trade which they approved during the course of the Review Session. [BISD 3S/224]

6. The Italian delegation considered that the General Agreement was a trade agreement and its scope was limited to measures governing trade; thus the text of paragraph 4 of Article III applied only to such laws, regulations and requirements which were concerned with the actual conditions for sale, transportation, etc., of the commodity in question and should not be interpreted in an extensive way. In particular, the Italian delegation stated that the commitment undertaken by the CONTRACTING PARTIES under that paragraph was limited to qualitative and quantitative regulations to which goods were subjected, with respect to their sale or purchase on the domestic market.

7. It was clear in their view that Law No. 949 which concerned the development of the Italian economy and the improvement in the employment of labor was not related to the questions of sale, purchase or transportation of imported and domestically produced products which were the only matters dealt with in Article III.

8. Moreover the Italian delegation considered that the text of Article III:4 could not be construed in such a way as to prevent the Italian Government from taking the necessary measures to assist the economic

development of the country and to improve the conditions of employment in Italy.

9. Finally, the Italian delegation, noting that the United Kingdom delegation recognized that the Italian Government would be entitled to grant subsidies exclusively to domestic producers, stressed it would not be logical to exclude this possibility in the case of credit facilities which had a far less pronounced effect on the terms of competition.

10. In the view of the Italian delegation it would be inappropriate for the CONTRACTING PARTIES to construe the provisions of Article III in a broad way since this would limit the rights of contracting parties in the formulation of their domestic economic policies in a way which was not contemplated when they accepted the terms of the General Agreement.

11. The Panel agreed that the question of the consistency of the effects of the Italian Law with the provisions of the General Agreement raised a problem of interpretation. It had the impression that the contention of the Italian Government might have been influenced in part by the slight difference of wording which existed between the French and the English texts of paragraph 4 of Article III. The French text which had been submitted to the Italian Parliament for approval provided that the imported products *ne seront pas soumis à un traitement moins favorable* whereas the English text read "the imported product shall be accorded treatment no less favorable". It was clear from the English text that any favorable treatment granted to domestic products would have to be granted to like imported products and the fact that the particular law in question did not specifically prescribe conditions of sale or purchase appeared irrelevant in the light of the English text. It was considered, moreover, that the intention of the drafters of the Agreement was clearly to treat the imported products in the same way as the like domestic products once they had been cleared through customs. Otherwise indirect protection could be given.

12. In addition, the text of paragraph 4 referred both in English and French to laws and regulations and requirements *affecting* internal sale, purchase, etc., and not to laws, regulations and requirements governing the conditions of sale or purchase. The selection of the word "affecting" would imply, in the opinion of the Panel, that the drafters of the Article intended to cover in paragraph 4 not only the laws and regulations which directly governed the conditions of sale or purchase but also any laws or regulations which might adversely modify the conditions of competition between the domestic and imported products on the internal market.

13. The Italian delegation alleged that the provisions of paragraph 8 (b) which exempted the granting of subsidies to producers from the

operation of this Article showed that the intention of the drafters of the Agreement was to limit the scope of Article III to laws and regulations directly related to the conditions of sale, purchase, etc. On the other hand, the Panel considered that if the Italian contention were correct and if the scope of Article III was limited in this way (which would, of course, not include any measure of subsidization) it would have been unnecessary to include the provisions contained in paragraph 8 (b) since they would be excluded *ipso facto* from the scope of Article III. The fact that the drafters of Article III thought it necessary to include this exemption for production subsidies would indicate that the intent of the drafters was to provide equal conditions of competition once goods had been cleared through customs.

14. Moreover, the Panel agreed with the contention of the United Kingdom delegation that in any case the provisions of paragraph 8 (b) would not be applicable to this particular case since the credit facilities provided under the Law were granted to the purchasers of agricultural machinery and could not be considered as subsidies accorded to the producers of agricultural machinery.

15. The Panel also noted that if the Italian contention were correct, and if the scope of Article III were limited in the way the Italian delegation suggested to a specific type of laws and regulations, the value of the bindings under Article II of the Agreement and of the general rules of non-discrimination as between imported and domestic products could be easily evaded.

16. The Panel recognized—and the United Kingdom delegation agreed with this view—that it was not the intention of the General Agreement to limit the right of a contracting party to adopt measures which appeared to it necessary to foster its economic development or to protect a domestic industry, provided that such measures were permitted by the terms of the General Agreement. The GATT offered a number of possibilities to achieve these purposes through tariff measures or otherwise. The Panel did not appreciate why the extension of the credit facilities in question to the purchasers of imported tractors as well as domestically produced tractors would detract from the attainment of the objectives of the Law, which aimed at stimulating the purchase of tractors mainly by small farmers and cooperatives in the interests of economic development. If, on the other hand, the objective of the Law, although not specifically stated in the text thereof, were to protect the Italian agricultural machinery industry, the Panel considered that such protection should be given in ways permissible under the General Agreement rather than by the extension of credit exclusively for purchases of domestically produced agricultural machinery.

IV. ALLEGED NULLIFICATION OR IMPAIRMENT OF BENEFITS ACCRUING TO THE UNITED KINGDOM UNDER THE GENERAL AGREEMENT

17. The Panel considered whether the operation of the Law No. 949 had caused injury to United Kingdom commercial interests, and whether such an injury represented an impairment of the benefits accruing to the United Kingdom under the General Agreement.

18. The Panel and the two parties agreed that under Article XXIII of the General Agreement a case of impairment or nullification may be brought before the CONTRACTING PARTIES whether the impairment was a result of a measure conflicting with the provisions of the Agreement or of a measure which was not inconsistent with the provisions of the Agreement.

19. The Panel had before it statistics relating to the imports of tractors from 1952 to 1957 as well as statistics of imports of agricultural machinery from 1950 to 1957. It also had before it statistics for the registration of tractors of domestic and foreign origin from 1950 to 1957. These statistics showed that total imports of tractors remained at a more or less stable level from 1952 to 1955 (with the exception of 1953 when the imports were abnormally high), and that there was a significant falling off of imports in 1956-1957. The figures for the imports of tractors from the United Kingdom followed approximately the same trend, in the first part of the period, but the decline in recent years was more marked. The Panel recognized that the fluctuations in the registrations of foreign tractors from 1952 to 1957 were less marked than for imports although the registrations in 1956 and 1957 were also smaller than in the preceding years.

20. The statistics showed that if the variations in absolute numbers were not very large in the case of registrations, the share of imported tractors in the total registrations steadily decreased from 1952 to 1957. The registration of national tractors on the other hand increased up to 1954, and had remained more or less stable from 1955 to 1957 in spite of a diminution in the total number of registrations.

21. The United Kingdom delegation contended that the diminution in the share of imported tractors in the total supply was to a large extent the result of the special credit facilities granted by the Italian Government for purchases of Italian tractors. The Italian delegation could not agree with this and maintained that the growing share of the national industry in the market was due to a better supply from that industry

following on its post-war reconstruction and to a better adaptation of Italian tractors to particular conditions of Italian agriculture. The Italian delegation produced figures of production which indicated that production of national tractors in 1952 had amounted to only 12,000 units and increased gradually to a figure of 25,000 units in 1955, 1956 and 1957. As regards reaper binders and other agricultural machinery the import figures indicated that there was a substantial increase in imports from 1952 to 1955 or even later. The reduction of imports of tractors during the last two years was in addition due, in the opinion of the Italian delegation, to a saturation of the market and not to effects of the credit facilities granted by the State to certain purchasers of Italian tractors. In this connexion it was to be noted that imports of other agricultural machinery were continuing to rise. The Italian delegation pointed out that in the years in question the credit facilities had only been applied in respect of some 44,000 domestic tractors or one half of total sales of the domestic product. The other half of sales of domestic tractors had competed on normal commercial terms with imported tractors. Thus the influence of these credit facilities extended to only a part of sales of domestic tractors. The Italian delegation stressed that, apart from the rate of interest, the loans under the Law did not differ from ordinary agricultural loans in Italy. Finally, the Italian delegation stressed that thanks to the credit facilities under the Law a large number of small farmers had been able to buy agricultural machinery which they would not be in a position to acquire in the absence of such measures.

22. On the basis of the statistics presented by the parties and the explanations given, the Panel came to the conclusion that the falling off in imports of tractors and, in particular, of the tractors from the United Kingdom, could not entirely be attributed to the operation of the credit facilities under the Law. It considered, however, that these credit facilities had probably influenced a number of purchasers in the selection of the tractors which they purchased. The Panel considered, furthermore, that if the considered view of the Italian Government was that these credit facilities had not influenced the terms of competition on the Italian market, there would not seem to be a serious problem in amending the operation of the Law so as to avoid any discrimination as regards these credit facilities between the domestic and imported tractors and agricultural machinery.

23. The Panel noted that in the course of the bilateral negotiations between Italy and the United Kingdom the Italian government mentioned that any modification of the present system might involve special difficulties. The Italian delegation pointed out in particular that if the

Law were operated in such a way as to apply to all tractors, whatever their origin, there would be budgetary implications because of the increased appropriations which would be required. Moreover it would be difficult for the government to justify the use of the proceeds of taxes levied on Italian nationals in a way which would work to the advantage of foreign producers. Finally the limitation of the credit facilities to tractors of domestic origin was necessary to assure national production of agricultural machinery.

24. The Panel considered that the application of the special credit facilities to both imported and domestic machinery need not involve any increase in budgetary appropriations since there could be a different application of the funds within a total already available. In this connexion it noted that the United Kingdom Government was not asking the Italian Government to increase the budgetary appropriation, but rather to extend the availability of the credit facility to permit a fair choice between purchases of tractors of domestic and foreign origin. Further, the Panel noted that the credit facilities were not granted to the Italian producers of agricultural machinery but to the Italian purchasers. Since these facilities were of advantage to Italian citizens the Panel questioned whether their extension to purchasers of imported machinery would be considered by public opinion as representing a benefit to foreign interests. Finally, as regards the need to assure national production of agricultural machinery, the Panel noted that the Italian industry already had the benefit of tariff protection (which in the case of the tractors under reference, amounted to 32 per cent ad valorem) and that the tariff was an accepted means of giving protection to domestic industry under the General Agreement.

V. CONCLUSIONS

25. In the light of the considerations set out above the Panel suggests to the CONTRACTING PARTIES that it would be appropriate for them to make a recommendation to the Italian Government in accordance with paragraph 2 of Article XXIII. The Panel considers that the recommendation should draw the attention of the Italian Government to the adverse effects on United Kingdom exports of agricultural machinery, particularly tractors, of those provisions of Law No. 949 limiting the prescribed credit facilities to purchasers of Italian produced machinery and suggest to the Italian Government that it consider the desirability of eliminating within a reasonable time the adverse effects of the Law on

the import trade of agricultural machinery by modifying the operation of that Law or by other appropriate means.

Recommendation adopted by the Contracting Parties on October 23, 1958
BISD 7S/23

Having examined in accordance with Article XXIII of the General Agreement, the complaint of the United Kingdom Government concerning those provisions of Italian Law No. 949 of July 25, 1952 which provide credit facilities for the purchase of tractors and other agricultural machinery of Italian, but not of foreign, origin;

The CONTRACTING PARTIES

Recommend that the Italian Government consider the desirability of eliminating within a reasonable time the adverse effects on imports of agricultural machinery of the provisions of Law No. 949, referred to above, by making available to the farmers and co-operatives eligible under that Law the same credit facilities for the purchase of agricultural machinery imported from other contracting parties as are now provided for the purchase of domestically produced agricultural machinery, or by other appropriate means.

FRENCH ASSISTANCE TO EXPORTS OF WHEAT AND WHEAT FLOUR

Report adopted on November 21, 1958
BISD 7S/46

I. INTRODUCTION

1. The Panel for Conciliation examined a complaint by the Government of Australia that as a result of subsidies being granted by the French Government on exports of wheat and wheat flour, inconsistently with the provisions of Article XVI:3, French exports have displaced Australian trade in these products particularly in its traditional wheat flour markets in Ceylon, Indonesia and Malaya, and have thus impaired the benefits which accrue to Australia under the General Agreement. At meetings held on April 29 and May 1, 1958 the Panel heard statements from both parties concerned and then decided to suspend consideration of the complaint pending the outcome of further bilateral discussions which were then to be resumed. In September the Australian Government reported that further bilateral discussions had led to no satisfactory outcome and accordingly the Panel was reconvened during the Thirteenth Session of the CONTRACTING PARTIES. The Panel heard further statements from the representatives of Australia and France and obtained additional information from them in order to clarify certain points in its further examination of the complaint. It also heard a statement by the representative of Japan who recorded his Government's concern in the situation which led to the Australian complaint in view of its interest in the export trade in wheat flour.

2. On the basis of these statements, together with statistical data provided by both parties and the secretariat, the Panel considered:

(a) whether or not the operation of the French price equalization system for wheat and flour amounted to the grant of subsidies on exports of those products;

(b) whether in fact this had resulted in France obtaining more than an equitable share in world trade for these products inconsistent with the provision of Article XVI:3; and

(c) further, whether and to what extent, the operation of the system had impaired the benefits accruing directly or indirectly to the Government of Australia under the General Agreement.

3. Finally, the Panel agreed on the text of a recommendation which, in its opinion, would assist the Australian and French Governments in arriving at a satisfactory adjustment of the case submitted by Australia to the CONTRACTING PARTIES to GATT.

II. FACTS OF THE CASE

(i) Operation of the French price stabilization system for wheat

4. Under French law the Office National Interprofessionnel des Céréales (ONIC) controls the production, collection, storage and domestic sale of cereals including wheat and flour and exercises a monopoly on imports and exports thereof. One of the main provisions of the legislation enforced by ONIC is the institution of a legal domestic price for wheat. A price is guaranteed to the producer each year for deliveries up to a maximum amount, or quantum. Quantities produced in excess of that quantum are not purchased at the basic guaranteed price and the producer receives only that price which ONIC can obtain either by selling on the world market or at concessional prices on the domestic market. The quantum includes not only quantities for anticipated domestic consumption but also a margin in excess of that for export. The producer does not, however, finally realize the basic guaranteed price since apart from taxes on all deliveries deducted to defray storage costs and other such expenses incurred by ONIC a surplus disposal tax (*taxe de résorption des excédents*) is levied on deliveries within the quantum at a highly progressive rate increasing in proportion to deliveries; the proceeds of that tax are utilized to cover ONIC's losses in the disposal of wheat surpluses either at home or exported abroad. Moreover, the ONIC receives repayments from traders and cooperatives based on the price differential for wheat delivered in excess of the quantum (*redevance hors du quantum*) and any deficit in the operations of the ONIC is financed out of budgetary appropriations.

5. With regard to exports of wheat and wheat flour the procedures are as follows:

(a) In view of the fact that world prices are lower than French guaranteed prices the ONIC makes a payment (*ristourne*) to the exporter designed to cover the difference.

(b) In the case of wheat the *ristourne* is paid on the basis of tenders submitted by exporters, the ONIC accepting the bid which involves the lowest payment; these tenders are not considered according to destination and the ONIC may reject tenders or make counter-proposals. The amount of the *ristourne* is in effect governed by current price trends in the world market for wheat.

(c) Insofar as exports of wheat flour are concerned the *ristourne* is based on the average *ristourne* paid in respect of wheat export bids during the week preceding the flour sale. Over and above this basic payment the exporter of flour also receives a bonus fixed from time to time which amounts at present to 200 francs per quintal of wheat utilized and is designed to make up for the price differential between wheat and flour in world markets and to defray additional expenses incurred in milling grain with a high moisture content. In addition a variable bonus is granted according to distance of the export market which is fixed from time to time. This bonus at present varies from 0 to 160 francs per quintal of wheat utilized.

(ii) The development of French exports of wheat and wheat flour

6. In both the inter-war period and the early post-war years, the volume of French exports of wheat and wheat flour respectively has been characterized by wide fluctuations. Since world exports of wheat and of wheat flour have fluctuated less, France's share in the world total has been quite unstable. However, it rose to much higher levels in 1954 and especially in 1955, as regards both wheat and wheat flour—particularly the latter. Disregarding effects of the crop failure of 1956, French exports of wheat now account for 7½ per cent of the world total and her exports of wheat flour represent 9 to 10 per cent of world exports.

7. Judging from export unit values, the prices charged for French exports of wheat flour (to destinations outside the franc zone) have in recent years been on the whole lower than those of other exporters. This is further confirmed by the import unit values recorded in Ceylon, Malaya (including Singapore) and Indonesia and by recent quotations for French wheat flour in these markets that were supplied by the Australian delegation and were not disputed by the French delegation.

III. ALLEGED INCONSISTENCY OF THE OPERATION OF THE FRENCH SYSTEM WITH THE PROVISIONS OF PARAGRAPH 3 OF ARTICLE XVI

(i) Consideration as to whether the French system involved a subsidy on exports within the terms of Article XVI:3

8. The Panel considered the contention of the Australian Government that the operation of the French system amounted to the grant of subsidies on the export of wheat and wheat flour. The Panel noted the view of the French representative that the French system was rather a scheme for the stabilization of domestic prices and returns to producers. In this connexion the Panel referred to an interpretative note to paragraph 3 of Article XVI, in which the CONTRACTING PARTIES had recognized that in certain circumstances a system for the stabilization of domestic prices would not be considered as involving a subsidy on exports within the meaning of that paragraph; it found that even if the French system had the characteristics described in paragraph 2 of the latter interpretative note the exemption provided from the provisions of paragraph 3 of Article XVI would be precluded if operations under such a system were "wholly or partly financed out of government funds in addition to funds collected from producers in respect of the products concerned". Accordingly the Panel addressed itself to a consideration of whether the operation of the French system involved financial contributions from the Government.

9. In the first instance the Panel noted that exporters of wheat and wheat flour were exempted from the tax of 235 francs per quintal of wheat and wheat equivalent in flour delivered on the domestic market which was levied for the financing of agricultural family allowances. Although it is questionable whether such an exemption was within the ambit of the preamble to the interpretative notes to Article XVI, the Panel did not think it necessary to make a judgement on this point since the *ristourne* which traders received represented a much higher amount.

10. According to data furnished by the French representative the average *ristourne* paid to wheat exporters during the 1957-58 crop season amounted to 1,566 francs per quintal. Exporters of flour received on the average 1,878 francs per quintal of wheat utilized, i.e. 2,608 francs per quintal of flour. As indicated in paragraph 5 (c) the former payment represented a basic *ristourne* plus a fixed and variable bonus. In the light of the above, therefore, and of the fact that the legal price for sales of wheat on the domestic market was 3,662 francs per quintal,

the Panel noted that traders could obtain wheat for export at a price approximately 1,800 francs per quintal lower than that prevailing on the domestic market and that in the case of wheat flour this difference was greater.

11. As indicated in paragraphs 4 and 5, the ONIC bears the losses resulting from payments to exporters and sales of wheat on the home market at reduced prices to cover domestic bread requirements and either direct sale as livestock feedstuff or costs of denaturation for such use. The 1957 wheat harvest yielded an excess over domestic requirements amounting to 30 million quintals of which 9 million quintals were denatured and sold for feeding purposes and the remaining 21 million quintals were exported in the form of wheat and flour. A percentage breakdown of ONIC's total expenditure for that crop year shows that 50 per cent was allocated in the form of *ristournes* to wheat exporters and 22 per cent to exporters of wheat flour. The remaining 28 per cent covered losses incurred from sales on the domestic market.

12. As stated, however, the ONIC receives its revenue from three main sources, namely the surplus disposal tax (*taxe de résorption des excédents*) and repayments for deliveries in excess of the quantum (*redevance hors du quantum*) with the balance being met by budgetary appropriations. For the 1957-58 crop year the first two items provided 20 and 45 per cent of receipts respectively and the balance of 35 per cent was contributed from Government funds.

13. The Panel noted that it was not possible to apportion or link the various sources of the ONIC's revenue directly to the items of expenditure and accordingly it would be difficult to assess with any precision the share of the budgetary appropriation in the financing of exports. If it was considered, however, that the receipts were uniformly divided under the various items of expenditure then it could be claimed that for the 1957-58 crop year 35 per cent of the payments on exports were derived from Government funds. Moreover, even if it was assumed that the export losses were primarily financed by sources of revenue other than budgetary appropriations then there would still have to be a part of these losses to be covered by the latter. This situation obtained even in the favorable circumstances of the 1957-58 crop year when funds collected from the producers were relatively high as compared with the 1955-56 crop year when budgetary appropriations represented 61 per cent of total revenue and payments on exports amounted to 94 per cent of ONIC's total expenditure. In that year, therefore, the bulk of payments made to exporters was covered by Government funds.

14. Accordingly, on the basis of these considerations, the Panel concluded that the operation of the French system did in fact result in the grant of subsidies on the export of wheat and wheat flour within the terms of paragraph 3 of Article XVI.

(ii) Consideration as to whether the operation of the French system resulted in France obtaining more than an equitable share of the world export trade in wheat and wheat flour

15. The Panel considered whether, in the terms of paragraph 3 of Article XVI, France had granted subsidies on the export of wheat and wheat flour in such a manner as to have resulted in France having obtained more than an equitable share of world export trade in these products. The Panel noted that there was no explicit definition in Article XVI of what constituted an "equitable" share in world markets. It was recalled, however, that at both Havana and the Review Session when the provisions of this paragraph were discussed it was implicitly agreed that the concept of "equitable" share was meant to refer to share in "world" export trade of a particular product and not to trade in that product in individual markets. It was understood, moreover, that in making such a determination the CONTRACTING PARTIES should not lose sight of the desirability of facilitating the satisfaction of world requirements of the commodity concerned in the most effective and economic manner, and that due account should be taken of any special factors affecting world trade in the products under reference with particular regard to the exporting country's share of world trade in those products during a previous representative period.

16. In the first instance, the French representative drew attention to France's established position in world trade as an exporter of wheat and wheat flour. Although curtailed in immediate post-war years as a result of damage incurred during the war, France was again assuming its traditional role. This *de facto* status of France as an exporter of wheat and wheat flour has been recognized by the International Wheat Agreement under which export quotas have been accorded to France. Moreover, France's share in the exports of wheat and wheat flour among the five major exporting countries (United States, Canada, Argentina, Australia and France) was considerably less in proportion to her production as compared with the others.

17. The Panel noted that French exports of wheat and wheat flour began to rise in 1954 in absolute quantity to levels exceeding substantially the quantities exported in any year since 1934 and have since

remained considerably higher than in pre-war or early post-war years. This increase in the absolute quantities of wheat and of wheat flour exported by France also represents an increase in France's share of world exports, especially as regards wheat flour.

18. The Panel further considered whether this increase in France's share of world exports, particularly of wheat flour, could be attributed to the operation of the French subsidy system. The facts above mentioned in paragraph 7 show that French exporters have been able to quote prices for wheat flour lower than those quoted by other exporters, whether at F.O.B. or C.I.F. values. Moreover, judging from export unit values, the price charged by French exporters for wheat flour has in recent years barely exceeded that charged for wheat. While this seems to be the practice followed also in some other European countries, e.g. in Germany, flour is exported even more cheaply than wheat, the export price for flour charged by Australia, Canada and the United States does exceed the export price of wheat by 30 to 50 per cent.

19. In these circumstances, it is reasonable to conclude that, while there is no statistical definition of an "equitable" share in world exports, subsidy arrangements have contributed to a large extent to the increase in France's exports of wheat and of wheat flour, and that the present French share of world export trade, particularly in wheat flour, is more than equitable.

IV. ALLEGED NULLIFICATION OR IMPAIRMENT OF BENEFITS ACCRUING TO AUSTRALIA UNDER THE GENERAL AGREEMENT

20. On the basis of statistical data before it the Panel considered whether and to what extent the operation of subsidies granted by France on the export of wheat and wheat flour had caused injury to Australia's normal commercial interests, and whether such an injury represented an impairment of benefits accruing to Australia under the General Agreement.

21. The Australian representative contended that the effect of the French subsidies had been such as to impair benefits Australia expected under the General Agreement, viz., the assurance that its export trade would not face subsidies going beyond the limits permissible under Article XVI. It was pointed out, in particular, that on the basis of statistical data French exports of wheat flour had displaced normal

Australian exports to markets in Southeast Asia, especially Ceylon, Malaya (including Singapore) and Indonesia. Furthermore, the losses suffered by Australia included not only direct damage to the flour milling industry, but also a reduction in the domestic supply of by-products, such as bran and pollard, and finally adverse effects upon Australia's transport facilities for exports of other goods to the Southeast Asian markets, since wheat flour was used as a "bottom cargo".

22. On the basis of statistics on the Australian wheat situation the French representative expressed the view that Australia's claim was not well founded since the deterioration in her position in Southeast Asian wheat flour markets was not due to French deliveries but to inability to supply as a result of two consecutive short crops. Even the reduced wheat and wheat flour exports of Australia could only be effected by reducing stocks to excessively low levels and even by recourse (though on a limited scale) to imports.

23. On the basis of the statistics submitted and of the explanations provided by the Australian and French representatives, the Panel arrived at the following conclusions:

(a) French exports of wheat flour to the three Southeast Asian countries rose substantially in recent years and accounted for a growing share in France's total wheat flour exports which rose from 13 per cent in 1953-54 to 34 per cent in 1957-58. Australia's exports to these markets fell substantially during this period and their share in Australia's total export of wheat flour declined from 64 per cent in 1953-54 to 50 per cent in 1957-58.

(b) In the three Southeast Asian markets combined, French supplies represented a greatly increased proportion of total imports of wheat flour, accounting for 0.7 per cent in 1954 and 46 per cent in the first half of 1958. The share of Australian supplies, on the other hand, fell from 83 per cent in 1954 to 37 per cent in the first half of 1958.

(c) While other suppliers of wheat flour have recently begun to play a larger part in the Southeast Asian markets, and although it is difficult to estimate to what extent such incursions as these are displacing traditional exporters, it is nevertheless clear that French supplies have in fact to a large extent displaced Australian supplies in the three markets.

(d) As regards the contention of the French representative that the reduction in Australia's exports to these markets was due to limited supplies, it is clear that Australia could not have maintained her combined exports of wheat *and* wheat flour at normal levels in 1957-58. However, Australia could have effected her traditional exports of wheat *flour* in spite of the crop failures, owing to measures taken by the Australian Wheat Board to set aside a quantity of wheat considered necessary to keep up normal exports of flour; this was substantiated by the declaration of the Australian representative that there were no contractual commitments for the export of wheat in the form of grain. Actually, the growth of French subsidized exports to Ceylon and other Southeast Asian countries and the consequent displacement of normal Australian flour exports resulted in the wheat thus available for transformation into flour being exported *as wheat* to other markets.

(e) Since it is obviously more profitable to export wheat flour rather than wheat, Australia has suffered a direct damage which could be evaluated by applying the price difference between wheat flour and wheat to the quantity of Australian exports that were displaced by French exports. It would, however, be difficult to assess this displacement quantitatively with any precision. In addition to this direct damage, there were other incidental adverse effects upon Australia which cannot be measured. Thus, Australia has suffered indirectly by the reduction in the domestic supply of the by-products of flour milling and by the reduction in transport facilities for other Australian export goods to the Southeast Asian markets.

24. The Panel then directed its attention to the question of whether the damage apparent in recent years was likely to recur or be prolonged. In this connexion it noted a statement by the French representative that France had concluded no important new contracts for sales of flour to this area since 1957 and that deliveries in 1958 were mostly the result of contracts entered into the previous year. Furthermore, it was estimated that the French wheat harvest for the year would not be as large as in previous years, and that there was a probability that there would be less available for export, whether as wheat or flour, in the near future. In this connexion the French representative stressed that his Government's policy was in fact to reduce wheat production in favor of coarse grains as feedstuffs to promote the livestock industry, and to that end regulations had been announced in October 1957 which would gradually lower the basic production price for wheat from 3,350 francs per quintal to 3,200 francs by 1961, and thus the quantities available for export should be

reduced. The Panel noted, however, the recent decision by the French Government to increase the quantum on which the guaranteed price is paid from 68 to 72 million quintals and considered that this decision might to a certain extent counteract the effects of its long-term policy.

25. Although the Panel recognized that the French Government's policy would tend to reduce the effects of the system on patterns of world trade, it considered, nevertheless, that the operation of the system was such that when climatic circumstances were favorable there might be substantial quantities of wheat in excess of normal domestic consumption requirements. Although the ONIC disposes of part of the surplus on the domestic market, the nature of French wheat was such that with its high moisture content, it was not capable of being stored for long periods. Moreover, storage and drying facilities were inadequate and it was inevitable that a substantial part of any sizeable surplus would have to be disposed of on the world markets. The French system appears very flexible in the sense that the amount of subsidy on wheat and flour exports may be increased without any government limitation in order to meet terms of competition on different markets. Also experience has shown that French wheat and flour exports have been regularly quoted at prices below those tendered by other suppliers and that there was no inherent guarantee in the system that it would operate in such a manner as to conform to the limits contemplated in Article XVI:3.

26. Before concluding its report the Panel wishes to draw the CONTRACTING PARTIES' attention to the general state of disequilibrium in the Southeast Asian flour markets, which its examination of the case before it has revealed. It had noted that substantial shifts had taken place as to source of supplies; France, for instance, had once exported large quantities of flour to what formerly constituted French Indochina. In the years 1951-54 that market had received 50,000-60,000 tons annually from France. For various reasons, particularly owing to non-commercial supplies from other sources, however, French flour exports to that market had fallen to zero by 1957. Accordingly, French exporters had been forced to seek alternative markets in the region, thus resulting in incursions on the traditional markets of other exporters. Moreover, other European countries became or returned as occasional and sporadic suppliers of substantial quantities of flour to those markets. This had further contributed towards the general state of disequilibrium which is apparent. In view of this situation, therefore, the Panel considered that so long as trade in flour with this region was likely to be affected by other than strict commercial considerations and the agriculture policy of a number of countries enabled exporters to obtain sub-

stantial assistance from their governments, it would be necessary for some arrangement to be arrived at to take due account of the interests of traditional suppliers. The most practical method of achieving this end thus avoiding any further disorganization of the flour markets in this region, appears to the Panel to be inter-governmental consultations.

27. In the light of the considerations set forth in Sections III and IV of this report, the Panel submits the following draft recommendation for the consideration of the CONTRACTING PARTIES.

Recommendation adopted by the Contracting Parties on November 21, 1958
BISD 7S/22

Having examined, in accordance with Article XXIII, of the General Agreement, the complaint of the Australian Government concerning the adverse effects on its trade arising from the assistance granted to French exporters of wheat, and more particularly of wheat flour, through the operation of the French wheat mononoly,

The CONTRACTING PARTIES

Recommend that the French Government consider appropriate measures to avoid, in the future, that the system of payments by the Office National Interprofessionnel des Céréales (ONIC) to exporters of wheat and wheat flour operates in such a manner as to create adverse effects on normal Australian exports of flour to Southeast Asian markets, and, more generally, on markets of wheat and wheat flour. These measures might consist of a revision of the methods applied by ONIC for the financing of French exports of wheat and more particularly of wheat flour, or of an agreement by the Government of France to enter into consultations with the Government of Australia before new contracts are entered into by French exporters of flour to the Southeast Asian markets, with a view to minimizing the impact of such contracts on normal Australian trade channels.

EXPORTS OF POTATOES TO CANADA

Report adopted on November 16, 1962
BISD 11S/88

I. INTRODUCTION

1. The Panel examined, in accordance with the provisions of paragraph 2 of Article XXIII, the question submitted to the CONTRACTING PARTIES by the Government of the United States concerning the application of values for duty on potatoes under the Canadian Customs Act on October 16, 1962. The Panel heard statements from both parties and obtained additional information from them to clarify certain points.

II. FACTS OF THE CASE

2. On October 16, 1962 the Canadian Government introduced a "value for duty" in respect of fresh potatoes imported into Western Canada of Can.$2.67 per 100 lbs. Under the Canadian legislation the difference between the lower export value and the "value for duty" would be levied by the Canadian customs authorities as "dumping duty" if the circumstances described in the legislation below were fulfilled. The United States Government complained against the imposition of this charge which would be levied in addition to a specific duty of Can.$0.375 per 100 lbs. which had been granted on April 5, 1957 by Canada as a tariff concession to the United States on potatoes.

III. HISTORY OF THE CASE

3. Due to their geographic location, there was considerable trade in fresh fruit and vegetables between the United States and Canada. Over 60 per cent of agricultural imports into Canada from the United States were made up of products in that group, including potatoes. Because of the variety of climate of the United States and their more southerly location, the season in many parts of that country was advanced on the Canadian production season. At the time Canadian producers were only beginning to market their fruit and vegetables, the United States' season

was often at its peak and, accordingly, prices were normally at their lowest level for the season. In order to meet such specific difficulties, which were particularly relevant to the fruit and vegetable trade sector, where the marketing season was often short and changes in supply could result in wide fluctuations in price over a very short period, in 1958 legislation was enacted whereby Article 40A(7) (b) of the Canadian Customs Act provided that "where the market price in the country of export of any fresh fruit or vegetable of a class or kind produced in Canada has, as a result of the advance of the season or the marketing period, declined to levels that do not reflect in the opinion of the Minister their normal price, the value for duty of such fresh fruit or vegetable, when imported into such region or part of Canada and during such period as the Minister may specify, shall be the amount determined and declared by him to be the average value, weighted as to quantity, at which like fresh fruits or vegetables were imported during the three-year period immediately preceding the date of shipment to Canada".

4. The Canadian delegation indicated that this was permissive legislation which was not intended to be concerned with normal trade but with unusual trade movements at critically low prices which could cause serious injury to Canadian producers in the shorter northern marketing season available to them.

5. Under this provision action had been taken for the first time in August 1961 whereby the value for duty of fresh potatoes imported into Western Canada had been determined at an amount of Can.$2.78 per 100 lbs. The United States Government had made representations to the Canadian Government against such action. The action was withdrawn only on April 30, 1962 towards the end of the marketing season.

6. On October 16, 1962 action was again taken under this provision and the value for duty of fresh potatoes imported into Western Canada was determined at Can.$2.67 per 100 lbs. The Canadian delegation stated that the action was taken because of the fact that potatoes were being imported into Western Canada from the United States at prices as low as Can.$1.13 per 100 lbs., while at the same time prices in the State of Washington ranged from US$1.50 to US$1.80 per 100 lbs. Those prices were to be compared with average prices over the preceding three years amounting to Can.$2.54 in the month of September and Can.$2.39 in the month of October. That was a clear case of application of the legislation in circumstances which threatened disruption in the Canadian market. The Canadian delegation stressed that the legislation had been used with the greatest restraint. The question now raised by the United States resulted from only the second application of the

relevant Customs Act provision. It had never been applied for the whole of Canada but only for the western part of the country.

IV. ALLEGED INCONSISTENCY OF THE APPLICATION OF "VALUE FOR DUTY" ON POTATOES UNDER THE CANADIAN CUSTOMS ACT WITH THE PROVISIONS OF THE GENERAL AGREEMENT

7. The United States delegation noted that Article VII of the General Agreement included provisions in respect of products subject to charges or restrictions on importation based upon or regulated in any manner by value. Paragraph 2(a) of this Article stated that the value for customs purposes of imported merchandise should be based on the actual value of the imported merchandise on which duty was assessed and should not be based on an arbitrary or fictitious value. In their view, the determination of the value for duties on potatoes at the average value, weighted as to quantity, at which potatoes were imported during the three-year period immediately preceding the date of shipment to Canada, constituted a determination based on arbitrary or fictitious value and was consequently inconsistent with the provisions of paragraph 2(a) of Article VII. The Canadian delegation stated that the relevant provision of the Canadian Customs Act did not contain arbitrary or fictitious evaluations but was based on the value of actual imports during the preceding three years and was less arbitrary than previously existing legislation.

8. The United States delegation indicated that the example given by the representative of Canada of imports at a price of Can.$1.13 per 100 lbs. was without reference to quality or to quantity moving at that price. Furthermore such figures, in their view, were not comparable to seasonal averages for three preceding years. The United States delegation furnished the Panel with information on prices. Prices of potatoes US No. 1, size A Russet, F.O.B. at the shipping point in the area of production, Idaho, amounted to:

For the week ending	29 September 1962 ..	US$2.08 per 100 lbs.
" " " "	27 October 1962	US$2.58 " " "

On the same basis prices in the State of Washington amounted to:

For the week ending	29 September 1962 ..	US$1.66 per 100 lbs.
" " " "	27 October 1962	US$1.98 " " "

The United States representative added that no distinction was made between prices of potatoes intended for exportation and for domestic consumption. It was clear, in the view of the United States delegation, that prices of exported products, as compared with domestic market prices in the United States were such that imports of potatoes from the United States into Canada could not be considered to take place at less than the normal value in the sense of Article VI. Any additional charge on imports of potatoes was consequently in their view inconsistent with the provisions of Article VI. The Canadian representative reiterated that the above market quotations were average prices for a specified quality and did not necessarily relate to the prices of actual imports into Canada.

9. The United States delegation indicated that their Government had negotiated a tariff concession with the Canadian Government under which import duties on potatoes were bound under the General Agreement at Can.$0.375 per 100 lbs. United States exports were now faced with a situation under which, apart from the normal customs duty of Can.$0.375, they were subject to an additional amount to make up for any difference between the export value indicated in the customs document and the value for duty determined under the Canadian Customs Act. In their view, the charge of such additional amount constituted an impairment of the concession provided in Schedule V to the General Agreement, as a result of the failure of Canada to carry out its obligations under Article II of the General Agreement.

V. ALLEGED NULLIFICATION OR IMPAIRMENT OF BENEFITS ACCRUING TO THE UNITED STATES UNDER THE GENERAL AGREEMENT

10. The Canadian delegation stated that a representation had been received from the United States regarding the value for potatoes only a few days before the present session of the CONTRACTING PARTIES. Generally it had been possible to solve problems of that nature through the process of discussion between the governments concerned.

11. The Panel noted that the United States Government had made representations to the Canadian Government when action in respect of potatoes had been taken for the first time in 1961. It noted further that when action had been taken on October 16, 1962, i.e. the week preceding the present session of the CONTRACTING PARTIES, the United States

Government had again made representations to the Canadian Government, but at the same time had referred the question to the CONTRACTING PARTIES at very short notice. The Panel noted the United States' explanation that, because of the seasonal character of such action, the present session provided the only opportunity for consideration of the matter by the CONTRACTING PARTIES.

12. The Canadian delegation considered that it would not be possible for the United States delegation to prove that action taken on October 16, 1962 involved an impairment of trade benefits. There were no statistics available over such a short period of time. On the other hand, statistics showed that in the 1961/62 marketing season, when the provision had been applied for the first time, Canada had imported from the United States 852,000 cwt. of potatoes at a value of Can.$1,949,000, while imports in 1960/61 had amounted to 715,900 cwt. at a total value of Can.$1,943,000. Both in volume and value imports had increased despite the application of value for duty on potatoes. In fact the United States exporters, by supplying more potatoes of a high quality and by exporting a greater proportion of potatoes in a more advanced stage of preparation, had in practice not suffered from the application of value for duty.

13. The United States delegation stated that according to their export statistics, the per unit value of potatoes exported to Canada had amounted in 1960 to US$2.90 per 100 lbs. and in 1961 to US$2.19 per 100 lbs. That was contrary to the Canadian statement that higher priced qualities of potatoes had been imported in 1961. In their view, irrespective of the variation in exports or prices, the imposition of any additional import charge on shipments below the fixed value for duty *ipso facto* constituted an impairment of the terms of trade which the United States Government had envisaged when negotiating for a tariff concession.

14. The Canadian delegation stated that the application of the provisions depended on the movement of prices. The application was announced when crops were being harvested and there was no indication to the producers in advance that the legislation would be applied. The application of a value for duty, therefore, had no effect on potato production. That was confirmed by the fact that in the four western provinces to which the value for duty applied, production in 1961 had increased in only one province as compared with the average of the three preceding years. Production had declined in two provinces and had remained at the same level in one province.

VI. CONSIDERATIONS OF THE PANEL

15. The Panel considered that by its terms of reference it was not called on to examine whether or not the requirement of a reasonable time as laid down in paragraph 2 of Article XXIII had been fulfilled.

16. The Panel, having heard the points of view of the parties concerned, considered that the concept of value for duty as applied presently on imports of potatoes under the Canadian Customs Act was different from the concept of value for customs purposes, which the CONTRACTING PARTIES had in mind in drafting the provisions of Article VII. The Panel, therefore, did not consider that the provisions of Article VII were relevant in the context of its examination.

17. The Panel further considered that there was no basic difference between the price, in the ordinary course of trade, of exported potatoes and potatoes intended for domestic consumption in the United States. The Panel felt that the problem for Canadian potato producers due to imports of potatoes from the United States was caused by specific climatic differences which could in certain years give rise to exceptional difficulties. The Panel concluded that the imposition of an additional charge could not be justified by Article VI of the General Agreement, since the main requirement laid down in paragraph 1(a) of this Article was not fulfilled, namely that the price of the product exported from one country to another was less than the comparable price, in the ordinary course of trade, for the like product when destined for consumption in the exporting country.

18. The Panel came to the conclusion that the measure introduced by the Canadian Government amounted to the imposition of an additional charge on potatoes which were imported at a price lower than Can.$2.67 per 100 lbs. The Panel considered that this charge was in addition to the specific import duty which had been bound at a rate of Can.$0.375 per 100 lbs. Since no provisions of the General Agreement had been brought forward for the justification of the imposition of an additional charge above the bound import duty, the Panel considered that the Canadian Government had failed to carry out its obligations under paragraph 1(a) of Article II.

19. The Panel suggests that the CONTRACTING PARTIES recommend to the Canadian Government the withdrawal of the additional charge under the Canadian Customs Act on imports of potatoes, or to effect any other satisfactory adjustment of the impaired benefit accruing to the United States.

20. The Panel did not consider the question whether the circumstances were serious enough to justify a recommendation to the CONTRACTING PARTIES authorizing the United States Government to suspend obligations or concessions. In view of the circumstances described in this report, and because of the fact that since the imposition of the additional charge adequate statistics covering trade in the product concerned were not available, the Panel had no basis for consideration of that question.

21. The Panel further suggests that the CONTRACTING PARTIES authorize the Council to deal with the matter if the United States, in the light of developments, considers it necessary to raise it again.

FRENCH IMPORT RESTRICTIONS

Report adopted on November 14, 1962
BISD 11S/94

1. The Panel was established by the CONTRACTING PARTIES in connexion with the request made by the Government of the United States that the CONTRACTING PARTIES consider, pursuant to paragraph 2 of Article XXIII of the General Agreement, import restrictions applied by the Government of France to products on which the European Economic Community had given tariff concessions to the United States in the recently concluded negotiations under GATT. The terms of reference of the Panel were:

"To examine the matter referred by the Government of the United States to the CONTRACTING PARTIES pursuant to paragraph 2 of Article XXIII relating to import restrictions maintained by France, and to make such findings as will assist the CONTRACTING PARTIES in making the recommendations or rulings provided for in paragraph 2 of Article XXIII."

2. The Panel heard statements by the representative of the United States and by the representative of France and obtained clarification on certain points from those representatives.

3. The Panel was informed by the French representative that his government did not contest that the restrictions under consideration were contrary to Article XI of the General Agreement. Moreover, in the course of the discussion, the French representative did not invoke any other provisions of the General Agreement in justification of the maintenance of the restrictions.

4. The Panel agreed that the maintenance by a contracting party of restrictions inconsistent with Article XI after the contracting party concerned had ceased to be entitled to have recourse to Article XII constituted nullification or impairment of benefits to which other contracting parties were entitled under GATT and the effects of such nullification or impairment were aggravated if such maintenance of restrictions continued for an extended period of time.

5. The Panel noted that the United States had claimed nullification or impairment in respect of benefits which it expected to receive from tariff

concessions on the particular products set out in the Annex to the Note by the United States delegation in document L/1899. It follows from the Panel's general finding in paragraph 4 above that the Panel considers that, as a result of the import restrictions maintained by France, there is nullification or impairment of benefits to which the United States is entitled under GATT.

6. The Panel therefore suggests that the CONTRACTING PARTIES could appropriately recommend to the French Government the withdrawal of restrictions inconsistent with Article XI, with particular reference to restrictions on the products which have been specifically referred to by the United States Government. In suggesting that recommendation the Panel has very much in mind the view expressed in its report by the Working Party on Organizational and Functional Questions, which met during the Review Session, namely that the first objective, in cases of this sort, should be to secure the withdrawal of the measures which are inconsistent with the General Agreement. The view of the Panel is that the making of such a recommendation by the CONTRACTING PARTIES and its fulfillment would be the most satisfactory way of resolving the question which is before the CONTRACTING PARTIES.

7. The Panel would therefore suggest that the CONTRACTING PARTIES recommend to the United States Government that it refrain, for a reasonable period, from exercising its right, under the procedures of paragraph 2 of Article XXIII, to propose suspension of the application of equivalent obligations or concessions. The Panel also suggests that the CONTRACTING PARTIES authorize the Council to deal with any proposals regarding such suspension put forward by the Government of the United States should it find it necessary to do so.

URUGUAYAN RECOURSE TO ARTICLE XXIII

Report adopted on November 16, 1962
BISD 11S/95

Terms of Reference and Membership

1. The Panel was appointed by the Council in February 1962 on the instructions of the CONTRACTING PARTIES given at the nineteenth session. Its terms of reference were:

> "In the light of the written submissions of Uruguay and in consultation with the contracting parties concerned, to examine the cases referred to it by Uruguay, in accordance with the provisions of paragraph 2 of Article XXIII, and to report thereupon to the Council."

2. It will be recalled that in October 1961 the representative of Uruguay drew the attention of the Council of Representatives (L/1572) to the trade problems concerning temperate primary producers such as Uruguay, both as regards the limited marketing opportunities available to them and the failure of the prices of their products to be maintained at a satisfactory level. He made certain proposals to overcome those problems, and distributed a table (Spec(61)294), showing the extent to which Uruguayan exports were confronted by restrictive measures in force in nineteen industrialized countries.

* * *

Proceedings of the Panel

7. Immediately after its appointment the Panel sought to determine the scope of its work by requesting the Uruguayan delegation definitively to identify the contracting parties, the products and the restrictive measures with respect to which action under Article XXIII:2 was taken. Uruguay was also requested to supply information on the circumstances which it considered had justified the invocation of Article XXIII:2, its view of the consistency or otherwise of the restrictive measures in question with the provisions of the General Agreement, the

effects of the measures on Uruguay's exports and the extent to which it considered benefits accruing to it under the General Agreement had been nullified or impaired.

8. In response to this request, the Uruguayan delegation submitted in June a general note in which it confirmed that the Uruguayan submissions related to all the fifteen contracting parties named by it at the Council meeting; stated that it would wish the Panel to review all the measures enumerated in document L/1662 (which were of twelve different types and applied to over thirty different products or groups of products); and generally reiterated the position it had taken as noted in the various previous statements. Subsequently, the Uruguayan delegation also supplied fifteen separate papers concerning the representations and consultations under Article XXII or XXIII:1 which had led to the cases being brought under Article XXIII:2. The receipt of these papers enabled the Panel to commence its consultations with the fifteen contracting parties concerned and Uruguay. These took place from July 17 to July 28, 1962. During these consultations the Panel examined each restrictive measure, the manner in which it was applied and its relationship with the provisions of the General Agreement and the relevant protocol. The Panel also discussed with the delegations of Uruguay and of the contracting parties concerned the question of nullification or impairment of benefits accruing to Uruguay under the Agreement as it was alleged to have arisen from the application of each measure. The records of these consultations were immediately transmitted to the delegations of Uruguay and of the contracting parties concerned in order that the Panel's recommendations might be drawn up after the records had been examined and accepted by both sides.

9. The Panel reconvened early in October 1962 immediately after comments on the records had been received from the contracting parties concerned and Uruguay. In the course of the meeting the Uruguayan delegation made it known that it wished to raise further questions with the fifteen contracting parties, and a second round of consultations was accordingly held from October 30 to November 5, 1962 with the fifteen delegations.

General Considerations

10. Paragraph 2 of Article XXIII provides that the CONTRACTING PARTIES shall promptly investigate any matter referred to them under that paragraph. From the context it is obvious, however, that before a "matter" can be so referred to the CONTRACTING PARTIES it must have been the subject of representations or proposals made pursuant to

paragraph 1 of the Article which have not resulted in a "satisfactory adjustment" (unless the difficulty is of the type described in paragraph 1(c) of the Article).[1] Under paragraph 1 representations or proposals can be made by a contracting party if it considers:

(i) that a benefit accruing to it directly or indirectly under the General Agreement is being nullified or impaired; or

(ii) that the attainment of any objective of the Agreement is being impeded.[2]

In referring the cases to the CONTRACTING PARTIES the Uruguayan delegation maintained that it had fulfilled those conditions for the invocation of paragraph 2 of Article XXIII.

11. Paragraph 2 of Article XXIII provides, apart from promptly investigating any matter so referred to them, for two kinds of action by the CONTRACTING PARTIES, namely:

(i) they shall make appropriate recommendations or give a ruling on the matter;

(ii) they may authorize the suspension of concessions or obligations.

The action stated under (i) is obligatory and must be taken in all cases where there can be an "appropriate" recommendation or ruling. The action under (ii) is to be taken at the discretion of the CONTRACTING PARTIES in defined circumstances.

12. The paragraph states that the CONTRACTING PARTIES "shall make appropriate recommendations to the contracting parties which they consider to be concerned or give a ruling on the matter, as appropriate". Whilst a "ruling" is called for only when there is a point of contention on fact or law, recommendations should always be appropriate whenever, in the view of the CONTRACTING PARTIES, they would lead to a satisfactory adjustment of the matter.

[1] However, at least in respect of quantitative import restrictions applied inconsistently with the General Agreement, it has been agreed by the CONTRACTING PARTIES that the holding of a consultation under paragraph 1 of Article XXII would fulfill the conditions of paragraph 1 of Article XXIII (see BISD, Ninth supplement, pages 19-20).

[2] The paragraph goes on to enumerate the circumstances under which either of these two contingencies could arise, under the three sub-headings (a), (b) and (c).

UNIV

13. The latter part of paragraph 2 of Article XXIII states that "if the CONTRACTING PARTIES consider the circumstances are serious enough to justify such action, they may authorize a contracting party or parties to suspend the application to any other contracting party or parties of such concessions or other obligations under this Agreement as they determine to be appropriate in the circumstances". In the view of the Panel the requirement that the situation must be serious enough limits the applicability of the provision to cases where there is nullification or impairment; it would at any rate be difficult to conceive a situation in which the suspension of concessions or obligations could be appropriate where nullification or impairment was not involved.

Nullification or Impairment

14. In most cases Uruguay claimed that the maintenance of the trade measures by the other contracting parties had nullified or impaired benefits accruing to Uruguay under the General Agreement. The Panel thought it essential to have a clear idea as to what would constitute a nullification or impairment. In its view impairment and nullification in the sense of Article XXIII does not arise merely because of the existence of any measures; the nullification or impairment must relate to benefits accruing to the contracting party "under the General Agreement".

15. In implementing the compensation provision of Article XXIII:2 the CONTRACTING PARTIES would therefore need to know what benefits accruing under the Agreement, in the view of the country invoking the provisions, had been nullified or impaired, and the reasons for that view. In cases where there is a clear infringement of the provisions of the General Agreement, or in other words, where measures are applied in conflict with the provisions of GATT and are not permitted under the terms of the relevant protocol under which the GATT is applied by the contracting party, the action would, *prima facie*, constitute a case of nullification or impairment and would *ipso facto* require consideration of whether the circumstances are serious enough to justify the authorization of suspension of concessions or obligations.[1] While it is not

[1] It may be noted in this connexion that the status of a measure (that is, whether or not it is consistent with GATT) is not to be affected by a waiver decision taken subsequently. In fact, decisions taken under Article XXV: 5 granting waivers from GATT obligations have normally expressly provided for the continued validity of the procedures of Article XXIII in respect of the otherwise "waived" obligations (cf. *inter alia*, BISD, Third Supplement, pages 35-41; Eighth Supplement, page 22).

precluded that a *prima facie* case of nullification or impairment could arise even if there is no infringement of GATT provisions, it would be in such cases incumbent on the country invoking Article XXIII to demonstrate the grounds and reasons for its invocation. Detailed submissions on the part of that contracting party on these points were therefore essential for a judgment to be made under this Article.

16. In a number of cases, the contracting party concerned maintained (a) that certain measures applied by it were consistent with the provisions of GATT, or (b) that the measures, while not consistent with the provisions of the General Agreement, were permitted under the terms of the Protocol of Provisional Application, the Annecy Protocol or the Torquay Protocol on account of their being applied pursuant to "existing legislation". In most of these cases, the contention was not questioned by the Uruguayan delegation. For practical purposes, the Panel has taken the position that in cases where the contention has not been challenged and is not contradicted by the available records of the CONTRACTING PARTIES, it would be beyond its competence to examine whether the contention was or was not justified.

17. The Panel was faced with a particular difficulty in considering the status of variable import levies or charges. It noted the discussion which took place at the nineteenth session of the CONTRACTING PARTIES on this subject during which it was pointed out that such measures raised serious questions which had not been resolved. In these circumstances the Panel has not considered it appropriate to examine the consistency or otherwise of these measures under the General Agreement.

18. Whilst the Panel was conducting its consultations, the EEC introduced its Regulation on cereals under the common agricultural policy, replacing the measures included in the original submission by Uruguay. The Panel noted the statement by the delegation of Uruguay that those new measures (which are described in COM.II/134) would have a significant impact on Uruguay's cereals trade. However, since the measures did not form part of Uruguay's original submission and since they were under consideration by the CONTRACTING PARTIES with the active participation of Uruguay, the Panel considered that it would not be appropriate for it to examine the compatibility or otherwise of the measures applied under that Regulation with the General Agreement.[1] The Panel also noted that the measures applying to certain other products might be replaced shortly with the extension of the application of

[1] These measures have been included in Section 1 of the relevant individual country reports merely in order to provide a complete list of measures which were considered by Uruguay to be confronting its export trade.

the common agricultural policy, but in the absence of any definite indication in that regard, the Panel deemed it advisable to treat such measures as they now existed.

19. For the reasons given in paragraphs 16 to 18 above, the Panel has not found itself in a position to sustain Uruguay's claim regarding nullification or impairment in respect of a number of cases.

Recommendations Based on Nullification or Impairment

20. Where the Panel finds that there is *prima facie* nullification or impairment of benefits accruing to Uruguay under the Agreement, it has proposed recommendations based on that finding. Where a measure affecting imports is maintained clearly in contradiction with the provisions of the General Agreement (and is not covered by the "existing legislation" clause of a Protocol), the Panel has in all cases recommended that the measure in question be removed. Reference is made in these recommendations based on nullification or impairment to the possibility of further action, in the event of non-fulfilment, by the CONTRACTING PARTIES under paragraph 2 of Article XXIII. In respect of these particular cases the Panel proposes the following procedure for adoption by the CONTRACTING PARTIES:

> The contracting parties concerned should be asked to report on their action taken to comply with the CONTRACTING PARTIES' recommendations or any other satisfactory adjustment (such as the provision of suitable concessions acceptable to Uruguay) by March 1, 1963. If by that date the recommendations are not carried out and no satisfactory adjustment is made, the circumstances shall be deemed to be "serious enough" to justify action under the penultimate sentence of Article XXIII:2 and Uruguay shall be entitled immediately to ask for the authorization of suspension of concessions or obligations. The CONTRACTING PARTIES should make arrangements for prompt determination as to what are the concessions or obligations the suspension of which should be authorized.

21. In recommending this two-stage procedure, the Panel had principally in mind, once again, the requirement stated in Article XXIII:2 that the situation must be "serious enough" before suspension can be authorized. It noted, as a report of the ninth session had made clear, that the action of authorization of suspension of concessions or obliga-

tions should never be taken except as a last resort; it also noted that the aim of Uruguay at this stage was to seek the prompt removal of the measures in question.

General Observations

22. In invoking the provisions of Article XXIII the Uruguayan delegation repeatedly referred to the general difficulties created for Uruguay by the prevalence of restrictive measures affecting its exports and to the resulting inequality in the terms on which temperate zone primary producers participated in world trade. The Panel noted that it was not charged with the examination of broader issues falling outside the purview of Article XXIII. It also noted that those broader issues were being actively discussed by the CONTRACTING PARTIES. The Panel is of the view that if the proposed recommendations, especially those relating to health regulations and those figuring in paragraph (c) of section 4 of the individual reports were fulfilled, an important contribution would have been made to the solution of the difficulties mentioned by Uruguay in bringing the cases before the CONTRACTING PARTIES under Article XXIII.

23. With these general considerations and observations, the Panel submits, for consideration and adoption by the CONTRACTING PARTIES, the attached fifteen reports on the Uruguayan recourse under Article XXIII with respect to the fifteen contracting parties.

[Editors' Note: The 15 country reports, which cover 46 pages of text, have been omitted. Generally, only a few quota and import permit systems and mixing requirements were found to nullify or impair Uruguay's GATT benefits.]

OMITTED

OMITTED

OMITTED

TURKEY—CONSULTATION UNDER ARTICLE XXII:2

Report of Working Party adopted on March 28, 1966
BISD 14S/59

A. INTRODUCTION

1. The terms of reference of the Working Party were "to carry out, under the provisions of paragraph 2 of Article XXII, a consultation in respect of the following question raised by the United Kingdom:

> 'The application by Turkey of Article XXIV:5 (a) and of Article XXIV:6 when, in the course of forming a customs union with the European Economic Community, the Turkish Government reduces its tariff in successive stages towards the Community on the one hand and towards other contracting parties on the other'."

2. The Working Party met under the Chairmanship of Mr. Donovan (Australia) on June 14 and 15 and on July 16, 1965.

B. OPENING STATEMENTS OF THE POSITION OF THE UNITED KINGDOM AND TURKEY

3. The representative of the United Kingdom recalled that, under a waiver, dated August 22, 1964, the Turkish Government was imposing duties on a number of imports in excess of rates bound to contracting parties to the General Agreement. It was in the meantime seeking to negotiate release from these concessions in accordance with Article XXVIII. The increases involved were sizeable; but the United Kingdom delegation wished to emphasize that there was full and sympathetic understanding of the development needs which had prompted the Turkish Government to make these increases and the United Kingdom authorities were not challenging the right of Turkey to seek negotiations with the object of securing appropriate protection for Turkish industry.

4. In February 1964, the Contracting Parties had been notified

of the terms of the Ankara Agreement, concluded between the Turkish Government on the one hand and the European Economic Community on the other, as an interim agreement preparatory to the formation of a customs union between the two parties.

5. The coincidence of these two sequences of events raised a point on which the United Kingdom and, it could be assumed, the rest of the contracting parties, would need clarification.

6. Bearing in mind the purpose of the Ankara Agreement, in the face of the tariff increases sought by Turkey what would be the position of contracting parties vis-à-vis each other as competitors in the Turkish market? So long as Turkish industry needed increased protection, would all contracting parties find themselves on an equal footing? It appeared to the United Kingdom delegation that it would be difficult to persuade any traders that these increases were justifiable if it became apparent that some of their competitors were in any sense to share the benefit with Turkish industry of new high levels of protection. This would be the case if Community exporters entered the Turkish markets at privileged rates while other contracting parties found themselves excluded by increased rates maintained on the grounds that Turkish industry was still not ready to lose the shelter which they afforded.

7. It was, therefore, important to know at what point and by what stages the Turkish Government intended to begin and to carry through its program of aligning its external tariff to the common external tariff of the Community and to reduce its tariff on imports from Community sources to zero.

8. The United Kingdom delegation naturally did not contest that a point would be reached when a preference would open up between the two rates. Since, however, it was its understanding that the present increases in the Turkish tariff had been made only as a protection for Turkish industry, it suggested that Article XXIV would be appropriately applied if the preference did not begin to appear until the most-favored-nation rate had, by whatever stages Turkey had found appropriate, returned to the present bound rates.

9. The representative of Turkey said the basis of the United Kingdom case seemed to be that there was some link between the Agreement of Association and the revision of the Turkish tariff and therefore between the operations of Articles XXIV and XXVIII. In fact there was no such link; the closeness of the two events in time was a matter of pure coincidence.

10. The revision in the Turkish tariff was part of a general fiscal reform to meet the requirements of the Turkish Development Plan and

an expert study of this by the Government had begun some considerable time before. Parliamentary action on the proposals submitted by the Government following this study had been slow and this was why the relevant legislation was, in the end, passed only in May 1964. The Turkish tariff came into force thereafter and the Turkish Government was, in August 1964, granted a waiver to authorize it to apply a new tariff before the conclusion of the necessary renegotiations under Article XXVIII. The new tariff, which included the compensatory adjustments proposed by the Turkish Government, applied to all countries, including those of the EEC.

11. In the meantime negotiations had been taking place with the Community, and the Agreement of Association had been signed in September 1963 but did not come into force until December 1964. From the legal point of view, the latter was the relevant date since until then the Ankara Agreement had no legal basis. The Turkish tariff had been modified and the waiver sought and granted well before that date.

12. As far as negotiations under Article XXVIII were concerned, Turkey had made, since November 1964, several approaches to the contracting parties which have had initial negotiation rights and endeavoured to bring negotiations to a mutually satisfactory conclusion. However, Turkey had encountered certain difficulties in negotiating with some of the industrialized countries, chiefly because of the fact that there existed great imbalances between concessions granted by Turkey and those received in return.

13. In the view of the Turkish Government, therefore, the provisions of Article XXIV were not relevant to the increase in the Turkish tariff and the only relevant provisions were those of Article XXVIII. The Turkish Government recognized its obligations under Article XXVIII and was prepared to meet them, but it was not prepared to assume additional obligations under Article XXIV arising out of considerations which it regarded as having no legal basis.

14. On this last point, the representative of the United Kingdom explained that it was not the United Kingdom's intention to ask the Turkish Government to assume new obligations. He had made a suggestion about the circumstances in which (though not the time when—this was entirely a matter for the Turkish Government) a preference in favor of imports from the Community might begin to appear in the Turkish tariff; but the main objective was to find out what Turkish intentions in fact were in this respect, since, without knowing these intentions, the United Kingdom could not form a view of what was, in its view, at issue in the Article XXVIII negotiations or what was the value to be placed on the offer Turkey had made in the Kennedy Round.

C. DISCUSSION IN THE WORKING PARTY

15. The representative of one member of the Working Party said that he had always assumed that the Turkish Government would in fact do what was suggested by the United Kingdom, that is that it would reduce the recently increased rates of duty to the pre-existing levels before opening a preference in favor of Community suppliers. In his view it was not possible to argue that, on the one hand, Turkish industry needed increased protection but that, on the other hand, it was possible for Turkey at the same time to give tariff preferences to a group of countries with a highly competitive and diversified export trade.

16. The representative of Turkey pointed out that the increase of the Turkish tariff could not be appreciated out of the context in which this measure had been taken. The tariff increase was only one feature of the long-term development plan which, as appeared from the Turkish submission for the waiver, was intended to accelerate economic growth, raise levels of employment and ensure economic stability, and the maintenance of balance-of-payments equilibrium, thus enabling Turkey to reduce reliance on direct import controls. He did not share the view that a contracting party which was in balance-of-payments difficulties and needed protection for its economy could not grant preferential tariff treatment; indeed there were many such instances among contracting parties in GATT. Moreover, the representative of Turkey said that Turkey was quite conscious of its own interest and would naturally act in accordance with the requirements of its economic development, but as sovereign State, Turkey strongly felt that no further guidance was required in this context.

17. Some other members of the Working Party pointed out that, while there may have been no connexion in intent between the Ankara Agreement and the tariff increase, in terms of practical effect the connexion existed and the way in which Turkey eventually moved towards customs union with the Community was of great interest to third countries, particularly in respect of duty rates on items presently bound in Schedule XXXVII of the General Agreement. These representatives found the United Kingdom suggestion an appropriate one.

18. Referring to the mention of Article XXIV in the terms of reference of the Group, the representative of the EEC enquired as to what juridical basis in the GATT could be invoked for asking to the Government of Turkey to accept a proposal whereby it would renounce rights which it had under Article XXIV. The provisions of this Article did not

impose on members of a customs union any obligation with respect to the time relationship to be observed between the adoption of the common external tariff and the movement towards free trade within the union. It appeared to him that, by asking the Turkish Government not to introduce preferential tariff treatment on certain items before a certain stage had been reached, the United Kingdom was in fact asking Turkey to assume new obligations which would restrict the freedom of action to which it was legally entitled under Article XXIV. He recalled that the increase in the Turkish tariff would be a temporary one since this tariff would, under the Ankara Agreement, be reduced to the level of the common external tariff of the Community and he noted that whereas the United Kingdom proposal contained in paragraph 8, if accepted, would prevent Turkey from introducing differential tariff treatment on certain items until the temporary increases had been eliminated, the United Kingdom, which imposed a surcharge which was also temporary, had not stopped the process of dismantling its tariffs within the framework of the EFTA arrangements until this surcharge was eliminated. The representative of the Community added that there was nothing unique about the coincidence between the Agreement of Association and the increase in the Turkish tariff; the increase in the Portuguese tariff at the time of the coming into force of the Stockholm Convention setting up the EFTA was another instance of such coincidence.

19. In reply to a question, the representative of the EEC explained that, except as provided for in the Ankara Agreement, the text of which had been submitted to and examined by the CONTRACTING PARTIES, the parties to it had complete freedom of action on the matter examined by the Group.

20. Some other member of the Working Party did not agree that the examples mentioned by the representative of the Community were relevant to the present issue. Among the points they made was that, in the case of Portugal, there was no question of bound duties; and in the case of the United Kingdom surcharge, what was at issue then was a very temporary measure introduced as an alternative to quantitative restrictions for solely balance-of-payments reasons.

21. There was some discussion in the Working Party of what the expectations of traders in the EEC could have been when the terms of the Ankara Agreement were finalized. The Working Party noted that, at that time, EEC traders could not have expected to enjoy preferences larger than could be given under the Turkish tariff as it stood before the recent increase.

CONCLUSIONS

22. The representative of Turkey said that his Government, although it maintained its previous position, had felt that a further effort should be made in order to foster goodwill and better understanding amongst contracting parties and in that spirit, and guided by the principle of equity, it had authorized him to offer the incorporation into agreements reached in the renegotiations under Article XXVIII of the following declaration:

> "The Turkish Government, having taken note of the problem raised by the United Kingdom delegation with respect to items previously bound, rates on which have been increased in the new Turkish tariff, declares herewith that, without prejudice to any rights which accrue to Turkey under the General Agreement, it will give due consideration to the equitable rights of contracting parties who are not members of the Ankara Agreement when it comes to implementing differential tariff treatment in favor of the EEC on these items."

23. The Working Party noted this statement.

24. With reference to that part of the declaration which explained that it was without prejudice to any rights which accrued to Turkey under the General Agreement, the Chairman said that it was his understanding that the declaration was without prejudice to the rights of contracting parties generally under the GATT.

25. Taking note of the declaration which the Government of Turkey envisaged to make on the completion of the negotiations under Article XXVIII, the representative of the EEC considered that the declaration was not incompatible with the provisions of the Ankara Agreement and he was glad to see that the solution had allowed the Working Party to fulfil its task.

26. The Working Party agreed that it could now report that the consultation it had been asked to carry out had been concluded.

UNITED KINGDOM TEMPORARY IMPORT CHARGES

Report of the Working Party adopted on November 17, 1966
BISD 15S/113

1. The fifth meeting of the Working Party on United Kingdom Temporary Import Charges was held on June 9. At that meeting the Working Party took note of the United Kingdom announcement that the surcharge was to be discontinued after November 30, 1966 (L/2651) and of a United Kingdom statement that it was not intended to replace the surcharge by any other measure of direct import restraint on the demise of the charge. Accordingly, the Working Party decided to prepare this final report to the Council for submission when the surcharge is no longer in effect. No recommendation is made, but the Working Party felt that it would be appropriate to record briefly the history of the surcharge and to set down certain understandings and views of members.

2. On October 27, 1964, the CONTRACTING PARTIES were informed by the United Kingdom (L/2285) that in order to safeguard the external financial position of the United Kingdom and to correct its balance of payments and as part of wider policies directed to the short-term and longer-term problems of the country's underlying economic situation it had been decided to impose a charge of 15 per cent *ad valorem* on all imports from all sources except for certain listed foods and raw materials. The United Kingdom invoked the provisions of Article XII of the General Agreement as justification for restricting imports, even though it recognized that the type of restraint on imports there envisaged was the use of quantitative restrictions. The United Kingdom authorities explained that in their view the elaborate administrative machinery required to re-establish import licensing would be unnecessarily disruptive of trade, especially as the surcharge was intended strictly as a temporary measure to be reduced and abolished as soon as the balance-of-payments situation might permit.

3. At the Council meeting at which this matter was first considered, on December 7, 1964 (C/M/23), widespread sympathy was expressed for the difficulties facing the United Kingdom Government and approval was expressed for the promptness with which the British Government

had acted to safeguard the balance of payments, even though many members were not able to support the use of this particular measure.

4. In order to provide an opportunity for full and if necessary repeated consultation with the United Kingdom, but bearing in mind that Article XII envisaged that any necessary restraint on imports would be by way of quantitative restrictions, a special Working Party was established which was given the following terms of reference:

> "Consultations shall be promptly initiated with the United Kingdom as to the nature of the balance-of-payments difficulties, the nature of the measures taken, alternative corrective measures which may be available and the possible effect of the measures taken on the economies of other contracting parties.
>
> "The Consultations shall be carried out promptly and a report shall be submitted to the Council which shall meet as soon as possible to consider such action as may be appropriate in the light of the report."

5. Beginning in December 1964, the Working Party carried on consultations with the United Kingdom at four separate meetings. Between the first and second meetings the United Kingdom announced a reduction of the surcharge from 15 to 10 per cent *ad valorem* effective in April 1965. At each of the first four meetings the Working Party consulted with the International Monetary Fund, which contributed background material and gave the Working Party the benefit of its judgment concerning the serious decline of United Kingdom monetary reserves and the measures taken to correct it. The announcement that the charge would lapse after November 30, 1966, made in May 1966, came some time after the fourth meeting of the Working Party.

6. For the fifth and final meeting, therefore, it did not appear appropriate to resume the consultation. Instead the Working Party confined itself to receiving the United Kingdom announcement and to giving instructions for the preparation of this report. At this meeting the United Kingdom representative also assured the Working Party that his Government has no intention of replacing the surcharge by any other measure of direct import restraint on the demise of the charge. This assurance was of course not to be interpreted as a hard and fast undertaking of indefinite duration or as a commitment not to use direct measures if for example the balance of payments once again deteriorated seriously.

7. Whilst it would serve no useful purpose to repeat in detail the debates which took place on the various issues involved, the Working Party felt that it might be useful to record the main issues which had been discussed and to set down certain understandings as to characteristics of this case.

8. Perhaps the most important consideration in reassuring members as to the consequences of the United Kingdom action was the fact that the surcharge had from the outset been justified only as a temporary transitional measure designed to give immediate help in a unique situation and that the United Kingdom had from the beginning emphasized the intention of reducing and eliminating the charge as soon as the balance-of-payments situation might permit. Many members remarked favorably at the fifth meeting on the decision of the United Kingdom to announce termination of the measure.

9. All of the United Kingdom statements to the Working Party and much of the questioning in the meetings emphasized the view that the underlying causes of the United Kingdom's recognized difficulties lay not so much in excess imports as in a lack of growth and modernization of the economy, particularly in the export sectors, and in inadequate efforts to divert increased resources into export industries and away from consumption. Hence, the most serious criticisms of the import surcharge raised questions about the appropriateness of a measure which addressed itself to what was regarded as a symptom only. In answer, the United Kingdom representative described an array of internal measures in hand but emphasized that while they were expected to restore equilibrium in due course none could be expected to produce the immediate stemming of outward payments that was required. All agreed in welcoming the end of the surcharge and reliance on internal measures as a means of completing the restoration of equilibrium, the more so as the importance of a strong United Kingdom economy to the international community at large was fully recognized.

10. The less-developed countries, throughout the meetings, advanced their special case for preferred treatment with respect to application of the surcharge. In their view, it had been agreed in the drafting of Part IV that less-developed countries should not be expected to bear as large a share as others in solving international trade problems, yet the United Kingdom measure, by making no exception for goods supplied by them, in effect forced them to pay their full share in resolving internal British problems by accepting reduced sales or reduced profit margins or both. They felt that the surcharge worked special hardship in

two particular situations. First they cited the case of cotton textiles already subject to special quantitative restrictions when imported into the United Kingdom and urged that application of the surcharge to such products amounted to a double penalty. Certain developed countries which export cotton textiles joined in the plea for special treatment in this sector. Further, the less-developed countries argued, there would be products of which they as a group were principal suppliers. Such products might be exempted from the surcharge, they felt, either when imported from less-developed countries only or regardless of source in recognition of their special need to maintain and expand their export earnings. As a minimum, they felt that the second case should be accepted as a basis for exemption from the surcharge. The United Kingdom representative stated that his government was reluctant to embark on a course which would necessarily have a discriminatory effect and which, to the extent that it favored more importation, would postpone the time when the surcharge could be reduced and removed. In this, he was strongly supported by the United States representative, who felt it most important that the measure be removed at the earliest possible moment and pointed out that final removal would be delayed by any exemptions from surcharge, of which the first might not necessarily be the last.

11. Another matter considered in the early stages was the inclusion within the scope of the surcharge of goods imported under contracts concluded prior to the imposition of the surcharge; representatives of many countries took exception to this feature. Members pointed out that the incidence of the surcharge was not uniform, depending as it did on the terms of the particular contract, and the time involved; distant suppliers were also being penalized more severely in that their contracts tended to be made farther ahead. The United Kingdom representative pointed out that any easement would inevitably lessen the effectiveness of the measure and that his Government considered it important to obtain a maximum impact in the shortest possible time.

12. In reviewing other measures taken by the United Kingdom to overcome the difficulties, reference was made to the export incentive measures instituted in the autumn of 1964, and at the last meeting interest was expressed in the new Selective Employment Tax. While on the one hand some doubts were expressed concerning the consistency of some of the export incentives with the provisions of the General Agreement, it was agreed on the other hand that any question of that kind fell outside the terms of reference of the Working Party.

13. In concluding the fifth meeting of the Working Party, note was also taken of the likely effect of the advance announcement by the United Kingdom of the ending of the surcharge. The reasons for the early announcement were appreciated but at the same time it was noted that a likely consequence would be a slowing of imports in the months between May and November, followed by a sudden increase once the surcharge is removed. Such an increase, it was hoped and expected, would not be followed by the institution of new obstacles to importation.

UNITED STATES SUBSIDY ON UNMANUFACTURED TOBACCO

Report of the Working Party on Article XXII:2 Consultations adopted on November 22, 1967
BISD 15S/116,122

LEGAL ISSUES

21. The representative of Malawi said that, in his view, Article XVI, read as a whole, was aimed at discouraging the use of export subsidies for primary products. To the extent that the Article condoned such practices, the operation of subsidies was limited by the provisions of paragraph 3 of Article XVI which provided that a subsidy "shall not be applied in a manner which results in the [subsidizing] contracting party having more than an equitable share of world export trade . . .". It was difficult to define the concept of equitability in this context but it was his view that it did not refer to the maintenance by the subsidizing contracting party of a predetermined proportionate share of a growing world market. Moreover, particularly in view of the provisions of an Interpretative Note to paragraph 3 which allowed for the entry of new exporters, there were grounds for maintaining that "equitable shares" could vary. He noted that the United States exports, whilst declining as a proportion of world trade, had not diminished in volume and had actually increased in value. The lack of clarity as regards the provisions of Article XVI:3 would seem to call for the establishment of some ground rules by the CONTRACTING PARTIES. Another member of the Working Party noted that the Working Party on Other Barriers to Trade, established to conduct the review of the General Agreement in 1954, had agreed "that in determining what are equitable shares of world trade the CONTRACTING PARTIES should not lose sight of the desirability of facilitating the satisfaction of world requirements of the commodity concerned in the most economic and effective manner . . .". (BISD, 3S, page 226). Other members of the Working Party also emphasized that the pattern of supply to world markets could not, particularly in the spirit of GATT, be regarded as static and should allow for changes in relative competitive positions.

22. The representative of the United States said that his Government regarded its action in introducing the subsidy as fully in conformity with

the provisions of Article XVI. The United States Government shared the view of the Malawi Government that it would not be desirable to assume that a particular country's share of a market should remain static. It was not the intention of the United States to increase its share beyond an "equitable level" but it could not be expected to accept the continued erosion of its relative position. He agreed it was not possible to determine precisely what constituted an "equitable share", but the United States share had by 1965 declined in comparison with any previous "representative period". The Food and Agriculture Organization in its recently revised *Agricultural Commodities—Projections for 1975 and 1985* had concluded that, ". . . this secular decline [in the United States share] has been due, on the one hand, to the strong competition offered by the larger supplies of cheaper leaf coming from developing countries, and on the other, to a change in manufacturers' requirements in importing countries. United States leaf is generally more expensive because of its better quality and also because of domestic farm price policies which aim at maintaining remunerative prices to producers. . . . It appears therefore that it may become increasingly difficult for the United States producers to keep up with foreign competition if there are no basic changes in their present price support policies, or in the commodity situation as such."

23. The representative of Malawi then referred to the provisions of Part IV of the General Agreement. He noted that Article XXXVI:3 provided that "there was need for positive efforts designed to ensure that less-developed contracting parties secure a share in the growth of international trade commensurate with the needs of their economic development". He suggested that this could be interpreted as meaning that the share of less-developed countries in world trade in a particular commodity could grow at a faster rate than world trade as a whole, and the rate of export growth by industrialized countries. The representative of Malawi also referred to the provisions of Article XXXVII:3(*c*) and, whilst noting that prior consultations were not explicitly required, they would enable a less-developed country concerned to express its views which might not otherwise be known to the industrialized country contemplating action. Other members of the Working Party expressed their support of this view.

24. The representative of the United States said that the action taken by his Government was fully in conformity with the provisions of Part IV. He noted, in this connexion, that the FAO study previously cited had found that the developing countries were competing successfully with the United States in the world tobacco market. As regards the provisions of Article XXXVII:3(*c*), the United States had carried out

a thorough examination of alternative remedies and had concluded that the alternatives were less desirable. In this examination, the special interests of developing countries were taken into account. Article XXXVII:3(*c*) did not obligate a contracting party to hold consultations prior to the introduction of the subsidy.

25. Certain representatives pointed out that the subsidy introduced by the United States raised an important point of general principle and precedent concerning the provisions of Part IV which went far beyond the implications of the present matter. The representative of Malawi suggested that it might be useful to establish some conventions with respect to products in which industrialized and developing countries were competing, particularly as it was necessary to demonstrate that the provisions of Part IV were effective in safeguarding the interests of developing countries.

CONCLUSIONS

26. The other members of the Working Party thanked the representative of the United States for the full and frank manner with which he had dealt with the questions they had posed. The representative of the United States thanked the other representatives for the friendly and constructive spirit in which they had put their views during the consultations.

27. Although it was not possible, on the basis of the available evidence and in view of the many factors which affect levels of exports and prices to demonstrate conclusively that the trade interests of Malawi and the other countries which had joined with her in the consultations had been adversely affected, the representatives of Malawi, Canada, India, Jamaica and Turkey nevertheless reiterated their apprehension concerning the effects which the United States subsidy could have on the international tobacco market. In view of what they considered to be the adverse effects of the United States subsidy on the incomes of their respective tobacco industries these representatives requested that the subsidy be removed. In making this request the representatives of Malawi, India, Jamaica and Turkey referred in particular to the requirements of Part IV of the General Agreement. The representative of the United States stated that he was not in a position to give any formal undertaking in this regard.

28. The representatives of Malawi, Canada, India and Turkey also repeated the second representation made to the United States

Government in February namely that, in the event of its considering the extension of the existing subsidy, it should consult, before taking action, with those governments whose export interests were chiefly affected. This representation was supported by certain other members of the Working Party. The representative of the United States stated that he was not in a position to give any formal undertaking in this regard, but would convey this request to the appropriate United States authorities with his recommendation that it be given sympathetic attention.

JAMAICA—MARGINS OF PREFERENCE

Report of the Panel adopted on February 2, 1971
BISD 18S/184

3. The Panel noted that in accordance with paragraph 2 of the Protocol of Provisional Application, the Government of the United Kingdom, by letter dated June 28, 1948, gave notice to the Secretary-General of the United Nations of its intention to apply the General Agreement provisionally to the territories for the international relations of which it was responsible. Jamaica, however, was explicitly excluded at that time. Only in 1962, the United Kingdom, in a communication received on July 2, notified the Secretary-General of the United Nations and the Director-General of GATT that the General Agreement was to be applied provisionally also in respect of Jamaica. In accordance with paragraph 2 of the Protocol of Provisional Application and paragraph 5 (*b*) of Article XXVI, this notification was effective as from August 1, 1962 (L/1809).

4. The Panel noted that on August 6, 1962 Jamaica achieved independence. On the sponsorship of the United Kingdom, the Recommendation providing for the *de facto* application of the General Agreement in relations with newly independent States became applicable to Jamaica (L/1823). At the same time, the Director-General entered into consultation with the Government of Jamaica informing it *inter alia* of the options open to it. Jamaica could either become a contracting party under Article XXVI:5(*c*), in which case Jamaica would assume the obligations involved in the application to it of the General Agreement by the United Kingdom before Jamaica became independent, or accede to the General Agreement under Article XXXIII. In reply, the Jamaican Government expressed its intention to apply the General Agreement on a reciprocal *de facto* basis pending a final decision on its membership in GATT.

5. The Panel noted that in 1963 the Government of Jamaica advised that it wished to become a full contracting party to the GATT under Article XXVI:5(*c*). In his letter of acknowledgement, the Director-General stated that in accepting the status of contracting party to the GATT, the Government of Jamaica had acquired the rights and obligations which had previously been accepted by the United Kingdom in respect of the territory of Jamaica. Subsequently, on December 31, 1963, a certification was issued (L/2111) declaring that the conditions

required by Article XXVI:5(*c*) were met, and Jamaica had become a contracting party; its rights and obligations dated from August 6, 1962.

6. The Panel noted that in the period before August 1962, when the General Agreement was not applicable to Jamaica, certain modifications had been made in the Jamaican tariff, as a result of which some preferential margins were reduced while some were increased, the majority of preferential margins, however, remaining unchanged. In June 1967, further modifications in the Jamaican Customs Tariff resulted in increased margins of preference on a much larger number of items. The Panel, therefore, was confronted with the task of expressing an opinion as to the consistency of these increases in margins of preference with the obligations of Jamaica under the General Agreement, and in particular, as to whether the base date of April 10, 1947, provided in paragraph 4 of Article I, was legally applicable to Jamaica.

* * *

13. The Panel held that since Jamaica had acceded to the General Agreement on Tariffs and Trade under the provisions of Article XXVI:5(*c*) it had acquired the rights and obligations which had previously been accepted by the United Kingdom in respect of the territory of Jamaica. This meant that Jamaica assumed the rights and obligations involved in the application to it of the General Agreement by the United Kingdom before Jamaica became independent. On August 6, 1962, the day Jamaica became independent, Article I:4 formed part of the General Agreement as it had been applied by the United Kingdom on behalf of the territory of Jamaica. The provision of Article I:4 establishing April 10, 1947 as the base date for permissible margins of preference was therefore applicable to Jamaica.

14. The Panel agreed, however, that it was important to find a solution which, on the one hand, would not require a strained interpretation of the General Agreement and which would leave the General Agreement intact, but which, on the other hand, would take into account the uniqueness of the Jamaican case and would therefore permit Jamaica to apply in a legally correct manner margins of preference as they were in effect on August 1, 1962, the date of the General Agreement was first applied to the territory of Jamaica.

15. The Panel therefore suggests that in the light of the exceptional circumstances the CONTRACTING PARTIES consider taking a decision in accordance with the provisions of paragraph 5 of Article XXV to change with respect to Jamaica the base date referred to in paragraph 4 of Article I from April 10, 1947 to August 1, 1962.

OMITTED

UNITED KINGDOM—DOLLAR AREA QUOTAS

Reports of the Panel adopted on July 30, 1973
BISD 20S/230

INTERIM REPORT

I. INTRODUCTION

* * *

4. The matter referred to the Panel related to the maintenance by the United Kingdom of quantitative restrictions on certain products when imported from the United States and certain other "dollar area" countries. [Bolivia, Canada, Colombia, Costa Rica, Cuba, Dominican Republic, Ecuador, El Salvador, Guatemala, Haiti, Republic of Honduras, Liberia, Mexico, Nicaragua, Panama, Philippines, United States, Venezuela.] The following products are subject to these restrictions:

BTN	Product
ex 08.01	Bananas
ex 08.02	Grapefruit, fresh
ex 08.10	Grapefruit (whether or not cooked), preserved by freezing not containing added sugar
ex 20.03	Grapefruit preserved by freezing, containing added sugar
ex 20.06	Grapefruit, otherwise prepared or preserved, whether or not containing added sugar or spirit
ex 20.07	Grapefruit juice and orange juice other than unpasteurized frozen orange and grapefruit juice concentrate
ex 22.09	Rum
ex 24.02	Cigars

5. The Dollar Area Quota restrictions had their origin in the exchange control and currency conservation measures taken by the United Kingdom during and immediately after the Second World War. Initially the Dollar Area countries were those whose exports to the United Kingdom required payment in United States dollars. It needs to be stressed that this is no longer the case and the term "Dollar Area" in no

way now implies a requirement for payment in dollars. While the restrictions originally applied to a wide range of products, most of the quotas were subsequently removed, leaving those on the products referred to in paragraph 4 above. The quotas on these products while initially introduced for balance-of-payments reasons are now maintained on the grounds that they are regarded as constituting valuable protection for the economic interests of the developing Commonwealth Caribbean countries.

* * *

III. CONSIDERATIONS OF THE PANEL

1. The Panel noted the contention of the United States delegation that the restrictions were in contravention of Articles XI and XIII of the General Agreement and that delegation's request that the restrictions be eliminated. The Panel also noted that the United Kingdom had never denied that the Dollar Area Quotas were in formal contravention of the provisions of the General Agreement on quantitative restrictions, and for the time being reserved its findings on this question. The Panel noted as well the argument put forward by the Caribbean countries and territories that the restrictions must be viewed in the context of the General Agreement as a whole and with particular regard to Part IV of the Agreement. According to these delegations, the continued application of the quotas was justified in the light of Part IV which was designed to deal with the special circumstances of developing countries.

2. In the course of its consultations, the Panel ascertained that the items of critical export interest to the United States were: fresh grapefruit (ex 08.02), citrus juices (ex 20.07), rum (ex 22.09) and cigars (ex 24.07). The Panel accordingly decided to concentrate its further deliberations on these four items.

3. With respect to these four items, the Panel noted that the products principally benefiting from the Dollar Area Quotas were fresh grapefruit (ex 08.02) and citrus juices (ex 20.07). Moreover, on the basis of recent statistical data, imports by the United Kingdom from these countries of fresh grapefruit accounted for no more than 3 per cent of total United Kingdom imports of this product; on the other hand virtually all of the exports by the Caribbean countries of this product go to the United Kingdom. Similarly, imports from these countries of grapefruit juice represent only about 10 per cent of total United Kingdom imports of this product while on the other hand 60 per cent of Jamaica's

exports of these products and 40 per cent of Trinidad and Tobago's exports go to the United Kingdom.

4. The Panel noted the contention of the United Kingdom delegation that the Dollar Area Quotas bring no trading advantage to the United Kingdom and are not linked to any reverse preferences or trading concessions granted on a reciprocal basis to the United Kingdom by the countries and territories concerned and, furthermore, that the quotas afforded no protection to any United Kingdom national industry or trading interest.

5. The Panel noted the possibility of assessing the damage which is inflicted by the Dollar Area Quota on United States exports of the commodities concerned to the United Kingdom market and the further possibility of suspending such concessions or other obligations under the General Agreement as is deemed to be appropriate in the circumstances.

6. The Panel considered and discussed with the parties concerned various possible solutions and, in this connexion, strongly requested the parties concerned to actively seek a mutually acceptable solution to the problem which especially would pay due regard to the importance to the Caribbean countries and territories of the two products referred to in paragraph 3 above, namely fresh grapefruit and grapefruit juice and orange juice.

7. In the light of the above, and taking into account the constructive spirit of the parties concerned, the Panel refrains from making formal recommendations at this stage. It will, however, revert to the matter and make appropriate recommendations, if after an interval of one month from the date of presentation of this Interim Report to the Council, the parties concerned have been unable to reach a mutually acceptable solution to the problem.

* * *

FINAL REPORT

5. On July 9, 1973, the Director-General of the GATT was informed in writing by the United States of the withdrawal, following the settlement between the United States and the United Kingdom, of the complaint brought under Article XXIII:2. Details of the settlement were subsequently communicated to the Panel in separate letters from the United States and the United Kingdom.

6. The Panel welcomes the fact that agreement has been reached between the parties to the dispute. The Panel understands, however, that the Commonwealth Caribbean countries do not consider the settlement reached between the United States and the United Kingdom as giving full satisfaction to their interests, especially in view of the importance of the products concerned to their export interests and to their economies in general, and bearing in mind Part IV of the General Agreement—as well as the repeated assurances given by both parties to the dispute that it was not their intention to harm the export interests of Caribbean countries in the products included in the settlement.

7. The Panel welcomes the assurances given by the Governments of the United Kingdom and the United States to continue to safeguard, as far as possible, the interests of the Caribbean countries.

CANADIAN IMPORT QUOTAS ON EGGS

Report of the Working Party adopted on February 17, 1976
BISD 23S/91

1. In a communication dated September 9, 1975 (L/4222) the Government of the United States request that a meeting of the Council of Representatives be held at the earliest possible date to discuss the establishment of a working party to make an advisory ruling on the consistency of Canada's import quotas on eggs with Article XI of the GATT. In a further communication dated September 10, 1975 (L/4223) the Government of the United States set out the points at issue and specified the following three questions on which it requested an advisory ruling:

(a) Does the Canadian supply management system on eggs conform to the requirements of GATT Article XI?

(b) Is the basis for determining the import quotas in accord with the requirements of the last paragraph of Article XI?

(c) Irrespective of findings under (*a*) and (*b*) above, does the imposition of the Canadian quotas under Article XI constitute nullification and impairment of a prior binding?

2. At the meeting of the Council on September 25, 1975, a Working Party was set up with the following terms of reference:

> "To examine the matters referred to the CONTRACTING PARTIES by the Government of the United States (L/4223) concerning the imposition of import quotas for eggs and egg products by the Government of Canada (L/4207), and to report thereon to the Council."

3. The Working Part held extensive discussions on October 9, 28 and 29 and December 8, 9 and 11 under the chairmanship of Mr. M. Eggert (Finland) and decided to provide the following answers to the three questions posed by the United States in document L/4223.

4. With regard to question (*a*) the members of the Working Party, except the United States, agreed with the Canadian view that the operation of the Canadian supply management program for eggs, as

described and explained to the Working Party, was in conformity with the requirements of Article XI:2(*c*)(i). The United States, while agreeing that Canada had a supply management system for eggs, did not agree that the present system was able to effectively control domestic production, and considered, therefore, that it would not be in conformity with Article XI:2(*c*)(i).

5. With regard to question (*b*) the Working Party was unable to decide which representative period was the correct one nor whether or not the one chosen by Canada was in conformity with the requirements of the last paragraph of Article XI. The other members of the Working Party proposed that the United States and Canada try to come to a pragmatic solution in bilateral discussions and that the countries be guided by the suggestion that annual fluctuations in trade in eggs were an important element, *inter alia*, to be taken into account in determining a proper balance.

These members suggested that the period from June 1, 1967 to May 31, 1973 might provide one basis for agreement.

6. With regard to question (*c*), whether the imposition of the Canadian quotas on eggs under Article XI constituted nullification or impairment of a prior binding, the Working Party did not come to any conclusion in this particular case.

UNITED STATES TAX LEGISLATION (*DISC*)

Report of the Panel presented to the Council of Representatives on November 12, 1976
BISD 23S/98, 99

FACTUAL ASPECTS OF THE *DISC* LEGISLATION

6. The following is a brief description of factual aspects of the DISC legislation as the Panel understood them.

7. The United States tax system finds its origin in the first income tax act, the Revenue Act of 1913. Under this system, corporations and their shareholders are separately taxed. The United States taxes the entire worldwide income of its domestic corporations, allowing a foreign tax credit against United States tax for income taxes paid abroad.

8. Prior to 1962 the United States did not tax the foreign-source income of a foreign corporation organized outside the United States. Taxes on that income were deferred until the income was repatriated. When "subpart F" was enacted in the Revenue Act of 1962, the United States began taxing currently to the United States shareholders of controlled foreign corporations the income from certain sales and services of these foreign subsidiaries.

9. Inter-company pricing rules, adopted first in 1924, follow the arm's-length principle.

10. The next major change was the introduction of the DISC system. The *Domestic International Sales Corporation* statute came into force on January 1, 1972 and was incorporated in the United States Internal Revenue Code as Sections 991 to 997.

11. To qualify as a DISC, a United States corporation must meet specific requirements, including requirements that it be a domestic corporation, that 95 per cent of the corporation's gross receipts for each taxable year consist of "qualified export receipts" and that 95 per cent of the corporation's assets at the close of the taxable year be "qualified export assets".

12. A United States corporation that qualifies as a DISC is not subject to United States federal income tax on its current or retained export earnings. However, one half of a DISC's earnings is deemed

distributed to the shareholders of the DISC and is taxable to those shareholders as a dividend. A liability of shareholders to taxation on the retained earnings arises when one of the following events occur: (*a*) there is an actual distribution of untaxed DISC earnings, (*b*) the DISC is liquidated, (*c*) a shareholder disposes of the DISC stocks, or (*d*) the corporation fails to qualify as a DISC for the taxable year.

13. Special inter-company pricing rules permit a rule-of-thumb allocation of export sales income between the parent company and the DISC. These rules provide that a DISC's profits are taken to be an amount which does not exceed the greater of: (*a*) 4 per cent of its export sales receipts, or (*b*) 50 per cent of the combined taxable income of the DISC and its related supplier, or (*c*) taxable income based upon the price actually charged to the DISC by its related supplier if that price is justifiable on an arm's-length basis. In the case of either (*a*) or (*b*) the DISC can earn an additional profit equal to 10 per cent of related export promotion expenses. The rules cannot be applied so as to create in the parent a loss on a sale.

14. In most cases, total profits of a manufacturing company and its DISC combined exceed 8 per cent and the 50-50 split of profits between the parent and the DISC is chosen. Since one half of the DISC's profits are deemed distributed to its parent, the net effect is as if 75 per cent of the export profits were allocated to the parent manufacturer and taxed currently. Twenty-five per cent is allocated to the DISC and tax on this is deferred, without attracting interest for the period involved, in contrast to the general practice in the case of late payment of corporation income tax.

15. The definition of "export promotion expenses" says *inter alia* that "such expenses shall also include freight expenses to the extent of 50 per cent of the cost of shipping export property aboard airplanes owned and operated by United States persons or ships documented under the laws of the United States in those cases where law or regulations does not require that such property be shipped aboard such airplanes or ships".

16. The number of companies electing for DISC treatment has developed as follows. By the end of March 1972, three months after the legislation came into effect, 1,136 DISCs had been created. By the end of 1972 the figure was 3,439; by the end of 1973 it was 4,825; by the end of 1974 it was 6,738 and by the end of 1975 it was 8,258. By the end of February 1976 the number of DISCs had reached 8,382. However, some DISCs are inactive, many companies have more than one DISC, and the data are not adjusted for DISCs that have been liquidated or have withdrawn their elections.

17. DISC exports accounted in DISC year 1974 for about $43.5 thousand million, or 61 per cent of total United States exports in calendar year 1973. According to the *International Economic Report of the President*, 70 per cent of United States exports went through DISCs in 1975 and it is estimated that DISC exports will account for approximately three quarters of total United States exports in 1976.

* * *

20. It is estimated that United States exports in DISC year 1974 were about $4.6 thousand million higher than they would have been without the DISC legislation. These additional exports may have provided about 230,000 jobs in the export sector in the DISC year 1974.

21. According to a statement of the Secretary of the United States Treasury on April 13, 1976, projections indicate that the effect of the DISC legislation on exports in 1976 could be as large as $9 thousand million.

* * *

CONCLUSIONS

67. The Panel started by examining the effects of the DISC legislation in economic terms. The Panel concluded that it conferred a tax benefit and that this benefit was essentially related to exports. The Panel considered that if the corporation income tax was reduced with respect to export-related activities and was unchanged with respect to domestic activities for the internal market this would tend to lead to an expansion of export activity. Therefore the DISC legislation would result in more resources being attracted to export activities than would have occurred in the absence of such benefits for exports.

68. The Panel noted that the United States Treasury had acknowledged that exports had increased as a result of the DISC legislation and the Panel considered that the fact that so many DISCs had been created was evidence that DISC status conferred a substantial benefit.

69. The Panel noted that the DISC legislation was intended, in its own terms, to increase United States exports and concluded that, as its benefits arose as a function of profits from exports, it should be regarded as an export subsidy.

70. The Panel examined whether a deferral of tax was "a remission"

in terms of item (*c*) or "an exemption" in terms of item (*d*) of the illustrative list of 1960.[1]

71. The Panel was not convinced that a deferral, *simply* because it was given for an indeterminate period, was equal to a remission or an exemption. In addition it noted that the DISC legislation provided for the termination of the deferral under specified circumstances. The Panel further noted, however, that the deferral did not attract the interest component of the tax normally levied for late or deferred payment and therefore concluded that, to this extent, the DISC legislation constituted a partial exemption which was covered by one or both of paragraphs (*c*) and (*d*) of the illustrative list.

72. The Panel noted that the contracting parties that had accepted the 1960 Declaration had agreed that the practices in the illustrative list were generally to be considered as subsidies in the sense of Article XVI:4. The Panel further noted that these contracting parties considered that, in general, the practices contained in the illustrative list could be presumed to result in bi-level pricing, and considered that this presumption could therefore be applied to the DISC legislation. The Panel concluded, however, from the words "generally to be considered" that these contracting parties did not consider that the presumption was absolute.

73. The Panel considered that, from an economic point of view, there was a presumption that an export subsidy would lead to any or a combination of the following consequences in the export sector: (*a*) lowering of prices, (*b*) increase of sales effort and (*c*) increase of profits per unit. Because the subsidy was both significant and broadly based it was to be expected that all of these effects would occur and that, if one occurred, the other two would not necessarily be excluded. A concentration of the subsidy benefits on prices could lead to substantial reductions in prices. The Panel did not accept that a reduction in prices in export markets needed automatically to be accompanied by similar reductions in domestic markets. These conclusions were supported by statements by American personalities and companies and the Panel felt that it should pay some regard to this evidence.

74. The Panel therefore concluded that the DISC legislation in some cases had effects which were not in accordance with the United States' obligations under Article XVI:4.

75. The Panel examined the significance of the various options under

[1] BISD 9S/186.

the DISC legislation for the allocation of profits from export sales between parent companies and DISCs, and concluded that these could influence the size of the exemption.

76. The Panel concluded that the provision allowing the deduction of certain shipping costs by DISCs (on the condition that exports be carried in United States vessels), and the provision allowing 10 per cent of export promotion expenses to be assigned as a deductible expense to a DISC would appear to confer additional pecuniary benefits.

77. The Panel considered that, as it had found the DISC legislation to constitute an export subsidy which had led to an increase in exports, it was also covered by the notification obligation contained in Article XVI:1.

78. While the Panel noted that primary product exports were eligible for DISC benefits and had been treated substantially through DISCs, it did not examine whether the benefits would result in the United States obtaining a disproportionate share of the world market in terms of Article XVI:3.

79. The Panel noted the United States argument that it had introduced the DISC legislation to correct an existing distortion created by tax practices of certain other contracting parties. However, the Panel did not accept that one distortion could be justified by the existence of another one and considered that, if the United States had considered that other contracting parties were violating the General Agreement, it could have had recourse to the remedies which the General Agreement offered. On the other hand, the fact that tax practices of certain other countries had been in force for some time without being the subject of complaints was not, in itself, conclusive evidence that there was a consensus that they were compatible with the General Agreement.

80. In the light of the above and bearing in mind the precedent set by the Uruguayan case, the Panel found that there was a *prima facie* case of nullification or impairment of benefits which other contracting parties were entitled to expect under the General Agreement.

COUNCIL ACTION
BISD 28S/114

At the meeting of the Council on December 7 and 8, 1981, the Council adopted the four Panel Reports in documents L/4422,[1] L/4423,[2] L/4424[3] and L/4425,[4] on the following understanding:

> "The Council adopts these reports on the understanding that with respect to these cases, and in general, economic processes (including transactions involving exported goods) located outside the territorial limits of the exporting country need not be subject to taxation by the exporting country and should not be regarded as export activities in terms of Article XVI:4 of the General Agreement. It is further understood that Article XVI:4 requires that arm's-length pricing be observed, i.e., prices for goods in transactions between exporting enterprises and foreign buyers under their [sic] or the same control should for tax purposes be the prices which would be charged between independent enterprises acting at arm's length. Furthermore, Article XVI:4 does not prohibit the adoption of measures to avoid double taxation of foreign source income."

Following the adoption of these reports the Chairman noted that the Council's decision and understanding does not mean that the parties adhering to Article XVI:4 are forbidden from taxing the profits on transactions beyond their borders, it only means that they are not required to do so. He noted further that the decision does not modify the existing GATT rules in Article XVI:4 as they relate to the taxation of exported goods. He noted also that this decision does not affect and is not affected by the Agreement on the Interpretation and Application of Articles VI, XVI and XXIII. Finally, he noted that the adoption of these reports together with the understanding does not affect the rights and obligations of contracting parties under the General Agreement.

[1] BISD 23S/98 [Case 31].
[2] BISD 23S/114 [Case 32].
[3] BISD 23S/127 [Case 33].
[4] BISD 23S/137 [Case 34].

INCOME TAX PRACTICES MAINTAINED BY FRANCE

Report of the Panel presented to the Council of Representatives on November 12, 1976
BISD 23S/114, 115

FACTUAL ASPECTS OF THE PRACTICES IN QUESTION

7. The following is a brief factual description of the tax practices complained of by the United States as the Panel understood them.

8. The French income tax system for corporations is based on the territoriality principle which, in general, taxes income earned in France but not income arising outside France. It is a principle deriving from the history of the French system dating back to the beginning of the century. French companies are liable to corporation tax solely in respect of profits made by enterprises operating in France and of profits taxable by France under an international double taxation agreement.

9. Under the territoriality rule as applied by France, profits generated by undertakings operated abroad are exempt from French taxation. On the other hand, a French company is not entitled to any foreign tax credit and cannot deduct losses suffered abroad, apart from exceptions specified below.

10. If a subsidiary is a purely fictitious corporation located abroad and all its activities are directed from France, tax is levied in France on total profits for the reason that all corporations, regardless of nationality or location of the statutory head office, which have an effective management headquarters in France are taxable in France.

11. Ninety-five per cent of dividends from the French or foreign subsidiaries of a French company is excluded from the profits of the parent corporation. Participation by the parent in the subsidiary must exceed 10 per cent. This arrangement stems from the desire to avoid double taxation of the dividends of subsidiaries.

12. Dealings between French companies and their branches, subsidiaries or associated companies in foreign countries must in principle be conducted as if the companies were independent enterprises, each being regarded as a separate distinct economic entity ("arm's-length" rela-

tionship). French tax authorities are empowered to make the necessary inspections and rectifications. The actual application of the principle was interpreted in administrative notes in 1959, 1972 and 1973, according to which officials are requested to take into consideration foreign competitive conditions and commercial operations as a whole, not a single transaction alone. The problems of international tax fraud and evasion are also dealt with in other parts of French law, notably Article 1649 quinquies B and Article 155A of the CGI.

13. In certain cases provision can be made for losses abroad and certain expenditures relating thereto. Since January 1, 1973 this treatment applies only to new establishments, is limited on account of the permitted amount of the reduction, and is limited to five years in time.

14. French companies are allowed to set up certain reserves to cover risks in respect of medium-term credit for sales or projects carried out abroad.

15. Exports are excluded from the application of the inflation levy introduced in France on January 1, 1975. The levy has not been applied in practice. After having been abolished from September 1, 1975, it was re-established in principle for 1976 and is to be applied if increases in prices of manufactures exceed 2 per cent over a period of three months.

16. An exporter's card system was in force between 1957 and 1973. The card was issued after an enquiry as to the circumstances and respectability of the company; card-holders could make purchases free of value-added tax without needing to make the ordinary security deposits. Card-holders could originally apply a 15 per cent supplementary depreciation to certain assets. This rule has been abolished in respect of assets acquired since January 1, 1965.

* * *

CONCLUSIONS

47. The Panel started by examining the effects of the income tax practices before it in economic terms. The Panel noted that the particular application of the territoriality principle by France allowed some part of export activities, belonging to an economic process originating in the country, to be outside the scope of French taxes. In this way France had forgone revenue from this source and created a possibility of a pecuniary benefit to exports in those cases where income and corporation tax provisions were significantly more liberal in foreign countries.

48. The Panel found that however much the practices may have been an incidental consequence of French taxation principles rather than a specific policy intention, they nonetheless constituted a subsidy on exports because the above-mentioned benefits to exports did not apply to domestic activities for the internal market. The Panel also considered that the fact that the practices might also act as an incentive to investment abroad was not relevant in this context.

49. The Panel also noted that the tax treatment of dividends from abroad ensured that the benefits referred to above were fully preserved.

50. In circumstances where different tax treatment in different countries resulted in a small total tax bill in aggregate being paid on exports than on sales in the home market, the Panel concluded that there was a partial exemption from direct taxes. The Panel further concluded that the practices were covered by one or both items (*c*) and (*d*) of the illustrative list of 1960.[1]

51. The Panel noted that the contracting parties that had accepted the 1960 Declaration had agreed that the practices in the illustrative list were generally to be considered as subsidies in the sense of Article XVI:4. The Panel further noted that these contracting parties considered that, in general, the practices contained in the illustrative list could be presumed to result in bi-level pricing and that this presumption could therefore be applied to the French practices. The Panel concluded, however, from the words "generally to be considered" that these contracting parties did not consider that the presumption was absolute.

52. The Panel considered that, from an economic point of view, there was a presumption that an export subsidy would lead to any or a combination of the following consequences in the export sector: (*a*) lowering of prices, (*b*) increase of sales effort, and (*c*) increase of profits per unit. Because France was an important supplier in certain export sectors it was to be expected that all of these effects would occur and that, if one occurred, the other two would not necessarily be excluded. A concentration of the subsidy benefits on prices could lead to substantial reductions in prices. The Panel did not consider that a reduction in prices in export markets needed automatically to be accompanied by similar reductions in domestic markets. The Panel added that the extent to which tax havens existed was well known and that they considered this some evidence of the extent to which bi-level pricing had probably occurred.

[1] BISD 9S/186

53. The Panel therefore concluded that the French tax practices in some cases had effects which were not in accordance with French obligations under Article XVI:4.

54. The Panel noted that the allocation of profits between companies and their foreign operations was made in accordance with the arm's-length pricing principle but that there were formal exceptions to this principle and concluded that the benefit would be increased to the extent that arm's-length pricing was not fully observed.

55. The Panel considered that deductions against domestic profits of certain costs and losses relating to certain specific foreign operations outside the scope of domestic taxation constituted an additional exemption which reinforced their conclusions. The Panel did not consider that the other specific practices, which had been raised relating to medium-term credit, the inflation levy and exporter's cards, altered the general picture outlined above.

56. The Panel considered that the fact that these arrangements might have existed before the General Agreement was not a justification for them and noted that France had made no reservation with respect to the standstill agreement or to the 1960 Declaration.[1]

57. The Panel was of the view that, given the size and breadth of the export subsidy, it was likely that it had led to an increase in French exports in some sectors and, although the possibility could not be ruled out that the tax arrangements would encourage production abroad and a decrease in exports in other sectors, nonetheless concluded that it was also covered by the notification obligation of Article XVI:1.

58. In the light of the above, and bearing in mind the precedent set by the Uruguayan case, the Panel found that there was a *prima facie* case of nullification or impairment of benefits which other contracting parties were entitled to expect under the General Agreement.

[The text of the understanding pursuant to which this report and the three other reports on tax legislation were adopted (Cases 31–34) is set out at the end of Case 31.]

[1] BISD 9S/32

INCOME TAX PRACTICES MAINTAINED BY BELGIUM

Report of the Panel presented to the Council of Representatives on November 12, 1976
BISD 23S/127, 128

FACTUAL ASPECTS OF THE PRACTICES IN QUESTION

7. The following is a brief factual description of the tax practices complained of by the United States as the Panel understood them.

8. The Belgian income tax system is based on the principle of world-wide taxation of residents and on the source principle as far as taxation of non-residents is concerned.

9. Therefore, non-residents are only taxed in Belgium on income obtained or collected by them there. Profits of foreign subsidiaries of Belgium-based corporations are not taxed by the Belgian authorities, but are subject to the tax jurisdiction of the foreign country in question.

10. In order to avoid double taxation of sales effected abroad by foreign sales establishments Belgium introduced the principle of tax relief in 1906; the measure was subsequently carried into law in 1919, when income tax was established in Belgium.

11. Income obtained from foreign establishments by resident corporations and which has been taxed abroad is assessed after deduction of foreign tax. Belgian tax is then applied to it at one quarter of the normal rate. Evidence that the profits are both obtained and taxed abroad must be produced. In practice, evidence of foreign taxation is not required in respect of profits obtained through an establishment located abroad, if it draws up separate accounts. The fact that certain constituent elements of income may not be taxable or may be tax free in the foreign country is not generally sufficient justification for refusing to grant the benefit of Belgian tax reliefs.

12. As far as sales through foreign sales subsidiaries (permanent equity holdings) are concerned, Belgium taxes foreign profits therefrom only to the degree that they are actually distributed to the parent corporation. However, in order to remedy the effects of cascading taxation of dividends, dividends derived from subsidiaries which would

normally have been taxed are deducted from the tax base of the recipient to the extent of 95 per cent (or 90 per cent for certain holding companies) of the net amount received, grossed up by a deemed movable prepayment of 5 per cent; this system is applicable regardless of the size of the Belgian corporation's equity holding generating dividends.

13. A provision in Belgium's Income Tax Code (Article 24), which is of general scope, lays down that transactions between Belgian enterprises directly or indirectly related to an enterprise abroad shall be governed by the arm's-length principle. The administration is given much latitude in its application of this provision.

* * *

CONCLUSIONS

34. The Panel started by examining the effects of the income tax practices before it in economic terms. The Panel noted that the particular application of the territoriality principle by Belgium allowed some part of export activities, belonging to an economic process originating in the country, to be outside the scope of Belgian taxes. In this way Belgium had forgone revenue from this source and created a possibility of a pecuniary benefit to exports in those cases where income and corporation tax provisions were significantly more liberal in foreign countries.

35. The Panel found that however much the practices may have been an incidental consequence of Belgian taxation principles rather than a specific policy intention, they nonetheless constituted a subsidy on exports because the above-mentioned benefits to exports did not apply to domestic activities for the internal market. The Panel also considered that the fact that the practices might also act as an incentive to investment abroad was not relevant in this context.

36. The Panel also noted that the tax treatment of dividends from abroad ensured that the benefits referred to above were fully preserved.

37. In circumstances where different tax treatment in different countries resulted in a smaller total tax bill in aggregate being paid on exports than on sales in the home market, the Panel concluded that there was a partial exemption from direct taxes. The Panel further concluded that

the practices were covered by one or both items (*c*) and (*d*) of the illustrative list of 1960.[1]

38. The Panel noted that the contracting parties that had accepted the 1960 Declaration had agreed that the practices in the illustrative list were generally to be considered as subsidies in the sense of Article XVI:4. The Panel further noted that these contracting parties considered that, in general, the practices contained in the illustrative list could be presumed to result in bi-level pricing and that this presumption could therefore be applied to the Belgian practices. The Panel concluded, however, from the words "generally to be considered" that these contracting parties did not consider that the presumption was absolute.

39. The Panel considered that, from an economic point of view, there was a presumption that an export subsidy would lead to any or a combination of the following consequences in the export sector: (*a*) lowering of prices, (*b*) increase of sales effort, and (*c*) increase of profits per unit. Because Belgium was an important supplier in certain export sectors it was to be expected that all of these effects would occur and that, if one occurred, the other two would not necessarily be excluded. A concentration of the subsidy benefits on prices could lead to substantial reductions in prices. The Panel did not consider that a reduction in prices in export markets needed automatically to be accompanied by similar reductions in domestic markets. The Panel added that the extent to which tax havens existed was well known and that they considered this some evidence of the extent to which bi-level pricing had probably occurred.

40. The Panel therefore concluded that the Belgian tax practices in some cases had effects which were not in accordance with Belgian obligations under Article XVI:4.

41. The Panel considered that deviations from the principle of arm's-length pricing might arise from the recognized flexibility in the administration of the rules in this area and that the benefit would be increased to the extent that arm's-length pricing was not fully observed.

42. The Panel considered that the possibility of allocating profits of foreign operations outside the scope of domestic taxation might be affected by the fact that branches and subsidiaries were not subject to the test that a material installation and an autonomous management existed.

[1] BISD 9S/186

43. The Panel considered that the fact that these arrangements might have existed before the General Agreement was not a justification for them and noted that Belgium had made no reservation with respect to the standstill agreement or to the 1960 Declaration.[1]

44. The Panel was of the view that, given the size and breadth of the export subsidy, it was likely that it had led to an increase in Belgian exports in some sectors and, although the possibility could not be ruled out that the tax arrangements would encourage production abroad and a decrease in exports in other sectors, nonetheless concluded that it was also covered by the notification obligation of Article XVI:1.

45. In the light of the above, and bearing in mind the precedent set by the Uruguayan case, the Panel found that there was a *prima facie* case of nullification or impairment of benefits which other contracting parties were entitled to expect under the General Agreement.

[The text of the understanding pursuant to which this report and the three other reports on tax legislation were adopted (Cases 31–34) is set out at the end of Case 31.]

[1] BISD 9S/32

INCOME TAX PRACTICES MAINTAINED BY THE NETHERLANDS

Report of the Panel presented to the Council of Representatives on November 12, 1976
BISD 23S/137, 138

FACTUAL ASPECTS OF THE PRACTICES IN QUESTION

7. The following is a brief factual description of the tax practices complained of by the United States as the Panel understood them.

8. The Netherlands system of levying income tax and corporation tax is that profits made by an individual or an enterprise should be taxed in the country where the profits were made. In principle, however, income tax on resident corporations and individuals is levied on the worldwide income. If a treaty provides for different tax treatment the treaty rules will prevail over Dutch national law, and if no treaty exists, unilateral relief will be granted through a proportional reduction in Dutch taxation for foreign-source profits if an income tax is in principle due in the foreign country. The portion of profits or income which is not taxable in the Netherlands is therefore important when determining the tax rate to be applied to the portion that is taxable in the Netherlands. This means in practice that for individuals who are subject to a progressive rate of income tax, the Dutch tax is affected by the amount not taxable in the Netherlands. For resident corporations this system has effects which are similar to those of the territoriality principle. One difference between the Dutch system and the territoriality system in its pure form is that foreign losses of a permanent establishment (the concept includes the location of the principal office of management) or dependent permanent representative are deductible when computing liability to Dutch tax, provided that tax is in principle due in the foreign country.

9. This method amounts to a credit, not for foreign, but for Dutch tax on foreign income, and is the principal method for avoiding double taxation (Royal Decree providing Unilateral Regulations for the Avoidance of Double Taxation of 1965).

10. In the Netherlands the taxation of dividends is governed by the territoriality principle applied to the residence of the person entitled to dividends. As a general rule, therefore, no relief from Dutch tax is

granted to dividends. However, the Decree provides a relief for all income earned by a permanent establishment, which in practice means that dividends can qualify for relief if they are channelled through a permanent establishment and are subject to tax in the other country. Under Dutch double taxation agreements these rules apply even if the other country does not make use of its taxation rights. A 1970 amendment to the Decree also introduced a special foreign tax credit for interest and royalties paid to Dutch residents from developing countries.

11. An "affiliation privilege", laid down in the Corporation Tax Act of 1969, constitutes an exemption for inter-company dividends and other profits connected with a substantial participation in ownership (normally 5 per cent) and was enacted to prevent double taxation of profits when a company receives dividends or other gains from a qualified company. This privilege is also applicable if a resident company participates in a foreign company which is formally subject to some kind of income tax under the laws of a foreign State. The rate of the foreign tax is immaterial, but liability to foreign local or regional taxes is not sufficient. In the case of participation in a foreign company, the tax inspector may refuse to grant the exemption on the grounds that it is a portfolio investment.

12. Under Dutch legislation the profits of an enterprise must be calculated in accordance with "sound business practice". There are no administrative guidelines for the application of the arm's-length principle.

* * *

CONCLUSIONS

34. The Panel started by examining the effects of the income tax practices before it in economic terms. The Panel noted that the particular application of the worldwide principle by the Netherlands, in conjunction with the qualified exemption in respect of foreign income, allowed some part of export activities, belonging to an economic process originating in the country, to be outside the scope of the Netherlands' taxes. In this way the Netherlands has forgone revenue from this source and created a possibility of a pecuniary benefit to exports in those cases where income and corporation tax provisions were significantly more liberal in foreign countries.

35. The Panel found that however much the practices may have been an incidental consequence of the Netherlands' taxation principles rather than a specific policy intention, they nonetheless constituted a subsidy on exports because the above-mentioned benefits to exports did not apply to domestic activities for the internal market. The Panel also considered that the fact that the practices might also act as an incentive to investment abroad was not relevant in this context.

36. The Panel also noted that the tax treatment of dividends from abroad ensured that the benefits referred to above were fully preserved.

37. In circumstances where different tax treatment in different countries resulted in a smaller total tax bill in aggregate being paid on exports than on sale in the home market, the Panel concluded that there was a partial exemption from direct taxes. This resulted from the fact that, even though it followed the worldwide taxation principle, the Netherlands did not levy a tax on profits from export sales by foreign branches or subsidiaries when these were subject to tax abroad irrespective of whether these tax rights were exercised. The Panel further concluded that the practices were covered by one or both items (*c*) and (*d*) of the illustrative list of 1960.[1]

38. The Panel noted that the contracting parties that had accepted the 1960 Declaration had agreed that the practices in the illustrative list were generally to be considered as subsidies in the sense of Article XVI:4. The Panel further noted that these contracting parties considered that, in general, the practices contained in the illustrative list could be presumed to result in bi-level pricing and that this presumption could therefore be applied to the Netherlands' practices. The Panel concluded, however, from the words "generally to be considered" that these contracting parties did not consider that the presumption was absolute.

39. The Panel considered that, from an economic point of view, there was a presumption that an export subsidy would lead to any or a combination of the following consequences in the export sector: (*a*) lowering of prices, (*b*) increase of sales effort, and (*c*) increase of profits per unit. Because the Netherlands was an important supplier in certain export sectors it was to be expected that all of these effects would occur and that, if one occurred, the other two would not necessarily be excluded. A concentration of the subsidy benefits on prices could lead to substantial reductions in prices. The Panel did not consider that a

[1] BISD 9S/186

reduction in prices in export markets needed automatically to be accompanied by similar reductions in domestic markets. The Panel added that the extent to which tax havens existed was well known and that they considered this some evidence of the extent to which bi-level pricing had probably occurred.

40. The Panel therefore concluded that the Netherlands' tax practices in some cases had effects which were not in accordance with Dutch obligations under Article XVI:4.

41. The Panel noted that the allocation of profits between companies and their foreign operations was made in accordance with the rule of sound business practice. This might not always coincide with arm's-length pricing. The Panel concluded that the benefit would be increased to the extent that arm's-length pricing was not fully observed.

42. The Panel noted the argument of the Netherlands that its tax practices were in part designed to ensure that they did not nullify tax incentive policies of developing countries. The Panel fully recognized this problem in relation to developing countries. The argument advanced did not, however, lead it to modify its conclusions in that the practices of the Netherlands did not differentiate between developed and developing countries.

43. The Panel considered that the fact that these tax arrangements might have existed before the General Agreement was not a justification for them and noted that the Netherlands had made no reservation with respect to the standstill agreement or to the 1960 Declaration.[1]

44. The Panel was of the view that, given the size and breadth of the export subsidy, it was likely that it had led to an increase in the Netherlands' exports in some sectors and, although the possibility could not be ruled out that the tax arrangements would encourage production abroad and a decrease in exports in other sectors, nonetheless concluded that it was also covered by the notification obligation of Article XVI:1.

45. In the light of the above, and bearing in mind the precedent set by the Uruguayan case, the Panel found that there was a *prima facie* case of nullification or impairment of benefits which other contracting parties were entitled to expect under the General Agreement.

[1] BISD 9S/32

[The text of the understanding pursuant to which this report and three other reports on tax legislation were adopted (Cases 31–34) is set out at the end of Case 31.]

EEC—MEASURES ON ANIMAL FEED PROTEINS

Report of the Panel adopted on March 14, 1978
BISD 25S/49, 50

II. FACTUAL ASPECTS

2.1 The following is a brief description of factual aspects of the EEC measures as the Panel understood them.

2.2 On March 15, 1976, the Council of the European Communities adopted Council Regulation (EEC) No. 563/76 on the compulsory purchase of skimmed milk powder held by intervention agencies for use in feedingstuffs.

* * *

2.3 The objective of the EEC measures was to allow for increased utilization of denatured skimmed milk powder as a protein source for use in feedingstuffs for animals other than calves, with a view to reducing by 400,000 tons the surplus stocks of skimmed milk powder held by governmental intervention agencies.

2.4 The EEC measures came into force on March 19, 1976 for imported products and on April 1, 1976 for domestically produced products. Their application was expressly intended to be of such a limited duration necessary to achieve the stated objective. They were terminated on October 25, 1976.

2.5 Under these measures, EEC domestic producers or importers of oilseeds, cakes and meals, dehydrated fodder and compound feeds and importers of corn gluten feeds had an obligation to purchase a certain quantity of skimmed milk powder held by intervention agencies and to have it denatured for use as feed for animals other than calves.

* * *

2.7 Compliance with the purchase obligation was enforced: (*a*) by making the granting of aid to domestic producers of oilseeds and dehydrated fodder, as provided for under the EEC common agricultural policy, conditional upon the presentation of a document providing proof of the purchase and the denaturing of the skimmed milk powder; (*b*) by making the free circulation in the EEC of imported oilseeds, cakes and meals, dehydrated fodder, corn gluten and compound feeds subject to the presentation of a protein certificate issued by member States upon the provision of a document of proof of the purchase and the denaturing of the skimmed milk powder.

2.8 In the case of both domestic and imported products subject to the measures, the EEC regulations allowed for the replacing of the document providing proof of the purchase and the denaturing of the skimmed milk powder by the deposit of a security or a bank guarantee, which was released upon production of the above-mentioned document and with regard to products not used in feedingstuffs. This security was refunded interest-free upon presentation of that document but forfeited if the obligation of purchase and denaturing of the skimmed milk powder was not carried out.

* * *

IV. CONCLUSIONS

4.1 The Panel began by examining whether all products used for the same purpose of adding protein to animal feeds should be considered as "like products" within the meaning of Articles I and III. Having noted that the General Agreement gave no definition of the concept of "like product" the Panel reviewed how it had been applied by the CONTRACTING PARTIES in previous cases.[2]

4.2 The Panel noted, in this case, such factors as the number of products and tariff items carrying different duty rates and tariff bindings, the varying protein contents and the different vegetable, animal and synthetic origins of the protein products before the Panel—not all of which were subject to the EEC measures. Therefore, the Panel concluded that these various protein products could not be considered as "like products" within the meaning of Articles I and III.

4.3 The Panel noted that the General Agreement made a distinction between "like products" and "directly competitive and substitutable" products. The Panel therefore also examined whether these products should be considered as directly competitive and substitutable within the meaning of Article III. In this regard the Panel noted that both the United States and the EEC considered most of these products to be substitutable under certain conditions. The Panel also noted that the

[2] For instance BISD II/188 [Case 5], BISD 1S/53 [Case 7], BISD II/181, 183 [Case 2].

objective of the EEC Regulation during the period of its application, in its own terms, was to allow for increased utilization of denatured skimmed milk powder as a protein source for use in feedingstuffs for animals other than calves. Furthermore the Panel noted that the security deposit had been fixed at such a level as to make it economically advantageous to buy denatured skimmed milk powder rather than to provide the security, thus making denatured skimmed milk powder competitive with these products. The Panel concluded that vegetable proteins and skimmed milk powder were technically substitutable in terms of their final use and that the effects of the EEC measures were to make skimmed milk powder competitive with these vegetable proteins.

4.4 The Panel examined the effects of the possibility for the buyers of vegetable proteins of providing a security as an alternative to the requirements of purchasing a certain quantity of skimmed milk powder. The Panel was of the opinion that the security deposit was not a fiscal nature because, if it had been, it would have defeated the stated purpose of the EEC Regulation which was to increase utilization of denatured skimmed milk powder. In addition the revenue from the security deposit accrued to EEC budgetary authorities only when the buyer of vegetable proteins had not fulfilled the purchase obligations. The Panel further noted that less than 1 per cent of the security deposits paid, were not released, indicating compliance with the purchase obligation. The Panel therefore considered that the security deposit, including any associated cost, was only an enforcement mechanism for the purchase requirement and, as such, should be examined with the purchase obligation.

4.5 The Panel examined the obligation under the EEC Regulation, to purchase a certain quantity of denatured skimmed milk powder from intervention agencies, in terms of the provisions of Article III:5, that is whether the EEC measures constituted an "internal quantitative regulation relating to the mixture, processing or use" within the meaning of Article III:5.

4.6 The Panel noted that the Council Regulation (EEC) No. 563/76 referred, in its stated considerations, to the considerable stocks of skimmed milk powder held by intervention agencies and to the objective of increasing the utilization of skimmed milk powder as a protein in feedingstuffs for animals other than calves. In other words, the Regulation was intended to dispose on the internal market ("utilization") of a given quantity ("stocks") of skimmed milk powder in a particular form ("denatured" i.e. utilizable only for the intended purposes). The Panel therefore considered that the EEC Regulation was an "internal quantitative regulation" in the sense of Article III:5. However, the Panel found that this "internal quantitative regulation" as such was not related to "the mixture, processing or use . . . in specified amounts or proportions within the meaning of Article III:5 because, at the level of its application, the EEC Regulation introduced basically an obligation to purchase a certain quantity of skimmed milk powder and the purchase obligation falls under Article III:1.

4.7 Given the reference in Article III:5, second sentence, to Article III:1, the Panel then examined the consistency of the EEC Regulation as an "internal quantitative regulation" with the provisions of Article III:1, particularly as to whether the Regulation afforded protection to domestic production. The Panel noted that the EEC Regulation considered, in its own terms, that denatured skimmed milk powder was an important source of protein which could be used in feedingstuffs. The Panel also noted that surplus stocks could originate either from domestic production or imports, but that the intervention agencies from which the buyers of vegetable proteins had to purchase a certain quantity of denatured skimmed milk powder only held domestically produced products. The Panel further noted that, although globally about 15 per cent of the EEC apparent consumption of vegetable protein was supplied from domestic sources, not all the individual products subject to the EEC measures were produced domestically in substantial quantities.

4.8 The Panel concluded that the measures provided for by the Regulation with a view to ensuring the sale of a given quantity of skimmed milk powder protected this product in a manner contrary to the principles of Article III:1 and to the provisions of Article III:5, second sentence.

4.9 The Panel was of the opinion that the requirement to denature the skimmed milk powder purchased from the intervention agencies was only an element designed to secure the final utilization of that product. In addition, the Panel did not consider it necessary to examine the legal implications arising from any temporary administrative difficulties initially associated with the introduction of the EEC measures.

4.10 The Panel also examined whether the EEC measures accorded imported protein products less favorable treatment than that accorded to like products of EEC origin within the meaning of Article III:4. In this regard the Panel noted the economic considerations, including the level of domestic production and of the applicable security deposit, put forward by the EEC to justify the application of the measures to corn gluten of foreign origin only. The Panel was not convinced that these considerations justified the non-application of these measures to domestic corn gluten and therefore concluded that the measures accorded imported corn gluten less favorable treatment than that accorded corn gluten of national origin in violation of Article III:4.

4.11 The Panel also examined whether the fact that the EEC measures were not applicable to animal, fish and synthetic proteins was consistent with the provisions of Article III:4. Having regard to its own conclusion with respect to "like products", the Panel was satisfied that animal, fish and synthetic proteins could not be considered as "like products" for the purpose of Article III:4. Since the obligations under Article III:4 relate to "like products", the Panel concluded that the non-application of the EEC measures to these products was not inconsistent with the EEC obligations under the Article.

4.12 The Panel examined whether the protein certificate requirement and other specific administrative requirements accorded to imported products treatment less favorable than that accorded to "like products" of EEC origin in respect of the purchase, sale and distribution of the products in the EEC within the meaning of Article III:4. The Panel was of the opinion that these requirements should be considered as enforcement mechanisms to ensure that the obligation, of either purchasing a certain quantity of denatured skimmed milk powder or of providing a security, had been complied with. The Panel noted that the protein certificate applied only to imports but that there was an equivalent document required for products of national origin except for a relatively short period at the beginning of the application of the EEC measures. The Panel concluded that the various administrative requirements, including the protein certificate, were not inconsistent with the EEC obligations under Article III:4.

4.13 The Panel also examined whether the EEC measures were consistent with the EEC obligations under Article II.

4.14 The Panel first noted the United States view that the EEC purchase obligation, the security deposit and the protein certificate; (*a*) constituted "charges of any kind" in excess of the bound duty rates within the meaning of Article II:1(*b*); and (*b*) were conditions which did not bear any relationship to the administration of the tariff bindings; and (*c*) could not have been reasonably foreseen at the time the duty rates were negotiated. The Panel also noted the view of the European Communities that, to the extent that the security deposit constituted a charge in excess of the bound duty rates, such a charge was covered by Article II:2(*a*) and that the protein certificate was not a condition imposed on the tariff bindings.

4.15 The Panel then considered the question of whether the EEC measures should be examined both as internal measures under Article III and border measures under Article II. In this regard, the Panel reviewed the drafting history of Articles II and III and their subsequent application by contracting parties, particularly with a view to ascertaining the relationship between these two Articles.

4.16 In the light of that review, the Panel noted the following:

(a) The note Ad Article III states that: "Any internal tax or other internal charge, or any law, regulation or requirement of the kind referred to in paragraph 1 which applies to an imported product and to the like domestic product and is collected or enforced in the case of the imported product at the time of importation, is nevertheless to be regarded as an internal tax or other internal charge, or a law, regulation or requirement of the kind referred to in paragraph 1, and is accordingly subject to the provisions of Article III."

(b) The Sub-Committee at the Havana Conference considered[1] that "certain charges . . . were import duties and not internal taxes because . . . (a) they are collected at the time of, and as a condition to, the entry of the goods into the importing country, and (b) they apply exclusively to imported products without being related in any way to similar charges collected internally on like domestic products".

(c) The wording of Article II:2(*a*) which refers to "charges equivalent to internal taxes" is different from that of Article III:2 which refers to "internal taxes and other charges of any kind", but it appeared to be the common understanding of the drafters of these articles that their scope should be the same as to the kind of measures being covered;

(d) The Panel established to consider charges imposed by Belgium on certain imported products[2] found as follows: "after examining the legal provisions regarding the methods of collection of that charge, the panel came to the conclusion that the . . . levy was collected only on products purchased by public bodies for their own use and not on imports as such, and that the levy was charged, not at the time of importation, but when the purchase

[1] Havana Reports, pp. 62–63, paragraphs 42–43, E/CONF.2/C.3/A/W.30, p. 2
[2] 1S/60, paragraph 2 [Case 10]

price was paid by the public body. In those circumstances, it would appear that the levy was to be treated as an "internal charge" within the meaning of paragraph 2 of Article III of the General Agreement", and not as an import charge within the meaning of paragraph 2 of Article II.

4.17 The Panel also recalled its own findings that (*a*) the EEC measures applied to both imported and domestically produced vegetable proteins (except in the case of corn gluten); (*b*) the EEC measures basically instituted an obligation to purchase a certain quantity of skimmed milk powder and, as an "internal quantitative regulation" fell under Article III:1; (*c*) the EEC security deposit and protein certificate were enforcement mechanisms for the purchase obligation.

4.18 Having regard to the legal considerations referred to above and taking account of its own findings in relation to Article III:5 and Article III:1 that the EEC measures were an "internal quantitative regulation", the Panel concluded that the EEC measures should be examined as internal measures under Article III and not as border measures under Article II.

4.19 The Panel examined whether the EEC measures discriminated against the exports of the United States within the meaning of Article I:1.

4.20 The Panel noted that the general most-favored-nation treatment provided for in Article I:1 applied to "like products" regardless of territorial origin but did not mention "directly competitive or substitutable products". In this regard the Panel did not consider animal, marine and synthetic proteins to be products like those vegetable proteins covered by the measures. The Panel also noted that a significant proportion of EEC imports of "like products", including soybeans, subject to the measures originated from contracting parties other than the United States.

4.21 Having heard no evidence that either the purchasing obligation, the security deposit or the protein certificate discriminated against imports of "like products" from any contracting party, the Panel concluded that the EEC measures were not inconsistent with the EEC obligations under Article I:1.

CANADA—WITHDRAWAL OF TARIFF CONCESSIONS

Report of the Panel on Lead and Zinc adopted on May 17, 1978
BISD 25S/42, 43

II. FACTUAL ASPECTS

6. The European Economic Community had in December 1972 invoked Article XXVIII:5 in order to reserve the right to modify its schedule of concessions during the forthcoming three-year period of validity of the concessions. In December 1974 the Community notified in GATT that it wished to enter into negotiations with interested parties in order to modify the specific duties on unwrought lead and unwrought zinc (ex 78.01 and ex 79.01), both of which had been bound in the Dillon Round at a rate of 1.32 units of account per 100 kgs. The object of the negotiations was to convert the specific duties of the items concerned to *ad valorem* rates of duty. Negotiations took subsequently place with Australia and Canada which had notified their interest in the matter. In addition, consultations were held with Norway and South Africa. Informal contacts, with a first exchange of statistics and discussion of data, took place between the negotiating partners during February 1975. Substantive negotiations were conducted in the following months and lasted until November 1975, with the first formal offer by the Community to Canada put forward at the end of June 1975. In December 1975 the Community submitted to the CONTRACTING PARTIES a final report on the negotiations which had resulted in agreement with Australia while no settlement had been arrived at with Canada. New rates of duty of 3.5 per cent *ad valorem* on both lead and zinc, as agreed with Australia, were introduced by the Community on January 1, 1976.

7. Canada notified to the CONTRACTING PARTIES in May 1976 that it considered the final offer of the Community, which had subsequently been implemented, to be unsatisfactory especially on zinc. It also notified, as provided for in paragraph 3 of Article XXVIII, the withdrawal of the bindings in the Canadian schedule of concessions on the following tariff items: canned meats, liqueurs, vermouth, aperitifs and cordial wines, and wire of iron and steel. No changes have until now been made in the actual rates of duty of these items. The trade coverage of the Canadian withdrawals was equivalent to the annual average figure for

Canada's total exports to the Community of zinc in the period 1973–75. The final Community *ad valorem* rate on lead was not contested by Canada.

* * *

IV. CONCLUSIONS

14. The Panel based its consideration of the case on Article XXVIII of the GATT which, as both parties agreed, was the applicable provision, *inter alia*, for negotiations which are undertaken with the aim of converting specific rates of duty into *ad valorem* rates. In this connexion, the Panel considered of special importance paragraph 2 of Article XXVIII which provides that the contracting parties concerned "shall endeavour to maintain a general level of reciprocal and mutually advantageous concessions not less favorable to trade than that provided for in this Agreement prior to such negotiations".

15. The Panel noted that as a general principle, Article XXVIII negotiations had in the past been based on the most recent three-year period for which trade statistics were available, for the purpose of determining principal or substantial supplier rights. It was also the understanding of the Panel that in past negotiations a three-year period had been used as an element in the determination of the value of tariff concessions. The Panel noted on the other hand that no clear precedent could be found as regards the selection of a base period for the purpose of converting specific into *ad valorem* rates of duty. In the absence of agreement between the parties on an appropriate base period, the Panel held that the general principle of using the most recent three-year period should be applied to this case as well in order to allow account to be taken of cyclical movements and random events.

16. The Panel took note of the fact that the Community had notified other contracting parties in a GATT document circulated on December 23, 1974 of its wish to enter into negotiations in order to modify certain concessions on lead and zinc. It further noted that while informal contacts had taken place between the Community and Canada in February 1975, concrete and substantial negotiations were initiated only thereafter and lasted until November 1975, with the first formal offer by the Community to Canada put forward at the end of June 1975. The Panel therefore concurs with the view expressed by both parties that 1974 was a period prior to the beginning of the negotiations.

17. The Panel does not consider that full statistics for the applicable base period must be available at the very beginning of the negotiations, provided these data become available later in the negotiations and the latter are not unduly delayed. By June 1975, Community statistics (on which Canada had agreed to conduct the negotiations) for the first ten or eleven months of 1974 became available (except for Ireland) for both lead and zinc. The offer of the Community in the negotiations on both lead and zinc, submitted to Canada in late June 1975, should therefore, in the Panel's view, have taken account of trade figures for 1974. The Panel came to the conclusion that a correct and reasonable interpretation of the GATT, in the particular circumstances applying in this case, would be to base the *ad valorem* equivalents on global trade statistics for the years 1972–74. The Panel, in basing its decision on figures relating to global Community imports of zinc rather than relating to imports from Canada only, took account of the provision of Article XXVIII:2 which refers to the maintenance of a "general level" of concessions, not less favorable to "trade", formulations which in the view of the Panel clearly indicate the requirement, in the absence of specific agreement between the parties, to base the *ad valorem* equivalent of a specific duty on total import figures. To take another view would, in the case of two or more principal or substantial suppliers with different price levels, result in different *ad valorem* rates which is inconceivable under the General Agreement. The 1972–74 figures submitted to the Panel by the Community indicate an *ad valorem* equivalent of 2.64 per cent for total Community imports of zinc. Consequently, the Panel considers that, as it was not the intention of the Community to modify the scope of the concession, the *ad valorem* duty rate of the Community for zinc should have been rebound, after conversion, at that level or at the closest round half-percentage point figure, rather than at 3.5 per cent.

18. In the Panel's view, this result would also be appropriate when considering lead and zinc together. Again, basing itself on statistics submitted by the Community, the Panel noted that the trade-weighted *ad valorem* equivalent for both products together for the years 1972–74 amount to 2.97 per cent, a figure indicating that a rebinding for lead of 3.5 per cent (as implemented by the Community) and for zinc at the lower level, as indicated in the previous paragraph, would have been in conformity with the requirement of Article XXVIII:2 of the GATT.

19. In light of the conclusions reached above, Canada was entitled, in the Panel's opinion, to proceed to a withdrawal of concessions. The Panel, however, was of the view that the withdrawal of concessions should have been less than the equivalent of the total export volume of

zinc to the Community as account should have been taken of the rebinding of the Community duty. Also, the right of retaliation should be related to the actual damage suffered by Canada and consequently the withdrawals should have been based on the difference between the *ad valorem* equivalent of the specific rate calculated on imports from Canada only and the new *ad valorem* rate. Finally, account should have been taken of the fact that the *ad valorem* duty on lead had been fixed at a level lower than the incidence in respect of Community imports from Canada. In view of the complexity of assessing the value of a tariff binding, irrespective of the rate of duty involved, the Panel abstained from making any quantitative assessment in this respect. In the interest of maintaining the highest possible general level of concessions the Panel finds that the Canadian retaliatory action should be withdrawn; i.e. that the previous Canadian tariff bindings should be re-established as soon as the Community proceeds either to decrease their tariff on zinc or to make tariff concessions on other products of export interest to Canada of an equivalent value.

OMITTED

EEC—PROGRAM OF MINIMUM IMPORT PRICES, LICENSES AND SURETY DEPOSITS FOR CERTAIN PROCESSED FRUITS AND VEGETABLES

Report of the Panel adopted on October 18, 1978
BISD 25S/68, 69

II. FACTUAL ASPECTS

2.1. The following is a brief description of the factual aspects of the Community measures as the Panel understood them.

2.2. On July 22, 1975, the Council of the European Communities adopted Regulation (EEC) No. 1927/75 which stated in Article 2 that a minimum import price for tomato concentrates falling within subheading 20.02 C of the Common Customs Tariff would be fixed each year before April 1 for the subsequent marketing year. This Article further stated the factors that were to be taken into account when the minimum price was established.

* * *

2.5. Article 4 of Council Regulation (EEC) 1927/75 stated that any imports into the Community of the products listed in the Annex [Tomato concentrates, peeled tomatoes, peaches in syrup, tomato juice, mushrooms, pears, prunes, peas, beans in pod, and raspberries] would be subject to the production of an import certificate, which would be issued by Member States to any interested party who applied for such a certificate, irrespective of his place of establishment within the Community, and that the certificate would be valid for an import transaction carried out within the Community.

2.6. The second paragraph of this Article stated that the issue of an import certificate would be conditional upon the following:

— with respect to all products, the lodging of a security to guarantee the undertaking to effect certain imports for as long as the certificate was valid, which security, except in cases of *force majeure*, would be forfeit in whole or in part if the imports were not effected or were effected only in part within the period;

— for tomato concentrates, the lodging of an additional security to guarantee that the free-at-frontier price of the products to be imported under cover of the certificate plus the customs duty payable thereon would together be equal to or more than the minimum price or the special minimum price, whichever was appropriate. The security would be forfeit in proportion to any quantities imported at a price lower than the minimum price or than the special minimum price; however, the lodging of such additional security would not be required for products originating in third countries which undertook, and were in a position, to guarantee that the price on import into the Community would not be less than the minimum price for the product in question, and that all deflection of trade would be avoided.

* * *

IV. ANALYSIS AND CONCLUSIONS

(a) Import Certificate and Associated Security System

Article XI:1

4.1. The Panel began by examining the import certificate and associated security system in relation to the Community's obligations under Article XI:1. In this regard, the Panel noted that Article 10 of Council Regulation (EEC) No. 516/77 stated that: "The issue of an import certificate shall be conditional upon the following:—with respect to all products, the lodging of a security to guarantee the undertaking to effect certain imports for as long as the certificate is valid . . ." The Panel further noted that, without prejudice to the application of safeguard measures, import certificates were to be issued on the fifth working day following that on which the application was lodged and that import certificates were to be valid for seventy-five days. The Panel considered that, pending results concerning automatic licensing in the Multilateral Trade Negotiations, this system did not depart from systems which other contracting parties claimed were justified as automatic licensing. The Panel also considered that automatic licensing did not constitute a restriction of the type meant to fall under the purview of Article XI:1. Therefore the Panel concluded that the import certificate and associated security system operated by the Community was not inconsistent with the Community's obligations under Article XI:1.

Article VIII

4.2. The Panel next examined the status of the interest charges and cost in connexion with the lodging of the security associated with the import certificate in relation to the Community's obligations under Article VIII:1(*a*). The Panel noted the complaint by the United States representative that the interest charges and costs associated with the lodging of the security were imposed as protection for domestic products contrary to the provisions of Article VIII:1(*a*). The Panel further noted that Article VIII:1(*a*) stated that: "All fees and charges of whatever character . . . shall be limited in amount to the approximate cost of services rendered and shall not represent an indirect protection to domestic products or a taxation of imports or exports for fiscal purposes." The Panel also noted the contention by the Community representative that the incidence of these charges did not exceed 0.005 per cent. The Panel considered that these interest charges and costs were limited in amount to the approximate costs of administration. The Panel further considered that the term "cost of services rendered" in Article VIII:1(*a*) would include these costs of administration. Therefore, the Panel concluded that the interest charges and costs associated with the lodging of the security were not inconsistent with the Community's obligations under Article VIII:1(*a*).

4.3. The Panel next examined the provisions for the forfeiture of the security associated with the import certificate in relation to the obligations of the Community under Article VIII. The Panel noted the argument by the United States representative that, when a security was forfeited because importation did not take place within the seventy-five day validity of the certificate, this forfeiture should be considered as a charge in connexion with importation" in violation of Article VIII:1(*a*), since the importation would likely take place later under a new licence. The Panel further noted the argument by the United States representative that the forfeiture of all or part of this security imposed "substantial penalties for minor breaches of customs regulations or procedural requirements" in violation of Article VIII:3. The Panel considered that such a forfeiture could not logically be accepted as a charge "in connexion with importation" within the meaning of Article VIII:1(*a*), since no importation had occurred, but only as a penalty to the importer for not fulfilling his obligation to complete the importation within the seventy-five day time-limit. The Panel further considered that such a penalty should be considered as part of an enforcement mechanism and not as a fee or formality "in connexion with importation" within the purview of Article VIII. As a result, the Panel considered that Article VIII was not relevant, and therefore concluded that the provision for the forfeiture of the security associated with the import certificate could not be inconsistent with the obligations of the Community under Article VIII.

4.4. The Panel next examined the obligations which the importer had to undertake when he applied for the import certificate in relation to the Community's obligations under Article VIII. The Panel noted that the importer, when applying for the certificate, must agree to complete the importation within the seventy-five day validity limit of the certificate and to import the quantity stated on the certificate plus or minus 5 per cent. The Panel further noted that the importer was not required to obtain an import certificate when a contract was signed, but could wait until the product was approaching the Community frontier. The Panel further considered that these obligations, which had to be assumed by the importer, were not onerous enough to violate Article VIII. Therefore, the Panel concluded that the obligations which had to be undertaken by the importer when he applied for the import certificate were not inconsistent with the Community's obligations under Article VIII.

4.5. The Panel then examined the relevant Community Regulations to determine if member States had the authority to arbitrarily suspend import certificates, and, if so, to examine this authority in relation to the Community's obligations under Article VIII. The Panel noted that the United States representative had argued that the uncertainty caused by the arbitrariness of member States to suspend import certificates was contrary to Article VIII. On examining the relevant Community Regulations, the Panel was unable to find any provision which allowed member States to arbitrarily suspend import certificates which had already been issued. The Panel noted the assertion of the Community representative that an import certificate, once issued, could not be revoked and could not be subject to any subsequent safeguard action. In this connexion, the Panel further noted that member States could totally or partially suspend the issuing of new import certificates, pending Community action in response to a request for safeguard action by a member State. The Panel also noted that such a request must be acted upon by the Community within twenty-four hours. The Panel considered that such a short delay would not cause any harmful disruption of trade. Therefore, the Panel concluded that the authority of member States to totally or partially suspend the issuing of import certificates, pending Community action in response to a request for safeguard action, was not inconsistent with the Community's obligations under Article VIII.

Article II

4.6. The Panel next examined the status of the interest charges and costs in connexion with the lodging of the security associated with the import certificate in relation to the obligations of the Community under Article II. The Panel noted the arguments by the representatives of the United States and Australia that these interest charges and costs were charges imposed on or in connexion with importation in excess of those allowed by Article II:1(*b*). The Panel accepted the argument that these interest charges and costs were in excess of the bound rate, but noted that they had been found to be limited in amount to the approximate costs of administration in accordance with the provisions of Article VIII:1(*a*). The Panel further noted that Article II-2(*c*) stated that: "Nothing in this Article shall prevent any contracting party from imposing at any time on the importation of any product: . . . fees or other charges commensurate with the cost of services rendered." The Panel considered that the term "fees or other charges commensurate with the cost of services rendered" in Article II:2(*c*) would include these costs of administration. Therefore, the Panel concluded that the interest charges and costs in connexion with the lodging of the security associated with the import certificate were not inconsistent with the obligations of the Community under Article II.

4.7. The Panel next examined the provision for the forfeiture of the security associated with the import certificate in relation to the Community's obligations under Article II:1(*b*). The Panel noted the arguments by the representatives of the United States and Australia that the forfeiture of a security was a charge imposed on or in connexion with importation in excess of those allowed by Article II:1(*b*). The Panel considered that such a forfeiture could not logically be accepted as a charge "imposed on or in connexion with importation" within the meaning of Article II:1(*b*), since no importation had occurred, but only as a penalty to the importer for not fulfilling the obligations which he had undertaken when he applied for the certificate. The Panel further considered that such a penalty should be considered as part of an enforcement mechanism and not as a charge "imposed on or in connexion with importation" within the purview of Article II:1(*b*). As a result, the Panel considered that Article II:1(*b*) was not relevant, and therefore concluded that the provision for the forfeiture of the security associated with the import certificate could not be inconsistent with the Community's obligations under Article II:1(*b*).

(b) Minimum Import Price and Associated Additional Security System

4.8. The Panel began its examination of the minimum import price and associated additional security system for tomato concentrates by noting that the representative of the United States had argued that this system was inconsistent with the Community's obligations under Articles I, II, VIII, and XI of the General Agreement. The Panel further noted that the representative of the Community had argued that this system was justified by the provisions of Article XI:2. Therefore, the Panel decided to examine the minimum import price system first in relation to the provisions of Article XI, and then in relation to the other Articles of the General Agreement taken up by the two parties.

Article XI:1

4.9. The Panel examined the minimum import price and associated additional security system for tomato concentrates in relation to the obligations of the Community under Article XI:1. The Panel noted that Article 3 of Council Regulation (EEC) No. 516/77, provided that "A minimum price for tomato concentrates falling within sub-heading 20.02 C of the Common Customs Tariff shall be fixed each year before April 1 for the subsequent marketing year". The Panel further noted that this minimum import price was enforced by the following provision of Article 10 of Council Regulation (EEC) No. 516/77: "The issue of an import certificate shall be conditional upon the following: . . .

— for tomato concentrates, the lodging of an additional security to guarantee that the free-at-frontier price of the products to be imported under cover of the certificate plus the customs duty payable thereon shall together be equal to or more than the minimum price . . . The security shall be forfeit in proportion to any quantities imported at a price lower than the minimum price . . ."

The Panel further noted the argument by the representative of the United States that this system prohibited importation of goods below a certain price and was, therefore, a restriction within the meaning of Article XI on the importation of those goods. The Panel also noted the argument by the representative of the Community that this system, as enforced by the additional security, was a non-tariff measure and that, in principle, imports of tomato concentrates into the Community were allowed, but not below the minimum price level. The Panel further noted the argument by the Community representative that, in view of the nature of the system itself, which resulted in importers complying with the minimum price obligation, the additional security had been forfeited in only a very limited number of cases. Finally, the Panel noted the assertion by the representative of the Community that this system was a measure which fell within the purview of Article XI and Article XI alone, and furthermore, that it qualified for the exemption from the provisions of Article XI:1 provided by Article XI:2(*c*)(i) and (ii). Having noted the foregoing, the Panel considered that the minimum import price system, as enforced by the additional security, was a restriction "other than duties, taxes or other charges" within the meaning of Article XI:1. Having noted, in particular, the claim by the representative of the Community that this system qualified for the exemption from the provisions of Article XI:1 provided by Article XI:2(*c*)(i) and (ii), the Panel concluded that the question of the system's consistency with the Community's obligations under Article XI could only be decided after an examination of the system in relation to the provisions of Article XI:2(*c*)(i) and (ii). One member of the Panel considered that the minimum import price system, as enforced by the additional security, could well be applied in a way which would qualify it as a restriction "other than duties, taxes or other charges" within the meaning of Article XI:1. However, having noted the explanation given with respect to the functioning of the system, this member considered that importation of tomato concentrate at a price lower than the minimum price could still be carried out by importers who had an interest in doing so. He further considered that the system operated in a way to levy an additional charge which raised the price of tomato concentrate imported at a price lower than the minimum price. Therefore, he concluded that the minimum import price system was not being enforced in a manner which would qualify it as a restriction within the meaning of Article XI.

Article XI:2(c)(i) and (ii)

4.10. The Panel then examined the minimum import price and associated additional security system in relation to the provisions of Article XI:2(*c*)(i) and (ii). The Panel began this examination by considering if tomato concentrate qualified as an "agricultural or fisheries product imported in any form" within the meaning of Article XI:2(*c*). The Panel noted the interpretative note on page 66 of Basic Instruments and Selected Documents (BISD), Volume IV, which stated "The term 'in any form' in this paragraph covers the same products when in an early stage of processing and still perishable, which compete directly with the fresh product and if freely imported would tend to make the restriction on the fresh product ineffective". The Panel considered that tomato concentrate was perishable because after a certain time it would decline in quality and value. The Panel also considered that tomato concentrate could compete directly with fresh tomatoes in so far as a large number of end-uses were concerned. Therefore, the Panel concluded that tomato concentrate qualified as an "agricultural or fisheries product, imported in any form" within the meaning of Article XI:2(*c*).

4.11. The Panel next examined if the minimum import price and associated additional security system for tomato concentrates was "necessary to the enforcement of" the intervention system for fresh tomatoes within the meaning of Article XI:2(*c*). The Panel noted the report of the ninth session of the Working Party on Quantitative Restrictions which stated that ". . . if restrictions of the type referred to in paragraph 2(*c*) of Article XI were applied to imports during that part of the year in which domestic supplies of the product were not available, such restrictions would be regarded as consistent with the provisions of the Article only to the extent that they were necessary to enforce or to achieve the objectives of the governmental measures relating to control of the domestic product". ". . . it would be an abuse of intent of the provisions under paragraph 2(*c*))(i) of Article XI if contracting parties were to apply restrictions to processed products exceeding those 'necessary' to secure enforcement of the actual measures restricting production or marketing of the primary product". The Panel further noted that the minimum import price and additional security system for tomato concentrates was permanent, i.e. in operation year round. The Panel also noted that the intervention system for fresh tomatoes, while being permanently in force, operated only at certain times of the year, i.e. when fresh tomatoes were being marketed in quantities in excess of commercial market requirements. The Panel found that the minimum import price and associated additional security system for tomato concentrates would be "necessary to the enforcement of" the intervention system for fresh tomatoes essentially during those periods when fresh tomatoes were being bought-in by the intervention organizations, and only to the extent that the system satisfied the other conditions contained in Article XI:2(*c*)(i) and (ii).

4.12. The Panel next examined the concept of "the like domestic product" within the meaning of Article XI:2(*c*)(i) and (ii), and attempted to determine which Community product should be considered as "the like domestic product" in relation to imported tomato concentrate. Having noted that the General Agreement provided no definition of the terms "the like domestic product" or "like product", the Panel reviewed how these terms had been applied by the CONTRACTING PARTIES in previous cases and the discussions relating to these terms when the General Agreement was being drafted. During this review, the Panel noted the League of Nations definition of "practically identical with another product" and the diverging interpretations of these terms by contracting parties in different contexts. The Panel further noted the definition of "like product" contained in the GATT Anti-Dumping Code and the definitions of "identical goods" and "similar goods" contained in the Customs Co-operation Council's Customs Valuation Explanatory Notes to the Brussels definition of value. On the basis of this review, the Panel considered that tomato concentrate produced within the Community would qualify as "the like domestic product" but was unable to decide if fresh tomatoes grown within the Community would also qualify. As a pragmatic solution, the Panel decided to proceed to determine if the other conditions set forth in Article XI:2(*c*)(i) and (ii) were satisfied by the Community system, on the basis that "the like domestic product" in this case could be domestically-produced tomato concentrate, fresh tomatoes or both.

4.13. The Panel next examined the Community's intervention system for fresh tomatoes to determine if it qualified as a governmental measure which operated "to restrict the quantities" of fresh tomatoes or tomato concentrates "permitted to be marketed or produced" or "to remove a temporary surplus" of fresh tomatoes "by making the surplus available to certain groups of domestic consumers free of charge or at prices below the current market level" within the meaning of Article XI:2(*c*)(i) and (ii). The Panel noted that paragraph 1 of Article 15 of the Council Regulation (EEC) No. 1035/72 provided that: ". . . producers' organizations or associations of such organizations may fix a withdrawal price below which the producers' organizations will not offer for sale products supplied by their members . . .". The Panel further noted that this paragraph also provided that: "The disposal of products thus withdrawn from the market shall be determined by the producers' organizations in such a way as not to interfere with normal marketing of the product in question." The Panel also noted that paragraph 1 of Article 19 of Council Regulation (EEC) No. 1035/72 provided that: "Where, for a given product on one of the representative markets referred to in Article 17(2), the prices communicated to the Commission pursuant to Article 17(1) remain below the buying-in price for three consecutive market days, the Commission shall without delay record that the market in the product in question is in a state of serious crisis." The Panel also noted that paragraph 2 of this Article stated that: "Upon such finding the member States shall, through the bodies or natural or legal persons appointed by them for the purpose, buy in products of Community origin offered to them, provided that these products satisfy the requirements of quality and sizing laid down by the quality standards and that they were not withdrawn from the market pursuant to Article 15(1)." The Panel also noted that paragraph 4 of this Article stated that: "Member States for whom the obligation laid down in paragraph 2 presents serious difficulties may be exempted therefrom. In order to claim exemption, member States shall inform the Commission of the existence of such difficulties. Member States claiming such exemption shall take all appropriate steps to set up producers' organizations which will intervene on the market under Article 15." Finally, the Panel noted that paragraph 1 of Article 21 of Council Regulation (EEC) No. 1035/72 provided that products withdrawn from the market would be disposed of *inter alia* by "free distribution to charitable organizations and foundations and to persons whose right to public assistance is recognized by their national laws, in particular because they lack the necessary means of subsistence". Having noted all of the foregoing provisions of the Community Regulations, the Panel considered that there was no effective Community or governmental enforcement of the withdrawals of fresh tomatoes by the producers' organizations; these organizations were merely encouraged to make such withdrawals. The Panel further considered that there was no requirement that tomato producers must create, join or market their production through such producers' organizations. In the case where member States were obligated to buy in tomatoes which had been offered to them, the Panel considered that the provision allowing member States to claim an exemption from this obligation was so liberal that it would constitute a lack of effective enforcement of the intent of this Article of the Regulation. The Panel further considered that, in addition, in light of the fact that the buying-in or withdrawal prices were fixed at about one half of the normal cost of production, the intervention system would not effectively restrict the marketing or production of fresh tomatoes, but simply remove any market surplus after all potential commercial markets, including processing into tomato concentrate, had been saturated. The Panel further considered that, since this system was not considered to be an effective restriction on the marketing or production of fresh tomatoes, then it could not be considered to be an effective restriction on the marketing or production of tomato concentrate. Therefore, the Panel concluded that, even if fresh tomatoes were considered to be the "like domestic product", the intervention system for fresh tomatoes did not qualify as a governmental measure which operated "to restrict the quantities of the like domestic product permitted to be marketed or produced", or "to remove a temporary surplus of the like domestic product by making the surplus available to certain groups of domestic consumers free of charge or at prices below the current market level", within the meaning of Article XI:2(*c*)(i) and (ii).

4.14. As a result of the conclusions contained in the preceding paragraphs, the Panel concluded that the minimum import price and associated additional security system for tomato concentrates did not qualify for the exemptions provided by Article XI:2(*c*)(i) and (ii) from the provisions of Article XI:1. Therefore, the Panel concluded that this system was inconsistent with the obligations of the Community under Article XI. One member recalled his earlier conclusion, in paragraph 4.9, that the minimum import price system was not being enforced in a manner which would qualify it as a restriction within the meaning of Article XI. As a result, this member of the Panel considered that Article XI was not relevant, and therefore concluded that this minimum import price system, as actually enforced by the additional security, could not be inconsistent with the obligations of the Community under Article XI.

Article II

4.15. The Panel next examined the status of the interest charges and costs in connexion with the lodging of the additional security associated with the minimum import price for tomato concentrates in relation to the obligations of the Community under Article II:1(*b*). The Panel noted the argument by the representative of the United States that the interest charges and costs associated with the lodging of the additional security were charges on or in connexion with importation in excess of those allowed by Article II:1(*b*). The Panel further noted that the minimum import price and additional security system for tomato concentrates had not been found to be consistent with Article XI, nor had any justification been claimed by the Community under any other provision of the General Agreement. The Panel considered that these interest charges and costs were "other duties or charges of any kind imposed on or in connexion with importation" in excess of the bound rate within the meaning of Article II:1(*b*). Therefore, the Panel concluded that the interest charges and costs in connexion with the lodging of the additional security associated with the minimum import price for tomato concentrates were inconsistent with the obligations of the Community under Article II:1(*b*).

4.16. The Panel next examined the provision for the forfeiture of all or part of the additional security associated with the minimum import price for tomato concentrates in relation to the obligations of the Community under Article II:1(*b*). The Panel noted the argument by the representative of the United States that the forfeiture of all or part of the additional security, if importation took place at a price below the minimum, was a charge imposed on or in connexion with importation in excess of the bound rate in violation of Article II:1(*b*). The Panel further noted the argument by the Community representative that, in view of the nature of the system itself, which resulted in importers complying with the minimum price obligation, the additional security had been forfeited in only a very limited number of cases. The Panel also noted that the forfeiture of the additional security was meant by the Community to be a penalty imposed on the importer for not fulfilling an obligation which he had undertaken when he applied for the import certificate. The Panel considered that such a forfeiture should be considered as part of an enforcement mechanism and not as a charge "imposed on or in connexion with importation" within the purview of Article II:1(*b*). As a result, the Panel considered that Article II:1(*b*) was not relevant, and therefore concluded that the provision for the forfeiture of all or part of the additional security associated with the minimum import price for tomato concentrates could not be inconsistent with the obligations of the Community under Article II:1(*b*). One member of the Panel recalled his earlier conclusion, in paragraph 4.9, that the minimum import price system was not being enforced in a manner which would qualify it as a restriction within the meaning of Article XI. He noted that no justification for this system had been claimed by the Community under any other provision of the General Agreement. He considered that importation of tomato concentrate at a price lower than the minimum price could still be carried out by importers who had an interest in doing so. He further considered that the system operated in a way so that the forfeiture of a security levied an additional charge which raised the price of tomato concentrate imported at a price lower than the minimum prices. He also considered that such a forfeiture qualified as "other duties or charges of any kind imposed on or in connexion with importation" in excess of the bound rate within the meaning of Article II:1(*b*). Therefore, he concluded that the provision for the forfeiture of all or part of the additional security associated with the minimum import price for tomato concentrates was inconsistent with the obligations of the Community under Article II:1(*b*).

Article VIII

4.17. The Panel next examined the status of the interest charges and costs associated with the lodging of the additional security which enforced the minimum import price for tomato concentrates in relation to the Community's obligations under Article VIII. The Panel noted the complaint by the representative of the United States that the interest charges and costs associated with the lodging of the additional security were imposed as protection for domestic products contrary to the provisions of Article VIII:1(*a*). The Panel recalled its earlier conclusions with regard to Article II and Article XI. As a result of these previous conclusions, the Panel considered that this minimum import price and associated additional security system could not also be considered merely as an administrative formality or fee falling under the purview of Article VIII. As a result, the Panel considered that Article VIII was not relevant, and therefore concluded that the interest charges and costs associated with the lodging of the additional security could not be inconsistent with the obligations of the Community under Article VIII.

4.18. The Panel next examined the provision for the forfeiture of all or part of the additional security associated with the minimum import price for tomato concentrates in relation to the obligations of the Community under Article VIII. The Panel noted the argument by the representative of the United States that such a forfeiture, if importation took place at a price below the minimum, imposed a substantial penalty for minor breaches of customs regulations or procedural requirements in violation of Article VIII:3. The Panel noted that the forfeiture of the additional security was a penalty imposed on the importer for not fulfilling an obligation which he had undertaken when he applied for the import certificate. The Panel considered that such a penalty should be considered as part of an enforcement mechanism and not as a fee or formality "in connexion with importation" within the purview of Article VIII. As a result, the Panel considered that Article VIII was not relevant, and therefore concluded that the provision for the forfeiture of all or part of the additional security associated with the minimum import price for tomato concentrates could not be inconsistent with the obligations of the Community under Article VIII.

Article I

4.19. The Panel next examined the provision for an exemption from the lodging of the additional security associated with the minimum import price for tomato concentrates in relation to the obligations of the Community under Article I:1. The Panel noted that Article 10 of Council Regulation (EEC) No. 516/77 stated that the "lodging of such additional security shall not be required for products originating in non-member countries which undertake, and are in a position, to guarantee that the price on import into the Community shall be not less than the minimum price for the product in question, and that all deflection of trade will be avoided". The Panel noted the argument by the representative of the United States that this provision amounted to conditional most-favoured-nation treatment inconsistent with Article I:1 of the General Agreement, since it removed one of the requirements for certain countries while leaving a burden on other countries. The Panel further noted the argument by the representative of the Community that this provision did not make any distinction based on the economic system or any other factor between third suppliers and, that the possibility to guarantee that the minimum price would be respected was open to all, unconditionally. The Panel considered that, regardless of whether a guarantee had to be provided by the importer or the government of the exporting country, so long as a guarantee was necessary for all imports from all potential third country suppliers, there would be no discrimination within the meaning of Article I:1. Therefore the Panel concluded that the provision for an exemption from the lodging of the additional security associated with the minimum import price for tomato concentrates was not inconsistent with the obligations of the Community under Article I:1.

(c) Nullification or impairment

Article XXIII

4.20. The Panel next examined the import certificate and associated security system and the minimum import price and associated additional security to determine if there had been any nullification or impairment of any benefit accruing to the United States under the General Agreement within the meaning of Article XXIII. The Panel noted that Article XXIII:1 provided that nullification or impairment could be the result of:

"(a) the failure of another contracting party to carry out its obligations under the Agreement, or

(b) the application by another contracting party of any measure, whether or not it conflicts with the provisions of this Agreement, or

(c) the existence of any other situation."

In accordance with established GATT practice[1], the Panel considered that where measures were applied which were judged to be inconsistent with the GATT obligations of the contracting party concerned, this action would *prima facie* constitute a case of nullification or impairment.

4.21. The Panel then recalled its previous conclusions with respect to the import certificate and associated security system that no inconsistency with the provisions of Articles II, VIII and XI of the General Agreement had been found. Therefore, the Panel concluded that no *prima facie* case of nullification or impairment existed. The Panel then examined if there had been any damage to trade serious enough to constitute nullification or impairment within the meaning of Article XXIII. The Panel recalled its earlier conclusions that the obligations which the importer had to undertake when he applied for the import certificate were not onerous enough to violate Article VIII. The Panel considered that this system, being a measure which was not inconsistent with the provisions of Article VIII, did not have trade effects which could be considered as a nullification or impairment within the meaning of Article XXIII. Therefore, the Panel concluded that the Community's import certificate and associated security system did not constitute a nullification or impairment of any benefit accruing to the United States under the General Agreement within the meaning of Article XXIII.

4.22. The Panel then recalled its conclusions with regard to the minimum import price and associated additional security system for tomato concentrates that this system was inconsistent with the provisions of Articles II and XI. Noting that the Community had claimed justification of this system under Article XI:*2*(c)(i) and (ii) only, the Panel concluded that there was a *prima facie* case of nullification or impairment of benefits accruing to the United States within the meaning of Article XXIII.

[1] BISD 11S/100, paragraph 15 [Case 20].

EUROPEAN COMMUNITIES—REFUNDS ON EXPORTS OF SUGAR

Report of the Panel adopted on November 6, 1979
BISD 26S/290

I. INTRODUCTION

1.1 In a communication dated September 25, 1978 and circulated to contracting parties, the Government of Australia presented a complaint that the refunds on exports of sugar applied by the European Communities were inconsistent with the European Communities' obligations under the GATT.

* * *

IV. FINDINGS

(a) Introduction

4.1 The Panel has carried out its considerations of the matter referred to it for examination in light of its terms of reference as expressed in paragraph 1.3. It has based its considerations on arguments presented to it by the parties to the dispute (Chapter II) and on various factual information which was available to it, notably that concerning the sugar market system of the European Communities and features of the world sugar market (Chapter III).

4.2 The Panel noted the provisions of Article XVI and also Notes and Supplementary Provisions concerning that Article, and in particular the last sentence of the Notes to Article XVI:3 which says:

> "Notwithstanding such determination by the CONTRACTING PARTIES, operations under such a system shall be subject to the provisions of paragraph 3 where they are wholly or partly financed out of government funds in addition to the funds collected from producers in respect of the product concerned."

4.3 When examining the Community system for granting refunds on exports of sugar, the Panel found that such refunds were granted to enable Community sugar to be exported and that the refunds thus granted were financed out of the European Agriculture Guidance and Guarantee Fund. The Panel considered this Fund to be a government fund of the type mentioned in the Note to Article XVI:3 quoted above.

4.4 The Panel therefore concluded that the Community system for granting refunds on exports of sugar must be considered to be a form of subsidy and which was subject to the provisions of Article XVI. The Panel found that the parties to the dispute were in agreement with this interpretation.

4.5 The Panel noted that under Article XVI, contracting parties had some basic obligations:

(a) to notify in writing to the CONTRACTING PARTIES the application of any subsidy. Moreover, contracting parties shall submit regularly responses to a questionnaire on subsidies giving details on the nature and extent of the subsidy and the effect of that subsidy[1] (Article XVI:1);

(b) to discuss (or consult) with another contracting party of parties concerned, or with the CONTRACTING PARTIES, the possibility of limiting the subsidization in cases in which it is determined that serious prejudice is caused or threatened to another contracting party (Article XVI:1);

(c) seek to avoid the use of subsidies on exports of primary products. If export subsidies are nevertheless applied to such products, the subsidized exports shall be kept within certain more or less strict limits, i.e. "shall not be applied in a manner which results in that contracting party having more than an equitable share of world export trade in that product" (Article XVI:3).

4.6 The Panel draws attention to the fact that the five points listed in the Australian complaint are to some extent interrelated and therefore the following considerations may not necessarily follow the structure of the complaint as set out above (paragraph 2.1).

(b) Consistency with Procedural Provisions of Article XVI:1

4.7 In examining the Australian complaint that the European Communities had not complied with the terms of Article XVI:1, the Panel

[1] BISD 9S/193, 194; BISD 11S/58, 59.

noted that the European Communities had notified, on a regular basis, its system of export refunds on sugar pursuant to Article XVI:1.

4.8 As both parties seemed to agree that bilateral consultations had taken place on the matter, apparently without concrete results, the Panel felt that it had not been requested to examine the question of whether or not the European Communities had met is obligations to discuss with other parties.

(c) Consistency with Article XVI:3

(i) World Export Trade

4.9 The Panel considered that its examination should be based not on the concept of "free market" introduced by Australia in presenting its contentions (see paragraph 2.20) but on the concept of "world export trade" mentioned in Article XVI:3 of the General Agreement. In that connexion the Panel referred back to various discussions that had taken place in the past regarding the term "world export trade" and its interpretation.[1] In the event, the Panel did not consider it necessary for the purpose of determining whether a market share was a "more than equitable share of world export trade" to establish market shares in relation to concepts other than those of total world exports, taking into account the fact that a consideration of shares of the free market involved methodological difficulties that would make any comparison difficult.

(ii) Time Periods Considered

4.10 The Panel noted that the Australian complaint referred to the post-1975 period. Regarding the years preceding the period subject to complaint, the Panel felt that 1975 did not appear to be sufficiently representative, as world market prices were abnormally high in 1974/1975. The strong rise in sugar prices in 1974 was mainly due to the fact that for the fourth successive year total world consumption exceeded world production and stocks were declining, and the supply situation was particularly bad in Europe. Mainly due to a bad crop in 1974, there was a shortage of sugar in the European Communities in 1974/1975, and some exports were delayed from 1975 to 1976. The Panel also had some

[1] Discussions at the ninth session of the CONTRACTING PARTIES (1955) (SR. 9/41, page 6) and those of the Panel on French assistance to exports of wheat and wheat flour (1958), (BISD, 7S/52).

doubts as to whether 1974 would qualify as a fully representative year, but nevertheless thought that the years 1972 to 1974 would still be an acceptable approach. The three most recent calendar years for which market conditions could be considered as normal were then 1971 to 1973, or with some reservations 1972 to 1974. Furthermore, 1977 could also be compared to an average of 1972, 1973 and 1976. In view of the difficulties involved in selecting what could be considered to be the "previous representative period", the Panel felt it necessary to consider various alternatives and to make a set of comparisons.

(iii) Equitable Share

4.11 The Panel noted that no definition of the concept "equitable share" had been provided, and neither had it in the past been considered absolutely necessary to agree upon a precise definition of the concept. The Panel felt that it was appropriate and sufficient in this case to try to analyse main reasons for developments in individual market shares, and to examine market and price developments, and then draw a conclusion on that basis.

(iv) Market Shares

4.12 Table 2 [omitted] shows the European Communities' share of world export trade in sugar for some previous representative periods and for periods subject to complaint. Table 3 [omitted] is a compilation of the comparisons the Panel made in order to determine the direction and magnitude of the changes in Community market shares. The Panel found that the final result was very much the same whichever of the previous representative periods was used for comparison. In any case it appeared that the Community market share had increased in 1976 and 1977 compared to previous periods. The increase in the Community market shares for both 1976 and 1977 was nevertheless rather small, in no case exceeding 2.1 percentage points, which was the increase for 1977 compared to 1972–1974.

4.13 In 1978, the Community export system with respect to sugar remained the same as in previous years. However, the Panel felt that this year constituted a special case, for the following two reasons: at the time when Australia presented its complaint, the year 1978 had not yet ended and the data for that year were not formally finalized at the time the Panel drew its conclusions; 1978 was also the year in which the International Sugar Agreement, 1977, came into operation modifying certain elements of the international sugar market. Despite these facts the Panel nevertheless felt that the year 1978 should be taken into consideration, be it on the basis of preliminary data noting that this would be in conformity with earlier practice.[1]

4.14 An examination of available data for 1978 indicated that Community sugar exports had increased from 2.7 million tons in 1977 to 3.6 million tons in 1978. The share of Community sugar exports in world exports in 1978 exceeded 14 per cent which meant a level 5–6 percentage points higher than the market shares in various reference periods considered. This increase in the Community market share corresponded to roughly 1.5 million tons of sugar.

4.15 With respect to the year 1978, the Panel, in addition, noted that the International Sugar Agreement, 1977 (ISA) came into operation on January 1, 1978. Australia limited its exports in accordance with obligations it had taken upon itself under that Agreement. The European Communities did not participate in the ISA.

4.16 The Panel therefore concluded that given the significant increase of Community exports in 1978 both in absolute and relative terms it was justified to examine more thoroughly the conditions under which this development took place.

(v) Displacement

4.17 The Panel was of the opinion that the term "more than an equitable share of world export trade" should include situations in which the effect of an export subsidy granted by a signatory was to displace the exports of another signatory, bearing in mind the developments in world markets. With regard to new markets, traditional patterns of supply of the product concerned to the world market, region or country, in which the new market is situated, should be taken into account in determining what would be "more than an equitable share of world export trade".

4.18 The Panel therefore proceeded to a detailed examination of sugar export statistics, notably in order to see if and to what extent the increased Community sugar exports had displaced Australian sugar exports.

4.19 The Panel noted that total Australian sugar exports had shown a fairly steady increase up to 1978, while Australia's share of world export

[1] BISD, 25S/48 [Case 36].

trade had on the average remained fairly stable with three-year averages for both 1971 to 1973 and 1972 to 1974 at 9.5 per cent and the average 1976 and 1977 at 11.1 per cent. For 1978, the Panel estimated the market share of Australia to be around 8 per cent. In the latter year, Australian export had been limited by obligations under the ISA. However, Australia had fulfilled, and even exceeded, its ISA quota in effect for 1978.

4.20 An examination of individual markets enabled the Panel to distinguish between the following five groups of markets, for which data are shown in Table 4 [omitted].

Group I:	Countries where both Australia and the European Communities sold sugar in recent years, directly competing with each other
Group II:	Australian exports to the European Communities
Group III:	Major outlets for Australian exports
Group IV:	Certain markets in the Mediterranean area, Middle East and Africa
Group V:	Other destinations.

4.21 Group I (countries where both Australia and the European Communities had sold sugar in recent years, directly competing with each other) in Table 4 consists mainly of China, the United States and the USSR. For this group as a whole, both Australian and Community sales increased in 1976 and 1977, but declined strongly in 1978 by 123,000 tons for the European Communities and by 428,000 tons for Australia. In the case of Australia, the decline in 1978 was due to a reduction in sales to China and the United States, while for the European Communities a strong decline in sales to the USSR was only partly compensated for by increased sales to China and the United States. In the case of the United States, Community exports increased for the third consecutive year, while Australian exports to that market showed a strong decline in 1978. However, the increase in Community exports to the United States for 1978 corresponded to less than 10 per cent of the decrease in Australian sugar exports to that market. In the case of China, Community sales which had been negligible until 1978, reached 93,000 tons or approximately 6 per cent of total imports into China in that year. This might have partly replaced Australian sales to this market, which fell by 138,000 tons from 1977 to 1978, but it must be noted that also supplies from other sources (e.g. Cuba and India) at the same time increased considerably.

4.22 Group II in Table 4 shows Australian exports to the European Communities. The Panel noted that following the enlargement of the European Communities in 1973, and the termination of the Commonwealth Sugar Agreement in 1974, Australian sugar exports to the Community market fell sharply and were negligible in 1978.

4.23 Group III (major outlets for Australian exports) in Table 4 consists of Canada, Japan, Malaysia, New Zealand, Singapore, the Republic of Korea and neighboring Pacific islands where Australian sugar exports had benefited from preferential tariffs or long-term trade agreements and which may have so far prevented damage from Community competition. These outlets accounted for more than 60 per cent of Australian sugar exports up to 1975 (i.e. before the Commonwealth Sugar Agreement was abolished), in 1975 to 1977 for 70 to 74 per cent and in 1978 for 85 per cent of total Australian exports. Australian exports to these markets showed a strong expansion from 1974 to 1977, when they were nearly doubled. The decline in Australian sales to these markets in 1978 should be seen in relation to Australian commitments under the ISA. Community sales to these markets remained insignificant throughout the period under consideration.

4.24 The increase in Community sugar exports in recent years was mainly due to increased sales to certain markets in the Mediterranean area, the Middle East and Africa (Group IV in Table 4) (i.e. Algeria, Iraq, Iran, Israel, Kuwait, Lebanon, Morocco, Nigeria, Persian Gulf, Saudi Arabia, Sudan, Syria, Tunisia, the Arab Republic of Yemen, and the People's Republic of Yemen). These markets accounted for almost one half of the Community sugar sales in 1976 and 1977 and the increase in sales to these markets accounted for 47 and 56 per cent respectively of total increase in Community exports. In 1978, these outlets accounted for more than 60 per cent of total Community sugar exports, and the increase in Community sales to these markets exceeded the total increase in Community sugar exports from 1977 to 1978. Apart from sales of 59,000 tons to Algeria, Morocco and Tunisia in 1972, Australia had not been exporting to any of these markets in the period under consideration.

4.25 Group V in Table 4 (other destinations) consists of about sixty markets where the European Communities had traditionally been the major, if not the only, supplier at least for refined sugar. The increase in Community exports to this group of markets was significant in the years 1976–1978, while Australian supplies to these markets had remained insignificant.

4.26 The Panel therefore found that there was not sufficient evidence to state that the increased Community exports in recent years had to a considerable extent directly displaced Australian exports from world markets although it should not be excluded that Community exports to China in 1978 could partly have replaced Australian supplies.

4.27 When considering a possible indirect displacement of Australian sugar exports by increased Community exports with refunds, the Panel noted that while Community exports consisted of refined white sugar, Australian exports were predominantly of raw sugar with only about 30,000 tons of refined sugar having been exported to neighboring Pacific islands. Australian exports of raw sugar had consequently been limited to markets where the sugar could be further refined, while Community exports of refined sugar were spread over a larger number of markets, often without local refining facilities or where the capacity of the local refining industry was insufficient to handle increased imports of raw sugar. However, in countries where refining facilities existed, raw sugar could nevertheless be replaced by white sugar.

4.28 The Panel noted some information concerning Community exports to markets which have traditionally been regarded as important outlets for raw sugar (Table 5) [omitted]. The figures in the table show a strong increase in Community exports of white sugar to these markets since 1976, i.e. when the world market prices for sugar were low, and the difference in quotations between white sugar and raw sugar did not constitute a reasonable margin for costs of refining, packaging and difference in sucrose content. The Panel felt that the figures shown in Table 5 indicated fairly clearly that Community exports of white sugar had expanded in some traditional raw sugar markets and that this could be related to the small difference between prices for white and raw sugar since 1976. Raw sugar displaced from these markets by Community white sugar might have exercised a pressure on residual raw sugar markets. Increased Community white sugar exports to the markets listed in Table 5 could therefore have resulted indirectly in some replacement of Australian raw sugar in other markets or in reduced opportunities for Australian sales in various markets. However, the Panel did not exclude the possibility that increased Community sales of white sugar might be a result of re-export of raw sugar imported by the European Communities under special arrangements (*trafic de perfectionnement*). It did not consider the information in Table 5 to constitute clear evidence that Australian raw sugar exports had thus been indirectly displaced by Community exports of white sugar. The Panel nevertheless felt that a continuation of subsidized Community sugar exports could constitute a menace or threat to Australian raw sugar exports in the future, for instance when current bilateral agreements between Australia and some importing countries expired.

(vi) Effects of the Operation of Community Regulations

4.29 The Panel proceeded to an examination of whether the increase in 1976 to 1978 in Community sugar exports, notably the increase in the Community share of world sugar export trade could be attributed to the operation of the Community regulations. With regard to production, the Panel noted that the Community system may put an economic but not necessarily legal limit to the size of the production.

4.30 Some basic data for production, trade, consumption and stocks of sugar, for Australia and the European Communities are shown in Annex Table I[1] and, for comparison, world totals for the same in Annex Table II.[1] A simple comparison of the figures in these tables indicates that the increase in the community sugar production corresponded roughly to the world average until 1978. For illustrative purposes, it can be mentioned that the Australian sugar production showed a stronger increase until 1978, when the area harvested was however reduced by 44,000 hectares, resulting in a reduction in production.

4.31 Graph 1[2] shows developments in Community sugar production, consumption and target prices since 1969. Up to 1977, the Community area under sugar beet increased with the increase in the Community target price, the price policy apparently being a stimulating factor. Although the increase in the target price was halted in 1977, and the area of sugar beet was reduced, total Community sugar production continued to increase because of higher average yields. It can be seen from Annex Table I and Graph 1 that there was a downwards shift in the Community sugar consumption in 1975 contributing, together with a continued growth in production, significantly to increased exportable surpluses of sugar.

4.32 The Panel noted that the fixing of production quotas was of decisive importance for the application of the price system for sugar in the European Communities. It also noted that in 1975 the basic quota was raised from 7.82 million tons to 9.14 million tons and the maximum quota was maintained at 145 per cent of the basic quota. The basic quota was then maintained in the following years, but the maximum quota was

[1] The Annex is not reproduced.
[2] The Graph is not reproduced.

reduced first in 1976 (to 135 per cent) and again in 1978 (to 127.5 per cent) (Annex Table VIII).[1] Furthermore, the Panel noted that sugar produced in excess of the basic quota, but within the limits of the maximum quota, was subject to a production levy of up to 30 per cent of the intervention price. Although this step resulted in a smaller area planted with sugar beets in 1977 and 1978, total production continued to increase, as yields were higher. The steps taken were therefore not sufficient to prevent the exportable surplus from increasing further in 1977 and 1978.

4.33 The Panel understood the Community system of regulations concerning the sugar markets to imply that the quantity exported from the European Communities with an export refund would be limited by the total of maximum production quotas, plus imports under special arrangements minus domestic consumption. Any sugar produced in excess of maximum quotas must be disposed of on external markets without benefiting from any refund. Table 6 [omitted] shows Community exports totally and with a breakdown into exports with refunds and exports without refunds in 1972–1978. A comparison of figures for 1976, 1977 and 1978 with averages for 1972–1974, indicates clearly that the increase in Community sugar exports in 1976-1978 mainly consisted of increased exports with export refunds, i.e. sugar produced within the maximum quota. Both in 1976 and 1977, exports without refunds were inferior to the average for 1972–1974. Although Community exports without refund (C—sugar) showed some increase in 1977 and 1978, the reduction in maximum quotas and the application of production levies had not prevented that exports with refund continued to increase even in 1978, and still counted for 76 per cent of Community sugar exports.

4.34 The Panel also noted the strong increase in the total amount spent by the European Communities on refunds of sugar in 1977 and 1978. This increase was partly due to larger exports entitled to refund and to falling world market prices, but the Panel noted that the increase was also partly due to an increase in the Community market intervention price for sugar. When examining the question of whether Community export refunds could be subject to budgetary limits, the Panel noted that if the appropriations originally allocated to the Guarantee Section of the European Agriculture Guidance and Guarantee Fund proved to be insufficient in any particular year, the Commission could have recourse to a supplementary budget during the financial year and there would thus be no legally fixed budgetary limits for how much could be spent on export refunds for sugar.

[1] The Annex is not reproduced.

4.35 The Panel felt that in those conditions neither exportable surpluses of sugar nor the amount of refund granted had been effectively limited as a result of the Community system or its application. There was no element in the system and its application that would prevent the European Communities from having more than an equitable share of world export trade in sugar.

(d) Effect on World Market Prices

4.36 In examining more in detail the granting of export refunds on sugar by the European Communities, the Panel noted that for the quasi-totality of exports with refunds, the refunds were granted under the tendering procedure (e.g. for 91 per cent in 1976, 97 per cent in 1977 and almost 100 per cent in 1978,—Table 6 [omitted]). Under the tendering procedure, the Commission fixed maximum amounts of refunds and for a given quantity, taking into account the supply situation and prices within the Community, prices and potential outlets on the world market, and costs incurred in exporting sugar. The Commission's determination of what were world market prices for sugar was based on the amount of refund proposed in the tenders, which were occasionally based on prices lower than the average quotations for white sugar published by the Paris Exchange.

4.37 The Panel noted that the weighted average of export refunds usually corresponded to the difference between the Community intervention price at F.O.B. stage and average spot quotations for white sugar on the Paris Exchange. However, towards the end of the crop years 1975/1976, 1976/1977 (and apparently also 1977/1978) the weighted average refund had tended to exceed that difference. The Panel also noted that from the middle of 1976 on, Community export refunds were increased sharply with only little difference between weighted average refunds and maximum refunds. These developments coincided with a sharp decline in world market prices. Furthermore, the premium for white sugar had diminished, and at times white sugar had been quoted at prices lower than those quoted for raw sugar.

4.38 The Panel felt that since the Community sugar exporters were leading the world market for white sugar, traditionally covering more than half of the world market for refined sugar, the availability of exportable Community surpluses of sugar combined with the possibility of non-limited amounts available to cover export refunds, may well have had a depressing effect on world market prices for sugar, both white and raw sugar.

V. CONCLUSIONS

In the light of the foregoing findings, the Panel reached the following conclusions:

(a) The Panel concluded that the Community system for granting refunds on exports of sugar must be considered as a form of subsidy which was subject to the provisions of Article XVI, and it noted that the European Communities had notified their system of export refunds on sugar pursuant to Article XVI:1.

(b) When examining whether or not the Community system of export refunds on sugar was consistent with Article XVI:3, the Panel first noted that, in spite of various measures taken to limit Community sugar production, the Community regulations on sugar and their operation had not prevented production from continuing to increase, and neither exportable surpluses of sugar entitled to export refunds nor the amount of refund granted had been reduced or limited.

(c) Examining next the Community share of world export trade in sugar, the Panel noted that that share had increased somewhat in 1976 and 1977, although that increase was not unusual in magnitude. In 1978, however, that share had increased in such proportions that the Panel felt that the situation justified a thorough examination as to whether the Community system of export refunds for sugar had been applied in a manner which had resulted in the European Communities having more than an equitable share in world export trade in sugar. It was evident that the increase in exports was effected through the use of subsidies.

(d) When examining the development of various sugar markets, the Panel found that, despite the increase in Community exports in 1978, Community sugar exports had directly displaced Australian exports only to a limited extent and in a few markets. Furthermore, increased Community white sugar exports may well have resulted indirectly in reduced opportunities for Australian raw sugar sales in various markets.

(e) The Panel noted that a substantial share of Australian exports had taken place under long-term bilateral agreements with importing countries. It also noted that the International Sugar Agreement, 1977 (ISA) came into operation in 1978 and that this for its members resulted in a certain contraction in their sugar trade.

(f) In the light of all the circumstances related to the present complaint, and especially taking into account the difficulties in establishing clearly the causal relationships between the increase in Community exports, the developments of Australian sugar exports and other developments in the world sugar market, the Panel found that it was not in a position to reach a definite conclusion that the increased share had resulted in the European Communities "having more than an equitable share of world export trade in that product", in terms of Article XVI:3.

(g) The Panel noted however that the Community system for granting refunds on sugar exports and its application had contributed to depress world sugar prices in recent years and that thereby serious prejudice had been caused indirectly to Australia, although it was not feasible to quantify the prejudice in exact terms.

(h) The Panel found that the Community system of export refunds for sugar did not comprise any pre-established effective limitations in respect of either production, price or the amounts of export refunds and constituted a permanent source of uncertainty in world sugar markets. It therefore concluded that the Community system and its application constitutes a threat of prejudice in terms of Article XVI:1.

(i) No detailed submission had been made as to exactly what benefits accruing to Australia under the General Agreement had been nullified or impaired or as to which objective of the General Agreement had been impeded, and the Panel did not consider these questions.

OMITTED

NORWAY—RESTRICTIONS ON IMPORTS OF CERTAIN TEXTILE PRODUCTS

Report of the Panel adopted on June 18, 1980
BISD 27S/119, 120

II. FACTUAL ASPECTS

5. The Panel based its deliberations principally on the following facts:

(a) Until the end of 1977, exports from Hong Kong to Norway of most of the textile products covered by Norway's present global quota system were subject to a bilateral restraint agreement concluded under the Arrangement Regarding International Trade in Textile (MFA). On October 7, 1977 Norway had requested Hong Kong to negotiate a further bilateral agreement for 1978. Consultations to this effect took place on December 12, 1977 but no agreement was reached.

(b) Effective from January 1, 1978, Norway introduced temporary unilateral control measures on imports of certain textile products from a number of countries including Hong Kong. During the first four months of 1978 Norway, with the aim of acceding to the extended MFA, concluded long-term bilateral arrangements with six textile-supplying developing countries, providing for export restraints on a retroactive basis from January 1, 1978; Hong Kong and Norway held further consultations on May 2–3, 1978 but were unable to determine a level of textile exports acceptable to both sides.

* * *

On July 20, 1978 Norway informed the CONTRACTING PARTIES that it had decided to invoke Article XIX and that is was preparing the introduction of global import quotas on nine textile items for 1979.

* * *

(e) Consultations under Article XIX:2 were held between the parties on September 6–8, 1978 during which Hong Kong was informed of the modalities regarding Norway's Article XIX action, including the fact that imports from the EEC and EFTA countries, together with the six developing countries with which Norway had concluded long-term bilateral arrangements, would not be covered by the action. Hong Kong requested that as a substantial supplier of the products concerned it be allocated for 1979, in accordance with the provisions of Article XIII, a share of the global quotas "similar" to the shares which in the opinion of Hong Kong had been allotted to the six countries with which Norway had signed bilateral agreements; for the year 1978, Hong Kong requested compensation for export trade lost. Again, agreement could not be reached.

* * *

IV. CONCLUSIONS

14. The Panel based its consideration of the case on Articles XIX and XIII of the GATT:

(a) The Panel noted that while both parties had advanced extensive data and arguments concerning the history of the case, i.e. especially the situation during 1978 prior to the invocation of Article XIX by Norway, Hong Kong had limited its formal request to a finding on Norway's Article XIX action. The Panel at the same time noted and consequently based its decision on the statements by Hong Kong that the latter was prepared to assume that Norway had the necessary justification for taking this action and that a finding concerning the exclusion from the quotas of the EEC and EFTA countries was not necessary.

(b) The Panel was of the view that the type of action chosen by Norway, i.e. the quantitative restrictions limiting the importation of the nine textile categories in question, as the form of emergency action under Article XIX was subject to the provisions of Article XIII which provides for non-discriminatory administration of quantitative restrictions. In this connexion, the Panel noted the introductory part of paragraph 2 which stipulates that in applying an import restriction on a product, a contracting party "shall aim at a distribution of trade in such product approaching as closely as possible the shares which the various contracting parties might be expected to obtain in the absence of such restrictions . . .". To this end, paragraph 2(*a*) of Article XIII further prescribes that wherever practicable, quotas representing the total amount of permitted imports (whether allocated among supplying countries or not) shall be fixed.

15. In the case before the Panel, Norway had in early 1978 concluded long-term bilateral arrangements with six textile-supplying countries. The Panel noted that Norway had concluded these agreements with the intention of acceding to the MFA and notifying the agreements to the TSB pursuant to the appropriate Article of the MFA. The Panel noted also, however, that in the event Norway had not acceded to the MFA and that for these arrangements no derogation or provision of Parts I–III of GATT had ever been invoked by Norway. While noting that provision for some developing exporting countries of assured increase in access to Norway's textile and clothing markets might be consistent for those countries with the spirit and objectives of Part IV of the GATT, this cannot be cited as justification for actions which would be inconsistent with a country's obligations under Part II of the GATT. The Panel held that Norway's reservation of market shares for these six countries therefore represented a partial allocation of quotas under an existing régime of import restrictions of the products in question and that Norway must therefore be considered to have acted under Article XIII:2(*d*). The Panel noted that had the reservation of market shares for the six countries been entered into pursuant to Article XIII:2(*d*), Norway could have been presumed to have acted under the first sentence of that provision.

16. Since Hong Kong has a substantial interest in supplying eight of the nine product categories in question to the Norwegian market, it had the right to expect the allocation of a share of the quotas in accordance with Article XIII:2(*d*). The Panel was of the view that to the extent that Norway had acted with effect to allocate import quotas for these products to six countries but had failed to allocate a share to Hong Kong, its Article XIX action was not consistent with Article XIII.

17. In accordance with established GATT practice, the Panel held that where a measure had been taken which was judged to be inconsistent with the provisions of the General Agreement, this measure would *prima facie* constitute a case of nullification or impairment of benefits which other contracting parties were entitled to expect under the General Agreement.

18. On the basis of the conclusions reached above, the Panel finds that Norway should immediately either terminate its action taken under Article XIX or make it consistent with the provisions of Article XIII.

19. The Panel expresses the hope that in the light of this report the parties will be able to arrive at a mutually acceptable agreement.

OMITTED

EEC RESTRICTIONS ON IMPORTS OF APPLES FROM CHILE

Report of the Panel adopted on November 10, 1980
BISD 27S/98, 99

II. FACTUAL ASPECTS

2.1 The following is a brief description of the factual aspects of the EEC measures as the Panel understood them.

2.2 The European Economic Community has a common organization for the marketing of apples which includes common quality standards, an internal price support and intervention system, and a levy system on imports. When market prices fall below a certain minimum in representative markets, for three successive marketing days, member States are authorized to buy up at a certain price apples offered for intervention. Producer groups may also be compensated for effecting market withdrawals. Offer prices of apples from third countries are compared daily to a fixed minimum price, called a reference price which is based, *inter alia*, on EEC average costs of production. If for any origin the offer price is below the reference price, a compensatory tax is applied to apples of that origin in addition to the normal customs duty. In case there is a disruption of the Community market or threat thereof from imports, or in case of heavy EEC interventions or market withdrawals, the EC Commission is authorized under EEC regulations to suspend imports totally or partially or impose a supplementary charge on them.

2.3 At the beginning of 1979, the EC Commission undertook consultations with Southern Hemisphere supplying countries (Argentina, Australia, Chile, New Zealand and South Africa) in order to achieve voluntary restrictions of their respective apple shipments to the Community. Negotiations for similar arrangements had been carried out with these countries in 1976. Agreements were reached between the EEC and Argentina, Australia, New Zealand and South Africa but negotiations broke down in March 1979 between the EEC and Chile. The EC Commission had proposed 42,000 m.t. which was considered insufficient by Chile in that its exporters had already negotiated commercial contracts with EEC importers for up to 60,500 m.t.

2.4 On April 5, 1979, the EC Commission issued Regulation No. 687/79 which suspended the free circulation into the Community of apples (Common External Tariff No. 08.06 AII) originating from Chile for the period April 25 to August 15, 1979.

* * *

2.6 * * * [T]he EEC financed the grubbing-up of 54,876 hectares of apple orchards in 1969 and 8,852 hectares in 1976.

* * *

IV. CONCLUSIONS

Article I

4.1 The Panel examined the consistency of the EEC measures with the most-favored-nation principles of the General Agreement. The Panel considered it more appropriate to examine the matter in the context of Article XIII which deals with the non-discriminatory administration of quantitative restrictions rather than Article I:1. (See paragraphs 4.11 to 4.21.)

Article II

4.2 The Panel examined the EEC measure in relation to Article II:1(*a*) and (*b*). The Panel considered that the EEC import suspension did affect the value of the EEC tariff binding to Chile on apples. With reference to II:1(*b*), however, the Panel considered that the EEC measure was not strictly speaking a duty or charge in excess of the tariff concession provided in the EEC schedule. Therefore, the Panel considered that it was more appropriate to examine the EEC measure in the context of Article XI.

Article XI

4.3 The Panel examined the EEC measure in relation to Article XI:1 and found that the measure was a prohibition or restriction in terms of that paragraph. The Panel next examined whether the EEC measure could qualify as an exception to Article XI:1 under the provisions of Article XI:2*c* (i) or (ii).

4.4 The Panel considered that the EEC measure concerned an agricultural product and that Chilean apples, although of different varieties, were "a like product" to Community apples for the purposes of Article XI:2*c*.

4.5 As regards XI:2*c* (i), the Panel considered that the EEC grubbing-up programs in 1969 and 1976 seemed to be isolated actions of production control rather than steps in a continuing long-term policy of the Community to restrict production. The Panel noted that the programs had not resulted in any significant drop in EEC apple production.

4.6 The Panel considered that the EEC did restrict quantities of apples permitted to be marketed, through its system of intervention purchases by member States and compensation to producer groups for withdrawing apples from the market. The Panel considered that although the EEC measures occurred outside the EEC domestic production season, imports could have affected the possibilities for the disposal or release of EEC apples out of intervention on to the EEC market at that time.

4.7 The Panel noted, however, that measures taken under XI:2*c* (i) must also meet the criteria expressed in the last paragraph of XI:2. The Panel noted that the EEC had not given public notice of the quantities or values to be imported under the voluntary restraint agreements it had negotiated with Argentina, Australia, New Zealand and South Africa as required by the first sentence of this paragraph. The Panel considered that the evidence before it suggested that the EEC measures did not fulfill the conditions of the second sentence of this paragraph. According to that sentence, any restrictions applied under XI:2*c*(i) "shall not be such as will reduce the total of imports relative to the total of domestic production as compared with the proportion which might reasonably be expected to rule between the two in the absence of restrictions". The Panel found that the EEC had not maintained this proportion.

4.8 In making this finding, the Panel looked at total imports into the EEC from Southern Hemisphere suppliers, including Chile, as these were the main EEC suppliers during the marketing season concerned when restraints were in effect. The Panel looked at the proportion of these imports to EEC production "prevailing during a previous representative period" as provided in the third sentence of the last paragraph of XI:2. In keeping with normal GATT practice, the Panel considered it appropriate to use as a "representative period" a three-year period previous to 1979, the year in which the EEC measures were in effect. Due to the existence of restrictions in 1976, the Panel held that that year could not be considered as representative, and that the year immediately preceding 1976 should be used instead. The Panel thus chose the years 1975, 1977 and 1978 as a "representative period". The Panel noted that the proportion between total imports of apples from the Southern Hemisphere to total EEC production had been 5.7 per cent on the average during 1975, 1977 and 1978, and would have been 4.9 per cent in 1979 based on estimated export intentions of the Southern Hemisphere countries before restraints were put into place. The levels the EEC fixed during its negotiations of voluntary restraint agreements with the Southern Hemisphere countries (including Chile) totalled 313,000 m.t. which meant a proportion of imports to EEC production of 4.5 per cent.

4.9 As regards XI:2*c*(ii), the Panel found that the EEC was "making the surplus available to certain groups of domestic consumers free of charge or at prices below the current market level", in so far as the apples withdrawn from the market during 1978/79 went into animal feed as well as were distributed freely to social organizations. However, the Panel had doubts as to whether the EEC apple surplus could be considered a "temporary surplus" in terms of XI:2*c*(ii). The Panel noted that the EEC production statistics indicated the EEC has constantly had a surplus of apples over the years. On the other hand, it appeared from the statistics on monthly stocks in the EEC, that the levels of stocks during 1979 were significantly higher than normal.

4.10 In concluding its examination of the EEC measures in relation to Article XI, the Panel found that they met some but not all of the criteria contained in :2*c*(i) and (ii) in order to qualify as an exception to :1. The Panel found the EEC measures could not qualify as an exception to XI:1 under XI:2*c*(i) in that they had not fulfilled the conditions of the last paragraph of Article XI:2. As regards XI:2*c*(ii) the Panel thought that the EEC surplus of apples could not be considered "temporary" as it appeared year after year. However, the Panel noted that the surplus in 1979 was significantly higher than normal and could be considered to be a temporary surplus above the recurring surplus. Therefore, the Panel could not conclude that the EEC did not meet the conditions of XI:2*c*(ii) and proceeded to examine the EEC measures in relation to Article XIII.

Article XIII

4.11 The Panel examined the EEC measure in relation to Article XIII:1. The Panel found that the EEC suspension applied to imports from Chile was not a restriction similar to the voluntary restraint agreements negotiated with the other Southern Hemisphere suppliers on the basis primarily that:

(a) there was a difference in transparency between two types of action;

(b) there was a difference in the administration of the restrictions, the one being an import restriction, the other an export restraint; and

(c) the import suspension was unilateral and mandatory while the other was voluntary and negotiated.

4.12 The Panel noted that the EEC held that it had observed the provisions of Article XIII:2(*d*) in allocating shares among the Southern Hemisphere suppliers. Notwithstanding the Panel's conclusions regarding the lack of similarity of the restrictions with reference to Article XIII:1, and in light of XIII:5, the Panel proceeded to consider the EEC import suspension against Chile and the voluntary restraint agreements with other Southern Hemisphere exporters as "quotas" for purposes of the Panel's examination of the EEC measure under XIII:2.

4.13 The Panel noted that the first sentence of XIII:2 stated that "in applying import restrictions to any product, contracting parties shall aim at a distribution of trade in such product approaching as closely as possible the shares which the various contracting parties might be expected to obtain in the absence of such restrictions".

4.14 The Panel noted that XIII:2*a* stipulated that "wherever practicable, quotas representing the total amount of permitted imports (whether allocated among supplying countries or not) shall be fixed". The Panel also noted that the EEC had issued regulations in the Official Journal regarding the suspension of imports from Chile but that there had not been public notice given of the quantity or value of permitted imports under the voluntary restraints agreements. Such notice is required by XIII:2*a* and :3*b* first sentence.

4.15 The Panel noted that the EEC had held bilateral consultations with each Southern Hemisphere supplier "with respect to the allocation of shares in the quota" in keeping with XIII:2(*d*) first sentence but that it had not been possible to reach agreement with Chile. The Panel noted that XIII:2(*d*) second sentence states that "the contracting party concerned shall allot to contracting parties having a substantial interest in supplying the product shares based upon the proportions supplied by such contracting parties during a previous representative period, of the total quantity or value of imports of the product, due account being taken of any special factors which may have affected or may be affecting the trade in the product".

4.16 In this context, the Panel examined the volume of imports of apples into the EEC from the Southern Hemisphere. For reasons previously cited the Panel considered 1975, 1977 and 1978 as a "representative period" (see paragraph 4.8). On the basis of this representative period, the Chilean share of total EEC imports from the Southern Hemisphere would be 13.6 per cent. Thus a Chilean share of a quota of 313,000 m.t. would have been 42,600 m.t. using this percentage. This figure is close what the EEC allocated to Chile.

4.17 However, the Panel noted the fact that exports from Chile into the EEC had been expanding rapidly. Chile had more than doubled its share among Southern Hemisphere suppliers into the EEC market over a recent period, accounting for 5 per cent in 1974, 10 per cent in 1975, 13 per cent in 1976, 14 per cent in 1977 and 17 per cent in 1978. The Panel believed that Chile's increased export capacity should have been taken into account by the EEC in its allocation of shares among the Southern Hemisphere suppliers. The Panel felt such a consideration was in line with the interpretative note to the term "special factors" as drafted in the Havana Charter, in particular with reference to "the existence of new or additional ability to export" as between foreign producers.[1] Moreover, the Panel considered that the fact that Chilean exporters had signed commercial contracts with EEC importers to the amount of 60,500 m.t. further demonstrated Chile's increased export capacity and that these contracts should have been taken into account as a "special factor" as well.

4.18 The Panel was unable to determine precisely what the Chilean share should have been. Nevertheless, the Panel believed that Chile should have received at any rate a greater quota share than 42,000 m.t. because of the special factors mentioned above.

4.19 The Panel noted that at the time of the suspension, Chilean exporters had signed commercial contracts for 60,500 m.t. of apples with EEC importers. The Panel reviewed the *Standard Practices for the Administration of Import and Export Restrictions and Exchange Controls*[2] that were approved by the CONTRACTING PARTIES in 1950. These guidelines specify, *inter alia*, that:

[1] Havana Charter Interpretative Note and Article 22, paragraphs 2(*d*) and 4.
[2] GATT/CP.5/30/Rev.1.

(a) "any new or intensified restrictions on importation or exportation should not apply to goods shown to the satisfaction of the control authority to have been en route at the time the change was announced or to have been paid for in substantial part or covered by an irrevocable letter of credit" and

(b) "goods proven to have been covered by adequate confirmed prior order at the time new or intensified restrictions are announced, and not marketable elsewhere without appreciable loss should receive special consideration on an individual case basis, provided their delivery can be completed within a specified period."

The Panel noted however that these standard practices "should be regarded as a code for the guidance of contacting parties and not as additional obligations imposed upon them under the General Agreement" and that individual contracting parties "should endeavour to adopt them to the maximum practicable extent".

4.20 With the above in mind, the Panel examined whether the EEC measure against Chile was "retroactive" in the context of XIII:3(*b*) second sentence. The Panel found the EEC to be consistent therewith, as the EEC had not excluded from entry Chilean apples on board and destined for the EEC, at the time the EEC regulation regarding the import suspension was published.

4.21 In sum, the Panel found the EEC measure to be in conformity with Article XIII:3(*b*) second sentence. The Panel found the EEC measure was not in conformity with the most-favored-nation type obligations of Article XIII as it had not fulfilled the requirements of paragraphs 1 and 2(*d*) thereof. The Panel also found that the EEC had not conformed to the provisions regarding public notice under :2(*a*) and :3(*b*) first sentence.

Part IV

4.22 The Panel examined the EEC measure in relation to the objectives and commitments embodied in Articles XXXVI and XXXVII; in particular, XXXVII:1(*b*) which states that "the developed contracting parties shall to the fullest extent possible . . . refrain from introducing, or increasing the incidence of, customs duties or non-tariff import barriers on products currently or potentially of particular export interest to less-developed contracting parties".

4.23 Although the EEC measure did affect the ability of a developing country to export into the EEC market, the Panel noted that the EEC had taken certain actions, including bilateral consultations in order to avoid suspending imports of apples from Chile. After a careful examination, the Panel could not determine that the EEC had not made serious efforts to avoid taking protective measures against Chile. Therefore the Panel did not conclude that the EEC was in breach of its obligations under Part IV.

Article XXIII

4.24 The Panel examined the EEC measure to determine if there had been any nullification or impairment of any benefit accruing to Chile under the General Agreement within the meaning of Article XXIII. The Panel noted that Article XXIII:1 provided that nullification or impairment could be the result of:

"(a) the failure of another contracting party to carry out its obligations under the Agreement, or

(b) the application by another contracting party of any measure, whether or not it conflicts with the provisions of this Agreement, or

(c) the existence of any other situation."

In accordance with established GATT practice[1], the Panel considered that where a measure was applied which was judged to be inconsistent with the GATT obligations of the contracting party concerned, this action would *prima facie* constitute a case of nullification or impairment.

4.25 The Panel recalled that it had found the EEC measure not to be in conformity with Article XIII:1, :2(*a*), :2(*d*) and :3(*b*) first sentence. Accordingly, the Panel concluded that there was a *prima facie* case of nullification or impairment of benefits accruing to Chile within the meaning of Article XXIII.

4.26 In light of the above, the Panel was of the view that the economic interests of Chile had been adversely affected. The Panel considered that the CONTRACTING PARTIES should recommend that the EEC and Chile consult bilaterally with a view to arriving at a mutually satisfactory solution.

[1] BISD 11S/100, [Case 20] paragraph 15

EUROPEAN COMMUNITIES—REFUNDS ON EXPORTS OF SUGAR— COMPLAINT BY BRAZIL

Report of the Panel adopted on November 10, 1980
BISD 27S/69

I. INTRODUCTION

1.1 In a communication dated November 10, 1978 and which was circulated to contracting parties in document L/4722, the Government of Brazil requested the CONTRACTING PARTIES to establish a panel to examine a dispute between Brazil and the European Communities over Community export refunds for sugar.

* * *

IV. FINDINGS

(a) Introduction

4.1 The Panel has carried out its considerations of the matter referred to it for examination in the light of its terms of reference as expressed in paragraph 1.3. It has based its considerations on arguments presented to it by the parties to the dispute (Chapter II) and on various factual information which was available to it, notably that concerning the sugar market system of the European Communities and features of the world sugar market (Chapter III).

4.2 When examining the Community system for granting refunds on exports of sugar, the Panel found that such refunds were granted to enable Community sugar to be exported and that the refunds thus granted were financed out of the European Agriculture Guidance and Guarantee Fund. The Panel considered this Fund to be a government fund of the type mentioned in the Notes and Supplementary Provisions concerning Article XVI:3.[1]

[1] "Notwithstanding such determination by the CONTRACTING PARTIES, operations under such a system shall be subject to the provisions of paragraph 3

4.3 The Panel therefore found that the Community system for granting refunds on exports of sugar must be considered to be a form of subsidy and which was subject to the provisions of Article XVI. The Panel noted that the parties to the dispute were in agreement with this interpretation.

(b) The Complaint

4.4 The Panel understood the complaint of the Government of Brazil to be that the application of the Community system for granting refunds on exports of sugar has resulted in that the European Communities had more than an equitable share of world export trade in sugar, in terms of Article XVI:3, had caused or threatened to cause serious prejudice to Brazilian interests in terms of Article XVI:1 and that the application of the Community system was not in conformity with the guidelines for joint action stipulated in Article XXXVIII to further the principles and objectives of Article XXXVI.

(c) Relevant GATT Provisions

4.5 The Panel therefore noted that the relevant GATT provisions concerned were the following:

(i) Article XVI:1, last sentence:
"In any case in which it is determined that serious prejudice to the interests of any other contracting party is caused or threatened by any such subsidization, the contracting party granting the subsidy shall, upon request, discuss with the other contracting party or parties concerned, or with the CONTRACTING PARTIES, the possibility of limiting the subsidization."

(ii) Article XVI:3, last sentence:
"If, however, a contracting party grants directly or indirectly any form of subsidy which operates to increase the export of any primary product from its territory, such subsidy shall not be applied in a manner which results in that contracting party having more than an equitable share of world export trade in that product, account being taken of the shares of the contracting

where they are wholly or partly financed out of government funds in addition to the funds collected from producers in respect of the product concerned." (BISD, Vol. IV, page 68.)

parties in such trade in the product during a previous representative period, and any special factors which may have affected or may be affecting such trade in the product."

(iii) Article XXXVI, paragraphs 2, 3, 4 and 9:

"2. There is need for a rapid and sustained expansion of the export earnings of the less-developed contracting parties."

"3. There is a need for positive efforts designed to ensure that less-developed contracting parties secure a share in the growth in international trade commensurate with the needs of their economic development."

"4. Given the continued dependence of many less-developed contracting parties on the exportation of a limited range of primary products, there is need to provide in the largest possible measure more favorable and acceptable conditions of access to world markets for these products, and wherever appropriate to devise measures designed to stabilize and improve conditions of world markets in these products, including in particular measures designed to attain stable, equitable and remunerative prices, thus permitting an expansion of world trade and demand and a dynamic and steady growth of the real export earnings of these countries so as to provide them with expanding resources for their economic development."

"9. The adoption of measures to give effect to these principles and objectives shall be a matter of conscious and purposeful effort on the part of the contracting parties both individually and jointly."

(iv) Article XXXVIII:1

"1. The contracting parties shall collaborate jointly, within the framework of the Agreement and elsewhere, as appropriate, to further the objectives set forth in Article XXXVI."

(d) "More Than Equitable Share"

(i) General

4.6 The Panel noted that no complete definition of the concept "more than equitable share" had been provided, and neither had it in the past been considered absolutely necessary to have an agreed precise definition of the concept. The Panel felt that it was appropriate and sufficient in this case to try to analyze main reasons for developments in individual market shares, and in light of the circumstances related to the present complaint try to determine any causal relationship between the increase in Community exports of sugar, the developments in Brazilian sugar exports and other developments in the world sugar market, and then draw a conclusion on that basis.

4.7 The Panel furthermore noted Article 10:2(*a*) and (*b*) of the Agreement on Interpretation and Application of Articles VI, XVI and XXIII of the General Agreement on Tariffs and Trade, and which has been accepted by the parties to the dispute:

> "2. For purposes of Article XVI:3 of the General Agreement and paragraph 1 above:
>
> (*a*)'more than an equitable share of world export trade' shall include any case in which the effect of export subsidy granted by a signatory is to displace the exports of another signatory bearing in mind the developments on world markets;
>
> (*b*) with regard to new markets traditional patterns of supply of the product concerned to the world market, region or country, in which the new market is situated shall be taken into account in determining 'equitable share of world export trade';"

4.8 The Panel also noted that Brazil had presented its complaint before final data for 1978 were available and that it would even at the conclusion of its work only have preliminary data for 1979 at its disposal. The Panel nevertheless felt that it was appropriate to include not only 1978, but to the extent possible, also 1979 in its considerations, as the Community export system with respect to sugar had remained the same as in previous years and the effects of the application of the system may have been even more significant than previously. Furthermore, the complaint by Brazil also covered threat of serious prejudice. The Panel therefore felt it appropriate to take into consideration any available information about developments in recent periods and that this would be in conformity with earlier practice.[1]

4.9 Table 4 [omitted] shows the shares of world export trade for the European Communities; Brazil and "Others" for the two periods which the Panel considered to qualify as "previous representative periods", namely 1971-73 and 1972-74 and for the years 1976 to 1979, to which the

[1] BISD 25S/48 [Case 36]. BISD 26S/309 [Case 39] paragraph 4.13.

complaint referred. The Panel found that whichever of the two previous representative periods is used for comparison, the outcome would be fairly similar.

4.10 For the years 1976 and 1977, the Community share of world export trade in sugar showed some increase compared to average shares in 1971-73 and 1972-74, the increase corresponding to 0.5 to 2.1 percentage points. The very low market share for Brazil in 1976 was mainly due to a certain lack of sugar available for export caused by a reduced crop in 1975, low carry-over stocks and a continued increase in domestic consumption. In 1977, Brazilian sugar exports showed a good recovery and corresponded in absolute terms to the average for previous representative periods, but the market share did not reach the previous level. However, the Panel felt that Brazilian sugar exports in 1977 corresponded roughly to the quantities of sugar available for export, and that the comparatively low market share for Brazil was not necessarily due to increased Community exports.

4.11 For 1978, subsidized Community sugar exports were increased further, resulting in a significant increase in the Community share of world export trade in sugar. Exports from Brazil could not be increased in spite of ample supplies available for export and which would in themselves permit larger shipments to have been made. In 1978, the market share of Brazil was comparable to that in 1977 but remained inferior to the averages for the years 1971-73 and 1972-74. Preliminary data for 1979, available to the Panel, confirmed that the situation of 1978 had persisted in 1979. It was evident that the increase in Community sugar exports had been effected through the use of subsidies. The Panel therefore felt that the Community share of world export trade in sugar had increased in such proportions that a thorough examination of the situation was required.

(ii) Displacement

4.12 The Panel undertook systematic analysis of data for imports of sugar into a number of countries and also examined these data in detail with the parties to the dispute. The cases thus examined were selected markets which the representative of Brazil claimed constituted traditional outlets for Brazilian sugar, or new country markets located in those regions where Brazilian sugar had traditionally been offered for sale (countries listed in Annex Table IX).[1] The purpose of the analysis

[1] The Annex is not reproduced.

and examination was to determine whether subsidized Community sugar exports had displaced Brazilian exports of sugar.

4.13 Table 5 [omitted] shows total Brazilian and Community shares and that for "Others" for a selection of markets examined (countries listed in Annex Table IX).[1] For this selection of markets as a whole, the Community share started to increase in 1976 and was for the years 1978 and 1979 around two and a half times of what it had been in previous representative periods. Brazil's share which had been extremely low in 1976 (for reasons mentioned above), showed a good recovery in 1977, and the share then attained was more or less kept in the following years, but nevertheless remained inferior to the Brazilian share of the market in 1971–73 and 1972–74. The Panel therefore found that there was a change in the relative positions of Brazil and the European Communities for this group of markets as a whole.

4.14 Systematical analysis of trade statistics for individual markets did not produce statistically significant conclusions, and it was evident that developments had also been influenced by factors such as particular trade relations, competition from other exporters and prevailing market prices. The size and destination of Brazilian sugar exports in 1978 and 1979 were apparently also influenced by national sugar export policy. As an illustration it can be mentioned that in the major outlet for Brazilian sugar, i.e. the United States market, Brazilian sales which had been very low in 1975 and 1976 reached a level comparable to that of 1971–73 in 1977 and 1978. In 1979, Brazilian sales of sugar to the United States market exceeded 1 million tons, nearly twice the sales in previous years, resulting in Brazil having a share of that market of almost one fourth.

4.15 An examination of individual markets indicated that there was simultaneously a decline in Brazilian sales and an increase in imports from the European Communities only in a few markets (e.g. Lebanon, Morocco, Sudan and Tunisia), but in the majority of markets examined it was not possible to establish a clear relationship between developments in imports of sugar from Brazil and developments in imports of sugar from the European Communities. This systematic analysis thus did not provide clear and general evidence that Brazilian supplies had been directly displaced by subsidized exports of Community sugar.

[1] The Annex is not reproduced.

(iii) Special Factors

4.16 The entering into force on January 1, 1978 of the International Sugar Agreement, 1977, apparently had a strong impact on the volume of world sugar trade in 1977 already. In 1977, total world exports of sugar exceeded 28 million tons, with an increase of one quarter from the previous year, the largest annual increase ever recorded. These developments were due to efforts made by exporters to ship as much sugar as possible before the entry into operation of export quotas under the ISA on January 1, 1978, and also to an expectation prevailing among refiners and importers that prices might increase with the entry into force of the ISA.

4.17 However, as supplies continued to be affluent, world market prices for sugar remained depressed throughout 1978 and most of 1979. With a situation of depressed prices for sugar in the world market, major exporting members were committed to limit their exports to 85 per cent or less of their basic export tonnages stipulated in the ISA[1]. For major sugar exporting countries having acceded to the ISA, the result was a substantial contraction in their exports. In practice this meant that nearly 2 million tons of sugar was withheld from world markets by these countries both in 1978 and 1979. However, these efforts did not immediately result in a better market equilibrium as total supplies offered in the world market remained in excess of demand, due to increased exports under special arrangements not subject to the limitations under the ISA and to increased exports from countries not being members of the ISA. Among the non-members to the ISA, the European Communities accounted for nearly three quarters of the total supplies coming from these countries in 1978.[2] As a consequence, supplies of sugar to the world market remained high in 1978 and 1979 and prices did not improve before late in 1979. Major exporting members of the ISA were thus unable to obtain any immediate benefits of their efforts to stabilize the world sugar market. Export quotas were maintained at their minimum level in 1978 and 1979, and it was impossible to increase basic export tonnages as well. In this situation, Brazil was committed to limit its exports to 81.5 per cent of its basic export tonnages under the ISA, but this reduced quota was filled and even exceeded slightly both in 1978 and 1979.

[1] Article 41 of the International Sugar Agreement, 1977.
[2] ISO Annual Report for the year 1978, page 32.

(iv) Effects of the Operation of Community Regulations

4.18 The Panel proceeded to an examination of whether the increase in 1976 to 1979 in Community sugar exports, notably the increase in the Community share of world sugar export trade could be attributed to the operation of the Community regulations. With regard to production, the Panel noted that the Community system may put an economic but not necessarily legal limit to the size of the production.

4.19 Some basic data for production, trade, consumption and stocks of sugar, for Brazil and the European Communities are shown in Annex Table I[1], and, for comparison, world totals for the same in Annex Table II[1]. A simple comparison of the figures in these tables indicates that the increase in the Community sugar production corresponded roughly to the world average until 1978. For illustrative purposes, it can be mentioned that the Brazilian sugar production showed a stronger increase over the same period.

4.20 Graph 1 shows developments in Community sugar production, consumption and target prices from 1969 to 1979. Up to 1977, the Community area under sugar beet increased with the increase in the Community target price, the price policy, apparently being a stimulating factor. Although the increase in the target price was halted in 1977, and the area of sugar beet was reduced, total Community sugar production continued to increase because of higher average yields. Preliminary data for 1979 indicated that area, yields and total production remained at a level comparable to that of 1978.

4.21 It can be seen from Annex Table I and Graph 1 that there was a downwards shift in the Community sugar consumption in 1975 contributing together with a continued growth in production, significantly to increase exportable surpluses of sugar.

4.22 The Panel noted that the fixing of production quotas was of decisive importance for the application of the price system for sugar in the European Communities. It also noted that in 1975 the basic quota was raised from 7.82 million tons to 9.14 million tons and the maximum quota was maintained at 145 per cent of the basic quota. The basic quota was then maintained in the following years, but the maximum quota was reduced to 135 per cent in 1976 and reduced further to 127.5 per cent in 1978 and maintained at that level for 1979/80 (Annex Table VIII).[1]

4.23 Furthermore, the Panel noted that sugar produced in excess of

[1] The Annex is not reproduced.

the basic quota, but within the limits of the maximum quota, was subject to a production levy of up to 30 per cent of the intervention price. Although this step was followed by a smaller area planted with sugar beets in 1977 and 1978, total production continued to increase, as yields were higher. The steps taken (i.e. reduced maximum quotas for 1978 and 1979 and the collection of production levies at their maximum level for 1977/78, 1978/79 and 1979/80) were therefore not sufficient to prevent the exportable surplus from increasing further in 1977 and 1978, and to remain at a high level in 1979.

4.24 The Panel understood the Community system of regulations concerning the sugar markets to imply that the quantity exported from the European Communities with an export refund would be limited by the total of maximum production quotas, plus imports under special arrangements minus domestic consumption. Any sugar produced in excess of maximum quotas must be disposed of on external markets without benefiting from any refund. Table 3 [omitted] shows Community exports totally and with a breakdown into exports with refunds and exports without refunds in 1972-1978. A comparison of figures for 1976, 1977 and 1978 with averages for 1972-1974, indicates clearly that the increase in Community sugar exports in 1976-1978 mainly consisted of increased exports with export refunds, i.e. sugar produced within the maximum quota. Both in 1976 and 1977, exports without refunds were inferior to the average for 1972-1974. Although Community exports without refund (C-sugar) showed some increase in 1977 and 1978, the reduction in maximum quotas and the application of production levies had not prevented that exports with refund continued to increase even in 1978, and still counted for 76 per cent of Community sugar exports.

4.25 The Panel noted the strong increase in the total amount spent by the European Communities on refunds of sugar in 1977, 1978 and 1979. This was partly due to larger Community exports entitled to refund and to falling world market prices, but partly also due to the annual increases in the Community market intervention price for sugar. When examining the question of whether Community export refunds could be subject to budgetary limits, the Panel noted that if the appropriations originally allocated to the Guarantee Section of the European Agriculture Guidance and Guarantee Fund proved to be insufficient in any particular year, the Commission could have recourse to a supplementary budget during the financial year and there would thus be no legally fixed budgetary limits for how much could be spent on export refunds for sugar.

4.26 The Panel felt that in those conditions neither exportable surpluses of sugar nor the amount of export refunds granted had been effectively limited as a result of the Community system or its application. There was no element in the system and its application that would prevent the European Communities from having more than an equitable share of world export trade in sugar.

(e) Effect on World Market Prices

4.27 In examining more in detail the granting of export refunds on sugar by the European Communities, the Panel noted that for the quasi-totality of exports with refunds, the refunds were granted under the tendering procedure (e.g. for 91 per cent in 1976, 97 per cent in 1977 and almost 100 per cent in 1978 and 1979). Under the tendering procedure, the Commission fixed maximum amounts of refunds and for a given quantity, taking into account the supply situation and prices within the Community, prices and potential outlets on the world market, and costs incurred in exporting sugar. The Commission's determination of what were world market prices for sugar was based on the amount of refund proposed in the tenders, which were occasionally based on prices lower than the average quotations for white sugar published by the Paris Exchange. In such situations, Brazilian sugar, (notably white sugar), which in the absence of long-term contracts was offered at prevailing world market prices (i.e. London and New York quotations), was at a disadvantage and had difficulties in competing with subsidized Community sugar (e.g. in Iran, Israel, Kuwait and Nigeria).

4.28 The Panel noted that the weighted average of export refunds usually corresponded to the difference between the Community intervention price at F.O.B. stage and average spot quotations for white sugar on the Paris Exchange (Annex Table VII).[1] However, towards the end of the crop years 1975/76, 1976/1977, and 1977/1978 the weighted average refund had tended to exceed that difference (Annex Table VII).[1] The Panel also noted that from the middle of 1976 on, Community export refunds were increased sharply with only little difference between weighted average refunds and maximum refunds. These developments coincided with a sharp decline in world market prices. Furthermore, the premium for white sugar had diminished, and at times white sugar had been quoted at prices lower than those quoted for raw sugar.

4.29 The Panel felt that since the Community sugar exporters were leading the world market for white sugar, traditionally covering more

[1] The Annex is not reproduced.

than half of the world market for refined sugar, the availability of exportable Community surpluses of sugar combined with the possibility of non-limited amounts available to cover export refunds, inevitably must have had an amplifying effect on the depressed world market prices for sugar, both white and raw sugar.

(f) Article XXXVI and XXXVIII

4.30 The Panel noted the principles and objectives stipulated in Article XXXVI and the guidelines for joint action given in Article XXXVIII to further the objectives set forth in Article XXXVI, and that Brazil being a developing country could expect to enjoy benefits in accordance with these provisions. In this connexion, the Panel also noted that the European Communities had made considerable efforts in favor of a number of developing countries and had pursued an active and constructive policy towards the setting-up of international agreements.

4.31 However, the Panel also noted that in the particular situation in the sugar market in 1978 and 1979, when Brazil and other developing countries took action through the ISA to improve the market situation, the European Communities increased its subsidized sugar exports to an extent that inevitably reduced significantly the effects of the measures taken by Brazil and other sugar exporters. It was evident that the magnitude of subsidized Community sugar exports together with the extensive use of maximum export refunds, tended to accentuate the detrimental effect on export earnings of other sugar exporters directly faced with the competition from Community sugar. The Panel felt that even though the European Communities was not a party to the ISA and not bound by the same obligations as members to that Agreement, it would nevertheless be appropriate to collaborate with other contracting parties in conformity with the guidelines given in Article XXXVIII and thus further the principles and objectives of Article XXXVI.

V. CONCLUSION

In the light of the foregoing, the Panel reached the following conclusions:

(a) The Panel found that the Community system for granting refunds on exports of sugar must be considered to be a form of subsidy and thus subject to the provisions of Article XVI, and it noted that the parties to the dispute were in agreement with this interpretation.

(b) The Panel noted that Brazilian sugar exports had been extremely low in 1976, but that this was due to other factors than competition from Community sugar and furthermore that Brazilian exports in 1977 corresponded roughly to the quantities available for export. The Panel therefore concluded that although the Community share of world export trade in sugar had increased somewhat in 1976 and 1977, this increase was not to be considered as unusual and did not explain the reduced market share of Brazil in these years.

(c) For the years 1978 and 1979 (according to preliminary figures), the Panel found that the Community share of world export trade in sugar was significantly higher than in previous representative periods, while the market share of Brazil was comparable to that of 1977, but remained inferior to averages for previous representative periods. The Panel furthermore found that for a group of markets where it was believed to have been a direct competition between Community and Brazilian sugar, the Community share had increased even stronger, while the share of Brazil basically maintained its level of 1977. Further expansion in Brazilian exports in 1978 and 1979 was limited by Brazilian commitments under the ISA, but Brazil filled and even exceeded slightly its reduced ISA export quotas in both years.

(d) A close examination of individual markets did not provide clear and general evidence that Community exports had directly displaced Brazilian exports. There was simultaneously a decline in Brazilian sales and an increase in imports from the European Communities in only a few markets of minor importance.

(e) Therefore, in light of all the circumstances related to the present complaint and especially taking into account the difficulties in establishing clearly the causal relationships between the increase in Community exports, the developments of Brazilian sugar exports and other developments in the world sugar market, the Panel found that on the basis of the evidence available to it in this particular case, it was not able to conclude that the increased share had resulted in the European Communities "having more than an equitable share of world export trade in the product", in terms of Article XVI:3.

(f) The Panel concluded that in view of the quantity of Community sugar made available for export with maximum refunds and the non-limited funds available to finance export refunds, the Community system of granting export refunds on sugar had been applied in a manner which in the particular market situation prevailing in 1978 and 1979, contributed to depress sugar prices in the world market, and that this constituted a serious prejudice to Brazilian interests, in terms of Article XVI:1.

(g) The Panel found that the Community system of export refunds for sugar did not comprise any pre-established effective limitations in respect of either production, price or the amounts of export refunds and that the Community system had not been applied in a manner so as to limit effectively neither exportable surpluses nor the amount of refunds granted. Neither the system nor its application would prevent the European Communities from having more than an equitable share of world export trade in sugar. The Panel, therefore, concluded that the Community system and its application constituted a permanent source of uncertainty in world sugar markets and therefore constituted a threat of serious prejudice in terms of Article XVI:1.

(h) The Panel recognized the efforts made by the European Communities in complying with the provisions of Articles XXXVI and XXXVIII. It nevertheless felt that increased Community exports of sugar through the use of subsidies in the particular market situation in 1978 and 1979, and where developing contracting parties had taken steps within the framework of the ISA to improve the conditions in the world sugar market, inevitably reduced the effects of the efforts made by these countries. For this time-period and for this particular field, the European Communities had therefore not collaborated jointly with other contracting parties to further the principles and objectives set forth in Article XXXVI, in conformity with the guidelines given in Article XXXVIII.

EUROPEAN ECONOMIC COMMUNITY—IMPORTS OF BEEF FROM CANADA

Report of the Panel adopted on March 10, 1981
BISD 28S/92, 97

IV. FINDINGS AND CONCLUSIONS

4.1 (*a*) The Panel examined the conformity of the EEC regulations [concerning high quality beef imports] with the provisions of *Article I, paragraph 1*. In this connexion the Panel noted that paragraph 1 provided for most-favored-nation treatment of like products irrespective of their origin.

(*b*) The Panel further noted: in order to implement the high quality grain fed beef concession that the EEC had granted during the Multilateral Trade Negotiations, the EEC Commission issued detailed rules for the importation of this meat; Commission Regulation (EEC) No. 2972/79 specified in its paragraph 1(*d*) of Article 1, the quality of meat to be imported under this concession, and provided that "Beef graded USDA 'choice' or 'prime' automatically meets the definition above".[1]

(*c*) The Panel also noted: the suspension of the import levy for the meat in paragraph 1(*d*) was subject to a certificate of authenticity, valid only if completed and endorsed by the appropriate issuing authority listed in Annex II; the "Food Safety and Quality Service (FSQS) of the United States Department of Agriculture (USDA)" was the only authority listed as certifying agency for the meat in question, it being specified that this agency was empowered to certify "meat originating in the United States, answering the definition of Article 1(1)(*d*)"; an import licence was needed for the meat referred to in Article 1(1)(*d*) of the Regulation.

[1] Article 1, paragraph 1(*d*) reads: "10,000 tons, product weight, of fresh, chilled or frozen meat, falling within subheadings 02.01 A II (*a*) and 02.01 A II (*b*) of the Common Customs Tariff and answering the following definition: Carcasses or any cuts from cattle not over thirty months of age which have been fed for 100 days or more on a nutritionally balanced, high energy feed concentration ration containing no less than 70 per cent grain and at least 20 pounds total feed per day. Beef graded USDA 'choice' or 'prime' automatically meets the definition above."

(*d*) The Panel also noted the assertion by Canada that it could certify that the meat Canada proposed to export to the EEC under this quota, met the exact product specifications required for access.

4.2 (*a*) The Panel found that products meeting the description in Article 1(1)(*d*) of Commission Regulation (EEC) 2972/79 were "like products" for the purposes of Article I of the General Agreement. The Panel further found that exports of like products of other origin than that of United States were in effect denied access to the EEC market considering that the only certifying agency authorized to certify the meat described in Article 1(1)(*d*), listed in Annex II of the Commission Regulation, was a United States agency mandated to certify only meat from the United States.

(*b*) The Panel further found that the mention "Beef graded USDA 'choice', or 'prime' automatically meets the definition above" could accord an advantage to products of United States' origin insofar as other like products were not mentioned in the same manner. The Panel found, however, that only the practical application of the Commission Regulation would make it possible to judge whether this mention in itself was inconsistent with Article I of the General Agreement.

4.3 The Panel *concluded* that Commission Regulation (EEC) No. 2972/79 and its Annex II, in their present form had the effect of preventing access of "like products" from other origin than the United States, thus being inconsistent with the most-favored-nation principle in Article I of the General Agreement.

4.4 (*a*) The Panel examined the conformity of the EEC regulations with the provisions of *Article II, paragraph 1* of the General Agreement. In this connexion the Panel noted that paragraph 1 stipulated that "Each contracting party shall accord to the commerce of the other contracting parties treatment no less favorable than that provided for . . . " in the "appropriate schedule . . . ". It also noted that products described in the schedules "shall, on their importation into the territory to which the Schedule relates, and subject to the terms, conditions or qualifications set forth in that Schedule, be exempt from ordinary customs duties in excess of those set forth and provided for therein".

(*b*) The Panel further noted: The levy-free tariff quota concerning 10,000 tons of high quality beef was bound in Schedule LXXII of the EEC, Part I, tariff sub-headings 02.01 A II (*a*) and 02.01 A II (*b*) at a rate of 20 per cent. In a footnote to the concession it was provided that "Entry under this subheading is subject to conditions to be determined by the competent authorities"; furthermore, in the Introductory Notes to Schedule LXXII the following paragraph was included, pertaining to the concession in question: "The implementation of this concession will follow strictly, as far as dates are concerned, that applied by the Community's partners in the same sector."

(*c*) The Panel also noted: The Concession was implemented by Council Regulation (EEC) No. 2957/79 whereas Regulation (EEC) No. 2972/79 provided detailed rules concerning the application of the import arrangements; the latter regulation provided for quite detailed rules and conditions as concerns formalities to be completed, such as providing a certificate of authenticity and an import licence.

4.5 (*a*) The Panel found that the European Economic Community had, by virtue of the footnote in the Schedule reserved its right to set conditions for the entry under the levy-free tariff quota in question. The Panel further found that the right to set conditions was presupposed in Article II:1(*b*) of the General Agreement. The Panel found, however, that the words "terms, conditions or qualifications" in paragraph 1(*b*) of Article II could not be interpreted to mean that countries could explicitly or by the manner in which a concession was administered actually limit a given concession to the products of a particular country.

(*b*) The Panel further found that the fact that in Annex II there was only one certifying agency for the meat in question and that this agency only certified meat of United States origin in effect prevented access of high quality meat as described in Article 1(1)(*d*) of Commission Regulation (EEC) 2972/79 from other countries.

4.6 Consequently, the Panel *concluded* that the manner in which the EEC concession on high quality beef was implemented accorded less favorable treatment to Canada than that provided for in the relevant EEC Schedule, thus being inconsistent with the provisions of paragraph 1 of Article II of the General Agreement.

4.7 The Panel noted the reference made by the European Economic Community to the importance of a *balance of concessions* and also its reference in this regard to paragraph 5 of the Tokyo Declaration. The Panel agreed that the achievement of a satisfactory balance was an important consideration of the participants in a negotiation. However the Panel did not find reason to consider the question of balance between the parties in relation to the matter before it. The Panel found that when a multilateral negotiation under the auspices of the GATT had been completed, the concessions granted would have to be implemented as laid down in the Schedules and on the basis of the relevant provisions of the General Agreement. Therefore, the Panel *concluded* that considerations pertaining to the balance between concessions could not modify its findings.

4.8 The Panel examined the conformity of the EEC regulations with the provisions of *Article XXIII*. It noted that nullification or impairment of a benefit accruing directly or indirectly under the General Agreement to a contracting party could be the result of:

"(a) the failure of another contracting party to carry out its obligations under this Agreement, or

(b) the application by another contracting party of any measure, whether or not it conflicts with the provisions of the Agreement, or

(c) the existence of any other situation."

4.9 The Panel found that the infringement of Articles I and II of the General Agreement, referred to in paragraphs 4.3 and 4.6 above, constituted *prima facie* nullification or impairment of benefits in the sense of Article XXIII, accruing directly or indirectly to Canada under the General Agreement. It *proposed*, therefore, that the CONTRACTING PARTIES should recommend to the authorities of the European Economic Community to take the necessary steps to make the implementation of the concession consistent with the provisions of the General Agreement.

OMITTED

OMITTED

SPAIN—TARIFF TREATMENT OF UNROASTED COFFEE

Report of the Panel adopted on June 11, 1981
BISD 28S/102, 103

II. FACTUAL ASPECTS

2.1 The following is a brief description of factual aspects of the matter under dispute as the Panel understood them.

2.2 On July 8, 1979, the Spanish authorities enacted the Royal Decree No. 1764/79 (B.O.E. of July 20) by which the tariff treatment and the sub-tariff classification applied to imports of unroasted, non-decaffeinated coffee (ex. CCCN 09.01) were modified and amended, effective by March 1, 1980. Imports of unroasted coffee, which prior to this last date entered Spain's customs territory under one and the same designation, was subdivided into five tariff lines to which duty rates applied as follows: [Colombian mild and other mild–free; unwashed Arabica, Robusta and other–7% ad valorem.]

* * *

IV. FINDINGS AND CONCLUSIONS

4.1 The Panel has carried out its consideration of the matter referred to it for examination in the light of its terms of reference and on the basis of various factual information which was available to it, and of arguments presented to it by the parties to the dispute.

4.2 The Panel considered that it was called upon to examine whether the Spanish tariff régime for unroasted coffee introduced by Spain through the Royal Decree 1764/79 (ref. paragraph 2.2) was consistent with Spanish obligations under the GATT, and more precisely whether it was in conformity with the most-favored-nation provision of Article I:1.

4.3 Having noted that Spain had not bound under the GATT its tariff rate on unroasted coffee, the Panel pointed out that Article I:1 equally applied to bound and unbound tariff items.

4.4 The Panel found that there was no obligation under the GATT to follow any particular system for classifying goods, and that a contracting party had the right to introduce in its customs tariff new positions or subpositions as appropriate.[1] The Panel considered, however, that, whatever the classification adopted, Article I:1 required that the same tariff treatment be applied to "like products".

4.5 The Panel, therefore, in accordance with its terms of reference, focused its examination on whether the various types of unroasted coffee listed in the Royal Decree 1764/79 should be regarded as "like products" within the meaning of Article I:1. Having reviewed how the concept of "like products" had been applied by the CONTRACTING PARTIES in previous cases involving, *inter alia*, a recourse to Article I:1[2], the Panel noted that neither the General Agreement nor the settlement of previous cases gave any definition of such concept.

4.6 The Panel examined all arguments that had been advanced during the proceedings for the justification of a different tariff treatment for various groups and types of unroasted coffee. It noted that these arguments mainly related to organoleptic differences resulting from geographical factors, cultivation methods, the processing of the beans, and the genetic factor. The Panel did not consider that such differences were sufficient reason to allow for a different tariff treatment. It pointed out that it was not unusual in the case of agricultural products that the taste and aroma of the end-product would differ because of one or several of the above-mentioned factors.

4.7 The Panel furthermore found relevant to its examination of the matter that unroasted coffee was mainly, it not exclusively, sold in the form of blends, combining various types of coffee, and that coffee in its end-use, was universally regarded as a well-defined and single product intended for drinking.

4.8 The Panel noted that no other contracting party applied its tariff régime in respect of unroasted, non-decaffeinated coffee in such a way that different types of coffee were subject to different tariff rates.

4.9 In the light of the foregoing, the Panel *concluded* that unroasted, non-decaffeinated coffee beans listed in the Spanish Customs Tariffs under CCCN 09.01 A.1a, as amended by the Royal Decree 1764/79,

[1] Provided that a reclassification subsequent to the making of a concession under the GATT would not be a violation of the basic commitment regarding that concession (Article II:5).

[2] BISD Vol. II/188 [Case 5]; BISD 1S/53 [Case 7]; BISD 25S/49 [Case 35]; BISD 27S/98 [Case 43].

should be considered as "like products" within the meaning of Article I:1.

4.10 The Panel further noted that Brazil exported to Spain mainly "unwashed Arabica" and also Robusta coffee which were both presently charged with higher duties than that applied to "mild" coffee. Since these were considered to be "like products", the Panel *concluded* that the tariff régime as presently applied by Spain was discriminatory vis-à-vis unroasted coffee originating in Brazil.

4.11 Having recalled that it found the tariff régime for unroasted coffee introduced by Spain through the Royal Decree 1764/79 not to be in conformity with the provision of Article I:1, the Panel further concluded that this constituted *prima facie* a case of impairment of benefits accruing to Brazil within the meaning of Article XXIII.

4.12 In the light of the above, the Panel suggest that the CONTRACTING PARTIES request Spain to take the necessary measures in order to make its tariff régime for unroasted coffee conform to Article I:1.

OMITTED

UNITED STATES—PROHIBITION OF IMPORTS OF TUNA AND TUNA PRODUCTS FROM CANADA

Report of the Panel adopted on February 22, 1982
BISD 29S/91, 105

IV. FINDINGS AND CONCLUSIONS

4.1 In accordance with its terms of reference as set out in paragraph 1.3, the Panel focused its work on an examination of the measures taken by the United States concerning imports of tuna and tuna products from Canada, in the light of relevant GATT provisions. It noted, however, that the dispute was part of a wider disagreement between Canada and the United States mainly related to fisheries and that the trade aspect constituted a part of a broader complex.

4.2 In the course of its work and in accordance with established practice[1], the Panel consulted regularly with the parties and repeatedly encouraged them in light of developments taking place to reach a mutually acceptable solution to the dispute. In this connection, the Panel noted that following continued bilateral discussions between the parties, an interim arrangement on albacore tuna fisheries between Canada and the United States was reached in August 1980. It also noted that the United States subsequently lifted the prohibition on imports of tuna and tuna products from Canada, with effect from September 4, 1980. The Panel furthermore noted that subsequent negotiations between the parties resulted in the establishment of the Treaty on Pacific Coast Albacore Tuna Vessels and Port Privileges which was signed on May 26, 1981 and ratified on July 29, 1981. This Treaty replaced the interim agreement of August 1980.

4.3 In light of these developments the Panel noted that according to prevailing GATT practice when a bilateral settlement to a dispute had been found, panels had usually confined their reports to a brief description of the case indicating that a solution had been reached.[2] However, it

[1] BISD 26S/210.

[2] BISD 25S/107 [Case 37]; BISD 26S/320 [Case 40]; BISD 28S/100 [Case 47]; BISD 28S/90 [Case 46]; BISD 28S/113 [Case 49].

also noted that in the past, panels had on occasion presented a complete report even if the measure giving rise to the dispute had been disinvoked.[1] It furthermore noted that the representative of Canada did not accept that the results obtained bilaterally constituted a satisfactory solution or settlement in terms of paragraph 17 of the Understanding Regarding Notification, Consultation, Dispute Settlement and Surveillance,[2] and that he argued that the damage caused by the action which gave rise to the dispute had not been satisfactorily repaired, and that the threat of the United States taking action under Section 205 of the Fishery Conservation and Management Act of 1976 continued to exist. He therefore requested the Panel to present a substantial report on the case. The Panel noted that the Canadian Embassy, in a diplomatic note to the Department of State of the United States (No. 423, Washington DC, August 21, 1980), indicated that the arrangements concerning fisheries for albacore tuna off the Pacific coasts of Canada and the United States were without prejudice to action brought before the GATT regarding import prohibition on tuna and tuna products. The Panel also noted that the representative of the United States, although expressing serious doubts about the usefulness of establishing a comprehensive report when a conciliation on the dispute had been achieved, nevertheless declared himself willing and ready to provide his full cooperation if the Panel wanted to establish a comprehensive report. The Panel consequently felt that in this particular case it had to consider itself what type of report it should present to the Council and decided to proceed with its work and establish a complete report.

4.4 The Panel started by examining the complaint by Canada that the United States import prohibition on tuna and tuna products from Canada was contrary to Article XI. The Panel noted the provisions of Article XI:1.[3] It found that the United States Government decision of 31 August 1979[4] to prohibit with immediate effect the entry for consumption or withdrawal from warehouse for consumption of tuna and tuna products from Canada constituted a prohibition in terms of Article XI:1. The Panel, therefore, examined the legal basis of the United States import

[1] BISD 25S/49 [Case 35].

[2] BISD 26S/213.

[3] "No prohibitions or restrictions other than duties, taxes or other charges, whether made effective through quotas, import or export licences or other measures, shall be instituted or maintained by any contracting party on the importation of any product of the territory of any other contracting party or on the exportation or sale for export of any product destined for the territory of any other contracting party." (BISD Volume IV, page 17).

[4] United States—Federal Register, Vol. 44, No. 178 (September 12, 1979).

prohibition on tuna and tuna products from Canada in light of the exceptions to the provisions of Article XI:1 listed in Article XI:2.

4.5 The Panel noted that the decision of the United States Government was based on Section 205 of the United States Fishery Conservation and Management Act of 1976. The Panel was informed that the purpose of the Fishery Conservation and Management Act of 1976 was to ensure that certain stocks of fish were properly conserved and managed, to support and encourage the implementation and enforcement of international fishery agreements for the conservation and management of highly migratory species, and to encourage the negotiation and implementation of such additional agreements as necessary. It furthermore noted that Section 205 of the Fishery Conservation and Management Act of 1976 contained provisions designed to discourage other countries from seeking to manage tuna unilaterally and from seizing United States fishing vessels which were fishing more than 12 miles off their coasts.

4.6 The Panel also noted that the United States had applied limitations on the catch of some species of tuna (e.g. Pacific and Atlantic yellowfin and Atlantic bluefin and bigeye), during the time the import prohibitions on tuna and tuna products from Canada had been in force. The Panel found, however, that even if an import restriction could, at least partly, have been necessary to the enforcement of measures taken to restrict the catches of certain tuna species, an import prohibition on all tuna and tuna products from Canada as applied by the United States from August 31, 1979 to September 4, 1980 would not sufficiently meet the requirements of Article XI:2, firstly because the measure applied to species for which the catch had not so far been restricted in the United States (such as albacore and skipjack) and secondly because it was maintained when restrictions on the catch were no longer maintained (e.g. Pacific yellowfin tuna in 1980). Furthermore the Panel noted the difference in language between Article XI:2(*a*) and (*b*) and Article XI:2(*c*), and it felt that the provisions of Article XI;2(*c*), could not justify the application of an import prohibition.[1]

4.7 The Panel noted that the representative of the United States based his arguments concerning the justification for the action taken against imports of tuna and tuna products from Canada entirely on Article XX(*g*).[2] The Panel therefore proceeded to an examination of the

[1] In Article XI:2(*a*) and (*b*) the words "prohibitions or restrictions" are used while in Article XI:2(*c*) mention is only made of "restrictions".

[2] "Subject to the requirement that such measures are not applied in a manner which would constitute a means of arbitrary or unjustifiable discrimination

arguments presented in respect of this Article by both the representatives of the United States and Canada.

4.8 The Panel noted the preamble to Article XX. The United States action of August 31, 1979 had been taken exclusively against imports of tuna and tuna products from Canada,[2] but similar actions had been taken against imports from Costa Rica, Ecuador, Mexico and Peru and then for similar reasons. The Panel felt that the discrimination of Canada in this case might not necessarily have been arbitrary or unjustifiable. It furthermore felt that the United States action should not be considered to be a disguised restriction on international trade, noting that the United States prohibition of imports of tuna and tuna products from Canada had been taken as a trade measure and publicly announced as such. The Panel therefore considered it appropriate to examine further the United States import prohibition of tuna and tuna products from Canada in light of the list of specific types of measures contained in Article XX, and notably in Article XX(*g*).

4.9 The Panel furthermore noted that both parties considered tuna stocks, including albacore tuna, to be an exhaustible natural resource in need of conservation management and that both parties were participating in international conventions aimed, *inter alia*, at a better conservation of such stocks. However, attention was drawn to the fact that Article XX(*g*) contained a qualification on measures relating to the conservation if they were to be justified under that Article, namely that such measures were made effective in conjunction with restrictions on domestic production or consumption.

4.10 The Panel noted that the action taken by the United States applied to imports from Canada of all tuna and tuna products, and that the United States could at various times apply restrictions to species of tuna covered by the IATTC and the ICCAT. However, restrictions on domestic production (catch) had so far been applied only to Pacific yellowfin tuna, from July to December 1979 under the Tuna Convention Act (related to the IATTC) and to Atlantic yellowfin tuna, bluefin and bigeye tuna under the Atlantic Tunas Convention Act (related to the

between countries where the same conditions prevail, or a disguised restriction on international trade, nothing in this Agreement shall be construed to prevent the adoption or enforcement by any contracting party of measures:

. . .

(*g*) relating to the conservation of exhaustible natural resources if such measures are made effective in conjunction with restrictions on domestic production or consumption". (BISD Volume IV, pages 37 and 38).

[2] United States—Federal Register, Vol. 44, No. 178 (September 12, 1979).

ICCAT), and no restrictions has been applied to the catch or landings of any other species of tuna, such as for instance albacore.

4.11 The Panel also noted that the United States representative had provided no evidence that domestic consumption of tuna and tuna products had been restricted in the United States.

4.12 The Panel could therefore not accept it to be justified that the United States prohibition of imports of all tuna and tuna products from Canada as applied from August 31, 1979 to September 4, 1980, had been made effective in conjunction with restrictions on United States domestic production or consumption on all tuna and tuna products.

4.13 The Panel also noted that the United States prohibition of imports of all tuna and tuna products from Canada had been imposed in response to Canadian arrest of United States vessels fishing albacore tuna. The Panel could not find that this particular action would in itself constitute a measure of a type listed in Article XX.

4.14 The Panel furthermore noted that the amount of trade in tuna and tuna products affected by the action taken by the United States was relatively small with annual totals varying between US$ 172 thousand [sic] to U$ [sic] 1.6 million in 1976-79 according to figures supplied by the representative of the United States. However, as the measure which gave rise to the dispute was lifted after one year, as subsequent negotiations between the parties had resulted in the establishment of a treaty on albacore tuna fisheries, and as no detailed submission had been made as to exactly what benefits accruing to Canada under the General Agreement had been nullified or impaired, the Panel did not consider the question of possible compensation.

4.15 In the light of the foregoing, the Panel *concluded* that the United States embargo on imports of tuna and tuna products from Canada as applied from August 31, 1979 to September 4, 1980 was not consistent with the provisions of Article XI. It *did not find* that the United States representative had provided sufficient evidence that the import prohibition on all tuna and tuna products from Canada as applied from August 31, 1979 to September 4, 1980 complied with the requirements of Article XX and notably sub-paragraph (*g*) of that article.

4.16 Finally, the Panel would stress that its findings and conclusions were relevant only for the trade aspects of the matter under dispute and were not intended to have any bearing whatsoever on other aspects including those concerning questions of fishery jurisdiction.

PANEL ON VITAMINS

Report of the Panel adopted on October 1, 1982
BISD 29S/110

II. FACTUAL ASPECTS

5. In the course of the Multilateral Trade Negotiations, the United States agreed to eliminate the American Selling Price (ASP) System of Valuation[1] upon the entry into force of the Agreement on the Implementation of Article VII of GATT (Valuation Code). Prior to the implementation of the new Valuation Code by the United States on July 1, 1980, both Vitamin B12 feedgrade and pharmaceutical qualities were subject to the ASP System of Valuation. They were classified under Tariff Line 407.85 at a nominal rate of duty of 1.7 cents per pound plus 12.5 per cent ad valorem.

6. Vitamin B12 feedgrade quality and Vitamin B12 pharmaceutical quality were subject to different charges resulting from the ASP valuation: during the period January 1, 1976-June 30, 1980 the feedgrade quality had an ASP of US$3.45 to US$3.50 per gram of active substance, resulting in an effective duty of approximately 21.4 per cent, whereas the pharmaceutical quality entered with an ASP of US$11.2 per gram of active substance, resulting in an effective duty of approximately 43.6 per cent (calculated on the basis of average duties collected and average invoice values in 1976, the base year for ASP conversions).

7. In the process of conversion of the ASP rates both qualities of Vitamin B12 were taken together and the rate of duty was converted from 1.7 cents per pound plus 12.5 per cent ad valorem to 1.7 cents per pound plus 40.4 per cent ad valorem (to be reduced to 16.2% in 1987). According to US calculations, this converted rate of duty represented the weighted average of the actual charges collected for both grades. After the conversion of the rate of duty for Vitamin B12 in the Tariff Schedules of the United States (TSUS), the tariff item number for all Vitamins B12 was 412.56.

[1] Under the ASP system "competitive" products imported were valued for customs purposes at the wholesale price of a competitive US product rather than at the invoice price of the imported product.

IV. CONCLUSIONS

22. The Panel reached the following conclusions:

(a) On the basis of the information supplied by the parties to the dispute, the Panel has not been able to determine with certainty whether the United States had made it clear to the Community negotiators, prior to June 30, 1979, that the United States was not prepared to continue the negotiations on Vitamin B12 after that date. The United States thought that it had made it clear that it was not prepared to continue the negotiations. The Community, on the other hand, reverted to the question of the conversion of the duty on Vitamin B12 on several occasions between June 1979 and April 1981 without receiving a final negative reply in written form from the United States until April 22, 1981. In these circumstances the Panel believes that the Community could not reasonably have been expected to make a reservation concerning Vitamin B12 with respect to the United States Tokyo Round Schedule. The existence of such a reservation would in any event, in the opinion of the Panel, not have been relevant for its further consideration of the dispute.

(b) By entering into the bilateral Understanding with the United States on March 2, 1979 concerning ASP Chemical Products, the Community—for which, the Panel holds, the abolition of the ASP valuation system represented one of the aims of the negotiations—accepted that the base rates for the tariff cuts to be negotiated in the Tokyo Round for Vitamin B12, as for other "competitive" ASP products, would be the converted rates offered by the United States without a need for renegotiations under Article XXVIII in respect of such products.

(c) In the ASP Chemical Products Understanding the United States undertook to examine, on a case by case basis, with a view to finding a mutually acceptable solution any specific cases raised by the Community on the ground that the Community in such case contested the method of conversion. The Panel noted that the only case concerning a "competitive" product raised by the Community related to Vitamin B12.

(d) It is clear in the opinion of the Panel that the ASP Chemical Products Understanding, while requiring the United States delegation to examine cases raised by the Community with a view to finding a mutually acceptable solution, did not create an obligation for the United States to meet the requests of the Community in each case it could raise.

(e) The Panel considers that the United States did not have an obligation to maintain the de facto tariff rate differentiation between feedgrade and pharmaceutical quality vitamins, provided that the method used for the conversion of the previous common bound rate was neutral and did not involve any arbitrary increase. The Panel believes the method used by the United States for the calculation of the level of the base rate—the weighted average of actual duties collected for feedgrade and pharmaceutical quality vitamins—to be in conformity with that proviso.

(f) The Panel notes that Community exports of feedgrade Vitamin B12 to the United States virtually ceased in the second half of 1980, after the abolition of the ASP valuation system on July 1, 1980, but that they recommenced in 1981, although at a lower level than in 1978 and 1979.

(g) Although the Panel, as indicated above, considers that the method used by the United States for the calculation of the base rate for Vitamin B12 was in principle fair and equitable, it felt that in this particular case, the result in respect of feedgrade quality vitamins had excessively negative effects for the suppliers of this product. The European Economic Community could reasonably have foreseen that the abolition of the ASP valuation system in some cases would lead to a less favorable tariff treatment for certain products, but it had in the opinion of the Panel no reason to assume that the tariff treatment of feedgrade quality vitamins would be modified in such a way that imports into the United States would decrease to the extent experienced.

(h) The Panel considers that the United States has not infringed its commitment under the General Agreement or under the ASP Chemical Products Understanding of March 2, 1979. Nevertheless, the Panel feels that in the light of the particular circumstances, the Council could invite the United States to advance the implementation of the Tokyo Round concession rate on feedgrade Vitamin B12 to such an extent that imported vitamins could again attain their traditional competitive position in the United States market.

UNITED STATES—IMPORTS OF CERTAIN AUTOMOTIVE SPRING ASSEMBLIES

Report of the Panel adopted on May 26, 1983
BISD 30S/107, 108

II. FACTUAL ASPECTS

The Panel based its deliberations on the following background:

a) Procedural Background

6. On August 10, 1981 the ITC issued an order excluding from importation into the United States automotive spring assemblies which had been found to infringe the claims of United States Letters Patent No. 3,782.708 and which would infringe claims of United States Letters Patent No. 3,866.287 were the process used to produce them practiced in the United States. The exclusion order was to remain in force for the remaining terms of the patents, except where such importation was licensed by the patent owner. The ITC also ordered that the articles to be excluded from entry into the United States should be entitled to entry under bond in the amount of 72 per cent of the C.I.F. value of the imported articles until such time as the President of the United States notified the ITC that he approved or disapproved this action, but, in any event, not later than 60 days after receipt. The order became final on October 10, 1981, after being reviewed by the President and not disapproved for policy reasons.

7. The exclusion order of the ITC was made under Section 337 of the United States Tariff Act of 1930 which declares unlawful "unfair methods of competition and unfair acts in the importation of articles into the United States, or in their sale by the owner, importer, consignee, or agent of either, the effect or tendency of which is to destroy or substantially injure an industry, efficiently and economically operated, in the United States, or to prevent the establishment of such an industry, or to restrain or monopolize trade and commerce in the United States." The legislation also requires the ITC to investigate alleged violations and provides procedures for its application, including a provision that the ITC should make its determination not later than one year, or in

complicated cases 18 months, after the date of publication of notice of such investigation. It also contains a provision that where the ITC determines that there is a violation, the determination shall have no effect if the President, for policy reasons, disapproves such determination within the 60-day review period.

* * *

IV. CONCLUSIONS

49. In accordance with its terms of reference, the Panel examined the exclusion of imports of certain automotive spring assemblies by the United States under Section 337 of the United States Tariff Act of 1930. The provisions of the GATT considered to be relevant were Articles II:1(*b*), III:1, 2 and 4, XI:1 and XX(*d*).

50. The Panel noted the arguments put forward by Canada and the United States as set out in Section III above and took these arguments fully into account. A further communication, with particular reference to the question of national treatment, was subsequently received from the Canadian authorities and this, together with arguments put forward orally in this context, was also taken fully into account. The Panel came to the conclusion that its first step should be to consider whether or not the exception provision of Article XX(*d*) applied in this case. The Panel considered that if Article XX(*d*) applied, then an examination of the question of the consistency of the exclusion order with the other GATT provisions cited above would not be required.

51. The Panel noted that, as far as it had been able to ascertain, this was the first time a specific case of patent infringement involving Article XX(*d*) had been brought before the CONTRACTING PARTIES.

52. The Preamble to Article XX and paragraph (*d*) of that Article, provide that "Subject to the requirement that such measures are not applied in a manner which would constitute a means of arbitrary or unjustifiable discrimination between countries where the same conditions prevail, or a disguised restriction on international trade, nothing in this Agreement shall be construed to prevent the adoption or enforcement by any contracting party of measures . . . (*d*) necessary to secure compliance with laws or regulations which are not inconsistent with the provisions of this Agreement, including those relating to . . . the protection of patents, trade marks and copyrights, and the prevention of deceptive practices."

53. The Panel noted that the GATT recognized, by the very existence of Article XX(*d*), the need to provide that certain measures taken by a contracting party to secure compliance with its national laws or regulations which otherwise would not be in conformity with the GATT obligations of that contracting party would, through the application of this provision under the conditions stipulated therein, be in conformity with the GATT provided that the national laws or regulations concerned were not inconsistent with the General Agreement. In this connection the Panel noted in particular that the protection of patents was one of the few areas of national laws and regulations expressly mentioned in Article XX(*d*).

54. Looking first at the Preamble, the Panel interpreted the word "measure" to mean the exclusion order issued by the United States International Trade Commission (ITC) under the provisions and procedures of Section 337 since, in the view of the Panel, it was the exclusion order which operated as the measure preventing the importation of the infringing product.

55. The Panel noted that the exclusion order was directed against imports of certain automotive spring assemblies produced in violation of a valid United States patent from all foreign sources, and not just from Canada. It found, therefore, that the exclusion order was "not applied in a manner which would constitute a means of arbitrary or unjustifiable discrimination against countries where the same conditions prevail."

56. The Panel then considered whether or not the exclusion order was "applied in a manner which would constitute . . . a disguised restriction on international trade". The Panel noted that the Preamble of Article XX made it clear that it was the application of the measure and not the measure itself that needed to be examined. Notice of the exclusion order was published in the Federal Register and the order was enforced by the United States Customs at the border. The Panel also noted that the ITC proceedings in this particular case were directed against the importation of automotive spring assemblies produced in violation of a valid United States patent and that, before an exclusion order could be issued under Section 337, both the validity of a patent and its infringement by a foreign manufacturer had to be clearly established. Furthermore, the exclusion order would not prohibit the importation of automotive spring assemblies produced by any producer outside the United States who had a licence from Kuhlman Corporation (Kuhlman) to produce these goods. Consequently, the Panel found that the exclusion order had not been applied in a manner which constituted a disguised restriction on international trade.

57. Turning to paragraph (*d*) of Article XX, the Panel concluded that the laws and regulations which were not inconsistent with the General Agreement and with which compliance was to be secured were the patent laws of the United States, since the case in question was based on the allegation of an infringement of patent rights under United States patent law.

58. The Panel considered whether the ITC action, in making the exclusion order, was "necessary" in the sense of paragraph (*d*) of Article XX to secure compliance with United States patent law. In this connection the Panel examined whether a satisfactory and effective alternative existed under civil court procedures which would have provided the patent holder Kuhlman with a sufficiently effective remedy against the violation of its patent by foreign producers including the Canadian producer Wallbank Manufacturing Co. Ltd (Wallbank).

59. The Panel noted that if Kuhlman had pursued the action it had commenced before the United States district court, it could have joined General Motors, Ford and possibly other known users of the automotive spring assemblies in the action and, once the patent had been found to be valid by the court, prevented these parties, but not unknown users, from utilizing the automotive spring assemblies produced by Wallbank by means of an injunction or a cease and desist order. The Panel decided, however, that such a remedy would not have been sufficient to protect Kuhlman's patent rights because, in practice, it would have been effective only in relation to the automotive spring assemblies produced by Wallbank and supplied to parties joined in the court action. The same remedy would not have been effective against other possible foreign infringers of the United States patent and potential users of the infringing product in the United States. Furthermore, in view of the relatively simple manufacturing process used to produce automotive spring assemblies, these could without major difficulties be produced by other foreign producers infringing Kuhlman's patent and subsequently imported for use in the United States.

60. Against the background of the above considerations, it was the view of the Panel that United States civil court action would not have provided a satisfactory and effective means of protecting Kuhlman's patent rights against importation of the infringing product. The Panel took the view that the only way in which, under existing United States law, Kuhlman's right to the exclusive use of its patent in the United States domestic market could be effectively protected against the importation of the infringing product would be to resort to the exclusion order procedure. For the above reasons, therefore, the Panel found that the

exclusion order issued by the ITC under Section 337 of the United States Tariff Act of 1930 was "necessary" in the sense of Article XX(*d*) to prevent the importation and sale of automotive spring assemblies infringing the patent, thus protecting the patent holder's rights and securing compliance with United States patent law.

61. In the light of the views and findings set out in the above paragraphs, the Panel came to the conclusion that, in the specific case before it, the exclusion order issued by the ITC against the importation of automotive spring assemblies fell within the provisions of Article XX(*d*) and was, therefore, consistent with the GATT. Since Article XX(*d*) had been found to apply, the Panel considered that an examination of the United States action in the light of the other GATT provisions referred to in paragraph 49 above was not required.

62. Under its terms of reference the Panel was also required to include in its examination "the issue of the use of Section 337 by the United States in cases of alleged patent infringement."

63. The Panel focused its attention on the possible conclusions it might be able to draw from its examination of the specific automotive spring assemblies case in the context of the use of Section 337 in cases of patent infringement generally.

64. The Panel took the view that its conclusion in the automotive spring assemblies case, namely that Article XX(*d*) applied, would in principle apply to many cases of alleged patent infringement and that the only effective remedy in such cases under existing United States law would be an exclusion order under Section 337 of the Tariff Act.

65. The Panel noted, however, that the substance of patent infringement cases could vary considerably, for example as regards the characteristics of the product which was the subject of the infringement and the simplicity or complexity involved in its manufacture. There might also be variations in the degree of difficulty which might be encountered in joining in a court action all possible users of the product which had been manufactured in violation of the patent, in the serving of process and enforcement of court judgements depending, among other things, on the legal and judicial court system in the country of the manufacturer infringing the patent.

66. The Panel did not, therefore, exclude the strong possibility that there might be cases, for example, involving high-cost products of an advanced technical nature and with a very limited number of potential users in the United States, where a procedure before a United States

court might provide the patent holder with an equally satisfactory and effective remedy against infringement of his patent rights. In such cases the use of an exclusion order under Section 337 might not be necessary in terms of Article XX(*d*) to secure compliance with laws and regulations (i.e. United States patent law) which were not inconsistent with the General Agreement. If therefore Article XX(*d*) were found not to be applicable, such use would be subject to the order relevant provisions of the General Agreement.

67. The Panel considered it appropriate and in accordance with its terms of reference to supplement the views expressed in paragraphs 63-66 above by means of some additional observations.

68. In the first place, the Panel pointed out that its finding in paragraph 60 above that the exclusion order issued by the ITC was "necessary" within the meaning of Article XX(*d*) had been made on the basis of existing United States law. It carried no implication that the use of Section 337 was an entirely satisfactory means of dealing with patent-based cases.

69. The Panel noted the frequent use that had been made of Section 337 in patent-based cases. Since 1975 these had made up 84 of the 100 cases completed by the ITC. The use of the Section had been a major factor in securing compliance with United States patent law in cases of infringement of a patent by a foreign product.

70. However, in the course of its examination of the automotive spring assemblies case, it became evident to the Panel that certain elements contained in Section 337, having a direct bearing on the use of the Section, appeared to be out of place in legislation used for the protection of private patent rights, where all that was strictly required was proof of the validity of the patent and a finding that the patent had been infringed.

71. One such element related to the words "unfair methods of competition and unfair acts" which were declared unlawful in terms of subsection (*a*) of Section 337. The Panel observed that these words might be capable of being widely interpreted and might be misconstrued as to their precise scope, purpose and application.

72. Another such element was the reference in subsection (*a*) of Section 337 to substantial injury to a United States industry which was efficiently and economically operated. The Panel recognized that this injury criterion could work to the advantage of a respondent in an ITC investigation, in that it represented an additional requirement to be

satisfied by the complainant. However, in the Panel's view, it could reasonably be said that in considering what were the essential elements in legislation dealing with patent-based cases an injury criterion could only be considered irrelevant.

73. The Panel also noted the system of dual procedures for dealing with cases involving a foreign patent infringer. In such cases, the United States patent holder, at his discretion, could take action through the ITC, through the civil court or, if he so wished, use both procedures. In respect of a domestic infringer the patent holder could take action against infringement of his patent only through the civil court. The Panel observed that there might be merit in consideration being given to simplifying and improving the legal procedures for patent infringement cases.

EEC—QUANTITATIVE RESTRICTIONS AGAINST IMPORTS OF CERTAIN PRODUCTS FROM HONG KONG

Report of the Panel adopted on July 12, 1983
BISD 30S/129, 130

II. FACTUAL ASPECTS

6. The case before the Panel concerned quantitative import restrictions maintained by France on the following product categories:

(1) knitwear other than of cotton, man-made fibres, and wool (ex 60.04, ex 60.05 A);

(2) clothing other than of cotton, man-made fibres, and wool (ex 61.01, ex 61.02, ex 61.03);

(3) umbrellas (ex 66.01);

(4) radios and radio parts (85.15 A ex III and 85.15 C);

(5) pleasure and sports boats for marine use (89.01 ex B);

(6) compound optical microscopes (ex 90.12);

(7) toys and toy parts (ex 97.03);

(8) electronic watches with piezo-electric quartz crystal regulating device (ex 91.01).

7. The French Decree of November 30, 1944, which is the fundamental text for French foreign trade regulations, lays down, *inter alia*, that:

> "Article 1. The entry of foreign goods into France under whatsoever customs régime shall be permitted only subject to production of an individual import permit issued by the Central Import and Export Licensing Service in the conditions laid down by the provisionally applicable law of February 22, 1944.
>
> Article 2. General derogations may nevertheless be authorized; they shall be published in the "Journal Officiel" in the form of notices to importers."

The text of the law referred to in the Decree (Law No. 98 of February 22, 1944) was supplied to the Panel.

8. Restrictions on all categories had been maintained *de jure* since 1944 even though certain adaptations had been made by way of a régime without quantitative limitations ("régime sans limitation de quantité") usually referred to as the SLQ régime, even though this expression had not been utilized in all cases. If, during certain periods, the import régime of certain products had been made more flexible, these imports had always been subject to the delivery of licences. The SLQ régime was described as a system which concerned imports of products subject in principle to quantitative restrictions but for which no quota amount had been set either in quantity or value, permit applications being granted on request. It could be defined as a suspension—which was provisional and could be revoked at any time—of strict quota limitation. At the present time, radio parts, boats and microscopes are subject to the SLQ régime. With respect to electronic watches, a previous SLQ régime was replaced by a quantitative quota restriction on October 23, 1981, consistent with the basic legal situation in France.

9. The European Community informed the Panel that for all the eight items, bilateral quotas or in some cases (boats, microscopes, radio parts) a SLQ régime was maintained with regard to Hong Kong. For six items (knitwear, clothing, umbrellas, radios, microscopes and toys), general restraints were also maintained for a specific group of countries, except in certain cases where specific quotas or a SLQ régime applied. For two items (boats and watches) general restraints were also maintained for all third countries except in certain cases where specific quotas or a SLQ régime applied.

10. All the product categories had been subject to consultations; the quantitative restrictions on the first seven product categories had been subject to informal talks prior to 1970 and following the introduction of quantitative restrictions on quartz watches, Hong Kong and the Commission of the European Communities had held Article XXIII:1 consultations on the measures examined by the Panel. Following those consultations, the French authorities unilaterally, with the exceptions of umbrellas and quartz watches, either increased quotas applicable to Hong Kong, or relaxed the import régime by introducing a SLQ régime. However, the matter had not been settled to the satisfaction of the Hong Kong authorities, which sought recourse to Article XXIII: 2 as set out in L/5362 dated September 3, 1982.

* * *

DD53/2

IV. FINDINGS AND CONCLUSIONS

24. The Panel considered the matter referred to it by the CONTRACTING PARTIES in connection with the request made by the Government of the United Kingdom on behalf of Hong Kong regarding quantitative restrictions maintained by the Government of France, and carried out an examination in accordance with the terms of reference as expressed in paragraph 1 of this Report.

25. The Panel noted that restrictions on all categories of products covered by the complaint had been maintained *de jure* since 1944, by virtue of French Decree of November 30 of that year. The Panel also observed that the said Decree had not been notified to the GATT as being covered by the Protocol of Provisional Application of the General Agreement on Tariffs and Trade. From time to time certain adaptations have been made, on the basis of a licensing system, including restrictions applicable to a number of countries, bilateral quotas, and an SLQ régime without quantitative limitation.

26. The Panel first considered the argument that it could only discharge its obligations by examining the issue before it in the light of all relevant GATT provisions and all other relevant discussions which have taken place in GATT. It recognized that situations might exist in which the maintenance of quantitative restrictions would be justified under the relevant GATT provisions. It noted, however, that no such provisions had been invoked by the European Community in the matter. It decided that in such circumstances it was not for the Panel to establish whether the present measures would be justified under any GATT provision or provisions.

27. The Panel considered the arguments put forward by the European Community regarding the social and economic conditions which prevailed in the various product categories under examination. The European Community did not claim any corresponding GATT provision in justification for these arguments. The Panel was of the opinion that such matters did not come within the purview of Articles XI and XIII of the GATT, and in this instance concluded that they lay outside its consideration.

28. With regard to Article XI the Panel considered the arguments advanced by both parties, and summarized above in paragraphs 15-19 of this Report. The Panel acknowledged that there exists quantitative restrictions which are maintained for other than balance-of-payments reasons. It recognized that restrictions had been in existence for a long

time without Article XXIII ever having been invoked by Hong Kong in regard to the products concerned, but concluded that this did not alter the obligations which contracting parties had accepted under GATT provisions. Furthermore the Panel considered it would be erroneous to interpret the fact that a measure had not been subject to Article XXIII over a number of years, as tantamount to its tacit acceptance by contracting parties. In fact, contracting parties and in particular Hong Kong have made it clear that the discussions on quantitative restrictions which have taken place in the GATT over the years were without prejudice to the legal status of the measures or the rights and obligations of GATT contracting parties. The Panel observed that, while most of the measures had been notified to the GATT in the past, the measures on watches had not been notified.

29. The Panel considered the argument put forward by the European Community that the principle referred to as "the law-creating force derived from circumstances" could be relevant in the absence of law. It found, however, that in the present case such a situation did not exist, and the matter was to be considered strictly in the light of the provisions of the General Agreement.

30. It will be apparent that a difference of opinion exists between the parties regarding the inclusion of item 85.15 C amongst the product categories under examination by the Panel. The Panel considered that just as the terms of reference must be agreed between the parties prior to the commencement of the Panel's examination, similarly the product coverage must be clearly understood and agreed between the parties to the dispute. The Panel considered that to allow the inclusion of an additional product item about which one party had not been formally advised prior to the commencement of proceedings would be to introduce an element of inequity. The Panel appreciates that in this instance the absence originally of item 85.15 C was an error of omission. However as the inclusion of the item is not a matter of crucial importance, and in any case peripheral to its conclusions, the Panel has chosen to disregard it.

31. In view of the above the Panel was able to conclude that all product categories were subject to quantitative restrictions within the meaning of the General Agreement[1]. The Panel noted that Hong Kong, under certain product categories, was subject to an SLQ régime as

[1] Official Journal of the European Communities, No. L 35 of February 9, 1982 and corrigendum in No. L 189 of July 1, 1982, as well as No. L 103 of April 21, 1983.

described in paragraph 8 above. The Panel observed that this régime had been described as a suspension—which was provisional and could be revoked at any time—of strict quota limitation but that the SLQ régime was an import licensing procedure which would amount to a quantitative restriction unless it provided for the automatic issuance of licences[1] and that the EC itself referred to the products concerned as subject to quantitative restrictions.

32. The Panel further noted that no GATT justification had been advanced for the quantitative restrictions referred to in paragraph 31 above, and concluded that the relevant provisions of Article XI were not complied with.

33. With regard to Article XIII the Panel considered the arguments advanced by both parties, and summarised above in paragraphs 20 and 21 of this Report. It was apparent to the Panel that the French measures were not applied uniformly to all contracting parties (e.g. there is a differentiation between suppliers depending on their categorization in different geographical zones, and in addition the French import régime included various measures which differed in scope and content for different suppliers). The Panel was of the opinion that the evidence presented by the parties raised questions regarding the consistency of the application of the French régime with the provisions of Article XIII. However, the Panel considered it unnecessary to go further into this question as it had already found that the relevant provisions of Article XI were not complied with.

34. In view of the above, the Panel found that there was an infringement of obligations assumed under the General Agreement in Article XI and that this infringement had to be considered *prima facie* to constitute a case of nullification or impairment of benefits accruing to Hong Kong under the General Agreement. The Panel suggests that the CONTRACTING PARTIES should recommend that France terminate the quantitative restrictions that are the subject of the complaint by Hong Kong.

[1] BISD 25S/95 [Case 38].

CANADA—ADMINISTRATION OF THE FOREIGN INVESTMENT REVIEW ACT

Report of the Panel adopted on February 7, 1984
BISD 30S/140, 142

2.2 *The Foreign Investment Review Act.* In December 1973 the Parliament of Canada enacted the Foreign Investment Review Act. According to Section 2(1) of this Act, the Parliament adopted the law "in recognition that the extent to which control of Canadian industry, trade and commerce has become acquired by persons other than Canadians and the effect thereof on the ability of Canadians to maintain effective control over their economic environment is a matter of national concern" and that it was therefore expedient to ensure that acquisitions of control of a Canadian business or establishments of a new business by persons other than Canadians be reviewed and assessed and only be allowed to proceed if the government had determined that they were, or were likely to be, of "significant benefit to Canada."

2.3 Section 2(2) lists five factors to be taken into account in assessing whether a proposed investment is or is likely to be of significant benefit to Canada. These are:

(a) the effect of the acquisition or establishment on the level and nature of economic activity in Canada, including, without limiting the generality of the foregoing, the effect on employment, on resource processing, on the utilization of parts, components and services produced in Canada, and on exports from Canada;

(b) the degree and significance of participation by Canadians in the business enterprise or new business and in any industry or industries in Canada of which the business enterprise or new business forms or would form a part;

(c) the effect of the acquisition or establishment on productivity, industrial efficiency, technological development, product innovation and product variety in Canada;

(d) the effect of the acquisition or establishment on competition within any industry or industries in Canada; and

(e) the compatibility of the acquisition or establishment with national industrial and economic policies, taking into consideration industrial and economic policy objectives enunciated by the government or legislature of any province likely to be significantly affected by the acquisition or establishment.

2.4 *Written undertakings given by investors.* The Act provides that investors may submit written undertakings on the conduct of the business they are proposing to acquire or establish, conditional on approval by the Canadian government of the proposed acquisition or establishment. The submission of undertakings is not required under the Act but, as the administration of the Act evolved, they are now routinely submitted in support of nearly all larger investment proposals. Many undertakings are the result of negotiations between the investor and the Canadian government. Undertakings given by investors may deal with any aspect of the conduct of a business, including employment, investment, research and development, participation of Canadian shareholders and managers, productivity improvements as well as practices with respect to purchasing, manufacturing and exports. There are no pre-set formulas or prescriptions for the undertakings.

2.5 *Purchase undertakings.* Undertakings with respect to the purchase of goods have been given in a variety of forms:

— some involve best efforts to seek Canadian sources of supply;

— some specify a percentage or amount of purchases of Canadian products;

— some envisage replacement of imports with Canadian-made goods in a specific dollar amount;

— some refer to the purchase of Canadian products, others only to the purchase from Canadian suppliers (whether of domestic or imported goods);

— some involve a commitment to set up a purchasing division in the Canadian subsidiary; and

— some involve a commitment to consult with federal or provincial industry specialists in drawing up tender lists.

Undertakings on purchases are often but not always conditional on goods being "available," "reasonably available" or "competitively available" in Canada with respect to price, quality, and delivery or other factors specified by the investor.

2.6 *Manufacturing undertakings.* Some firms have given undertakings to manufacture in Canada products or components of a product used or sold by the firm.

2.7 *Export undertakings.* The undertakings involving the export of goods have been given in a variety of forms:

— some involving development of natural resources are predicated on the development of offshore markets;

— some involve a specific export target, expressed as a percentage of output or sales, often to be achieved within a specified time frame;

— some involve assigning to the Canadian business exclusive rights to export either all its products to certain countries or specified products on a world basis;

— some involve a commitment by the investor to assist the Canadian subsidiary in selling its products in foreign markets; and

— some involve commitments that the Canadian business will not be restricted from seeking out and taking advantage of any export opportunities.

2.8 *Statistics on the undertakings.* The Act came into force on April 9, 1974 with respect to acquisitions and on October 15, 1975 with respect to new businesses. From April 1974 to September 1982, the Government of Canada has rendered decisions on 4,103 investment proposals, of which 2,448 were from the United States. Approximately 90 per cent of the reviewable investment proposals on which the government has taken a decision have been judged to be of significant benefit to Canada and have, therefore, been allowed. The Panel asked questions about the frequency with which the various types of undertakings have been given. In order to answer these questions the Canadian government reviewed a sample of 181 investments allowed in the month of November in the years 1980, 1981 and 1982. (November was the latest month for which data were available). In this sample, 55 of the investors or 30 per cent of the total gave no undertakings relating to sourcing. The remaining 126 investors gave a total of 178 sourcing undertakings. (Some investors gave more than one sourcing undertaking). Of those 178 sourcing undertakings, 65 per cent referred to the purchase of goods and services from Canadian suppliers or words to that effect, 15 per cent referred to purchase of Canadian produced goods. The remaining 20 per cent were sourcing commitments of other kinds, e.g. to set up a Canadian purchasing division, or to consult with a government body to identify potential Canadian suppliers. This latter 20 per cent also includes undertakings relating solely to the purchase of services. 71 per cent of the undertakings to purchase in Canada or to purchase Canadian produced goods carried a qualification with respect to the availability of goods on competitive terms.

2.9 With respect to export undertakings in the same sample of 181 investments, 97 investors or 54 per cent of the total gave no export undertakings of any kind. The remaining 84 investors gave 96 export undertakings. (Again some investors gave more than one undertaking relating to exports). Of the 96 export undertakings, 32 per cent referred to a quantifiable level of exports, e.g. target value of exports or a percentage of output. The remaining 68 per cent were export undertakings of other kinds, such as an undertaking not to restrict the export activities of the Canadian business, or to actively pursue export opportunities.

2.10 *Enforcement of the undertakings.* Written undertakings given by firms are legally binding on the investor if the investment is allowed. According to Section 21 of the Act the Minister responsible for the administration of the Act may apply to the courts for a remedial order in the event an investor fails to implement undertakings he has given. The Minister responsible for the Act made the following statement in the Canadian Parliament in 1973 on the enforcement of undertakings:

> "In normal circumstances the inability to fulfill undertakings will lead to discussions with the Minister and perhaps to the negotiation of new undertakings. Like any contract, an undertaking can be modified with the consent of both parties. If, however, the failure to comply with an undertaking is clearly the result of changed market conditions—for example, the undertaking to export frisbees is followed by the collapse of the frisbee market—the person would not be held accountable. It should be remembered, however, that some undertakings may be tailored to a range of market expectations."

2.11 All investments that are allowed subject to the Act are monitored by the government of Canada. If the investment involves specific undertakings the investor is asked at regular intervals for a progress report on the implementation of his undertakings. All undertakings are monitored at least once before the file is closed, normally after the fifth anniversary of the date on which the permission to invest was granted. If the investor's progress report reveals a variation from the undertakings, or non-fulfilment of them, the investor is asked to provide a more detailed explanation. Depending on the circumstances, performance of unfulfilled undertakings has so far always been either postponed or waived, or the undertakings have been replaced by revised undertakings. To date, the Minister responsible for the administration of the Act has not applied to the courts to enforce an investor's written undertaking.

* * *

5. Findings

(a) General

5.1 In view of the fact that the General Agreement does not prevent Canada from exercising its sovereign right to regulate foreign direct investments, the Panel examined the purchase and export undertakings by investors subject to the Foreign Investment Review Act of Canada solely in the light of Canada's trade obligations under the General Agreement. This approach is in accordance with the Chairman of the Council's conclusions at the close of the discussion of this question at the Council meeting of November 2, 1982.

5.2 In its statement before the Panel, Argentina also pointed out that the provisions and arguments invoked against Canada in this case were not necessarily those which could be legitimately invoked against less-developed contracting parties, given rights to protect national industries which these contracting parties enjoyed under the General Agreement. The Panel recognizes that in disputes involving less-developed contracting parties full account should be taken of the special provisions in the General Agreement relating to these countries (such as Article XVIII:C). The Panel did not examine the issues before it in the light of these provisions since the dispute only involved developed contracting parties.

5.3 The Panel considered that the examination of undertakings to *manufacture* goods which would be imported otherwise, as requested by the United States (paragraphs 3.1 (*b*), and 3.17 to 3.19 above), was not covered by its terms of reference which only refer to "the *purchase* of goods in Canada and/or the *export* of goods from Canada." Accordingly the Panel did not examine this question.

(b) Undertakings to Purchase Goods of Canadian Origin in Preference to Imported Goods or in Specified Amounts or Proportions, or to Purchase Goods from Canadian Sources

5.4 *Article III:4.* The Panel first examined whether the purchase undertakings are to be considered "laws, regulations or requirements" within the meaning of Article III:4. As both parties had agreed that the Foreign Investment Review Act and the Foreign Investment Review Regulations—whilst providing for the possibility of written undertakings—did not make their submission obligatory, the question remained whether the undertakings given in individual cases are to be considered "requirements" within the meaning of Article III:4. In this respect the Panel noted that Section 9(*c*) of the Act refers to "any written undertakings . . . relating to the proposed or actual investment given by any party thereto conditional upon the allowance of the investment" and that Section 21 of the Act states that "where a person who has given a written undertaking . . . fails or refuses to comply with such undertaking" a court order may be made "directing that person to comply with the undertaking." The Panel further noted that written purchase undertakings—leaving aside the manner in which they may have been arrived at (voluntary submission, encouragement, negotiation, etc.)—once they were accepted, became part of the conditions under which the investment proposals were approved, in which case compliance could be legally enforced. The Panel therefore found that the word "requirements" as used in Article III:4 could be considered a proper description of existing undertakings.

5.5 The Panel could not subscribe to the Canadian view that the word "requirements" in Article III:4 should be interpreted as "mandatory rules applying across-the-board" because this latter concept was already more aptly covered by the term "regulations" and the authors of this provision must have had something different in mind when adding the word "requirements." The mere fact that the few disputes that have so far been brought before the CONTRACTING PARTIES regarding the application of Article III:4 have only concerned laws and regulations does not in the view of the Panel justify an assimilation of "requirements" with "regulations." The Panel also considered that, in judging whether a measure is contrary to obligations under Article III:4, it is not relevant whether it applies across-the-board or only in isolated cases. Any interpretation which would exclude case-by-case action would, in the view of the Panel, defeat the purposes of Article III:4.

5.6 The Panel carefully examined the Canadian view that the purchase undertakings should be considered as private contractual obligations of particular foreign investors vis-à-vis the Canadian government. The Panel recognized that investors might have an economic advantage in assuming purchase undertakings, taking into account the other conditions under which the investment was permitted. The Panel felt, however, that even if this was so, private contractual obligations entered into by investors should not adversely affect the rights which contracting parties, including contracting parties not involved in the dispute, possess under Article III:4 of the General Agreement and which they can exercise on behalf of their exporters. This applies in particular to the rights deriving from the national treatment principle, which—as stated in Article III:1—is aimed at preventing the use of internal measures "so as to afford protection to domestic production."

5.7 The Panel then examined the question whether less favorable treatment was accorded to imported products than that accorded to like products of Canadian origin in respect of requirements affecting their purchase. For this purpose the Panel distinguished between undertakings to purchase goods of Canadian origin and undertakings to use Canadian sources or suppliers (irrespective of the origin of the goods), and for both types of undertakings took into account the qualifications "available," "reasonably available," or "competitively available."

5.8 The Panel found that undertakings to purchase *goods of Canadian origin* without any qualification exclude the possibility of purchasing available imported products so that the latter are clearly treated less favorably than domestic products and that such requirements are therefore not consistent with Article III:4. This finding is not modified in cases where undertakings to purchase goods of Canadian origin are subject to the qualification that such goods be "available." It is obvious that if Canadian goods are not available, the question of less favorable treatment of imported goods does not arise.

5.9 When these undertakings are conditional on goods being "competitively available" (as in the majority of cases) the choice between Canadian or imported products may frequently coincide with normal commercial considerations and the latter will not be adversely affected whenever one or the other offer is more competitive. However, it is the Panel's understanding that the qualification "competitively available" is intended to deal with situations where there are Canadian goods available on competitive terms. The Panel considered that in those cases where the imported and domestic product are offered on equivalent terms, adherence to the undertaking would entail giving preference to the domestic product. Whether or not the foreign investor chooses to buy Canadian goods in given practical situations, is not at issue. The purpose of Article III:4 is not to protect the interests of the foreign investor but to ensure that goods originating in any other contracting party benefit from treatment no less favorable than domestic (Canadian) goods, in respect of the requirements that affect their purchase (in Canada). On the basis of these considerations, the Panel found that a requirement to purchase goods of Canadian origin, also when subject to "competitive availability," is contrary to Article III:4. The Panel considered that the alternative qualification "reasonably available" which is used in some cases, is *a fortiori* inconsistent with Article III:4, since the undertaking in these cases implies that preference has to be given to Canadian goods also when these are not available on entirely competitive terms.

5.10 The Panel then turned to the undertakings to buy from *Canadian suppliers*. The Panel did not consider the situation where domestic products are not available, since such a situation is not covered by Article III:4. The Panel understood the choice under this type of requirement to apply on the one hand to imported goods if bought through a Canadian agent or importer and on the other hand to Canadian goods which can be purchased either from a Canadian "middleman" or directly from the Canadian producer. The Panel recognized that these requirements might in a number of cases have little or no effect on the choice between imported or domestic products. However, the possibility of purchasing imported products *directly* from the foreign producer would be excluded and as the conditions of purchasing imported products through a Canadian agent or importer would normally be less advantageous, the imported product would therefore have more difficulty in competing with Canadian products (which are not subject to similar requirements affecting their sale) and be treated less favorably. For this reason, the Panel found that the requirements to buy from Canadian suppliers are inconsistent with Article III:4.

5.11 In case undertakings to purchase from Canadian suppliers are subject to a "competitive availability" qualification, as is frequent, the handicap for the imported product is alleviated as it can be obtained directly from the foreign producer if offered under more competitive conditions than via Canadian sources. In those cases in which Canadian sources and a foreign manufacturer offer a product on equivalent terms, adherence to the undertaking would entail giving preference to Canadian sources, which in practice would tend to result in the purchase being made directly from the Canadian producer, thereby excluding the foreign product. The Panel therefore found that requirements to purchase from Canadian suppliers, also when subject to competitive availability, are contrary to Article III:4. As before (paragraph 5.9), the Panel considered that the qualification "reasonably available" is *a fortiori* inconsistent with Article III:4.

5.12 The Panel considered the Canadian view expressed in paragraph 3.9 above that the word "requirements" in article III:4 of the General Agreement should be interpreted in the light of Article 12 of the Havana Charter, the general principles of which the contracting parties, in Article XXIX of the General Agreement, agreed to observe to the fullest extent of their executive authority. The Panel noted that the deletion of Article XXIX of the General Agreement was proposed in 1955 and accepted by all but one contracting party[1], and that—although this Article is technically still in force—it refers to an instrument which itself has never been implemented and the acceptance of which is no longer pending as is assumed in Article XXIX. This leaves considerable doubt as to the manner in which its provisions would have been interpreted if they had entered into force. The Panel further noted that paragraph 1 (*c*) of Article 12 of the Charter was to apply "without prejudice to existing international agreements to which Members are parties," and that paragraph 1(*a*), (*b*) and (*d*) as well as paragraphs 2 and 3 of this Article tended to encourage international investments (including international cooperation in this field). It is therefore doubtful whether paragraph 1(*c*) which reserved the rights of Members to prescribe "reasonable requirements" should by itself be considered as a "general principle" in the sense of Article XXIX:1 of the General Agreement. The wording of this latter provision suggests that it was not the intention of its drafters that contracting parties should "undertake to observe to the fullest extent of their executive authority" what they would in any case judge to be in their own interest, nor that they should invoke the Charter to detract from their obligations under the General Agreement, but rather that they should observe general principles which reinforced or added to these obligations. In the light of the foregoing facts and considerations the Panel could not subscribe to the assumption that the drafters of Article III had intended the term "requirements" to exclude requirements connected with the regulation of international investments and did not find anything in the negotiating history, the wording, the objectives and the subsequent application of Article III which would support such an interpretation.

[1] Protocol Amending Part I and Articles XXIX and XXX of the General Agreement on Tariffs and Trade, annexed to the Final Act adopted at the Ninth Session of the CONTRACTING PARTIES, published March 10, 1955. This protocol did not enter into force (see Status of Legal Instruments, page 2-7.1).

5.13 *Article III.5.* The Panel then considered the United States contention that purchase undertakings which obliged the investor to purchase in Canada a specified amount or proportion of his requirements were also contrary to Article III:5. The Panel noted that these cases had been characterized by both parties as *purchase* undertakings (paragraph 2.5) and had also been presented as such by the United States (paragraphs 3.1(*a*) and 3.12). In this regard the Panel noted that in paragraph 5 of Article III the conditions of purchase are not at issue but rather the existence of internal quantitative regulations relating to the mixture, processing or use of products (irrespective of whether these are purchased or obtained by other means). On the basis of the presentations made, the Panel (which was unable to go into a detailed examination of individual cases where purchase undertakings referred to percentages or specific amounts) therefore did not find sufficient grounds to consider the undertakings in question in the light of Article III:5, but came to the conclusion that they fell under the purchase requirements that had been found inconsistent with Article III:4.

5.14 *Article XI.* The United States further asked the Panel to find that the purchase undertakings operate as restrictions on the importation of products into Canada and are therefore contrary to Article XI:1. The Panel shares the view of Canada that the General Agreement distinguishes between measures affecting the "importation" of products, which are regulated in Article XI:1, and those affecting "imported products," which are dealt with in Article III. If Article XI:1 were interpreted broadly to cover also internal requirements, Article III would be partly superfluous. Moreover, the exceptions to Article XI:1, in particular those contained in Article XI:2, would also apply to internal requirements restricting imports, which would be contrary to the basic aim of Article III. The Panel did not find, either in the drafting history of the General Agreement or in previous cases examined by the CONTRACTING PARTIES, any evidence justifying such an interpretation of Article XI. For these reasons, the Panel, noting that purchase undertakings do not prevent the importation of goods as such, reached the conclusion that they are not inconsistent with Article XI:1.

5.15 *Article XVII:1(c).* The United States requested the Panel to find that the purchase undertakings obliging investors to give less favorable treatment to imported products than to domestic products prevent the investors from acting solely in accordance with commercial considerations and that they therefore violate Canada's obligations under Article XVII:1(*c*).

5.16 The Panel takes the view that, through its reference to sub-paragraph (*a*), paragraph 1(*c*) of Article XVII of the General Agreement imposes on contracting parties the obligation to act in their relations with state-trading and other enterprises "in a manner consistent with the general principles of non-discriminatory treatment prescribed in this Agreement for governmental measures affecting imports or exports by private traders." This obligation is defined in sub-paragraph (*b*), which declares, *inter alia,* that these principles are understood to require the enterprises to make their purchases and sales solely in accordance with commercial considerations. The fact that sub-paragraph (*b*) does not establish a separate general obligation to allow enterprises to act in accordance with commercial considerations, but merely defines the obligations set out in the preceding sub-paragraph, is made clear through the introductory words "The provisions of sub-paragraph (*a*) of the paragraph shall be understood to require. . ." For these reasons, the Panel considers that the commercial considerations criterion becomes relevant only after it has been determined that the governmental action at issue falls within the scope of the general principles of non-discriminatory treatment prescribed by the General Agreement. The Panel saw great force in Canada's argument that only the most-favored-nation and not the national treatment obligations fall within the scope of the general principles referred to in Article XVII:1(*a*). However, the Panel did not consider it necessary to decide in this particular case whether the general reference to the principles of non-discriminatory treatment referred to in Article XVII:1 also comprises the national treatment principle since it had already found the purchase undertakings at issue to be inconsistent with Article III:4 which implements the national treatment principle specifically in respect of purchase requirements.

(c) Undertakings to Export Specified Quantities or Proportions

5.17 The United States requested the Panel to find that the undertakings which oblige investors to export specified quantities or proportions of their production are inconsistent with Article XVII:1*(c)* because the export levels of companies subject to such undertakings cannot be assumed to be the result of a decision-making process based on commercial considerations.

5.18 As explained in paragraph 5.16 above, Article XVII:1(*b*) does not establish a separate obligation to allow enterprises to act in accordance with commercial considerations but merely defines the obligation of the enterprises, set out in sub-paragraph (*a*) of Article XVII:1, to "act in a manner consistent with the general principles of non-discriminatory treatment" prescribed in the General Agreement. Hence, before applying the commercial considerations criterion to the export undertakings, the Panel first had to determine whether Canada, in accepting investment proposals on the condition that the investor export a certain quantity or proportion of his production, acts inconsistently with any of the general principles of non-discriminatory treatment prescribed in the General Agreement. The Panel found that there is no provision in the General Agreement which forbids requirements to sell goods in foreign markets in preference to the domestic market. In particular, the General Agreement does not impose on contracting parties the obligation to prevent enterprises from dumping. Therefore, when allowing foreign investments on the condition that the investors export a certain amount or proportion of their production, Canada does not, in the view of the Panel, act inconsistently with any of the principles of non-discriminatory treatment prescribed by the General Agreement for governmental measures affecting exports by private traders. Article XVII:1(*c*) is for these reasons not applicable to the export undertakings at issue.

(e) Article XX(d)

5.19 Canada contended that, in the event that the Panel were to consider the purchase undertakings to be inconsistent with Article III:4, these would fall within the exception provided for in Article XX(*d*) of the General Agreement because, within the meaning of that provision, the Foreign Investment Review Act constitutes "a law which is not inconsistent with the provisions of the General Agreement" and the purchase undertakings are "measures necessary to secure compliance" with that law.

5.20 Since Article XX(*d*) is an exception to the General Agreement it is up to Canada, as the party invoking the exception, to demonstrate that the purchase undertakings are necessary to secure compliance with the Foreign Investment Review Act. On the basis of the explanations given by Canada the Panel could not, however, conclude that the purchase undertakings that were found to be inconsistent with Article III:4 are necessary for the effective administration of the Act. The Panel is in particular not convinced that, in order to achieve the aims of the Act, investors submitting applications under the Act had to be bound to purchasing practices having the effect of giving preference to domestic products. It was not clear to the Panel why a detailed review of investment proposals without purchasing requirements would not be sufficient to enable the Canadian government to determine whether the proposed investments were or were likely to be of significant benefit to Canada within the meaning of Section 2 of the Foreign Investment Review Act.

(f) Other Undertakings

5.21 To avoid any misunderstanding the Panel wishes to underline that some of the undertakings mentioned in paragraph 2.5 above, such as undertakings to set up a purchasing division in the Canadian subsidiary or to consult with Canadian industry specialists in drawing up tender lists,—although related to the purchase of goods in Canada—have not been the subject of United States contention in the Panel proceedings and were therefore not examined. The Panel also wishes to stress that the considerations relating to the purchase undertakings examined in paragraphs 5.1 to 5.20 remain strictly without prejudice to the status of other undertakings agreed upon in the context of the Foreign Investment Review Act and referred to in paragraph 2.4 but pertaining to employment, investment, research and development and other subjects which clearly fall outside the scope of the General Agreement.

6. Conclusions

6.1 In the light of the considerations set out in paragraphs 5.4 to 5.12, the Panel concluded that the practice of Canada to allow certain investments subject to the Foreign Investment Review Act conditional upon written undertakings by the investors to *purchase* goods of Canadian origin, or goods from Canadian sources, is inconsistent with Article III:4 of the General Agreement according to which contracting parties shall accord to imported products treatment no less favorable than that accorded to like products of national origin in respect of all internal requirements affecting their purchase. The Panel further concluded that in relation to Article III:5, there were insufficient grounds to consider the purchase undertakings which refer to specific amounts or proportions under its provisions (paragraph 5.13). Noting that purchase undertakings do not prevent the importation of goods as such, the Panel reached the conclusion that they are not inconsistent with Article XI:1 (paragraph 5.14). Further, having reached a decision on purchase requirements in relation to Article III:4, the Panel did not consider it necessary to make a specific finding on the interpretation of Article XVII:1(*c*) in the context of this case, and therefore did not reach a separate conclusion regarding the consistency of purchase requirements with this provision (paragraphs 5.15 and 5.16). On the basis of the evidence before it, the Panel could not conclude that the purchase undertakings that were found to be inconsistent with Article III:4 are necessary within the meaning of Article XX(*d*) for the effective administration of the Foreign Investment Review Act (paragraphs 5.19 to 5.20).

6.2 For the reasons set out in paragraphs 5.17 and 5.18, the Panel found that Canada does not act inconsistently with Article XVII:1(*c*) of the General Agreement when allowing certain investments subject to the Foreign Investment Review Act conditional upon undertakings by investors to *export* a specified amount or proportion of their production. Finally, the Panel considered that the examination of undertakings to *manufacture* goods which would be imported otherwise was not covered by its terms of reference (paragraph 5.3).

6.3 The Panel is aware that inconsistency with Article III:4 was not intended by the Foreign Investment Review Act, which does not require the submission of undertakings, but that this practice developed as the administration of the Act evolved, to the point that "they are now routinely submitted in support of nearly all larger investment proposals" (paragraph 2.4 above). This evolution may partly reflect the need for foreign investors to demonstrate, by this and other means, to the Canadian administration that their proposed investment would be of significant benefit to Canada. The Panel sympathizes with the desire of the Canadian authorities to ensure that Canadian goods and suppliers would be given a fair chance to compete with imported products. However, the Panel holds the view that the purchase requirements under examination do not stop short of this objective but tend to tip the balance in favor of Canadian products, thus coming into conflict with Article III:4.

6.4 The Panel recognizes that purchase requirements may reflect plans which the investors would have carried out also in the absence of the undertakings; that undertakings with such provisos as "competitive availability" have an adverse impact on imported products only in those cases in which imported and Canadian goods are offered on equivalent terms; and that the undertakings are enforced flexibly. Many of the undertakings, though technically in violation with the General Agreement, therefore possibly do not nullify or impair benefits accruing to the United States under the General Agreement. However, understanding GATT practice, a breach of a rule is presumed to have an adverse impact on other contracting parties[1], and the Panel also proceeded on this assumption.

[1] BISD 26S/216.

6.5 As to the extent to which purchase requirements reflect plans of the investors, the Panel does not consider it relevant nor does it feel competent to judge how the foreign investors are affected by the purchase requirements, as the national treatment obligations of Article III of the General Agreement do not apply to foreign persons or firms but to imported products and serve to protect the interests of producers and exporters established on the territory of any contracting party. Purchase requirements applied to foreign investors in Canada which are inconsistent with Article III:4 can affect the trade interests of all contracting parties, and impinge upon their rights.

6.6 The Panel carefully considered the effects of the purchase requirements on trade. The Panel concluded that an evaluation of these effects would entail scrutiny and analysis of the implementation of several thousands of often differently worded undertakings as well as speculation on what the purchasing behaviour of foreign investors would have been in their absence. The Panel could not undertake such an evaluation and it is therefore not in a position to judge how frequently the purchase requirements cause investors to act differently than they would have acted in the absence of the undertakings and how frequently they therefore adversely affect the trade interests of other contracting parties. The Panel, however, believes that an evaluation of the trade effects was not directly relevant to its findings because a breach of a GATT rule is presumed to have an adverse impact on other contracting parties (see paragraph 6.4 above).

6.7 Taking into account all the above considerations, the Panel considered what scope might exist for modifications of administrative practices under the Foreign Investment Review Act so as to bring them into conformity with Canada's obligations under the General Agreement. In this connection, the Panel considered the following Canadian submission contained in paragraph 3.6 of particular relevance:

> "Since both the investor and the Canadian government had to act in the context of markets in which the investor's competitors were not subject to undertakings, it was highly unlikely that purchase undertakings would either be offered or sought that departed significantly from the purchasing practices the investor would follow in the absence of the undertaking."

On the face of it, this statement and the above-mentioned considerations seem to suggest that there may be scope for adapting the administration of the Foreign Investment Review Act in such a way as to remove the implication that imported products are treated less favorably than domestic products. The Panel notes that in a previous case another Panel had been confronted with a somewhat similar situation and had suggested a solution along these lines.[1] In the case at issue, the Panel considers that the Canadian authorities might resolve the problem by ensuring that any *future* purchase undertakings will not provide more favorable treatment to Canadian products in relation to imported products. The Panel's findings also apply to *existing* purchase undertakings. However, the Panel recognizes that an immediate application of its findings to these undertakings might cause difficulties in the administration of the Foreign Investment Review Act. Consequently, the Panel suggests that the CONTRACTING PARTIES recommend that Canada bring the existing purchase undertakings as soon as possible into conformity with its obligations under the General Agreement, and invite Canada to report on the steps taken to that effect before the end of 1985.

[1] BISD 7S/66-67 [Case 16]: "The Panel considered, furthermore, that if the considered view of the Italian Government was that these credit facilities had not influenced the terms of competition on the Italian market, there would not seem to be a serious problem in amending the operation of the Law so as to avoid any discrimination as regards these credit facilities between the domestic and imported tractors and agricultural machinery."

UNITED STATES—IMPORTS OF SUGAR FROM NICARAGUA

Report of the Panel adopted on March 13, 1984
BISD 31S/67, 73

4. FINDINGS AND CONCLUSIONS

4.1 The Panel noted that the measures taken by the United States concerning sugar imports from Nicaragua were but one aspect of a more general problem. The Panel, in accordance with its terms of reference as set out in paragraph 1.4, examined those measures solely in the light of the relevant GATT provisions, concerning itself only with the trade issue under dispute.

4.2 Nicaragua claimed that the United States sugar quota system was contrary to *Article XI* of the General Agreement and not covered by the decision of the CONTRACTING PARTIES of March 5, 1955 which waived, *inter alia,* the obligations of the United States under this Article to permit actions under Section 22 of the Agricultural Adjustment Act. The Panel noted that its terms of reference defined the matter before it as "the measures taken by the United States concerning imports of sugar from Nicaragua," and referred to document L/5492 in which Nicaragua had asked for consultations under Article XXIII:1 on "the announcement by the United States Government of the modification regarding the allocation of the sugar import quota on Nicaragua." The Panel concluded, therefore, that the task assigned to it by the Council was to examine not the United States sugar quota system as such but the reduction in the quota allocated to Nicaragua within that system, and that any consideration of the sugar quota system in the light of Article XI fell outside its terms of reference.

4.3 Nicaragua argued that the United States measures were inconsistent with the provisions of *Article XIII* of the General Agreement and in particular with paragraph 2 of that Article, according to which "in applying import restrictions to any product, contracting parties shall aim at a distribution of trade in such product approaching as closely as possible the shares which the various contracting parties might be expected to obtain in the absence of such restrictions, . . ." The Panel noted that under the sugar quota system established by the United

States on May 5, 1982 the share of each supplying country corresponded to its share in the total sugar imports of the United States during a previous representative period, and that Nicaragua had, on this basis, been allocated 2.1 per cent of the total import quota, which amounted in the fiscal year 1982/83 to 58,000 short tons. Nicaragua's quota for the fiscal year 1983/84 had been reduced to 6,000 short tons, or about one-tenth of its prior allocation, and this reduction had not been motivated by any factor which might have affected or might be affecting trade in sugar. The Panel therefore concluded that the sugar quota allocated to Nicaragua for the fiscal year 1983/84 was inconsistent with the United States' obligations under Article XIII:2.

4.4 The Panel noted that the United States had not invoked any of the exceptions provided for in the General Agreement permitting discriminatory quantitative restrictions contrary to Article XIII. The Panel therefore did not examine whether the reduction in Nicaragua's quota could be justified under any such provision.

4.5 Having found the reduction of the quota to be inconsistent with the obligations of the United States under Article XIII, the Panel did not deem it necessary to examine whether the action was also inconsistent with any other obligations on quota allocations which the United States might have assumed under *Article II* in its schedule of concessions.

4.6 Moreover, having found the quota reduction to be inconsistent with a specific obligation of the United States under Part II of the General Agreement, the Panel saw no need to pursue the question whether the action was also contrary to the United States' more general commitments under *Part IV*.

4.7 For the reasons set out above the Panel concluded that in allocating to Nicaragua for the fiscal year 1983/84 an import quota of 6,000 short tons the United States had failed to carry out its obligations under the General Agreement. The Panel suggests that the CONTRACTING PARTIES recommend that the United States promptly allocate to Nicaragua a sugar import quota consistent with the criteria set out in Article XIII:2.

UNITED STATES MANUFACTURING CLAUSE

Report of the Panel adopted on May 15/16, 1984
BISD 31S/74, 76

II. FACTUAL ASPECTS

4. The Manufacturing Clause—Section 601 of Title 17 of the United States Code, as extended by Public Law 97-215 of July 13, 1982—prohibits, with certain exceptions, the importation into or public distribution in the United States of a copyrighted work consisting preponderantly of non-dramatic literary material in the English language, the author of which is a United States domiciliary, unless the portions consisting of such material have been manufactured in the United States or Canada. The law defines "manufacture" as including typesetting if the materials are produced directly from type or plates made from type, making lithographic or photo-engraved plates, and printing and binding. The United States Customs Service may seize materials imported in violation of the Section. In addition, an infringer of a copyright has a complete defense in court if the infringer produced the infringing materials in the United States and can show that the copyright owner imported materials in violation of the Manufacturing Clause. The text of the Manufacturing Clause is reproduced in the annex to this report.

5. The Chace Act of March 3, 1891, that permitted foreign nationals to obtain copyright protection in the United States for the first time, added the original Manufacturing Clause to United States copyright law. Fearing that the then infant United States printing and publishing industries would be overwhelmed by foreign competition, the United States Congress specified that copyright protection in the United States would only be granted if manufacture took place in the United States. The Congress ensured adherence to the Manufacturing Clause by prohibiting for the term of the copyright importation of all copyrighted materials produced abroad.

6. As a result of amendments in 1909, 1919, 1949, 1952 and 1976, the coverage of the Manufacturing Clause has been progressively reduced. The Manufacturing Clause was given its present form in 1976 by Public Law 94-553, a comprehensive revision of the United States copyright

law. Among the amendments then made, manufacture in Canada was for the first time treated as meeting the manufacturing requirements of the Clause. The 1976 amendment also provided for the first time an expiry date for the Manufacturing Clause by specifying that it was to be applied "prior to July 1, 1982."

7. On June 30, 1982, both Houses of the United States Congress passed a bill changing the date prior to which the Manufacturing Clause was to be applied from July 1, 1982 to July 1, 1986. The United States President returned the unsigned bill to Congress on July 8, 1982 with a statement of his objections to its enactment. On July 13, 1982, each of the Houses of Congress repassed the bill by the two-thirds majority necessary to enact a bill notwithstanding the objections of the President. The bill thus became law (Public Law 97-215) on July 13, 1982.

* * *

IV. FINDINGS

(a) Article XI

34. The Panel first considered whether the Manufacturing Clause was consistent with Article XI of the General Agreement. It found that the prohibition of imports of certain printed matter provided for in the Manufacturing Clause was inconsistent with paragraph 1 of Article XI. The Panel noted that the United States had neither contested this nor attempted to justify the Manufacturing Clause under any of the exceptions to Article XI:1 contained in the General Agreement.

(b) The Protocol of Provisional Application

35. The Panel then examined whether this inconsistency with Article XI could be justified under the Protocol of Provisional Application, under which the United States applies the General Agreement[1]. It noted that, according to paragraph 1(b) of the Protocol, Part II of the General Agreement is to be applied "to the fullest extent not inconsistent with existing legislation," that is mandatory legislation in force on October 30, 1947[2]. It also noted that the central point of difference between the

[1] BISD Vol. IV/77
[2] BISD Vol. II/35 [Case 4] and 62 [Case 3]

two parties to the dispute related to whether the Manufacturing Clause, despite the postponement by legislation of July 1982 of the expiry date of July 1, 1982 inserted in the Clause in 1976, could still qualify as "existing legislation" under the Protocol of Provisional Application.

36. In order to examine the arguments advanced by the two parties on this matter (see paragraphs 12-18 above), the Panel, noting that the Manufacturing Clause had been amended on July 13, 1982, first asked itself whether the mere fact that the Clause had been amended after October 30, 1947 meant that it had lost the cover of the "existing legislation" provision of the Protocol of Provisional Application. The Panel noted that in the case of the Brazilian internal taxes[1] the CONTRACTING PARTIES had accepted that legislation inconsistent with Part II of the GATT could be modified without losing its status of "existing legislation" provided the degree of inconsistency with the General Agreement was not increased. The Panel further noted that one of the basic purposes of the provisional application of Part II of the GATT had been to ensure that the value of tariff concessions was not undermined by new protective legislation. To permit changes to "existing legislation" that did not increase the degree of inconsistency of such legislation with the General Agreement would thus be in accordance with this purpose of the Protocol of Provisional Application. The Panel therefore considered that changes to the Manufacturing Clause that did not alter its degree of inconsistency with the General Agreement, or which constituted a move towards a greater degree of consistency, would not cause it to cease to qualify as "existing legislation" in terms of paragraph 1(b) of the Protocol of Provisional Application. In this regard, the Panel noted with satisfaction that certain of the amendments made by the United States since 1947 to the Manufacturing Clause had reduced its degree of inconsistency with the General Agreement.

37. The Panel then asked itself whether or not the legislation of July 13, 1982 postponing the expiry date of the Manufacturing Clause had merely amended the Manufacturing Clause without increasing its degree of inconsistency with the General Agreement. The Panel considered that the answer to this question depended on whether the introduction by the United States in 1976 of an expiry date of July 1, 1982 for the Manufacturing Clause had constituted a move towards GATT conformity, which had been reversed by the 1982 legislation, or whether the 1976 amendment had represented only an announcement of the possibility of a future move. The Panel considered that the response to this

[1] BISD Vol. II/181

question depended in turn on whether, in the circumstance of the particular case, the insertion of the expiry date could justifiably have been considered by trading partners as a change in United States policy (with delayed implementation) or merely as the announcement of the possibility of a future change in policy. After a careful evaluation of the evidence before it, in particular of the evidence in paragraphs 24-29, and having regard to the fact that the expiry date inserted in the Clause in 1976 was the first such provision introduced since the legislation came into force in 1891, the Panel found that the European Communities had been justified in reaching the conclusion that the expiry date inserted in 1976 had constituted a policy change. The Panel therefore found that the insertion of the expiry date of July 1, 1982 for the Manufacturing Clause by Public Law 94-553 had represented a move towards greater GATT conformity. In consequence, the Panel further found that the legislation of July 13, 1982 postponing this expiry date had, in the circumstances of this particular case, constituted a reversal of this move towards greater GATT conformity and, therefore, increased the degree of inconsistency with the General Agreement of the Manufacturing Clause.

38. The Panel then considered whether this increase in the degree of inconsistency with the General Agreement of the Manufacturing Clause could be justified in terms of paragraph 1(b) of the Protocol of Provisional Application because the postponement of the expiry date had not increased the degree of inconsistency to a level in excess of that which had existed on October 30, 1947. The Panel was of the view that the basic issue in this respect was whether the "existing legislation" provision of the Protocol of Provisional Application should be interpreted as opening a "one-way street" permitting only movements from the situation on October 30, 1947 to the situation required by Part II of the GATT or a "two-way street" permitting also movements back towards the 1947 situation.

39. Since the text of the Protocol itself and previous decisions of the CONTRACTING PARTIES concerning the Protocol are not clear on this point, the Panel examined which of these two interpretations would be in accordance with the purposes of the Protocol of Provisional Application and of the General Agreement. It noted that the Protocol had been conceived of as providing a temporary dispensation to enable contracting parties to apply Part II of the General Agreement without changing existing legislation or acting inconsistently with it. Given this purpose of the Protocol, the Panel believed that, once a contracting party had reduced the degree of inconsistency of "existing legislation" with the

General Agreement, there could be no justification for a subsequent move to increase the degree of GATT inconsistency of such legislation, albeit to a level not exceeding that which had existed on October 30, 1947. The Panel further noted that one of the basic aims of the General Agreement was security and predictability in trade relations among contracting parties. The Panel believed that it would not be consistent with this aim if contracting parties were free to reverse steps that had brought legislation inconsistent with GATT and justified under the Protocol of Provisional Application into line with the provisions of the General Agreement. The Panel therefore found that the Protocol of Provisional Application did not authorize contracting parties to enact legislation increasing the degree of GATT inconsistency of "existing legislation," even if that degree of inconsistency remained not in excess of that which had obtained on October 30, 1947. The Panel therefore found that the United States legislation of July 13, 1982 postponing the expiry date of the Manufacturing Clause could not be justified under the Protocol of Provisional Application.

(c) Other Arguments Presented to the Panel

40. In the light of the above findings, the Panel considered that it was unnecessary to examine the arguments presented to it relating to Article XIII and the balance of Tokyo Round concessions.

41. The Panel noted that the United States had argued that, even if the Panel were to find nullification or impairment of a benefit accruing to the European Communities under the General Agreement, the circumstances would not be serious enough to justify authorization of a suspension of obligations or concessions under Article XXIII:2, since the European Communities had suffered no economic harm. The Panel decided not to examine this argument, because the complaining party, the European Communities, had not requested the Panel to make findings concerning the authorization of suspension of obligations or concessions under Article XXIII (see paragraph 30 above).

V. CONCLUSIONS

42. The Panel *found* that:

(i) the Manufacturing Clause was inconsistent with Article XI of the General Agreement;

(ii) the extension of the Manufacturing Clause beyond July 1, 1982 could not be justified under the Protocol of Provisional Application;

(iii) the United States was therefore acting in this respect inconsistently with its obligations under the General Agreement, as applied pursuant to the Protocol of Provisional Application; and

(iv) the extension of the Manufacturing Clause beyond July 1, 1982 consequently had to be considered *prima facie* to nullify or impair benefits accruing to the European Communities under the GATT.

43. In the light of the above, the Panel *suggests* that the CONTRACTING PARTIES recommend that the United States bring the Manufacturing Clause into line with its obligations under the General Agreement.

PANEL ON JAPANESE MEASURES ON IMPORTS OF LEATHER

Report of the Panel adopted on May 15/16, 1984
BISD 31S/94, 110

V. FINDINGS AND CONCLUSIONS

40. The Panel considered the matter referred to it by the CONTRACTING PARTIES regarding restrictions maintained by Japan on the import of certain semi-processed and finished leather, in accordance with its terms of reference set out in paragraph 2 above. It considered the arguments put forward by the parties to the dispute, as well as the points made by other delegations indicating an interest in the matter to the extent that these points bore on the case before it.

41. The Panel noted that the approach of the two parties had important differences. The United States approach was based essentially on legal arguments. Its main contention was that the Japanese restrictions were in contravention of Article XI and that, in addition, the restrictions also contravened Articles X:1 and 3 and XIII:3 and adversely affected tariff bindings. Japan's case, on the other hand, rested almost entirely on considerations resulting from the particular problems connected with the population group known as the Dowa people.

42. The Panel first considered the United States' complaint that quantitative restrictions maintained by Japan on the leather in question (see paragraph 7), were inconsistent with Article XI of the General Agreement which prohibits the use of quantitative restrictions.

43. The Panel appreciated the difficult socio-economic situation of the Japanese leather industry and the particularly sensitive problem of the Dowa population. The Panel appreciated the fact that leather and leather footwear were the only manufactured items which were subject to residual restrictions in Japan. This, in the Panel's view, bore witness to the difficulties which were involved in this case. The Panel also noted the fact that Japan had, despite its problem, increased the volume of leather imports permitted under its import régime and had continued to pursue a policy of expanding quotas over an extended period of time.

44. The Panel noted that Article XI:1 prohibits the use of quantita-

tive restrictions. It recognized that situations might exist in which the maintenance of such restrictions would be justified under the relevant GATT provisions. It noted, however, that Japan had not invoked any provision of the General Agreement to justify the maintenance of the import restrictions on leather. The Panel decided that in such circumstances it was not for it to establish whether the present measures would be justified under any GATT provision or provisions. The Panel considered that the special historical, cultural and socio-economic circumstances referred to by Japan could not be taken into account by it in this context since its terms of reference were to examine the matter "in the light of the relevant GATT provisions" and these provisions did not provide such a justification for import restrictions. It noted that a panel report[1] adopted by the CONTRACTING PARTIES in 1983 had, in a similar situation, concluded "that [such matters] did not come within the purview of Articles XI and XIII of the GATT and . . . lay outside its consideration." The Panel therefore found that the Japanese import restrictions at issue, made effective through quotas and import licences, contravened Article XI:1.

45. The Panel noted that Japan had ceased to invoke Article XII regarding balance-of-payments difficulties in 1963. It noted that the Panel report referred to above had also concluded that the fact that "restrictions had been in existence for a long time . . . did not alter the obligations which contracting parties had accepted under GATT provisions."[2] The Panel found this to be valid also in the present case.

46. In accordance with established GATT practice,[3] the Panel therefore found that the Japanese restrictions on the products under consideration constituted a *prima facie* case of nullification or impairment of benefits which the United States was entitled to expect under the General Agreement.

47. The Panel noted that its terms of reference in this case explicitly required it "to make findings on the question of nullification and impairment." It also noted that since a *prima facie* case had been established, according to the established GATT practice,[4] it was up to Japan to rebut the presumption that nullification or impairment had actually occurred.

[1] Panel report on Quantitative Restrictions against Imports of Certain Products from Hong Kong (L/5511, paragraph 27)

[2] L/5511, paragraph 28

[3] Annex to Understanding Regarding Notification, Consultation, Dispute Settlement and Surveillance (BISD, 26S/216, paragraph 5).

[4] Annex to Understanding Regarding Notification, Consultation, Dispute Settlement and Surveillance (BISD, 26S/216, paragraph 5)

48. Against this background the Panel considered Japan's argument that the existence of the quotas themselves did not necessarily mean that nullification or impairment of benefits accruing to the United States had actually been caused, but that this depended solely upon whether or not the allocation system and its implementation functioned so as to hinder United States' trade.

49. The Panel examined the trade figures supplied by Japan in support of this contention, which related to the period from 1978 (before conclusion of the bilateral agreement) to 1982. It noted that these figures showed that, while United States' total exports of bovine and equine leather had increased from about US$113 million to about US$213 million, or approximately 88 per cent, its export to Japan had increased by about 350 per cent, from US$2 million to about US$9 million. In comparison, United States' exports to the Federal Republic of Germany and Italy had, taken together, increased from about US$2.6 million to about US$8.5 million, i.e. a growth of only 227 per cent, and United States' exports to France and the United Kingdom had actually declined by 36 per cent in the same period from about US$7.7 million to about US$4.9 million.

50. On the other hand, the Panel noted that, according to figures supplied by the United States, whilst United States bovine and equine leather exports to Japan had increased by about US$7 million—more than twice as much as the growth of exports to the four member States of the European Community referred to—they had increased by about US$82 million, from about US$38 million to US$120 million, to three other East Asian markets taken together, each of which, since 1980, had imported more such leather from the United States than had Japan. The Panel also noted that while United States' bovine and equine leather exports to Japan in 1982 represented about 67 per cent of its exports to the four European Community countries, they were equivalent to less than 8 per cent of its exports of such leather to the three East Asian markets.[1] The Panel further noted that United States exports to Japan of the two other leather categories in question, i.e. sheep and lamb and goat and kid leather, were small and would not change the picture presented above.

51. The Panel then considered the Japanese argument that the quota did not limit United States' exports to Japan because United States' exporters had not filled the large quota opened for them and that the limiting factors were the recession of the Japanese leather market and

[1] The People's Republic of China, Hong Kong and the Republic of Korea.

lack of efforts by United States' suppliers in research and development, in improving quality and in responding to the specific needs of the Japanese market. It also took into account Japan's arguments that the licensing system was not an obstacle.

52. It noted the United States' arguments that its industry had exported the same type of leather to Japan as to any other country, that it could have filled the quota were it not for the accompanying administrative obstacles in the licensing system and that it could have exported more leather than provided for under the quota, if the Japanese régime had not existed.

53. The Panel found that the United States' exports of bovine and equine leather to Japan had increased considerably both in percentage terms and in absolute figures in the period under consideration and that this might be attributed to the relaxation of Japanese restrictions, as Japan had claimed. However, the Panel could not escape the conclusion that the import restrictions were maintained in order to restrict imports, including imports from the United States. Its noted that, while the Japanese market was not fully comparable to other markets in East Asia, the evidence relating to these markets still tended to support the view that the Japanese restrictions limited United States' exports of leather to its market.

54. The Panel then turned to the arguments based on the fact that the United States had not filled its quotas. It noted that these consisted of contradictory assertions by the two parties that, by their nature, were difficult to evaluate. It did, however, consider that the fact that the United States was able to export large quantities of leather to other markets, and that other supplying countries had supported the arguments of the United States, tended to confirm the assumption that the existence of the restrictions had adversely affected United States' exports.

55. In any event, the Panel wished to stress that the existence of a quantitative restriction should be presumed to cause nullification or impairment not only because of any effect it had had on the volume of trade but also for other reasons e.g., it would lead to increased transaction costs and would create uncertainties which could affect investment plans.

56. The Panel therefore found that the arguments advanced by Japan were not sufficient to rebut the presumption that the quantitative restrictions on imports of leather had nullified or impaired benefits accruing to the United States under Article XI of the General Agreement.

57. The Panel noted that the United States had, as a subsidiary matter, argued that Japan had also nullified or impaired benefits under Articles II, X:1, X:3 and XII:3. In view of the findings set out in the paragraphs above, the Panel found that it was not necessary for it to make a finding on these matters.

58. The Panel noted that some of the delegations which had indicated an interest in the matter before it and which had made statements to the Panel had argued that Japan's import régime on leather contained discriminatory elements and therefore contravened Article XIII:1 and 2. The Panel did not make a finding on this matter as it had not been raised by the United States and was not, therefore, within its terms of reference. It wishes however to draw the attention of the Council to the fact that this point was raised.

59. On the basis of the findings reached above, the Panel suggests that the CONTRACTING PARTIES recommend that Japan eliminate its quantitative restrictions maintained on the import of the products subject of the United States' complaint (see paragraph 7) and thus conform with the GATT provisions.

60. The Panel noted that Japan had indicated that it would not be possible for it to eliminate its quantitative restrictions on leather immediately. The Panel recognized the difficulties faced by Japan but noted that "the first objective of the CONTRACTING PARTIES is usually to secure the withdrawal of the measures concerned if these are found to be inconsistent with the General Agreement.[1]" The Panel felt that the Council might wish to consider whether or not Japan should be given a certain amount of time progressively to eliminate the import restrictions in question and, in this context, to consider the factors referred to above, in particular those in paragraph 43.

[1] Annex to Understanding Regarding Notification, Consultation, Dispute Settlement and Surveillance (BISD, 26/216, paragraph 4)

PANEL ON VALUE-ADDED TAX AND THRESHOLD

Report of the Panel adopted by the Committee on Government Procurement on May 16, 1984
BISD 31S/247, 254

IV. FINDINGS AND CONCLUSIONS

18. The Panel examined whether the European Economic Community's practice of excluding the value-added tax (VAT) from the contract price in relation to the determination of whether government purchases fall under the Agreement was in conformity with Article I:1(b) of the Agreement, according to which this Agreement applies to "any procurement contract of a value of SDR 150,000 or more."

19. The Panel noted that the case before it dealt with the value of contracts as estimated for the purpose of determining whether a procurement contract would fall above or below the threshold of the Agreement on Government Procurement or, in other words, whether a contract was to be advertised and subsequently awarded under the terms of the Agreement.

20. The Panel noted that no reference was made in Article I:1(b) or elsewhere in the Agreement to the inclusion or exclusion of value-added taxes in the calculation of the value of a procurement contract for the purpose of threshold determinations.

21. The Panel considered the case before it in the light of the drafting background of Article I:1(b). The Panel noted that the question of how the VAT should be treated in the calculation of the contract value had not been specifically raised in the negotiations.

22. The Panel found that the case before it depended on an interpretation of the term contract value. In view of the silence of the Agreement and the absence of a negotiating history concerning this term, the Panel analyzed the meaning of the term contract value. The Panel first noted that the value of a contract, as signed between a procuring entity and a winning supplier, might or might not include the element of indirect taxes, depending on how the procurement was carried out. However, for the purchasing entity, what counted was the

total price which the entity would have to pay in order to obtain the product in question. If the entity was to pay the VAT, this element would form part of the total price whether it was included in the supplier's bill or whether it would be paid in another way by the entity. Against this background and as Article I:1(b) did not expressly provide for the deduction of any taxes, the Panel found that the natural interpretation of the term contract value would be the full cost to the entity, taking into account all the elements that would normally enter into the final price, and would therefore include any VAT payable, unless the entity was exempted from paying VAT.

23. In this context, the Panel also noted that most Parties to the Agreement had, from the outset, included indirect taxes such as VAT when making threshold determinations.

24. The Panel asked itself what the intentions of the drafters had been with regard to the question before it in the light of the objectives of the Agreement. Whether any VAT payable was included or excluded in the context of threshold determination would, in the view of the Panel, make a clear difference to the number of contracts to which the Agreement would be applied. The Panel believed that it must have been the intention of the drafters that the obligations should be interpreted in a uniform way by all Parties with respect to this question.

25. The fact that the present EEC legislation excluding VAT for threshold determinations had already existed at the time of the negotiations was, in the Panel's view, not a decisive argument. Although the negotiating partners might have been aware of this particular element in the EEC's legislation, the Panel did not consider it reasonable to presume that it was in fact known to all negotiating partners nor that these partners foresaw and accepted that the EEC would exclude the VAT for the purpose of threshold determinations under the Agreement. The Panel further noted that, while Article I:1(b) was silent on the question of how to treat value-added taxes for this purpose, the corresponding part of the relevant EEC Directive had explicitly excluded the VAT. The Panel considered that the EEC legislation on this point could be taken as an indication that the term contract value in Article I:1(b) did not automatically exclude the VAT element.

26. The Panel also considered the argument that threshold determinations had to be based on estimates which by their nature were imprecise and that several erratic factors would be at play which lead to variations in the threshold. The figure of SDR 150,000 was, for instance, converted into national currencies once a year, whereas exchange rates

could fluctuate considerably over the year. Furthermore, the accuracy of the estimate would depend on the skill and experience of the officials responsible. The Panel was of the opinion that the acceptance of certain erratic factors which applied to all Parties and which could affect the threshold in both directions, could not mean that Parties might make a unilateral deduction of certain cost elements like VAT, which would have the effect of raising the threshold for the Party in question. The inevitable uncertainty resulting from the need to estimate the contract value and from currency variations was no reason to create this further difference. Regarding the currency conversions, the Panel also noted that the Committee had decided, at its January 1981 meeting, to examine any significant problem with regard to the application of the Agreement due to a major currency change in the course of the year.

27. The Panel considered the argument that the inclusion of the VAT would lead to differences among the various EC member States, caused by the absence of uniform VAT rates within the Community, and recognized that the Community considered this to be a problem. The Panel also recognized that arguments could be made for a net of VAT rule, in particular in the context of a common market such as the European Community which aimed at harmonizing conditions of competition. The Panel did not go further into a discussion of the merits or demerits of such a rule as it found that this would not change its interpretation of Article I:1(b). The Panel also considered that the existence of different VAT rates in the Community was not of decisive relevance for the interpretation of the provisions of the Agreement applying between the Parties to it. The Panel noted in this context that VAT rates as well as other elements that went into the total contract price differed between the Parties to the Agreement other than the EEC. The Panel considered that the fact that elements which went into the total contract price differed from Party to Party was no justification for excluding particular cost elements in the absence of provisions specifically excluding them.

28. Considering these various aspects and arguments, the Panel found that the term contract value in Article I:1(b) should be interpreted to be the full cost to the entity, taking into account all the elements that would normally enter into the final price, and would therefore include any VAT payable, unless the entity was exempted from paying VAT. The Panel concluded, therefore, that the present EEC practice of excluding the VAT was not in conformity with this interpretation of the existing Agreement when the entity was not exempted from paying VAT.

PANEL ON NEWSPRINT

Report of the Panel adopted on November 20, 1984
BISD 31S/114, 130

V. FINDINGS AND CONCLUSIONS

47. The Panel considered the matter referred to it by the CONTRACTING PARTIES regarding the complaint by Canada, in accordance with its terms of reference, set out in paragraph 2 above, which are limited to the duty-free quota of 1.5 million tonnes within the EC tariff concession on newsprint (see paragraph 9 above). It considered the arguments put forward by the parties to the dispute, as well as the points made by the delegations of the Nordic countries (Finland, Norway, Sweden) and New Zealand which appeared before the Panel.

48. The Panel noted that in its Regulation No. 3684/83 of December 22, 1983, the European Communities have, for the year 1984, opened a duty-free tariff quota of 500,000 tonnes for newsprint, whereas the commitment of the EC in its GATT Schedule LXXII provides for an annual duty-free quota of 1.5 million tonnes. The Panel also noted that in an introductory paragraph to the Regulation as well as in the EC communication to the contracting parties (document L/5599), reference is made to the volume of 500,000 tonnes to be fixed "at a provisional level;" Article 1:1 of the Regulation itself, however, makes no reference to the provisional nature of this quota.

49. The Panel also noted the EC statement that Schedule LXXII had not been modified, that the action taken by the EC was merely a change in the administration or management of the tariff quota which was permissible under Article XIII of the GATT, and that therefore renegotiations under Article XXVIII were not called for.

50. The Panel could not share the argument advanced by the EC that their action did not constitute a change in their GATT tariff commitment. It noted that under long-standing GATT practice, even purely formal changes in the tariff schedule of a contracting party, which may not affect the GATT rights of other countries, such as the conversion of a specific to an *ad valorem* duty without an increase in the protective effect of the tariff rate in question, have been considered to require renegotiations. By the same token, the EC action would, in the Panel's

view, have required the EC to conduct such negotiations. The Panel also noted that in granting the concession in 1973, the EC had not made it subject to any qualification or reservation in the sense of Article II:1(b) although at the time the concession was made, it was known that agreement had already been reached that the EFTA countries would obtain full duty-free access to the Community market for newsprint from January 1, 1984 onward. The Panel therefore found that although in the formal sense the EC had not modified its GATT concession, it had *in fact* changed its GATT commitment unilaterally, by limiting its duty-free tariff quota for M.F.N. suppliers for 1984 to 500,000 tonnes.

51. The Panel considered the arguments advanced by the EC relating to Article XIII, but concluded that the conditions for its application had not been fulfilled. In examining the EEC Regulation 3684/83, the Panel found that it did not in fact constitute a change in the administration or management of the tariff quota from a global quota system to a system of country shares, as had been asserted by the EC. The Regulation in its Article 1.1 simply opens a quota of 500,000 tonnes and stipulates in Article 1.3 that imports shall not be charged against this quota if they are already free of customs duties under other preferential tariff treatment. It does not provide an allocation of country shares to individual M.F.N. suppliers, nor has a separate quota (global or otherwise) for the EFTA countries been established, as Article XIII requires. The Panel also noted that the EC Regulation contains no basis for the contention that it was simply meant to bring about a change in the management of the quota. Rather, in one of its introductory provisions, the Regulation, in referring to the tariff quota of 1.5 million tonnes, states that this volume must be reduced to allow for imports from EFTA countries which by virtue of the free-trade agreements can be effected duty-free as from January 1, 1984. In this connection the Panel found relevant the wording of the text of the EC communication (contained in document L/5599) in which the EC stated: "An appropriate reduction in the level of the bound quota was decided in certain similar cases in the past (L/4537, paragraph 5), and the European Community considers that this could also be the right approach in the case of newsprint."

52. Taking all factors mentioned above into account, the Panel concluded that the EC, in unilaterally establishing for 1984 a duty-free quota of 500,000 tonnes, had not acted in conformity with their obligations under Article II of the GATT. The Panel shared the view expressed before it relating to the fundamental importance of the security and predictability of GATT tariff bindings, a principle which constitutes a central obligation in the system of the General Agreement.

53. In light of the foregoing and in accordance with established GATT practice (paragraph 5 of the Framework Understanding, BISD 26S/216), the Panel found that the EC action constituted a *prima facie* case of nullification or impairment of benefits which Canada was entitled to expect under the General Agreement.

54. While holding that the right of Canada to compete within a duty-free tariff quota of 1.5 million tonnes has been impaired by the EC action, the Panel recognized, however, that as a result of newsprint imports from EFTA countries entering the EC market duty-free since January 1, 1984 under the terms of the free-trade agreements, the *value* of the EC concession had greatly increased for non-EFTA suppliers and especially for Canada as the most important M.F.N. supplier. The Panel concluded that this increased value of the concession justifies the EC engaging in renegotiations under Article XXVIII, in accordance with the customary procedures and practices for such negotiations, with the objective of achieving some reduction in the size of the tariff quota. In the view of the Panel, such a reduction would, in a case like the one before the Panel where the increased value of the concession derives from an action by the EC to grant duty-free access to newsprint imports from the EFTA countries, be without payment of compensation. In this connection, the Panel found that although the statistical data before it did not differentiate between imports entering duty-free under the GATT quota and those under the autonomous régime, the fact that the GATT quota was filled while total Canadian exports never exceeded half that quota is evidence that the EFTA countries did participate in the GATT quota up until the end of 1983.

55. The Panel carefully noted and examined the statement by the EC that, should the Panel consider the action taken by the EC as not being in conformity with the GATT, they might proceed to option (b) under which the tariff quota would be maintained at 1.5 million tonnes but that imports from all sources, including the EFTA countries, would be recorded against that quota; once the latter had been filled, the Community's formal contractual obligations would have been met. While the Panel could find no specific GATT provision forbidding such action and no precedents to guide it, it considered that this would not be an appropriate solution to the problem and would create an unfortunate precedent. It is in the nature of a duty-free tariff quota to allow specified quantities of imports into a country duty-free which would otherwise be dutiable, which is not the case for EFTA imports by virtue of the free-trade agreements. Imports which are already duty-free, due to a preferential agreement, cannot by their very nature participate in an M.F.N.

duty-free quota. The situation in this respect could only change if the free-trade agreements with the EFTA countries were to be discontinued; in this case these countries would be entitled to fall back on their GATT rights vis-à-vis the EC, which rights continue to exist.

56. On the basis of the findings and conclusions reached above, the Panel suggests that the CONTRACTING PARTIES recommend that the European Communities engage promptly in renegotiations under the procedures of Article XXVIII of the GATT with regard to the tariff quota on newsprint in Schedule LXXII. Further, the Panel suggests that the CONTRACTING PARTIES recommend to the European Communities that, pending the termination of such renegotiations, the duty-free tariff quota of 1.5 million tonnes for M.F.N. suppliers be maintained.

57. In the light of the suggested recommendations contained in paragraph 56 above, the Panel saw no need to express itself on the request by Canada that it be authorized to suspend the application of appropriate concessions or other obligations under the GATT.

NEW ZEALAND—IMPORTS OF ELECTRICAL TRANSFORMERS FROM FINLAND

Report of the Panel adopted on July 18, 1985
BISD 32S/55, 66

IV. CONCLUSIONS

4:1. The Panel based its consideration of the case before it on Article VI of the General Agreement, in particular its paragraphs 1, 2 and 6(a). It noted that paragraph 1 of Article VI defined dumping as the introduction of products of one country into the commerce of another country at less than their normal value, but condemned dumping as such only in case material injury had been caused. In this connection, Article VI:6(a) prohibited the levying of an anti-dumping duty by a contracting party on the importation of any product of another contracting party unless it determined that the effect of the dumping was such as to cause or threaten material injury to an established domestic industry.

4:2 The first question which the Panel addressed was whether the Finnish exporter, in its sale of the two transformers in question to New Zealand, had engaged in dumping in terms of Article VI. The Panel noted that—in the absence of a domestic price in Finland for custom-built transformers of this kind—the New Zealand authorities had based their determination of normal value on the cost-of-production method foreseen in Article VI:1(b)(ii). The Panel also noted that Finland, while not objecting to the use of this method as such, had contested the individual elements of the calculation as being too high, resulting in a constructed price much higher than the actual price of the Finnish exporter. In the Finnish view, the New Zealand authorities should have instead used the cost elements provided by the exporter. The Panel, having heard the arguments put forward by both sides and having perused the documents submitted, concluded that the Finnish exporter, whether through its own fault or not, had not provided all of the necessary cost elements which would have enabled the New Zealand authorities to carry out a meaningful cost-of-production calculation on the basis of the information supplied by the exporter alone. This was true especially for the 4.5 MVA transformer but also to a large degree for the 12.5 MVA unit. In the view of the Panel, the New Zealand authorities were therefore justified in making a cost calculation, where necessary, on the basis of price elements obtained from other sources.

4:3. The Panel then considered the evidence put forward by both sides as to the appropriateness of the cost elements used by the New Zealand authorities in arriving at their decision that dumping had occurred. The Panel noted that this evidence was of a highly technical nature, especially because it related to complicated custom-built products. It also noted that Article VI did not contain any specific guidelines for the calculation of cost-of-production and considered that the method used in this particular case appeared to be a reasonable one. In view of this and having noted the arguments put forward by both sides as regards the costing of certain inputs used in the manufacture of the transformers, the Panel considered that there was no basis on which to disagree with the New Zealand authorities' finding of dumping and proceeded to the question of whether the imports in question had caused or threatened to cause injury to the New Zealand transformer industry.

4:4. The Panel noted the view expressed by the New Zealand delegation that the determination of material injury was a matter specifically and expressly reserved, under the terms of Article VI:6(a), for the decision of the contracting party levying the anti-dumping duty. It also noted the contention that other contracting parties might inquire as to whether such a determination had been made, but that the latter could not be challenged or scrutinized by other contracting parties nor indeed by the CONTRACTING PARTIES themselves. The Panel agreed that the responsibility to make a determination of material injury caused by dumped imports rested in the first place with the authorities of the importing contracting party concerned. However, the Panel could not share the view that such a determination could not be scrutinized if it were challenged by another contracting party. On the contrary, the Panel believed that if a contracting party affected by the determination could make a case that the importation could not in itself have the effect of causing material injury to the industry in question, that contracting party was entitled, under the relevant GATT provisions, in particular Article XXIII, that its representations be given sympathetic consideration and that eventually, if no satisfactory adjustment was effected, it might refer the matter to the CONTRACTING PARTIES, as had been done by Finland in the present case. To conclude otherwise would give governments complete freedom and unrestricted discretion in deciding anti-dumping cases without any possibility to review the action taken in the GATT. This would lead to an unacceptable situation under the aspect of law and order in international trade relations as governed by the GATT. The Panel in this connection noted that a similar point had been raised, and rejected, in the report of the Panel on Complaints relating to Swedish anti-dumping duties (BISD 3S/81). The Panel fully shared the view expressed by that panel when it stated that "it was clear from the wording of Article VI that no anti-dumping duties should be levied until certain facts had been established. As this represented an obligation on the part of the contracting party imposing such duties, it would be reasonable to expect that the contracting party should establish the existence of these facts when its action is challenged" (paragraph 15).

4:5. The Panel accepted the argument put forward by New Zealand that the complaining company represented the New Zealand transformer industry in terms of Article VI of the GATT since its output accounted for 92 per cent of the total domestic production. It found support for this view in the report of the Group of Experts on Anti-Dumping and Countervailing Duties (BISD 8S/145, paragraph 18) which had discussed the term "industry" in relation to the concept of injury and had concluded that as a general guiding principle, "judgements of material injury should be related to total national output of the like commodity concerned or a significant part thereof." In this connection, the Group of Experts did refer to a single firm that was an important or significant part of the industry.

4:6. In its examination whether the New Zealand transformer industry had suffered injury from the imports in question, the Panel subsequently dealt with the argument put forward by New Zealand that this industry was structured in such a way that there existed four distinguishable ranges of transformers, i.e. transformers between 1-5 MVA, 5-10 MVA, 10-20 MVA, and 20 MVA and above, which for purposes of injury determination had to be considered separately. The Panel was of the view that this was not a valid argument, especially in light of the fact that the complaining company, representing—as indicated above—the New Zealand transformer industry, in the year 1982/83 produced the whole range of transformers, most of which in a range (i.e. above 20 MVA) which was not at all affected by the imports from Finland. In its own submission to the Panel, the New Zealand delegation conceded that the segmentation according to MVA ratings might not coincide with that in other countries and underlined that each segment of the industry's operation made a contribution to the overall viability and profitability of a producer of transformers. It was thus, in the Panel's view, the overall state of health of the New Zealand transformer industry which must provide the basis for a judgement whether injury was caused by dumped imports. To decide otherwise would allow the possibility to grant relief through anti-dumping duties to individual lines of production of a particular industry or company—a notion which could clearly be at variance with the concept of industry in Article VI in a case like the present one where both the Finnish exporter and the New Zealand industry were engaged in the manufacture and distribution of power transformers.

4:7. In its examination, the Panel then turned to the question whether the New Zealand transformer industry had suffered material injury as a result of the imports of the two transformers from Finland. The Panel did not question that this industry had been in a poor economic situation, due to lack of new orders, diminishing orders on hand in certain product categories, declining profitability, a large increase in imports and considerable uncertainty as to new orders. The Panel noted, on the other hand, that the Finnish imports in question of about $NZ 175.000 (C & F NZ Port) represented only 2.4 per cent of total sales of the New Zealand transformer industry in 1983. In terms of MVA ratings, the data submitted to the Panel indicated that in the year 1982/83, total New Zealand production and imports taken together represented 1.130 MVA, of which 700 MVA were imported transformers; these figures should be compared with the 17 MVA of the two Finnish transformers taken together. The latter thus represented 1.5 per cent of the sum of domestic production and imports, or 2.4 per cent of total imports. The Panel also considered it significant that imports increased from 1981/82 to 1982/83 by 250 per cent in MVA terms, i.e. from 200 MVA to 700 MVA, and that the imports from Finland represented only 3.4 per cent of this increase. In view of these facts, the Panel concluded that while the New Zealand transformer industry might have suffered injury from increased imports, the cause of this injury could not be attributed to the imports in question from Finland, which constituted an almost insignificant part in the overall sales of transformers in the period concerned. In this connection, the Panel rejected the contention advanced by the New Zealand delegation that, at least as far as material injury in terms of Article VI was concerned, "any given amount of profit lost" by the complaining firm was in some sense an "injury" to a domestic industry.

4:8. The Panel noted that while the decision of the New Zealand Minister of Customs to impose anti-dumping duties was based solely on material injury having been caused by the imports in question, the New Zealand delegation had also alleged before the Panel the existence of threat of material injury. In view of the high import penetration of the

New Zealand transformer market, the significant increase in imports from all sources over one single year and the minimal impact of the actual Finnish imports in question, the Panel saw no reason to assume that imports from Finland would in the future change this picture significantly. The Panel noted in addition that at the time the ministerial decision was taken, the Finnish exporter had not attempted to make any further sales to the New Zealand market. The Panel could therefore not agree that the imposition of anti-dumping duties could have been based on threat of material injury in terms of Article VI.

4:9. In view of the reasons contained in the preceding paragraphs, the Panel came to the conclusion that New Zealand had not been able to demonstrate that any injury suffered by its transformer industry had been material injury caused by the imports from Finland. The Panel therefore found that the imposition of anti-dumping duties on these imports was not consistent with the provision of Article VI:6(a) of the General Agreement.

4:10. In accordance with established GATT practice, the Panel held that where a measure had been taken which was judged to be inconsistent with the provisions of the General Agreement, this measure would *prima facie* constitute a case of nullification or impairment of benefits which other contracting parties were entitled to expect under the General Agreement.

4:11. The Panel proposes to the Council that it addresses to New Zealand a recommendation to revoke the anti-dumping determination and to reimburse the anti-dumping duty paid.

OMITTED

UNITED STATES—TAXES ON PETROLEUM AND CERTAIN IMPORTED SUBSTANCES

Report of the Panel adopted on June 17, 1987
BISD 34S/136, 138

2. FACTUAL ASPECTS

2.1 The "United States Superfund Amendments and Reauthorization Act of 1986" (hereinafter referred to as the "Superfund Act") was signed into law on October 17, 1986. The Superfund Act reauthorized a program to clean up hazardous waste sites and deal with public health programs caused by hazardous waste. It provided for excise and corporate income taxes and appropriations to pay for the cost of these programs. The Superfund Act introduced in particular a new broad-based corporate income tax and authorized yearly appropriations from general government revenues. It further (a) re-imposed an excise tax on petroleum at higher rates, (b) re-imposed a tax on certain chemicals ("feedstock chemicals"), and (c) imposed a new tax on certain imported substances produced or manufactured from taxable feedstock chemicals.

2.2 The tax on petroleum, which had been imposed at the rate of 0.79 cent per barrel for both domestic and imported products, was increased to 8.2 cents per barrel for "crude oil received at a United States refinery" and 11.7 cents a barrel for "petroleum products entered into the United States for consumption, use or warehousing." The term "crude oil" is defined to include crude oil condensate and natural gasoline. The term "petroleum products" is defined to comprise not only the products defined as "crude oil" but also refined gasoline, refined and residual oil, and certain other liquid hydrocarbon products. The tax increases went into effect on January 1, 1987.

2.3 The Superfund Act reimposed a *tax on certain chemicals* with which effect from January 1, 1987. The taxable chemicals and the applicable tax rates are listed in Annex I. The tax rates were set at the lower of either $4.87 per ton for petrochemicals and $4.45 per ton for inorganic chemicals or a dollar amount equivalent to 2 per cent of the 1980 wholesale price of the chemical. The tax is borne by the chemicals whether they are sold by the manufacturer, producer or importer thereof. The tax is not imposed if the manufacturer or producer of the taxable chemical sells it for export or for resale by the purchaser to a second purchaser for export.

2.4 The Superfund Act further imposes a new *tax on certain imported substances* sold or used by the importer thereof. This tax enters into effect on January 1, 1989. The Superfund Act establishes an initial list of taxable substances, which is reproduced in Annex II. The taxable substances are derivatives of the chemicals subject to the tax on certain chemicals described in the preceding paragraph. A substance shall be added to the list if the Secretary of the Treasury, in consultation with the Administrator of the Environmental Protection Agency and the Commissioner of Customs, determined that chemicals subject to the tax on certain chemicals constitute more than 50 per cent of the *weight* of the materials used to produce such substance (determined on the basis of the predominant method of production). He may also, to the extent necessary to carry out the purposes of the legislation, add any substance to the list if the *value* of the taxable chemicals constitutes more than 50 per cent of the total value of the materials used to produce the substance. The Secretary of the Treasury may also withdraw items from the list of taxable substances as necessary to carry out the purposes of the legislation.

2.5 The amount of tax on any of the imported substances equals in principle the amount of the tax which would have been imposed under the Superfund Act on the chemicals used as materials in the manufacture or production of the imported substance if the taxable chemicals had been sold in the United States for use in the manufacture or production of the imported substance.

2.6 Importers will be required to provide sufficient information regarding the chemicals inputs of taxable substances to enable the tax authorities to determine the amount of tax to be imposed. If the importer fails to furnish such information a tax shall be imposed equivalent to five per cent of the appraised value of the product at the time it was entered into the United States for consumption, use, or warehousing. However, the Secretary of the Treasury may prescribe by regulation, in lieu of the five per cent rate, a rate which would equal the amount that would be imposed if the substance were produced using the predominant method of production.

* * *

5. FINDINGS AND CONCLUSIONS

5.1 *Tax on petroleum*

5.1.1 The Panel examined the tax on petroleum in the light of the obligations the United States assumed under the General Agreement and found the following: The tax on petroleum is an excise tax levied on imported and domestic goods. Such taxes are subject to the national treatment requirement of Article III:2, first sentence, which reads:

> "The products of the territory of any contracting party imported into the territory of any other contracting party shall not be subject, directly or indirectly, to internal taxes or other internal charges of any kind in excess of those applied, directly or indirectly, to like domestic products."

The CONTRACTING PARTIES have not developed a definition of the term "like products" in the above provision. In the report of the Working Party on Border Tax Adjustments, adopted by the CONTRACTING PARTIES in 1970, it was suggested that the problems arising from the interpretation of this term should be examined on a case-by-case basis and that one of the possible methods for determining whether two products were like products was to compare their end-uses in a given market (BISD 18S/102). The domestic products subject to the tax are: crude oil, crude oil condensates, and natural gasoline. The imported products subject to the tax are: crude oil, crude oil condensates, natural gasoline, refined and residual oil, and certain other liquid hydrocarbon products. The imported and domestic products are thus either identical or, in the case of imported liquid hydrocarbon products, serve substantially identical end-uses. The imported and domestic products subject to the tax on petroleum are therefore in the view of the Panel "like products" within the meaning of Article III:2. The rate of tax applied to the imported products is 3.5 cents per barrel higher than the rate applied to the like domestic products. Article III:2, first sentence, applies whether or not the products concerned are subject to a tariff concession and whether or not adverse trade effects occurred (see paragraph 5.1.9 below). The tax on petroleum is for these reasons inconsistent with the United States obligations under Article III:2, first sentence.

5.1.2 The United States did not present to the Panel any arguments to support a legal conclusion different from the one set out above. Its main contention was that the tax differential was so small that its trade effects were minimal or nil and that the tax differential—whether it conformed to Article III:2, first sentence, or not—did not nullify or impair benefits accruing to Canada, the EEC and Mexico under the General Agreement. Canada, the EEC and Mexico considered this defense to be neither legally valid nor factually correct (paragraphs 3.1.1-3.1.11 above). As both sides to the dispute considered this issue to be the central legal question to which the tax on petroleum gives rise, the Panel examined it in particular detail. It reached the following conclusions.

5.1.3 Under Article XXIII of the General Agreement contracting parties may bring complaints, *inter alia,* if they consider that benefits accruing to them under that Agreement are nullified or impaired. According to established GATT practice, described in the Annex to the 1979 Understanding on dispute settlement,

> "where there is an infringement of the obligations assumed under the General Agreement, the action is considered *prima facie* to constitute a case of nullification or impairment" (BISD 26S/216).

The question raised by the case before the Panel is whether the presumption that a measure inconsistent with the General Agreement causes a nullification or impairment of benefits accruing under that Agreement is an absolute or a rebuttable presumption and, if rebuttable, whether a demonstration that a measure inconsistent with Article III:2, first sentence, has no or insignificant effects on trade is a sufficient rebuttal.

5.1.4 According to Article XXIII:2 there are two decisions the Contracting Parties may take after a claim of nullification or impairment, unresolved through consultations, has been referred to them. First, they may make recommendations or give a ruling on the matter. As to such a decision paragraph 4 of the Annex to the 1979 Understanding on dispute settlement states:

> "In the absence of a mutually agreed solution, the first objective of the Contracting Parties is usually to secure the withdrawal of the measures concerned if these are found to be inconsistent with the General Agreement. The provision of compensation should be resorted to only if the immediate

withdrawal of the measure is impracticable and as a temporary measure pending the withdrawal of the measures which are inconsistent with the General Agreement" (BISD 26S/216).

The impact of the inconsistent measure is not mentioned in the above paragraph. This suggests that the practice of the CONTRACTING PARTIES is to make recommendations and rulings on measures found to be inconsistent with the General Agreement independent of the impact of such measures.

5.1.5 The second category of decisions the CONTRACTING PARTIES may take under Article XXIII:2 are decisions to authorize a suspension of concessions or other obligations if they "consider that the circumstances are serious enough to justify such an action." Paragraph 5 of the Annex to the 1979 Understanding on dispute settlement indicates how the CONTRACTING PARTIES are to deal with requests for such an authorization in the case of an infringement of the obligations assumed under the General Agreement. The relevant part of this paragraph reads:

> "A *prima facie* case of nullification or impairment would *ipso facto* require consideration of whether the circumstances are serious enough to justify the authorization of suspension of concessions or obligations, if the contracting party bringing the complaint so requests. This means that there is normally a presumption that a breach of the rules has an adverse impact on other contracting parties, and in such cases, it is up to the contracting parties against whom the complaint has been brought to rebut the charge" (BISD 26S/216).

Thus, the 1979 Understanding does not refer to the adverse impact of a measure, and the possibility of a rebuttal, in connexion with the power of the CONTRACTING PARTIES to make recommendations or give rulings on measures inconsistent with the General Agreement; it does so only in connection with the authorization of compensatory action. This, in the view of the Panel, supports the conclusion that the impact of a measure inconsistent with the General Agreement is not relevant for a determination of nullification or impairment by the CONTRACTING PARTIES.

5.1.6 The Panel examined how the CONTRACTING PARTIES have reacted in previous cases to claims that a measure inconsistent with the General Agreement had no adverse impact and therefore did not nullify or impair benefits accruing under the General Agreement to the contracting party that had brought the complaint. The Panel noted such claims had been made in a number of cases but that there was no case in the history of the GATT in which a contracting party had successfully rebutted the presumption that a measure infringing obligations causes nullification and impairment. In a case involving credit facilities granted to farmers that purchase domestically-produced machinery the Panel considered that:

> "If the considered view of the Italian Government was that these credit facilities had not influenced the terms of competition on the Italian market, there would not seem to be a serious problem in amending the operation of the Law so as to avoid any discrimination as regards these credit facilities between the domestic and imported tractors and agricultural machinery" (BISD 7S/66-67).

In a case involving undertakings to purchase domestic products, given by foreign visitors to obtain a governmental authorization to invest, the Panel concluded:

> "The Panel carefully considered the effects of the purchase requirements on trade. The Panel concluded that an evaluation of these effects would entail scrutiny and analysis of the implementation of several thousands of often differently worded undertakings as well as speculation on what the purchasing behaviour of foreign investors would have been in their absence. The Panel could not undertake such an evaluation and it is therefore not in a position to judge how frequently the purchase requirements cause investors to act differently than they would have acted in the absence of the undertakings and how frequently they therefore adversely affect the trade interests of other contracting parties. The Panel, however, believes that an evaluation of the trade effects was not directly relevant to its findings because a breach of a GATT rule is presumed to have an adverse impact on other contracting parties" (BISD 30S/167).

In the case of an import quota on leather which allegedly had not been fully utilized by the complaining country the Panel stated:

> "The Panel wished to stress that the existence of a quantitative restriction should be presumed to cause nullification or impairment not only because of any effect it had had on the volume of trade but also for other reasons e.g., it would lead to increased transaction costs and would create uncertainties which could affect investment plans" (BISD 31S/113).

The remarks made by the panels in these cases apply, *mutatis mutandis,* also to the case before the present Panel.

5.1.7 The Panel concluded from its review of the above and other cases, that while the CONTRACTING PARTIES had not explicitly decided whether the presumption that illegal measures cause nullification or impairment could be rebutted, the presumption had in practice operated as an irrefutable presumption.

5.1.8 The Panel then examined whether—even assuming that the presumption could be regarded as rebuttable in the present case—a demonstration that the trade effects of the tax differential were insignificant would constitute a proof that the benefits accruing to Canada, the EEC and Mexico under Article III:2, first sentence, had not been nullified or impaired.

5.1.9 An acceptance of the argument that measures which have only an insignificant effect on the volume of exports do not nullify or impair benefits accruing under Article III:2, first sentence, implies that the basic rationale of this provision—the benefit it generates for the contracting parties—is to protect expectations on export volumes. That, however, is not the case. Article III:2, first sentence, obliges contracting parties to establish certain competitive conditions for imported products in relation to domestic products. Unlike some other provisions in the General Agreement, it does not refer to trade effects. The majority of the members of the Working Party on the "Brazilian Internal Taxes" therefore correctly concluded that the provisions of Article III:2, first sentence, "were equally applicable, whether imports from other contracting parties were substantial, small or non-existent" (BISD Vol. II/185). The Working Party also concluded that "a contracting party was bound by the provisions of Article III whether or not the contracting party in question had undertaken tariff commitments in respect of the goods concerned" (BISD Vol. II/182), in other words, the benefits under Article III accrue independent of whether there is a negotiated expectation of market access or not. Moreover, it is conceivable that a tax consistent with the national treatment principle (for instance, a high but non-discriminatory excise tax) has a more severe impact on the exports of other contracting parties than a tax that violates that principle (for instance a very low but discriminatory tax). The case before the Panel illustrates this point: the United States could bring the tax on petroleum in conformity with Article III:2, first sentence, by raising the tax on domestic products, by lowering the tax on imported products or by fixing a new common tax rate for both imported and domestic products. Each of these solutions would have different trade results, and it is therefore logically not possible to determine the difference in trade impact between the present tax and one consistent with Article III:2, first sentence, and hence to determine the trade impact resulting from the non-observance of that provision. For these reasons, Article III:2, first sentence, cannot be interpreted to protect expectations on export volumes; it protects expectations on the competitive relationship between imported and domestic products. A change in the competitive relationship contrary to that provision must consequently be regarded *ipso facto* as a nullification or impairment of benefits accruing under the General Agreement. A demonstration that a measure inconsistent with Article III:2, first sentence, has no or insignificant effects would therefore in the view of the Panel not be a sufficient demonstration that the benefits accruing under that provision had not been nullified or impaired even if such a rebuttal were in principle permitted.

5.1.10 For the reasons given in the paragraphs above, the Panel decided not to examine the submissions of the parties on the trade effects of the tax differential. This decision was based on legal grounds only and should therefore not be interpreted as endorsing either the views of the United States or those of Canada, the EEC and Mexico on the trade effects of the tax differential.

5.1.11 The Panel noted that Canada had raised concerns regarding the taxation of imported products made from synthetic petroleum (paragraph 3.1.12 above). However, since the Superfund Act, according to the United States, is silent on the treatment of such products, the Panel did not specifically examine these concerns. Canada's right to request an investigation of this matter under Article XXIII:2 is therefore in no way affected by the present report.

5.1.12 *In the light of the considerations set out in paragraphs 5.1.1-5.1.9 above, the Panel concluded that the tax on petroleum was inconsistent with Article III:2, first sentence and consequently constituted a prima facie case of nullification and impairment and that an evaluation of the trade impact of the tax was not relevant for this finding. The Panel therefore suggests that the* CONTRACTING PARTIES *recommend that the*

United States bring the tax on petroleum in conformity with its obligations under the General Agreement.

5.2 Tax on certain imported substances

5.2.1 The Panel noted that the United States objected to an examination of this tax because it did not go into effect before January 1, 1989, and—having no immediate effect on trade and therefore not causing nullification or impairment—fell outside the framework of Article XXIII. The Panel examined this point and concluded the following.

5.2.2 The Panel on "Japanese Measures on Imports of Leather" examined the contention of Japan that an import quota had not been filled and considered that

> "the existence of a quantitative restriction should be presumed to cause nullification or impairment not only because of any effect it had had on the volume of trade but also for other reasons e.g. it would lead to increased transaction costs and would create uncertainties which could affect investment plans" (BISD 31S/113).

The reasoning endorsed by the CONTRACTING PARTIES on that occasion applies also in the present case. The general prohibition of quantitative restrictions under Article XI, which the Panel on Japanese Measures on Imports of Leather examined, and the national treatment obligation of Article III, which Canada and the EEC invoked in the present case, have essentially the same rationale, namely to protect expectations of the contracting parties as to the competitive relationship between their products and those of the other contracting parties. Both articles are not only to protect current trade but also to create the predictability needed to plan future trade. That objective could not be attained if contracting parties could not challenge existing legislation mandating actions at variance with the General Agreement until the administrative acts implementing it had actually been applied to their trade. Just as the very existence of a regulation providing for a quota, without it restricting particular imports, has been recognized to constitute a violation of Article XI:1, the very existence of mandatory legislation providing for an internal tax, without it being applied to a particular imported product, should be regarded as falling within the scope of Article III:2, first sentence. The Panel noted that the tax on certain imported substances had been enacted, that the legislation was mandatory and that the tax authorities had to apply it after the end of next year and hence within a time frame within which the trade and investment decisions that could be influenced by the tax are taken. The Panel therefore concluded that Canada and the EEC were entitled to an investigation of their claim that this tax did not meet the criteria of Article III:2, first sentence.

5.2.3 The Panel noted that the United States justified the tax on certain imported substances as a border tax adjustment corresponding in its effect to the internal tax on certain chemicals from which these substances were derived (paragraph 3.2.5 above). The Panel further noted that the EEC considered the tax on certain chemicals not to be eligible for border tax adjustment because it was designed to tax polluting activities that occurred in the United States and to finance environmental programmes benefiting only United States producers. Consistent with the Polluter-Pays Principle, the United States should have taxed only products of domestic origin because only their production gave rise to environmental problems in the United States. The United States denied the legal relevance of EEC's arguments and their applicability to the tax on certain chemicals (paragraphs 3.2.7- 3.2.11 above). The Panel therefore first examined whether the tax on certain chemicals was eligible for border tax adjustments.

5.2.4 The report of the Working Party on Border Tax Adjustments, adopted by the CONTRACTING PARTIES in 1970, concluded the following on the rules of the General Agreement relating to tax adjustments applied to goods entering into international trade:

> "There was convergence of views to the effect that taxes directly levied on products were eligible for tax adjustment. Examples of such taxes comprised specific excise duties, sales taxes and cascade taxes and the tax on value added . . . Furthermore, the Working Party concluded that there was convergence of views to the effect that certain taxes that were not directly levied on products were not eligible for tax adjustment. Examples of such taxes comprised social security charges whether on employers or employees and payroll taxes" (BISD 18S/100-101).

As these conclusions of the CONTRACTING PARTIES clearly indicate, the tax adjustment rules of the General Agreement distinguish between taxes on products and taxes not directly levied on products; they do not distinguish between taxes with different policy purposes. Whether a sales tax is levied on a product for general revenue purposes or to encourage the rational use of environmental resources, is therefore not relevant for the determination of the eligibility of a tax for border tax adjustment. For these reasons the Panel concluded that the tax on certain chemicals, being a tax directly imposed on products, was eligible for border tax adjustment independent of the purpose it served. The Panel therefore did not examine whether the tax on chemicals served environmental purposes and, if so, whether a border tax adjustment would be consistent with these purposes.

5.2.5 The Panel wishes to point out, however, that the Working Party on Border Tax Adjustment agreed that the provisions of the General Agreement on tax adjustment

> "set maxima limits for adjustment (compensation) which were not to be exceeded, but below which every contracting party was free to differentiate in the degree of compensation applied, provided that such action was in conformity with other provisions of the General Agreement" (BISD 18S/100).

Consequently, if a contracting party wishes to tax the sale of certain domestic products (because their production pollutes the domestic environment) and to impose a lower tax or no tax at all on like imported products (because their consumption or use causes fewer or no environmental problems), it is in principle free to do so. The General Agreement's rules on tax adjustment thus give the contracting party in such a case the possibility to follow the Polluter-Pays Principle, but they do not oblige it to do so.

5.2.6 The mandate of the Panel is to examine the case before it "in the light of the relevant GATT provisions" (paragraph 1.4 above) The Panel therefore did not examine the consistency of the revenue provisions in the Superfund Act with the environmental objectives of that Act or with the Polluter-Pays Principle. The Panel notes that the CONTRACTING PARTIES established in 1972 a Group on Environmental Measures and International Trade with the task

> "to examine, upon request, any specific matters relevant to the trade policy aspects of measures to control pollution and protect human environment, especially with regard to the application of the provisions of the General Agreement, taking into account the particular problems of developing countries" (L/3622/Rev.1 and C/M/74).

This Group has never met but still exists. The EEC would thus have a forum available in the GATT in which to pursue the environmental issues which the Panel, because of its limited mandate, could not address.

5.2.7 The Panel, having concluded that the tax on certain chemicals was in principle eligible for border tax adjustment, then examined whether the tax on certain imported substances meets the national treatment requirement of Article III:2, first sentence. This provision permits the imposition of an internal tax on imported products provided the like domestic products are taxed, directly or indirectly, at the same or a higher rate. Such internal taxes may be levied on imported products at the time or point of importation (Note ad Article III). Paragraph 2(a) of Article II therefore clarifies that a tariff concession does not prevent the levying of

> "a charge equivalent to an internal tax imposed consistently with the provisions of paragraph 2 of Article III in respect of the like domestic product or in respect of an article from which the imported product has been manufactured or produced in whole or in part."

The drafters of the General Agreement explained the word "equivalent" used in this provision with the following example:

> "If a charge is imposed on perfume because it contains alcohol, the charge to be imposed must take into consideration the value of the alcohol and not the value of the perfume, that is to say the value of the content and not the value of the whole" (EPCT/TAC/PV/26, page 21).

5.2.8 The Tax on certain imported substances equals in principle the amount of the tax which would have been imposed under the Superfund Act on the chemicals used as materials in the manufacture or production of the imported substance if these chemicals had been sold in the United States for use in the manufacture or production of the imported substance. In the words which the drafters of the General Agreement used in the above perfume-alcohol example: The tax is imposed on the imported substances because they are produced from chemicals subject to an excise tax in the United States and the tax rate is determined in principle in relation to the amount of these chemicals used and not in relation to the value of the imported substance. The Panel therefore concluded that, to the extent that the tax on certain imported substances was equivalent to the tax borne by like domestic substances as a result of the tax on certain chemicals, the tax met the national treatment requirement of Article III:2, first sentence.

5.2.9 According to the Superfund Act, the tax on certain imported substances will however not necessarily be equal to the tax on the chemicals used in their production. If an importer fails to furnish the information necessary to determine the amount of tax to be imposed, a penalty tax of 5 per cent of the appraised value of the imported substance shall be imposed. Since the tax on certain chemicals subjects some of the chemicals only to a tax equilvant to 2 per cent of the 1980 wholesale price of the chemical, the 5 per cent penalty tax could be much higher than the highest possible tax that the importer would have to pay if he provided sufficient information (paragraph 2.3 above). The imposition of a penalty tax on the basis of the appraised value of the imported substance would not conform with the national treatment requirement of Article III:2, first sentence, because the tax rate would in that case no longer be imposed in relation to the amount of taxable chemicals used in their production but the value of the imported substance. Thus it would not meet the requirement of equivalence which the drafters explained in the perfume-alcohol example mentioned in the preceding paragraph. However, the Superfund Act permits the Secretary of the Treasury to prescribe by regulation, in lieu of the 5 per cent rate, a rate which would equal the amount that would be imposed if the substance were produced using the predominant method of production (paragraph 2.6 above). These regulations have not yet been issued. Thus, whether they will eliminate the need to impose the penalty tax and whether they will establish complete equivalence between domestic and imported products, as required by Article III:2, first sentence, remain open questions. From the perspective of the overall objectives of the General Agreement it is regrettable that the Superfund Act explicitly directs the United States tax authorities to impose a tax inconsistent with the national treatment principle but, since the Superfund Act also gives them the possibility to avoid the need to impose that tax by issuing regulations, the existence of the penalty rate provisions as such does not constitute a violation of the United States obligations under the General Agreement. The Panel noted with satisfaction the statement of the United States that, given the tax authorities' regulatory authority under the Act, "in all probability the 5 per cent penalty rate would never be applied" (paragraph 3.2.13 above).

5.2.10 *The Panel concluded that the tax on certain imported substances constituted a tax adjustment corresponding to the tax on certain chemicals that was in principle consistent with Article III:2, first sentence, and that the existence of the penalty rate provisions as such did not constitute an infringement of Article III:2, first sentence, since the tax authorities had regulatory power to eliminate the need for the imposition of the penalty rate. The Panel recommends that the CONTRACTING PARTIES take note of the statement by the United States that the penalty rate would in all probability never be applied.*

JAPAN—CUSTOMS DUTIES, TAXES AND LABELLING PRACTICES ON IMPORTED WINES AND ALCOHOLIC BEVERAGES

Report of the Panel adopted on November 10, 1987
BISD 34S/83, 85

2. FACTUAL ASPECTS

Liquor Tax System of Japan

2.1 In 1940, the Liquor Tax Law was enacted in Japan. It classified alcoholic beverages into 9 categories and set the tax rates on each category of alcoholic beverages. The "grading system" was introduced to miscellaneous liquors in 1943. Although liquor taxes were basically specific taxes based on quantity, an *ad valorem* tax was introduced in 1962 to some of the special grade saké, wines and special grade whiskies, of which the price exceeded a certain threshold. This *ad valorem* tax system was expanded to apply to the 1st grade and 2nd grade whiskies in 1971. The revenue from the liquor tax was the third most important revenue source after the income tax and corporation tax in 1985, amounting to 4.9% of total tax revenue.

2.2 The tax system in Japan pursues the objective that taxation should be made according to the ability, on the part of tax bearers, to pay tax ("tax-bearing ability"). In the case of the liquor tax, the tax rates of various liquors are determined not only in accordance with their alcohol contents and other qualities but also by taking into account the tax-bearing ability of prospective consumers. The Japanese Liquor Tax Law classifies liquors into 10 categories. Six categories are further classified into 13 sub-categories and, in the case of saké and whisky/brandy, into three additional grades (see Annex I). The various categories have been defined in Article 3 of the Japanese Liquor Tax Law (see Annex II). Higher tax rates are applied to what are considered to be high-quality high-priced liquors, while lower rates are applied to what are considered low-quality low-priced liquors mainly consumed by those in the lower income brackets (see Annex III reproducing the specific tax rates on the main liquors). The same tax rate is applied to the liquors of the same quality, regardless whether imported or produced in Japan.

There is no category where only imported products are subject to taxation. For most of the categories or grades, the standard alcohol content and corresponding standard specific tax rate are set. To the extent that the alcohol content exceeds the standard level, they are subject to increased rates. In certain categories, reduced rates can be applied if alcohol content is below the standard.

2.3 Distilled liquors are comprised of three categories: shochu, whisky/brandy, and spirits (such as vodka, gin and rum). These classifications are based on criteria such as raw materials used and manufacturing method applied. For each category, the current tax rates are determined by taking account, *inter alia,* of their quality and alcohol content, the pattern and trend of consumption, the tax burden between different categories of liquors, and the objective of imposing higher rates on high-quality high-priced products so that consumers bear a tax burden commensurate with their tax-bearing ability.

2.4 Saké, whisky and brandy are classified into three different grades: special, first and second grade. The grading system for whisky and brandy is based on standards such as the mixture ratio of malt whisky, grain whisky, pure brandy, and the alcohol content of whisky and brandy. The grading system pursues the objective of levying a high tax for high-quality and high-priced whiskies/brandies and an appropriately lower tax in regard to low quality and low priced whiskies/brandies largely drunk by people in the lower income bracket. The grades apply regardless of whether whiskies/brandies are domestic or imported. In fiscal year 1985, 83% of special grade whiskies/brandies, 99.9% of first grade whiskies/brandies and 100% of second grade whiskies/brandies taxed in Japan were Japanese products.

2.5 *Ad valorem* taxes are applied on special grade saké, special, first and second grade whiskies/brandies, wines, spirits and liqueurs in cases where the price exceeds a certain threshold set for each category of alcoholic beverage (the thresholds and tax rates are reproduced in Annex IV). The *ad valorem* tax is not levied on liquors in five categories out of ten, such as mirin and beer. The non-taxable threshold of the *ad valorem* tax is determined based on the manufacturer's selling price for domestic products or the CIF and customs duty amount for imported products. For the main alcoholic beverages, the *ad valorem* tax is applied to 6.5% of special grade saké, 8.7% of wine and 9.2% of special grade whisky, respectively in volume terms.

* * *

Labelling

2.7 Japanese bottles of wines, whiskies and brandies currently bear labels using English, French or German terms, such as "Chateau" or "Reserve" or "Village." Japan has enacted various legal regulations in order to prevent the use of trade names in such a manner as to misrepresent the true origin of a product, including the Law for the Prevention of Unfair Competition, the Act against Unjustifiable Premiums and Misleading Representations, a range of "fair competition codes" voluntarily laid down by each industry concerned pursuant to Article 10 of the latter Act and approved by the Fair Trade Commission, and the Law concerning Liquor Business Association and Measures for Securing Revenue of Liquor Tax.

* * *

5. FINDINGS AND CONCLUSIONS

5.1 The Panel began the examination of the matter referred to it by noting that the dispute over Japanese taxes on imported wines and alcoholic beverages was due to the diverging views of the European Communities and Japan on the interpretation of GATT Article III:1 and 2, which reads:

> "1. The contracting parties recognize that internal taxes and other internal charges, and laws, regulations and requirements affecting the internal sale, offering for sale, purchase, transportation, distribution or use of products, and internal quantitative regulations requiring the mixture, processing or use of products in specified amounts or proportions, should not be applied to imported or domestic products so as to afford protection to domestic production."
>
> "2. The products of the territory of any contracting party imported into the territory of any other contracting party shall not be subject, directly or indirectly, to internal taxes or other internal charges of any kind in excess of those applied, directly or indirectly, to like domestic products. Moreover, no contracting party shall otherwise apply internal taxes or other internal charges to imported or domestic products in a manner contrary to the principles set forth in paragraph 1."

The interpretative note to Article III:2 adds as follows:

> "A tax conforming to the requirements of the first sentence of paragraph 2 would be considered to be inconsistent with the provisions of the second sentence only in cases where competition was involved between, on the one hand, the taxed product and, on the other hand, a directly competitive or substitutable product which was not similarly taxed."

5.2 The Panel noted that this part of the complaint by the European Communities consisted of a cluster of complaints relating to a large number of alcoholic beverages, liquor categories and subcategories, liquor tax rates and taxation methods. The examination of these complaints in the light of Article III raised certain general questions relating to the interpretation of this GATT Article, on the answering of which the Panel findings would necessarily depend. The Panel considered it therefore appropriate to clarify first certain general questions common to these various complaints regarding Article III:2.

5.3 The Panel noted the view of the European Communities that Article III:2 should be construed in accordance with its clear wording to the effect that it required, first, a product comparison so as to determine what are "like products" or "directly competitive or substitutable products," and, second, a fiscal comparison in order to determine whether imported products were taxed in excess of like domestic products or were subject to internal taxes affording protection to domestic production of directly competitive or substitutable products.

5.4 The Panel then considered the contrary view argued by Japan that, because each contracting party remained free to classify products for tax purposes, the "likeness" or "directly competitive or substitutable" relationship of imported and domestic products were legally not relevant to the interpretation of Article III:2 if

a) imported and domestic products were taxed in a non-discriminatory manner, regardless of their origin, within one and the same product category defined by a contracting party for tax purposes, and

b) there was both domestic production and importation of products within the product category defined for tax purposes.

5.5 The Panel carefully examined these two divergent interpretations of Article III:2 and reached the following conclusions:

a) The *text of the first sentence of Article III:2* clearly indicates that the comparison to be made is between internal taxes on imported products and "those applied . . . to like domestic products." The wording "like" products (in the French text: "produits similaires") has been used also in other GATT Articles on non-discrimination (*e.g.* Article I:1) in the sense not only of "identical" or "equal" products but covering also products with similar qualities (see, for instance, the 1981 Panel Report on Tariff Treatment by Spain of Imports of Unroasted Coffee, BISD 28S/102, 112).

b) The *context of Article III:2* shows that Article III:2 supplements, within the system of the General Agreement, the provisions on the liberalization of custom duties and of other charges by prohibiting discriminatory or protective taxation against certain products from other GATT contracting parties. The Panel found that this context had to be taken into account in the interpretation of Article III:2. For instance, the prohibition under GATT Article I:1 of different tariff treatment for various types of "like" products (such as unroasted coffee, see BISD 28S/102, 112) could not remain effective unless supplemented by the prohibition of different internal tax treatment for various types of "like" products. Just as Article I:1 was generally construed, in order to protect the competitive benefits accruing from reciprocal tariff bindings, as prohibiting "tariff specialization" discriminating against "like" products, only the literal interpretation of Article III:2 as prohibiting "internal tax specialization" discriminating against "like" products could ensure that the reasonable expectation, protected under GATT Article XXIII, of competitive benefits accruing under tariff concessions would not be nullified or impaired by internal tax discrimination against like products. It had therefore been correctly stated in another Panel Report recently adopted by the CONTRACTING PARTIES that "Article III:2, first sentence, obliges contracting parties to establish certain competitive conditions for imported products in relation to domestic products" (L/6175 [Case 62], paragraph 5.1.9). And it had been for similar reasons that, during the discussion in the GATT Council of the panel report on Spain's restrictions on the domestic sale of soybean oil which had *not* been adopted by the Council, several contracting parties, including Japan, had emphasized "with regard to Article III:4 that the interpretation of the term 'like products' in the Panel Report as meaning 'more or less the same product' was too strict an intrepretation" (C/M/152 at page 16).

c) The *drafting history* confirms that Article III:2 was designed with "the intention that internal taxes on goods should not be used as a means of protection" (see: UN Conference on Trade and Employment, Reports of Committees, 1948, page 61). As stated in the 1970 Working Party Report on Border Tax Adjustments in respect of the various GATT provisions on taxation, "the philosophy behind these provisions was the ensuring of a certain trade neutrality" (BISD 18S/99). This accords with the broader objective of Article III "to provide equal conditions of competition once goods had been cleared through customs" (BISD 7S/64 [Case 16]), and to protect thereby the benefits accruing from tariff concessions. This *object and purpose of Article III:2* of promoting non-discriminatory competition among imported and like domestic products could not be achieved if Article III:2 were construed in a manner allowing discriminatory and protective internal taxation of imported products in excess of like domestic products.

d) *Subsequent GATT practice* in the application of Article III further shows that past GATT panel reports adopted by the CONTRACTING PARTIES have examined Article III:2 and 4 by determining, firstly, whether the imported and domestic products concerned were "like" and, secondly, whether the internal taxation or other regulation discriminated against the imported products (see, for instance, BISD 25S/49, 63 [Case 35]; L/6175 [Case 62], paragraph 5). Past GATT practice has clearly established that "like" products in terms of Article III: 2 are not confined to identical products but cover also other products, for instance if they serve substantially identical end-uses (see L/6175, paragraph 5.1.1).

The Panel concluded that the ordinary meaning of Article III:2 in its context and in the light of its object and purpose supported the past GATT practice of examining the conformity of internal taxes with Article III:2 by determining, firstly, whether the taxed imported and domestic products are "like" or "directly competitive or substitutable" and, secondly, whether the taxation is discriminatory (first sentence) or protective (second sentence of Article III:2). The Panel decided to proceed accordingly also in this case.

5.6 The CONTRACTING PARTIES have never developed a general definition of the term *"like products"* in Article III:2. Past decisions on this question have been made on a case-by-case basis after examining a number of relevant factors. The working party report on border tax adjustments, adopted by the CONTRACTING PARTIES in 1970, concluded that problems arising from the interpretation of the terms "like" or "similar" products, which occurred some sixteen times throughout the General Agreement, should be examined on a case-by-case basis using, *inter alia,* the following criteria: the product's end-uses in a given market; consumers' tastes and habits, which change from country to country; and the product's properties, nature and quality (BISD 18S/102, paragraph 18). The GATT drafting history confirms that "the expression had different meanings in different contexts of the Draft Charter" (EPCT/C II/65, page 2). Subsequent GATT practice indicates that, as stated in respect of GATT Article I:1 in the 1981 Panel Report on the Tariff Treatment applied by Spain to Imports of Unroasted Coffee, "neither the General Agreement nor the settlement of previous cases gave any definition of such concept" (BISD 28S/102, III). The Panel was aware of the more specific definition of the term "like product" in Article 2:2 of the 1979 Antidumping Agreement (BISD 26S/172) but did not consider this very narrow definition for the purpose of antidumping proceedings to be suitable for the different purpose of GATT Article III:2. The Panel decided, therefore, to examine the table of "like products" submitted by the EEC (see Annex V) on a product-by-product basis using the above-mentioned criteria as well as others recognized in previous GATT practice (see BISD 25S/49, 63), such as the Customs Cooperation Council Nomenclature (CCCN) for the classification of goods in customs tariffs which has been accepted by Japan. The Panel found that the following alcoholic beverages should be considered as "like products" in terms of Article III:2, in view of their similar properties, end-uses and usually uniform classification in tariff nomenclatures:

— imported and Japanese-made *gin*;

— imported and Japanese-made *vodka*;

— imported and Japanese-made *whisky* (including all grades classified as "whisky" in the Japanese Liquor Tax Law) and "spirits similar to whisky in color, flavor and other properties" as described in the Japanese Liquor Tax Law;

— imported and Japanese-made *grape brandy* (including all grades classified as "brandy" in the Japanese Liquor Tax Law);

— imported and Japanese-made *fruit brandy* (including all grades classified as "brandy" in the Japanese Liquor Tax Law);

— imported and Japanese-made *"classic" liqueurs* (not including, for instance, medicinal liqueurs);

— imported and Japanese-made unsweetened *still wine*;

— imported and Japanese-made *sparkling wines*.

The Panel agreed in this respect with the arguments submitted to it not only by the European Communities but also by other important producing countries of wines and distilled spirits that gin, vodka, whisky, grape brandy, other fruit brandy, certain "classic" liqueurs, still wine and sparkling wine, respectively, were recognized not only by governments for purposes of tariff and statistical nomenclature, but also by consumers to constitute "each in its end-use . . . a well defined and single product intended for drinking" (BSID 28S/102, 112, paragraph 4.7). The Panel also agreed in this respect with the finding of an earlier panel report adopted by the CONTRACTING PARTIES that minor differences in taste, color and other properties did not prevent products qualifying as "like products" (BISD 28S/102, 112).

5.7 The Panel did not exclude that also other alcoholic beverages could be considered as "like" products. Thus, even though the Panel was of the view that the "likeness" of products must be examined taking into account not only objective criteria (such as composition and manufacturing processes of products) but also the more subjective consumers' viewpoint (such as consumption and use by consumers), the Panel agreed with the arguments submitted to it by European Communities, Finland and the United States that Japanese shochu (Group A) and vodka could be considered as "like" products in terms of Article III:2 because they were both white/clean spirits, made of similar raw materials, and their end-uses were virtually identical (either as straight "schnaps" type of drinks or in various mixtures). Since consumer habits are variable in time and space and the aim of Article III:2 of ensuring neutrality of internal taxation as regards competition between imported and domestic like products could not be achieved if differential taxes could be used to crystallize consumer preferences for traditional domestic products, the Panel found that the traditional Japanese consumer habits with regard to shochu provided no reason for not considering vodka to be a "like" product. The Panel decided not to examine the "likeness" of alcoholic beverages beyond the requests specified in the complaint by the European Communities (see Annex V). The Panel felt justified in doing so also for the following reasons: Alcoholic drinks might be drunk straight, with water, or as mixes. Even if imported alcoholic beverages (e.g. vodka) were not considered to be "like" to Japanese alcoholic beverages (e.g. shochu Group A), the flexibility in the use of alcoholic drinks and their common characteristics often offered an alternative choice for consumers leading to a competitive relationship. In the view of the Panel there existed—even if not necessarily in respect of all the economic uses to which the product may be put—direct competition or substitutability among the various distilled liquors, among various liqueurs, among unsweetened and sweetened wines, and among sparkling wines. The increasing imports of "Western-style" alcoholic beverages into Japan bore witness to this lasting competitive relationship and to the potential products substitution through trade among various alcoholic beverages. Since consumer habits vis-à-vis these products varied in response to their respective prices, their availability through trade and their other competitive interrelationships, the Panel concluded that the following alcoholic beverages could be considered to be *"directly competitive or substitutable products"* in terms of Article III:2, second sentence:

— imported and Japanese-made distilled liquors, including all grades of whiskies/brandies, vodka and shochu Groups A and B, among each other;

— imported and Japanese-made liqueurs among each other;

— imported and Japanese-made unsweetened and sweetened wines among each other; and

— imported and Japanese-made sparkling wines among each other.

5.8 Having compared the imported and domestic alcoholic beverages in order to determine their "likeness" or "directly competitive or substitutable" relationship, the Panel next proceeded to a comparison of the fiscal burdens on these products. The Panel noted that the first sentence of Article III:2 prohibited the direct or indirect imposition of "internal taxes or other internal charges of any kind in excess of those applied, directly or indirectly, to like domestic products." The Panel noted that the wording of this prohibition of tax discrimination was strict. It had been applied in GATT practice also in a strict manner, for instance as prohibiting even very small tax differentials amounting to US dollar 0.0002 per litre of imported petroleum (see the panel report adopted by the CONTRACTING PARTIES on US taxes on petroleum, L/6175) and as excluding a *de minimis* argument based on allegedly minimal trade effects (see L/6175, paragraphs 5.1.2 to 5.1.9). The Panel further found that the wording "directly or indirectly" and "internal taxes . . . *of any kind*" implied that, in assessing whether there is tax discrimination, account is to be taken not only of the rate of the applicable internal tax but also of the taxation methods (e.g. different kinds of internal taxes, direct taxation of the finished product or indirect taxation by taxing the raw materials used in the product during the various stages of its production) and of the rules for the tax collection (e.g. basis of assessment).

5.9 The Panel then examined the European Communities' contention (see above paragraph 3.5) that Japanese internal taxes on whiskies, brandies, still wines, sparkling wines, spirits and liqueurs imported from the EEC were in excess of those applied to like Japanese products, and reached the following conclusions:

a) *Whiskies and brandies subject to the grading system:* The Panel noted that the Japanese specific tax rates on imported and Japanese whiskies/brandies special grade (2,098,100 yen/kl) were considerably higher than the Japanese specific tax rates on whiskies/brandies first grade (1,011,400 yen/kl) and second grade (296,200 yen/kl). The Panel was unable to find that these tax differentials corresponded to objective differences of the various distilled liquors, for instance that they could be explained as a non-discriminatory taxation of their respective alcohol contents. The Panel further found that, as a result of this differential taxation of "like products," almost all whiskies/brandies imported from the EEC were subject to the higher rates of tax whereas more than half of whiskies/brandies produced in Japan benefited from considerably lower rates of tax. The Panel concluded, therefore, that (special and first grade) whiskies/brandies imported from the EEC were subject to internal Japanese taxes "in excess of those applied . . . to like domestic products" (i.e. first and second grade whiskies/brandies) in the sense of Article III:2, first sentence.

b) *Wines, spirits and liqueurs subject to the "mixed" system of specific tax and ad valorem tax:* The Panel noted that imported and domestic wines, whiskies, brandies, spirits and liqueurs were subject to *ad valorem* taxes in lieu of the specific tax when the manufacturer's selling price (CIF and customs duty for imported products) exceeded a specified threshold (see Annex IV). The Panel was of the view that a "mixed" system of specific and *ad valorem* liquor taxes was as such not inconsistent with Article III:2, which prohibits only discriminatory or protective taxation of imported products but not the use of differentiated taxation methods as such, provided the differentiated taxation methods do not result in discriminatory or protective taxation.

The Panel noted that the *ad valorem* taxes were not applied to all liquor categories such as the traditional Japanese products shochu, mirin and saké (first and second grades). The Panel was unable to find that the differences as to the applicability and non-taxable thresholds of the *ad valorem* taxes were based on corresponding objective product differences (e.g. alcohol contents) and formed part of a general system of internal taxation equally applied in a trade-neutral manner to all like or directly competitive liquors (e.g. "alcohol taxes" equally applied to all alcoholic beverages). The Panel was of the view that "like" products do not become "unlike" merely because of differences in local consumer traditions within a country (e.g. consumption of shochu mainly in specific regions within Japan) or differences in their prices, which were often influenced by external government measures (e.g. customs duties) and market conditions (e.g. supply and demand, sales margins). The Panel was convinced that such an interpretation would run counter to the objective of Article III:2 to avoid that discriminatory or protective internal taxation of imported products would distort price competition with domestic like or directly competitive products, for instance by creating different price and consumer categories and hardening consumer preferences for traditional home products.

The Panel concluded from the preceding findings that—since liquors above the non-taxable thresholds were subjected to *ad valorem* taxes in excess of the specific taxes on "like" liquors below the threshold (e.g. *ad valorem* tax rates up to 8 times higher than the specific tax rates on wines, 4 times higher than the specific tax rates on liqueurs and 2 times higher than the specific tax rates on spirits)—the imposition of *ad valorem* taxes on wines, spirits and liqueurs imported from the EEC, which are considerably higher than the specific taxes on "like" domestic wines, spirits and liqueurs, was inconsistent with Article III:2, first sentence.

c) *The different methods of calculating ad valorem taxes on imported and domestic liquors:* The Panel shared the view expressed by both parties that Article III:2 does not prescribe the use of any specific method or system of taxation. The Panel was further of the view that there could be objective reasons proper to the tax in question which could justify or necessitate differences in the system of taxation for imported and for domestic products. The Panel found that it could be also compatible with Article III:2 to allow two different methods of calculation of price for tax purposes. Since Article III:2 prohibited only discriminatory or protective tax burdens on imported products, what mattered was, in the view of the Panel, whether the application of the different taxation methods actually had a discriminatory or protective effect against imported products. The Panel could therefore not agree with the European Community's view that the mere fact that the so-called "fixed subtraction system" was available only for domestic liquors constituted in itself a discrimination contrary to Article III:2 or 4. Nor could the Panel agree with the EEC submission that the mere possibility of exceptional tax rates available only for domestic whiskies/brandies provided sufficient evidence of tax discrimination contrary to Article III:2. The Panel shared the doubts expressed by the European Community that the deduction from the retail price of a uniform 30% non-taxable allowance (designed to cover trade profits, manufacturer's rebate and manufacturer's delivery charges) must not necessarily result in what would have been the manufacturer's selling price. Yet, the Panel did not dispose of sufficient evidence for concluding that the application of this simplified method of tax base assessment had actually resulted, or was likely to result, in tax discrimination against liquors imported into Japan.

d) *Taxation according to extract content:* The Panel recalled its earlier finding that imported and Japanese-made sparkling wines, as well as imported and Japanese-made "classic" liqueurs, were "like products," respectively and that minor differences in taste, color and other properties (including different alcohol contents) did not prevent products qualifying as "like products." It followed from the clear wording of Article III:2 that imported liquors "shall not be subject . . . to internal taxes . . . in excess of those applied . . . to like domestic products." The Panel was of the view that this unqualified wording must not necessarily mean that there could never be any circumstances in which different tax treatment of "like products" was compatible with the General Agreement. The Panel noted, for instance, that GATT Article II:2,a permitted the non-discriminatory taxation "of an article from which the imported product has been manufactured or produced in whole or in part," and that such a non-discriminatory alcohol tax on like alcoholic beverages with different alcohol contents could result in differential tax rates on like products. The Panel further noted that, pursuant to the "general exceptions" listed in Article XX, Article III:2 must not be construed "to prevent the adoption or enforcement by any contracting party of measures . . . (b) necessary to protect human, animal or plant life or health" (Article XX:(b)); non-discriminatory measures under this exception clause might also entail differential tax rates on like products. The Panel noted that Japan's specific and *ad valorem* tax rates on liqueurs and sparkling wines differed according to alcohol and extract contents and that Japan considered these differential taxes to be compatible with Article III:2 regardless of their justifiability as a non-discriminatory internal taxation of these ingredients equally applied to all products with such ingredients, and regardless of their justifiability under any of the exception clauses of GATT Article XX. The Panel noted also the contrary view of the EEC "that taxation according to extract content is artificial and irrational and discriminates against imports contrary to Article III:2" because it ensured "that almost all Community liqueurs are subject to the higher rate of specific tax whilst some Japanese liqueurs are able to benefit from a lower specific rate (one third of the rate on most Community liqueurs) together with a lower *ad valorem* rate (50% as opposed to 100%) and a much lower increment per degree of alcohol (9.780 yen per 1% over 13% compared with 24.5 yen per 1% over 15% in the higher rate category)." Having found that

— liqueurs and sparkling wines with high raw material contents, imported into Japan, were subject to internal taxes in excess of those applied to like domestic liqueurs and sparkling wines with lower raw material contents (see Annexes III and IV), and that

— this differential taxation of like products depending on their extract and raw material content had not been, and apparently could not be, justified as resulting from a non-discriminatory internal tax on the raw material content concerned or as justifiable under any of the exception clauses of the General Agreement,

the Panel concluded that this imposition of higher taxes on "classic" liqueurs and sparkling wines with higher raw material content was inconsistent with Article III:2, first sentence.

5.10 The Panel next turned to examining the European Community's contention (see above paragraph 3.7) that the Japanese liquor taxes were inconsistent with Article III:2, second sequence, because

— distilled liquors (whisky, brandy, gin, vodka, etc) which were directly competitive with shochu were affected by the system of categorization which permitted shochu to benefit from extremely favorable taxation in comparison with other spirits; and

— Community products in categories which were subject to *ad valorem* taxation were at a disadvantage in comparison with Japanese "traditional" products which were only obliged to be subject to specific taxes.

5.11 The Panel recalled its findings that distilled liquors, including all grades of shochu types A and B, were "directly competitive or substitutable products" in terms of the interpretative note to Article III:2 (see above paragraph 5.7). The Panel noted that shochu was not subject to *ad valorem* taxes and that the specific tax rates on shochu were many times lower than the specific tax rates on whiskies, brandies and other spirits. The Panel noted that, whereas under the first sentence of Article III:2 the tax on the imported product and the tax on the like domestic product had to be equal in effect, Article III:1 and 2, second sentence, prohibited only the application of internal taxes to imported or domestic products in a manner "so as to afford protection to domestic production." The Panel was of the view that also small tax differences could influence the competitive relationship between directly competing distilled liquors, but the existence of protective taxation could be established only in the light of the particular circumstances of each case and there could be a *de minimis* level below which a tax difference ceased to have the protective effect prohibited by Article III:2, second sentence. The Panel found that the following factors were sufficient evidence of fiscal distortions of the competitive relationship between imported distilled liquors and domestic shochu affording protection to the domestic production of shochu:

— the considerably lower specific tax rates on shochu than on imported whiskies, brandies and other spirits (see Annex III);

— the imposition of high *ad valorem* taxes on imported whiskies, brandies and other spirits and the absence of *ad valorem* taxes on shochu;

— the fact that shochu was almost exclusively produced in Japan and that the lower taxation of shochu did "afford protection to domestic production" (Article III:1) rather than to the production of a product produced in many countries (say, butter) in relation to another product (say, oleomargarine, as in the example referred to by Japan in paragraph 3.11 above);

— the mutual substitutability of these distilled liquors, as illustrated by the increasing imports into Japan of "Western-style" distilled liquors and by the consumer use of shochu blended in various proportions with whisky, brandy or other drinks.

Since it has been recognized in GATT practice that Article III:2 protects expectations on the competitive relationship between imported and domestic products rather than expectations on trade volumes (see L/6175, paragraph 5.1.9), the Panel did not consider it necessary to examine the quantitative trade effects of this considerably different taxation for its conclusion that the application of considerably lower internal taxes by Japan on shochu than on other directly competitive or substitutable distilled liquors had trade-distorting effects affording protection to domestic production of shochu contrary to Article III:1 and 2, second sentence.

5.12 The Panel next examined the contention of the EEC that wines, whiskies, brandies, other spirits and liqueurs imported from the EEC and subject to *ad valorem* tax were at a disadvantage in comparison with Japanese "traditional" products which were only subject to specific taxes. The Panel noted that the "traditional" Japanese liquors saké (first and second grade), saké compound, shochu and mirin were not subject to *ad valorem* taxes and that the grading of saké was voluntary so that less than 0.1% of all saké were subject to *ad valorem* taxation. The Panel recalled its findings that shochu and other distilled liquors were "directly competitive or substitutable" products in terms of the interpretative note to Article III:2. The Panel further recalled its finding that the application of higher internal taxes on imported whiskies, brandies and other spirits than on shochu afforded protection to the domestic production of shochu contrary to Article III:1 and 2, second sentence.

The Panel noted that the European Communities had not specified whether and why they considered saké, saké compound and mirin to be "directly competitive or substitutable" products in relation to wines of fresh grapes or to distilled spirits and liqueurs imported from the EEC. The Panel noted that rice wine (saké) and wines of fresh grapes were classified under separate headings in the CCCN nomenclature. The Panel did not exclude that there could be a "directly competitive or substitutable" relationship between saké, saké compound, mirin and liquors imported from the EEC into Japan. The Panel did, however, consider it neither necessary nor appropriate to decide on this question because, in any case, the Panel had not been presented sufficient evidence to determine whether and to what extent wines and other liquors imported from the EEC had actually been subjected to higher tax burdens than domestic saké, saké compound or mirin affording protection to the domestic production of these latter products.

5.13 Having concluded that whiskies, brandies, other distilled spirits, liqueurs, still wines and sparkling wines imported into Japan were subject to discriminatory or protective Japanese taxes contrary to Article III:2, the Panel examined whether these discriminatory or protective taxes could be justified by the argument submitted by Japan that the tax differentials were designed to realize the basic Japanese tax policy objective of "taxation according to tax-bearing ability" of the respective consumers. The Panel agreed with the submissions of both parties that

Article III:2 does not impose an obligation on contracting parties to adopt a specific tax system or specific taxation methods. Nor does a finding of an inconsistency of a tax with Article III:2 oblige the contracting party to reduce the tax on the imported product, as it could also remove any discriminatory or protective effect by raising the tax on the domestic product concerned. The General Agreement also explicitly permits "imposing at any time on the importation of any product . . . a charge equivalent to an internal tax imposed consistently with the provisions of paragraph 2 of Article III in respect of the like domestic product or in respect of an article from which the imported product has been manufactured or produced in whole or in part" (Article II:2,a), for instance a charge on the alcohol component of imported liquors equivalent to a non-discriminatory internal alcohol tax. The "general exceptions" provided for in GATT Article XX might also justify internal tax differentiations among like or directly competitive products, for instance if "necessary to protect human . . . or plant life or health" (Article XX,b). The Panel found, therefore, that the General Agreement reserved each contracting party a large degree of freedom to decide autonomously on the objectives, level, principles and methods of its internal taxation of goods.

The Panel noted the Japanese submission that, for instance, the grading system for whisky was "based on the circumstances of production and consumption of whiskies in Japan," and that generally "taxes on liquors are levied according to the tax-bearing ability on the part of consumers of each category of liquor." The Panel was of the view that the use of product and tax differentiations with the view of maintaining or promoting certain production and consumption patterns could easily distort price-competition among like or directly competitive products by creating price differences and price-related consumer preferences which would not exist in case of non-discriminatory internal taxation consistent with Article III:2. The Panel noted that the General Agreement did not make provision for such a far-reaching exception to Article III:2, and that the concept of "taxation according to tax-bearing ability of prospective consumers" of a product did not offer an objective criterion because it relied on necessarily subjective assumptions about future competition and inevitably uncertain consumer responses. The Panel was of the view that a national policy of "taxation according to tax-bearing ability" did not necessitate discriminatory or protective taxation of imported products and could be pursued by each contracting party in many ways in compliance with Article III:2. A national policy of promoting the domestic production of certain goods could likewise be pursued in conformity with the General Agreement (e.g. by means of production subsidies) without discriminatory or protective taxation of imported goods. The Panel concluded therefore from the text, system and objectives of the General Agreement that, even though each contracting party retained broad freedom as to its internal tax policy also in respect of its internal taxation of goods, the General Agreement did not provide for the possibility of justifying discriminatory or protective taxes inconsistent with Article III:2 on the ground that they had been introduced for the purpose of "taxation according to the tax-bearing ability" of domestic consumers of imported and directly competitive domestic liquors.

5.14 The Panel then examined the European Community's claim that Japan had violated its obligation under GATT Article IX:6 to "cooperate . . . with a view to preventing the use of trade names in such manner as to misrepresent the true origin of a product, to the detriment of such distinctive regional or geographical names of products of the territory of a contracting party as are protected by its legislation," and to "accord full and sympathetic consideration to such requests or representations as may be made by any other contracting party regarding the application of the undertaking set forth in the preceding sentence to names of products which have been communicated to it by the other contracting party." The Panel noted from the drafting history relating to Article IX:6 that it had been agreed that the text of Article IX:6

> "should not have the effect of prejudicing the present situation as regards certain distinctive names of products, provided always that the names affixed to the products cannot misrepresent their true origin. This is particularly the case *when the name of the producing country is clearly indicated.* It will rest with the governments concerned to proceed to a joint examination of particular cases which might arise if disputes occur as a result of the use of distinctive names of products which may have lost their original significance through constant use permitted by law in the country where they are used." (Reports of Committees and Principal Sub-Committees, UN Conference on Trade and Employment, 1948, p. 79).

The Panel noted that the Japanese Law and Cabinet Order concerning Liquor Business Association and Measures for Securing Revenue of Liquor Tax stipulated that "Any manufacturer of liquors must indicate, at a legible location of the container of liquors . . . which are shipped out from the manufacturing premise . . . , the name of the manufacturer, the place of the manufacturing premise . . . , the capacity of the container . . ., the category of liquors . . . , the grade of liquors and the following matters according to the category of liquors, in a conspicuous manner," including the alcohol content in the case of wine, whisky, brandy, spirits and liqueurs. The Panel examined a large number of labels, photos, wine bottles and packages submitted by the EEC as evidence. *The Panel found that this evidence seemed to confirm the Japanese submission to the Panel that the labels on liquor bottles manufactured in Japan indicated their Japanese origin.*

5.15 The Panel examined the view of the European Community that the use of French words, French names, of other European languages and European label styles or symbols by Japanese manufacturers continued to mislead Japanese consumers as to the origin of the liquors, and that the indication of a Japanese manufacturer did not clarify his precise activities because, for instance, wines bottled in Japan could contain as much as 95% imported bulk wine. The Panel inferred from the wording of Article IX:6 that it was confined to an obligation to "cooperate with each other with a view to preventing the use of trade names in such manner as to misrepresent the true origin of a product, to the detriment of such distinctive regional or geographical names of products of the territory of a contracting party as are protected by its legislation." The Panel noted that there was no definition of a "trade name" in the General Agreement, and that there were differences in the laws of various countries as to what might constitute a trade name. The Panel did not consider it necessary to define the term "trade name" in this case for the following reasons: Article IX:6 was designed to protect "distinctive regional or geographical names of products of the territory of a contracting party as are protected by its legislation." The Panel did not dispose of evidence and was unable to find that the use by Japanese manufacturers of labels written partly in English (in the case of whisky and brandy) or in French (in the case of wine), the use of names of varieties of grapes (such as "Riesling" or "Sémillon"), or the use of foreign terms to describe Japanese spirits ("whisky," "brandy") or Japanese wines ("château," "réserve," "vin rosé") had actually been to the detriment of "distinctive regional or geographical names of products" produced and legally protected in the EEC. *Nor could the Panel find that Japan*—given, for example, its participation in the Madrid Agreement for the Repression of False or Deceptive Indications of Source of Goods and its internal laws and regulations on labelling and on the protection of distinctive regional or geographical names (such as "Armagnac" or "Chianti")—*had failed to meet its obligation to cooperate pursuant to GATT Article IX:6.*

DD63/18

5.16 The Panel recalled the established GATT principle that "where there is an infringement of the obligations assumed under the General Agreement, the action is considered prima facie to constitute a case of nullification or impairment" (BISD 26S/216). Having found that whiskies, brandies, other distilled spirits, liqueurs, still wines and sparkling wines imported into Japan were subject to discriminatory or protective Japanese taxes contrary to Article III:2, the Panel concluded that these taxes inconsistent with Article III:2 had to be presumed to cause nullification or impairment of benefits accruing to the European Community under the General Agreement. The Panel noted the Japanese submission that imports of these liquors into Japan had considerably increased since the 1960's. The Panel shared, however, the view expressed in another panel report adopted by the CONTRACTING PARTIES that an increase in imports could not refute the presumption that discriminatory or protective taxes inconsistent with Article III:2 had impaired the competitive benefits protected under Article III:2 because, *inter alia,* an increase in imports did say nothing about what the trade might have been in the absence of the inconsistent trade restrictions (see the Panel Report on US Taxes on Petroleum, L/6175, paragraphs 5.1.6 to 5.1.10).

5.17 *The Panel therefore suggests that the CONTRACTING PARTIES recommend that Japan bring its taxes on whiskies, brandies, other distilled spirits (such as gin and vodka), liqueurs, still wines and sparkling wines in conformity with its obligations under the General Agreement.*

UNITED STATES—CUSTOMS USER FEE

Report of the Panel adopted on February 2, 1988
BISD 35S/245, 247

II. FACTUAL ASPECTS

7. The term "customs user fee" refers to a number of fees imposed by the United States for the processing by the US Customs Service of passengers, conveyances and merchandise entering the United States. Only one of these fees is at issue in this dispute. It is the "merchandising processing fee," an *ad valorem* charge imposed for the processing of commercial merchandise entering the United States. The merchandise processing fee was enacted on October 21, 1986 in the Omnibus Budget and Reconciliation Act of 1986 (OBRA) (Public Law 99-509). It was enacted as an amendment to an earlier provision, Section 13031(a) of the Consolidated Omnibus Budget Reconciliation Act of 1985 (COBRA) (Public Law 99-272). As first enacted, Section 13031(a) had imposed a series of eight other customs user fees, for the arrival of passengers and conveyances, for customs broker permits, and for certain dutiable mail. The October 1986 amendment added the merchandise processing fee, which went into effect on December 1, 1986.

8. From December 1, 1986 until September 30, 1987, the end of the 1987 fiscal year, the merchandise processing fee was 0.22 per cent of the customs value of the merchandise being entered. In fiscal years 1988 and 1989, the fee will be either 0.17 per cent or a lesser *ad valorem* rate determined by the Secretary of the Treasury to be sufficient to provide the amount of revenue needed to fund "commercial operations" of the United States Customs Service for the upcoming fiscal year. According to the authoritative explanation of the legislation by the legislative committee that drafted it, this "special formula would allow reduction of the fee if that became necessary to ensure that the fee structure and revenue derived therefrom in the [subsequent years] of the program are consistent with the international obligations of the United States."

* * *

V. FINDINGS AND CONCLUSIONS

68. Having reviewed the arguments made by Canada and the European Economic Community, the Panel considered that it would be possible to cover the points raised be each party in a single set of findings and conclusions, and that it would be neither necessary nor helpful to try to separate the frequently overlapping positions of the two parties in order to be able to give separate responses to them.

69. Before tuning to the specific questions raised by the parties, the Panel first addressed the general meaning of Articles II:2(c) and VIII:1(a), and their relationship to each other. Article VIII:1(a) states a rule applicable to all charges levied at the border, except tariffs and charges which serve to equalize internal taxes. It applies to all such charges, whether or not there is a tariff binding on the product in question. The rule of Article VIII:1(a) prohibits all such charges unless they satisfy the three criteria listed in that provision:

(a) the charge must be "limited in amount to the approximate cost of services rendered";

(b) it must not "represent an indirect protection to domestic products";

(c) it must not "represent . . . a taxation of imports . . . for fiscal purposes".

The first requirement is actually a dual requirement, because the charge in question must first involve a "service" rendered, and then the level of the charge must not exceed the approximate cost of the "service".

70. Article II:2(c) is a provision of somewhat narrower scope. Its function is to permit the imposition of certain non-tariff border charges on products which are subject to a bound tariff. Paragraph 1(b) of Article II establishes a general ceiling on the charges that can be levied on a product whose tariff is bound; it requires that the product be exempt from all tariffs in excess of the bound rate, and from all other charges in excess of those (i) in force on the date of the tariff concession, or (ii) directly and mandatorily required by legislation in force on that date. Article II:2 permits governments to impose, above the ceiling, three types of non-tariff charges, of which the third, permitted by subparagraph (c), is "fees or other charges commensurate with the cost of services rendered".

71. In order to help clarify the meaning of Articles II:2(c) and VIII:1(a), the Panel examined the origins and the drafting history of these provisions. During the drafting of General Agreement, the previous legal instrument referred to most frequently in connection with these provisions was the *International Convention Relating to the Simplification of Customs Formalities* of November 3, 1923[1]. One of the major purposes of the 1923 convention had been to reduce the number and the level of fees imposed in connection with importation. Governments had agreed to limit certain fees to the actual cost of the government activity in question. Article 10 stated, "When a visa [for commercial travelers] is required, its cost shall be as low as possible and shall not exceed the cost of the services." Article 11(8) stated, "The cost of the [consular] visa must be as low as possible, and must not exceed the cost of issue, especially in the case of consignments of small value." Article 12 stated, "The cost of a visa for Consular invoices shall be a fixed charge, which should be as low as possible." The Convention's two provisions on consular fees were reaffirmed in the recommendations of the World Economic Conference of 1927, which restated them as follows:

> (1) Consular fees should be a charge, fixed in amount and not exceeding the cost of issue, rather than an additional source of revenue. Arbitrary or variable consular fees cause not only an increase of charges, which is at times unexpected, but also an unwarrantable uncertainty in trade.[2]

72. The Panel was unable to find specific antecedents to Articles II:2(c) and VIII:1(a). In particular, no such provisions could be found in the United States bilateral trade agreements of 1934-1942, from which the United States had drawn many of the texts proposed for adoption in the General Agreement. Those bilateral agreements had contained no general limitation on non-tariff charges as in Article VIII:1(a), nor had their definition of tariff bindings permitted the imposition of new "service" fees as in Article II:2(c).

73. According to the detailed negotiating history of GATT Articles II:2(c) and VIII:1(a) provided by the United States, proposals to permit

[1] League of Nations Treaty Series, vol. 30, p. 372 (1925). The treaty, which was negotiated under League of Nations auspices, entered into force on November 27, 1924.

[2] League of Nations Document C.356.M.129.1927.II., paragraph 5(1).

such fees, characterized as fees for "services rendered," appeared in the earliest stages of the GATT/ITO negotiations.[1] The criteria stated in the initial draft texts submitted to the negotiating conference[2] were almost identical to those adopted in the final texts, with the result that the actual negotiations presented no occasions for further elaboration of their meaning.

74. When the General Agreement was first adopted in 1947, the requirements of Article VIII:1(a) were merely hortatory, reading "should" rather than "shall." Article VIII:1(a) was made mandatory in the Review Session amendments to Part II of the General Agreement (3S/214), which were adopted in March 1955 and which entered into force in October 1957. Article II:2(c) was included in the original 1947 text of the General Agreement in its present form.

75. Two questions of general interpretation had to be answered before addressing the specific issues raised by the complainants. First, it was necessary to decide whether there was any legal significance in the slight difference in wording between the two "cost of services" limitations stated in Articles II:2(c) and VIII:1(a), i.e. "commensurate with the cost of services rendered" and "limited in amount to the approximate cost of services rendered." The words themselves suggested no immediately apparent difference in meaning. After reviewing both the drafting history and the subsequent application of these provisions, the Panel concluded that no difference of meaning had been intended. The difference in wording appears to be explained by the somewhat different paths by which each provision entered the General Agreement. The text which was to become Article VIII:1(a) appeared in the very first draft submitted to the negotiating conference by the United States, whereas the text of Article II:2(c) originated as a standard term to be incorporated in each contracting party's schedule of concessions

[1] According to negotiation records in the United States archives, the earliest reference occurred in a document titled "Agenda Resulting from Informal Exploratory Discussions between Officials of the United Kingdom and of the United States . . .", dated 16 October 1943.

[2] Article VIII:1(a) first appeared as Article 13, *Suggested Charter for an International Trade Organization of the United Nations*, submitted by the United States in September 1946. The first document found by the Panel containing the text of what was to become Article II:2(c) was E/PC/T/153 of August 1947. See also E/PC/T/201 of September 1947.

(see E/PC/T/153) and was not raised to the text of Article II until some time later (E/PC/T/201).[1]

76. Second, it was necessary to determine what type of fees were incorporated within the basic concept of "services rendered" in Article II:2(c) and VIII:1(a). The Panel concluded that there was a rather well established general understanding of this concept, demonstrated more by practice than by the actual text of the General Agreement. In its original form, as found in Article 13 of the United States' *Suggested Charter* of September, 1946, Article VIII was explicitly addressed to "fees, charges, formalities and requirements relating to all customs matters," and this definition was followed by an illustrative list which is virtually the same as the list now included in Article VIII:4. The illustrative list includes various aspects of the customs process such as "consular transactions," "statistical services," and "analysis and inspection." The text of Article VIII was later changed to enlarge the scope of that provision. Notwithstanding the fact that the enlarged scope gave a different meaning to the illustrative list in paragraph 4, GATT practice since 1948 has tended to interpret that illustrative list according to its original meaning, as a list of those customs-related government activities which the draftsmen meant when they referred to "services rendered." Thus, GATT proceedings have treated the following types of import fees as being within Articles II:2(c) or VIII:1(a): consular fees (CP.2/SR.11 (pages 7-8); 1S/25), customs fees (L/245; SR.9/28 (pages 4-5)), and statistical fees (18S/89).

77. In referring to these customs-related government activities as "services rendered," the drafters of Article II and VIII were clearly not employing the term "services" in the economic sense. Granted that

[1] A collateral issue which the Panel considered but was not required to answer was whether the form of words utilized in Article II:2(c) might not have been intended as a reference to exactly the same fees permitted by Article VIII:1(a)—in other words, whether Article II:2(c) incorporates all three of the criteria in Article VIII:1(a). The following considerations had raised the issue: (i) The text of Article II:2(c) was in fact developed after the draft text of Article VIII:1(a) had been established. (ii) Article II:2(c) sets the standards for determining when "service" fees may be imposed in excess of tariff bindings, whereas Article VIII:1(a) is a general provision relating to fees on all products. (iii) At least two Article XXIII complaints in the past had claimed that an import fee used for a "fiscal purpose" had constituted a violation of Article II, and in both cases the contracting party complained against had agreed and had withdrawn the fee (L/64; SR.8/7 (page 10); L/410; SR.10/5 (pages 51-52).

some government regulatory activities can be considered as "services" in an economic sense when they endow goods with safety or quality characteristics deemed necessary for commerce, most of the activities that governments perform in connection with the importation process do not meet that definition. They are not desired by the importers who are subject to them. Nor do they add value to the goods in any commercial sense. Whatever governments may choose to call them, fees for such government regulatory activities are, in the Panel's view, simply taxes on imports. It must be presumed, therefore, that the drafters meant the term "services" to be used in a more artful political sense, i.e., government activities closely enough connected to the processes of customs entry that they might, with no more than the customary artistic license accorded to taxing authorities, be called a "service" to the importer in question. No other interpretation can make Articles II:2(c) and VIII:1(a) conform to their generally accepted meaning.

(i) To What Extent Does the "Cost of Services" Limitation in Articles II:2(c) and VIII:1(a) Require That the Amount of the Fee Not Exceed the Approximate Cost of the Government Activities Performed with Respect to the Individual Customs Entry for Which the Fee is Imposed?

78. The Panel began its consideration of the legal issues by addressing the primary issue raised by Canada and the European Economic Community: whether the structure of the United States merchandise processing fee, in the form of an *ad valorem* charge without upper limits, was consistent with the "cost of services" limitation in Articles II and VIII. The complainants stressed that they did not intend to question the *ad valorem* method itself. They suggested, for example, that they would not object to an *ad valorem* fee that had a ceiling limitation equal to the average cost of processing an individual customs entry. The aspect of the United States fee the complainants wished to challenge was its tendency to impose fees exceeding the average cost of processing an individual entry. When the rate of an *ad valorem* fee is calculated by dividing the total costs of customs processing by the total value of the imports processed, the fee will, when imposed without upper limits, automatically exceed the average cost of processing whenever it is applied to entries of greater-than-average value.

79. The Panel agreed with the parties that the GATT consistency of this type of *ad valorem* fee turned on the meaning of the "cost of

services" limitation in Article II:2(c) and Article VIII:1(a). The Panel understood the central contentions of the parties to be as follows: Canada and the EEC had argued that "cost of services rendered" should be interpreted to mean the cost of the customs processing activities ("services") actually rendered to the individual importer with respect to the customs entry in question, or, at least, the average cost of such processing activities for all customs entries of a similar kind. Both complainants had stressed that the normal practice with respect to service fees was to require persons to pay only for the services rendered to them. The United States had argued that the "cost of services" limitation did not require exact conformity between fees and costs, but only that the fee be "commensurate with" the cost (Article II:2(c)), or limited to the "approximate" cost (Article VIII:1(a)). It had argued that, stated in these terms, the "cost of services" requirements would be satisfied if the total revenues from the fee did not exceed the total cost of the government activities in question, and if the fee were otherwise fair and equitable in its application. The United States had stressed that the *ad valorem* structure of the merchandise processing fee was the most equitable and least protective method by which such a fee could be imposed.

80. The Panel agreed with Canada and the EEC that the ordinary meaning of the term "cost of services rendered" would be the cost of those services rendered to the individual importer in question. That meaning was also in keeping with general practice when "services" are charged for, which is to charge the same fee for the same service received. And, finally, the origins of these provisions in the "cost of issue" requirements of the 1923 Convention pointed to this meaning as well.

81. The United States interpretation, by contrast, presented serious difficulties. Granted that the terms "commensurate with" and "approximate" were intended to confer a certain degree of flexibility in the requirement that fees not exceed costs, the range of fees permitted under the US merchandise processing fee could by no stretch of language be considered a matter of mere flexibility. Moreover, the United States contention that "cost of services rendered" referred only to the total cost of the relevant government activities would leave Articles II:2(c) and VIII:1(a) without any express standard for apportioning such fees among individual importers, thereby committing the issue of apportionment, at best, to an implied requirement of equitable (or non-protective) apportionment that would be neither predictable nor capable of objective application. Finally, if "cost of services

rendered" meant the total cost of customs operations, the "fiscal purposes" criterion of Article VIII:1(a) would be rendered largely redundant.

82. While the Panel thus found that the text of the General Agreement supported the interpretation advocated by Canada and the EEC, it recognized that this interpretation did not yield a result that was completely satisfying from a policy standpoint. A standard which requires the same fee for the same service would be an appropriate method of charging for government activities which were actually "services" in the economic sense. As noted above, however, most of the import fees covered by these provisions do not involve any such services. They are ordinary taxes on imports.

83. Viewing the US merchandise processing fee as an ordinary tax on imports, the Panel found itself in agreement with the United States argument that the *ad valorem* structure of that fee was the least distortive means of levying such a tax. That structure would have the lowest *ad valorem* impact for whatever amount was being collected,[1] it would create no distortion in relative prices between imports, it would be the most predictable for traders and investors, and it would be the simplest and least costly to administer. The United States had represented that the importers affected by the merchandise processing fee preferred its present method to all others. The Panel had no difficulty in believing that this was so.

84. The Panel was of the view, however, that the interpretation proposed by the United States presented an equally serious problem with regard to the policy objectives of the General Agreement. The problem was that the United States interpretation would enlarge the "service fee" authority granted by Articles II:2(c) and VIII:1(a), more importantly the former. Article II:2(c) is a rather extraordinary exception. It authorizes governments to impose new charges on imports in excess of the ceiling established by a tariff binding. Given the central importance assigned by the General Agreement to protecting the commercial value of tariff bindings, any such exceptions would require strict interpretation. The exception stated in Article II:2(c) requires partic-

[1] The complainants had observed that the *ad valorem* impact of a flat-charge user fee can be reduced to minimal levels by simply not trying to collect the entire cost of the "service" in question. While this may be true, it is also true that, given the same revenue target for both kinds of tax, collecting that amount by means of an *ad valorem* tax without upper limits will produce lower upper rates than any other.

ularly strict interpretation, however, because it does not conform to the policy justification normally given for such exceptions. In the words of an explanation of Article II:2 contained in a 1980 proposal by the Director-General (27S/24), the policy justification for the three types of border charges permitted by Article II:2 was that they did not "discriminate against imports." If the import fees authorized by Article II:2(c) were in fact fees for beneficial services, this justification would be valid. But given the reality that most such fees are simply an ordinary tax on imports, it cannot be said that such fees do not disadvantage imports vis-à-vis domestic products. In simple terms, Article II:2(c) authorizes governments to impose new protective charges in addition to the bound tariff rate. As such, it is an exception which should be doubly guarded against enlargement by interpretation.

85. In the Panel's view, the interpretation advocated by the United States would expand the scope of Articles II:2(c), as well as VIII:1(a). It would permit a broader variety of import fees to be imposed, and the greater availability and convenience of such fees would, the Panel believed, lead to an increase in both the number and the level of such fees. The Panel was convinced that the attainment of GATT policy objectives would not be furthered by such an interpretation. Thus, even though the requirement that import fees not exceed the cost of individual entries might increase the protective effect of such fees in a particular case, the Panel was unable to accept the United States argument that such consequences justified a more flexible interpretation. The Panel was satisfied that the text of the General Agreement did impose such a requirement, and that it would not promote the objectives of the General Agreement to relax it in the manner proposed by the United States.

86. *The Panel concluded that the term "cost of services rendered" in Articles II:2(c) and VIII:1(a) must be interpreted to refer to the cost of the customs processing for the individual entry in question, and accordingly that the* ad valorem *structure of the United States merchandise processing fee was inconsistent with the obligations of Articles II:2(c) and VIII:1(a) to the extent that it caused fees to be levied in excess of such costs.*

87. In reaching this conclusion, the Panel had also given careful consideration to another United States' argument based on the GATT's prior legal experience with *ad valorem* customs fees. The United States had argued that *ad valorem* service fees had been widely used throughout GATT's history, and that the absence of any previous challenge to their *ad valorem* character during this long period demonstrated that

most contracting parties considered *ad valorem* fees to be consistent with Articles II and VIII. The United States had cited several instances in which the CONTRACTING PARTIES had examined particular *ad valorem* fees without objecting to their *ad valorem* character, and had placed particular stress upon the fact that, notwithstanding the large number of *ad valorem* fees in force in 1955, the governments maintaining such fees had agreed to make Article VIII:1(a) mandatory in the 1955 Review Session amendments.

88. The Panel had examined all of the instances cited by the United States, as well as others that came to light during the course of its research. This examination had persuaded the Panel that the evidence did not support the conclusion advocated by the United States. The Panel believed it would be of assistance to include the results of this examination in its report.

89. The Panel first noted that a substantial number of the service fees reported in GATT documents appeared to have had excessively high rates, a problem that would normally have led to legal challenges far more readily than questions of *ad valorem* structure. The fact that, for the most part, these rather obvious legal shortcomings also appeared not to have been challenged suggested that many of these fees had simply not been subject to the rules of Articles II and VIII, or had otherwise escaped attention. The Panel found some support for the former hypothesis in the fact that most service fees existing on the date of a government's accession to GATT were immune from legal scrutiny under both Articles II and VIII. Article II:1(b) states that tariff bindings do not prevent governments from continuing to impose any non-tariff border charges existing at the time tariff concessions were made.[1] Article VIII:1(a) imposed no legal obligations at all from 1947 to 1957 when the Review Session amendments went into force, and thereafter the obligations of Article VIII were subject to the reservation for existing mandatory legislation in the Protocol of Provisional Application.[2] The relative importance of such legal immunity was indicated in a 1962 working party report on customs formalities:

[1] Article II:1(b) also exempted border charges imposed subsequently if they were required by laws in force at the time bindings were made. *Ad valorem* charges in this category would also have been exempt from challenge.

[2] The decision stating that Review Session amendments to Part II of the General Agreement are subject to the Protocol reservation is found at 6S/13; for an explanation of the decision, see John H. Jackson, World Trade and the law of GATT (1968) pages 74-75.

> The question was raised whether the levying of substantial consular fees by the importing country was in conformity with the obligations of Article VIII of GATT since the rates exceeded the costs of the services rendered and were not the equivalent of an internal charge. It was noted, however, that Article VIII being in Part II of GATT involved obligations only within the arrangements for provisional application of the Agreement. [11S/216]

90. This same legal immunity would also have made it possible for governments with pre-accession service fees to accept the Review Session amendments making Article VIII:1(a) mandatory for post-accession service fees. Once again, the most evident legal problem at the time would have been the excessive rate of many existing fees, and the fact that the new legal obligation was accepted in spite of these more obvious legal shortcomings would tend to support that conclusion. In addition, it is not accurate to say that all governments accepting the Review Session amendment of Article VIII did so in the belief that their fees were in compliance with it. The working party report recommending the amendment also recommended that "the Agreement . . . contain a general provision allowing time for governments to bring their legislation into conformity with the rules." (3S/214-215) The same report went on to note that five governments had reserved their position, proposing instead that the amendment should become effective "at the earliest practicable date."

91. The Panel found five cases in which individual *ad valorem* service fees had been investigated by the CONTRACTING PARTIES.[1] The Panel found that in three of the cases the *ad valorem* method had not been challenged, but that in each case the failure to challenge it could be accounted for by reasons other than an assumption of its validity, either because the fee was immune from legal attack on that issue, or because the government imposing the fee had promptly agreed to remove it for other reasons.[2] In the fourth case, the report of the working party contained a phrase which could have been a criticism of the *ad valorem*

[1] Articles II:2(c) and VIII:1(a) had also been considered in a sixth case, "EEC Program of Minimum Import Prices, Licenses and Surety Deposits for Certain Processed Fruits and Vegetables" (25S/68 (pages 95-98)), but the Panel concluded that nothing in that discussion was relevant to the present case.

[2] In 1948, the Netherlands brought a complaint concerning a discriminatory consular tax imposed by Cuba in which a rate of 5 per cent *ad valorem* was charged on goods from the Netherlands while a rate of 2 per cent *ad valorem* was

method, although the text was not clear.[3] In the fifth case, the legal consistency of the *ad valorem* method had been expressly questioned.

92. The fifth case involved a 1954 complaint by the United States concerning an increase in the rate of a French stamp tax. The stamp tax was calculated as a percentage of the customs duty; the increase in question raised the rate from 1.7% of the customs duty to 2%, an increase said to equal about 0.1% *ad valorem* . France defended the increase on the ground that the tax had been provided for in its consolidated schedule and had not actually been changed in gold or dollar value (in essence, that it was exempt under Article II:1(b)). France also defended the fee on the ground that its current level was commensurate with the cost of customs services rendered, and was thus authorized by Article II:2(c).[4] The reply of the United States delegation was as follows:

charged on others. Cuba agreed to remove the discriminatory element (CP.2/9; CP.2/SR.11). Given the early date of the complaint, the tax itself almost certainly antedated Cuba's accession, and so would not have been open to challenge under Article II. Article VIII was not then in force.

In 1952, the United States brought a complaint concerning a French statistical tax of 0.4 per cent *ad valorem,* on the ground that it was being used to fund social payments to agricultural workers. France agreed that this purpose constituted a violation of Article II, and agreed to remove the tax, thereby rendering moot any other claim of legal inconsistency. (L/64; SR.8/7, page 10).

In 1955, the United States brought a complaint concerning the increase of a French stamp tax, from 2 per cent of the customs duties to 3 per cent; the revenues from the additional 1 per cent were used to fund social payments to agricultural workers. France immediately agreed that the added 1 per cent was inconsistent with GATT obligations because it was not used to fund customs services, thereby rendering moot any other claim of legal inconsistency. (L/410; SR.10/5, pages 51-52). (As is explained more fully below, the United States had already challenged the *ad valorem* character of the original 2 per cent tax in a 1954 proceeding.)

[3] A 1971 working party report on the accession of Zaire stated that a statistical tax of 3 per cent *ad valorem* was "not commensurate with the service rendered and was contrary to the provisions of Article VIII:1(a)." The report did not specify the specific violation or violations in question. Although Zaire's reply to this finding concentrated on the excessive rate of the tax, the working party's eventual recommendation also asked Zaire to "re-examine its present method of application of the statistical tax . . ." a form of expression which was more appropriate to a concern over the form of the tax than to concern over the excessive rate. (18S/89, pages 89-90).

[4] Compliance with Article VIII:1(a) was not issue, because in 1954 it was not mandatory.

> Mr. Brown (United States) thanked the French delegate for his report. The United States Government was particularly concerned with the principle that the maintenance of an *ad valorem* charge alone would not satisfy the requirements of Article II. After the statement and explanation of the intentions and attitude of the French Government, and since there was no substantial injury to United States exports, his delegation was prepared to withdraw the complaint from the Agenda. (SR.9/28, page 5)

93. Finally, to give a more complete view of GATT legal experience on the issue of *ad valorem* service fees, the Panel considered it relevant to note that the *ad valorem* method had in fact been expressly attacked in 1952 and 1957, in two formal recommendations concerning consular fees. (1S/25; 6S/25.) Although these recommendations were initiated at a time when Article VIII:1(a) was merely hortatory, and thus were not a legal ruling as such, they were expressly intended to implement the standards of Article VIII:1(a). In its preamble, the 1952 recommendation noted the "cost of services" standard stated in Article VIII:1(a), and then observed that "the [consular] fee charged is in many cases a high percentage of the value of the goods." The operative part of the recommendation then stated, "Any consular fee should not be a percentage of the value of the goods but should be a flat charge." The 1957 recommendation, issued one month after the effective date of the protocol making Article VIII:1(a) mandatory, restated the 1952 recommendation in similar terms. While it is probable that the primary concern with the *ad valorem* method in these recommendations had been its tendency to encourage excessive rates, the text of these recommendations is also consistent with a parallel objection to its cost apportionment consequences. In either event, governments were on notice from an early date that the CONTRACTING PARTIES did not necessarily consider the *ad valorem* method an acceptable structure for the type of fees covered by Article VIII.

94. Considering the historical evidence as a whole, the Panel could not agree with the United States argument that the GATT's legal experience with *ad valorem* service fees evidenced a widespread belief that the *ad valorem* method as such was consistent with the obligations of Article II and VIII. Whether considered individually or as a whole, the events which constitute that history simply do not demonstrate any such understanding. If anything, these events tend to show that the *ad valorem* method has been questioned in those few cases where it has been put in issue.

(ii) Do All the Costs Included in the "Commercial Operations" Budget of the United States Customs Service Constitute "Cost of Services Rendered" to the Commercial Importers Subject to the Merchandise Processing Fee within the Meaning of Articles II:2(c) and VIII:1(a)?

95. After having dealt with the primary issue raised by the complaining parties, the Panel next considered several additional arguments by Canada and the European Economic Community claiming that various costs included in the "commercial operations" budget of the US Customs Service could not be considered "services rendered" to those commercial importers who were required to pay the fee. These arguments and the conclusions following from them were separate from the issue raised in the previous section. They would apply to any fee based on a calculation of total costs of customs processing, whether the fee was levied on an *ad valorem* basis or as a flat charge per entry. For convenience of analysis, the present report divides the arguments relating to different costs into three categories.

96. (a) *The cost of certain Customs Service activities.* The first category of costs to be challenged were the costs of certain Customs Service operations which, in the view of the complainant governments, could not be considered as "services rendered" within the meaning of Articles II:2(c) and VIII:1(a), and thus could not be charged to commercial importers under these provisions. Under this first heading, the parties questioned the inclusion of costs for the following activities of the Customs Service: airport passenger processing, activities related to exports, investigation of commercial fraud, investigation of counterfeit goods, collection of antidumping and countervailing duties, legal rulings on customs matters, technical laboratories, "clearance of carriers," and the *pro-rata* share of Executive Management activities called International Affairs, Internal Affairs, and Chief Counsel.

97. As noted in the previous section of this report, the Panel was of the view that Articles II:2(c) and VIII:1(a) contained a limitation upon the type of charges that could be imposed under these two provisions, a limitation to be found in the term "services rendered." Stated generally, the type of government activities deemed to be "services" were those activities closely enough connected to the processes of customs entry that they might, with no more than the customary artistic license accorded to taxing authorities, be called "services" to the importer in question.

98. The Panel was aware that, in applying this standard, its capacity to make judgements about the nature and functioning of particular

government operations would of necessity be limited by the quality of the information presented to it. The Panel was of the view that the government imposing the fee should have the initial burden of justifying any government activity being charged for. Once a *prima facie* satisfactory explanation had been given, it would then be upon the complainant government to present further information calling into question the adequacy of that explanation.

99. In the course of reaching its conclusions on these issues, the Panel also took into account that the United States Government had made a substantial effort to conform to GATT requirements when calculating the basis of the fee. The fact that the entire budget for the US Customs Service had been restructured in order to create a separate "commercial operations" account testified to the seriousness of that effort.

100. The Panel found that two of the challenged activities could not under any circumstances be regarded as "services rendered" to the commercial importers in question. The first was the activity of airport passenger processing. The cost of passenger processing was a large item in the "commercial operations" budget of the Customs Service, accounting for approximately ten percent. According to the information furnished to the Panel, the customs clearance of passengers was a wholly separate operation from the clearance of commercial cargoes, and the expenditures for the two processes are budgeted separately. Thus, passenger processing could not be considered a government activity "serving" those commercial importers who pay the merchandise processing fee.

101. The second item found not to qualify was the collecting and transmission of export documentation. No argument was made that export-related activities were properly chargeable to commercial importers. The United States sought to defend the failure to exclude the cost of this activity on the ground that the costs were *de minimis*. The Panel accepted that any system of cost allocation would of necessity require certain consolidations of minor functions within larger general categories, and that on balance such consolidations would probably not distort costs to any significant degree, especially since improper costs included in one case were likely to be offset by the exclusion of proper costs in another. On the other hand, the Panel also noted that the cost of adjusting budgets to reallocate any improper costs that were challenged would not be very great. Consequently, the Panel was of the view that, where affected governments consider particular cost items important enough to be challenged, the better solution would be to adhere to the legal requirements and to recommend that the government in question make the necessary budgetary correction. If costs were known well

enough to support a claim of *de minimis,* they should be known well enough to permit moving the estimated cost of the challenged activity to another budget item.

102. The remaining "commercial operations" activities questioned by the complainants were all activities that had some relationship to the processing of commercial imports, but in each case one or both of the complainants had raised a question whether the activity was of sufficient proximity to the normal process of customs clearance to be considered a "service" rendered to the importer. A second and related issue raised by the complainants was whether, assuming that a particular activity (e.g., a customs fraud investigation) were considered a "service" to the directly affected importer, that activity could also be considered a "service" to all other importers who were not in fact directly affected by it.

103. With respect to all but one of these remaining activities, the Panel was satisfied that the challenged activities were both proximate enough, and of sufficiently general applicability, that their costs could be included in the fee applicable to all commercial importers. In reaching these conclusions, the Panel gave considerable weight to the United States explanation that customs processing in the United States had increasingly moved away from hands on processing of incoming shipments, towards a highly centralized process which focused on identifying problem transactions and concentrating on them. Under such a system, centralized and specialized activities far removed from the ordinary importer were in fact as essential ingredient to the more rapid handling of the ordinary entry, the ultimate objective of the "service" that importers were being made to pay for.

104. Taking into account this system of customs administration, the Panel was persuaded that investigations of customs fraud and counterfeit goods were activities that directly affected the manner in which all entries were processed. The Panel concluded that collection of anti-dumping and countervailing duties were also normal customs activities, and that, taken as a group with the administration of other special border measures that affect varying goods at varying times, they are of a sufficiently general character that they might properly be considered a part of general customs "services" applicable to all commercial importers. The Panel was likewise of the view that both technical laboratories and the service of providing legal rulings on customs matters were resources of general applicability to the entire customs process, and that their cost could be allocated among all commercial importers and did

not have to be charged solely to the specific importers who happened to be beneficiaries of their "services" at the time in question. With respect to the "clearance of carriers" item, the Panel noted that this activity involved the examination of manifests which was the first step in discharging commercial cargo, and thus was clearly a part of the normal process of customs clearance.

105. Finally, with regard to the cost of those Executive Management functions challenged by the complainants, the Panel was satisfied that the United States was justified in including the *pro rata* cost of Internal Affairs and Chief Counsel, but it was unable to conclude that the International Affairs item had been properly allocated. Unlike the other functions in this category, which were described as involving centralized administrative functions, International Affairs was described as involving a variety of activities of Customs officers stationed in other countries, activities that were not identical and only some of which appeared to be related to the process of customs clearance. The Panel considered that the costs of such activities could not be allocated on the same *pro rata* basis as the other items. Since the United States supplied no other basis for allocating these costs, the Panel could not find that their inclusion was justified.

106. *The Panel's conclusion under this first category of challenged costs was that the cost of passenger processing and the cost of handling export documentation could not be included in the cost base of the merchandise processing fee, and that the inclusion of the cost of International Affairs had not been justified.*

107. (b) *The cost of customs processing for exempt imports.* The second category of costs challenged by the complainants was the cost of customs processing for imports that were exempt from the merchandise processing fee. Exemptions from the fee had been provided to imports from US insular possessions, imports from least developed developing countries, imports from developing countries designated as beneficiaries under the Caribbean Basin Economic Recovery Act (CBERA), and imports classified under Schedule 8 of the Tariff Schedules of the United States. The information provided to the Panel made clear that the rate of the merchandise processing fee was calculated in a manner which assured that the revenues from the fee would cover the cost of customs processing for all commercial imports, including the cost of processing exempt imports. In short, those who paid the fee were paying not only the cost of processing their own entries, but also the costs of exempt entries. According to information supplied by the United States, the

costs attributable to exempt imports were substantial. Out of total 1986 imports of $369 billion, the total value of imports exempted from the fee would have been approximately $102 billion, or about 28% if measured by value.

108. The United States gave a full explanation of the reasons for making these exemptions. In the Panel's view, however, none of the reasons for exempting a particular class of imports could provide any justification for the decision to make other importers pay the costs attributable to those imports.

109. *The Panel concluded that processing exempted imports could not be considered as "services rendered" to the commercial importers paying the merchandise processing fee.*

110. (c) *The cost of "commercial operations" for the first two months of Fiscal Year 1987.* The third category of costs challenged by the complainants concerned the cost of all "commercial operations" during the first two months of Fiscal Year 1987, a period when the fee was not in force. During the last ten months of FY 1987 when the merchandise processing fee had been in force, the rate had been set high enough to produce revenues sufficient to cover the "commercial operations" budget for the entire fiscal year. The complainants argued that the costs for the first two months could not be regarded as "cost of services rendered" to the importers paying the fee in the last ten months. The United States offered the view that the higher rate during the last ten months of the initial fiscal year of the fee was permissible, in view of the essential similarity between services rendered in the last ten months and those rendered during the entire fiscal year.

111. The Panel could not accept the justification presented by the United States. The Panel found nothing in Articles II or VIII which would authorize retroactive imposition of customs fees. The only plausible reading of the link required between costs and revenues was that revenues must be measured against the costs of the period in which the revenues are collected.

112. *The Panel concluded, therefore, that the receipts from the last ten months of FY 1987 had to be measured against the costs of customs operations during that period, or, at least, against 10/12 of the total cost of "commercial operations" for FY 1987. Costs in excess of this amount could not be attributed to the commercial importers paying the fee.*

(iii) To What Extent, under Articles II:2(c) and VIII:1(a), Can Total Charges in Excess of the Total "Cost of Services Rendered" be Rectified by Sequestering Revenues from the Fee in an Account That Can Only be Expended for Customs Services in Subsequent Years?

113. Viewing the United States merchandise processing fee as a whole, Canada and the European Economic Community contended that the fee had resulted in an overcharge, for two basic reasons. The first reason was the inclusion in the base of the fee of the improper charges described above: (a) charges for the cost of airport passenger processing, export-related activities, and International Affairs, (b) charges for the cost of processing exempt imports, and (c) charges for the cost of "commercial operations" for the two months prior to December 1986. The second reason for the overcharge, argued the complainants, was that the rate of the fee had been set too high, generating more revenue than needed to cover all the costs (proper or improper) contained in the "commercial operations" budget. The rate of 0.22 per cent *ad valorem* applied in the last ten months of FY 1987 had yielded approximately $536 million in revenue, against estimated costs of approximately $505 million for Customs "commercial operations" during all of FY 1987. Revenues for FY 1988 from the statutory rate of 0.17 percent *ad valorem* were projected to be $540 million, against projected costs of $535 million for the same period.

114. In response to the general problem of overcharges, the United States argued that the problem was essentially self-correcting under the US law, because funds from the merchandise processing fee were sequestered in a separate account that could only be expended for the "commercial operations" budget of the Customs Service. Excess revenues in one year simply constituted a surplus that must be used to reduce the fee in years following.

115. With regard to overcharges due to the second reason, i.e. incorrect rates, the Panel recognized that the "cost of services" limitation was a legal standard that could not be applied with precision in advance, at least not at the upper limit. Under any method of assessment seeking total reimbursement for the costs in question, governments would of necessity have to set the level of the fee on the basis of cost and revenue estimates, with a procedure for correcting overcharges when they occurred. The Panel considered that the United States system of sequestered accounts was a reasonable solution to the problem of over-

charges due to incorrect estimates. The Panel noted the complainants' argument that the size of the overcharge in FY 1987 due to an incorrect rate (i.e. revenues of $535 million for costs of $505 million) exceeded normal tolerances. The Panel was not provided with the data on which the 1987 calculations were made, but, having been supplied by the parties with an array of differing cost and revenue estimates made *during* FY 1987, the Panel did not consider this six percent error to be outside the normal range of error for such forecasts.

116. The Panel could not agree, however, that sequestered accounts alone were sufficient to cure the overcharge due to the first reason, improper charges. The amount of the overcharge in FY 1987 due to such improper charges had been substantial. Based on the data accepted for the purpose of the present report, the Panel found that the $505 million allocated to the "commercial operations" budget in FY 1987 exceeded the proper amount by over $230 million.[1] The projected costs of $535 million for "commercial operations" in FY 1988 would also exceed proper costs by a similarly substantial sum, approximately $185 million, so long as it included charges for airport passenger processing and exempt imports.[2]

117. As long as such improper costs remained in the "commercial operations" budget, sequestering of accounts would do nothing at all to correct the overcharge, because the revenues collected for such costs would be used to pay them and would never create a surplus to be carried over into future years. Even if such sums were treated as surplus, however, the carrying forward of sums of such magnitude, for credit in future years, could not be considered a satisfactory implemen-

[1] Setting aside possible corrections for export-related activities and International Affairs, for which the Panel had no data, the Panel made the following calculations: The total cost, $505 million, was first reduced by approximately $51 million, representing the amount budgeted for passenger processing. The resulting sum of $454 million was then further reduced to exclude the share of these costs attributable to exempt imports. The Panel did not have the data to calculate the percentage of exempt imports by number of entries, but using the percentage of exempt imports by value (28 per cent) it arrived at a figure of $127 million that would have to be excluded. And finally, this sum of $327 million was reduced by a further 2/12 (55 million) to exclude the cost of the two months prior to the imposition of the fee. The total chargeable amount under these calculations was $272 million.

[2] For FY 1988, the projected cost of passenger processing in the data submitted to the Panel was $53 million. Removing this item reduced the total to $482. Using the 1986 percentage by value (28 per cent) to calculate the necessary exclusion for exempt imports, a further reduction of approximately $135 million was required. Once again, the Panel's calculation did not include possible corrections for export-related activities and International Affairs.

tation of the legal obligations in question. Compliance with these obligations would require the removal of such costs from the basis of the present tax so that no further excess revenues are collected.

(iv) Does the US Merchandising Processing Fee Represent Either "An Indirect Protection to Domestic Products" or "A Taxation of Imports . . . for Fiscal Purposes" within the Meaning of Article VIII:1(a)?

118. Having considered at some length the issues raised by the parties under the "cost of services" limitation in Articles II:2(c) and VIII:1(a), the Panel then considered whether the arguments of the parties had raised any further issues concerning the US merchandise processing fee under the second and third criteria stated in Article VIII:1(a).

119. The only issue raised by the parties under the third criterion prohibiting "taxation of imports . . . for fiscal purposes" was the question of whether total revenues exceeded total attributable costs, an issue which the Panel dealt with fully under the "cost of services" requirement.

120. The only specific issue raised by the parties under the second criterion was whether the 0.22 and 0.17 percent *ad valorem* charges constituted "an indirect protection to domestic products" due to their effect on certain classes of price-sensitive imports. It was not necessary for the Panel to decide whether the "indirect protection" criterion actually involved a requirement of no adverse trade effects. The Panel concluded that, even if it did, it had not been demonstrated that these *ad valorem* charges had had a trade distorting effect.

(v) Were the Exemptions from the US Merchandise Processing Fee Granted to Imports from Certain Countries Inconsistent with the MFN Obligation of Article I:1?

121. In a submission to the Panel, India, appearing as a intervening party, requested the Panel to consider whether the exemption contained in the merchandise processing fee legislation in favor of imports from least developed countries was consistent with the MFN obligations of Article I:1. Two other interveners, Australia and Singapore, also referred to this issue, mentioning in addition the exemption for beneficiaries of the CBERA. The two complainants had not raised this matter but reserved their right on the issue. They indicated that they had no objection to the Panel dealing with the issue.

122. The Panel understood the argument that these exemptions were inconsistent with the obligations of Article I to be as follows: The merchandise processing fee was a "charge imposed on or in connection with importation" within the meaning of Article I:1. Exemptions from the fee fell within the category of "advantage, favor, privilege or immunity" which Article I:1 required to be extended unconditionally to all other contracting parties. Such preferential exemptions therefore constituted a breach of the obligation of non-discrimination of Article I:1. The exemption from the fee granted to beneficiaries of the CBERA was not authorized by the waiver granting the US authority to extend duty-free treatment to these beneficiaries (31S/20). Nor was it authorized by the Enabling Clause of November 28, 1979 (26S/203), the relevant provisions of which authorized preferential tariff and non-tariff measures for the benefit of developing countries only if such measures conformed to the Generalized System of Preferences or to instruments multilaterally negotiated under GATT auspices. Nor, finally, did the Enabling Clause, cited above, authorize the preferential exemption from the merchandise processing fee for products from least developed developing countries. Under the Enabling Clause, special measures for least developed developing countries were permitted only if taken "in the context of any general or specific measures in favor of developing countries."

123. No answer in opposition to these legal claims was given, nor was the Panel aware of any that could be given.

124. Nevertheless the Panel concluded that it would not be appropriate to make a formal finding on this issue. GATT practice has been for panels to make findings only on those issues raised by the parties to the dispute. The Panel believed that this was sound legal practice and should be followed in this case. It was, of course, open to any contracting party who wished to raise this issue, or any other issue pertaining to the US merchandise processing fee, to commence dispute settlement proceedings in its own right under the General Agreement.

VI. SUMMARY

125. The Panel *found* that:

(a) The term "cost of services rendered" in Articles II:2(c) and VIII:1(a) must be interpreted to refer to the approximate cost of customs processing for the individual entry in question, and that consequently the *ad valorem* structure of the United States merchandising processing fee was inconsistent with the obligations of Articles II:2(c) and VIII:1(a) to the extent it caused fees to be levied in excess of these approximate costs.

(b) The United States merchandise processing fee, as applied in Fiscal Year 1987 and as established for Fiscal Year 1988, also exceeded the "cost of services rendered" within the meaning of Articles II:2(c) and VIII:1(a) to the extent it included charges for the cost of the following activities of the US Customs Service:
   (i) airport passenger processing;
   (ii) collecting and forwarding of export documentation;
   (iii) the International Affairs item in the "commercial operations" budget;
   (iv) customs processing of imports exempt from the merchandise processing fee;
   (v) all activities within the present definition of "commercial operations" for the first two months of Fiscal Year 1987.

(c) Accordingly, to the extent it had caused fees to be levied in excess of the "cost of services rendered" within the meaning of Articles II:2(c) and VIII:1(a), the United States merchandise processing fee had to be considered *prima facie* to nullify or impair benefits accruing to Canada and to the European Economic Community under the General Agreement.

126. In the light of the above, the Panel *suggests* that the CONTRACTING PARTIES recommend that the United States bring the merchandise processing fee into conformity with its obligations under the General Agreement.

CANADA—IMPORT, DISTRIBUTION AND SALE OF ALCOHOLIC DRINKS BY CANADIAN PROVINCIAL MARKETING AGENCIES

Report of the Panel adopted on March 22, 1988
BISD 35S/37, 38

2. FACTUAL ASPECTS

2.1 In Canada, constitutional authority to control import and export transactions across national or provincial boundaries is within the exclusive legislative authority of the Federal Parliament under Section 91 of the Canadian Constitution Act, 1867 (formerly the British North America Act). This "trade and commerce" power of the federal authorities essentially excludes any authority over the distribution of imported or local products within provinces. Legislation of either level of government which is determined to have encroached on areas within the exclusive legislative authority of another level of government, is *ultra vires* and therefore null and void. Only a Canadian court of competent jurisdiction is empowered to make such a determination.

2.2 All liquor boards in Canada are created by provincial statutes and their monopoly position with respect to the supply and distribution of alcoholic beverages within their provincial borders is based on provincial legislation. The provinces are constitutionally empowered to enact such legislation under Section 92 of the *Constitution Act, 1867,* in particular the heads referring to 'Property and Civil Rights' and 'Local Matters within the Province.' The importation of liquor into Canada is, on the other hand, regulated by federal legislation. By means of the 1928 Importation of Intoxicating Liquors Act (now R.S.C, 1970) the Canadian Parliament restricted the importation of liquor except under the provisions established by a provincial agency vested with the right to sell liquor. This has resulted in a monopoly on the importation of alcoholic beverages by provincial liquor boards. The federal statute restricts the importation of liquor except under provisions established by a provincial monopoly of supply and distribution. By virtue of the Act importers and consumers in Canada cannot bypass the intermediary of the provincial liquor boards by making direct imports.

2.3 The distribution of alcoholic beverages in Canada is controlled or conducted by the provincial marketing agencies, or "liquor boards." All provinces have government liquor stores situated throughout their territory. Some provinces also permit off-premise sales, sales through hotels, restaurants, grocery stores and "beer" or "wine" stores at prices and under conditions determined by the provincial authorities (liquor commissions). The objectives of the provincial liquor monopolies include (i) profit maximization for revenue generating purposes (fiscal objectives) and (ii) limitation, for moral and health reasons, of the potential abuse of alcoholic drinks (social objectives).

2.4 The retail price of an alcoholic beverage sold in a Canadian province is established by adding applicable federal customs duties and taxes, provincial mark-ups and taxes to the base price. The provincial mark-ups are applied in addition to customs duties at the rates bound under Canada's GATT tariff schedule. All duties on beer, wines and spirits are bound in this schedule. The European Communities or its particular member States have initial negotiating rights on a number of concessions. Several other Contracting Parties, including the United States, also have initial negotiating rights on a number of concessions granted by Canada on alcoholic beverages.

2.5 The mark-up is the percentage increase over the base price. The base price is defined, both for imported and domestic products, as invoice price plus standard freight to a pre-set destination plus federal charges, including customs duties. The mark-ups being imposed, in part, for fiscal reasons constitute an important source of revenue for provincial governments. Most Canadian provinces have had a long-standing policy of differential mark-ups for provincial and imported alcoholic beverages, the mark-ups applied by the provincial liquor boards to imported products being frequently, but in degrees which vary from province to province and with respect to the type of alcoholic drink, higher than those applied to domestic products. Certain provinces apply differential mark-ups to some products from other provinces, as well.

2.6 While the situation varies somewhat from province-to-province, generally any supplier of beer, wine or spirits, domestic or imported, wishing to sell the products in a province must first obtain a "listing" from the provincial marketing agency. A listing request (which may vary by province and by product) is assessed on the basis of criteria such as quality, price marketability, relationship to other products of the same type already listed, performance in other markets, etc. If the listing is granted, it can be subject to conditions under which the product in question may be sold in the province (e.g. minimum sales quotas, bottle/package sizes). Moreover, factors such as space limitations, and revenue maximization also affect listing and delisting practices of the various liquor commissions and their marketing agency outlets, which endeavour to operate as commercial enterprises with a certain degree of autonomy. In certain provinces (e.g. British Columbia, Ontario, Quebec) the conditions and formalities to be respected for an imported product to be admitted to the list of items available for sale by a liquor board are more onerous than those applying to domestic wines, spirits and beer. Certain of these practices are to be terminated by January 1, 1988. Moreover, in a number of provinces additional outlets—such as grocery stores, or "licensed retail stores"—are available for sales of the domestic products or domestically bottled products and are denied for imported products. Several provinces' liquor boards also differentiate between domestic and imported alcoholic beverages through listing and delisting practices and other conditions and formalities.

2.7 The practices described in paragraphs 2.5 and 2.6 are referred to in the "Provincial Statement of Intentions with Respect to Sales of Alcoholic Beverages by Provincial Marketing Agencies in Canada" (see Annex). The Statement which should be fully implemented by January 1, 1988, was negotiated by Canada on behalf of its provinces in the context of the Tokyo Round of Multilateral Trade Negotiations with the European Communities and sets out specific undertakings with respect to mark-ups, listing and distribution practices. Similar statements were also negotiated by Canada with the United States, Australia, New Zealand and Finland.

2.8 The Statement refers to policies and practices affecting all alcoholic beverages imported by Canada from the EC. It stipulates, *inter alia,* that any differential in mark-up between domestic and imported wines will not in future be increased beyond current levels, except as might be justified by normal commercial considerations. The Statement also provides that by January 1, 1988 "any differential in mark-up between domestic and imported distilled spirits will reflect normal commercial considerations, including higher costs of handling and marketing which are not included in the basic delivery price." A number of letters relating to the Statement were exchanged between Canada, on behalf of the Canadian provinces, and the European Communities in April 1979 (see Annex I). In the letter of April 5, 1979, Canada informed the European Communities that the Statement was "necessarily non-contractual in nature." The text of Statement of Intentions, was realised by the Government of Canada and included in a document of the EC Commission reporting on the Tokyo Round. Specific reference to the Statement of Intentions was also included from 1982 on in Canada's notification to GATT on state trading pursuant to Article XVII:4(a). However, the Statement is not an integral part of Canada's GATT tariff schedule, neither had it been notified to all participants in the Multilateral Trade Negotiations nor to the CONTRACTING PARTIES. In many instances mark-up differentials between imported and domestic alcoholic beverages were reduced or eliminated since April 1979. In a number of cases, mark-up differentials between imported and domestic wines were increased since that date.

* * *

4. FINDINGS

4.1 The Panel noted that two questions were posed in its terms of reference, namely "whether certain practices of provincial agencies which market alcoholic beverages (i.e. liquor boards) are in accordance with the provisions of the General Agreement" and "whether Canada has carried out its obligations under the General Agreement." It decided to deal with the first question before examining the second.

Practices of Provincial Liquor Boards

4.2 The Panel recalled that the practices complained of related to mark-up practices, including restaurant discounts on domestic alcoholic beverages; and restrictions on points of sales and listing/delisting procedures.

Mark-Ups

4.3 Since Canada's Schedule of Concessions included tariff bindings on all imported alcoholic beverages, the Panel first examined the European Communities' contention that the mark-up practices were not in conformity with Article II of the General Agreement.

4.4 The Panel recalled that Canada and the European Communities agreed on the fact that Canada had, through the Importation of Intoxicating Liquors Act, authorized a monopoly of the importation of alcoholic beverages. The Panel noted therefore that the amount of protection admissible under Article II:4 was thus either the amount provided for in the Canadian Schedule or "as otherwise agreed between the parties which had initially negotiated the concession."

4.5 The panel recalled in this context its terms of reference, which requested the Panel to take into account, "in carrying out its examination . . . , *inter alia,* the provincial statement of intentions concluded in the context of the Tokyo Round of multilateral trade negotiations with respect to sales of alcoholic beverages by provincial marketing agencies in Canada." The Panel examined, therefore, whether the parties had, by the Provincial Statement of Intentions and the related exchange of letters, "otherwise agreed" in the sense of Article II:4, as claimed by Canada, on an amount of protection different from that provided for in the Canadian Schedule.

4.6 The Canadian government's letter of April 5, 1979 made it clear that the Provincial Statement of Intentions was put forward on behalf of the provincial authorities. The title and wording of the Provincial Statement of Intentions indicated that it expressed "intentions" and was, as confirmed in the letter, "necessarily non-contractual in nature." The only undertaking expressed by the Government of Canada in the letter of April 5, 1979 was that it "will be prepared to use its good offices with the provincial authorities concerned regarding any problem which may arise with respect to the application of provincial policies and practices set forth in the statement." Canada's emphasis on the non-binding nature of the undertaking seemed to indicate that it was not meant to affect Canada's rights and obligations under Article II:4. Nor did the letters of the EC Commission, dated April 5 and June 29, 1979, express an acceptance of an agreement concerning its rights and obligations under Article II:4. The first of these letters restricted itself to acknowledging the receipt of the Canadian letter and the second only expressed "some disquiet" concerning the terms "normal commercial considerations" in the Provincial Statement of Intentions.

4.7 The Panel noted that the Provincial Statement of Intentions and related letters had not been included among the texts listed in the Procès-Verbal embodying the results of the Tokyo Round, that the letters were classified as confidential and had not been notified to the CONTRACTING PARTIES. While the Council has stated in the terms of reference of the Panel that the Provincial Statement had been "concluded in the Tokyo Round of Multilateral Trade Negotiations" it appeared to the Panel that for the Statement to satisfy the conditions of Article II:4, it would have had to be binding to the same extent as the concession in the Schedule which it was intended to supersede.

4.8 The Panel therefore *concluded* that the Provincial Statement of Intentions and the related exchange of letters could not be held to constitute an agreement in terms of Article II:4 and did not, therefore, modify Canada's obligations arising from the inclusion of alcoholic beverages in its GATT Schedule.

4.9 The Panel then proceeded to examine whether the mark-ups imposed on imported alcoholic beverages plus the import duties, which were collected at the bound rate, afforded protection on the average in excess of the amount of protection provided for in Canada's Schedule contrary to Article II:4, as claimed by the European Communities, the Panel noted that according to the interpretative note to Article II:4. the paragraph was to be applied "in the light of the provisions of Article 31 of the Havana Charter." The text of Article 31, including its interpretative note, is contained in Annex II.

4.10 The Panel noted that Article II:4, applied in the light of Article 31:4, prohibited the charging of prices by the provincial liquor boards for imported alcoholic beverages which (regard being had to average landed costs and selling prices over recent periods) exceeded the landed costs; *plus* customs duties collected at the rates bound under Article II; *plus* transportation, distribution and other expenses incident to the purchase, sale or further processing; *plus* a reasonable margin of profit; *plus* internal taxes conforming to the provisions of Article III.

4.11 The Panel also noted that the retail prices charged by the provincial liquor boards for imported alcoholic beverages were composed of the invoice price; *plus* federal customs duties collected at the bound rates; *plus* standard freight to a set destination; *plus* additional price increases ("mark-ups") which were sometimes higher on imported than on like domestic alcoholic beverages ("differential mark-ups"); *plus* federal and provincial sales taxes.

4.12 The Panel proceeded to examine the Canadian contention that such differential mark-ups generally reflected higher transportation, distribution and other expenses associated with imported products, such as storage, as well as a reasonable margin of profit, and were therefore in accordance with the provisions of the General Agreement.

4.13 The Panel considered that differential mark-ups could be justified to offset any additional costs of transportation, distribution and other expenses incident to the purchase, sale or further processing, such as storage, necessarily associated with importing products and that such calculations could be made on the basis of average costs over recent periods.

4.14 The Panel noted Canada's statement that, in some instances, the differential mark-ups also reflected a policy of revenue maximization on the part of the provincial liquor boards, which charged higher mark-ups on imported than on domestic alcoholic beverages because they marketed imported products as premium products and exploited less price elastic demand for these products, and that this policy was in accordance with the General Agreement because revenue maximization was justified by normal commercial considerations.

4.15 The Panel considered that a monopoly profit-margin on imports resulting from policies of revenue maximization by provincial liquor boards could not normally be considered as a "reasonable margin of profit" in the sense of Article II:4, especially if it were higher on imported products than on domestic products.

4.16 The Panel considered that the phrase "a reasonable margin of profit" should be interpreted in accordance with the normal meaning of these words in their context of Article II and Article 31 of the Havana Charter, and that "a reasonable margin of profit" was a margin of profit that would be obtained under normal conditions of competition (in the absence of the monopoly). The margin of profit would have on the average to be the same on both domestic and the like imported products so as not to undermine the value of tariff concessions under Article II.

4.17 The Panel also noted Canada's argument that the drafting history implied that a reasonable margin of profit was a margin which "should not be so excessive as to restrict the volume of trade in the product concerned.," and that since the volume of imports from the European Communities of the products in question had not declined, the margin of profit was a reasonable one. The Panel noted that the fact that these imports had not declined did not say anything about what they would had been in the absence of a policy of monopolistic profit maximization by the provincial liquor boards.

4.18 The Panel examined Canada's reference to normal commercial considerations and noted that the term "commercial considerations" was mentioned in Article XVII:1(b). It considered that this reference was not relevant to its examination of Article II:4 as the context in which the term 'commercial considerations' had been used was different.

4.19 The Panel therefore *concluded* that the mark-ups which were higher on imported than on like domestic alcoholic beverages (differential mark-ups) could only be justified under Article II:4, to the extent that they represented additional costs necessarily associated with marketing of the imported products, and that calculations could be made on the basis of average costs over recent periods. The Panel also *concluded* that the burden of proof would be on Canada if it wished to claim that additional costs were necessarily associated with marketing of the imported products.

4.20 The Panel noted that Article 31:6 of the Havana Charter provided that "in applying the provisions of this Article, due regard shall be had for the fact that some monopolies are established and operated mainly for social, cultural, humanitarian or revenue purposes." While the drafting history indicated that Article 31 should be applied to the extent that it was relevant to the context of the General Agreement, the Panel considered that Canada had the right to use import monopolies to raise revenue for the provinces, consistently with the relevant provisions of the General Agreement. The Panel also considered that its conclusions on Article II:4 did not affect this right, because Article II:4, applied in the light of Article 31:4 of the Charter, permitted the charging of internal taxes conforming to the provisions of Article III. It noted that federal and provincial sales taxes were levied on alcoholic beverages and asked itself whether the fiscal elements of mark-ups, which produced revenue for the provinces, could also be justified as "internal taxes conforming to the provisions of Article III," noting that Article III:2 itself referred, not only to internal taxes, but also to "other internal charges." The Panel was of the view that to be so considered, the fiscal element of mark-ups must of course meet the requirements of Article III, e.g. they must not be applied to imported or domestic products so as to afford protection to domestic production. The Panel also considered it important that, if fiscal elements were to be considered as internal taxes, mark-ups would also have to be administered in conformity with other provisions of the General Agreement, in particular Article X dealing with the Publication and Administration of Trade Regulations.

4.21 The Panel noted the view put forward by the European Communities as well as by Canada that the EC's complaint did not necessitate—at least not at this stage of the proceedings—a detailed factual analysis by the Panel of the cost differentials calculated by individual liquor boards for individual imported products in this respect. The Panel did not therefore pursue the matter.

Restrictions on the Points of Sale and on Listing

4.22 The Panel then examined the contention of the European Communities that the application by provincial liquor boards of practices concerning listing/delisting requirements and the availability of points of sale which discriminate against imported alcoholic beverages was inconsistent with Canada's obligations under Article III:4, XI or XVII of the General Agreement.

4.23 The Panel first examined the arguments relating to the relevance of Article XI to these requirements. The Panel noted Canada's claim that the practices referred to were not "restrictions" in the sense of Article XI because they were not associated with the "importation" of the products, because they were provincial measures and because they were consistent with the Provincial Statement of Intentions.

4.24 The Panel observed that the note to Articles XI, XII, XIII, XIV and XVIII provided that throughout these Articles "the terms import restrictions" and 'export restrictions' include restrictions made effective through state-trading operations." The Panel considered it significant that the note referred to "restrictions made effective through state-trading operations" and not to "import restrictions." It considered that this was a recognition of the fact that in the case of enterprises enjoying a monopoly of both importation and distribution in the domestic market, the distinction normally made in the General Agreement between restrictions affecting the importation of products and restrictions affecting imported products lost much of its significance since both types of restriction could be made effective through decision by the monopoly. The Panel considered that systematic discriminatory practices of the kind preferred to should be considered as restrictions made—effective through "other measures" contrary to the provisions of Article XI:1. It also noted that an agreement or arrangement would have to be consistent with the General Agreement. The Panel noted that the relevance of the fact that the measures concerned were provincial measures would be examined in the second part of its findings.

4.25 The Panel therefore *concluded* that the practices concerning listing/delisting requirements and the availability of points of sale which discriminate against imported alcoholic beverages were restrictions made effective through state-trading operations contrary to Article XI:1. The Panel considered that it was not necessary at this stage to make a detailed factual analysis by the Panel of the restrictions on points of sale and the discriminatory listing/delisting practices by the individual provincial liquor boards.

4.26 The Panel then examined the contention of the European Communities that the practices complained of were contrary to Article III. The Panel noted that Canada did not consider Article III to be relevant to this case, arguing that the interpretative note to Articles XI, XII, XIII, XIV and XVIII made it clear that provisions other than Article

XVII applied to state-trading enterprises by specific reference only. The Panel considered that it was not necessary to decide in this particular case whether the practices complained of were contrary to Article III:4 because it had already found that they were inconsistent with Article XI. However, the Panel saw great force in the argument that Article III:4 was also applicable to state-trading enterprises at least when the monopoly of the importation and monopoly of the distribution in the domestic markets were combined, as was the case of the provincial liquor boards in Canada. This interpretation was confirmed *e contrario* by the wording of Article III:8(a).

4.27 The Panel next turned its attention to the relevance of Article XVII and in particular to the contention of the European Communities that the practices under examination contravened a national treatment obligation contained in paragraph 1 of that Article. The Panel noted that two previous panels had examined questions related to this paragraph. The Panel report on Belgian Family Allowances (BISD 1S/60) said that "as regards the exception contained in paragraph 2 of Article XVII, it would appear that it referred only to the principle set forth in paragraph 1 of that Article, i.e. the obligation to make purchases in accordance with commercial considerations and did not extend to matters dealt with in Article III." The Panel on Canada—Administration of the Foreign Investment Review Act (BISD 30S/163) "saw great force in Canada's argument that only the most-favored-nation and note [sic] the national treatment obligations fall within the scope of the general principles referred to in Article XVII:1(a). The Panel considered, however, that it was not necessary to decide in this particular case whether the practices complained of were contrary to Article XVII because it had already found that they were inconsistent with Article XI.

4.28 The Panel recalled Canada's claim that the Importation of Intoxicating Liquors Act of 1928 constituted existing legislation within the meaning of paragraph 1(b) of the Protocol of Provisional Application which provided that Part II was applied to the fullest extent not inconsistent with existing legislation. The Panel noted that the CONTRACTING PARTIES had decided in August 1949 that this paragraph only referred to legislation of a mandatory character (BISD II/62 [Case 3]) and that this decision had been confirmed on many subsequent occasions, most recently in 1984 (BISD 31S/88 [Case 56]). The Panel *concluded* that the Importation of Intoxicating Liquors Act did not make mandatory restrictions on points of sale and discriminatory listing requirements.

4.29 The Panel wished to stress that nothing in its conclusions on restrictions on points of sale and discriminatory listing requirements affected the right of Canada to use import monopolies for purposes foreseen in the General Agreement, such as the protection of health of its population (Article XX), provided that it was done consistently with the relevant provisions of the General Agreement.

Notification Requirements

4.30 The Panel examined the European Communities' contention that Canada had not fully complied with its notification obligations under Article XVII:4(a), which should be interpreted in the light of the CONTRACTING PARTIES' decisions of 1960 and 1962 (BISD, 9S/182,11S/58). The Panel found that these decisions did not interpret Article XVII:4(a), but were separate instruments. The Panel found that Canada had complied with its obligations under Article XVII:4(a), but that it should supply the information called for by the decisions of 1960 and 1962 to the extent that it had not already done so.

Canada's Obligations

4.31 The Panel then turned to the second question raised in its terms of reference, namely "whether Canada has carried out its obligations under the General Agreement."

4.32 The Panel noted that the main question related to the interpretation of Article XXIV:12 which states: "Each contracting party shall take such reasonable measures as may be available to it to ensure observance of the provisions of this Agreement by the regional and local governments and authorities within its territory."

4.33 The Panel noted that there was no dispute that the provincial liquor boards were "regional authorities" within the meaning of Article XXIV:12.

4.34 The Panel noted that Canada had taken the position that the only authority that could judge whether all reasonable measures had been taken under Article XXIV:12 was in this case the Canadian government. While noting that in the final analysis it was the contracting party concerned that would be the judge as to whether or not specific measures could be taken, the Panel *concluded* that Canada would have to demonstrate to the CONTRACTING PARTIES that it had taken all reasonable measures available and that it would then be for the CONTRACTING PARTIES to decide whether Canada had met its obligations under Article XXIV:12.

4.35 The Panel noted that the Government of Canada considered that it had already taken such reasonable measures as were available to it to ensure observance of the provisions of the General Agreement by the provincial liquor boards. The Panel, however, also noted that the efforts of the Canadian federal authorities had been directed towards ensuring the observance of these provisions as they themselves interpreted them and not as interpreted in these findings. The Panel therefore *concluded* that the measures taken by the Government of Canada were clearly not all the reasonable measures as might be available to it to ensure observance of the provisions of the General Agreement by the provincial liquor boards, as provided in Article XXIV:12 and that therefore the Government of Canada had not yet complied with the provisions of that paragraph. The Panel was of the view, however, that in the circumstances the Government of Canada should be given a reasonable period of time to take such measures to bring the practices of the provincial liquor boards into line with the relevant provisions of the General Agreement.

5. CONCLUSIONS

4.36 In the light of the findings set out above, the Panel *recommends* that the CONTRACTING PARTIES request Canada:

(a) to take such reasonable measures as may be available to it to ensure observance of the provisions of Articles II and XI of the General Agreement by the provincial liquor boards in Canada;

(b) to report to the CONTRACTING PARTIES on the action taken before the end of 1988, to permit the CONTRACTING PARTIES to decide on any further action that might be necessary.

CANADA—MEASURES AFFECTING EXPORTS OF UNPROCESSED HERRING AND SALMON

Report of the Panel adopted on March 22, 1988
BISD 35S/98, 111

4. FINDINGS

(a) The Issue before the Panel

4.1 The Panel noted that the basic issue before it was the following: Canada prohibits the export of sockeye and pink salmon that is not canned, salted, smoked, dried, pickled or frozen (hereinafter referred to as "certain unprocessed salmon") and of food herring, roe herring, herring roe and herring spawn on kelp that is not canned, salted, dried, smoked, pickled or frozen (hereinafter referred to as "unprocessed herring"). The parties to the dispute and the Panel agree that such prohibitions on the exportation of any product destined for the territory of any other contracting parties [sic: to the dispute and the Panel agree that such prohibitions] are contrary to Article XI:1 of the General Agreement according to which contracting parties shall not institute or maintain prohibitions on the exportation of any product destined for the territory of any other contracting party. Canada invokes as justifications for the prohibitions two exceptions in the General Agreement: first, Article XI:2(b) permitting "export prohibitions . . . necessary to the application of standards or regulations for the classification, grading or marketing of commodities in international trade" and, second, Article XX(g) permitting any measure "relating to the conservation of exhaustible natural resources . . . made effective in conjunction with restrictions on domestic production or consumption." The United States denies that the export prohibitions are "necessary to the application of standards or regulations" within the meaning of Article XI:2(b) and that they are "related to the conservation of exhaustible natural resources" within the meaning of Article XX(g).

(b) Article XI:2(b)

4.2 The Panel first examined whether the export prohibitions maintained by Canada are justified by Article XI:2(b). The Panel noted that Canada considered it necessary to prohibit the export of certain unprocessed salmon and unprocessed herring to maintain its quality standards for these fish, including the standards for frozen salmon exported from Canada (cf. paragraphs 3.16-3.18 above). The Panel noted that Canada applied quality standards to fish and that it prohibited the export of fish not meeting these standards. The Panel further noted, however, that Canada prohibited export of certain unprocessed salmon and unprocessed herring even if they could meet the standards generally applied to fish exported from Canada. The Panel therefore found that these export prohibitions could not be considered as "necessary" to the application of standards within the meaning of Article XI:2(b).

4.3 The Panel then examined the Canadian contention that the prohibition of exports of certain unprocessed salmon and unprocessed herring was necessary for the international marketing of processed salmon and herring. Canada had argued that, without these prohibitions, Canadian processors would not have been able to develop a superior quality fish product for marketing abroad and would not have been able to maintain their share of the market for herring roe in Japan (cf. paragraphs 3.16-3.18 above). The question before the Panel therefore was thus whether the export restrictions on certain unprocessed salmon and unprocessed herring constituted marketing regulations on processed salmon and herring within the meaning of Article XI:2(b). The Panel noted that this provision referred to ". . . regulations . . . for the marketing of commodities in international trade," which suggests that the regulations covered by the provisions are not all regulations that facilitate foreign sales but only those that apply to the marketing as such. The drafters of Article XI.2(b) agreed that this provision would cover export restrictions designed to further the marketing of a commodity by spreading supplies of the restricted product over a longer period of time.[1] During the drafting mention was made only of export restrictions designed to promote foreign sales of the restricted product but not of export restrictions on one commodity designed to promote sales of another commodity. The broad interpretation of the term "marketing regulation" implied in Canada's argument would have the consequence that any import or export restriction protecting a domestic industry and enabling it to sell abroad would be exempted from the

[1] E/PC/T/A/PV/19, page 8

General Agreement's prohibition of import and export restrictions. Such interpretation would therefore expand the scope of the provision far beyond its purpose. The Panel found for these reasons that the export prohibitions on certain unprocessed salmon and unprocessed herring were not "regulations for the marketing" of processed salmon and herring in international trade within the meaning of Article XI:2(b). In the light of the considerations set out above, the Panel concluded that the export prohibitions were not justified by Article XI:2(b).

(c) Article XX(g)

4.4 The Panel then turned to the question of whether Article XX(g) justified the imposition of the export prohibitions on certain unprocessed salmon and unprocessed herring. The Panel noted that both parties agreed that Canada maintains a variety of measures for the conservation of salmon and herring stocks and imposes limitations on the harvesting of salmon and herring. The Panel agreed with the parties that salmon and herring stocks are "exhaustible natural resources" and the harvest limitations "restrictions on domestic production" within the meaning of Article XX(g). Having reached this conclusion the Panel examined whether the export prohibitions on certain unprocessed salmon and unprocessed herring are "relating to" the conservation of salmon and herring stocks and whether they are made effective "in conjunction with" the restrictions on the harvesting of salmon and herring.

4.5 Article XX(g) does not state how the trade measures are to be related to the conservation and how they have to be conjoined with the production restrictions. This raises the question of whether *any* relationship with conservation and *any* conjunction with production restrictions are sufficient for a trade measure to fall under Article XX(g) or whether a *particular* relationship and conjunction are required. The Panel noted that the only previous case in which the CONTRACTING PARTIES took a decision on Article XX(g) was the case examined by the Panel on "United States—Prohibition of Imports of Tuna and Tuna Products from Canada" but that Panel had found that the party invoking Article XX(g) did not maintain restrictions on the production or consumption of tuna and thus had not been required to interpret the terms "relating to" and "in conjunction with."[1] The Panel therefore decided to analyze the meaning of these terms in the light of the context in which Article XX(g) appears in the General Agreement and in the light of the purpose of that provision.

[1] BISD 29S/91

4.6 The Panel noted that some of the subparagraphs of Article XX state that the measure must be "necessary" or "essential" to the achievement of the policy purpose set out in the provision [cf. subparagraphs (a), (b), (d) and (j)] while subparagraph (g) refers only to measures "relating to" the conservation of exhaustible natural resources. This suggests that Article XX(g) does not only cover measures that are necessary or essential for the conservation of exhaustible natural resources but a wider range of measures. However, as the preamble of Article XX indicates, the purpose of including Article XX(g) in the General Agreement was not to widen the scope for measures serving trade policy purposes but merely to ensure that the commitments under the General Agreement do not hinder the pursuit of policies aimed at the conservation of exhaustible natural resources. The Panel concluded for these reasons that, while a trade measure did not have to be necessary or essential to the conservation of an exhaustible natural resource, it had to be primarily aimed at the conservation of an exhaustible natural resource to be considered as "relating to" conservation with the meaning of Article XX(g). The Panel, similarly, considered that the terms "in conjunction with" in Article XX(g) had to be interpreted in a way that ensures that the scope of possible actions under that provision corresponds to the purpose for which it was included in the General Agreement. A trade measure could therefore in the view of the Panel only be considered to be made effective "in conjunction with" production restrictions if it was primarily aimed at rendering effective these restrictions.

4.7 Having reached these conclusions the Panel examined whether the export prohibitions on certain unprocessed salmon and unprocessed herring maintained by Canada were primarily aimed at the conservation of salmon and herring stocks and at rendering effective the restrictions on the harvesting of salmon and herring. The Panel noted Canada's contention that the export prohibitions were not conservation measures *per se* but had an effect on conservation because they helped provide the statistical foundation for the harvesting restrictions and increase the benefits to the Canadian economy arising from the Salmonid Enhancement Program. The Panel carefully examined this contention and noted the following: Canada collects statistical data on many different species of fish, including certain salmon species, without imposing export prohibitions on them. Canada maintains statistics on all fish exports. If certain unprocessed salmon and unprocessed herring were exported, statistics on these exports would therefore be collected. The Salmonid Enhancement Program covers salmon species for which export prohibitions apply and other species not subject to export prohibitions. The export prohibitions do not limit access to salmon and herring supplies in general but only to certain salmon and herring supplies in unprocessed form. Canada limits purchases of these unprocessed fish only by foreign processors and consumers and not by domestic processors and consumers. In light of all these factors taken together, the Panel found that these prohibitions could not be deemed to be primarily aimed at the conservation of salmon and herring stocks and at rendering effective the restrictions on the harvesting of these fish. The Panel therefore concluded that the export prohibitions were not justified by Article XX(g).

5. CONCLUSIONS

5.1 *For the reasons set out in paragraphs 4.2-4.7 above, the Panel found that the export prohibitions on certain unprocessed salmon and unprocessed herring were contrary to Article XI:1 and were justified neither by Article XI:2(b) nor by Article XX(g). The Panel therefore suggests that the CONTRACTING PARTIES recommend that Canada bring its measures affecting exports of certain unprocessed salmon and unprocessed herring into conformity with the General Agreement.*

5.2 The United States asked the Panel to suggest that Canada be requested to refrain from replacing the export prohibitions by other measures having equivalent effects. The Panel considered that its mandate was limited to the examination of Canada's present measures and it therefore did not examine whether other measures with equivalent effects would be inconsistent with Canada's obligations under the General Agreement.

5.3 Canada referred in its submissions to international agreements on fisheries and the Convention of the Law of the Sea. The Panel considered that its mandate was limited to the examination of Canada's measures in the light of the relevant provisions of the General Agreement. This report therefore has no bearing on questions of fisheries jurisdiction.

JAPAN—RESTRICTIONS ON IMPORTS OF CERTAIN AGRICULTURAL PRODUCTS

Report of the Panel adopted on March 22, 1988
BISD 35S/163, 220

5. FINDINGS

The Panel noted that the United States claims that Japan maintains quantitative import restrictions on twelve product categories inconsistent with the general prohibition of quantitative restrictions in Article XI:1 of the General Agreement and that Japan invoked Article XI:2(c)(i) and Article XX(d) to justify the restrictions on these categories. The Panel first examined the general legal considerations applicable to all the products in question, and then proceeded to a product-by-product examination, and then to the examination of other issues before the Panel.

5.1 Article XI:2(c)(i)

5.1.1 Text and Notes

The part of Article XI relevant in this dispute reads as follows:

> "1. No prohibitions or restrictions other than duties, taxes or other charges, whether made effective through quotas, import or export licences or other measures, shall be instituted or maintained by any contracting party on the importation of any product of the territory of any other contracting party or on the exportation or sale for export of any product destined for the territory of any other contracting party.
>
> 2. The provisions of paragraph 1 of this Article shall not extend to the following:
>
> . . . .
>
> (c) Import restrictions on any agricultural or fisheries product, imported in any form, necessary to the enforcement of governmental measures which operate:

(i) to restrict the quantities of the like domestic product permitted to be marketed or produced, or, if there is no substantial domestic production of the like product, of a domestic product for which the imported product can be directly substituted;

. . . .

Any contracting party applying restrictions on the importation of any product pursuant to sub-paragraph (c) of this paragraph shall give public notice of the total quantity or value of the product permitted to be imported during a specified future period and if any change in such quantity or value. Moreover, any restrictions applied under (i) above shall not be such as will reduce the total of imports relative to the total of domestic production, as compared with the proportion which might reasonably be expected to rule between the two in the absence of restrictions. In determining this proportion, the contracting party shall pay due regard to the proportion prevailing during a previous representative period and to any special factors which may have affected or may be affecting the trade in the product concerned."

An interpretative note ad Article XI (which, according to Article XXXIV of the General Agreement, is an integral party of that Agreement) specifies the following:

"Paragraph 2(c)

The term in any form in this paragraph covers the same products when in an early stage of processing and still perishable, which compete directly with the fresh product and if freely imported would tend to make the restriction on the fresh product ineffective.

Paragraph 2, last sub-paragraph

The term special factors includes changes in relative productive efficiency as between domestic and foreign producers, or as between different foreign producers, but not changes artificially brought about by means not permitted under the Agreement."

5.1.2 Drafting History and General Considerations

A provision corresponding to Article XI:2(c)(i) was included in the "Suggested Charter for an International Trade Organization of the United Nations" proposed by the United States in 1946. The subsequent negotiations led to a refinement of the proposal but not to any basic changes except for the addition of fisheries products. It was stated that Article XI:2(c)(i) was required because:

> ". . . *in agriculture and fisheries you have to deal with the capricious bounty of nature, which will sometimes give you a huge catch of fish or a huge crop,* which knocks the bottom out of prices.
>
> You also have the phenomenon peculiar to agriculture and fisheries of *a multitude of small unorganized producers that cannot organize themselves.* It often happens that the Government has to step in and organize them. But if it does so, it cannot allow the results of its organization to be frustrated by uncontrolled imports." (EPCT/A/PV/19, emphasis added)

The drafters agreed that the exception:

> "*was not intended to provide a means of protecting domestic producers against foreign competition,* but simply to permit, in appropriate cases, the enforcement of domestic governmental measures necessitated by the special problems relating to the production and marketing of agricultural and fisheries products (Havana Reports, p. 89, emphasis added).

They also agreed that the exception:

> "should *not be construed as permitting the use of quantitative restrictions as a method of protecting* the *industrial processing* of agricultural or fisheries products." (Havana Reports, p. 93, emphasis added)

5.1.3 With this background in mind, the panel proceeded to a detailed examination of Article XI:2(c)(i). The Panel noted that each of the import controls maintained by Japan for which it invoked Article XI:2(c)(i) had to meet each and every one of the following seven conditions to be covered by that provision.

5.1.3.1 The Measure Must Constitute an Import Restriction

The Panel on "United States - Prohibition of Imports of Tuna and Tuna Products from Canada" noted that:

> "in Article XI:2(a) and (b) the words "prohibitions and restrictions" are used while in Article XI:2(c) mention is made only of restrictions."

and it therefore concluded that:

> "the provisions of Article XI:2(c)(i) could not justify the application of an import prohibition" (BISD 29S/91).

5.1.3.2 The Import Restriction Must be on an Agricultural or Fisheries Product

The General Agreement does not define the term "agricultural product". In the past rounds of trade negotiations it was accepted that the products falling under Chapters 1 to 24 in the Customs Cooperation Council Nomenclature could in principle be regarded as agricultural products. In the light of this long-standing practice of the GATT, the Panel decided to use the same concept in the case before it and therefore found that all the products at issue in this case were agricultural products within the meaning of Article XI:2(c).

5.1.3.3 There Must be a Governmental Measure Which Operates to Restrict the Quantities of a Product Permitted to be Marketed or Produced

> "To restrict" means, according to the drafters, to "keep output below the level which [would have been] allowed in the absence of restrictions". The drafters rejected the proposal that *regulation* of production, through price stabilization programmes, also be an accepted criterion (EPCT/A/PV/19). They agreed that subsidies were *not* "necessarily inconsistent with restrictions on production and that in some cases they might be necessary features of a governmental program for restricting production" (Havana Reports, p. 90). According to the note to Article XI the proportion between imports and domestic production is to be determined by taking into account "special factors" that may have affected or may be affecting the trade in the product concerned. The note specifically excludes from the definition of the term "special factors" changes

"artificially brought about by means not permitted under the [General] Agreement", but not changes artificially brought by legal means such as production subsidies or tariff protection granted within the bounds of Article II. It is thus clear that the production restrictions applied under Article XI:2(c)(i) may in principle coexist with production subsidies. This means that it is not necessary to restrict the level of production below the level that would exist in the absence of all government support. It also means that production which exists only because of production subsidies may be effectively restricted by imposing quantitative limits on the availability of subsidies. Other than requiring a governmental measure, Article XI:2(c)(i) does not specify how the production restriction is to be imposed.

It was agreed that:

". . . in interpreting the term 'restrict' for the purposes of paragraph 2(c), the essential point was that the measures of domestic restriction must effectively keep output below the level which it would have attained in the absence of restrictions." (Havana Reports, page 89)

5.1.3.4 The Import Restriction and the Domestic Supply Restriction Must in Principle Apply to "Like" Products (or Directly Substitutable Products if There is No Substantial Production of the Like Product)

In the preparatory work reference was made to the definition of the term "like products" adopted by the League of Nations which was "practically identical with another product", but it was also stated that the term had different meanings in different contexts and that the exact definition should be left to subsequent decisions. (EPCT/C.II/65,—/A/PV/41—C.II/36). It was further stated that the words "like products" in Article XI:2(c):

"definitely do not mean what they mean in other contexts—merely a competing product. In other words, to take an extreme case, if a country restricted its output of apples, it could not restrict importation of bananas because they only compete with them." (EPCT/C.II/PV.12).

Thus the mere fact that a product is competitive with another does not in and of itself make them like products. As noted in the following paragraph, Article XI:2(c) and the note supplementary to it regarding "in any form" establish different requirements for (a) restrictions on the importation of products that are "like" the product subject to domestic supply restrictions and (b) restrictions on the importation of products that are *processed* from a product that is "like" the product subject to domestic supply restrictions. This differentiation would be lost if a product in its original form and a product processed from that product were to be considered to be "like" products with the meaning of Article XI:2(c).

For those products which are not "like" products but are processed from the like product, the term *"in any form"* also permits import restrictions provided the conditions of the Note Ad Article XI are met, that is:

(a) the product is in an early stage of processing; *and*

(b) still perishable; *and*

(c) the processed product competes directly with the fresh product; *and*

(d) the product, if freely imported, would tend to make the restriction on the fresh product ineffective.

One of the purposes of Article XI:2(c)(i) was to allow governments to intervene in situations in which there was an unexpected excess of supplies of agricultural products that could not be stored under normal conditions until the market had improved (paragraph 5.1.2 above). In discussing the term "in any form", the drafters stated that it was not the intention ". . . to extend the [import] control . . . to things like *tinned* fish and sardines . . ." and further that ". . . what we have in mind here is the perishable kind of processed product, *not the kind which is capable of being stocked*" (EPCT/A/PV/19, emphasis added). The Panel observed that this requirement had been redrafted in the Havana Charter to read:

> ". . . imported 'in any form' means the product in the form in which it is originally sold by its producer and such processed forms of the product as are so closely related to the original product as regards utilization that their unrestricted importation would make the restriction on the original product ineffective." (Note to Article 20.)

However, this extension to cover also products which were not perishable was not incorporated into the General Agreement and the condition of perishability therefore remained in force.

5.1.3.5 The Import Restriction Must Be Necessary to the Enforcement of the Domestic Supply Restriction

In relation to this requirement the report of the ninth Session of the Working Party on Quantitative Restrictions (BISD 3S/190) states that:

> ". . . if restrictions of the type referred to in paragraph 2(c) of Article XI were applied to imports during that part of the year in which domestic supplies of the product were not available, such restrictions would be regarded as consistent with the provisions of the Article only to the extent that they were necessary to enforce or to achieve the objectives of the governmental measures relating to control of the domestic product."

The report further states that:

> ". . . it would be an abuse of intent of the provisions under paragraph 2(c)(i) of Article XI if contracting parties were to apply restrictions to processed products exceeding those 'necessary' to secure enforcement of the actual measure restricting production or marketing of the primary product."

5.1.3.6 Public Notice Must Be Given of the Total Quantity or Value of the Quota for Each Product

The last sub-paragraph of Article XI:2 requires that if a contracting party applies an import restriction pursuant to provisions of sub-paragraph (c), it must give public notice of the total quantity or value of a product permitted to be imported during a specified future period, and of any changes in such quantity or value. This requirement implies that under Article XI:2(c) only those quotas can be applied which define the quantity or value for each product subject to quota.

5.1.3.7 The Restriction on Imports Must Not Reduce the Total of Imports Relative to the Total of Domestic Production, as Compared with the Proportion Which Might Reasonably Be Expected to Rule Between the Two in the Absence of Restrictions

The last sentence of Article XI:2 prescribes the minimum size of the import quotas that contracting parties may establish in accordance with sub-paragraph (c)(i) of that provision. The quotas must be such as not to reduce the total of imports relative to domestic production as compared with the proportion which might reasonably be expected to rule between the two in the absence of restrictions. In order to determine the size of the import quota the contracting party thus has to estimate what the amount of domestic production and of imports would be during the quota period in the absence of supply and quantitative import restrictions. The General Agreement states that in making this determination contracting parties shall pay "due regard" to the proportions that prevailed during a previous representative period and to "special factors" that affected or may be affecting the trade in the product concerned. Among the special factors to which due regard should be paid are changes in relative productive efficiency, but not changes resulting from measures not permitted under the General Agreement.

The Panel noted that in the case before it the import restrictions maintained by Japan had been in place for decades and there was, therefore, no previous period free of restrictions in which the shares of imports and domestic supplies could reasonably be assumed to resemble those which would prevail today. The Panel further noted that the CONTRACTING PARTIES recognized in a previous case that a contracting party invoking an exception to the General Agreement had the burden of demonstrating that rule requirements of the exception were fulfilled.[1] The Panel realized that a strict application of this burden of proof rule had the consequence that Article XI:2(c)(i) could in practice not be invoked in cases in which restrictions had been maintained for such a long time that the proportion between imports and domestic supplies that would prevail in the absence of restrictions could no longer be determined on the basis of a previous representative period. The Panel therefore, examined whether it would be possible to change the burden of proof in such a way that the provision could be resorted to also in such a situation. The Panel noted that one among the possible ways of achieving this aim would be to consider a demonstration that the size of the quota is equivalent to a certain percentage of the quantities marketed or produced in the importing country as a sufficient proof that the proportionality requirement had been met. The Panel however also noted that the practical consequence of such a change in the burden of proof would be to turn the requirement of Article XI:2(c)(i) to fix the size of the import quotas in relation to the *reduction in the quantities marketed or produced* into a requirement to determine the size of the quota in relation to the *quantities actually marketed or produced.* The Panel found that the above or any other change in the burden of proof to make Article XI:2(c)(i) operational in the case of long-term import and/or supply restrictions would have consequences equivalent to those

[1] Report of the Panel on Canadian Administration of the Foreign Investment Review Act (BISD) 30S/140)

of an amendment of this provision and could therefore seriously affect the balance of tariff concessions negotiated among contracting parties. The Panel noted in this context that Article XI:2—unlike some other provisions of the General Agreement permitting restrictive trade measures, such as Articles XVIII:C, XXVIII or XIX—does not provide for compensation for contracting parties adversely affected by the measures taken under it. The Panel considered for these reasons that the burden of providing the evidence that all the requirements of Article XI:2(c)(i), including the proportionality requirement, had been met must remain fully with the contracting party invoking that provision.

5.2 Import Monopolies

5.2.1 Text and Notes

The Panel noted that Japan justified its import restrictions on prepared and preserved beef and certain dairy products on the basis of its monopoly import system for certain beef and dairy products. The parts of the General Agreement relevant in this dispute read as follows:

Note Ad Articles XI, XII, XIII, XIV and XVIII

"Throughout Articles, XI, XII, XIII, XIV and XVIII, the terms "import restrictions" or "export restrictions" include restrictions made effective through state-trading operations."

Article II

" . . .

4. If any contracting party establishes, maintains or authorizes, formally or in effect, a monopoly of the importation of any product described in the appropriate Schedule annexed to this Agreement, such monopoly shall not, except as provided for in that Schedule or as otherwise agreed between the parties which initially negotiated the concession, operate so as to afford protection on the average in excess of the amount of protection provided for in that Schedule. The provisions of this paragraph shall not limit the use by contracting parties of any form of assistance to domestic producers permitted by other provisions of this Agreement."

Note Ad Article II at paragraph 4

"Except where otherwise specifically agreed between the contracting parties which initially negotiated the concession, the provisions of this paragraph will be applied in the light of the provisions of Article 31 of the Havana Charter."

(Article 31:5 of the Havana Charter reads as follows:

. . .

"5. With regard to any product to which the provisions of this article apply, the monopoly shall, wherever this principle can be effectively applied and subject to the other provisions of this Charter, import and offer for sale such quantities of the products as will be sufficient to satisfy the full domestic demand for the imported product, account being taken of any rationing to consumers of the imported and like domestic product which may be in force at that time.")

Article XX

"Subject to the requirement that such measures are not applied in a manner which would constitute a means of arbitrary or unjustifiable discrimination between countries where the same conditions prevail, or a disguised restriction on international trade, nothing in this Agreement shall be construed to prevent the adoption or enforcement by any contracting party of measures:

*   *   *

(d) necessary to secure compliance with laws or regulations which are not inconsistent with the provisions of this Agreement, including those relating to . . . the enforcement of monopolies operated under paragraph 4 of Article II and Article XVII, . . . ;"

5.2.2 Drafting History and General Considerations

5.2.2.1 The Panel noted the view of Japan that Article XI:1 did not apply to import restrictions made effective through an import monopoly. According to Japan, the drafters of the Havana Charter for an International Trade Organization intended to deal with the problem of quantitative trade limitations applied by import monopolies through a provision under which a monopoly of the importation of any product for which a concession had been negotiated would have "to import and offer for sale such quantities of the product as will be sufficient to satisfy the full domestic demand for the imported product" (Article 31:5 of the Havana Charter). Japan contended that the provision had not been inserted into the General Agreement and that quantitative restrictions made effective through import monopolies could therefore not be considered to be covered by Article XI:1 of the General Agreement (paragraph 3.3.3 above).

5.2.2.2 The Panel examined this contention and noted the following: Article XI:1 covers restrictions on the importation of any product, "whether made effective through quotas, import . . . licences *or other measures*" (emphasis added). The wording of this provision is comprehensive, thus comprising restrictions made effective through an import monopoly. This is confirmed by the note to Articles XI, XII, XIII, XIV and XVIII, according to which the term "import restrictions" throughout these Articles covers restrictions made effective through state-trading operations. The basic purpose of this note is to extend to state-trading the rules of the General Agreement governing private trade and to ensure that the contracting parties cannot escape their obligations with respect to private trade by establishing state-trading operations. This purpose would be frustrated if import restrictions were considered to be consistent with Article XI:1 only because they were made effective through import monopolies. The note to Article II:4 of the General Agreement specifies that that provision "will be applied in the light of the provisions of Article 31 of the Havana Charter". The obligation of a monopoly importing a product for which a concession has been granted "to import and offer for sale such quantities of the product as will be sufficient to satisfy the full domestic demand for the imported product" is thus part of the General Agreement. The Panel could therefore not follow the arguments of Japan based on the assumption that Article 31:5 of the Havana Charter was *not* included in the General Agreement. The Panel found for these reasons that the import restrictions applied by Japan fell under Article XI independent of whether they were made effective through quotas or through import monopoly operations.

5.2.2.3 The Panel further examined whether Article XX(d) of the General Agreement justified import restrictions made effective through import monopolies. The Panel noted that Article XX(d) permits measures necessary to the enforcement of monopolies. Article XX(d) therefore permits measures necessary to enforce the exclusive possession of the trade by the monopoly, such as measures limiting private imports that would undermine the control of the trade by the monopoly. However, Article XX(d) only exempts from the obligations under the General Agreement measures necessary to secure compliance with those laws and regulations "which are not inconsistent with the provisions of [the General] Agreement". Article XX(d) therefore does not permit contracting parties to operate monopolies inconsistently with the other provisions of the General Agreement. The General Agreement contains detailed rules designed to preclude protective and discriminatory practices by import monopolies (cf. in particular Article II:4, the note to Articles XI, XII, XIII, XIV and XVIII, and Article XVII). These rules would become meaningless if Article XX(d) were interpreted to exempt from the obligations under the General Agreement protective or discriminatory trading practices by such monopolies. the Panel therefore found that the enforcement of laws or regulations providing for an import restriction made effective through an import monopoly inconsistent with Article XI:1 was not covered by Article XX(d).

5.3 Product Specific Findings

The Panel then proceeded to examine the restrictions maintained on each of the items subject of the complaint against the background and drafting history of Article XI:2(c)(i) and Article XX(d) and in light of the considerations noted above. In order for an import restriction to be justified under Article XI:2(c)(i) all of the conditions noted above must be fulfilled. Therefore, in those cases in which the Panel found that one condition was not met, it did not consider it necessary to examine the restriction further in the light of the other conditions, except in those cases in which the unfulfilled condition could be met by changing the administration of the restriction. In these cases the Panel further examined whether such a change in administration would in itself be sufficient to fulfill the conditions of Article XI:2(c)(i).

5.3.1.1 The Panel noted that certain dairy products included in this complaint were subject to an import monopoly and that Japan maintained that import monopoly operations were not subject to the provisions of Article XI:1 and furthermore that restrictions on the importation of all dairy products under consideration by the Panel were necessary to the operation of the import monopoly. On the basis of its considerations in paragraphs 5.2 above, the Panel found that Article XI was also applicable to these dairy products. The Panel thus proceeded to examine the dairy products in question in light of the conditions set out in Article XI:2(c)(i) (paragraph 5.1.3 above).

5.3.1.2 With regard to *prepared and preserved milk and cream (04.02),* the Panel recalled that for certain products contained in this tariff category, namely *evaporated milk (04.02-1),* an import quota was available only for imports for use in Okinawa or for use in international tourist hotels and for international shipping vessels traveling between Japan and foreign countries. Imports of *sweetened condensed milk (04.02-1)* were permitted only for hotel and shipping vessel use. It considered that this resulted in a *de facto* prohibition of imports of evaporated milk and sweetened condensed milk into the general customs tariff territory of Japan. The Panel recalled a previous panel conclusion that " . . . the provisions of Article XI:2(c)(i) could not justify the application of an import prohibition" (paragraph 5.1.3.1 above), and found that ruling to be applicable also in the present case.

5.3.1.3 The Panel further observed that *prepared whey (04.02-3)* for use in processing prepared milk powder for infants was subject to the Japanese Miscellaneous Import Quota. This single quota contained many and diverse products. The Panel recalled the notification requirement of the last sub-paragraph of Article XI:2 which implies that under Article XI:2(c) only those quotas can be applied which define the particular quantity or value for each product subject to quota (paragraph 5.1.3.6 above). The Panel found that import restrictions made effective through a miscellaneous "basket" quota for which only a global value or quantity was announced could not satisfy the requirements of Article XI:2(c).

5.3.1.4 The Panel further examined whether the establishment of a planned quota for the products contained in the tariff category *prepared and preserved milk and cream (04.02)* would satisfy the requirements of Article XI:2(c)(i). The Panel, thus examined whether fresh milk for manufacturing use and the products prepared from it, particularly evaporated milk, sweetened condensed milk, skimmed milk powder, whole milk powder, prepared whey, and whey powder were "like products" in the sense of Article XI:2(c)(i), (paragraph 5.1.3.4 above). The Panel recalled that as different requirements were established for restrictions on like products and on the importation of those products processed from a like product, a product in its original form and a product processed from it could not be considered to be "like products". The Panel thus found that these prepared and preserved milk and cream products were not "like" fresh milk for manufacturing use in terms of Article XI:2(c)(i), but were processed from the like product. It thus examined whether they met the requirements of products "in any form", that is, whether these milk products were in an early stage of processing and still perishable, which competed directly with fresh milk and if freely imported would render ineffective the restrictions on fresh milk, as required by the interpretative note to Article XI:2(c). It noted that fresh milk as such was rarely traded internationally because of its bulk and perishability, but rather it was processed into (among other things) the canned, powdered or otherwise prepared milk and cream products in question which rendered it capable of being transported and stocked. The Panel considered that the difficulties regarding transport into Japan of a perishable milk product were such that it was highly unlikely that imports of such a product would of themselves render ineffective the government restriction on the production of fresh milk, nor that restriction of its importation would be necessary to the enforcement of the government program. Thus, although the Panel considered that some of these products might meet some of the requirements of being products in an early stage of processing and still perishable which could compete directly with fresh milk for manufacturing use and whose free importation might render ineffective the domestic measures on fresh milk, the Panel did not find that any of the products under consideration in tariff category 04.02 met all of the conditions of Article XI:2(c)(i), particularly that regarding perishability.

5.3.2.1 The Panel next examined the restrictions applied to *processed cheese (04.04 ex)*. The Panel observed that imports of processed cheese were subject to special quotas which limited their availability only to Okinawa, and to tourist hotel and shipping vessel use. It considered that this resulted in a *de facto* prohibition on the importation of processed cheese into the general customs territory of Japan. The Panel found that such prohibition was not permitted under the provisions of Article XI:2(c)(i) (paragraph 5.1.3.1 above).

5.3.2.2 The Panel examined whether if a quota were to be established for processed cheese permitting import into the general customs territory of Japan, the other requirements of Article XI:2(c)(i) would be met. The Panel considered that under the definition of "like product" to be applied under that provision (paragraph 5.1.3.4 above), imported processed cheese and Japanese-produced fresh milk were not "like products". It thus examined whether processed cheese met the requirements of a product "in any form", that is whether it was a product in an early stage of processing and still perishable, which competed directly with fresh milk for manufacturing use and if freely imported would render ineffective the restriction on the fresh milk. Processed cheese is made by the mixing of one or more natural cheeses with the addition of emulsifying agents and often of flavoring and coloring materials. It is a product not generally intended for further processing. The Panel also noted that processed cheese was capable of being stocked. The Panel further observed that imports of natural cheese into Japan were not subject to quantitative restriction and that substantial quantities were indeed imported. Natural cheese, the principle ingredient in processed cheese, was at an earlier stage of processing than the latter and more likely to compete directly with fresh milk for manufacturing use. The Panel considered that if imports of natural cheese did not render ineffective the domestic restriction on fresh milk for manufacturing use, the imports of a higher processed product could not be considered to do so. It further noted that there was a duty-free tariff quota in effect for natural cheese imported into Japan for use in the production of processed cheese. The Panel thus found that even if imports of processed cheese were permitted into the general customs territory of Japan, restrictions on these imports would not satisfy the conditions of Article XI:2(c)(i) as processed cheese was not an item in an early stage of processing and still perishable which competed directly with fresh milk and whose free importation would render ineffective the restriction on fresh milk.

5.3.3 The Panel then examined the restriction maintained on *lactose (17.02 ex)*. The Panel noted the restriction was applied only to "crude" lactose and recalled Japan's argument that import restrictions on crude lactose were required because it was virtually identical to whey powder subject to LIPC monopoly import control. In this regard, the Panel recalled its findings in paragraph 5.2 above. It also observed that lactose was subject to the Miscellaneous Import Quota, and recalled its findings on such restrictions (paragraph 5.3.1.3 above). The Panel then examined whether the establishment of a specific quota for crude lactose would be sufficient for the requirements of Article XI:2(c)(i) to be met. The Panel considered that crude lactose was not "like" fresh milk for manufacturing use within the meaning of that provision, but was a by-product resulting from the production of cheese and other dairy products. As it was virtually indistinguishable from the whey powder examined by the Panel in paragraph 5.3.1.4 above, the Panel considered that its findings with regard to whey powder were equally applicable to crude lactose.

5.3.4 The Panel proceeded to examine the restriction applied to *food preparations, not elsewhere specified, consisting mainly of dairy products (21.07 ex)*. The Panel noted that these products were also subject to the Miscellaneous Import Quota and recalled its findings on such restrictions (paragraph 5.3.1.3 above). The Panel further examined whether the establishment of a specific quota for these dairy food preparations would be sufficient to fulfill the requirements of Article XI:2(c)(i). The Panel considered that these items were not "like" fresh milk for manufacturing use but could be processed from fresh milk or other dairy products. The Panel thus examined whether dairy food preparations met the requirements of products "in any form", that is whether, they were products in an early stage of processing and still perishable, which competed directly with the fresh milk and if freely imported would render ineffective the restrictions on the fresh milk. It noted that a large number of items were included in this basket category, only a few of which had been specifically identified, i.e., frozen yogurt base, ice cream powder, prepared milk powder for infants. For this quota to meet the requirements of Article XI:2(c)(i), the Panel considered that all of the products within it would have to meet these conditions. The Panel noticed that many of the products in tariff classification 21.07 were consumer-ready prepared foods as opposed to products which had undergone only initial processing. The Panel thus found that not all of the dairy food preparations under consideration here could be considered as items in an early stage of processing and still perishable which competed directly with fresh milk for manufacturing use, and whose free importation would render ineffective the restrictions on the production of fresh milk.

5.3.5.1 The Panel then reviewed the facts and arguments presented on *dried leguminous vegetables (07.05 ex)*. It noted that imported dried leguminous vegetables were "like" legumes produced in Japan within the meaning of Article XI:2(c)(i). The Panel then proceeded to examine whether there was a Japanese governmental measure in effect which restricts the quantities of legumes permitted to be produced or marketed in Japan. It noted in this respect the operation of the directive on Planned Production of Legumes in Hokkaido, where virtually all commercial production was concentrated. The Panel considered that restrictions on cultivated acreage, even if they effectively reduced planted area, could not in themselves be considered as restrictions on production or marketing, as increased yields brought about by improved varieties, increased fertilizer use, or improvements in other inputs could result in expanded output even from reduced area. The Panel further recalled that a previous panel[1] had also examined the enforcement of the governmental measures in evaluating their effectiveness. In this regard, the Panel noted that there was no penalty or charge imposed on Japanese producers whose cultivation exceeded the target area, but rather a benefit or subsidy could be withheld from them. The Panel considered that, as indicated by the drafting history of Article XI:2(c)(i), the important factor was not the methods used by governments but their effectiveness. The Panel thus examined the effectiveness of the Japanese measures and found not only that the targets for area reduction had been met and planted area had been reduced, but also that the actual quantity produced had declined since the 1984 directive. The Panel

[1] Report of the Panel on EEC Program of Minimum Import Prices, Licences and Surety Deposits for Certain Processed Fruits and Vegetables (BISD 25S/101).

examined the arguments presented by Japan and the United States with respect to the level of output which would have been attained in the absence of restrictions. The Panel considered that in light of the number of contradictory factors which affected historic and current output, including the long-standing application of import restrictions, the provision of subsidies or loans for production, the changing pattern of agricultural production, and improved varieties, cultivation methods and yields, in this situation was virtually impossible to objectively determine what the level of production would have been in the absence of restrictions. The Panel noted, however, the consistent decline in past production both in the short and longer term, and found that the Japanese measures in the past had in practice been effective in restricting production. On this basis the Panel considered that it could reasonably be assumed that the current production measures were capable of effectively limiting production.

5.3.5.2 The Panel then examined whether the restrictions on imports of dried leguminous vegetables could be considered as "necessary" to secure the enforcement of the production restrictions. In this regard, it noted that the Japanese production restrictions were applied to all categories of dried leguminous vegetables and that the various dried legumes were substitutable in terms of the principal form of their consumption in Japan, namely sweetened bean paste. The Panel, therefore, considered that the restrictions maintained by Japan could be reasonably considered as "necessary" in terms of Article XI:2(c)(i).

5.3.5.3 The panel then considered whether Japan fulfilled the requirements of the last sub-paragraph of Article XI:2, with respect to maintaining the proportion of imports to domestic production as might reasonably be expected to rule between the two in the absence of restrictions. The Panel considered that the burden of proof that this proportionality had been maintained rested with Japan and that such proof had not been provided (paragraph 5.1.3.7 above).

5.3.6.1 The Panel examined the restrictions maintained by Japan on imports of *starch and inulin (11.08)*. The Panel observed that starch and inulin for special use were subject to the Miscellaneous Import Quota and recalled its finding on such restrictions (paragraph 5.3.1.3 above). It observed that the import restrictions were applied to all starches (except modified starch) and inulin and therefore considered that the Japanese "like product" in this case would be all starches produced in Japan. The Panel then examined whether there were governmental measures in effect which operated to restrict the production of all fresh products which could be processed into starch. It found that such restrictions existed only for potatoes and sweet potatoes and potato starches, which represented a minor and declining proportion of total Japanese starch production.

5.3.6.2 The Panel then examined whether the limitation of the import restriction to only potato and sweet potato starches or whether restriction of domestic production of other raw materials for starch processing would be sufficient to meet the requirements of Article XI:2(c)(i). It thus examined whether starches and inulin satisfied the requirements of products "in any form", that is whether they were products in an early stage of processing and still perishable, which competed directly with the fresh product and if freely imported would render ineffective the restrictions on the fresh products. With regard to perishability, the Panel noted that starch was a stable product which was capable of being stocked. The Panel further observed that imports into Japan of the raw materials from which starch could be processed, such as potatoes, corn and manioc, were not restricted and that substantial amounts were actually imported for starch production. The Panel considered that if restrictions on imports of these fresh products were not considered necessary to ensure the operation of restrictions on potato and sweet potato production, then import restrictions on the processed product were not necessary.

5.3.7 With regard to *glucose and other sugars (17.02 ex)* and *food preparations, not elsewhere specified, consisting mainly of sugar (21.07 ex),* the Panel noted that these products were also subject to the Miscellaneous Import Quota and recalled its previous finding on such restrictions (paragraph 5.3.1.3 above). The Panel further examined whether the establishment of a specific quota for these sugars and sugar food preparations would be sufficient to fulfil the requirements of Article XI:2(c)(i). It noted that a large number of items were included in this basket category, only a few of which were specifically identified, i.e., chewing gum and bases for beverages. It also noted that some of the sugars in question could be processed from potato starch, and then used in the production of sugar food preparations. In light of its findings on potatoes and on starches (paragraphs 5.4.6 above), the panel considered that these products, which were further processed from a processed product, were not in an early stage of processing and still perishable and that import restrictions on these processed product categories could not be considered as necessary to the enforcement of the limitation of production of potatoes and sweet potatoes.

5.3.8.1 With respect to *groundnuts (12.01 ex),* the Panel noted that groundnuts produced in Japan and imported groundnuts were identical in all respects and were, therefore, like products. The Panel examined the Japanese measures applied to groundnuts to determine whether these constituted a governmental measure which restricts the quantities of groundnuts permitted to be produced or marketed. It noted in this regard the MAFF directive to the Principal Groundnut-Producing Prefectures Liaison Council regarding limitation of area planted to groundnuts. The Panel considered that restrictions on planted area could not be considered the equivalent of restrictions on production or marketing unless they demonstrably had that effect. Another panel[1] had also examined the enforcement of governmental measures in evaluating their effectiveness. In this regard, the Panel noted that there was no penalty or charge imposed on Japanese producers who exceeded their target cultivation area, but rather they could lose eligibility to receive a benefit in the form of a subsidy or loan. The Panel considered that, as indicated by the drafting history of Article XI:2(c)(i), the important factor was not the methods used in restricting production but their effectiveness. The Panel further found that there were many factors, including the long-standing application of import restrictions, the provision of subsidies or loans for production, the changing pattern of agricultural production and varieties, cultivation methods and improved yields, which affected historic and current output in often contradictory ways, rendering it virtually impossible to objectively determine what the level of production would have been in the absence of restrictions. The Panel considered, therefore, the actual pattern of quantities produced. It found that production exhibited a long-term trend of decline, and on an in-shell basis, had further declined since the reinforcement of the governmental measures in 1984. The Panel found, therefore, that the Japanese measures in the past had in practice been effective in restricting the quantity of groundnuts produced or marketed. On this basis the Panel considered that it could reasonably be assumed that the current production measures were capable of effectively limiting production.

5.3.8.2 The Panel then examined whether the restrictions on imports of groundnuts could be considered as "necessary" to secure the enforcement of the production restrictions. It noted that Japanese groundnuts and imported groundnuts were essentially identical and perfectly substitutable in terms of their use. It further observed that the marketing period for Japanese groundnuts was not limited to a few weeks or months, but was essentially the entire year. The Panel considered that

[1] Report of the Panel on EEC Program of Minimum Import Prices, Licences and Surety Deposits for Certain Processed Fruits and Vegetables (BISD 25S/101).

the absence of restrictions on imports of processed groundnut products was not relevant to this consideration. The Panel found, therefore, that the restrictions maintained by Japan on imports of groundnuts could be reasonably considered as "necessary" in terms of Article XI:2(c).

5.3.8.3 The Panel then considered whether Japan fulfilled the requirements of the last sub-paragraph of Article XI:2, with respect to maintaining the proportion of imports to domestic production that might reasonably be expected to rule between the two in the absence of restrictions. The Panel considered that the burden of proof that this proportionality had been maintained rested with Japan and that such proof had not been provided (paragraph 5.1.3.7 above).

5.3.9 The Panel noted the existence of quantitative restrictions on imports of *meat of bovine animals, prepared or preserved (16.02 ex)*. The Panel further observed that Japan did not invoke Article XI:2(c)(i) with regard to this category but considered these restrictions necessary to the operation of the import monopoly for beef. The Panel recalled its findings with regard to this contention as contained in paragraph 5.2 above, and found that Article XI:2(c)(i) was applicable to this product. The Panel observed that certain prepared and preserved beef products were subject to the Miscellaneous Import Quota and recalled its finding on these restrictions (paragraph 5.3.1.3 above). The Panel further found that there did not exist any governmental measures which operated to restrict the production of beef in Japan.

5.3.10.1 The Panel then examined the restrictions applied to *fruit purée and paste (20.05 ex)*, to *fruit pulp (20.06 ex)* and to certain *fruit juices (20.07 ex)*. The Panel observed that certain fruit purées and paste and fruit juices were subject to the Miscellaneous Import Quota (see paragraphs 2.7.3 and 2.7.4). The Panel recalled its previous finding on such restrictions (paragraph 5.1.3 above).

5.3.10.2 The Panel also noted that imports of single-strength pineapple, grape and apple juice were subject to a special quota which limited their availability only to hotel, airline and shipping vessel use. It considered that this resulted in a *de facto* prohibition on the importation of these types of juices into the general customs territory of Japan. The Panel found that such prohibition was not permitted under the provisions of Article XI:2(c)(i) (paragraph 5.1.3.1 above).

5.3.10.3 The Panel then examined whether those restrictions placed on imports of fruit products under planned quotas were consistent with the provisions of Article XI:2(c)(i). The Panel noted that measures were in place which could affect the production of certain fresh fruits and possibly of apple juice. It considered that imported fruit purée and paste, fruit pulp and fruit juice were not "like" Japanese produced fresh fruit in terms of Article XI:2(c)(i) (paragraph 5.1.3.4 above). The Panel therefore proceeded to examine whether these fruit products met the requirements of products "in any form", that is whether they were products in an early stage of processing and still perishable which competed directly with fresh fruit and if freely imported would render ineffective the domestic restrictions on fresh fruit. The Panel then noted that the information available to it did not permit a finding of whether all the fruit products under consideration were imported in a perishable form, but it observed that some of the products in these categories were not perishable, such as fruit juices and those fruit products entering in a canned form. The Panel further observed that by far the greater proportion of the fresh fruit produced in Japan was consumed in its fresh form and was not processed. Imports into Japan of most fresh fruit, including fresh apples, peaches, grapes and pineapples, were not subject to quantitative restrictions. International trade in fresh apples, grapes and pineapples was substantial and distance to markets did not appear to be a barrier to this trade. Japan actually imported substantial quantities of fresh pineapple, and some, albeit small, quantities of fresh grapes and apples. Imports of frozen apples and pineapples suitable for further processing were also unrestricted. The Panel considered that given the proportion of Japanese produced fresh fruit under consideration, other than pineapples, which was consumed fresh and was marketed only during the time and immediately following its harvest, processed fruit products could not be considered to directly compete with the fresh fruit other than possibly during this brief period. Japanese import restrictions, however, were applied all during the year and not just seasonally. The Panel thus found that in light of the proportion of Japanese fresh fruit which was destined for processing, the absence of restrictions on imports of fresh fruit, and the differing uses of fresh fruit and processed fruit products, the quantitative restrictions on imports of the indicated fruit purée and paste, fruit pulp, and fruit juices were not necessary to the enforcement of governmental measures which might operate to restrict the production or marketing of fresh fruit.

5.3.11 The Panel next reviewed the facts and arguments presented with regard to *prepared and preserved pineapple (20.06 ex)*. The Panel did not consider that prepared and preserved pineapple was "like" fresh pineapple in terms of Article XI:2(c)(i) (paragraph 5.1.3.4 above). The Panel thus examined whether prepared and preserved pineapple met the requirements of a product "in any form", that is whether it was a product in the early stage of processing and still perishable, which competed directly with fresh pineapple and if freely imported would render ineffective the restriction on fresh pineapple. In this regard, the Panel noted that the imported product was primarily canned pineapple. The canning of pineapple enabled it to be stocked for a considerable length of time and therefore rendered it no longer perishable in terms of Article XI:2(c)(i). The Panel then noted that imports of fresh and frozen pineapple were not restricted, and substantial quantities of the latter were imported for processing into canned pineapple. The Panel considered that if imports of frozen pineapple for processing into canned pineapple were presumed not to render ineffective the domestic measures relating to production of fresh pineapples, the importation of the further processed canned pineapple could not have such an effect. The Panel found, therefore, that restrictions on the importation of canned pineapple were not necessary for the operation of the domestic measures for fresh pineapples.

5.3.12.1 The Panel proceeded to examine the restrictions maintained on *tomato juice (20.07 ex), tomato sauce and tomato ketchup (21.04 ex).* The Panel noted that target levels of production of tomato juice, sauce and ketchup were established as a means to enforce the production restrictions on fresh tomatoes for processing, through the contractual arrangements between growers and processors and penalties for excess shipment of the fresh tomatoes. The Panel considered that under the definition of "like product" under Article XI:2 (paragraph 5.1.3.4 above), fresh tomatoes and these particular processed tomato products were not like products. The Panel then proceeded to examine whether the import restrictions on tomato juice, sauce and ketchup could be justified on the basis of the restriction of production of fresh tomatoes for processing, the like product to that from which they were processed.

5.3.12.2 With respect to *tomato juice,* the Panel noted that although Japanese-produced tomato juice was "fresh pack" and perhaps was perishable, the Japanese quota made no distinction with regard to whether the imported juice was "fresh pack" or in some other form and the tomato juice actually imported into Japan was primarily canned juice, capable of being stocked. The Panel recognized that tomato juice was a product in an early stage of processing which could compete directly with fresh tomatoes for processing and whose free importation might render ineffective the government measures on fresh tomatoes for processing, however, the Panel found that tomato juice in the canned form primarily imported into Japan was not perishable.

5.3.12.3 With regard to *tomato sauce* and *ketchup,* the Panel also noted the long shelf-life of these products when stored under normal conditions. Furthermore, in terms of the normal processing chain of tomato products, tomato juice, tomato paste and ketchup were not normally subject to further processing but rather were consumer-ready products. The Panel also observed that imports of tomato purée and paste (20.02 ex), which were equally processed tomato products and used frequently as inputs into the manufacture of tomato sauce and ketchup, were not restricted. The Panel considered that if unrestricted imports of these earlier stage processed products were not deemed to impair the domestic production restrictions on fresh tomatoes for processing, then imports of higher processed products such as tomato sauce and ketchup would not have that effect. The Panel thus found that tomato sauce and tomato ketchup were not products in an early stage of processing and still perishable, which competed directly with fresh tomatoes and whose free importation would render ineffective the domestic restrictions on fresh tomatoes for processing.

5.4 Other Issues Before the Panel

5.4.1 Other "Pertinent" Elements

The Panel noted that its terms of reference indicated that ". . . In examining the matter, the Panel may take into account all pertinent elements including the Council's discussion on the matter at its meeting on October 27, 1986". The Panel thus considered the record of the discussion of that meeting (C/M/202, pages 6-9) as well as Japan's arguments regarding the practices of other countries, the status of the multilateral negotiations and the special characteristics of Japanese agriculture.

5.4.1.1 The Panel recognized that quantitative restrictions and other trade barriers were still widespread in international trade in agricultural products but noted that only a few contracting parties had justified their restrictions under Article XI:2(c)(i) and that such justification had thus far only been challenged in one case. The Panel noted that the requirements of this provision had often been described as rigid and restrictive by Japan and other contracting parties.[1] Because of the difficulty of meeting these requirements a number of contracting parties had invoked other exceptions in the General Agreement or had sought waivers. In this context the Panel noted that Japan had on accession to the

[1] Reflected in AG/W/9/Rev.3, AG/W/14 and various summaries of main points raised at the Committee's meetings.

GATT notified its import restrictions under Article XII, and after disinvoking this Article in 1963 had notified a number of residual restrictions, which had since been gradually reduced.

5.4.1.2 The Panel also noted that a modification of Article XI:2 has been proposed in the Uruguay Round and that in the Ministerial Declaration of 1986 participants in the Uruguay Round had undertaken the commitment to phase out or bring into conformity all trade restrictive or distorting measures inconsistent with the provisions of the General Agreement or instruments negotiated within the framework of GATT. The Panel noted that it was generally understood that neither this commitment nor the possible modification of provisions of the General Agreement in the course of the negotiations curtailed the rights and obligations of contracting parties under Article XXIII of the General Agreement.

5.4.1.3 The Panel recalled that the purpose of GATT panels to assist CONTRACTING PARTIES in taking a decision under Article XXIII:2 and that according to the Ministerial Declaration of 1982, "it is understood that decisions [in the dispute settlement process] cannot add or diminish the rights and obligations provided in the General Agreement."[1] What was pertinent, therefore, in a panel's conclusions were findings regarding the conformity of the measures under examination with the General Agreement, and their effects on the benefits accruing from the General Agreement. These benefits arose, in part, from the obligations assumed by Japan under the General Agreement. Consequently, the Panel found that Japan's actions could, appropriately, be judged only against its obligations under the General Agreement and not against the practices of others, nor did the Panel consider it appropriate to prejudge the outcome of the multilateral negotiations.

5.4.1.4 As regards the vital role the twelve items under considerations played in Japan's agricultural and regional economies and their underlying social and political as well as economic background, the Panel—while aware of their significance in the Japanese context—found that previous panels had established that such circumstances could not provide a justification for import restrictions under the General Agreement.[2] However, in one respect the Panel took into account the special circumstances prevailing in Japan. This concerns the interpretation of

[1] BISD 29S/16

[2] Report of the Panel on Quantitative Restrictions against Imports of Certain Products from Hong Kong (BISD 30S/129), paragraph 27; and Report of the Panel on Japanese Measures on Imports of Leather (BISD 31S/94), paragraph 44.

the term "the enforcement of governmental measures" in Article XI:2(c)(i). As indicated in paragraph 5.1.3.3 above, the text of this provision does not specify how the domestic production or marketing restrictions are to be imposed, except that they have to be governmental and the drafting history suggests that the drafters were primarily concerned with the effectiveness of the measures. Although the Panel had some difficulty during its initial proceedings in establishing the exact nature of the domestic restrictions, Japan fully cooperated in providing the necessary detailed information, from which it became clear that the measures did in fact emanate from the government. As regards the method used to enforce these measures the Panel found that the practice of "administrative guidance" played an important role. Considering that this practice is a traditional tool of Japanese Government policy based on consensus and peer pressure, the Panel decided to base its judgements on the effectiveness of the measures in spite of the initial lack of transparency. In view of the special characteristics of Japanese society the Panel wishes, however, to stress that its approach in this particular case should not be interpreted as a precedent in other cases where societies are not adapted to this form of enforcing government policies.

5.4.1.5 The Panel found, therefore, that the practices of other countries, the existence of multilateral negotiations and the special characteristics of Japanese agriculture, could not, under the circumstances, be considered "pertinent elements" which could be taken into account when considering whether measures taken by Japan were in conformity with Japan's obligations under the General Agreement.

5.4.2 Articles X and XIII

The Panel noted that the United States had, as a subsidiary matter, argued that Japan had also nullified or impaired benefits under Articles X:1, X:3, and XIII:3. Since these provisions dealt with the administration of quotas that may be applied consistently with the General Agreement, the Panel decided that it was not necessary for it to make a finding on these matters with regard to quantitative restrictions maintained contrary to that Agreement.

5.4.3 Nullification and Impairment

The Panel was specifically asked "to make findings . . . on the question of nullification or impairment". Japan contended that there "was no proof of actual nullification or impairment supported by facts or statistics for individual items". In this respect, the Panel noted the following: the CONTRACTING PARTIES decided in the 1979 Understanding on dispute settlement that a measure inconsistent with the General Agreement was presumed to nullify or impair the benefits accruing under that Agreement.[1] The CONTRACTING PARTIES agreed in two previous cases[2] that Article XI protected expectations on competitive conditions, not on export volumes, and that the presumption that a measure inconsistent with Article XI caused nullification or impairment could therefore not be refuted with arguments relating to export volumes.

6. CONCLUSIONS

6.1 In the light of the findings set out in paragraphs 5.1-5.4 above, the Panel reached the following conclusions on the import restrictions maintained by Japan on the agricultural products subject to this complaint.

6.2 Article XI:1 of the General Agreement provides for the elimination of all import restrictions, including those "made effective through quotas" and those "made effective through state-trading operations" (paragraph 5.2 above). Article XX(d) of the General Agreement permits measures necessary to enforce the exclusive trading rights of import monopolies but not measures applied by such monopolies inconsistently with the other provisions of the General Agreement. The Panel therefore concludes that the import restrictions maintained by Japan are inconsistent with Article XI:1 of the General Agreement independent of whether they are made effective through quotas or through import monopoly operations.

6.3 Article XI:2(c) establishes several exceptions from the general prohibition of quantitative import restrictions for agricultural and fisheries products. Sub-paragraph (i) of that provision permits, *inter alia,* import restrictions on any agricultural or fisheries product, imported in any form, necessary to the enforcement of governmental measures which operate to restrict the quantities of the like domestic product permitted to be marketed or producted. To prevent the use of this

[1] Annex to Understanding Regarding Notification, Consultation, Dispute Settlement and Surveillance (BISD 26S/216, paragraph 5).

[2] Report of the Panel on United States Taxes on Petroleum and Certain Imported Substances (L/6175); and Report of the Panel on Japanese Measures on Imports of Leather (BISD 31S/94)).

provision for import restrictions that have the effect of expanding the domestic production of agricultural products or of protecting domestic industries processing such products, Article XI:2(c)(i) imposes a number of strict conditions. The Panel examined the restrictions at issue in the light of these conditions and concluded the following.

6.4 The Panel notes that Article XI:2(c)(i) does not permit the prohibition of imports but only their restriction. It finds that Japan maintains a *de facto* prohibition on the importation of *evaporated milk (04.02 ex), sweetened condensed milk (04.02 ex), processed cheese (04.04 ex)* and *certain single-strength fruit juices (20.07 ex)* into its general customs territory. The Panel concludes that these prohibitions maintained by Japan are contrary to Article XI.

6.5 The Panel notes that Article XI:2(c)(i) requires the existence of a governmental measure which restricts domestic production. In this regard, the Panel recalls its findings that Japanese production of all starches or the raw materials thereof, the like product to the restricted import, is not restricted. The Panel further recalls that Japan provided no evidence of governmental measures which operate to restrict the production of beef in Japan. The Panel concludes, therefore, that Japanese import restrictions on *starches and inulin (11.08)* and on *prepared and preserved meat of bovine animals (16.02 ex)* are not justified under Article XI:2(c)(i).

6.6 The Panel notes that Article XI:2(c)(i) permits restrictions not only on fresh products but also on those processed agricultural and fishery products that are in the early stages of processing and still perishable which compete directly with the fresh product and, if freely imported, would render ineffective the restrictions on the fresh product. It concludes, on the basis of its findings presented above, that the import restrictions maintained by Japan on the following items do not meet *all* of these conditions and are thus not justified under Article XI:2(c)(i): *prepared and preserved milk and cream (04.02), processed cheese (04.04 ex), starch and inulin (11.08), glucose, lactose and other sugars and syrups (17.02 ex), prepared or preserved pineapple (20.06 ex), certain fruit juice and tomato juice (20.07 ex), tomato ketchup and sauce (21.04),* and *certain food preparations, not elsewhere specified, consisting mainly of milk or of sugar (21.07 ex).*

6.7 The Panel observes that import restrictions applied under Article XI:2(c)(i) cannot exceed those "necessary" for the operation of the domestic governmental measure concerned. Such restrictions can thus not normally be justified if applied to imports during that time of year in which domestic supplies of the product are not available (paragraph 5.1.3.5 above). The Panel further considers that a restriction on imports of a processed product can in general not be considered as necessary if importation of more directly competitive forms of the product, i.e. the fresh product (when economically feasible) or earlier-stage products processed from the fresh product, are not also restricted. For these reasons and in light of its findings in paragraph 5.3.10 above, the Panel concludes that Japanese import restrictions on *fruit purées and pastes (20.05 ex), prepared or preserved fruit pulp (20.06 ex),* and *certain fruit juices (20.07 ex)* are not justified under Article XI:2(c)(i).

6.8 The Panel recalls that under the last sub-paragraph of Article XI:2(c) a contracting party applying an import restriction must give public notice of the total quantity or value of each product permitted to be imported during a specified future period. This requirement implies that under Article XI:2(c) only those quotas can be applied which define the particular quantity or value for each product subject to quota. The Panel finds that the Miscellaneous Import Quota maintained by Japan precludes the identification of the quantity or value of permitted imports of each product included therein. The Panel therefore concludes that those import restrictions maintained by Japan through the Miscellaneous Import Quota on *prepared whey powder (04.02 ex), starch and inulin for special use (11.08 ex), certain prepared and preserved bovine meat products (16.02 ex), lactose, glucose and other sugars and sugar syrups (17:02 ex), certain fruit purées and pastes (20.05 ex), certain fruit juices (20.07 ex),* and *food preparations not elsewhere specified mainly consisting of dairy or sugar (21.07 ex),* are not justified under the provisions of Article XI:2(c).

6.9 The Panel observes that a further requirement of Article XI:2 is that the restrictions applied can not be such as would reduce the level of imports relative to domestic production below the proportion which would be expected to exist in the absence of restrictions. The Panel notes that the burden of proof that such a proportion has been maintained in principle rests with the country invoking the exception to the General Agreement, and that under the circumstances Japan is not able to provide such evidence with respect to its import restrictions on *dried leguminous vegetables (07.05 ex)* and on *groundnuts (12.01 ex).* The Panel concludes, however, that the import restrictions maintained by Japan on these two particular products are otherwise justified under the provisions of Article XI:2(c)(i).

6.10 On the basis of the above conclusions, the Panel suggests that the CONTRACTING PARTIES recommend that Japan eliminate or otherwise bring into conformity with the GATT provisions its quantitative restrictions maintained on the import of the products subject to this complaint.

JAPAN—TRADE IN SEMI-CONDUCTORS

Report of the Panel adopted on May 4, 1988
BISD 35S/116, 117

II. BACKGROUND

A. Developments Leading to the Japan/US Arrangement in Semi-conductor Trade

10. The United States and Japan are the largest producers and exporters of semi-conductors. The United States was the largest producer during the 1970's, but Japan became increasingly important as both a producer and exporter of semi-conductor products at the beginning of the 1980's. In 1981, its exports exceeded those of the United States for the first time. In February 1983, the United States' industry began to express concerns to the Government of the United States about the lack of access of non-Japanese companies to the Japanese market and possible unfair trade practices of Japanese companies in the US market.

11. On June 14, 1985, the United States Semi-conductor Industry Association filed a petition under Section 301 of the Trade Act of 1974 against the Government of Japan, alleging that Japan was restricting access to the domestic semi-conductor market for United States producers. This industry-wide action was followed by several complaints brought under the anti-dumping law. On June 24, 1985, an anti-dumping petition concerning 64K DRAMs from Japan was filed by Micron Technology Inc. Also, on September 30, 1985, a petition concerning the alleged dumping of EPROMs from Japan was filed by Intel Corporation, Advanced Micro-Devices, Inc. and by National Semiconductor Corporation. Finally, on December 6, 1985 the United States Department of Commerce initiated an anti-dumping investigation to determine whether DRAMs of 256K and above from Japan were sold at less than fair value. Protracted negotiations between the governments of Japan and the United States led to the conclusion of a bilateral agreement in September 1986.

12. On September 2, 1986, Japan and the United States formally concluded an Arrangement concerning Trade in Semi-Conductor Products (hereinafter called "the Arrangement") which was subsequently notified to the GATT on November 6, 1986 in document L/6076. The

Arrangement was linked to the suspension of anti-dumping procedures initiated in the United States against imports of certain categories of Japanese semi-conductors and to the suspension of the Section 301 proceedings on access to the Japanese market for US-made semi-conductors.

B. Main Provisions of the Arrangement

13. The Arrangement contains three main sections. The first section relates to market access. It provides that the Government of Japan will impress upon the Japanese producers and users of semi-conductors the need to aggressively take advantage of increased market access opportunities in Japan for foreign-based firms which wish to improve their actual sales performance and position. Specifically, the Government of Japan will provide further support for expanded sales of foreign-produced semi-conductors in Japan through the establishment of an organization which will provide sales assistance, quality assessment, research fellowship programs, exhibitions, etc., for foreign semi-conductor producers, and through promotion of long-term relationship between Japanese buyers and foreign producers including joint product development programs. On the other hand, the Government of the United Sates will impress upon the U.S. semi-conductor producers the need to aggressively pursue every sales opportunity in the Japanese market and will also provide support for the activities of the organization mentioned above. The section further provides that there should be full and equitable access for foreign companies to patents resulting from government-sponsored research and development, and that both Governments should refrain from policies or programs which stimulate inordinate increases in semi-conductor production capacity.

14. The second main section of the Arrangement contains three sub-sections dealing with prevention of dumping. The first sub-section concerns the suspension of present anti-dumping cases on two types of semi-conductors: Erasable Programmable Ready Only Memory (EPROM) and 256 Kilobits and above Dynamic Random Access Memory (DRAM). The second sub-section provides that, in order to prevent dumping, the Government of Japan will monitor cost and prices on a list of semi-conductor products exported to the United States. The format of the data report concerning company and product-specific cost and export price data on monitored products is contained in an appendix to the Arrangement. It has 35 entries, seeking information on production costs, packaging costs, freight, insurance, duty, commissions and re-

bates, charges, other expenses, and finally, net prices. This sub-section also provides that if any monitored product is being sold or exported at prices less than company-specific fair value, the Government of the United States may request immediate consultations. Based on monitoring and/or consultation, the Government of Japan will take appropriate actions available under laws and regulations in Japan to prevent such exports to the United States. The third sub-section relates to monitoring of third-country markets. It is stated that both governments recognize the need to prevent dumping in accordance with relevant provisions of the GATT and encourage respective industries to conform with the above principles. It is also stated that in order to prevent dumping, the Government of Japan will monitor, as appropriate, cost and export prices on the products exported by Japanese semi-conductor firms from Japan to certain markets.

15. The Third section contains general provisions on periodic and emergency consultations, on the conditions of amending and terminating the Arrangement, and on the preservation of GATT rights and the interests of third countries. The duration of the Arrangement is five years, ending on July 31, 1991.

C. Implementation of the Arrangement by Japan

16. According to information provided by the Japanese delegation, the following measures had been taken to implement the Arrangement.

(a) Access to the Japanese Market

17. To promote the sales of foreign semi-conductors in Japan, the Japanese government encouraged Japanese users to purchase foreign semi-conductors from all sources on the whole range of semi-conductor products. Specifically, the Director-General of the Machinery and Information Industries Bureau sent letters in September 1986 and July 1987 to major domestic users or purchasers of semi-conductors, requesting their cooperation in increasing the purchase of foreign-based products. The Minister of the Ministry of International Trade and Industry (MITI) also organized meetings with the top ten major users of semi-conductors in March and May of 1987 to make the same request. Relevant governmental departments also made similar requests to users' associations and individual companies. In addition, surveys of the procurement situation of foreign-based semi-conductors were carried out regularly by MITI.

18. The International Semi-conductor Cooperation Centre, an organization to promote the sales of foreign semi-conductors, was established in March 1987. The activities of the Centre were open to all foreign companies. The Centre held exhibitions, conducted survey, offered sales-related information and organized other activities helpful to the promotion of sales of foreign semi-conductors. The Centre's first exhibition was held on April 13 to 16, 1987. A symposium was held on October 6, 1987.

(b) Monitoring

19. The third Country Market Monitoring measures could be discussed under two headings: (i) requests by Government to producers and exporters; (ii) export approval and monitoring costs and export prices.

(i) Requests by Government to Producers and Exporters

20. The Director-General of the Machinery and Information Industries Bureau and the Minister of MITI organized meetings with producers and exporters (in September 1986, March and May 1987) to request that dumping should be avoided. These requests were general appeal, not legally binding. The likely consequences of disregarding these requests were pointed out. If requests were not complied with, they were repeatedly made by MITI [sic].

(ii) Export Approval and Monitoring Costs and Export Prices

21. The export approval system for semi-conductors, based on the Foreign Exchange and Foreign Trade Control Law, was introduced for the purpose of COCOM enforcement. Since November 1986, this system had been used to monitor export prices of semi-conductors. Exporters of items subject to COCOM enforcement, including all semi-conductors, to be monitored under the Arrangement, were required to submit licence applications which were screened according to COCOM considerations and export licences were approved or rejected by MITI according to these considerations.

22. The threshold for shipments of semi-conductors requiring export licences was reduced from Y1 million to Y50,000 in January 1987. As a result of this change, the number of applications almost doubled, causing delay in the processing of certain licence applications. Incomplete information in applications also caused delay in some cases. There was

no limit of processing time for export licence applications, whether maximum or minimum. Depending on various factors relating to individual applications, the time taken to process them ranged from a couple of weeks to several months.

23. Manufacturers and exporters were required to report data on export prices, and periodically on costs to MITI. The data collection procedures for prices were established in accordance with Article 67 of the Foreign Exchange and Foreign Trade Control Law and Article 10 of the Export Trade Control Order. Failure to report or submission of false reports were liable to penal servitude not exceeding six months or a fine not exceeding two hundred thousand yen. However, non-compliance in this regard would not lead to denial of export licence or prohibition of exports. When MITI found cases in which export prices were "extremely below costs", it would inform the companies concerned of the facts and of MITI's concern. MITI did not set minimum prices for exports and the communications by MITI to the companies were not legally binding. Companies were expected to understand that it was in their own self-interest to prevent dumping, and to take action accordingly.

24. The existence or non-existence of injury in foreign importing countries was not taken into consideration by MITI when watching costs and export prices.

25. Effective from November 10, 1987, the revised Foreign Exchange and Foreign Trade Control Laws to strengthen the regulations on reporting COCOM-related commodities had separated export approval from monitoring as far as semi-conductors were concerned. Under the new system, the licensing procedure was separated from the monitoring procedure. Exporters could either apply for licences and report on price information to MITI simultaneously or separately, but in any case prior to customs clearance. On receipt of a licence application and a report (in two separate documents), the licence application would be processed by the office dealing with COCOM screening. The report on prices would be processed in consideration of cost information obtained separately by the Monitoring Office. In cases where export prices were "extremely below cost", MITI would express its concern to the companies concerned. As with COCOM screening, the approval or rejection of export licences was not affected by the contents of the reports. Under the old system, an export licence was approved only after the two consecutive processes of COCOM screening and monitoring, hence it took a longer time for processing and some misunderstanding seemed to have been created among exporters that delays had been caused by inappropriate

pricing. The new system would eliminate such misunderstandings. MITI could not disapprove applications due to inappropriate pricing.

(c) Supply and Demand Forecasts

26. In relation to monitoring and improvement of market access, MITI compiled on a quarterly basis Semi-Conductor Supply-Demand Forecasts. It sent out questionnaires to all manufacturers and major users of various semi-conductors to seek data on production, demand and other information. Based on the results of the surveys, and taking into account information from foreign markets and various research organizations, a report was drafted for the deliberation of the Semi-conductor Supply-Demand Forecast Committee, composed of users, manufacturers, academics and experts. The report was then issued to the press and in MITI's public report. MITI also distributed it freely upon request.

27. The forecast was formulated as a reference for manufacturers in their production schedules. MITI explained its objective to manufacturers and impressed upon them the need to reflect real demand in their production. Individual companies were expected voluntarily to bring their production almost in line with the forecasts, taking into account the appropriate total production. The forecasts were not legally binding and the Government did not allocate production volume to individual companies. For manufacturers to conspire on production volume was against the anti-trust laws in Japan.

* * *

VII. FINDINGS

96. The Panel understood the complaint of the EEC to be that:

— the measures applied by the Japanese Government to exports of semi-conductors at prices below company-specific costs to certain third countries to implement its Arrangement concerning Trade in Semi-Conductor Products with the United States, restricted exports of semi-conductors and therefore contravened Articles VI and XI; and also Articles I and XVII;

— the measures taken by the Japanese Government to improve access to the Japanese market for semi-conductors pursuant to that Arrangement favored United States' products and therefore contravened Article I;

— the measures applied to exports of semi-conductors to third country markets and the measures to improve access to the Japanese market lacked transparency and therefore contravened Article X.

97. The Panel further noted that the EEC had alleged that, even if the above measures were considered to be consistent with the General Agreement, they nullified or impaired benefits accruing to the EEC under the General Agreement and impeded the attainment of the objectives of the General Agreement.

98. The Panel examined each of these issues in accordance with its terms of reference. In accordance with past GATT practice and the understanding reached in the Council on April 15, 1987 about the participation of the United States, the Panel took into consideration points made by the United States and interested third parties on issues raised by the parties to the dispute, but did not make findings on issues raised solely by the United States or interested third parties.

A. The Third Country Market Monitoring

99. The Panel considered the following facts as central to its examination of this part of the EEC's complaint. After having concluded the Arrangement with the United States concerning Trade in Semi-Conductors, the Japanese Government:

— requested Japanese producers and exporters of semi-conductors covered by the Arrangement not to export semi-conductors at prices below company-specific costs;

— collected data on company and product-specific costs from producers; introduced a statutory requirement, reinforced by penal servitude not exceeding six months or a fine not exceeding Y 200,000, for exporters of semi-conductors to report data on export prices;

— systematically monitored company and product-specific cost and export price data on semi-conductors which were sold for export to certain contracting parties other than the United States;

— instituted quarterly supply and demand forecasts and communicated to manufacturers its concern about the need to accommodate their production levels to the forecasts as compiled by MITI.

100. Up to November 10, 1987 the cost and price data had been reviewed within the framework of the screening of exports for COCOM purposes. An export licence for semi-conductors had been granted only after the Japanese Government had examined the information on costs and export prices. As a result of this monitoring, export licences had been granted with delays, sometimes amounting to several months. As of November 10, 1987 the COCOM screening and the monitoring of costs and export prices had been administratively separated. Producers and exporters of semi-conductors were now still obliged to supply the Government with information on costs and export prices before shipment and the Government still examined this information systematically, but the granting of the export licence within the framework of the COCOM regulations was no longer dependent on the examination of costs and prices.

101. The Panel noted that the complaint by the EEC started with arguments on Article VI. It decided, however, to examine Article XI before addressing other Articles.

102. The Panel understood the main contentions of the parties to the dispute on the consistency of the measures set out in paragraph 99 with Article XI:1 of the General Agreement to be the following. The EEC considered that such measures constituted restrictions on the sale for export of semi-conductors at prices below company-specific costs through measures other than duties, taxes or charges within the meaning of Article XI:1. Japan contended that there were no governmental measures limiting the right of Japanese producers and exporters to export semi-conductors at any price they wished. The Government's measures to avoid sales at dumping prices were not legally binding and therefore did not fall under Article XI:1. Exports were limited by private enterprises in their own self-interest and such private action was outside the purview of Article XI:1.

103. As for the export approval system, the EEC did not ask the Panel to examine the COCOM export controls as such but the delays in the issuing of export licences resulting from the monitoring of costs and export prices. The EEC considered that these delays constituted restrictions on exportation made effective through export licences within the meaning of Article XI:1. Japan maintained that the delays in the granting of export licences resulting from the monitoring of costs and export prices had occurred for purely administrative reasons and did not constitute restrictions within the meaning of Article XI:1, since no export licence had ever been denied for reasons related to export pricing.

104. The Panel examined the parties' contentions in the light of Article XI:1, the relevant part of which stated that:

> "No prohibitions or restrictions other than duties, taxes or other charges, whether made effective through quotas . . ., export licences or other measures, shall be instituted or maintained by any contracting party . . . on the exportation or sale for export of any product destined for the territory of any other contracting party".

The Panel noted that this wording was comprehensive: it applied to all measures instituted or maintained by a contracting party prohibiting or restricting the importation, exportation or sale for export of products other than measures that take the form of duties, taxes or other charges.

105. The Panel noted that the CONTRACTING PARTIES had decided in a previous case that the import regulation allowing the import of a product in principle, but not below a minimum price level, constituted a restriction on importation within the meaning of Article XI:1 (BISD 25S/99 [Case 38]). The Panel considered that the principle applied in that case to restrictions on imports of goods below certain prices was equally applicable to restrictions on exports below certain prices.

106. The Panel then examined the contention of the Japanese Government that the measures complained of were not restrictions within the meaning of Article XI:1 because they were not legally binding or mandatory. In this respect the Panel noted that Article XI:1, unlike other provisions of the General Agreement, did not refer to laws or regulations but more broadly to measures. This wording indicated clearly that any measure instituted or maintained by a contracting party which restricted the exportation or sale for export of products was covered by this provision, irrespective of the legal status of the measure.

107. Having reached this finding on the basis of the wording and purpose of the provision, the Panel looked for precedents that might be of further assistance to it on this point. It noted that the CONTRACTING PARTIES had addressed a case relating to the interpretation of Article XI:2(c) in the report of the Panel on "Japan — Restrictions on Imports of Certain Agricultural Products" (L/6253). Under Article XI:2(c), import restrictions might be imposed if they were necessary to the enforcement of "governmental measures" restricting domestic supplies. The complaining party argued in the earlier panel proceedings that some of the measures which Japan had described as governmental measures were in fact "only an appeal for private measures to be taken

voluntarily by private parties" and could therefore not justify the import restrictions. Japan replied that "to the extent that governmental measures were effective, it was irrelevant whether or not the measures were mandatory and statutory", that the governmental measures "were effectively enforced by detailed directives and instructions to local governments and/or farmers' organizations" and that "such centralised and mutually collaborative structure of policy implementation was the crux of government enforcement in Japan" (L/6253, paragraph 29). The Panel which examined that case had noted that "the practice of 'administrative guidance' played an important role" in the enforcement of the Japanese supply restrictions, that this practice was "a traditional tool of Japanese government policy based on consensus and peer pressure" and that administrative guidance in the special circumstances prevailing in Japan could therefore be regarded as a governmental measure enforcing supply restrictions. The Panel recognized the differences between Article XI:1 and Article XI:2(c) and the fact that the previous case was not the same in all respects as the case before it, but noted that the earlier case supported its finding that it was not necessarily the legal status of the measure which was decisive in determining whether or not it fell under Article XI:1.

108. The Panel recognized that not all non-mandatory requests could be regarded as measures within the meaning of Article XI:1. Government-industry relations varied from country to country, from industry to industry, and from case to case and were influenced by many factors. There was thus a wide spectrum of government involvement ranging from, for instance, direct government orders to occasional government consultations with advisory committees. The task of the Panel was to determine whether the measures taken in this case would be such as to constitute a contravention of Article XI.

109. In order to determine this, the Panel considered that it needed to be satisfied on two essential criteria. First, there were reasonable grounds to believe that sufficient incentives or disincentives existed for non-mandatory measures to take effect. Second, the operation of the measures to restrict export of semi-conductors at prices below company-specific costs was essentially dependent on Government action or intervention. The Panel considered each of these two criteria in turn. The Panel considered that if these two criteria were met, the measures would be operating in a manner equivalent to mandatory requirements such that the difference between the measures and mandatory requirements was only one of form and not of substance, and that there could be therefore no doubt that they fell within the range of measures covered by Article XI.1.

110. On the first criterion, the Panel considered the background against which the measures operated. The Panel noted that the Government of Japan had formally concluded in September 1986 an Arrangement with the Government of the United States, one of the main provisions of which was for the Japanese Government to monitor costs and export prices to third country markets in order to prevent dumping. Following bilateral consultations, the Government of Japan assured the United States in April 1987 that it had taken "appropriate action to ensure that Japanese semi-conductor exports are being sold at not less than their costs in third country markets". In the light of this, the Panel considered that at least by April 1987, there would certainly have been no doubt in the minds of relevant Japanese producers and exporters that the Japanese Government had made an undertaking to the United States to ensure that a certain class of sales did not take place. They would also have known that any such action would have led to the Government of Japan being unable to fulfil a commitment which it had given to the United States, and therefore would have adverse consequences for Japan. They would also have been aware that the Government had the fullest information available to identify any producers or exporters selling at prices below costs.

111. The Panel considered that, in the above circumstances, the Japanese Government's measures did not need to be legally binding to take effect, as there were reasonable grounds to believe that there were sufficient incentives or disincentives for Japanese producers and exporters to conform. The Panel did not consider that these circumstances were, of themselves, sufficient to ensure compliance. Indeed, events showed that despite the existence of the Arrangement, a certain number of Japanese producers and exporters had pursued their original course of production and sales. What was required to ensure compliance were additional Government measures.

112. The Panel went on to consider the second criterion regarding the manner in which the measures operated in this case. To begin with, the Panel noted the Japanese Government's own description of its measures as provided to the United States in its Position Paper of April 1987, notably that "Japan exercised administrative guidance to achieve production cut-backs and adopted more stringent export licensing practises" and that "actions have been taken aimed at reducing supplies and squeezing out grey market transactions". It referred also to the measures taken as "recently-ordered production cut-backs", and that "the measures (i.e. those relating to production and export administration) taken by the Japanese Government have as their exclusive purpose and effect avoiding below cost sales of semi-conductors in third country markets."

113. The Panel further examined the structure and elements of the measures adopted. It noted that Japanese producers were required to submit detailed information on costs on a regular basis. It also noted the importance of the statutory requirement for exporters to supply information on export prices and of the heavy penalties attached for failure to comply with that requirement. The objective of identification in the monitoring measures was clear. For instance, in cases where the exporter was not a producer, the origin of the transaction had to be declared and identified. The Panel noted that this gave the Japanese Government a comprehensive basis for precise identification of the source of any below cost pricing. It also observed that any producer or exporter would have been aware that the Japanese Government would be in a position to have this information. The preparedness of the Japanese Government to request, and to continue requesting, for below cost sales to cease was also evident.

114. The Panel examined the operation of the supply and demand forecasts. It noted that MITI had instituted regular meetings of the Supply and Demand Forecasts Committee, involving producers, upon which its forecasts were drawn up. The Panel considered that the Government of Japan played a decisive role in the entire operation. Indeed it was stated by Japan that "the Japanese Government, in consideration of large inventories of products, made an attempt to restore balance in supply and demand." Thus in the first and second quarters of 1987, the Government of Japan compiled the supply and demand forecasts" to get production levels reflective of actual demand." The Panel recalled the statement quoted in paragraph 112 above concerning the production cut-backs and the avoidance of below cost sales of semi-conductors in third country markets. On the basis of these, the Panel considered that the Government of Japan had intervened to facilitate the reduction of the production levels of semiconductors through the operation of the supply and demand forecasts. The Panel further considered that if Japanese producers and exporters were subject to any measure restricting the exportation or sale for export of semi-conductors, they would have to adjust their production levels accordingly. The Panel therefore considered that the operation of the supply and demand forecasts had facilitated the reduction of the production levels, strengthening the effectiveness of the other measures adopted.

115. The Panel then considered whether the operation of the measures was essentially dependent on Government action. The complex of measures was, in the Panel's view, so dependent. The period between

September 1986 and January 1987 gave an interesting indication of how Japanese firms were disposed to operate where they were subject to less constraint. It was apparent that they had been prepared to produce and sell up to a quantity which included what was later termed "false demand" in the context of the revised supply or demand forecast in February 1987. The Panel considered that the disposition to produce and sell was what the Government of Japan by its complex of measures intended to control, by the strengthening of the monitoring measures, lowering of the minimum export amount requiring an export license to 50,000 yen, requests to producers not to export at prices below company-specific costs, and the revisions of the supply and demand forecasts.

116. The Panel also considered that the series of statements quoted in paragraph 112 above were relevant in this context. In addition to these, the Panel noted that Japan had stated in the proceedings of the Panel that "although monitoring by MITI was limited in scope, it was still meaningful because MITI represented a neutral and objective figure overseeing the entire industry while taking into account costs and prices among competing companies in Japan. Monitoring also helped to stamp out suspicion among companies that others were cheating or resorting to dumping". Japan had further stated that "if the semi-conductor manufacturers were to pursue their own profits and ignore MITI's concern, the whole dumping prevention mechanism would collapse", and that "the administration presents (firms) with objective facts and considerations and others that are usually not obtainable by one firm alone". The Panel considered that these statements concerning the way in which the Government exercised its authority were a further confirmation of the fact that the Government's involvement was essential to the prevention of sales below company-specific costs.

117. All these factors led the Panel to conclude that an administrative structure had been created by the Government of Japan which operated to exert maximum possible pressure on the private sector to cease exporting at prices below company-specific costs. This was exercised through such measures as repeated direct requests by MITI, combined with the statutory requirement for exporters to submit information on export prices, the systematic monitoring of company and product-specific costs and export prices and the institution of the supply and demand forecasts mechanism and its utilization in a manner to directly influence the behavior of private companies. These measures operated furthermore to facilitate strong peer pressure to comply with requests by MITI and at the same time to foster a climate of uncertainty as to the

circumstances under which their exports could take place. The Panel considered that the complex of measures exhibited the rationale as well as the essential elements of a formal system of export control. The only distinction in this case was the absence of formal legally binding obligations in respect of exportation or sale for export of semi-conductors. However, the Panel concluded that this amounted to a difference in form rather than substance because the measures were operated in a manner equivalent to mandatory requirements. The Panel concluded that the complex of measures constituted a coherent system restricting the sale for export of monitored semi-conductors at prices below company-specific costs to markets other that the United States, inconsistent with Article XI:1.

118. The Panel then reverted to the issue raised by the EEC concerning the delays of up to three months in the issuing of export licences that had resulted from the monitoring of costs and export prices of semi-conductors destined for contracting parties other than the United States. It examined whether the measures taken by Japan constituted restrictions on exportation or sale for export within the meaning of Article XI:1. It noted that the CONTRACTING PARTIES had found in a previous case that automatic licensing did not constitute a restriction within the meaning of Article XI:1 and that an import licence issued on the fifth working day following the day on which the licence application was lodged could be deemed to have been automatically granted (BISD 25S/95 [Case 38]). The Panel recognized that the above applied to import licences but it considered that the standard applicable to import licences should, by analogy, be applied also to export licences because it saw no reason that would justify the application of a different standard. The Panel therefore found that export licensing practices by Japan, leading to delays of up to three months in the issuing of licences for semi-conductors destined for contracting parties other than the United States, had been non-automatic and constituted restrictions on the exportation of such products inconsistent with Article XI:1.

119. The Panel examined the data on export prices provided by the two parties, by the United States and by interested parties. It noted that these prices were influenced by a large number of factors, including the elasticity of demand for the final product, the seasonal demand and the product life cycle of the particular type of semi-conductors, exchange fluctuations, initiation of anti-dumping investigations and other factors. It was therefore understandable that these data did not present a clear picture, but the Panel noted that there was some evidence to indicate that the export price of Japanese semi-conductors had risen after the

measures had been taken, especially for 256K DRAMs and 256K EPROMs.

120. The Panel then considered Article VI and arguments advanced by the two parties concerning that Article. Having found Japan to have acted inconsistently with Article XI:1, the Panel examined Japan's contention that its measures, being designed to prevent dumping, were justified by the spirit of Article VI, which condemned dumping. The Panel noted that Article VI:1 declared that dumping was to be condemned if it caused or threatened material injury to an established industry or materially retarded the establishment of an industry and that Article VI:2 allowed contracting parties to levy a duty on dumped products, subject to certain specified conditions. The provision was silent on actions by exporting countries. The Panel therefore found that Article VI did not provide a justification for measures restricting the exportation or sale for export of a product inconsistently with Article XI:1.

121. The Panel proceeded to examine the contention of the EEC that the measures maintained by Japan to prevent dumping were contrary to Article VI because that provision gave the exclusive right of preventing dumping to the importing countries. The Panel noted that Article VI provided importing countries with the right to levy anti-dumping duties subject to certain specific conditions but was silent on actions by exporting countries.

122. The Panel further examined the contention of the EEC that the measures by the Japanese Government were in violation of the most-favored-nation provision of Article I because the Third Country Market Monitoring system was applied not to all exports but only to those to selected countries. The Panel, having found the Japanese measures to be inconsistent with Article XI:1, did not consider it necessary to make a finding on whether or not their administration was contrary to Article I:1. The Panel considered that, once a measure had been found to be inconsistent with the General Agreement whether or not it was applied discriminatorily, the question of its non-discriminatory administration was no longer legally relevant. The Panel noted that another Panel had also refrained from examining the alleged discriminatory aspects of a restriction after having found it to be inconsistent with Article XI (BISD 30S.140).

123. The Panel then turned to the contention of the EEC that the measures by the Japanese Government were contrary to Article XVII:1(c), according to which "no contracting party shall prevent any

enterprise under its jurisdiction from acting in accordance with the general principles of non-discriminatory treatment prescribed in [the General] Agreement." The Panel considered that, once a measure had been found to be inconsistent with a specific provision of the General Agreement, it was no longer meaningful to address the question of whether or not the measure was also contrary to principles underlying that Agreement and therefore the Panel, having already found the Japanese measures to be inconsistent with Article XI, did not consider it necessary to examine them in the light of Article XVII:1(c).

B. Access to the Japanese Market

124. The Panel then turned to the EEC's allegation that the measures taken by the Japanese Government to improve access to the Japanese market favored United States' products and therefore contravened Article I. It examined the activities conducted by the Japanese Government to promote sales of foreign semi-conductors and the contents of the MITI "guidance" to users and importers in this regard, in the context of the Arrangement between Japan and the United States. It took into consideration other related elements, such as trade figures and the retaliatory measures taken by the United States against Japan.

125. The Panel noted the Japanese statement that its policy was to improve access to its semi-conductor market on a non-discriminatory basis and that the Japanese Government had denied that it granted preferential market access to the producers of the United States. It further noted the statement by the United States in the Panel proceedings that there was no secret understanding on preferential access for US companies and that the subject of preferential access had never been discussed during the negotiations leading to the conclusion of the Arrangement. The Panel examined the Arrangement and concluded that nothing in it would prevent Japan from implementing its market opening provisions on a most-favored-nation basis. The Panel also examined the contents of the MITI "guidance" to users and importers in this regard and could not detect any evidence of preferences accorded to United States products. Import statistics supplied by Japan showed that the growth of sales of semi-conductors in Japan from sources other than the United States had been higher than that of the sales originating in the United States. It also noted the announcement by the United States' authorities on the retention of sanctions against certain Japanese goods on the grounds that United States' sales in the Japanese market had not increased as expected.

126. The Panel noted the EEC's argument that, unless preferential treatment was involved, there was no need for two governments to enter into a formal bilateral arrangement. The Panel considered this argument not valid as there were bilateral agreements which provided for non-discriminatory treatment. The Panel noted that the EEC had also argued that Japan's commitment under the Arrangement with the United States to take measures in respect of "foreign capital affiliated" companies in Japan could be taken as an indication of an intent to favor imports from the United States because there was only one such company and that was of United States' origin. The Panel did not consider that argument to be decisive: no evidence had been submitted to it demonstrating that companies from other countries were prevented from establishing themselves in Japan on the same terms as the United States company. It also noted the EEC argument that the general perception of the Japanese users and importers of semi-conductors might, under these special circumstances, be that they were expected to accord preference to United States products and would do so accordingly. The Panel considered this as a conjecture which therefore did not provide facts as evidence that preferences were accorded.

127. Taking into account all of the above, the Panel found that the information submitted to it did not demonstrate that the Japanese measures to improve access to its market for semi-conductors favored United States products inconsistently with Article I of the General Agreement.

C. Transparency

128. The Panel considered the contention of the EEC that the measures applied to exports of semi-conductors to third countries and the measures to improve access to the Japanese market lacked transparency and therefore contravened Article X. The Panel felt, however, that the present case did not call for a decision on that point. The measures under examination had been found to be inconsistent with Article XI. At issue was thus their elimination or bringing them into conformity with GATT, not their publication.

129. As for the measures to improve access to the Japanese market, the Panel, on the basis of the evidence analyzed in paragraphs 125 and 126 above, was unable to identify any measure constituting a requirement, restriction or prohibition on imports required to be published by Article X.

D. Nullification and Impairment

130. The Japanese measures relating to exports of semi-conductors to third country markets had been found to be inconsistent with Article XI:1. They were therefore, according to GATT practice, presumed to have nullified or impaired the benefits accruing to the EEC under the General Agreement (BISD 26S/216).

131. The Panel had not found that the measures relating to the access to the Japanese market were inconsistent with the provisions of the General Agreement. The Panel noted that the EEC had alleged that, even if the Japanese measures relating to exports and imports of semi-conductors were considered to be consistent with the General Agreement, they nullified or impaired benefits accruing to the EEC under the General Agreement and impeded the attainment of objectives of the General Agreement within the meaning of Article XXIII. According to the dispute settlement procedures adopted on November 28, 1979 (BISD 26S/216), a contracting party claiming that benefits accruing to it under the General Agreement had been nullified or impaired as a result of a measure consistent with the General Agreement would be called upon to provide a detailed justification. The Panel considered that the evidence submitted by the EEC relating to access to the Japanese market did not permit it to identify any measure by the Japanese Government that put EEC exporters of semi-conductors at a competitive disadvantage vis-à-vis those of the United States and that might therefore nullify or impair benefits accruing to the EEC under the General Agreement and impede the attainment of objectives of the General Agreement within the meaning of Article XXIII.

VIII. CONCLUSIONS

132. On the basis of the findings set out above, the Panel reached the following conclusions:

A. The requests not to export semi-conductors at prices below company-specific costs to contracting parties other than the United States which the Japanese Government addressed to Japanese producers and exporters of semi-conductors, combined with the statutory requirement for exporters to submit information on export prices and the systematic monitoring of company and product-specific costs and export prices by the Government, back-ed up with the use of supply and demand forecasts to impress on manufacturers the need to align their production to appropriate levels, constituted a coherent system restricting the sale for export of monitored semi-conductors at prices below company-specific costs to markets other than the United States, inconsistent with Article XI:1. The Panel suggests that the CONTRACTING PARTIES recommend that Japan bring its measures relating to the sale for export of semi-conductors to contracting parties other than the United States into conformity with the General Agreement.

B. The delays of up to three months in the issuing of export licences that resulted from the monitoring of costs and export prices of semi-conductors destined for contracting parties other than the United States constituted restrictions on exportation inconsistent with Article XI:1. The Panel suggests that the CONTRACTING PARTIES note that Japan had changed in November 1987 its export procedures to avoid such delays.

C. The evidence submitted to the Panel did not demonstrate that Japan's measures to improve access to the market for semi-conductors discriminate in favor of products originating in the United States. The Panel suggests that the CONTRACTING PARTIES take note of the statement of the Japanese Government that its policy was to improve the access to the Japanese market for semi-conductors in conformity with the General Agreement's most-favored-nation principle.

EUROPEAN ECONOMIC COMMUNITY—RESTRICTIONS ON IMPORTS OF DESSERT APPLES—COMPLAINT BY CHILE

Report of the Panel adopted on June 22, 1989
BISD 36S/93

2. FACTUAL ASPECTS

2.1 The common organization of the EEC market for dessert apples (and for other fruit and vegetables) is based on Council Regulation 1035 of 1972 (Official Journal L 118 of 5.20.72), as subsequently amended.

* * *

These regulations were described in an earlier panel report in 1980.[1] Despite a number of amending regulations since 1980 the essential features of the systems established under Regulation 1035/72 have not changed.

* * *

Prices and Intervention System

Before the start of each marketing year, the EEC Council of Ministers fixes a basic price and a buying-in price under Article 16 of Regulation 1035/72. The basic price is a guide price which determines the buying-in and withdrawal prices, explained below.

* * *

The buying-in price is fixed at between 40 and 55 per cent of the basic price.

* * *

2.2 Market intervention takes the form of withdrawal from the dessert apple market of apples meeting certain quality standards. Commu-

[1] Report of the Panel on "EEC Restrictions on Imports of Apples from Chile", BISD 27S, pp. 98-117, paragraph 2.2

nity regulations prescribe two possible methods; "buying-in" by member state authorities and "withdrawal" by producer organizations.

(a) Buying-in

During the period when the basic and buying-in prices are in force, member States notify the Commission daily of actual prices recorded on representative markets. If these remain below the buying-in price for three consecutive market days the Commission must, on member state request, record that the market in question is in a state of serious crisis. The member states are then required to buy apples of Community origin offered to them at a price equivalent to the buying-in price.

(b) Withdrawal by producer groups

When it appears to producer organizations that market prices are likely to fall substantially because of surplus supply, they may ask the member state authorities for permission to initiate withdrawal operations, at a withdrawal price not exceeding the public buying-in price plus 10 per cent of the basic price. (Article 15a of Regulation 1035/72 also enables member states to authorize "preventive withdrawals" by producer groups early in the marketing year in the light of the production outlook.) The member states, through their local representatives, verify that withdrawals have taken place and grant financial compensation, paid by the Community, to the producer groups for the withdrawal payments, less net receipts from the disposal of withdrawn apples.

Withdrawals by producer organizations, offering a somewhat higher price, account in practice for the major share of apples withdrawn. It is also Community policy to encourage the development of producer organizations and their role in market intervention.

2.3 Under Article 21 of Regulation 1035/72, member states shall ensure that products withdrawn are used for:

— free distribution;
— non-food purposes;
— animal feed;
— processing into alcohol;
— industrial processing.

2.4 The EEC has not enacted restrictions on the planting of apple trees. It did not operate a grubbing-up program for apple orchards during the period in which the import restrictions in question were applied.

* * *

2.11 By Regulation 962/88 of April 12, 1988 (OJ L 95 of April 13) the EEC Commission suspended the issue of import licences for (dessert) apples originating in Chile for the period April 15 to 22, 1988. Any applications pending on April 18 were to be rejected and the relevant securities released.

* * *

2.14 Then, on April 20 the Commission adopted Reg. 1040/88 (OJ L 102 of 4.21.88) which suspended until August 31, 1988 the issue of import licences for third-country imports in respect of tonnages which exceeded a prescribed quantity. In the case of Chile that "reference quantity", fixed at 142,131 tons, was deemed to have been already exceeded in terms of licences applied for, and therefore the suspension in place under Regulations 962/88 and 984/88 was continued through to August 31.

12. FINDINGS

Introduction

12.1 The Panel first examined the EEC's system of restrictive licensing applied to imports of apples from April through August 1988 under Article XI, as consistency with this Article was the primary determinant of the conformity of the EEC's system with the General Agreement, before proceeding to consider the measures under Articles XIII and X and Part IV of the Agreement. In considering the facts and arguments relating to Article XI in particular, the Panel took note of the fact that a previous Panel, in 1980[1], had reported on a complaint involving the same product and the same parties as the present matter and a similar set of GATT issues. The Panel noted carefully the arguments of the parties concerning the precedent value of this Panel's and other previous panels' recommendations, and the arguments on the legitimate expectations of contracting parties arising out of the adoption of panel reports. The Panel construed its terms of reference to mean that it was

[1] BISD 27S/98-117 [Case 43]

authorized to examine the matter referred to it by Chile in the light of *all* relevant provisions of the General Agreement and those related to its interpretation and implementation. It would take into account the 1980 Panel report and the legitimate expectations created by the adoption of this report, but also other GATT practices and panel reports adopted by the CONTRACTING PARTIES and the particular circumstances of this complaint. The Panel, therefore, did not feel it was legally bound by all the details and legal reasoning of the 1980 Panel report. The Panel communicated this decision to the parties early in its proceedings to assist them in the presentation of their arguments.

Article XI:1

12.2 The Panel found that the system of restrictive licensing applied by the EEC to imports of apples from April through August 1988 constituted an import restriction or prohibition inconsistent with Article XI:1 of the General Agreement. The Panel noted that the EEC had presented no arguments to refute this conclusion.

Article XI:2(c)(i)

12.3 The relevant sections of Article XI:2 read:

> "2. The provisions of paragraph 1 of this Article shall not extend to the following: . . .
> (c) Import restrictions on any agricultural or fisheries product, imported in any form, necessary to the enforcement of governmental measures which operate:
> (i) to restrict the quantities of the like domestic product permitted to be marketed or produced . . ."

The Panel noted that the EEC invoked Article XI:2 to justify its import restrictions on apples. The Panel recalled that a contracting party invoking an exception to the General Agreement bears the burden of proving that it has met all of the conditions of that exception.[1] In the present case, therefore, it was incumbent upon the EEC to demonstrate that the measures applied to imports of apples met each and every one

[1] Report of the Panel on "Canada—Administration of the Foreign Investment Review Act" (BISD 30S/140, 164); and Report of the Panel on "Japan—Restrictions on Imports of Certain Agricultural Products" (L/6253, p. 64)

of the conditions under Article XI:2(c)(i) and XI:2(c) last paragraph, in order to qualify in terms of these provisions for exemption from Article XI:1. These conditions were:

— the measure on importation must constitute an import restriction (and not a prohibition);

— the import restriction must be on an agricultural or fisheries product;

— the import restriction and the domestic marketing or production restriction must apply to "like" products in any form (or directly substitutable products if there is no substantial production of the like product);

— there must be governmental measures which operate to restrict the quantities of the domestic product permitted to be marketed or produced;

— the import restriction must be necessary to the enforcement of the domestic supply restriction;

— the contracting party applying restrictions on importation must give public notice of the total quality or value of the product permitted to be imported during a specified future period; and

— the restrictions applied under (i) must not reduce the proportion of total imports relative to total domestic production, as compared with the proportion which might reasonably be expected to rule between the two in the absence of restrictions.

12.4 The Panel observed that the requirements of Article XI:2(c)(i) for invoking an exception to the general prohibition on quantitative restrictions made this provision extremely difficult to comply with in practice. Indeed no contracting party had to date been found by a Panel to comply with all its requirements. The Panel was also aware that there existed widespread dissatisfaction with this provision and that its revision was under discussion. The Panel recalled, however, that it was not the function of panels to propose changes to the provisions of the General Agreement but to make findings regarding their interpretation and application.[1] With these general considerations in mind, the Panel proceeded to examine the EEC's import restrictions on apples in the light of the conditions set out above.

[1] Ministerial Declaration of 1982, BISD 29S/16

The Measure on Importation Must Constitute an Import Restriction

12.5 The Panel followed the view that prohibitions on imports were not permitted under this part of Article XI.[1] It considered that Article XI:2 (last paragraph) established conditions regarding the minimum quantity of imports that must be permitted; it did not regulate the distribution of that quantity of imports among supplying countries. As the EEC had at no time prohibited all imports of apples, its measures therefore constituted an import restriction, rather than an import prohibition in terms of Article XI:2(c)(i). The question of whether the EEC measures had operated as an effective prohibition of imports from Chile was examined under Article XIII of the General Agreement, which regulated the non-discriminatory administration of quantitative restrictions.

The Import Restriction Must be on an Agricultural or Fisheries Product

12.6 The Panel took account of longstanding GATT practice which classed as agricultural or fisheries products items specified in Chapters 1-24 of the CCCN, and concurred with both parties that the measures involved in this case applied to an agricultural product.

The Import Restriction and the Domestic Supply Restriction Must Apply to Like Products, in Any Form (or Directly Substitutable Products If There is No Substantial Production of the Like Product).

12.7 The Panel examined carefully the arguments of the parties on this issue, including the argument that differences in price, variety and quality between Chilean and EEC apples were such as to make them unlike products in terms of this GATT provision. It concluded that while such differences did exist, as they might for many products, they were not such as to outweigh the basic likeness. Dessert apples whether imported or domestic performed a similar function for the consumer and were both marketed as apples, i.e., as substantially similar products. The Panel therefore

[1] Report of the Panel on "United States—Prohibition of Imports of Tuna and Tuna Products from Canada" (BISD 29S/91)

found that EEC and Chilean dessert apples were like products for the purposes of Article XI:2(c)(i).

There Must be Governmental Measures Which Operate to Restrict the Quantities of a Domestic Product Permitted to be Marketed or Produced

12.8 The Panel proceeded by examining first whether the EEC did have "governmental" measures consistent with Article XI:2(c)(i), and second whether such measures did operate to restrict domestic supply in terms of the same provision. The Panel noted that the EEC did not claim that it restricted production of apples, but that it effectively restricted their marketing, through a system of market withdrawals carried out mainly by producer groups. The Panel also took note of the argument that these could not be considered "governmental" measures in terms of Article XI:2(c) because of the voluntary basis of the organization and the non-obligatory method of their operation. The Panel recalled that the concept of "governmental" measure had been previously examined on a number of occasions in respect of different articles of the General Agreement. A 1960 Panel, examining the question of whether subsidies financed by non-governmental levy were notifiable under Article XVI, expressed the view that ". . . the question . . . depends upon the source of the funds and the extent of government action, if any, in their collection".[1] Another Panel found that the informal administrative guidance used by the Japanese Government to restrict production of certain agricultural products could be considered to be a governmental measure within the meaning of Article XI:2 because it emanated from the Government and was effective in the Japanese context.[2] A third Panel considered that legally non-mandatory measures could constitute restrictions within the meaning of Article XI:1 if "sufficient incentives or disincentives existed for non-mandatory measures to take effect [and] the operation of the measures . . . was essentially dependent on Government action or intervention [because in that case] . . . the measures would be operating in a manner equivalent to mandatory requirements such that the difference between the measures and mandatory requirements was only one of form and not of substance.[3]

[1] Report of the Panel on "Review pursuant to Article XVI:5" (BISD 9S/192)
[2] Report of the Panel on "Japan—Restrictions on Imports of Certain Agricultural Products" (L/6253, p. 79)
[3] Report of the Panel on "Japan—Trade in Semi-Conductors" (L/6309, p. 40)

12.9 The Panel examined the EEC measures in the light of these decisions by the CONTRACTING PARTIES. It noted that the EEC internal régime for apples was a hybrid one, which combined elements of public and private responsibility. Legally there were two possible systems, direct buying-in of apples by Member State authorities and withdrawals by producer groups. Under the system of withdrawals by producer groups, which was the EEC's preferred option, the operational involvement of public authorities was indirect. However, the régime as a whole was established by Community regulations which set out its structure. Its operation depended on Community decisions fixing prices, and on public financing; apples withdrawn were disposed of in ways prescribed by regulation. The Panel therefore found that both the buying-in and withdrawal systems established for apples under EEC Regulation 1035/72 (as amended) could be considered to be governmental measures for the purposes of Article XI:2(c)(i).

12.10 Having made the above finding, the Panel went on to examine whether these governmental measures "operated to restrict the quantities of [EEC apples] permitted to be marketed". The Panel noted that the 1980 Panel had reached the conclusion that:

> "the EEC did restrict quantities of apples permitted to be marketed through its system of intervention purchases by member States and compensation to producer groups for withdrawing apples from the market".[1]

That Panel did not, however, explain the basis for this conclusion. The Panel also noted that a 1978 Panel[2] had come to the opposite conclusion about the consistency with Article XI:2(c)(i) of the EEC system set up under the same Regulation 1035/72 as it applied to tomatoes. While taking careful note of the earlier panel reports, the Panel did not consider they relieved it of the responsibility, under its terms of reference, to carry out its own thorough examination on this important point.

12.11 The Panel's scrutiny of the EEC market intervention scheme for apples led it to distinguish a number of features particularly relevant to the application of Article XI:2(c)(i). The system's operation and targets were essentially price-related; it was activated or suspended according to market price movements in relation to target prices fixed

[1] BISD 27S/112
[2] Report of the Panel on "EEC—Program of Minimum Import Prices, Licences and Surety Deposits for Certain Processed Fruits and Vegetables" (BISD 25S/68-107)

by the EEC. This was true of both direct intervention (buying-in) by members states and the decentralized withdrawal of apples from the dessert apple market by producers' organizations which could take place at a slightly higher price level than the former. The systems thus operated to provide a price floor to EEC producers. In certain years it had resulted in the withdrawal of substantial quantities of apples from the consumer market for dessert apples; but there was no quantitative target or limit defined by the EEC either for these withdrawals or for the overall quantity marketed. The overall quantity withdrawn in any year was a residual amount, resulting from the interplay of market forces instead of being determined by the EEC authorities. Likewise there was no quantitative restriction on supply by producers—i.e., the quantity they could offer for sale. The EEC regime, in assuring producers a minimum price but prescribing no ceiling on the quantity eligible for this guarantee, could in fact act as an incentive for producers operating at the margin of profitability and thereby increase the total amount of apples offered for sale. As noted in paragraph 12.8 above, marketing restrictions under Article XI:2(c)(i) may be implemented and enforced in various ways; but the Panel considered that the above features of the EEC system raised the more basic issue of whether it constituted a marketing restriction within the meaning of Article XI:2(c)(i) at all.

12.12 The Panel considered it necessary to examine a basic interpretative issue involved in this GATT requirement—i.e., did Article XI:2(c)(i) cover only schemes which set quantitative limits on the amount producers could offer for sale, or did it also cover schemes which could result in a reduction of products reaching the consumer through withdrawals activated by reference to a floor price without quantitative targets? The Panel examined this interpretative issue in the light of the wording of Article XI:2(c)(i), the context in which this provision appears in the General Agreement, the purpose of the General Agreement and the intentions of the drafters.

12.13 The Panel noted that Article XI:2(c)(i) referred to governmental measures which "operated to restrict the quantities" of the domestic products "permitted to be marketed or produced". Given the ordinary meanings of "to permit" (to authorize or allow) and "to market" (to expose for sale in a market or to sell) the *wording* of the provision suggested in the view of the Panel that the governmental measures must include an effective limitation on the quantity that domestic producers are authorized or allowed to sell. Measures which simply prevented consumers from buying products below certain prices would not appear to be covered by this wording. If the withdrawal of a product from the market without any governmental limitation on the amount that could be sold was included within the purview of Article XI:2(c)(i), the words "permitted to be" would not have any function. The Panel took into consideration, however, the argument that in the official languages of the General Agreement this provision could possibly be interpreted in a way which concentrated more on the market effects than on the government policy direction. It had been argued, for example, that the fact that a quantity of apples had been withdrawn from the dessert apple market as a result of governmental measures amounted, in effect, to a marketing restriction in terms of Article XI:2(c)(i). This interpretation would involve a more flexible reading of "permitted to be marketed". The Panel recalled the legal principle that exceptions were to be interpreted narrowly and considered that this argued against such a flexible interpretation of Article XI:2(c)(i).

12.14 As to the *context* in which the provision appears, the Panel noted that the final paragraph of Article XI:2 stipulated that imports may be restricted under Article XI:2(c)(i) only in proportion to domestic *production,* whether the government has chosen to restrict the quantities permitted to be *marketed* or those permitted to be *produced.* It is thus clear that in the case of marketing restrictions, also, imports may only be reduced to the extent that production declines. Schemes which operate to prevent, or effectively discourage, producers from selling their products beyond fixed amounts can reasonably be expected to have an effect on production because producers will tend to produce only up to the quantitative ceiling set. By contrast, a scheme which imposes no limitations on what producers may sell cannot, by itself, bring about a restriction of production. It therefore follows from the context of the provision that such a scheme would not be covered by Article XI:2(c)(i). The Panel also noted that, unlike Article XI:2(c)(i), Article XI:2(c)(ii), which concerned the removal of a temporary surplus, did not stipulate any restriction on domestic output in order to justify import restrictions. A withdrawal program not capable of limiting production could possibly come under Article XI:2(c)(ii), provided that the specific requirements of the provision were met. The difference between the two sub-paragraphs was a further contextual indication that Article XI:2(c)(i) could not be interpreted as widely as argued by the EEC.

12.15 Concerning the *purpose* of Article XI:2(c)(i), the Panel recalled that the title of Article XI was "General Elimination of Quantitative Restrictions". Article XI:2(c)(i) made an exception to this general rule. It permitted governments, under certain conditions, to enforce domestic output restrictions at the border. The Panel furthermore considered that, as one of the basic functions of the General Agreement was to provide a legal framework for the exchange of tariff concessions, great care had to be taken to avoid an interpretation of Article XI:2(c)(i) which would impair this function. The Panel noted that Article XI:2(c)(i)—unlike all provisions of the General Agreement specifically permitting actions to protect domestic producers[1]—did not provide either for compensation to be granted by the contracting parties adversely affected by the invocation. This reflected the fact that Article XI:2(c)(i) was not intended to be a provision permitting protective actions. If Article XI:2(c)(i) could be used to justify import restrictions which were not the counterpart of any governmental measure capable of limiting production, the value of the General Agreement as a legal frame-work for the exchange of tariff concession in the agricultural field would be seriously impaired.

12.16 The Panel also noted that during the *drafting* of the provision it had been agreed that the exception under Article XI:2(c)(i):

> ". . . was not intended to provide a means of protecting domestic producers against foreign competition, but simply to permit, in appropriate cases, the enforcement of domestic governmental measures . . ."[2] The drafters had also given some guidance as to the nature of the governmental measures intended to be covered by the provision. They recognized that output limitation might co-exist with subsidies[3], but that:
>
> ". . . in interpreting the term "restrict" for the purposes of paragraph 2, the essential point was that the measures of domestic restriction must effectively keep output below the level which it would have attained in the absence of restrictions."[4]

12.17 In the light of the considerations set out above, the Panel found that the EEC measures taken under the intervention system for apples did not constitute marketing restrictions of a type which could justify import restrictions under Article XI:2(c)(i).

12.18 Having made the above finding, the Panel did not consider it needed to continue its examination under the remaining Article

[1] E.g., Articles XVIII:A and C, XIX and XXVIII
[2] Havana Reports, p. 89, paragraph 16
[3] Havana Reports, p. 90, paragraph 22
[4] Havana Reports, p. 89, paragraph 17

XI:2(c)(i) criteria, in particular the question of whether the import restrictions were "necessary" in terms of this provision. It then proceeded to examine the EEC restrictions under Article XI:2(c)(ii).

Article XI:2(c)(ii)

12.19 Article XI:2(c)(ii) provides an exception to Article XI:1 for "import restrictions . . . necessary to the enforcement of government measures which operate to remove a temporary surplus of the like domestic product . . . by making the surplus available to certain groups of domestic consumers free of charge or at prices below the current market level". The Panel also took note of the views of the 1980 Panel on this point, noting that that Panel's finding of a "temporary surplus above the recurring surplus" related only to the situation in 1979. Article XI:2(c)(ii) clearly required the Panel to consider whether the EEC's surplus at the time the import restrictions were imposed, i.e. April 1988, had been demonstrated to be temporary. The Panel considered that the only practicable way to reach a finding on this point was to compare the EEC's apple surplus in 1988 with that in the previous years. From the statistics available to it, it observed that while amounts withdrawn had varied in the years up to and including the 1987-88 marketing year, stocks had remained relatively stable at levels which indicated a substantial structural surplus. The Panel thus found that the 1988 surplus could not be considered a temporary one, and that therefore the EEC did *not* meet the conditions for imposing import restrictions under Article XI:2(c)(ii). In the light of this finding the Panel did not consider it necessary to examine whether the EEC measures were in conformity with the other requirements of this provision.

Article XIII

Non-discriminatory Administration of Quantitative Restrictions

12.20 The Panel recognized that, given its findings that the EEC measures were a violation of Article XI:1 and not justified by Article XI:2(c)(i) or (ii), no further examination of the administration of the measure would normally be required. Nonetheless, and even though the Panel was concerned with measures which had already been eliminated, in view of the questions of great practical interest raised by both parties it considered it appropriate to examine the administration of the EEC measures in respect of Article XIII.

12.21 The first paragraph of the Article established the general obligation of non-discrimination in the administration of quantitative restrictions. The Panel noted that Commission Regulation 984/88 of April 12, 1988 suspended the issue of import licences in respect only of apples originating in Chile, eight days before the publication of import quotas. The Panel found that this measure constituted a prohibition in terms of Article XIII:1, and that it was applied contrary to that provision since the like products of all third countries had not been similarly prohibited. The Panel then proceeded to consider the EEC administration of the import quotas under Regulation 1040/88 in light of the subsequent provisions which delineated more specific requirements to achieve the aim of Article XIII:1.

Article XIII:2

12.22 The Panel noted that the first sentence of Article XIII:2 committed contracting parties applying import restrictions to any product to "aim at a distribution of trade in such product approaching as closely as possible the shares which the various contracting parties might be expected to obtain in the absence of such restrictions", and sub-paragraph (d) provided more specific requirements for the allocation of quota shares. The Panel considered that it would not be useful for it to make a finding regarding the actual size of quota shares. It observed that the previous three years were normally considered to be the appropriate reference period, with due account taken of relevant special factors. The Panel did not construe "special factors" applicable to only one, or some, exporters as a sufficient reason to change the base period which applied to all—though these special factors should be taken into account in considering individual quota allocations. Therefore the Panel found that the reference period applied by the EEC for the purpose of allocating quota shares—i.e., the previous three years—was consistent with its obligations under Article XIII.

12.23 Concerning "special factors", the Panel took into account the Interpretative Note to paragraph 4 of Article XIII, which refers to the Note relating to "special factors" in connection with the last sub-paragraph of Article XI:2. This reads:

> "The term "special factors" includes changes in relative productive efficiency as between domestic and foreign producers, or as between different foreign producers, but not changes artificially brought about by means not permitted under the Agreement".

Though not included in the General Agreement, the following interpretative note had been added at Havana to the Charter[1]:

> "The term "special factors" as used in Article 22 [XIII] includes among other factors the following changes, as between the various foreign producers, which may have occurred since the representative period:
>
> (1) changes in relative productive efficiency;
> (2) the existence of new or additional ability to export; and
> (3) reduced ability to export."

It was also agreed at Havana that "changes artificially brought about . . . by means not permissible under other provision of the Charter were not to be regarded as special factors for the purposes of paragraph 2(c) and Article 22 [XIII]".

12.24 The Panel further recalled that Article XIII:4 permits the party applying the restriction to initially select the representative period and appraise the special factors. It should subsequently consult, upon their request, with contracting parties seeking reappraisal of these factors. The Panel considered that this requirement for consultation was designed to ensure that due account was taken of special factors in terms of Article XIII:2(d) and in the light of the interpretation noted above. The Panel found that the overall trend towards an increase in Chile's relative productive efficiency and export capacity had not been duly taken into account, nor had the temporary reduction in export capacity caused by the 1985 earthquake. On the other hand the Panel did not find any basis in the General Agreement for the EEC taking into account as special factors the "restraint" alleged to have been exercised in previous years by other suppliers. Therefore the Panel found that the account taken of special factors by the EEC in allocating Chile's quota share did not meet the requirements of Article XIII:2(d).

Article XIII:3(b) and (c)

12.25 Concerning the notification of quotas and quota shares, the Panel noted that Article XIII:3(b) requires that "in the case of import restrictions involving the fixing of quotas, the contracting party applying the restrictions shall give public notice of the total quantity or value of the product or products which will be permitted to be imported during a

[1] Havana Reports, p. 95, paragraph 52; Havana Charter Interpretative Note ad Article 22

specified future period . . ." . And Article XIII:3(c) requires that "in the case of quotas allocated among supplying countries, the contracting party applying the restrictions shall promptly inform all other contracting parties having an interest in supplying the product concerned of the shares in the quota currently allocated, by quantity or value, to the various supplying countries and shall give public notice thereof". The Panel also took into account the requirement of Article X:1 to publish trade regulations, including prohibitions or restrictions on imports, promptly in such a manner as to enable governments and traders to become acquainted with them. In the context of Article XIII's overall concern with the non-discriminatory application of quantitative restrictions, it interpreted Article XIII:3(b) and (c) together as requiring that both the total quota and shares allocated in it be publicly notified for a specified *future* period. The Article XIII:3(c) requirement to promptly notify other contracting parties with an interest in supplying the product would otherwise be meaningless, as would the Article XIII:3(b) provision for supplies en route to be counted against quota entitlement.

12.26 The Panel therefore considered that the allocation of back-dated quotas, that is, quotas declared to have already been filled at the time of their announcement, did not conform to the requirements of Article XIII:3(b) and Article XIII:3(c). It found that EEC Commission Regulation 1040/88 constituted a back-dated quota in respect of Chile, since although it published a quota share for Chile it simultaneously declared that share to be filled and, in fact, continued the suspension of imports from Chile enacted eight days before quotas were published. The EEC had therefore not observed the notification requirements of Article XIII:3(b) and (c). Moreover, the fact that such a back-dated quota was allocated to only one supplying country, Chile, resulted in the discriminatory administration of the restriction in violation of Article XIII:1.

12.27 The Panel went on to examine the EEC's treatment of goods en route, in the light of Article XIII:3(b)'s stipulation that "any supplies of the product in question which were en route at the time at which public notice was given shall not be excluded from entry". The Panel also took note of the (non-obligatory) Standard Practices for the Administration of Import and Export Restrictions approved by the CONTRACTING PARTIES in 1950.[1] These state in part that "any new or intensified restrictions should not apply to goods shown to the satisfaction of the control authority to have been en route at the time the

[1] GATT/CP.5/Rev.1

change was announced . . . " The Panel noted that the EEC, in the preamble to Regulation 962/88, suspending the issue of import licences for Chilean apples, had stated that ". . . no account should be taken of goods being transported to the Community other than those for which import licences have been issued" but the issue of import licences before sailing was not mandatory under EEC Regulations. The Panel found that by allowing entry only to those goods en route for which an import licence had been issued prior to the Regulation's entry into force the EEC had added a requirement for which there was no basis in Article XIII. The wording of the Article clearly meant that apples en route—i.e., on board and destined for the EEC—at the time the suspension of Chilean import licences was published should have been admitted to the EEC. The Panel was also aware of the interim decision of the President of the European Court of Justice, dated June 10, 1988, which suspended the operation of the EEC regulations enacting the measures in question in respect of 89,514 cartons of Chilean apples which had been in transit but for which an import licence had not been issued at the time the issue of such licences was suspended for Chile.

Article I

12.28 The Panel considered it more appropriate to examine the consistency of the EEC measures with the most-favored-nation principles of the General Agreement in the context of Article XIII (see above). This provision deals with the non-discriminatory administration of quantitative restrictions and is thus the *lex specialis* in this particular case.

Article X

12.29 The Panel found that the EEC had observed the requirement of Article X:1 to publish the measures under examination "promptly in such a manner as to enable governments and traders to become acquainted with them" through their publication in the Official Journal of the European Communities. It noted that no time limit or delay between publication and entry into force was specified by this provision. However it interpreted the requirements of this provision as clearly prohibiting the use of back-dated quotas, whose use by the EEC in the case of Chile had already been the subject of a finding under Article XIII (above).

12.30 The Panel further noted that the EEC Commission Regulations in question were directly applicable in all of the ten Member States concerned in a substantially uniform manner, although there were some minor administrative variations, e.g. concerning the form in which licence applications could be made and the requirement of pro-forma invoices. The Panel found that these differences were minimal and did not in themselves establish a breach of Article X:3. The Panel therefore did not consider it necessary to examine the question whether the requirement of "uniform" administration of trade regulations was applicable to the Community as a whole or to each of its Member States individually.

Part IV

12.31 The Panel examined the EEC measures in relation to the objectives and commitments embodied in Articles XXXVI and XXXVII of Part IV of the General Agreement, particularly XXXVII:1(b) which states that "the developed contracting parties shall to the fullest extent possible . . . refrain from introducing, or increasing the incidence of, customs duties or non-tariff import barriers on products currently or potentially of particular export interest to less developed contracting parties"; and XXXVII:3(c), which requires developed contracting parties to "have special regard to the trade interests of less-developed contracting parties when considering the application of other measures permitted under this Agreement to meet particular problems and explore all possibilities of constructive remedies before applying such measures where they would affect essential interests of those contracting parties".

12.32 The Panel found that the EEC's import measures on dessert apples did affect a product of particular export interest to less-developed contracting parties. It noted that the EEC had held consultations with affected suppliers and had amended its regulations, but these consultation and amendments had been general in scope and had not related specifically to the interests of less-developed contracting parties in terms of Part IV. Following a careful examination of this issue, the Panel could not find that the EEC had made appropriate efforts to avoid taking protective measures on apples originating in Chile. However, the Panel noted that the commitments entered into by contracting parties under Article XXXVII were additional to their obligations under Parts I-III of the General Agreement, and that these commitments thus applied to measures which were permitted under Parts I-III. As the Panel had found the EEC's import restrictions to be inconsistent with specific obligations of the EEC under Part II of the General Agreement, it therefore did not consider it necessary to pursue the matter further under Article XXXVII.

Standstill

12.33 The Panel regarded the Standstill Commitment of the Punta del Este Declaration as outside its mandate. The Punta del Este Declaration contained commitments in the context of a plan for continuing negotiations whose outcome was yet to be decided. The Punta del Este Standstill commitments had their own special forum—the Surveillance Body established by the Committee on Trade Negotiations—to which any complaint concerning them should be taken. These commitments could therefore not be considered to be obligations within the meaning of Article XXIII:1(a).

Compensation

12.34 The Panel considered carefully Chile's arguments for a recommendation of compensation against the EEC, and the EEC's opposing arguments.

12.35 The Panel observed that it was customary for a panel examining complaints under paragraph 2 of Article XXIII to make a finding regarding nullification or impairment of benefits and to recommend the termination of measures found to be inconsistent with the General Agreement. It noted that there was no provision in the General Agreement obliging contracting parties to provide compensation, and that the Annex to the 1979 Understanding Regarding Notification, Consultation, Dispute Settlement and Surveillance indicated that:

> ". . . The provision of compensation should be resorted to only if the immediate withdrawal of the measure is impracticable and as a temporary measure pending the withdrawal of the measures which are inconsistent with the General Agreement.[1]

[1] BISD 26S/216

The Panel further recalled that a 1965 Secretariat note discussed this issue in relation to residual quantitative restrictions affecting developing countries. This note indicated:

> ". . . Where a proposal for compensation has been made, it would appear that it is open to the CONTRACTING PARTIES to make an assessment of the loss sustained . . . and to make a recommendation that pending elimination of these restrictions the country applying such restrictions should consider the establishment of other appropriate concessions which would serve to compensate this loss. There are, however, two points which need to be noted in this connection. Firstly, any such recommendation under the provisions of the present Article XXIII can be implemented only to the extent that it proves acceptable to the contracting party to whom it is addressed. If such contracting party is not in a position to accept the recommendation, the final sanction must remain the authority for withdrawing equivalent obligations as provided in paragraph 2 of Article XXIII.
>
> Secondly, the nature of the compensatory concession and the items on which these are offered would have to be determined by the contracting party to whom the recommendation is directed and would have to be a matter of agreement between the parties concerned. It would not be possible for a panel or other body set up by the CONTRACTING PARTIES to adjudicate on the specific compensations that should be offered . . . "[1]

12.36 The Panel endorsed the views contained in this note. It recognized that it would be possible for the EEC and Chile to negotiate compensation consistent with the provisions of the General Agreement; however the Panel did not consider that it would be appropriate for it to make a recommendation on this matter.

13. CONCLUSIONS

13.1 The main conclusions of the Panel were that:

— the EEC restrictions on imports of apples were inconsistent with Article XI:1 and were not justified by Article XI:2;

[1] COM.TD/5, March 1965

— the administration of the quotas resulted in a discriminatory application of import restrictions contrary to Article XIII; and

— the operation of a back-dated import restriction in respect of Chile was inconsistent with Articles X and XIII.

OMITTED

NORWAY—RESTRICTIONS ON IMPORTS OF APPLES AND PEARS

Report of the Panel adopted on June 22, 1989
BISD 36S/306

5. FINDINGS

5.1 The Panel noted that Norway maintained a system of restrictive licensing for import of apples and pears which was claimed by the United States to be inconsistent with Article XI:1 of the General Agreement. It also noted that Norway claimed that this system was covered by paragraph 1(b) of the Protocol of Provisional Application of the General Agreement of October 30, 1947 (hereinafter referred to as "the Protocol"), according to which the signatory contracting parties undertake to apply Part II of the General Agreement

> "to the fullest extent not inconsistent with existing legislation" (hereinafter referred to as "the existing legislation clause") (BISD Vol. IV/77).

5.2 According to Norway, the system of restrictive licensing was covered by the existing legislation clause because it implemented parliamentary acts predating the Protocol, namely Act No. 5 of June 12, 1934 Relating to the Provisional Ban on Imports etc. (Annex I), the Common Political Program adopted in 1945 by the parties represented in the Storting (the Norwegian Parliament) (Annex III) and some principles on agricultural policies endorsed by the Storting in connection with the adoption of the 1947 National Budget (Annex IV).

5.3 Norway did not contest the contention of the United States that the system of restrictive licensing was inconsistent with Article XI:1. The sole issue before the Panel was therefore whether Norway's system of restrictive licensing for import of apples and pears was covered by the existing legislation clause.

5.4 The Panel began its examination by analysing the historical origin of the Protocol and relevant decisions of the CONTRACTING PARTIES relating to the existing legislation clause.

5.5 The Panel noted in the first place that paragraph 1(b) of the Protocol served a well determined purpose in a particular historical situation. It was to enable, in 1947, governments to accept the obligations of Part II of the General Agreement without having to adjust their domestic legislation. The drafters of the Protocol expected the General Agreement to be superseded soon by the ITO Charter and they felt that legislative changes should not be required at that time because such changes would have delayed the acceptance of the obligations under the General Agreement and could have prejudged the outcome of the negotiations on the Charter (see Summary Record of the Preparatory Committee of the United Nations Conference on Trade and Employment, E/PC/T/TAC/SR 1, 2 and 6). In the light of this purpose of the existing legislation clause, the Panel considered that it would not be justified to give this clause four decades after the entry into force of the Protocol an interpretation that would extend its functions beyond those it was originally designed to serve.

5.6 The Panel further recalled that paragraph 1(b) of the Protocol had in various circumstances in the past been interpreted by the CONTRACTING PARTIES so as to further the full application of the General Agreement. The following decisions of the CONTRACTING PARTIES were particularly relevant in this respect.

(a) In a report approved by the CONTRACTING PARTIES on August 10, 1949, a Working Party agreed that the existing legislation clause applied only to:

> "legislation which is of a mandatory character or by its terms or expressed intent—that is, it imposes on the executive authority requirements which cannot be modified by executive action" (BISD II/49, paragraph 99, at 62).

This position was on several occasions reconfirmed by the CONTRACTING PARTIES (see Report of a Working Party adopted on February 28, March 5 and 7, 1955, BISD 3S/231, paragraph 58 at 249/250; Report of a Working Party on Import Restrictions Maintained by the Federal Republic of Germany, adopted on May 2, 1958, BISD 7S/99, paragraph 18, at 106; Panel Report on United States Manufacturing Clause, adopted on May 15/16, 1974, BISD 31S/74, paragraph 35, at 88).

The Panel noted that the parties to the present dispute agreed that this interpretation applied in the present case.

(b) In a Panel report adopted by the CONTRACTING PARTIES on the Manufacturing Clause in the US copyright legislation, the scope of paragraph 1(b) of the Protocol was extensively considered. The basic issue before that Panel was whether the existing legislation clause should be interpreted as opening a one-way street permitting only movements from the situation on October 30, 1947 to the situation required by Part II of the General Agreement or a two-way street permitting also movements back to the 1947 situation. The Panel decided in favor of the "one-way street" principle arguing that the Protocol was designed to provide only a temporary dispensation from Part II, that the basic aim of the General Agreement was security and predictability in trade relations and that it would be inconsistent with that aim if contracting parties were free to reverse, at any time and at their discretion, the steps they have taken to bring their legislation into conformity with the General Agreement (BISD 31S/74, at 90).

5.7 It follows from the foregoing that to be eligible as "existing legislation" under the Protocol, such legislation must:

(a) be legislation in a formal sense,

(b) predate the Protocol and

(c) be mandatory in character by its terms or expressed intent.

The Panel then proceeded to examine the 1934 Act and the other declarations cited by Norway in the light of these criteria.

5.8. The Panel recalled that *Norway* argued that, under the constitutional system of Norway, the executive authorities had no option but to restrict imports of apples and pears on the basis of the 1934 Act, after the agricultural policies to be followed by the executive authorities had been defined in the Common Political Program of 1945 and the Government's principles of agricultural policies had been endorsed in the Storting in 1947. The *United States* doubted that the Norwegian executive authorities were legally bound to restrict apple and pear imports under the 1934 Act and the parliamentary declarations referred to. In any case an obligation to do so was in its view not apparent from the text of the documents put forward; thus, even assuming the existence of such an obligation, the Act and the declarations surely were not mandatory by their terms or expressed intent.

5.9 The Panel further recalled that when in 1955 and 1958 the Contracting Parties requested notification of legislation eligible under paragraph 1(b) of the Protocol, six contracting parties (Canada, Denmark, Germany, the United Kingdom, the United States and the Union of South Africa) notified legislative acts, whereas seven contracting parties (Australia, Ceylon, Finland, Japan, Pakistan, Rhodesia and Nyasaland) declared that they had no such legislation (see document L/2375/Add.1). Although the Panel recognized that there was no legal obligation to make such notification, it did note that Norway did not avail itself of the opportunity to notify on that occasion the Acts and declarations cited in the present dispute.

5.10 In relation to the legislative measures relied upon by Norway, the Panel noted that the application of the 1946 Act (Annex II), which had prohibited all imports save those for which the King had granted express dispensation, was discontinued on the occasion of the introduction of a revised system of import licensing in 1958. The 1934 Act (Annex I) was then revived as the basis for import licensing. The relevant part of the 1934 Act provided that the "King can decide that . . . it should be prohibited to import from abroad . . . articles or goods, indicated by the King, . . ." . Under the terms of this Act, the King had discretion to prohibit the import of any commodity. The Panel found nothing in the text of the 1934 Act expressing the intent of rendering the institution of such restrictions mandatory. The Panel recalled that in fact no import restrictions relating to apples and pears had been based on the 1934 Act before the year 1958, restrictions in force before that period having resulted from the 1946 Act. According to its terms, the 1934 Act is enabling, not mandatory in character and can for this reason not be considered as being covered by the existing legislation clause.

5.11 As for the Common Political Programme of 1945 (Annex III) and the Government's White Paper No. 10 (Annex IV), endorsed by the Storting on the occasion of the adoption of the National Budget in 1947, the Panel concluded from the documents and from the explanations provided by Norway that these documents and the discussion which ensued in the Storting had in fact no bearing on import restrictions as such and contained no reference to the subject matter of the present dispute, i.e. import restrictions to be imposed on apples and pears. Though political guidelines could possibly be inferred from them, they could not be considered to be legislation conforming to the criteria enumerated in paragraph 5.7 above, and therefore could not fall within the meaning of the Protocol.

5.12 As for the various developments in the field of agricultural policy which took place after 1947, such as the "Basic Agricultural Agreement" concluded in 1950 and supplemented since by periodic medium-term agreements, several White Papers presented by the Government and recommendations of a Storting Committee, which have been relied upon by Norway (see Annexes V, VI, VII and XII), the Panel noted that these should have no relevance to the application of the existing legislation clause, since they occurred after the date of the Protocol.

5.13 For the reasons stated above, the evidence presented by Norway on the state of the legislation that existed on October 30, 1947 did not show that the Norwegian system of restrictive licensing of the import of apples and pears was based on legislation eligible under the paragraph 1(b) of the Protocol.

6. CONCLUSIONS

6.1 In the light of the considerations set out in Section 5 above, the Panel concluded that Norway's restrictions on imports of apples and pears were not covered by the existing legislation clause of the Protocol of Provisional Application.

6.2 The Panel *recommends* that the CONTRACTING PARTIES request Norway to bring its measures applying to imports of apples and pears into conformity with its obligations under the General Agreement.

UNITED STATES—RESTRICTIONS ON IMPORTS OF SUGAR

Report of the Panel adopted on June 22, 1989
BISD 36S/331

5. FINDINGS

5.1 The Panel noted that the basic issue before it was as follows. The United States maintains quantitative restrictions on the importation of certain sugars described in its GATT Schedule of Concessions (Schedule XX). The maintenance of quantitative restrictions is inconsistent with Article XI:1 of the General Agreement which provides, *inter alia*, that:

> "No restrictions . . . made effective through quotas . . . shall be . . . maintained by any contracting party on the importation of any product of the territory of any other contracting party."

Article II:1(b) of the General Agreement provides that the products described in the Schedules of Concessions of the contracting parties

> "shall, on their importation into the territory to which the Schedule relates, *and subject to the terms, conditions or qualifications set forth in that Schedule,* be exempt from ordinary customs duties in excess of those set forth and provided for therein." (emphasis added).

The *United States* argues that the proviso "subject to the terms, conditions or qualification set forth in that Schedule" in Article II:1(b) permits contracting parties to include qualifications relating to quantitative restrictions in their Schedule. The United States had made use of this possibility by reserving in its Schedule of Concessions the right to impose quota limitations on imports of sugar in certain circumstances. Since the restrictions on the importation of sugar conformed to the qualifications set out in the Schedule of the United States, and the Schedules of Concessions were, according to Article II:7, an integral part of the General Agreement, the restrictions were consistent with the

United States obligations under that Agreement. *Australia* argues that qualifications to concessions made in accordance with Article II:1(b) cannot justify measures contrary to other provisions of the General Agreement, in particular not quantitative restrictions inconsistent with Article XI:1 (for a complete description of the parties' arguments, see Section 3 above).

5.2 The Panel first examined the issue in the light of the wording of Article II. It noted that in Article II:1(b), the words "subject to the . . . qualification set forth in that Schedule" are used in conjunction with the words "shall . . . be exempt from ordinary customs duties in excess of those set forth in [the Schedule]". This suggests that Article II:1(b) permits contracting parties to qualify the obligation to exempt products from customs duties in excess of the levels specified in the Schedule, not however to qualify their obligations under other Articles of the General Agreement. The Panel further noted that the title of Article II is "Schedules of Concession" and that the ordinary meaning of the word "to concede" is "to grant or yield". This also suggests in the view of the Panel that Article II permits contracting parties to incorporate into their Schedules acts yielding rights under the General Agreement but not acts diminishing obligations under that Agreement.

5.3 The panel then examined the issue in the light of the purpose of the General Agreement. It noted that one of the basic functions of the General Agreement is, according to its Preamble, to provide a legal framework enabling contracting parties to enter into "reciprocal and mutually advantageous arrangements directed to the substantial reduction of tariffs and other barriers to trade". Where the General Agreement mentions specific types of negotiations, it refers to negotiations aimed at the reduction of barriers to trade (Articles IV(d), XVII:3 and XXVIII bis). This supports in the view of the Panel the assumption that Article II gives contracting parties the possibility to incorporate into the legal framework of the General Agreement commitments additional to those already contained in the General Agreement and to qualify such additional commitments, not however to reduce their commitments under other provisions of that Agreement.

5.4 The Panel then examined the issue in the context of the provisions of the General Agreement related to Article II. It noted that negotiations on obstacles to trade created by the operation of state-trading enterprises may be conducted under Article XVII:3 and that a note to that provision provides that such negotiations "may be directed towards the reduction of duties and other charges on imports and exports or towards the conclusion of *any other mutually satisfactory arrangement consistent with the provisions of this Agreement* (See paragraph 4 of Article II and the note to that paragraph)." (emphasis added).

The negotiations foreseen in Article XVII:3 are thus not to result in arrangements inconsistent with the General Agreement, in particular not quantitative restrictions made effective through state-trading that are not justified by an exception to Article XI:1. The Panel saw no reason why a different principle should apply to quantitative restrictions made effective by other means.

5.5 The Panel then examined the issue in the light of the practice of the CONTRACTING PARTIES. The Panel noted that the CONTRACTING PARTIES adopted in 1955 the report of the Review Working Party on Other Barriers to Trade, which had concluded that:

"there was nothing to prevent contracting parties, when they negotiate for the binding or reduction of tariffs, from negotiating on matters, such as subsidies, which might affect the practical effects of tariff concessions, and from incorporating in the appropriate schedule annexed to the Agreement the results of such negotiations; *provided that the results of such negotiations should not conflict with other provisions of the Agreement.*" (emphasis added) (BISD 3S/225).

Whether the proviso in this decision is regarded as a policy recommendation, as the United States argues, or as the confirmation of a legal requirement, as Australia claims, it does support, in the view of the Panel, the conclusion that the CONTRACTING PARTIES did not envisage that qualifications in Schedules established in accordance with Article II:1(b) could justify measures inconsistent with the other Articles of the General Agreement.

5.6 The Panel finally examined the issue in the light of the drafting history. It noted that the reference to "terms and qualifications" was included in a draft of the present Article II:1(b) during the Second Session of the Preparatory Committee of the United Nations Conference on Trade and Employment. The original draft had referred only to "conditions". This amendment was proposed and adopted "in order to provide more generally for the sort of qualifications actually provided in the form of notes in the specimen Schedule. A number of these notes are, in effect, additional concessions rather than *conditions* governing the tariff bindings to which they relate" (E/PC/T/153 and E/PC/T/W/295). Schedule provisions qualifying obligations under the General Agreement were not included in the specimen Schedule nor was the possibility of such Schedule provisions mentioned by the drafters. The Panel therefore found that the drafting history did not support the interpretation advanced by the United States.

5.7 For the reasons stated in the preceding paragraphs, the Panel found that Article II:1(b) does not permit contracting parties to qualify their obligations under other provisions of the General Agreement and that the provision in the United States GATT Schedule of Concessions can consequently not justify the maintenance of quantitative restrictions on the importation of certain sugars inconsistent with the application of Article XI:1.

5.8 Australia claimed that the reallocation of a portion of Guyana's sugar quota to Belize, Jamaica and Trinidad and Tobago in December 1988 was inconsistent with the application of Article XIII:2 of the General Agreement. The United States argued that this matter was not covered by the Panel's terms of reference because it had arisen after the establishment of the Panel by the Council in September 1988. The Panel considered that it had to interpret its terms of reference not only in the light of the interest of the parties to the dispute, but also in the light of the rights of third contracting parties. The Panel noted that, according to paragraph 15 of the Understanding on Dispute Settlement (BISD 26S/210), "any contracting party having a substantial interest in the matter before a Panel, and having notified this to the Council, should have an opportunity to be heard by the panel". The Panel concluded from this that only those issues which interested third contracting parties could reasonably have expected to be part of the proceedings when the Panel was established by the Council could be considered to be part of the matter referred to the Panel by the Council [sic]. The issue raised by Australia involves directly two contracting parties (Jamaica and Trinidad and Tobago); it also has implications for other contracting parties. Since the matter raised by Australia had arisen only after the establishment of the Panel by the Council in September 1988, contracting parties had no reason to expect that the reallocation of the sugar quotas among Caribbean countries would be an issue before the Panel. The Panel therefore decided that this reallocation was not part of its mandate. The Panel however recalled in this context that it had found *all* restrictions imposed by the United States on the importation of sugar under the authority of the Headnote in the Tariff Schedules of the United States to be inconsistent with the General Agreement independent of the quota allocation to specific countries. It also recalled its finding that Article II:1(b) does not permit contracting parties to qualify their obligations under other provisions of the General Agreement and that this could not justify inconsistencies with any article of the General Agreement, including Article XIII.

5.9 The Panel noted that the EEC, in its submission as an interested third party, argued that the restrictions on the importation of sugar were contrary to the terms of the waiver granted in 1955 by the CONTRACTING PARTIES in connection with import restrictions imposed under Section 22 of the United States Agricultural Adjustment Act (of 1933) as amended (BISD 3S/32). The Panel noted that the matter referred to the CONTRACTING PARTIES by Australia were restrictions maintained under the authority of the Headnote in the Tariff Schedules of the United States, and not restrictions taken under Section 22 of the Agricultural Adjustment Act (of 1933) as amended (see paragraph 1.2 above). Therefore the issue raised by the EEC could not be examined by the Panel. The Panel also recalled in this context that the practice has been for panels to make findings only on those issues raised by the parties to the dispute, not on those related solely by third parties (L/6264, page 43 [Case 64] and L/6309, page 37 [Case 68]).

6. CONCLUSIONS

6.1. In the light of the considerations set out in Section 5 above, the Panel has concluded that the restrictions on the importation of certain sugars maintained by the United States under the authority of the Headnote in the Tariff Schedule of the United States are inconsistent with Article XI:1 and cannot be justified under the provisions of Article II:1(b).

6.2 The Panel therefore *recommends* that the CONTRACTING PARTIES request the United States either to terminate these restrictions or to bring them into conformity with the General Agreement.

JAPAN—TARIFF ON IMPORT OF SPRUCE-PINE-FIR (SPF) DIMENSION LUMBER

Report of the Panel adopted on July 19, 1989
BISD 36S/167

V. FINDINGS

5.1 Under its terms of reference established by the Council the Panel had to examine a complaint by Canada that the application of a tariff duty of 8 per cent on imports of spruce-pine-fir (SPF) dimension lumber by Japan is not in conformity with the provisions of Article I:1 of the General Agreement and nullifies and impairs benefits accruing to Canada under the General Agreement, SPF dimension lumber being a "like product" as compared to other types of dimension lumber entering Japan with zero duty.

5.2 The Panel noted that Heading No. 4407.10 of the Japanese Tariff was defined in conformity with the International Convention on the Harmonized Commodity Description and Coding System of June 14, 1983 (hereinafter called the Harmonized System) as follows:

4407 "Wood sawn or chipped lengthwise, sliced or peeled, whether or not planed, sanded or finger-jointed, of a thickness exceeding 6 mm":

4407.10 "Coniferous"

5.3 The Panel further noted that the dispute before the Panel largely focused on the consistency with Article I:1 of the 8 per cent tariff imposed by Japan under sub-position 4407.10-110 of the Japanese Tariff:

4407.10-110 1. "Of *Pinus spp.*, *Abies spp.* (other than California red fir, grand fir, noble fir and pacific silver fir) or *Picea spp.* (other than Sitka spruce), not more than 160mm in thickness,

(1) planed or sanded."

5.4 According to Canada, Article I:1 required Japan to accord also to SPF dimension lumber the advantage of the zero tariff granted by Japan, under sub-position 4407.10-320 of its Tariff, to planed and sanded lumber of "other" coniferous trees, including the genera cedar and other *Chamaecyparis*, hemlock (*Tsuga*), and douglas-fir (*Pseudotsuga*), and five species excluded from sub-position No. 4407.10-110.

5.5 The Panel noted that the tariff classification for 4407.10-110 had been established autonomously by Japan, without negotiation.

5.6 The terms of Article I:1, as far as they are relevant to the issue, read as follows:

> *General Most-Favored Nation Treatment*
> "With respect to customs duties . . . imposed on . . . imports . . . any advantage . . . granted by any contracting party to any product originating in . . . any other country . . . shall be accorded . . . to the like product originating in . . . all other contracting parties."

5.7 In view of analysing the factual situation submitted to it under its terms of reference, the Panel had first to consider the legal framework in which the Canadian complaint had been raised. In substance, Canada complains of the fact that Japan had arranged its tariff classification in such a way that a considerable part of Canadian exports of SPF dimension lumber to Japan was submitted to a customs duty of 8 per cent, whereas other comparable types of dimension lumber enjoy the advantage of a zero-tariff duty. The Panel considered it impossible to appreciate fully the Canadian complaint if it had not in a preliminary way clarified the bearing of some principles of the GATT-system in relation to tariff structure and tariff classification.

5.8 The Panel noted in this respect that the General Agreement left wide discretion to the contracting parties in relation to the structure of national tariffs and the classification of goods in the framework of such structure (see the report of the Panel on Tariff Treatment of Unroasted Coffee, BISD 28S/102, at 111, paragraph 4.4). The adoption of the Harmonized System, to which both Canada and Japan have adhered, had brought about a large measure of harmonization in the field of customs classification of goods, but this system did not entail any obligation as to the ultimate detail in the respective tariff classifications. Indeed, this nomenclature has been on purpose structured in such a way that it leaves room for further specifications.

5.9 The Panel was of the opinion that, under these conditions, a tariff classification going beyond the Harmonized System's structure is a legitimate means of adapting the tariff scheme to each contracting party's trade policy interests, comprising both its protection needs and its requirements for the purposes of tariff and trade negotiations. It must however be borne in mind that such differentiations may lend themselves to abuse, insofar as they may serve to circumscribe tariff advantages in such a way that they are conducive to discrimination among like products originating in different contracting parties. A contracting party prejudiced by such action may request therefore that its own exports be treated as "like products" in spite of the fact that they might find themselves excluded by the differentiations retained in the importing country's tariff.

5.10 Tariff differentiation being basically a legitimate means of trade policy, a contracting party which claims to be prejudiced by such practice bears the burden of establishing that such tariff arrangement has been diverted from its normal purpose so as to become a means of discrimination in international trade. Such complaints have to be examined in considering simultaneously the internal protection interest involved in a given tariff specification, as well as its actual or potential influence on the pattern of imports from different extraneous sources. The Canadian complaint and the defense of Japan will have to be viewed in the light of these requirements.

5.11 "Dimension lumber" as understood by *Canada* is defined by its presentation in a standard form of measurements, quality-grading and finishing. It appears from the information provided by Canada that this type of lumber is largely used in platform-house construction in Canada as well as in the United States and that it has found also widespread use in Japan, as is testified by the existence of a Japanese technical standard known under the name of "JAS 600".

5.12 *Japan* objected to this claim on different grounds. Japan explained that dimension lumber was only one particular type of lumber among many other possible presentations and that house-building is only one of the many possible uses of this particular kind of lumber. From the legal point of view, Japan contended that the concept of "dimension lumber" is not used either in any internationally accepted tariff classification, or in the Japanese tariff classification. In accordance with the Harmonized System, position No. 4407.10 embraces all types of coniferous wood "sawn or chipped lengthwise . . . exceeding 6mm". Apart from the thickness and the grade of finishing, customs treatment of lumber according to the Japanese Tariff was determined exclusively on the basis of a distinction established between certain biological genera or species. Dimension lumber was therefore not identified as a particular category in the framework of the Japanese tariff classification.

5.13 *The Panel* considered that the tariffs referred to by the General Agreement are, quite evidently, those of the individual contracting parties. This was inherent in the system of the Agreement and appeared also in the current practice of tariff negotiations, the subject matter of which were the national tariffs of the individual contracting parties. It followed that, if a claim of likeness was raised by a contracting party in relation to the tariff treatment of its goods on importation by some other contracting party, such a claim should be based on the classification of the latter, i.e. the importing country's tariff.

5.14 The Panel noted in this respect that "dimension lumber" as defined by Canada was a concept extraneous to the Japanese Tariff. It was a standard applied by the Canadian industry which appeared to have some equivalent in the United States and in Japan itself, but it could not be considered for that reason alone as a category for tariff classification purposes, nor did it belong to any internationally accepted customs classification. The Panel concluded therefore that reliance by Canada on the concept of dimension lumber was not an appropriate basis for establishing "likeness" of products under Article I:1 of the General Agreement.

5.15 At the same time, the Panel felt unable to examine the Canadian complaint in a broader context, as Canada had declared expressly that the issue before the Panel should not be confused by broadening the scope of the Panel's examination beyond 'dimension lumber' to planed lumber generally. Canada's compliant was limited to the specific product known in North America, and also in Japan, as dimension lumber. Canada did not contend that different lumber species *per se* should be considered like products, regardless of the product-form they might take (see para. 3.15 above). Thus there appeared to be no basis for examining the issue raised by Canada in the general context of the Japanese tariff classification.

5.16 In these circumstances the Panel was not in a position to pursue further the questions relating to the concept of "like products" in the framework of Article I:1 of the General Agreement.

VI. CONCLUSIONS

6.1 In the light of the considerations set out in Section V above, the Panel could not establish that the tariff treatment of Canadian dimension lumber applied by Japan under its tariff number 4407.10-110 was inconsistent with Article I:1 of the General Agreement.

UNITED STATES—SECTION 337 OF THE TARIFF ACT OF 1930

Report of the Panel adopted on November 7, 1989
BISD 36S/345

II. FACTUAL ASPECTS

(i) Section 337

* * *

2.2 Under Section 337 of the United States Tariff Act of 1930 unfair methods of competition and unfair acts in the importation of articles into the United States, or in their sale, are unlawful if these unfair acts or methods of competition have the effect or tendency to (i) destroy or to substantially injure an industry efficiently and economically operated in the United States, (ii) prevent the establishment of such an industry, or (iii) restrain or monopolise trade and commerce in the United States. The unfair acts and methods of competition in question include the importation or sale of goods that infringe valid United States patents. Section 337a specifically applies Section 337 [sic] to the importation or sale of products produced abroad by a process covered by a United States patent. Since if was revised in the Trade Act of 1974, the majority of investigations under the Section 337 have concerned alleged infringements of patents. The text of Section 337 as of October 1987 is reproduced at Annex I to this report.

2.3 Remedies available under Section 337, in the event of a violation of the Section, consist of orders excluding the articles concerned from importation into the United States (exclusion orders) and/or cease and desist orders directing parties violating Section 337 to stop the act or method of competition found to be unfair. The exclusion order may be a general order covering all imports that, in a patent-based case, infringe the United States patent in question, or may be limited to goods produced by a respondent in the case.

(ii) The USITC and the Decision-making Process in Section 337 Cases

2.4 Investigations under Section 337 are carried out by the United States International Trade Commission (USITC). The USITC is an independent administrative agency of the United States Government. The USITC is not created as a court under Article III of the United States Constitution, but is authorised and directed by Congress to conduct proceedings under Section 337 which are similar to court proceedings. Section 337 proceedings are subject to the Administrative Procedure Act, which governs similar "quasi-judicial proceedings" conducted by numerous agencies of the United States Federal Government.

* * *

V. FINDINGS

(i) Scope of Findings

5.1 The Panel's terms of reference refer both to the application of Section 337 in general and to its application in the case concerning Certain Aramid Fibre which promoted the European Economic Community to submit its complaint to the CONTRACTING PARTIES. During the course of the Panel's proceedings, the parties to the Certain Aramid Fibre case reached a settlement (see paragraph 2.9 above), and thereafter the Community withdrew its request to the Panel to make findings in respect of that case. The Panel therefore limited its examination to Section 337 as such, plus the related Section 337a which the Council clearly intended to be covered by the Panel's term of reference since it was the provision applicable in the Certain Aramid Fibre case. (Hereinafter references to Section 337 should therefore be understood as references to both Section 337 and Section 337a.)

5.2 During the course of the Panel's work, Section 337 was amended by the Omnibus Trade and Competitiveness Act of 1988. The Panel's findings are based on Section 337 as it was at the time that the Panel was established by the Council, in October 1987. A summary of the main changes made to Section 337 by the 1988 Act is contained in Annex II to this report.

5.3 Section 337 is not limited to patent disputes; indeed, except in Section 337a, it does not even mention patents but merely speaks of "unfair methods of competition and unfair acts in the importation of articles into the United States". It has also been used in disputes concerning alleged infringement by imported products of other United States intellectual property rights, including trademarks and copyrights, as well as in disputes outside the field of intellectual property. While many of the observations that follow may be relevant to such cases as well, the complaint in this case, as well as the submissions of the parties, concentrated on the application of Section 337 to patent-based cases, and the Panel's findings and conclusions are limited to such cases.

5.4 The central and undisputed facts before the Panel are that, in patent infringement cases, proceedings before the USITC under Section 337 are only applicable to imported products alleged to infringe a United States patent; and that these proceedings are different, in a number of respects, from those applying before a federal district court when a product of United States origin is challenged on the grounds of patent infringement. The Community maintained that the differences between the two proceedings are such that the treatment accorded to imported products is less favorable than that accorded to like products of United States origin, inconsistently with Article III:4 of the General Agreement, and that this less favorable treatment cannot be justified under Article XX(d) of the General Agreement. The United States maintained that Section 337 is justifiable under Article XX(d) and, in any event, is not inconsistent with Article III:4 since it does not accord imported products less favorable treatment than that accorded to like products of United States origin.

5.5 The United States suggested that the scope of the complaint was confined to matters of legal procedure, and that the issues raised by the Community concerning *in rem* general exclusion orders and the possibility of imported products being subject to simultaneous proceedings under Section 337 and in federal district courts are not matters of procedure. However, the Panel noted that its terms of reference refer without limitation to "the different rules applicable under Section 337" to which imported products are subject. Accordingly, it determined that these issues fall within its terms of reference. The term "procedure" is used hereinafter in a broad sense that encompasses these issues.

5.6 In its deliberations, the Panel took into account the Report of the Panel on United States Imports of Certain Automotive Springs Assemblies (BISD 30S/107), in the light of the understanding on which it had been adopted by the Council that its adoption "shall not foreclose future examination of the use of Section 337 to deal with patent infringement cases from the point of view of consistency with Articles III and XX of the General Agreement" (C/M/168, item 7).

(ii) Relevant Provisions of the General Agreement

5.7 The main provisions invoked by the parties to the dispute are Article III:4 and Article XX(d). The relevant part of *Article III:4* reads:

> "The products of the territory of any contracting party imported into the territory of any other contracting party shall be accorded treatment no less favorable than that accorded to like products of national origin in respect of all laws, regulations and requirements affecting their internal sale, offering for sale, purchase, transportation, distribution or use."

This provision is supplemented by an *interpretative note*, the relevant part of which reads:

> ". . . any law, regulation or requirement . . . which applies to an imported product and to the like domestic product and is . . . enforced in the case of the imported product at the time or point of importation, is . . . subject to the provisions of Article III."

The relevant part of *Article XX(d)* reads:

> "Subject to the requirement that such measures are not applied in a manner which would constitute a means of arbitrary or unjustifiable discrimination between countries where the same conditions prevail, or a disguised restriction on international trade, nothing in this Agreement shall be construed to prevent the adoption or enforcement by any contracting party of measures: . . . (d) necessary to secure compliance with laws or regulations which are not inconsistent with the provisions of this Agreement, including those relating to . . . the protection of patents, trade marks and copyrights. . . "

(iii) Relation of Article III to Article XX(d)

5.8 The parties to the dispute agreed that Article III:4 applies to substantive patent law, since such law affects the "internal sale, offering for sale, purchase, transportation or use" of imported and domestic products. They also agreed that the consistency of the substantive provisions of United States patent law with the General Agreement is not at issue. Further, the parties agreed that Section 337, when applied in cases of alleged patent infringement, is a means to secure compliance with United States patent law in respect of imported products. They disagreed, however, on the question of whether a measure to secure compliance with patent laws—in contrast to the substantive patent law itself—is covered by Article III:4. In the view of the United States, measures to secure compliance with patent legislation are covered only by Article XX(d). The Community took the position that Article III:4 requires national treatment also for procedures designed to enforce internal legislation, and that Article XX(d) provides for an exception to be considered only after conduct inconsistent with another provision of the General Agreement has been established.

5.9 The Panel noted that Article XX is entitled "General Exceptions" and that the central phase in the introductory clause reads: "nothing in this Agreement shall be construed to prevent the adoption or enforcement . . . of measures . . . " . Article XX(d) thus provides for a limited and conditional exception from obligations under other provisions. The Panel therefore concluded that Article XX(d) applies only to measures inconsistent with another provision of the General Agreement, and that, consequently, the application of Section 337 has to be examined first in the light of Article III:4. If any inconsistencies with Article III:4 were found, the Panel would then examine whether they could be justified under Article XX(d).

(iv) Article III:4

(a) Meaning of "Laws, Regulations and Requirements" in Article III:4

5.10 The Panel then examined Section 337 in the light of Article III:4. The Panel first addressed the issue of whether only substantive laws, regulations and requirements or also procedural laws, regulations and requirements can be regarded as "affecting" the internal sale of imported products. The positions of the United States and the Community on this were different (paragraphs 3.6 to 3.10 above). The Panel noted that the text of Article III:4 makes no distinction between substantive and procedural laws, regulations or requirements and it was not aware of anything in the drafting history that suggests that such a distinction should be made. A previous Panel had found that "the selection of the word 'affecting' would imply . . . . . . that the drafters of the Article intended to cover in paragraph 4 not only the laws and regulations which directly governed the conditions of sale or purchase but also any laws or regulations which might adversely modify the conditions of competition between the domestic and imported products on the internal market."[1] In the Panel's view, enforcement procedures cannot be separated from the substantive provisions they serve to enforce. If the procedural provisions of internal law were not covered by Article III:4, contracting parties could escape the national treatment standard by enforcing substantive law, itself meeting the national treatment standard, through procedures less favorable to imported products than to like products of national origin. The interpretation suggested by the United States would therefore defeat the purpose of Article III, which is to ensure that internal measures "not be applied to imported or domestic products so as to afford protection to domestic production" (Article III:1). The fact that Section 337 is used as a means for the enforcement of United States patent law at the *border* does not provide an escape from the applicability of Article III:4; the interpretative note to Article III states that any law, regulation or requirement affecting the internal sale of products that is enforced in the case of the imported product at the time or point of importation is nevertheless subject to the provisions of Article III. Nor could the applicability of Article III:4 be denied on the ground that most of the procedures in the case before the Panel are applied to persons rather than products, since the factor determining whether persons might be susceptible to Section 337 proceedings or federal district court procedures is the source of the challenged products, that is whether they are of United States origin or imported. For these reasons, the Panel found that the procedures under Section 337 come within the concept of "laws, regulations and requirements" affecting the internal sale of imported products, as set out in Article III of the General Agreement.

(b) The "No Less Favorable" Treatment Standard of Article III:4

5.11 The Panel noted that, as far as the issues before it are concerned, the "no less favorable" treatment requirement set out in Article III:4, is unqualified. These words are to be found throughout the General Agreement and later agreements negotiated in the GATT framework as an expression of the underlying principle of equality of treatment of imported products as compared to the treatment given either to other foreign products, under the most favored nation standard, or to domestic products, under the national treatment standard of Article III. The

[1] Panel on Italian Discrimination Against Imported Agricultural Machinery (BISD 7S/60, paragraph 12), adopted on October 23, 1958.

words "treatment no less favorable" in paragraph 4 call for effective equality of opportunities for imported products in respect of the application of laws, regulations and requirements affecting the internal sale, offering for sale, purchase, transportation, distribution or use of products. This clearly sets a minimum permissible standard as a basis. On the one hand, contracting parties may apply to imported products different formal legal requirements if doing so would accord imported products more favorable treatment. On the other hand, it also has to be recognised that there may be cases where application of formally identical legal provisions would in practice accord less favorable treatment to imported products and a contracting party might thus have to apply different legal provisions to imported products to ensure that the treatment accorded them is in fact no less favorable. For these reasons, the mere fact that imported products are subject under Section 337 to legal provisions that are different from those applying to products of national origin is in itself not conclusive in establishing inconsistency with Article III:4. In such cases, it has to be assessed whether or not such differences in the legal provisions applicable do or do not accord to imported products less favorable treatment. Given that the underlying objective is to guarantee equality of treatment, it is incumbent on the contracting party applying differential treatment to show that, in spite of such differences, the no less favorable treatment standard of Article III is met.

5.12 The Panel noted the differing views of the parties on how an assessment should be made as to whether the differences between Section 337 and federal district court procedures do or do not accord imported products less favorable treatment than that accorded to products of United States origin (paragraphs 3.15-3.20 above). In brief, the United States believed that this determination could only be made on the basis of an examination of the *actual results* of past Section 337 cases. It would follow from this reasoning that any unfavorable elements of treatment of imported products could be offset by more favorable elements of treatment, provided that the results, as shown in past cases, have not been less favorable. The Community's interpretation of Article III:4 would require that Section 337 not be *capable* of according imported products less favorable treatment; elements of less and more favorable treatment could thus only be offset against each other to the extent that they always would arise in the same cases and necessarily would have an offsetting influence on each other.

5.13 The Panel examined these arguments carefully. It noted that a previous Panel had found that the purpose of the first sentence of

Article III:2, dealing with internal taxes and other internal charges, is to protect "expectations on the competitive relationship between imported and domestic products".[1] Article III:4, which is the parallel provision of Article III dealing with the "non-charge" elements of internal legislation, has to be construed as serving the same purpose. Article III:4 would not serve this purpose if the United States interpretation were adopted, since a law, regulation or requirement could then only be challenged in GATT after the event as a means of rectifying less favorable treatment of imported products rather than as a means of forestalling it. In any event, the Panel doubted the feasibility of an approach that would require it to be demonstrated that differences between procedures under Section 337 and those in federal district courts had actually caused, in a given case or cases, less favorable treatment. The Panel therefore considered that, in order to establish whether the "no less favorable" treatment standard of Article III:4 is met, it had to assess whether or not Section 337 in itself may lead to the application to imported products of treatment less favorable than that accorded to products of United States origin. It noted that this approach is in accordance with previous practice of the CONTRACTING PARTIES in applying Article III, which has been to base their decisions on the distinctions made by the laws, regulations or requirements themselves and on their potential impact rather than on the actual consequences for specific imported products.[2]

5.14 The Panel further found that the "no less favorable" treatment requirement of Article III:4 has to be understood as applicable to each individual case of imported products. The Panel rejected any notion of balancing more favorable treatment of some imported products against less favorable treatment of other imported products. If this notion were accepted, it would entitle a contracting party to derogate from the no less favorable treatment obligation in one case, or indeed in respect of one contracting party, on the ground that it accords more favorable

[1] Report of Panel on United States—Taxes on Petroleum and Certain Imported Substances (L/6175, paragraph 5.1.9), adopted by the Council on June 17, 1987.

[2] For example: Working Party on Brazilian Internal Taxes (BISD II/184-5, paragraph 13-16); Panel on Italian Discrimination against Imported Agricultural Machinery (BISD 7S/63-64, paragraphs 11-12); Panel on EEC—Measures on Animal Feed Proteins (BISD 25S/65, paragraph 4.10); Panel on Canada—Administration of the Foreign Investment Review Act (BISD 30S/167, paragraph 6.6); Panel on the United States—Taxes on Petroleum and Certain Imported Substances (L/6175, paragraphs 5.1.1-5.1.9).

treatment in some other case, or to another contracting party. Such an interpretation would lead to great uncertainty about the conditions of competition between imported and domestic products and thus defeat the purposes of Article III.

(c) Appraisal of Section 337 in Terms of Article III:4

Contentions by the United States that More Favorable Treatment is Accorded to Imported Products

5.15 The United States contended [paragraphs 3.47-3.54; see also paragraphs 2.8(e), (i), (j) and (k)] that Section 337 accords imported products more favorable treatment than that accorded to domestic products in district court proceedings because of:

— the substantive economic elements relating to injury and industry that a Section 337 complainant has to prove and that do not have to be proved in patent litigation in federal district courts;

— the possibility that relief under Section 337 might be modified or not applied on public interest or policy grounds, which possibility does not exist in federal district courts; and

— certain procedural differences from federal district court procedures that accord Section 337 respondents more favorable treatment.

The Panel examined whether these elements of claimed more favorable treatment could within the meaning of Article III:4 offset any elements of less favorable treatment of imported products alleged by the Community.

5.16 As has already been stated above, an element of more favorable treatment would only be relevant if it would always accompany and offset an element of differential treatment causing less favorable treatment. The Panel had no difficulty in recognising that the economic requirements and the possibility of denial or limitation of relief on public interest or policy grounds could decisively influence the outcome of certain Section 337 cases in favor of imported products, as might the requirement on a complainant to make a *prima facie* case in a default situation, and that no equivalent advantages are enjoyed by defendants in federal district court litigation in respect of products of United States origin.[1] However, the Panel found, on the one hand, that these requirements may involve the respondent in litigation, defense and discovery of business secrets unrelated to the underlying patent issue; and, on the other hand, there is no reason to believe that such dispositive influences would always operate in each individual case where a negative effect on the respondent might result from the operation of an element of less favorable treatment claimed by the Community. Further, the Panel noted that, in each case over which both the USITC and federal district courts have jurisdiction, the complainant has the choice whether to proceed before the USITC or before the regular courts (see paragraph 5.18 below).

5.17 The Panel noted that some of the procedural advantages that, according to the United States (paragraph 3.54), are given to respondents could operate in all cases. The Panel also recognised that the substantive economic requirements put procedural burdens not only on the respondent but also on the complainant, which has the burden of proof on these matters, and that these procedural burdens could operate in all cases. The Panel took these factors into account to the extent that they might be capable of exerting an offsetting influence in each individual case of less favorable treatment resulting from an element cited by the Community.

Contentions by the Community that Less Favorable Treatment is Accorded to Imported Products

5.18 In cases concerning imported products over which both federal district courts and the USITC have jurisdiction, the complainant has the choice of which forum to use, or possibly to initiate a complaint in both fora; no equivalent choice of forum is available to a plaintiff in a case concerning products of United States origin. This option was referred to on numerous occasions by the Community and by third contracting parties making submissions. The Panel found that, given the differences between the proceedings of the USITC and of federal courts, to provide the complainant with the choice of forum where imported products are concerned and to provide no corresponding choice where domestically-

[1] The Panel noted that several of the elements said to give advantages to respondents—notably the requirement that a complainant must show injury to an industry and the requirement that a complainant must show that the industry was being "efficiently and economically operated"—were repealed, at least as far as certain intellectual property based cases are concerned, by the Omnibus Trade and Competitiveness Act adopted by the United States in the Summer of 1988 (see Annex II).

produced products are concerned is in itself less favorable treatment of imported products and is therefore inconsistent with Article III:4. It is also a reason why in practice Section 337 is more likely to be employed in those cases where the specific elements that might accord less favorable treatment to imported products are significant. The complainant will tend to avoid recourse to Section 337 in cases where elements of more favorable treatment of the respondent than that accorded in federal district court litigation might play a role, for example where public interest or policy considerations might be expected to intervene.

5.19 The Panel considered the specific differences between Section 337 proceedings and those in federal district courts referred to by the Community to assess whether they accord less favorable treatment to imported products than that accorded to products of United States origin in patent-based cases:

— *Time limits* (paragraphs 2.8(f) and (n) and 3.29-3.34). The Panel found that the relatively short and fixed time-limits for the completion of proceedings under Section 337 could put the respondent in a significantly less favorable position than it would have been in before a federal district court where no fixed time-limits apply, both because the complainant has a greater opportunity than the respondent to prepare his case before bringing the complaint and because defense in general benefits from delay. It is true that the short time-limits might benefit the respondent in cases where a negative finding is made, since any damage to his business resulting from the uncertainty generated by the litigation would be ended more quickly, but this does not justify the less favorable treatment in other cases. The Panel did not accept the argument of the United States that the appropriate comparison with Section 337 time-limits is the time taken for issuing preliminary injunctions in federal district courts. A Section 337 final order is not comparable to a preliminary injunction since it is not subject to review by the same forum nor is it accompanied by the safeguards usually attached to preliminary orders to protect the legitimate interests of defendants. The Panel noted the arguments of the United States that a complainant was required to provide more detailed information in a Section 337 complaint—a point contested by the Community—and that an additional ten days was given to foreign respondents for service by mail, but concluded that these factors could not significantly offset the disadvantage that the respondent could suffer from the tighter Section 337 time-limits.

— *Inadmissibility of counterclaims* (paragraphs 2.8(h) and 3.21-3.23). The Panel found that the inability of the respondent to make counterclaims in a Section 337 action—a right that the defendant has in federal district court proceedings—deprives the respondent of an option that is available where products of United States origin rather than imported products are concerned. Moreover, the existence of this option, which applies to unrelated as well as related counterclaims, could act as a dissuasive factor on a potential complainant in filing a complaint in the first place. The Panel noted the observation of the United States that many of the points that might be the subject of a related counterclaim in court proceedings could be made in USITC proceedings by way of defense. However, the complainant runs no risk of an affirmative adverse finding on these points, or of adverse findings or need to litigate in respect of unrelated issues, and in the Panel's view this gives complainants before the USITC advantages that might well be significant. The Panel therefore found that the non-availability of the opportunity to raise counterclaims constitutes less favorable treatment of imported products within the meaning of Article III:4.

— *In rem exclusion orders* (paragraphs 2.8(l) and (m) and 3.43-3.44). The Community and some third contracting parties raised two issues concerning *in rem* exclusion orders. One of these issues—enforcement of orders—concerns both *limited* exclusion orders (orders directed only to products produced by respondents and found to be infringing—the more common type of exclusion order) and *general* exclusion orders (orders applicable to products found to be infringing produced by any person). While such exclusion orders are automatically enforced by the United States Customs Service, enforcement of an injunction ordered by a federal district court, the equivalent relief in respect of products of United States origin, requires individual proceedings brought by the successful plaintiff. The Panel found that this difference results in less favorable treatment of imported products within the meaning of Article III:4 of the GATT. In respect of the second issue, which concerns *general* exclusion orders only, the Panel noted that relief against persons other than the parties to a proceeding is not generally available to successful plaintiffs in action against domestic infringers. This difference therefore results in less favorable treatment of imported products within the meaning of Article III:4 of the General Agreement.

— *Double proceedings* (paragraphs 2.8(d) (iii) and 3.41-3.42). The Community raised the question of the possibility of simultaneous proceedings. Canada and Korea raised similar points (paragraphs 4.2 and 4.5). Under United States law, where a product patent is involved and the jurisdictional requirements of federal district court litigation and Section 337 investigations are met, imported products might be faced with double proceedings under Section 337 and before federal district courts, whereas like products of United States origin can only be challenged in proceedings in federal district courts.[1] The Panel found that, while the likelihood of having to defend imported products in two fora is small, the existence of the possibility is inherently less favorable than being faced with having to conduct a defense in only one of those fora. It therefore subjects imported products to less favorable treatment within the meeting of Article III:4 of the General Agreement.

— *Treatment of Confidential Information* (paragraphs 2.8(g) and 3.24-3.28). Apart from what has been said in paragraph 5.16, the Panel did not find that the techniques used under Section 337 to protect confidential information are effectively different from those generally employed in federal district courts in the United States. It therefore did not find that they disadvantage imported products.

— *Decision-making under Section 337* (paragraphs 2.4-2.5 and 3.35-3.40). The Community contended that USITC Commissioners are less qualified than federal district court judges to adjudicate legal issues in patent disputes. The Panel examined this contention but did not find that the difference in decision-makers between the USITC and federal district courts is such as to lead intrinsically to less-favorable treatment of imported products in respect of patent adjudication. The Panel noted also that there is at least a nominal difference in the standard used by the Court of Appeals for the Federal Circuit to review, on the one hand, findings of fact by the USITC, which like findings by juries in federal district courts can only be overturned if not supported by "substantial evidence", and on the other hand findings of fact by federal judges, which can be set aside if found to be "clearly erroneous". However, the Panel did *not* find that this difference in

[1] As a result of the Omnibus Trade and Competitiveness Act of 1988, this possibility now also applies where process patents are concerned. See Annex II for details.

the standard of review in itself results in less favorable treatment of imported products in terms of Article III:4.

(d) Summary of Findings Under Article III:4

5.20 The Panel *found* that Section 337, inconsistently with Article III:4 of the General Agreement, accords to imported products alleged to infringe United States patents treatment less favorable than that accorded under federal district court procedures to like products of United States origin as a result of the following factors:

(i) the availability to complainants of a choice of forum in which to challenge imported products, whereas no corresponding choice is available to challenge products of United States origin;

(ii) the potential disadvantage to producers or importers of challenged products of foreign origin resulting from the tight and fixed time-limits in proceedings under Section 337, when no comparable time-limits apply to producers of challenged products of United States origin;

(iii) the non-availability of opportunities in Section 337 proceedings to raise counterclaims, as is possible in proceedings in federal district court;

(iv) the possibility that general exclusion orders may result from proceedings brought before the USITC under Section 337, given that no comparable remedy is available against infringing products of United States origin;

(v) the automatic enforcement of exclusion orders by the United States Customs Service, when injunctive relief obtainable in federal court in respect of infringing products of United States origin requires for its enforcement individual proceedings brought by the successful plaintiff;

(vi) the possibility that producers or importers of challenged products of foreign origin may have to defend their products both before the USITC and in federal district court, whereas no corresponding exposure exists with respect to products of United States origin.

5.21 The Panel considered whether all these differences of treatment could be traced back to one common cause, this being the structure of the USITC which is fundamentally not a court of law but an administrative agency, and whether this structural difference could be said to entail in itself treatment incompatible with the requirements of Article III. The Panel however reached no conclusion in this respect, as this question had not been raised in such general terms by the Community.

(v) Article XX(d)

(a) The Conditions Attached to the Use of Article XX(d)

5.22 Having found the elements of Section 337 summarised in paragraph 5.20 above to be inconsistent with Article III:4, the Panel considered whether these inconsistencies can be justified under Article XX(d). The Panel noted that the parties to the dispute agreed that, for the purpose of Article XX(d), Section 337 can be considered as "measures . . . to secure compliance with" United States patent law. It then examined whether, in respect of the elements of Section 337 found to be inconsistent with Article III:4 of the General Agreement, the conditions specified in Article XX(d) to justify measures otherwise inconsistent with the GATT are met. These are:

— that the "laws or regulations" with which compliance is being secured are themselves "not inconsistent" with the General Agreement;

— that the measures are "necessary to secure compliance" with those laws or regulations;

— that the measures are "not applied in a manner which would constitute a means of arbitrary or unjustifiable discrimination between countries where the same conditions prevail, or a disguised restriction on international trade".

5.23 The Panel noted that each of these conditions must be met if an inconsistency with another GATT provision is to be justifiable under Article XX(d). A measure which does not meet any of these conditions, for example the condition that it must be "necessary to secure compliance" with a law consistent with the GATT, cannot be justified under Article XX(d).

5.24 The Panel noted that in the dispute before it the "laws or regulations" with which Section 337 secures compliance are the substantive patent laws of the United States and that the conformity of these laws with the General Agreement is not being challenged. The Panel then considered whether the inconsistencies with Article III:4 are "necessary" to secure compliance with these laws, this being the issue on which the discussion had mainly concentrated.

(b) The "Necessary to Secure Compliance" Condition

5.25 The Panel noted that the United States and the Community interpret the term "necessary" differently. They differ as to whether it requires the use of the least trade-restrictive measure available. They also differ as to whether "necessity" to use measures that accord less favorable treatment to imported products can be created by a contracting party's choice, in its national legislation, of enforcement measures against domestic products that would not be effective against imports (paragraphs 3.59—3.61).

5.26 It was clear to the Panel that a contracting party cannot justify a measure inconsistent with another GATT provision as "necessary" in terms of Article XX(d) if an alternative measure which it could reasonably be expected to employ and which is not inconsistent with other GATT provisions is available to it. By the same token, in cases where a measure consistent with other GATT provisions is not reasonably available, a contracting party is bound to use, among the measures reasonably available to it, that which entails the least degree of inconsistency with other GATT provisions. The Panel wished to make it clear that this does not mean that a contracting party could be asked to change its substantive patent law or its desired level of enforcement of that law, provided that such law and such level of enforcement are the same for imported and domestically-produced products. However, it does mean that, if a contracting party could reasonably secure that level of enforcement in a manner that is not inconsistent with other GATT provisions, it would be required to do so.

5.27 Bearing in mind the foregoing and that it is up to the contracting party seeking to justify measures under Article XX(d) to demonstrate that those measures are "necessary" within the meaning of that provision[1], the Panel considered whether the inconsistencies that it had found with Article III:4 can be justified as "necessary" in terms of Article XX(d). The Panel first examined the argument of the United States that the Panel should consider not whether the individual elements of Sec-

[1] See Report of the Panel on Canada—Administration of the Foreign Investment Review Act, paragraph 5.20 (BISD 30S/164), adopted on February 7, 1984.

tion 337 are "necessary" but rather whether Section 337 as a system is "necessary" for the enforcement of United States patent laws (paragraphs 3.57-3.58). The Panel did not accept this contention since it would permit contracting parties to introduce GATT inconsistencies that are not necessary simply by making them part of a scheme which contained elements that are necessary. In the view of the Panel, what has to be justified as "necessary" under Article XX(d) is each of the inconsistencies with another GATT Article found to exist, i.e. in this case, whether the differences between Section 337 and federal district court procedures that result in less favorable treatment of imported products within the meaning of Article III:4, as outlined above (paragraph 5.20), are necessary.

(c) The Necessity of the Specific Inconsistencies with Article III:4

5.28 The United States suggested that Section 337 can be justified because, under United States law, it provides the only means of enforcement of United States patent rights against imports of products manufactured abroad by means of a process patented in the United States (paragraph 3.62). The Panel considered that, even if it were accepted that a different scheme for imports alleged to infringe process patents is necessary, this could not in itself justify as "necessary" in terms of Article XX(d) any of the specific inconsistencies with Article III:4 summarised in paragraph 5.20 above. In any event, the Panel did not consider that a different scheme for imports alleged to infringe process patents is necessary, since many countries grant to their civil courts jurisdiction over imports of products manufactured abroad under processes protected by patents of the importing country. The Panel noted that, in the 1988 Omnibus Trade and Competitiveness Act, the United States has in fact amended its law to this effect (see Annex II).

5.29 The United States also suggested that certain features of Section 337 are necessary in order to permit Presidential review, which is in the interests of respondents (paragraph 3.66). The Panel did not believe that this provided an argument for necessity in terms of Article XX(d), since Presidential review is not necessary in order to secure compliance with United States patent legislation; it is not, of course, available in United States patent litigation involving challenged products of domestic origin.

5.30 The United States suggested that Section 337 is needed because of difficulties with service of process on and enforcement of judgments against foreign manufacturers (paragraphs 3.63-3.65). As regards service of process, the difference in procedures between Section 337 and federal district courts was not itself alleged to be inconsistent with any GATT provision; and the Panel did not see why any of the inconsistencies with Article III:4 are a necessary accompaniment of arrangements for effective service of process where imported products are concerned. However, as noted in paragraph 5.19 above, the Panel found the differences in procedures for the enforcement of judgments to be inconsistent with Article III:4 in that they provide for the possibility of *in rem* general exclusion orders against imported products when no equivalent remedy is available against products of United States origin; and that they provide for automatic customs enforcement of exclusion orders while the enforcement of a court injunction requires the initiation of proceedings by the successful party.

5.31 The United States stressed the importance to its system of enforcement of *in rem* orders, and the Panel considered this question at some length. The Panel agreed with the United States that taking action against infringing products at the source, that is at the point of their production, would generally be more difficult in respect of imported products than in respect of products of national origin: imported products are produced outside the jurisdiction of national enforcement bodies and it is seldom feasible to secure enforcement of the rulings of a court of the country of importation by local courts in the country of production. *In personam* action against importers would not in all cases be an adequate substitute for action against the manufacturer, not only because importers might be very numerous and not easily brought into a single judicial proceeding, but also, and more importantly, because as soon as activities of known importers were stopped it would often be possible for a foreign manufacturer to find another importer. For these reasons the Panel believed that there could be an objective need in terms of Article XX(d) to apply limited *in rem* exclusion orders to imported products, although no equivalent remedy is applied against domestically-produced products.

5.32 A limited *in rem* order applying to imported products can thus be justified, for the reasons presented in the previous paragraph, as the functional equivalent of an injunction enjoining named domestic manufacturers. However, these reasons do not justify as "necessary" in terms of Article XX(d) the inconsistency with Article III:4 found in respect of general exclusion orders; this is that such orders apply to products produced by persons who have not been named as respondents in the litigation, while no equivalent measure applicable to non-parties is available where products of United States origin are concerned. The

United States informed the Panel that the situations which under Section 337 could justify a general exclusion order against imported products are a widespread pattern of unauthorised use of the patented invention or process and a reason to infer that manufacturers other than respondents to the investigation might enter the United States market with infringing products. However, the Panel saw no reason why these situations could not also occur in respect of products produced in the United States. Nevertheless, the Panel did not rule out entirely that there could sometimes be objective reasons why general *in rem* exclusion orders might be "necessary" in terms of Article XX(d) against imported products even though no equivalent measure was needed against products of United States origin. For example, in the case of imported products it might be considerably more difficult to identify the source of infringing products or to prevent circumvention of orders limited to the products of named person, than in the case of products of United States origin. Of course, the United States could bring the provision of general exclusion orders into consistency with Article III:4 by providing for the application in like situations of equivalent measures against products of United States origin.

5.33 As noted above, the Panel found an inconsistency with Article III:4 in the fact that Section 337 exclusion orders are automatically enforced by the Customs Service, whereas the enforcement of injunctions against products of United States origin requires the successful plaintiff to bring individual proceedings. However, in this case the Panel accepted the argument of necessity in terms of Article XX(d). A United States manufacturer which has been enjoined by a federal district court order can normally be expected to comply with the injunction, because it would know that failure to do so would incur the risk of serious penalties resulting from a contempt proceeding brought by the successful plaintiff. An injunction should therefore normally suffice to stop enjoined activity without the need for subsequent action to enforce it. As far as imported products are concerned, enforcement at the border by the customs administration of exclusion orders can be considered as a means necessary to render such orders effective.

5.34 The Panel considered the argument of the United States that many of the procedural aspects of Section 337 reflect the need to provide expeditious prospective relief against infringing imports (paragraph 3.66). The Panel understood this argument to be based on the notion that, in respect of infringing imports, there would be greater difficulty than in respect of infringing products of domestic origin in collecting awards of damages for past infringement, because foreign manufacturers are outside the jurisdiction of national courts and importers might have little by way of assets. In the Panel's view, given the issues at stake in typical patent suits, this argument could only provide a justification for rapid *preliminary* or conservatory action against imported products, combined with the necessary safeguards to protect the legitimate interests of importers in the event that the products prove not to be infringing. The tight time-limits for the *conclusion* of Section 337 proceedings, when no comparable time-limits apply in federal district court, and the other features of Section 337 inconsistent with Article III:4 that serve to facilitate the expeditious completion of Section 337 proceedings, such as the inadmissibility of counterclaims, cannot be justified as "necessary" on this basis.

5.35 The United States did not advance, nor was the Panel aware of, any other arguments that might justify as necessary any of the elements of Section 337 that had been found to be inconsistent with Article III:4 of the General Agreement. On the basis of the preceding review and analysis, the Panel *found* that the system of determining allegations of violation of United States patent rights under Section 337 of the United States Tariff Act cannot be justified as necessary within the meaning of Article XX(d) so as to permit an exception to the basic obligation contained in Article III:4 of the General Agreement. The Panel, however, repeats that, as indicated in paragraphs 5.32 and 5.33 above, some of the inconsistencies with Article III:4 of individual aspects of procedures under Section 337 could be justified under Article XX(d) in certain circumstances.

VI. CONCLUSIONS

6.1 To avoid any misunderstanding as to the scope and implications of the above findings, the Panel stresses that neither Article III:4 nor Article XX(d) puts obligations on contracting parties specifying the level of protection that they should accord to patents or the effectiveness of procedures to enforce such protection. The only task entrusted to the Panel was to see whether the treatment accorded to imported products under Section 337 is compatible with the rules of the General Agreement.

6.2 The Panel also wishes to state that, although it found that some elements of Section 337 are inconsistent with the GATT obligations of the United States, it found no evidence that these elements had been deliberately introduced so as to discriminate against foreign products.

6.3 On the basis of the findings set out in paragraphs 5.1—5.35 above the Panel *concluded* that Section 337 of the United States Tariff Act of 1930 is inconsistent with Article III:4, in that it accords to imported products challenged as infringing United States patents treatment less favorable than the treatment accorded to products of United States origin similarly challenged, and that these inconsistencies cannot be justified in all respects under Article XX(d).

6.4 The Panel *recommends* that the CONTRACTING PARTIES request the United States to bring its procedures applied in patent infringement cases bearing on imported products into conformity with its obligations under the General Agreement.

DD74/21

UNIV DUNELM

REPUBLIC OF KOREA—RESTRICTIONS ON IMPORTS OF BEEF— COMPLAINT BY THE UNITED STATES

Report of the Panel adopted on November 7, 1989
BISD 36S/268

FINDINGS AND CONCLUSIONS

110. The Panel noted that the United States claimed that the Republic of Korea had banned imports of beef between 1984/85 and 1988, and since August 1988 maintained quantitative restrictions and other measures on beef imports, in violation of the provisions of Article XI:1. The United States further claimed that the LPMO was an import monopoly that applied mark-ups on imported beef in contravention of the provisions of Article II. The Panel noted that while Korea had claimed the provisions of Article XVIII:B as a general justification for its beef import restrictions, it had also stated that the measures introduced in 1984/85 had not been taken for balance-of-payments reasons. Furthermore, Korea claimed that the operations of the LPMO were consistent with the provisions of Articles II and XIII.

Article XI

111. The Panel considered that there were essentially two sets of restrictions on beef imports maintained by Korea:

(a) measures amounting to a virtual suspension of imports introduced in November 1984 and May 1985 and subsequently amended in August 1988. These measures were neither notified to, nor reviewed by, the Balance-of-Payments Committee;

(b) restrictions on beef existing since Korea's accession to the General Agreement in 1967, which were notified to, and reviewed by, the Balance-of-Payments Committee.

112. Article XI:1 did not permit the use of either import restrictions or import prohibitions; exemptions from this general proscription had to be specifically justified under other provisions of the General Agree-

ment. Korea claimed such justification under Article XVIII:B for the restrictions referred to in paragraph 111(b) above; this issue is examined in paragraphs 120-123 below.

113. In examining the measures in paragraph 111(a) above, the Panel noted that Korea's beef import measures introduced in 1984-1985 were taken for the purpose of protecting Korea's domestic cattle industry and not for balance-of-payments reasons, and were therefore not notified to the Balance-of-Payments Committee. Korea also had not notified the amended restrictions maintained since August 1988 to the Balance-of-Payments Committee. Korea did not contest that these measures were contrary to the provisions of Article XI:1. Moreover, Korea did not offer any justification for these measures under Article XI:2. The Panel concluded that the import measures and restrictions, introduced in 1984/85 and amended in 1988, were not consistent with the provisions of Article XI and were not taken for balance-of-payments reasons.

114. The Panel then examined the further claim by the *United States* that the existence, or use, of producer-controlled import monopolies to restrict imports was inconsistent with the provisions of Articles XI:1 and XVII. *Korea* contested that the existence of a producer-controlled import monopoly in itself constituted an additional barrier to trade. *The Panel* noted that the LPMO had been granted exclusive privileges as the sole importer of beef. As such, the LPMO had to comply with the provisions of the General Agreement applicable to state-trading enterprises, including those of Articles XI:1 and XVII.

115. Article XI:1 proscribed the use of "prohibitions or restrictions other than duties, taxes or other charges", including restrictions made effective through state-trading activities, but Article XVII permitted the establishment or maintenance of state-trading enterprises, including enterprises which had been granted exclusive or special privileges. The mere existence of producer-controlled import monopolies could not be considered as a separate import restriction inconsistent with the General Agreement. The Panel noted, however, that the activities of such enterprises had to conform to a number of rules contained in the General Agreement, including those of Article XVII and Article XI:1. The Panel had already found that the import restrictions presently administered by the LPMO violated the provisions of Article XI:1. As the rules of the General Agreement did not concern the organization or management of import monopolies but only their operations and effects on trade, the Panel concluded that the existence of a producer-controlled monopoly could not in itself be in violation of the General Agreement.

Article XVIII

(a) Procedural Aspects

116. The Panel examined Korea's contention that its import restrictions, referred to under paragraph 111(b) above, were justified under the provisions of Article XVIII:B. The Panel noted Korea's view that the compatibility with the General Agreement of Korea's import restrictions could not be challenged under Article XXIII because of the existence of special review procedures in paragraphs 12(b) and 12(d) of Article XVIII:B, and the adoption by the CONTRACTING PARTIES of the results of the paragraph 12(b) reviews in the Balance-of-Payments Committee. The Panel decided first to consider whether the consistency of restrictive measures with Article XVIII:B could be examined within the framework of Article XXIII.

117. The Panel considered the various arguments of the parties to the dispute concerning past deliberations by the CONTRACTING PARTIES on the exclusivity of special review procedures under the General Agreement. However, the Panel was not persuaded that any of these earlier deliberations in the GATT were directly applicable to the present dispute. Moreover, the Panel had a clear mandate to examine Korea's beef import restrictions under Article XXIII. The Panel's terms of reference, as agreed by Korea and the United States, and approved by the Council, required the Panel, however, to examine the beef import restrictions "in the light of the relevant GATT provisions", which included Article XVIII:B.

118. The Panel examined the drafting history of Article XXIII and Article XVIII, and noted that nothing was said about priority or exclusivity of procedures of either Article. The Panel observed that Article XVIII:12(b) provided for regular review of balance-of-payments restrictions by the CONTRACTING PARTIES. Article XVIII:12(d) specifically provided for consultations of balance-of-payments restrictions at the request of a contracting party where that party established a *prima facie* case that the restrictions were inconsistent with the provisions of Article XVIII:B or those of Article XIII, but the Article XVIII:12(d) provision had hitherto not been resorted to. In comparison, the wording of Article XXIII was all-embracing; it provided for dispute settlement procedures applicable to all relevant articles of the General Agreement, including Article XVIII:B in this case. Recourse to Article XXIII procedures could be had by all contracting parties. However, the Panel noted that

in GATT practice there were differences with respect to the procedures of Article XXIII and Article XVIII:B. The former provided for the detailed examination of individual measures by a panel of independent experts[37] whereas the latter provided for a general review of the country's balance-of-payments situation by a committee of government representatives.

119. It was the view of the Panel that excluding the possibility of bringing a complaint under Article XXIII against measures for which there was claimed balance-of-payments cover would unnecessarily restrict the application of the General Agreement. This did not preclude, however, resort to special review procedures under Article XVIII:B. Indeed, either procedure, that of Article XVIII:12(d) or Article XXIII, could have been pursued by the parties in this dispute. But as far as this Panel was concerned, the parties had chosen to proceed under Article XXIII.

(b) Justification for Restrictions

120. The Panel proceeded to examine Korea's Article XVIII:B justification for its import restrictions referred to in paragraph 111(b) above. The United States contended that the import restrictions on beef imposed for balance-of-payments reasons were not justified because Korea no longer had balance-of-payments problems. The Panel noted that Korea had maintained import restrictions on beef on balance-of-payments grounds since 1967. The Panel noted the condition in paragraph 9 of Article XVIII that "import restrictions instituted, maintained or intensified shall not exceed those necessary: (a) to forestall the threat of, or to stop, a serious decline in its monetary reserves, or (b) in the case of a contracting party with inadequate monetary reserves, to achieve a reasonable rate of increase in its reserves". The Panel noted further that paragraph 11 required the progressive relaxation of such restrictions "as conditions improve" and their elimination "when conditions no longer justify such maintenance".

121. Article XV:2 of the General Agreement provided that "[i]n all cases in which the CONTRACTING PARTIES are called upon to consider

[37] See paragraph 10 of 1979 Understanding on Notification, Consultation, Dispute Settlement and Surveillance (BISD 26S/212):

"It is agreed that if a contracting party invoking Article XXIII:2 requests the establishment of a panel to assist the CONTRACTING PARTIES to deal with the matter, the CONTRACTING PARTIES would decide on its establishment in accordance with standing practice."

or deal with problems concerning monetary reserves, balances of payments or foreign exchange arrangements, they shall consult fully with the International Monetary Fund." The latest full consultation concerning Korea's balance-of-payments situation in the Balance-of-Payments Committee had taken place in November 1987, the report of which had been adopted by the CONTRACTING PARTIES in February 1988. The next full consultation was scheduled for June 1989. The Panel considered that it should take into account the conclusions reached by the Balance-of-Payments Committee in 1987.

122. At the full consultation in the Balance-of-Payments Committee with Korea in November 1987, "[t]he prevailing view expressed in the Committee was that the current situation and outlook for the balance of payments was such that import restrictions could no longer be justified under Article XVIII:B".[38] Moreover, the full Balance-of-Payments Committee had "stressed the need to establish a clear timetable for the early, progressive removal of Korea's restrictive trade measures maintained for balance-of-payments purposes" and had expressed the expectation that "Korea would be able in the meantime to establish a timetable for the phasing-out of balance-of-payments restrictions, and that Korea would consider alternative GATT justification for any remaining measures, thus obviating the need for such consultations".[39]

123. The Panel noted that all available information, including figures published by the Korean authorities and advice provided to it in February 1989 by the International Monetary Fund, had shown that the reserve holdings of Korea had increased in 1988, that Korea's balance-of-payments situation had continued to improve at a good pace since the November 1987 consultations, and that the current economic indicators of Korea were very favorable. According to information provided to the Panel by the International Monetary Fund, the Korean gross official reserves had increased by 9 billion dollars to 12 billion dollars (equivalent to three months of imports) by end 1988. The Panel concluded that in the light of the continued improvement of the Korean balance-of-payments situation, and having regard to the provisions of Article XVIII:11, there was a need for the prompt establishment of a timetable for the phasing-out of Korea's balance-of-payments restrictions on beef, as called for by the CONTRACTING PARTIES in adopting the 1987 Balance-of-Payments Committee report.

[38] BOP/R/171, paragraph 22

[39] *Idem*, paragraph 23. The full text of the Balance-of-Payments Committee's conclusions is contained in Annex I.

Article II

124. The Panel noted that the LPMO was a beef import monopoly established in July 1988, with exclusive privileges for the administration of both the beef import quota set by the Korean Government and the resale of the imported beef to wholesalers or in certain cases directly to end users such as hotels. The Panel examined whether the mark-ups imposed on imported beef, in combination with the import duties collected at the bound rate, afforded "protection on the average in excess of the amount of protection provided for" in the Korean Schedule in violation of the provisions of paragraph 4 of Article II, as claimed by the United States. The Panel noted Korea's view that the operation of the LPMO was consistent with the provisions of Article II:4.

125. The LPMO bought imported beef at world market prices through a tender system and resold it either by auction to wholesalers or directly to end users. A minimum bid price at wholesale auction, or derived price for direct sale, was set by the LPMO with reference to the wholesale price for domestic beef.

126. In examining Article II:4, the Panel noted that, according to the interpretative note to Article II:4, the paragraph was to be applied "in the light of the provisions of Article 31 of the Havana Charter".[40] Two provisions of the Havana Charter, Articles 31:4 and 31:5, were relevant. Article 31:4 called for an analysis of the import costs and profit margins of the import monopoly. However, Article 31:5 stated that import monopolies would "import and offer for sale such quantities of the product as will be *sufficient to satisfy the full domestic demand* for the imported product . . ." (emphasis added). In the view of the Panel, Article 31:5 clearly implied that Article 31:4 of the Havana Charter and by implication Article II:4 of the General Agreement were intended to cover import monopolies operating in markets *not* subject to quantitative restrictions.

127. Bearing in mind Article 31:5 of the Havana Charter, the Panel considered that, in view of the existence of quantitative restrictions, it would be inappropriate to apply Article II:4 of the General Agreement in the present case. The price premium obtained by the LPMO through the setting of a minimum bid price or derived sale price was directly afforded by the situation of market scarcity arising from the quantitative restrictions on beef. The Panel concluded that because of the presence of the quantitative restrictions, the level of the LPMO's mark-up of the

[40] The text of Article 31, and its interpretative note, is contained in Annex III.

price for imported beef to achieve the minimum bid price or other derived price was not relevant in the present case. Furthermore, once these quantitative restrictions were phased out, as recommended by the Panel in paragraph 131 below, this price premium would disappear.

128. The Panel stressed, however, that in the absence of quantitative restrictions, an import monopoly was not to afford protection, on the average, in excess of the amount of protection provided for in the relevant schedule, as set out in Article II:4 of the General Agreement. Furthermore, in the absence of quantitative restrictions, an import monopoly was not to charge on the average a profit margin which was higher than that "which would be obtained under normal conditions of competition (in the absence of the monopoly)". See paragraph 4.16 of the report of the Panel on Import, Distribution and Sale of Alcoholic Drinks by Canadian Provincial Marketing Agencies (L/6304) adopted by the CONTRACTING PARTIES in March 1988. The Panel therefore expected that once Korea's quantitative restrictions on beef were removed, the operation of the LPMO would conform to these requirements.

129. The Panel then examined the United States contention that Korea imposed surcharges on imported beef in violation of the provisions of paragraph 1(b) of Article II and noted that Korea claimed that it did not impose any surcharges in violation of Article II:1(b). The Panel was of the view that, in the absence of quantitative restrictions, any charges imposed by an import monopoly would normally be examined under Article II:4 since it was the more specific provision applicable to the restriction at issue. In this regard, the Panel recalled its findings in paragraph 127 above. It concluded, therefore, that it was not necessary to examine this issue under Article II:1(b).

Articles X and XIII

130. The Panel noted that the United States had, as a subsidiary matter, claimed that Korea had not met its obligations under Articles X and XIII by not providing proper public notice of the import restrictions. It also noted that Korea had stated that the withdrawal of the measures imposed in 1984/85 and the import levels in 1988 had been widely publicized. In view of the Panel's determinations as concerned the consistency of the Korean measures with Articles II and XI, the Panel did not find it necessary to address these subsidiary issues. The Panel noted, however, the requirement in Article X:1 that "laws, regulations, judicial decisions and administrative rulings of general applica-

tion, made effective by any contracting party, pertaining to . . . rates of duty, taxes or other charges, or to requirements, restrictions or prohibitions on imports . . ., shall be published promptly in such a manner as to enable governments and traders to become acquainted with them". It also noted the provision in Article XIII:3(b) that "[i]n the case of import restrictions involving the fixing of quotas, the contracting party applying the restrictions shall give public notice of the total quantity or value of the product or products which will be permitted to be imported during a specified future period and of any change in such quantity or value".

RECOMMENDATIONS

131. In the light of the findings above, the Panel suggests that the CONTRACTING PARTIES recommend that:

(a) Korea eliminate or otherwise bring into conformity with the provisions of the General Agreement the import measures on beef introduced in 1984/85 and amended in 1988; and,

(b) Korea hold consultations with the United States and other interested contracting parties to work out a timetable for the removal of import restrictions on beef justified since 1967 by Korea for balance-of-payments reasons and report on the result of such consultations within a period of three months following the adoption of the Panel report by the Council.

CANADA—IMPORT RESTRICTIONS ON ICE CREAM AND YOGHURT

Report of the Panel adopted on December 4, 1989
BISD 36S/68

FINDINGS

Introduction

57. The Panel noted that the issue before it concerned restrictions maintained by Canada on imports of yoghurt and various ice cream products. The Panel observed that the quotas applied by Canada were prohibited by Article XI:1. This was not contested by the parties; at issue was whether these measures could be justified under Article XI:2(c)(i), and if so, whether the restrictions were administered in conformity with the provisions of Articles X and XIII. A further issue raised by the United States was whether the permit system *per se* operated as a restriction on imports in contravention of Article XI:1.

58. The Panel proceeded to examine whether Canada's import restrictions on ice cream and yoghurt could be justified under Article XI:2(c)(i). The text of this paragraph provides that:

> "2. The provisions of paragraph 1 of this Article shall not extend to the following: . . . .
> (c) Import restrictions on any agricultural or fisheries product, imported in any form, necessary to the enforcement of governmental measures which operate:
> (i) to restrict the quantities of the like domestic product permitted to be marketed or produced, or, if there is no substantial domestic production of the like product, of a domestic product for which the imported product can be directly substituted;"

and further (in last sub-paragraph) that:

> "Any contracting party applying restrictions on the importation of any product pursuant to sub-paragraph (c) of this paragraph shall give public notice of the total quantity or value

of the product permitted to be imported during a specified future period and of any change in such quantity or value. Moreover, any restrictions applied under (i) above shall not be such as will reduce the total of imports relative to the total of domestic production, as compared with the proportion which might reasonably be expected to rule between the two in the absence of restrictions. In determining this proportion, the contracting party shall pay due regard to the proportion prevailing during a previous representative period and to any special factors which may have affected or may be affecting the trade in the product concerned."

59. The Panel recalled that it had previously been concluded that a contracting party invoking an exception to the General Agreement bore the burden of proving that it had met all of the conditions of that exception.[5] It also noted, as had previous panels, that exceptions were to be interpreted narrowly and considered that this argued against flexible interpretation of Article XI:2(c)(i).[6] The Panel was aware that the requirements of Article XI:2(c)(i) for invoking an exception to the general prohibition on quantitative restrictions made this provision extremely difficult to comply with in practice.[7] However, any change in the burden of proof could have consequences equivalent to amending Article XI, seriously affecting the balance of tariff concessions negotiated among contracting parties, and was therefore outside the scope of the Panel's mandate.

60. The Panel also noted that there existed dissatisfaction with Article XI:2(c)(i) and that its revision was under discussion. The focus of this provision was limited to a fresh product restricted by the domestic measures and the competition this product faced from imports. The provision was not designed to address the difficulties of a domestic processing industry that, as a consequence of the domestic restrictions on the fresh product, faced higher raw material costs, making it less

[5] Report of the Panel on "Canada—Administration of the Foreign Investment Review Act", BISD 30S/140, 164; Report of the Panel on "Japan Restrictions on Imports of Certain Agricultural Products", L/6253, p. 64; and Report of the Panel on "European Economic Community—Restrictions on Imports of Dessert Applies—Complaint by Chile", L/6491, p. 37.

[6] See, for example, Report of the Panel on "Japan—Restrictions on Imports of Certain Agricultural Products", L/6253, p. 65 and Report of the Panel on "EEC—Restrictions on Imports of Apples—Complaint by the United States", L/6513, p. 33.

[7] See, e.g., Report of the Panel on "EEC—Restrictions on Imports on Dessert Apples—Complaint by Chile", L/6491.

competitive with imports. To the extent that Article XI:2(c)(i) could be applied to imports of processed products, it was solely on the basis of their relationship to the fresh product under domestic restriction. This was evident from the text of the provision and its interpretative notes. The drafters had expressly indicated, with regard to the application of the exception to processed products that ". . . [i]n particular, it should not be construed as permitting the use of quantitative restrictions as a method of protecting the industrial processing of agricultural or fisheries products" (Havana Reports, ICITO/I/8, p. 94). Although the Panel recognized that there could be concern over the practicability of applying the criteria of Article XI:2(c)(i) with respect to processed products, it was not the function of panels to propose changes to the provisions of the General Agreement but to make findings regarding their interpretation and application.[8]

61. The Panel considered the arguments presented by the parties with regard to the relevance of previous panel reports, and in particular that on Japan—Restrictions on Imports of Certain Agricultural Products (L/6253). That panel had also examined the application of quantitative restrictions to various processed dairy products. The Panel recognized that although the circumstances of the cases were quite different, some of the Japanese Agriculture Panel's considerations were relevant to this case. At the same time, however, on some issues of particular importance before this Panel, the report of the Japanese Agriculture Panel was useful but could not provide definitive guidance. The Panel thus thoroughly examined the questions before it in light of the relevant provisions of the General Agreement, taking account of all relevant previous panel findings.

62. As the party invoking an exception, it was incumbent upon Canada to demonstrate that the measures applied to imports of ice cream and yoghurt met each of the conditions under Article XI:2(c)(i) and XI:2(c) last sub-paragraph, in order to qualify in terms of these provisions for exemption from Article XI:1.

These conditions are:

— the measure on importation must constitute an import restriction (and not a prohibition);

— the import restrictions must be on an agricultural or fisheries product;

[8] Ministerial Declaration of 1982, BISD 29S/16.

— the import restriction and the domestic marketing or production restriction must apply to "like" products in any form (or directly substitutable products if there is no substantial production of the like product);

— there must be governmental measures which operate to restrict the quantities of the domestic product permitted to be marketed or produced;

— the import restriction must be necessary to the enforcement of the domestic supply restriction;

— the contracting party applying restrictions on importation must give public notice of the total quantity or value of the product permitted to be imported during a specified future period; and

— the restrictions applied must not reduce the proportion of total imports relative to total domestic production, as compared with the proportion which might reasonably be expected to rule between the two in the absence of restrictions.

63. The Panel concurred with the two parties that the first of these conditions had been met: Canada's measures constituted a restriction and not a prohibition of trade.

The Import Restriction must be on an Agricultural or Fisheries Product

64. The Panel observed that the Parties had not made detailed arguments with regard to this criterion of Article XI:2(c)(i). The term "agricultural product" is not defined in the General Agreement. The long-standing practice of the GATT, as evident in past rounds of trade negotiations and previous panel reports, was to accept that products falling under Chapters 1 to 24 in the Customs Cooperation Council Nomenclature could in principle be regarded as agricultural products.[9] The Panel further noted that ice cream and yoghurt were food products generally regarded by consumers and the industry to be agricultural products. The Panel thus found that ice cream and yoghurt were agricultural products within the meaning of Article XI:2(c).

[9] See, e.g., Report of the Panel on "Japan—Restrictions on Imports of Certain Agricultural Products", L/6253, p. 61.

Like Products Imported in any Form

65. The Panel then proceeded to examine whether the import restrictions and the domestic production restrictions applied to "like" products "in any form". The first issue was to determine the relevant "fresh" Canadian product. Although Canada maintained that it effectively restricted the production of all milk, its arguments had primarily made reference to industrial milk. Yet the differentiation of "fluid" milk (raw milk used for processing into table milk and cream) and "industrial milk" (raw milk used for processing into other dairy products) was recognized to be merely an administrative differentiation, based on the intended use of the milk and not any intrinsic differences.

66. The Panel recalled that in the drafting of the General Agreement, it was argued that Article XI:2(c)(i) was necessary due to ". . . the capricious bounty of nature, which will sometimes give you a huge catch of fish or a huge crop . . ." and because of the existence ". . . of a multitude of small unorganized producers that cannot organize themselves" (EPCT/A/PV/19). It was clear, therefore, that the domestic product subject to restrictions had to be the product produced by farmers. In this case the farmers were producing raw milk, not "industrial" or "fluid" milk. The Panel found that the relevant Canadian "fresh" product subject to restriction was total raw milk.

67. The Panel next considered whether ice cream and yoghurt were "like" products to raw milk. In the drafting of this provision it had been stated that the words "like products" in Article XI:2(c) ". . . definitely do not mean what they mean in other contexts—merely a competing product" (EPCT/C.II/PV.12). The Japanese Agriculture Panel had observed that Article XI:2(c)(i) and the note supplementary to it regarding "in any form" established different requirements for (a) restrictions on the importation of products that are "like" the product subject to domestic supply restrictions and (b) restrictions on the importation of products that are processed from a product that is "like" the product subject to domestic supply restrictions.[10] The Japanese Agriculture Panel had considered that this differentiation would be lost if a product in its original form and a product processed from the original one were to be considered to be "like" products within the meaning of Article XI:2(c). This Panel concurred with that observation. It further noted that there was virtually no international trade in raw milk.

[10] Report of the Panel on "Japan—Restrictions on Imports of Certain Agricultural Products", L/6253, p. 62.

68. The Panel therefore considered whether ice cream and yoghurt were "like" products "in any form" to raw milk. It was recognized in Article XI:2(c)(i) that it might be necessary to restrict not only the fresh product, but also some of its processed forms. However, the scope of this exception from the general prohibition on quantitative restrictions was limited by the interpretative note Ad Article XI:

> "Paragraph 2(c)
>
> The term "in any form" in this paragraph covers the same products when in an early stage of processing and still perishable, which compete directly with the fresh product and if freely imported would tend to make the restriction on the fresh product ineffective."

Thus, the exception could not be extended to all processed forms of the fresh product but only to those which met the specified criteria.

69. In the Havana Charter this provision had been redrafted to read:

> ". . . imported "in any form" means the product in the form in which it is originally sold by its producer and such processed forms of the product as are *so closely related to the original product as regards utilization* that their unrestricted importation would make the restriction of the original product ineffective" (Note to Article 20, emphasis added).

It was this close relationship with regard to use that justified extension of the exception to some forms of processed products. While the interpretative note to the General Agreement focused more on defining the acceptable *forms* of the processed product, i.e. those that were in an early stage of processing and still perishable, the concept of a close relationship in terms of use was nonetheless retained in the requirements that the processed product compete directly with the fresh one to the extent that its free importation would render ineffective the restrictions on the fresh product. There was no evidence in either the drafting history nor the texts of the General Agreement itself that the exception was ever meant to apply to all, or even most, of the processed forms of any particular fresh product.

70. In light of these considerations, the Panel examined whether ice cream and yoghurt met all the conditions for "like" products "in any form": that they were in an "early stage of processing", "still perishable", "directly competitive" with raw milk and if freely imported

would "make the restriction on the fresh product ineffective". The exception to Article XI:1 could be applied only to those processed products which met all of these conditions.

Early Stage of Processing

71. With regard to "early stage of processing", the Panel did not find sufficient the Canadian argument that products resulting from a direct continuous processing method should be considered *ipso facto* as in an early stage of processing. "Continuous" processing could theoretically be continued until a highly processed product (e.g. powdered cake mix) resulted. Neither could the Panel accept the implication of the US argument that any consumer-ready processed product could *not* be considered as in an early stage of processing. Drinking milk, having been pasteurized and homogenized, was a "processed", consumer-ready product, yet it would be difficult not to consider drinking milk to be "in an early stage of processing." The Panel noted that not all ice cream and yoghurt products were at the same stage of processing. For example, it appeared that fresh yoghurt was less processed than frozen yoghurt mix, and bulk ice cream less processed than individually packaged, chocolate-coated, moulded ice cream bars. A finding with respect to the "early stage of processing" criterion would thus require an examination of the processing of each type of product subject to the import restrictions. Given the variety of modern production methods and the rapid changes in technology, the Panel also had doubts whether the concept "early stage of processing" could provide much guidance as to the interpretation of Article XI:2(c). In light of its findings on the other requirements of Article XI:2(c)(i), the Panel did not consider it necessary to make a finding in this regard.

Still Perishable

72. With regard to "still perishable", the Panel observed that both parties agreed that ice cream and yoghurt required special handling and storage conditions, and that the shelf life of fresh yoghurt was approximately three weeks. Canada had stated that ice cream made according to Agriculture Canada standards had a three-month shelf life. The United States had provided evidence that the ice cream it exported could be stored for 12 months. The United States further argued that a product which had undergone processing to make it less perishable than the raw product could no longer be considered to meet the requirements of this provision. The Panel did not agree with this interpretation; the interpretative note required only that the product be "still perishable",

not "as perishable as the fresh product". The Panel recognized that there were considerable differences in perishability between products such as fresh yoghurt with its two to three week shelf life, and frozen yoghurt mix or some ice cream products which could be stored for up to one year. The Panel observed that there was no agreed definition of perishability in the General Agreement and little guidance provided by the drafting history. The drafters had stated that ". . . what we have in mind here is the perishable kind of processed product, not the kind which is capable of being stocked" (EPCT/A/PV/19). A previous panel had found that a product was still perishable because it would decline in quality and value after a certain time.[11] However, as virtually all agricultural products declined in quality and value after a certain time, the Panel did not believe that this previous finding provided sufficient guidance for clearly distinguishing between perishable and non-perishable items. As with the concept "early stage of processing", the Panel observed that rapid changes in technology since the General Agreement was drafted raised doubts as to the practicability of using the concept of "still perishable" to distinguish the items that fell within the scope of Article XI:2(c) from those that did not. The Panel recalled that compliance with Article XI:2(c)(i) required that all of its conditions be met. The Panel did not feel that it was therefore necessary to make a finding with regard to perishability.

Directly Competitive

73. The Panel then proceeded to examine whether ice cream and yoghurt "compete directly" with fresh raw milk. Canada argued that imported ice cream and yoghurt competed directly with Canadian produced ice cream and yoghurt and thus displaced the raw milk which would have been processed into these products. The United States argued that ice cream and yoghurt were neither substitutable for nor destined for the same markets as raw milk. The Panel considered that the term "compete *directly* with . . ." imposed a more limiting requirement than merely "compete with". As stated in the US arguments, the concept of "displacement" was apparently not intended by this provision. The essence of direct competition was that a buyer was basically indifferent if faced with the choice between one product or other and viewed them as substitutable in terms of their use. Only limited competition existed between raw milk and ice cream and yoghurt. Their

[11] Report of the Panel on "EEC—Programme of Minimum Import Prices, etc," BISD 25S/100.

marketing was quite different, and as we implied in the Canadian arguments the competition which did exist was related to displacement of raw milk used in Canadian ice cream and yoghurt production. The Panel recalled that this provision was not designed to protect the processing industry. It further recalled its consideration concerning the narrow interpretation of exceptions (paragraph 59 above). The Panel did not consider it appropriate to broaden the scope of this requirement to include the concept of displacement or indirect competition. The Panel thus found that imports of ice cream and yoghurt did *not* compete directly with raw milk in terms of Article XI:2(c)(i).

Would Make the Restrictions Ineffective

74. The exception to Article XI:1 is further limited by its application only to those processed products whose free importation would render ineffective the restrictions on the fresh product. The drafters agreed that the exception ". . . should *not* be construed as permitting the use of quantitative restrictions as a method of protecting the industrial processing of agricultural or fisheries products" (Havana Reports, ICITO/I/8, p. 94). Canada argued that developments in the United States dairy situation encouraged the expansion of US exports. Uncontrolled imports of these products could displace close to 11 per cent of its industrial milk production (on a butterfat basis). As the United States had pointed out, the current Canadian dairy restriction program had been in force since 1976, and although many other diary products had been subject to quotas since that time, it had not previously been considered necessary to restrict imports of ice cream and yoghurt. Unrestricted imports of ice cream and yoghurt in the five years previous to the 1988 imposition of restrictions averaged, respectively, two-tenths of one per cent and three-tenths of one per cent of Canadian production of these products. Their impact upon total raw milk production in Canada could be considered as minuscule.

75. The Panel recognized that Canada's concern was with regard to potential import levels, rather than historic ones, and with the accumulated effects of imports of various dairy products and the consequential effects on its domestic milk program. Prior to the imposition of the quantitative restrictions, imports of ice cream and yoghurt into Canada had been very small compared to Canadian production of these items, and these imports amounted to less than ten one-thousandths of one per cent of Canadian raw milk production. The factors cited by Canada could potentially lead to an increase in this import level; however,

Canada had not provided evidence sufficient to convince the Panel that there existed an immediate threat of imports at such significantly increased levels as could render ineffective the Canadian dairy supply program. Article XI:2(c)(i) did *not* provide for the imposition of quantitative restrictions on imports at current levels merely on the basis of some hypothetical future situation. The Panel did not find that the evidence submitted by Canada justified the conclusion that unrestricted imports of ice cream and yoghurt would presently render ineffective the Canadian domestic restrictions on raw milk production.

76. The exception to Article XI:1 can be applied only to those processed products which meet all the conditions for "like" products "in any form" of the interpretative note Ad Article XI:2(c)(i): are in "an early stage of processing", "still perishable", "compete directly" with the fresh product and if freely imported would "make the restriction on the fresh product ineffective". The Panel found that ice cream and yoghurt *did not* compete directly with raw milk, and that their free importation would *not* render ineffective the Canadian production measures for raw milk. The Panel did not find it necessary to make findings with regard to the criterion of early stage of processing or perishability.

Governmental Measures to Restrict Domestic Production

77. The *raison d'être* of Article XI:2(c)(i) is to permit the operation of governmental measures that restrict the quantity of some fresh agricultural product permitted to be produced or marketed. The drafters indicated that "to restrict" means to ". . . keep output below the level which it would have attained in the absence of restrictions".[12] Proposals to make the *regulation* of production, through price stabilization programs, an accepted criterion were rejected.[13] The Panel further observed that other than requiring a governmental measure, Article XI:2(c)(i) did not specify how the production or marketing restriction was to be imposed.

78. Canada had described in detail its domestic milk marketing programs, noting that the programs covered all producers and all milk produced in Canada. Canada argued that over quota levies, which resulted in returns below the farmer's cash cost of production, ensured that production did not exceed the established market sharing quota. According to Canada, existing excess capacity for production indicated

[12] Havana Reports, ICITO/I/8, p. 89 para. 17
[13] EPCT/A/PV/19

that in the absence of the government restrictions production would be higher. It presented econometric analyses indicating that the increase in production would be on the order of 31 to 39 per cent. The United States argued that the only limitation on fluid milk sales was what the market could bear, and there was no penalty for producers exceeding their fluid milk "quota". Furthermore, the United States contended that the method of calculating support payments on in-quota milk was such as to perhaps provide some financial incentive to overproduce. In fact, in the past six years total industrial milk production had consistently exceeded the established Market Sharing Quota.

79. The Panel recalled that the requirement was for the effective *restriction* of production, not merely its *regulation*. A major element of the requirement of restricted production was that the measure, regardless of how operated, had to reduce production below the level it would otherwise have attained. The Panel observed that this concept was difficult to apply in practice. In situations such as the Canadian one, where the government measures had been in place for many years and were interrelated with price support and other production incentives, it was virtually impossible to determine what production levels would be in their absence. This determination would be necessary in order to have an objective basis for comparison with current production levels. In light of its findings in paragraphs 73 to 76 above, the Panel *did not* consider it necessary to further examine this issue. The Panel, therefore, did not make a finding with regard to whether the Canadian dairy management scheme constituted a government measure which effectively restricted total raw milk production in Canada.

Necessary

80. A further requirement of Article XI:2(c)(i) is that the import restrictions be "necessary to the enforcement" of the supply-restricting governmental measures. The Panel observed that although the term "necessary" had never been defined, the 1955 Working Party on Quantitative Restrictions had concluded "it would be an abuse of intent of the provisions under Article XI:2(c)(i) if the contracting parties were to apply restrictions to processed products exceeding those necessary to secure enforcement of the actual measures restricting production or marketing of the primary products".[14] There were also further interpretations with regard to seasonal restrictions. When restrictions on

[14] BISD 3S/189, 190

processed products were involved, the Panel found it difficult to separate completely the criterion of "necessary to the enforcement" from that regarding ". . . would render ineffective the restriction on the fresh product". If unrestricted imports would render a government measure ineffective, it would be difficult not to conclude that some restriction of the imports was necessary. The arguments of the parties had essentially been the same for these two criteria. Canada had expressed concern that potential future imports could replace Canadian production of ice cream and yoghurt, and thus displace that proportion of Canadian milk normally used in their processing. The United States stated that ice cream and yoghurt had been freely imported over the many years during which Canada had a supply management system without causing any apparent difficulties to the operation of that program. Furthermore, unrestricted imports of these products had attained a very limited market share, amounting to a minuscule proportion of total Canadian milk production.

81. The Panel recognized the merits of Canada's argument that for a product which is traded almost exclusively in its processed form, such as milk, restrictions on the imports of the processed products might in some sense be "necessary" to ensure that the restriction on the production of the raw material was not undermined. This consequential result was, as the Panel had previously noted (paragraph 73), indirect. Canadian processors, whose access to dairy ingredient inputs was limited to higher priced domestic supplies, might not be able to compete effectively with imported processed products, and subsequently would reduce their production of these processed goods and hence their demand for the raw milk input. At this time, however, there was not sufficient evidence to believe that future imports of ice cream and yoghurt would achieve such levels as to significantly affect Canadian producers ability to market raw milk. In the past, unrestricted imports had gained less than a half a percent share of the Canadian ice cream and yoghurt market, and accounted for less than ten one-thousandths of one per cent of total raw milk production. Against this background and in the absence of an imminent threat to the Canadian dairy system, the Panel found that the criterion of "necessary" to the operation of the governmental restrictions could *not* be met.

Public Notice, Level of Imports

82. The Panel observed that the remaining provisions of Article XI:2(c), as concerned public notice and the level of imports, as well as those contained in Articles X and XIII, concerned the operation of the

quota. As the Panel had found that the Canadian import quotas for ice cream and yoghurt could not be justified under Article XI:2(c)(i), it *did not* consider it necessary to examine whether the administration of these quotas was in conformity with the General Agreement.

Permit System

83. The Panel considered the United States arguments that the permit system operated as a quantitative restriction *in addition to the quotas*, as permits were not freely available and had limited validity. Given the Panel's findings that the quotas could not be justified under the General Agreement, to the extent that the permit system was a mechanism for the administration of the quota system, it had no justifiable basis and the Panel did not consider it necessary to further examine its operation. The Panel was aware that in 1988, having announced the restriction of imports of ice cream and yoghurt, Canada had not established a quota but had nonetheless required import permits. The Panel recognized that this was an exceptional measure, which had been taken in the past and not repeated since 1988, and did not consider it necessary to further examine its conformity with the General Agreement. It did observe, however, that restrictions applied through discretionary licensing could not meet the requirement in Article XI:2(c) of prior public notice of the quantity or value permitted to be imported.

CONCLUSIONS

84. In light of the considerations set out in paragraphs 57 to 81 above, the Panel concluded that Canada's restrictions on the importation of ice cream and yoghurt are inconsistent with Article XI:1 and cannot be justified under the provisions of Article XI:2(c)(i). In particular, the Panel found that ice cream and yoghurt do not meet the requirements of Article XI:2(c)(i) for "like products" "in any form" to Canadian raw milk because they do *not* compete directly with raw milk nor would their free importation be likely to render ineffective the Canadian measures on raw milk production. The Panel found further that the restriction of imports of ice cream and yoghurt is not necessary to the enforcement of the Canadian program for raw milk.

85. The Panel, therefore, *recommends* that the CONTRACTING PARTIES request Canada either to terminate these restrictions or to bring them into conformity with its obligations under the General Agreement.

EEC—PAYMENTS AND SUBSIDIES PAID TO PROCESSORS AND PRODUCERS OF OILSEEDS AND RELATED ANIMAL-FEED PROTEINS

Report of the Panel adopted on January 25, 1990
BISD—S/—
(L/6627)

FINDINGS

Introduction

131. The legal issues before the Panel arise essentially from the following facts. In 1962, as an outcome of tariff negotiations with the United States and other contracting parties in the framework of the Dillon Round, the Community included in its Schedule of Concessions in accordance with Article II of the General Agreement duty-free tariff bindings for oilseeds and oilcakes (hereinafter referred to as "oilseeds"). The bindings were the result of general negotiations on the reduction of tariffs and of negotiations rendered necessary under Article XXIV:6 as a result of the creation of a common external tariff by the Community replacing the tariffs of the individual member States. On the occasion of each of its successive enlargements the Community conducted negotiations based on Article XXIV:6 and established a new Schedule of Concessions replacing the previous Community Schedule and the Schedules of the new member States, most recently in 1986/1987. The duty-free tariff bindings for oilseeds were maintained after each of these negotiations.

132. In 1966 the Community established a common organization of the market for rapeseed and sunflowerseed under Regulation No. 136/66. This Regulation has since been amended and complemented on numerous occasions but its principles have remained unchanged. The introductory clauses in Regulation No. 136/66 state that access to imported oilseeds duty free had made it easier for the Community processing industries to obtain raw materials at reasonable prices but that the Community producers of oils and fats "would be adversely affected if the effects of the removal of import barriers were not offset by other

measures." The market organization for the oilseeds concerned is based on a price system, but it does not provide, in contrast to other market organizations, for any import levies. Under the Regulation the Community fixes a "target price" and an "intervention price" for oilseeds. The target price is established at a level which, according to Article 23 of the Regulation, "is fair to producers, account being taken of the need to keep the Community production at the required level". The intervention price determines the price level at which the intervention agencies established in the framework of the market organization have the obligation of buying domestic oilseeds. The intervention price, according to Article 24 of the Regulation, must be "as close as possible to the target price", allowing however for certain reductions to take account of adaptation to general and local market fluctuations and transport costs within the Community.

133. Article 27 of the same Regulation provides for subsidies to be paid on rapeseed and sunflowerseed harvested and processed within the Community, to make up for the difference between the target price and the world market price whenever the target price is higher than the world market price, which has generally been the case. According to Article 29, the world market price is "calculated" on the basis of the most favorable purchasing opportunities and may be adjusted to take the prices of competing products into account. In practice the amount of the subsidy is calculated using reconstructed prices and adjustment factors because, as explained by the Community, world market prices for these products are either unreliable or do not exist. Eligibility of oilseeds for the benefit of the subsidy provided for by Article 27 is currently determined by Council Regulation No. 1594/83, as amended. Under this Regulation subsidies are paid to oil processors and producers of animal feeds (hereinafter referred to as "processors") whenever they establish by documentary evidence that they have transformed oilseeds of Community origin. It appeared from the information provided to the Panel that the oilseeds market has functioned on the basis of the payment to processors, which has rendered intervention purchases largely superfluous.

134. In 1974, a guide/minimum price scheme based on the same principles was introduced for soyabeans under Regulation No. 1900/74. This scheme was subsequently replaced or amended and the relevant rules are found at present in Regulation No. 1491/85. In the introductory clauses of Regulation No. 1900/74 it was stated that appropriate measures of support should be provided to promote the development of the production of soyabeans which was subjected to direct competition

from soyabeans imported from third countries duty free. Under Regulation No. 1491/85 subsidies are provided to make up for the difference between the "guide price" determined by the Community and the world market price of soyabeans. The payment of the subsidy to processors or first purchasers is conditional on the conclusion of contracts with Community producers providing for the payment of a price at least equal to the "minimum price".

135. The United States claims that the payments to processors are made on conditions that give them an incentive to purchase domestic rather than imported oilseeds. The United States considered this to be contrary to Article III:4 of the General Agreement which provides that:

> "the products of the territory of any contracting party shall be accorded treatment no less favorable than that accorded to like products of national origin in respect of all . . . regulations . . . affecting their internal . . . purchase . . .".

The United States further claims that most of the economic benefits generated by the payments to processors accrue to the producers of oilseeds and that the resulting incentive to produce oilseeds in the Community has impaired benefits it could reasonably expect to accrue to it under the tariff concessions for oilseeds. The United States therefore considered that it was entitled to redress under the provisions of Article XXIII:1(b) and 2 dealing with the impairment of benefits accruing under the General Agreement. The Community considers both claims to be unfounded.

National Treatment: Article III

136. The Panel first examined the United States' claim that the payments to processors generate an incentive to purchase domestic rather than imported oilseeds inconsistently with Article III:4. The Panel noted that the Community considers the payments made to processors to be covered by Article III:8(b) which provides that Article III ". . . shall not prevent the payment of subsidies exclusively to domestic producers . . .". The Community argues that the payments to processors are made conditional upon the transformation or purchase of domestic oilseeds sold at prices determined by the Community Regulations, are therefore passed on to the producers of domestic oilseeds and consequently constitute producer subsidies within the meaning of that provision.

137. The Panel noted that Article III:8(b) applies only to payments made *exclusively* to domestic producers and considered that it can reasonably be assumed that a payment not made directly to producers is not made "exclusively" to them. It noted moreover that, if the economic benefits generated by the payments granted by the Community can at least partly be retained by the processors of Community oilseeds, the payments generate a benefit conditional upon the purchase of oilseeds of domestic origin inconsistently with Article III:4. Under these circumstances Article III:8(b) would not be applicable because in that case the payments would not be made exclusively to domestic producers but to processors as well. The Panel noted that the payments may constitute the grant of a benefit to processors conditional upon the purchase of domestic oilseeds in two situations:

(a) the payments to the processors are based on prices determined by the Community authorities higher than the prices the processors actually pay to producers; and

(b) the payments to the processors are based on import prices determined by the Community authorities lower than the prices that the processors would actually have to pay if they bought imported instead of domestic oilseeds.

138. As to the first point it appeared from the evidence before the Panel that under the Community's intervention schemes for rapeseed and sunflowerseed, processors receive a subsidy based on a target price but they need not demonstrate that they in fact paid the target price to a Community producer. In all cases in which processors are able to purchase Community oilseeds at a price below the target price or the market price objective aimed at by the Commission (Annex B, Sections I and II, paragraph 5), the subsidy payments are based on prices higher than the prices processors actually pay to producers. In the case of soyabeans the subsidy paid to producers is based on a "guide" price; however the processors obtain the subsidy whenever they demonstrate that they paid a price at least equal to a "minimum price" (Article 2 of Regulation No. 1491/85). Whenever the guide price is higher than the minimum price the subsidy payment creates an incentive to purchase Community rather than imported soyabeans. The minimum price is fixed "at a level guaranteeing sales for producers at a price as close as possible to the guide price, allowing in particular for market fluctuations and the cost of transporting the beans" (Article 2:3 of Regulation No. 1491/85) and must therefore be generally below the guide price. For these reasons the Panel concluded that the Community Regulations do

not ensure that the payments to processors are based on prices processors actually have to pay when purchasing Community oilseeds.

139. As to the second point, the Panel noted that the prices which the Community authorities determine to be the import prices are those that prevailed in certain markets at a certain time. These prices are not necessarily the prices that prevail at the time the subsidy recipients decide to purchase domestic rather than imported products. The Community recognized this when it replied as follows to a question by the Panel: "It is true that there may always be some uncertainty relating to the difference between, on the one hand, the case-by-case decisions taken by an individual operator (who may furthermore take anticipatory or indeed speculative positions) and, on the other, an evaluation made by the public authorities based on market prices (involving the approximation inherent in the concept of prices)". The Panel further noted that for rapeseed and sunflowerseed the Community uses reconstructed prices to determine the subsidy payments and that the "world market price" implicit in the amount of the payment (namely the market price objective aimed at by the Commission less the subsidy payment) would not necessarily in all cases be the same as the price at which competing imports of these oilseeds are available to processors. The Panel found that due to these various factors, the Community Regulations do not ensure that the subsidy payments are based on prices that the subsidy recipients would actually have paid had they chosen to buy imported rather than domestic products.

140. For the reasons indicated in the preceding paragraphs, the Panel found that subsidy payments made to processors can be greater than the difference between the price processors actually pay to producers and the price that processors would have to pay for imported oilseeds. Whether such over-compensation creating an incentive to purchase domestic rather than imported products takes place depends on the circumstances of the individual purchase. The Community Regulations are thus capable of giving rise to discrimination against imported products though they may not necessarily do so in the case of each individual purchase.

141. Having made this finding the Panel examined whether a purchase regulation which does not necessarily discriminate against imported products but is capable of doing so is consistent with Article III:4. The Panel noted that the exposure of a particular imported product to a *risk* of discrimination constitutes, by itself, a form of discrimination. The Panel therefore concluded that purchase regulations creating such a risk must be considered to be according less favorable treatment within

the meaning of Article III:4. The Panel found for these reasons that the payments to processors of Community oilseeds are inconsistent with Article III:4.

Nullifcation or Impairment of Tariff Concessions: Article II

142. The Panel then turned to the complaint by the United States that the grant of subsidies to Community producers of oilseeds had nullified or impaired benefits accruing to the United States under the Community's tariff concessions for oilseeds. The Panel first examined whether its finding that the payments to the processors are inconsistent with the General Agreement might make an examination of the question of the nullification or impairment of the tariff concessions unnecessary. The Panel noted that this would be the case if compliance by the Community with the finding on Article III:4 would necessarily remove the basis of the United States claim of nullification or impairment. The Panel noted that the subsidies the Community presently grants to producers of oilseeds result from the maintenance of producer prices at levels generally exceeding the price of competing imports through payments to processors conditional upon the purchase or transformation of domestic oilseeds. The finding of the Panel under Article III:4 does not relate to the benefits accruing to the Community producers under the Community subsidy schemes but only to the benefits accruing to processors. The Panel further noted that the Community could comply with the Panel's finding on Article III and still make available in the Community market oilseeds produced with the benefit of producer prices maintained at levels exceeding the price of competing imports. Compliance with the finding on Article III thus could, but would not necessarily, eliminate the basis of the United States complaint that the benefits accruing to the Community producers of oilseeds impair the Community's tariff concessions for oilseeds. The Panel therefore decided that it had to examine that complaint as well.

143. The Panel noted that the tariff concessions for oilseeds were originally made in 1962 following negotiations with the United States and other contracting parties in the Dillon Round and under Article XXIV:6 after the Community had established a common external tariff. The United States bases its case on expectations it claims to have had in 1962 when the concessions for oilseeds were first incorporated into the Community Schedule. The Community argues that the United States can base its claim only on expectations it could reasonably have had when the Schedule of Concessions currently in force was negotiated,

namely in 1986 when the production subsidies had already been introduced.

144. The first issue the Panel examined in this context was therefore whether the benefits accruing to the United States under the tariff concessions on oilseeds presently in force include the protection of expectations that prevailed in 1962 when the tariff concessions on oilseeds were originally incorporated in the Schedule of Concessions of the Community. The Panel, noting that there is no explicit rule nor a precedent to guide it in this matter, considered the issue in the light of the purpose of the provisions of Article XXIII relating to the impairment of benefits accruing under the General Agreement. The Panel noted that these provisions, as conceived by the drafter and applied by the CONTRACTING PARTIES, serve mainly to protect the balance of tariff concessions.[11] The idea underlying them is that the improved competitive opportunities that can legitimately be expected from a tariff concession can be frustrated not only by measures proscribed by the General Agreement but also by measures consistent with that Agreement. In order to encourage contracting parties to make tariff concessions they must therefore be given a right of redress when a reciprocal concession is impaired by another contracting party as a result of the application of any measure, whether or not it conflicts with the General Agreement.

145. The Panel concluded from the above that the answer to the question of whether the expectations of 1962 continue to be protected depends on whether the concessions on oilseeds resulting from the subsequent renegotiations under Article XXIV:6 were part of a new balance of concessions or whether the reinstitution of the concessions at the same rate after the successive enlargements of the Community meant that the balance of concessions originally negotiated in 1962 was to be continued. The Panel noted that the result of the initial Article XXIV:6 negotiations of the Community in 1962 was the creation of a Schedule of Concessions for its common external tariff that had replaced the tariffs of the six founding member States. In these negotiations, the trading partners of the Community compared the benefits accruing to them under the previous tariff concessions of the individual member States with the benefits accruing to them under the common

[11] EPCT/A/PV6, page 5; "The Australian Subsidy on Ammonium Sulphate", report adopted on April 3, 1950 (BISD, Vol. II/188, 194-5); "Treatment by Germany of Imports of Sardines", report adopted on October 31, 1952 (BISD 1S/53, 58-59); "Operation of the Provisions of Article XVI", report adopted on November 21, 1961 (BISD 10S/201, 209).

external tariff in the whole territory of the Community. The result of the Article XXIV:6 negotiations following the successive enlargements of the Community was not the creation of a new common external tariff but the extension of the existing tariff concessions of the Community to the new member States.[12] On the occasion of these negotiations pre-existing concessions of the Community were renegotiated as well but such modifications remained exceptional. Except where such modifications were specifically renegotiated, the partners of the Community could confine themselves to comparing the benefits accruing to them under the previous tariff concessions of the new member States with the benefits accruing to them as a result of the application of the Community's tariff concessions by the new member States. They had no reason to proceed to a global reassessment of the value of all the Community's concessions in the whole of the Community's territory.

146. In these circumstances, the partners of the Community in the successive renegotiations under Article XXIV:6 could legitimately assume, in the absence of any indications to the contrary, that the offer to continue a tariff commitment by the Community was an offer not to change the balance of concessions previously attained. The Panel noted that nothing in the material submitted to it indicated that the Community had made it clear to its negotiating partners that the withdrawal and reinstitution of the tariff concessions for oilseeds as part of the withdrawal of the whole of the Community Schedule meant that the Community was seeking a new balance of concessions with respect to these items. There is in particular no evidence that the Community, in the context of these negotiations, offered to compensate its negotiating partners for any impairment of the tariff concessions through production subsidies or that it accepted compensatory tariff withdrawals by its negotiating partners to take into account any such impairment. The balance of concessions negotiated in 1962 in respect of oilseeds was thus not altered in the successive Article XXIV:6 negotiations. The Panel therefore found that the benefits accruing to the United States under the oilseed tariff concessions resulting from the Article XXIV:6 negotiations of 1986/87 include the protection of reasonable expectations the United States had when these concessions were initially negotiated in 1962.

[12] "Article XXIV:6 Negotiations: Communication from the Commission of the European Communities", document L/3807 dated January 11, 1973; "Negotiations Under the Provisions of Article XXIV:6: Communications from the Commission of the European Communities", document TAR/16 dated May 20, 1961; "Enlargement of the European Economic Community: Accession of Portugal and Spain", document L/5936, Add.2 and Third Geneva (1987) Protocol, Schedule LXXX.

147. The Panel carefully analysed the price mechanism established in the framework of the Community's market organization for oilseeds and found that the production subsidy schemes of the Community protect Community producers completely from the movement of prices for imports and hence prevent the lowering of import duties from having any impact on the competitive relationship between domestic and imported oilseeds. The Panel examined whether it was reasonable for the United States to expect that the Community would not introduce subsidy schemes systematically counteracting the price effect of the tariff concessions. The essential argument of the United States on this point was that the CONTRACTING PARTIES had already recognized in 1955 the legitimacy of such expectations when they decided that:

> "a contracting party which has negotiated a concession under Article II may be assumed, for the purpose of Article XXIII, to have a reasonable expectation, failing evidence to the contrary, that the value of the concession will not be nullified or impaired by the contracting party which granted the concession by the subsequent introduction or increase of a domestic subsidy . . .".[13]

The essential argument of the Community in this respect was that it is not legitimate to expect the absence of production subsidies even after the grant of a tariff concession because Articles III:8(b) and XVI:1 explicitly recognize the right of contracting parties to grant production subsidies. This right would be effectively eliminated if its exercise were assumed to impair tariff concessions.

148. The Panel examined in detail the implications of these arguments and found the following: the case before it does not require the Panel to address the question of whether the assumption created by the 1955 decision of the CONTRACTING PARTIES applies to all production subsidies, including generally available subsidies serving broad policy objectives of the kind mentioned in Article 11:1 of the Subsidies Code. At issue in the case before it are product-specific subsidies that protect producers completely from the movement of prices for imports and thereby prevent tariff concessions from having any impact on the competitive relationship between domestic and imported oilseeds. The Panel considered that the main value of a tariff concession is that it provides an assurance of better market access through improved price competition. Contracting parties negotiate tariff concessions primarily to obtain

[13] "Other Barriers to Trade", Report adopted on March 3, 1955 (BISD 3S/222, 224).

that advantage. They must therefore be assumed to base their tariff negotiations on the expectation that the price effect of the tariff concessions will not be systematically offset. If no right of redress were given to them in such a case they would be reluctant to make tariff concessions and the General Agreement would no longer be useful as a legal framework for incorporating the results of trade negotiations. The Panel does not share the view of the Community that the recognition of the legitimacy of such expectations would amount to a re-writing of the rules of the General Agreement. The CONTRACTING PARTIES have decided that a finding of impairment does not authorize them to request the impairing contracting party to remove a measure not inconsistent with the General Agreement; such a finding merely allows the contracting party frustrated in its expectation to request, in accordance with Article XXIII:2, an authorization to suspend the application of concessions or other obligations under the General Agreement.[14] The recognition of the legitimacy of an expectation thus essentially means the recognition of the legitimacy of such a request. The recognition of the legitimacy of an expectation relating to the use of production subsidies therefore in no way prevents a contracting party from using production subsidies consistently with the General Agreement; it merely delineates the scope of the protection of a negotiated balance of concessions. For these reasons the Panel found that the United States may be assumed not to have anticipated the introduction of subsidies which protect Community producers of oilseeds completely from the movement of prices for imports and thereby prevent tariff concessions from having any impact on the competitive relationship between domestic and imported oilseeds, and which have as one consequence that *all* domestically-produced oilseeds are disposed of in the internal market notwithstanding the availability of imports.

149. Having made this finding the Panel examined whether the Community had submitted any evidence to rebut that assumption. The Panel noted that the evidence submitted by the Community showed that the United States was aware that there existed in 1962 subsidies for oilseeds in some of the member States of the Community and that a common agricultural policy was being elaborated by the Community. Nothing in the evidence submitted by the Community, however, indicates that the Community had made it known at that time that it planned to introduce subsidy schemes insulating oilseed producers completely from import

[14] "The Australian Subsidy on Ammonium Sulphate", report adopted on April 3, 1950 (BISD Vol.II/188, 195); and "Reports of Committees and Principal Sub-Committees", Geneva, September 1948 (ICITO I/8, page 155).

competition. The evidence thus showed that the United States must reasonably have expected the transformation of national producer support measures into a Community support scheme but that it could not reasonably have anticipated the introduction of subsidy schemes which protect producers completely from the movement of prices for imports and thereby prevent the tariff concessions from having any impact on the competitive relationship between domestic and imported oilseeds.

150. The Community claims that the subsidy schemes for oilseeds, even if they could not reasonably have been anticipated, did not actually impair the concessions because they did not displace or impede imports, as imports of rapeseed, sunflowerseed and soyabeans had risen from 4.5 million tons in 1966 (EC-6) to 20.4 million tons in 1988 (EC-12) on a meal equivalent basis. The United States' view is that they did impair the tariff concessions because they upset the competitive relationship between domestic and imported oilseeds. These arguments of the parties raise the question of the nature of the benefit accruing under Article II: does that benefit consist of the protection of expectations on competitive conditions or on trade flows? The Panel noted that the CONTRACTING PARTIES have consistently interpreted the basic provisions of the General Agreement on restrictive trade measures as provisions establishing conditions of competition. Thus they decided that an import quota constitutes an import restriction within the meaning of Article XI:1 whether or not it actually impeded imports and that an internal tax on imported products does not meet the national treatment requirement of Article III whether or not the tax is actually applied to imports.[15] A previous panel pointed out that Articles III and XI are "to protect expectations of the contracting parties as to the competitive relationship between their products and those of other contracting parties. Both articles are not only to protect current trade but also create the predictability needed to plan future trade".[16] In the past Article XXIII:1(b) cases, the CONTRACTING PARTIES have adopted the same approach: their findings of nullification or impairment were based on a finding that the products for which a tariff concession had been granted were subjected to an adverse change in competitive conditions. In none of these cases did they consider the trade impact of the change in competitive conditions to be determining. In one case they specifically rejected the relevance of statistics on trade flows for a finding on nullification and

[15] "Panel on Japanese Measures on Imports of Leather", report adopted on May 15/16, 1984 (BISD 31S/113); "Brazilian Internal Taxes", report adopted on June 30, 1949 (BISD Vol.II/184-185).

[16] "United States-Taxes on Petroleum and Certain Imported Substances", report adopted on June 17, 1987 (BISD 34S/160).

impairment.[17] It is of course true that, in the tariff negotiations in the framework of GATT, contracting parties seek tariff concessions in the hope of expanding their exports, but the commitments they exchange in such negotiations are commitments on conditions of competition for trade, not on volumes of trade.

151. The approach of the CONTRACTING PARTIES reflects the fact that governments can often not predict with precision what the impact of their interventions on import volumes will be. If a finding of nullification or impairment depended not only on whether an adverse change in competitive conditions took place but also on whether that change resulted in a decline in imports, the exposure of the contracting parties to claims under Article XXIII:1(b) would depend on factors they do not control; the rules on nullification and impairment could consequently no longer guide government policies. Moreover, the contracting parties facing an adverse change in policies could make a claim of nullification or impairment only after that change has produced effects. Such claims could consequently not be made to prevent adverse effects; they could only be made to obtain redress *ex post*. If Article II were considered to be protecting expectations on trade flows it would be necessary for the CONTRACTING PARTIES to determine what export volumes a contracting party can reasonably expect after having obtained a tariff concession. The Panel is not aware of any criteria or principles that could be applied to make such a determination. The Panel further noted that changes in trade volumes result not only from government policies but also other factors, and that, in most circumstances, it is not possible to determine whether a decline in imports following a change in policies is attributable to that change or to other factors. The provisions of Article XXIII:1(b) could therefore in practice hardly be applied if a contracting party claiming nullification or impairment had to demonstrate not only that an adverse change in competition has taken place but also that the change has resulted in a decline in imports.

152. For these reasons the Panel found that benefits accruing to the United States under Article II of the General Agreement in respect of the zero tariff bindings for oilseeds in the Community Schedule of Concessions were impaired as a result of subsidy schemes which operate to protect Community producers of oilseeds completely from the movement of prices of imports and thereby prevent the oilseeds tariff concessions from having *any* impact on the competitive relationship between domestic and imported oilseeds.

[17] "Treatment by Germany of Imports of Sardines", panel report adopted on October 31, 1952 (BISD 1S/53, 56).

153. The Panel took note of the arguments of the Community relating to the embargo imposed on exports of soyabeans by the United States in 1973. The Panel considered that this embargo, though it may have understandably aroused concern in the Community about the security of its supplies, could provide no justification for measures adversely affecting the competitive position of imports originating not only in the United States but in any one of the contracting parties benefiting under Article II from the Community's tariff binding. It was open to the Community to bring this matter before the CONTRACTING PARTIES at the appropriate time and to seek the remedies provided for under the General Agreement.

154. The Panel was established to make findings "in the light of the relevant GATT provisions"; it therefore does not have the mandate to propose interpretations of the provisions of the Subsidies Code which the Community invokes to justify its position. However, the following may be noted in this respect. The Subsidies Code states in Article 8:4 that a nullification or impairment may arise through "the effects of the subsidy in displacing or impeding imports of like products into the market of the subsidizing country". The Community takes the position that its production subsidies for oilseeds were followed by a rise in imports of oilseeds; they therefore neither displaced nor impeded imports and consequently did not cause nullification or impairment. The Community's position implies that Article 8:4 redefines the benefit accruing under a tariff concession as being no longer the protection of expectations on conditions of competition but the protection of expectations on the level of trade volumes even though the CONTRACTING PARTIES have consistently decided otherwise. It is to be recalled that the CONTRACTING PARTIES considered in 1960 that "it is fair to assume that a subsidy which provides an incentive to increased production will, in the absence of offsetting measures, e.g., a consumption subsidy, either increase exports or reduce imports".[18] The implication of the Community's position is that, under the Subsidies Code, this assumption could no longer be made. The Panel noted that the purpose of the Subsidies Code is, according to its preamble, "to apply fully and interpret" provisions of the General Agreement. In the view of the Panel this speaks in favor of interpreting Article 8:4 in conformity with the decisions of the CONTRACTING PARTIES rather than, as the Community suggests, revising these decisions in the light of a particular interpretation of a Code accepted by a portion of the contracting parties.

[18] "Review Pursuant to Article XVI:5", report adopted on May 24, 1960 (BISD 9S/188, 191).

CONCLUSIONS

155. The Panel found that the Community Regulations providing for payments to seed processors conditional on the purchase of oilseeds originating in the Community are inconsistent with Article III:4 of the General Agreement, according to which imported products shall be given treatment no less favorable than that accorded to like domestic products in respect of all regulations affecting their internal purchase. The Panel recommends that the CONTRACTING PARTIES request the Community to bring these Regulations into conformity with the General Agreement.

156. The Panel further found that benefits accruing to the United States under Article II of the General Agreement in respect of the zero tariff bindings for oilseeds in the Community Schedule of Concessions were impaired as a result of the introduction of production subsidy schemes which operate to protect Community producers of oilseeds completely from the movement of prices of imports and thereby prevent the tariff concessions from having any impact on the competitive relationship between domestic and imported oilseeds. The Panel recommends that the CONTRACTING PARTIES suggest that the Community consider ways and means to eliminate the impairment of its tariff concessions for oilseeds.

157. The Panel finally considered that, as the inconsistency with Article III:4 and the impairment of the tariff concessions arise from the same Community Regulations, a modification of these Regulations in the light of Article III:4 could also eliminate the impairment of the tariff concessions. The Panel therefore recommends that the CONTRACTING PARTIES take no further action under Article XXIII:2 in relation to the impairment of the tariff concessions until the Community has had a reasonable opportunity to adjust its Regulations to conform to Article III:4.

[OMITTED]

EEC—REGULATION OF IMPORTS OF PARTS AND COMPONENTS

Report of the Panel adopted on May 16, 1990
BISD —S/—
(L/6657)

V. FINDINGS

Introduction

5.1 The Panel noted that the issues before it arise essentially from the following facts and arguments: In June 1987, the EEC included in its anti-dumping regulation, Council Regulation No. 2176/84, a provision intended to prevent the circumvention of anti-dumping duties on finished products through the importation of parts or materials for use in the assembly or production of like finished products within the EEC. The provision was subsequently incorporated in Article 13:10 of Council Regulation No. 2423/88 adopted on July 11, 1988 which states, *inter alia*, that

> "Definitive anti-dumping duties may be imposed . . . on products that are introduced into the commerce of the Community after having been assembled or produced in the Community, provided that:

— assembly or production is carried out by a party which is related or associated to any of the manufacturers whose exports of the like product are subject to a definitive anti-dumping duty,

— the assembly or production operation was started or substantially increased after the opening of the anti-dumping investigation.

— the value of parts or materials used in the assembly or production operation and originating in the country of exportation of the product subject to the anti-dumping duty exceeds the value of all other parts of materials used by at least 50%."

Article 13:10(d) of the same Regulation states that the provisions of the Regulation concerning investigation, procedure and undertakings apply to all questions arising under Article 13:10. Under these provisions, the EEC made the suspension of proceedings under Article 13:10 conditional on undertakings by assemblers and producers in the EEC to limit the use of imported parts and materials. During the period between the adoption of Article 13:10 in June 1987 and the establishment of the Panel in October 1988, investigations under Article 13:10 resulted in the imposition of duties on products produced or assembled in the EEC in eight cases and in the acceptance of undertakings in seven cases. During this period there were four cases in which the acceptance of undertakings led to the revocation of the duties initially imposed. All investigations initiated and measures taken during this period under Article 13:10 involved products assembled or produced in the EEC by parties related to or associated with Japanese manufacturers whose exports of the finished like products were subject to definitive anti-dumping duties in the EEC (for further details, see Annex I).

5.2 The Panel further noted that Japan considers

— the duties imposed under Article 13:10,

— the acceptance of undertakings under Article 13:10, and

— the provisions of Article 13:10 as such,

to be inconsistent with the EEC's obligations under Articles I and II or III, and not justified by Article VI of the General Agreement. The EEC considers both the application of Article 13:10 and the Article itself to be justified by Article XX(d). Japan disagrees that Article XX(d) justifies the measures at issue. Japan further considers that the administration of Article 13:10 contravenes Article X of the General Agreement concerning the publication and administration of trade regulations, *inter alia*, because the EEC has failed to publish criteria for accepting undertakings and to determine the origin of parts in a uniform manner. The EEC considers that it has acted in conformity with that provision.

5.3 The Panel decided to examine successively:

(a) the imposition of duties under Article 13:10 of the EEC's Council Regulations No. 2176/84 and No. 2423/88 (hereinafter referred to as "anti-circumvention duties");

(b) the acceptance of undertakings under Article 13:10 of Regulations No. 2176/84 and No. 2423/88 (hereinafter referred to as "parts undertakings");

(c) Article 13:10 of Regulations No. 2176/84 and No 2423/88 itself (hereinafter referred to as "anti-circumvention provision"); and

(d) the non-publication of criteria for accepting parts undertakings and the administration of the rules of origin for parts and materials.

The Panel further decided that it would examine each of the above issues first in the light of the provisions of the General Agreement which Japan claims to have been violated by the EEC and then, if it were to find an inconsistency with any of the provisions invoked by Japan, in the light of the exception in the General Agreement invoked by the EEC.

Anti-circumvention Duties

5.4 *Categorization as customs duties (Article II:1(b)) or internal taxes (Article III:2)*. The Panel noted that Japan argued that the anti-circumvention duties could be considered to be *either* duties imposed on or in connection with importation within the meaning of Article II:1(b) *or* internal taxes within the meaning of Article III:2. The EEC considered that the duties do not fall under Article III:2. The Panel recalled that the distinction between import duties and internal charges is of fundamental importance because the General Agreement regulates ordinary customs duties, other import charges and internal taxes differently: the imposition of "ordinary customs duties" for the purpose of protection is allowed unless they exceed tariff bindings; all other duties or charges of any kind imposed on or in connection with importation are in principle prohibited in respect of bound items (Article II:1(b)). By contrast, internal taxes that discriminate against imported products are prohibited, whether or not the items concerned are bound (Article III:2). The Panel therefore first examined whether the duties constitute customs or other duties imposed on or in connection with importation falling under Article II:1(b) or internal taxes falling under Article III:2.

5.5 The Panel noted that the anti-circumvention duties are levied, according to Article 13:10(a), "on products that are introduced into the commerce of the Community after having been assembled or produced in the Community". The duties are thus imposed, as the EEC explained before the Panel, not on imported parts or materials but on the finished products assembled or produced in the EEC. They are not imposed conditional upon the importation of a product or at the time or point of importation. The EEC considers that the anti-circumvention duties should, nevertheless, be regarded as customs duties imposed "in connection with importation" within the meaning of Article II:1(b). The main arguments the EEC advanced in support of this view were: firstly, that the purpose of these duties was to eliminate circumvention of anti-dumping duties on finished products and that their nature was identical to the nature of the anti-dumping duties they were intended to enforce; and secondly, that the duties were collected by the customs authorities under procedures identical to those applied for the collection of customs duties, formed part of the resources of the EEC in the same way as customs duties and related to parts and materials which were not considered to be "in free circulation" within the EEC.

5.6 In the light of the above facts and arguments, the Panel first examined whether the *policy purpose of a charge* is relevant to determining the issue of whether the charge is imposed in "connection with importation" within the meaning of Article II:1(b). The text of Articles I, II, III and the Note to Article III refers to charges "imposed on importation", "collected . . . at the time or point of importation" and applied "to an imported product and to the like domestic product". The relevant fact, according to the text of these provisions, is not the policy purpose attributed to the charge but rather whether the charge is due on importation or at the time or point of importation or whether it is collected internally. This reading of Articles II and III is supported by their drafting history and by previous panel reports (e.g. BISD 1S/60 [Case 10]; 25S/49, 67 [Case 35]). A recent panel report which has examined the provisions of the General Agreement governing tax adjustments applied to goods entering into international trade (among them Articles II and III) stated that

> "*the tax* adjustment *rules of the General Agreement* distinguish between taxes on products and taxes not directly levied on products; they *do not distinguish between taxes with different policy purposes*" (BISD 34S/161 [Case 62], emphasis added).

The Panel further noted that the policy purpose of charges is frequently difficult to determine objectively. Many charges could be regarded as serving both internal purposes and purposes related to the importation of goods. Only at the expense of creating substantial legal uncertainty could the policy purpose of a charge be considered to be relevant in determining whether the charge falls under Article II:1(b) or Article III:2. The Panel therefore concluded that the policy purpose of the charge is not relevant to determine the issue of whether the charge is imposed in "connection with importation" within the meaning of Article II:1(b).

5.7 The Panel proceeded to examine whether the mere *description or categorization of a charge under the domestic law* of a contracting party is relevant to determining the issue of whether it is subject to requirements of Article II or those of Article III:2. The Panel noted that if the description or categorization of a charge under the domestic law of a contracting party were to provide the required "connection with importation", contracting parties could determine themselves which of these provisions would apply to their charges. They could in particular impose charges on products after their importation simply by assigning the collection of these charges to their customs administration and allocating the revenue generated to their customs revenue. With such an interpretation the basic objective underlying Articles II and III, namely that discrimination against products from other contracting parties should only take the form of ordinary customs duties imposed on or in connection with importation and not the form of internal taxes, could not be achieved. The same reasoning applies to the *description or categorization of the product subject to a charge*. The fact that the EEC treats imported parts and materials subject to anti-circumvention duties as not being "in free circulation" therefore cannot, in the view of the Panel, support the conclusion that the anti-circumvention duties are being levied "in connection with importation" within the meaning of Article II:1(b).

5.8 In the light of the above, the Panel found that the anti-circumvention duties are not levied "on or in connection with importation" within the meaning of Article II:1(b), and consequently do not constitute customs duties within the meaning of that provision.

5.9 *Article III:2.* The Panel proceeded to examine the anti-circumvention duties in the light of Article III:2, first sentence, according to which

> "the products of the territory of any contracting party imported into the territory of any other contracting party shall not be subject, directly or indirectly, to internal taxes or other internal charges of any kind in excess of those applied, directly or indirectly, to like domestic products."

The Panel noted that, in the cases in which anti-circumvention duties had been applied, the EEC followed sub-paragraph (c) of the anti-circumvention provision, according to which "the amount of duty collected shall be proportional to that resulting from the application of the rate of the anti-dumping duty applicable to the exporter of the complete products on the C.I.F. value of the parts or materials imported". The Panel further noted that like parts and materials of domestic origin are not subject to any corresponding charge. The Panel therefore found that the anti-circumvention duties on the finished products subject imported parts and materials indirectly to an internal charge in excess of that applied to like domestic products and that they are consequently contrary to Article III:2, first sentence.

5.10 Having found that the anti-circumvention duties are inconsistent with Article III:2, first sentence, the Panel saw no need for examining whether the anti-circumvention duties are also inconsistent with the obligations of the EEC under Article III:2, second sentence, and Article I:1. The Panel proceeded to examine the question of whether the inconsistency of the duties with Article III:2, first sentence, can be justified under the exception in the General Agreement invoked by the EEC.

5.11 *Article VI.* The Panel noted that, in the proceedings before the Panel, the EEC had not defended the anti-circumvention duties as anti-dumping duties within the meaning of Article VI of the General Agreement but as measures designed to prevent what it considered to be circumvention of anti-dumping duties through the importation and subsequent assembly of parts and components. The legal basis of these measures, in the view of the EEC, was Article XX(d) of the General Agreement which permits contracting parties to take measures necessary to secure compliance with laws or regulations which are not inconsistent with the General Agreement. The Panel further noted that the United States, as an interested third party, had argued that Article VI of the General Agreement provided to a certain extent a legal basis for measures to prevent what it considered to be circumvention of anti-dumping duties. At one point in the proceedings the EEC stated that, if the Panel were to find that the anti-circumvention duties were justifiable under Article VI, "it would not disagree" with such an approach (*supra* paragraph 3.76). However, the EEC presented no arguments in support of a justification of its measures under Article VI; on the contrary, in the subsequent proceedings the EEC continued to present various arguments to the effect that measures under Article 13:10 were "necessary" within the meaning of Article XX(d) because Article VI did *not* provide a basis for the application of measures to prevent circumvention of anti-dumping duties (*supra* paragraphs 3.86-89). In conformity with the practice of panels not to examine exceptions under the General Agreement which have not been invoked by the contracting party complained against (see, e.g. BISD 31S/74 [Case 56]) and not to examine issues brought only by third parties (cf.L/6514, page 15 and the references therein [Case 72]), the Panel decided not to examine whether the anti-circumvention duties could be justified under Article VI of the General Agreement.

5.12 *Article XX(d)*. The Panel proceeded to examine whether Article XX(d), which the EEC did invoke, can justify the imposition of the anti-circumvention duties. The Panel noted that the relevant part of Article XX(d) provides that

> . . . "nothing in this Agreement shall be construed to prevent the adoption or enforcement by any contracting party of measures:
>
> . . .
>
> (d) necessary to secure compliance with laws or regulations which are not inconsistent with the provisions of this Agreement . . ."

The Panel noted that Article XX refers to "measures" in its introductory sentence and to "laws and regulations" in sub-paragraph (d). The Panel considered that the "*measure*" referred to in Article XX is the measure requiring justification under Article XX and that, therefore, the imposition of anti-circumvention duties inconsistent with Article III:2 is the "measure" in the present case. It further considered that the "*laws or regulations*" to be examined under sub-paragraph (d) are the laws or regulations the contracting party invoking Article XX(d) claims to secure compliance with, in the present case the Council Regulations Nos. 2176/84 and 2423/88 (except for the anti-circumvention provision) and the individual Council regulations imposing definitive anti-dumping duties on finished products from Japan.

5.13 The Panel then considered whether Council Regulations Nos. 2176/84 and 2423/88 (except for the anti-circumvention provision) and the individual EEC anti-dumping regulations imposing definitive anti-dumping duties on finished products imported from Japan could be considered as laws or regulations "*which are not inconsistent*" with the provisions of the General Agreement. The Panel recalled Japan's doubts as to whether these laws and regulations are "not inconsistent" with the provisions of the General Agreement. However, the Panel noted that its terms of reference and the submissions by both parties have been limited to the anti-circumvention provision and its application. The Panel therefore decided to assume that, for the purpose of its proceeding, Council Regulations Nos. 2176/84 and 2423/88, with the exception of the anti-circumvention provision, and the individual EEC regulations imposing definitive anti-dumping duties on imports from Japan are "laws or regulations which are not inconsistent with the provisions of this Agreement" in terms of Article XX(d). The Panel emphasizes that this assumption applies only to its proceeding and is consequently without prejudice to any examination of these regulations in any other dispute settlement proceeding.

5.14 The Panel noted that, in order for a measure to be covered by Article XX(d), it must "*secure compliance with*" laws or regulations that are not inconsistent with the General Agreement. The Panel therefore proceeded to examine the question of whether the imposition of anti-circumvention duties inconsistent with Article III:2 is a measure "to secure compliance with" the EEC's general anti-dumping regulations and the individual regulations imposing definitive anti-dumping duties. The essential argument of Japan on this point was that Article XX(d) permits contracting parties to take only measures to enforce the obligations provided for in the laws or regulations consistent with the General Agreement. The only part of the EEC's anti-dumping regulations that requires enforcement is the part establishing the obligation to pay anti-dumping duties. The anti-circumvention duties do not serve to secure the payment of these duties and can therefore in the view of Japan not be considered to be securing compliance with the EEC's anti-dumping regulations. The essential argument of the EEC was that the terms "to secure compliance with" should be interpreted more broadly to cover not only the enforcement of laws and regulations *per se* but also the prevention of actions which have the effect of undermining the objectives of laws and regulations. In the view of the EEC, the anti-circumvention duties, being levied only in narrowly defined circumstances in which the objectives of the EEC's anti-dumping regulations are clearly being undermined, therefore secure compliance with these regulations within the meaning of Article XX(d).

5.15 The Panel concluded from the above that the interpretative issue before it was: Does the qualification "to secure compliance with laws or regulations" mean that the measure must prevent actions inconsistent with the obligations set out in laws or regulations, or does it support a more expansive interpretation according to which it would also cover a measure which prevents actions that are consistent with laws or regulations but undermine their objectives?

5.16 The Panel first examined this interpretative issue in the light of the *text of Article XX(d)*. The Panel noted that this provision does not refer to objectives of laws or regulations but only to laws or regulations. This suggests that Article XX(d) merely covers measures to secure compliance with laws and regulations as such and not with their objectives. The examples of the laws and regulations indicated in Article XX(d), namely "those relating to customs *enforcement*, the *enforcement* of monopolies . . . , the *protection* of patents . . . and the *prevention* of deceptive practices" (emphasis added) also suggest that Article XX(d) covers only measures designed to prevent actions that would be illegal under the laws or regulations. This conclusion is further supported by the fact that the provision corresponding to Article XX(d) in the 1946 Suggested Charter for an International Trade Organization used the terms "to *induce* compliance with" while Article XX(d) of the General Agreement uses the stricter language "to *secure* compliance with" (emphasis added).

5.17 The Panel then examined the alternative interpretations in the light of the *purpose of Article XX(d)* and found the following. If the qualification "to secure compliance with laws and regulations" is interpreted to mean "to enforce obligations under laws and regulations", the main function of Article XX(d) would be to permit contracting parties to act inconsistently with the General Agreement whenever such inconsistency is necessary to ensure that the obligations which the contracting parties may impose consistently with the General Agreement under the laws or regulations are effectively enforced. If the qualification "to secure compliance with laws and regulations" is interpreted to mean "to ensure the attainment of the objectives of the laws and regulations", the function of Article XX(d) would be substantially broader. Whenever the objective of a law consistent with the General Agreement cannot be attained by enforcing the obligations under that law, the imposition of further obligations inconsistent with the General Agreement could then be justified under Article XX(d) on the grounds that this secures compliance with the objectives of that law. This cannot, in the view of the Panel, be the purpose of Article XX(d): Each of the exceptions in the General Agreement—such as Articles VI, XII or XIX—recognizes the legitimacy of a policy objective but at the same time sets out conditions as to the obligations which may be imposed to secure the attainment of that objective. These conditions would no longer be effective if it were possible to justify under Article XX(d) the enforcement of obligations that may not be imposed consistently with these exceptions on the grounds that the objective recognized to be legitimate by the exception cannot be attained within the framework of the conditions set out in the exception.

5.18 For the reasons indicated in the preceding paragraphs, the Panel found that Article XX(d) covers only measures related to the enforcement of obligations under laws or regulations consistent with the General Agreement. The Panel noted that the general anti-dumping Regulation of the EEC does not establish obligations that require enforcement; it merely establishes a legal framework for the authorities of the EEC. Only the individual regulations imposing definitive anti-dumping duties give rise to obligations that require enforcement, namely the obligation to pay a specified amount of anti-dumping duties. The Panel noted that the anti-circumvention duties do not serve to enforce the payment of anti-dumping duties. The Panel could, therefore, not establish that the anti-circumvention duties "secure compliance with" obligations under the EEC's anti-dumping regulations. The Panel concluded for these reasons that the duties could not be justified under Article XX(d).

Acceptance of Parts Undertakings

5.19 *Article III:4.* The Panel proceeded to examine whether, as contended by Japan, the acceptance of undertakings to limit the use of imported parts and materials constituted a "requirement" that accords treatment to imported products less favorable than that accorded to domestic products contrary to Article III:4.

5.20 The Panel recalled that, during the period June 1987 to October 1988, eleven undertakings by parties related to or associated with Japanese manufacturers had been accepted by the EEC in investigations under the anti-circumvention provision and that, according to the relevant Commission decisions published in the Official Journal of the European Communities, these undertakings related, *inter alia*, to changes in the sourcing of parts and materials used in assembly or production operations in the Community. The Panel noted that there is no obligation under the EEC's anti-dumping Regulation to offer parts undertakings, to accept suggestions by the EEC Commission to offer such undertakings and to maintain the parts undertakings given. However, the consequence of not offering an undertaking, or of withdrawing an existing undertaking, can be the continuation of procedures that may lead to the imposition of the anti-circumvention duties. Article 10 of Regulation No 2324/88 states that "where an undertaking has been withdrawn or where the Commission has reason to believe that it has been violated . . . it may . . . apply . . . antidumping . . . duties forthwith on the basis of the facts established before the acceptance of the undertaking".

5.21 The Panel noted that Article III:4 refers to "all laws, regulations or requirements affecting (the) internal sale, offering for sale, purchase, transportation, distribution or use". The Panel considered that the comprehensive coverage of "*all* laws, regulations or requirements *affecting*" (emphasis added) the internal sale, etc. of imported products suggests that not only requirements which an enterprise is legally bound to carry out, such as those examined by the "FIRA Panel" (BISD 30S/140, 158), but also those which an enterprise voluntarily accepts in order to obtain an advantage from the government constitute "requirements" within the meaning of that provision. The Panel noted that the EEC made the grant of an advantage, namely the suspension of proceedings under the anti-circumvention provision, dependent on undertakings to limit the use of parts or materials of Japanese origin without imposing similar limitations on the use of like products of EEC or other origin, hence dependent on undertakings to accord treatment to imported products less favorable than that accorded to like products of national origin in respect of their internal use. The Panel therefore concluded that the decisions of the EEC to suspend proceedings under Article 13:10 conditional on undertakings by enterprises in the EEC to limit the use of parts or materials originating in Japan in their assembly or production operations are inconsistent with Article III:4.

5.22 Having found the acceptance by the EEC of parts undertakings limiting the use of imported parts and components to be inconsistent with Article III:4, the Panel saw no need for examining whether the acceptance of such undertakings is also inconsistent with Article I:1 of the General Agreement.

5.23 *Article VI*. The Panel recalled that the EEC had, in the course of the Panel proceeding, not invoked Article VI as a justification of its anti-circumvention duties (see paragraph 5.11 above). As the EEC had also not invoked Article VI as a justification of its parts undertakings, the Panel decided not to examine whether the acceptance of undertakings inconsistent with Article III:4 of the General Agreement could be justified under Article VI.

5.24 *Article XX(d)*. The Panel recalled its finding that the imposition of anti-circumvention duties inconsistent with Article III:2 could not be justified under Article XX(d) because the duties did not "secure compliance with" the EEC's anti-dumping regulations within the meaning of that provision (see above paragraph 5.18). The Panel found that this implies that the acceptance of parts undertakings, which functioned as a substitute for the anti-circumvention duties, could likewise not be considered to "secure compliance with" the EEC's anti-dumping regulations.

Article 13:10 of the EEC Council Regulation

5.25 Japan considers not only the measures taken under the anti-circumvention provision but also the provision itself to be violating the EEC's obligations under the General Agreement. Japan therefore asked the Panel to recommend to the CONTRACTING PARTIES that they request the EEC not only to revoke the measures taken under the provision but also to withdraw the provision itself. The Panel therefore examined whether the mere existence of the anti-circumvention provision is inconsistent with the General Agreement. The Panel noted that the anti-circumvention provision does not mandate the imposition of duties or other measures by the EEC Commission and Council; it merely authorizes the Commission and the Council to take certain actions. Under the provisions of the General Agreement which Japan claims to have been violated by the EEC contracting parties are to avoid certain measures; but these provisions do not establish the obligation to avoid legislation under which the executive authorities may possibly impose such measures. The Panel further noted that it has been recognized in a previous panel report adopted by the CONTRACTING PARTIES that legislation mandatorily requiring the executive authority to impose internal taxes discriminating against imported products is inconsistent with Article III:2 whether or not an occasion for its actual application has as yet arisen (BISD 34S/160), but that legislation merely giving the executive authorities the possibility to act inconsistently with Article III:2 cannot, by itself, constitute a violation of that provision (BISD 34S/160, 164). At issue in that case was, *inter alia*, a provision in the Superfund Act of the United States which directs the United States tax authorities to impose a tax on certain chemical substances but allows these authorities not to impose the tax provided they issue certain regulations. The panel which examined that case noted that the levying of the tax would be inconsistent with Article III:2 and that the regulations eliminating the need to impose that tax had not yet been issued. The panel then concluded:

> "From the perspective of the overall objectives of the General Agreement it is regrettable that the Superfund Act explicitly directs the United States tax authorities to impose a tax inconsistent with the national treatment principle but, since the Superfund Act also gives them the possibility to avoid the need to impose that tax by issuing regulations, the existence of the penalty rate provisions as such does not constitute a violation of the United States obligations under the General Agreement" (BISD 34S/163).

5.26 In the light of the above the Panel found that the mere existence of the anti-circumvention provision in the EEC's anti-dumping Regulation is not inconsistent with the EEC's obligations under the General Agreement. Although it would, from the perspective of the overall objectives of the General Agreement, be desirable if the EEC were to withdraw the anti-circumvention provision, the EEC would meet its obligations under the General Agreement if it were to cease to apply the provision in respect of contracting parties.

Publication of Criteria for the Acceptance of Parts Undertakings and Administration of the Rules of Origin for Parts and Materials

5.27 The Panel considered the argument of Japan that, in the administration of the anti-circumvention provision, the EEC violated its obligations under Article X:1 and X:3 of the General Agreement, in particular in respect of the criteria for the acceptance of undertakings and the methodology for determining the origin of imported parts and components. Given that the Panel found the anti-circumvention duties and the acceptance of parts undertakings to be inconsistent with Article III:2 and 4, and not justifiable under Article XX(d), and that any further imposition of such duties or acceptance of related undertakings would therefore be inconsistent with the General Agreement, the issue of whether the administration of the anti-circumvention provision is consistent with Article X is no longer relevant.

Concluding Comment by the Panel

5.28 The Panel was aware that a number of participants in the ongoing multilateral trade negotiations consider that the increased internationalization of production processes has led to certain problems in the administration of their anti-dumping laws, and that these issues are presently the subject of these negotiations. The Panel would like to underline that its task was limited to an examination of the measures taken by the EEC in the light of the existing provisions of the General Agreement invoked by the parties to the dispute.

VI. CONCLUSIONS

6.1 The duties imposed by the EEC under Article 13:10 of Council Regulations Nos. 2176/84 and 2423/88 on products assembled or produced within the EEC by enterprises related to Japanese manufacturers of products subject to anti-dumping duties are inconsistent with Article III:2, first sentence, and are not justified by Article XX(d) of the General Agreement.

6.2 The decisions of the EEC to suspend proceedings under Article 13:10 conditional on undertakings by enterprises in the EEC to limit the use of parts or materials originating in Japan in their assembly or production operations are inconsistent with Article III:4 and not justified by Article XX(d) of the General Agreement.

6.3 The Panel *recommends* that the CONTRACTING PARTIES request the EEC to bring its application of Article 13:10 into conformity with its obligations under the General Agreement.

BIBLIOGRAPHY

BIBLIOGRAPHY

SELECT BIBLIOGRAPHY

Books

Benedek, Wolfgang, *Die Rechtordnung des GATT aus völkerrechtlicher Sicht,* Max-Planck-Institut für ausländiches öffenliches Recht und Völkerrecht, Beiträge, Band 100 (1990)

Hudec, Robert E., *The GATT Legal System and World Trade Diplomacy* (2nd ed. 1990) (1st ed. 1975)

Hudec, Robert E., *Adjudication of International Trade Disputes* (Thames Essay No. 16) (London: Trade Policy Research Institute 1978)

Jackson, John H., *World Trade and the Law of GATT* ch. 8 (1969)

Jackson, John H., *The World Trading System* ch. 4 (1989)

Long, Olivier, *Law and Its Limitations in the GATT Multilateral Trade System* (1985)

Articles

Bliss, J.C., "GATT Dispute Settlement Reform in the Uruguay Round: Problems and Prospects," 23 *Stanford Journal of International Law* 31 (1987)

Davey, William J., "Dispute Settlement in GATT," 11 *Fordham International Law Journal 51* (1987)

Flory, Thiebaut, "Les accords du Tokyo Round du GATT et la réforme des procédures de règlement des différends dans le système commercial interétatique," 86 *Revue Générale de Droit International Public* 235 (1982)

Harris, Kevin M., "The Post-Tokyo Round GATT Role in International Trade Dispute Settlement," 1 *International Tax and Business Lawyer* 142 (1983)

Hudec, Robert E., "GATT Dispute Settlement After the Tokyo Round: An Unfinished Business," 13 *Cornell International Law Journal* 145 (1980)

Jackson, John H., "Governmental Disputes in International Trade Relations: A Proposal in the Context of GATT," 13 *Journal of World Trade Law* 13 (1979)

Petersmann, Ernst-Ulrich, "Strengthening GATT Procedures for Settling Trade Disputes," 11 *The World Economy* 55 (1988)

Petersmann, Ernst-Ulrich, "The GATT Dispute Settlement System and the Uruguay Negotiations on its Reform," in *Legal Issues in International Trade* (Sarcevic & Van Houtte eds. 1990)

United States International Trade Commission, "Review of the Effectiveness of Trade Dispute Settlement under the GATT and Tokyo Round Agreements," Publication No. 1793 (1985)

Waincymer, Jeffrey M., "GATT Dispute Settlement: An Agenda for Evaluation and Reform," 13 *North Carolina Journal of International Law and Commercial Regulation* 81 (1989)

Dissertation

Canal-Forgues, Eric, L'institution de la conciliation dans le cadre du GATT (Paris I, 1990)

UNIV DUNELM

DURHAM UNIVERSITY LIBRARY
3 0104 00638748 8

25 MAY 1993
18 JAN 1994
30 SEP 1994
20 FEB 1995
28 MAY 1996
27 MAY 1997
-6 MAY 1997
16 MAR 1998
-5 MAY 1998